Worlds of Islam

Worlds of Islam

A Global History

JAMES McDOUGALL

ALLEN LANE

an imprint of

PENGUIN BOOKS

ALLEN LANE

UK | USA | Canada | Ireland | Australia
India | New Zealand | South Africa

Allen Lane is part of the Penguin Random House group of companies
whose addresses can be found at global.penguinrandomhouse.com.

Penguin Random House UK
One Embassy Gardens, 8 Viaduct Gardens, London sw11 7bw

penguin.co.uk

First published in the United States of America by Basic Books 2026
First published in Great Britain by Allen Lane 2026

001

Typeset by Jouve (UK), Milton Keynes
Printed and bound in Great Britain by Clays Ltd, Elcograf S.p.A.

The authorized representative in the EEA is Penguin Random House Ireland,
Morrison Chambers, 32 Nassau Street, Dublin D02 YH68

A CIP catalogue record for this book is available from the British Library

ISBN: 978-0-241-52848-8

Penguin Random House is committed to a sustainable future
for our business, our readers and our planet. This book is made from
Forest Stewardship Council® certified paper.

For my students at Princeton, SOAS,
and Oxford, who've taught me a lot

.

CONTENTS

Part 4 Muslims' Modern Worlds, 1950-2020 CE

NOTE ON ARABIC NAMES

Most Muslims are not Arabs, or Arabic speakers, and many Arabs are not (and never have been) Muslims. But because of the particular status of Arabic as the language of Islamic revelation, and the centrality of Arabic-speaking peoples to Islam's early history, reading the history of Islam means coming across many Arabic names. This is not confined to the early and classical periods in which Islamic history is known to us mostly from sources originally written in Arabic, or to those parts of Muslim history that concern the modern Arab Middle East; it is common for converts to Islam today to adopt an Arabic name as a sign of their new Muslim identity.

Rather than consisting of just a forename and a surname, traditional Arabic personal names often have several elements. While a man's personal name could be one word, such as Muhammad, Ali, Hasan or Husayn, it too could often be made up of several separate words, including the Arabic word for God, Allah, or one of the names of God (such as al-Karim, the kind, al-Rahman, the compassionate, al-Qadir, the powerful) or the word al-Din (religion), and a word relating to this, such as Abd (slave), or (less modestly) Sayf (sword), Jalal (glory) or Zayn (beauty, adornment): Abd al-Karim, Abd-Allah, Sayf al-Din, Jalal al-Din. So "Abd al-Qadir," for example, is one name: "Abdul" and "Qadir" are not separate names, although in Britain (Abdul) or France (Kader) today they are often used as standalone forenames. This name would often be followed by a patronymic, Ibn (sometimes written Ben or Bin) or Bint, meaning *son* or *daughter of*, and finally another name indicating a profession, an ancient clan affiliation, a place name suggesting family origin, or a place where someone had been educated or lived part of their life. Many of these names, like Haddad (blacksmith) and Nahhas (coppersmith), Baghdadi (from Baghdad) and Masri (Egyptian), Huwaytat and Harb (ancient Arabian tribal names), survive today as family names.

Women's personal names did not completely follow this model of men's names: an Abd al-Qadir would always be male, though some, especially elite, women, particularly in the Persianate and Indian Ocean worlds, might have names made of several elements on the Arabic model, like Khair un-Nisa (best among women) or Safiyyat ud-Din (purity of the faith). Personal names were more often drawn instead from notable women of Islamic history or poetry, like Asma, Fatima, Zayneb, Aisha, or Layla, or words with conventional connotations of femininity: Farida (pearl), Anissa (kind), Jamila (beautiful). Their other names, though, worked the same way as men's names, for example, Fatima Bint Muhammad al-Fihri (Fatima, daughter of Muhammad, of the Fihr family—an ancient clan from Mecca). On becoming parents, both men and women might acquire familiar names combining the word Abu (father) or Umm (mother) with the name of a first-born child, as in Abu Ammar (Ammar's father) or Umm Kulthum (Kulthum's mother). Abu might also be combined with a characteristic to make a nickname, as in Abu Nuzzara (the man with spectacles).

COLOR ILLUSTRATIONS

1. The Dome of the Rock, Jerusalem. © RooM the Agency/Alamy Stock Photo.
2. The Dome of the Rock, interior, Jerusalem. © Erich Lessing/ Bridgeman Images.
3. The caliph Abd al-Malik depicted on a gold dinar struck in Damascus, 697 CE. © Ashmolean Museum/Bridgeman Images.
4. Folio from a Qur'an Manuscript [29.160.23]. Ink, opaque watercolor, and gold on paper, ca. 1180. The Metropolitan Museum of Art Open Collection, New York.
5. The investiture of Ali Ibn Abi Talib at Ghadir Khumm, according to Shi'i tradition. (Il-Khanid manuscript illustration, fourteenth cent., Special Collections, Edinburgh University Library, Arab. MS 161).
6. *The Prophet Muhammad Ascends to the Heavens* (detail). 17th century. Ink, opaque watercolor, and gold on paper. Yale University Open Community Collections: Visual Resources of the Middle East.
7. Photograph showing a view of Mecca with al-Masjid al-Haram, the holiest site in Islam, and the Ka'ba in the foreground. 1899. Abd al-Ghaffar, al-Sayyid, Physician of Mecca. Library of Congress Prints and Photographs Division Washington, D.C.
8. The al-Azhar Mosque in Cairo, built ca. 10th/11th century. © hemro/Shutterstock.
9. Interior of the great mosque (*mezquita*), Cordoba. Alvaraujo, licensed under Creative Commons Attribution-Share Alike 3.0 Unported license.

10. Monumental gate of the 15th century madrasa of Ulugh Bey, Samarqand. Arian Zwegers, licensed under Creative Commons Attribution 2.0 Generic license.
11. The Suleymaniyye Mosque, Istanbul. Hunanuk, licensed under Creative Commons CC0 1.0 Universal Public Domain Dedication.
12. Venetian portrait of Sultan Sulayman I "the Magnificent" as a young man, ca. 1520. Public Domain, via Wikimedia Commons.
13. Hurrem Sultan, known as "Roxelana," consort and wife of Sulayman I, 16th century. Public Domain, via Wikimedia Commons.
14. Alexander the Great conversing with the philosophers Socrates, Plato, and Aristotle. Detail from illustration from a Persian book of poetry, 18th century. Acquired by Henry Walters, Walters Art Museum, Maryland, 1931, by bequest.
15. *The Angel Surush Rescues Khusrau Parviz from a Cul-de-sac*, detail from folio 708v from the *Shahnama* (Book of Kings) of Shah Tahmasp. Painting attributed to Muzaffar 'Ali, 1530–35. Gift of Arthur A. Houghton Jr., 1970. The Metropolitan Museum of Art, New York.
16. A gold coin depicting the Mughal Emperor Jahangir, seated on a throne and holding a goblet, 1614. © Ashmolean Museum/ Bridgeman Images.
17. Illuminated letter from the sultan of Aceh, Iskandar Muda, to King James I of England, 1615. Bodleian Libraries, University of Oxford. MS Laud Or. Rolls B1.
18. "Timbuktu, from the terrace of the traveller's house." Frontispiece to *Travels and discoveries in North and Central Africa: being a journal of an expedition undertaken under the auspices of H.B.M.'s Government, in the years 1849–1855* (Volume 4), by Heinrich Barth. Smithsonian Institution Libraries. The Russell E. Train Africana Collection.
19. *Sheikh Amadou Bamba Praying on the Waters*. Reverse-glass painting by Mor Gueye, 1998. 99x13x13. Fowler Museum at UCLA. Photography by Don Cole.

20. Imam Shamil, leader of resistance to Russia in Chechnya and the Caucasus, 1850s. Public Domain, via Wikimedia Commons.

21. Prince Dipanagara, a Javanese prince who opposed Dutch colonial rule. 1835 lithograph, after an original pencil drawing by A.J. Bik, 1830. Public Domain, via Wikimedia Commons.

22. Emir Abd al-Qadir al-Jaza'iri photographed in Cairo between 1860 and 1883. Library of Congress Prints and Photographs Division Washington, D.C. 20540 USA.

23. Sultan Abdülhamid II, photographed ca. 1890. Library of Congress Prints and Photographs Division Washington, D.C. 20540 USA.

24. Sayyid Jamal al-Din al-Afghani. Date unknown. Public Domain, via Wikimedia Commons.

25. Muhammad Abduh, ca. 1906. Public Domain, via Wikimedia Commons.

26. Sir Sayyid Ahmad Khan, 1907. Public Domain, via Wikimedia Commons.

27. Ali Abd al-Raziq. Date unknown. Public Domain, via Wikimedia Commons.

28. Egyptian women at a nationalist demonstration, May 1919. *The Madison Journal*, June 28, 1919, Image 1. Public Domain, via Wikimedia Commons.

29. Prince Faisal Ibn Husayn and his advisors at the Versailles Conference, 1919. From the Marist Lowell Thomas Papers Collection with ID LTP.1580.06.09. Public Domain, via Wikimedia Commons.

30. Algerian political leader Ferhat Abbas, ca. 1950. Photo by © Hulton-Deutsch Collection/Corbis via Getty Images.

31. Shakib Arslan. Date unknown. Public Domain.

32. Muhammad Ali Jinnah, founder and first governor-general of Pakistan, ca. 1945. Public Domain, via Wikimedia Commons.

33. Muhammad Rashid Rida, ca. 1934. Public Domain, via Wikimedia Commons.

34. Hassan al-Banna, date unknown. Alamy Stock Photo.

35. Abu'l-A'la Maududi, leader of the Jamaat-i Islami Party, at London Airport, 1968. © UKIM.

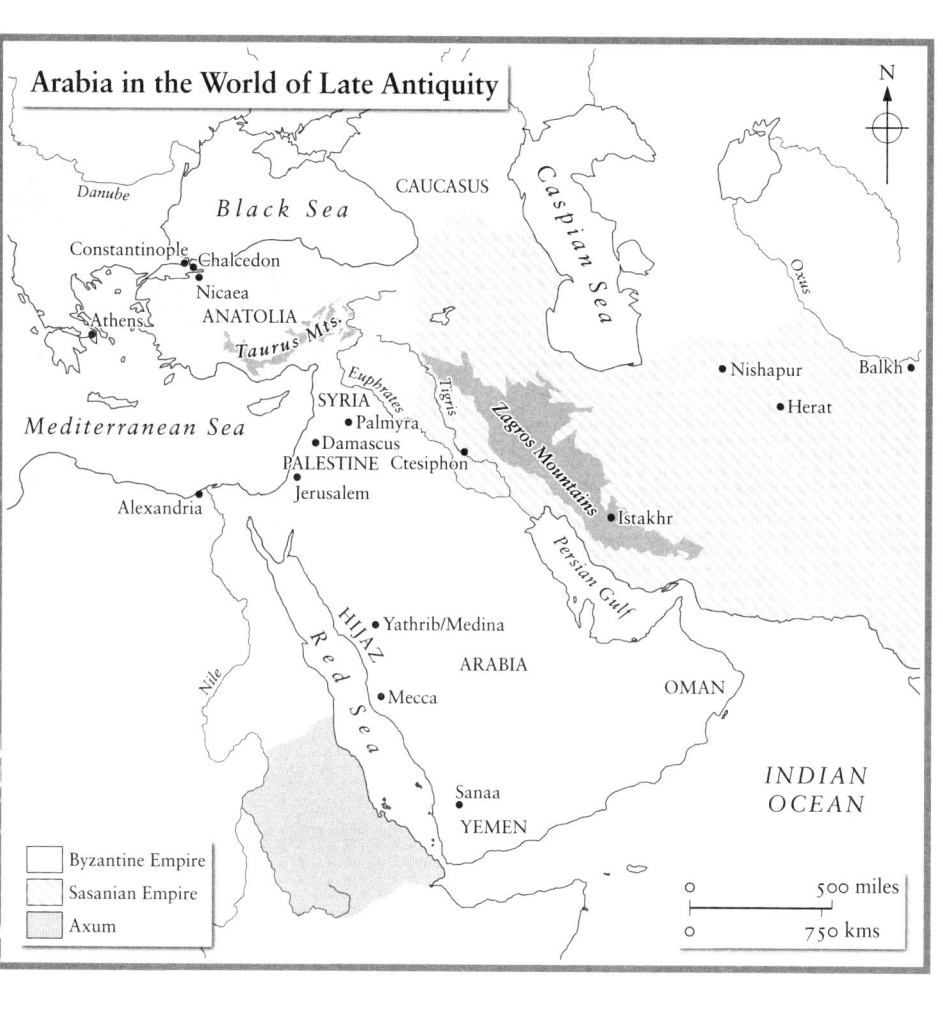

Arabia in the World of Late Antiquity

N

Danube
Black Sea
CAUCASUS
Caspian Sea
Oxus
Constantinople Chalcedon
Nicaea
Athens ANATOLIA
Taurus Mts.
Nishapur   Balkh
Herat
Euphrates
SYRIA
Palmyra
Tigris
Zagros Mountains
Mediterranean Sea
Damascus
PALESTINE Ctesiphon
Jerusalem
Alexandria
Istakhr
Persian Gulf
HIJAZ
Yathrib/Medina
Nile
Red Sea
ARABIA
Mecca
OMAN
INDIAN
OCEAN
Sanaa
YEMEN

Byzantine Empire
Sasanian Empire
Axum

0   500 miles
0   750 kms

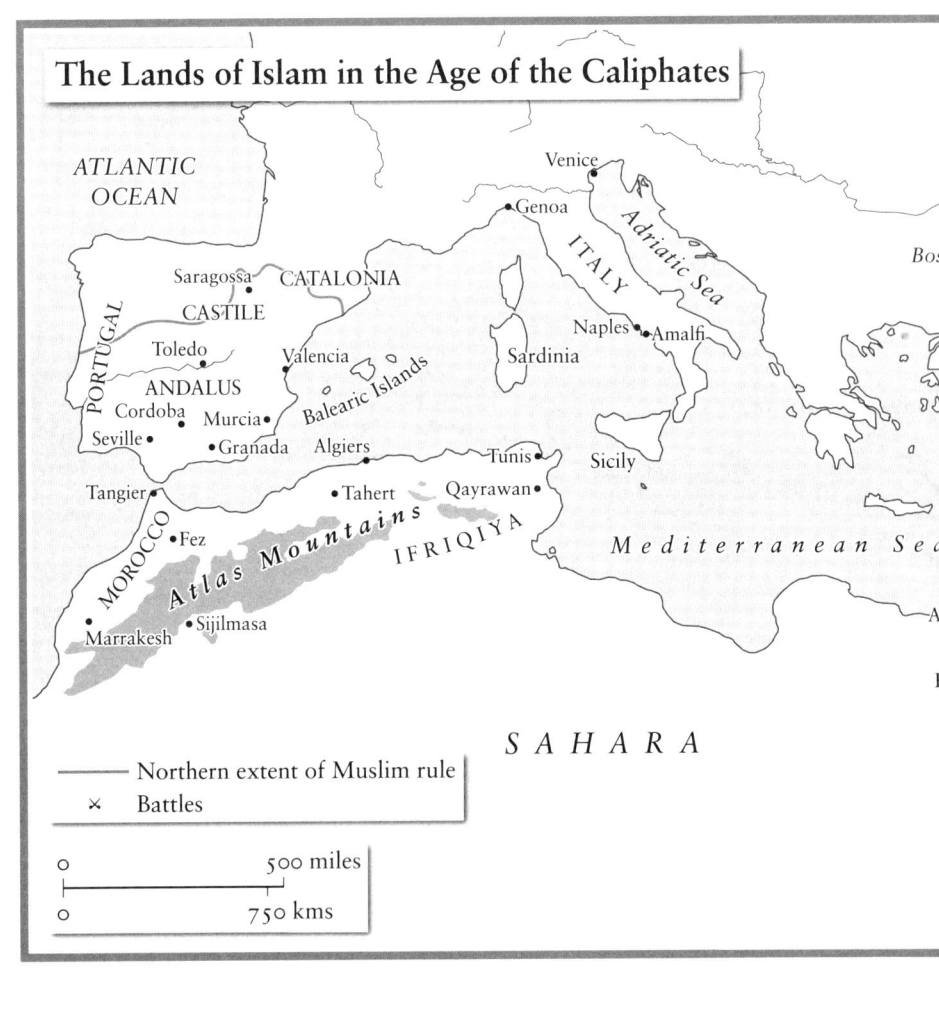

The Lands of Islam in the Age of the Caliphates

ATLANTIC
OCEAN

Venice
Genoa

Bos

Saragossa CATALONIA
CASTILE
Toledo
Valencia
Sardinia
ANDALUS
Cordoba Murcia
Balearic Islands
Seville
Granada Algiers
Tunis
Sicily

ITALY

Adriatic Sea

Naples Amalfi

PORTUGAL

Tangier
Tahert
Qayrawan
Fez
Atlas Mountains
IFRIQIYA

MOROCCO

Marrakesh Sijilmasa

Mediterranean Sea

Al

E

SAHARA

——— Northern extent of Muslim rule
× Battles

○ ——————————— 500 miles
○ ——————————— 750 kms

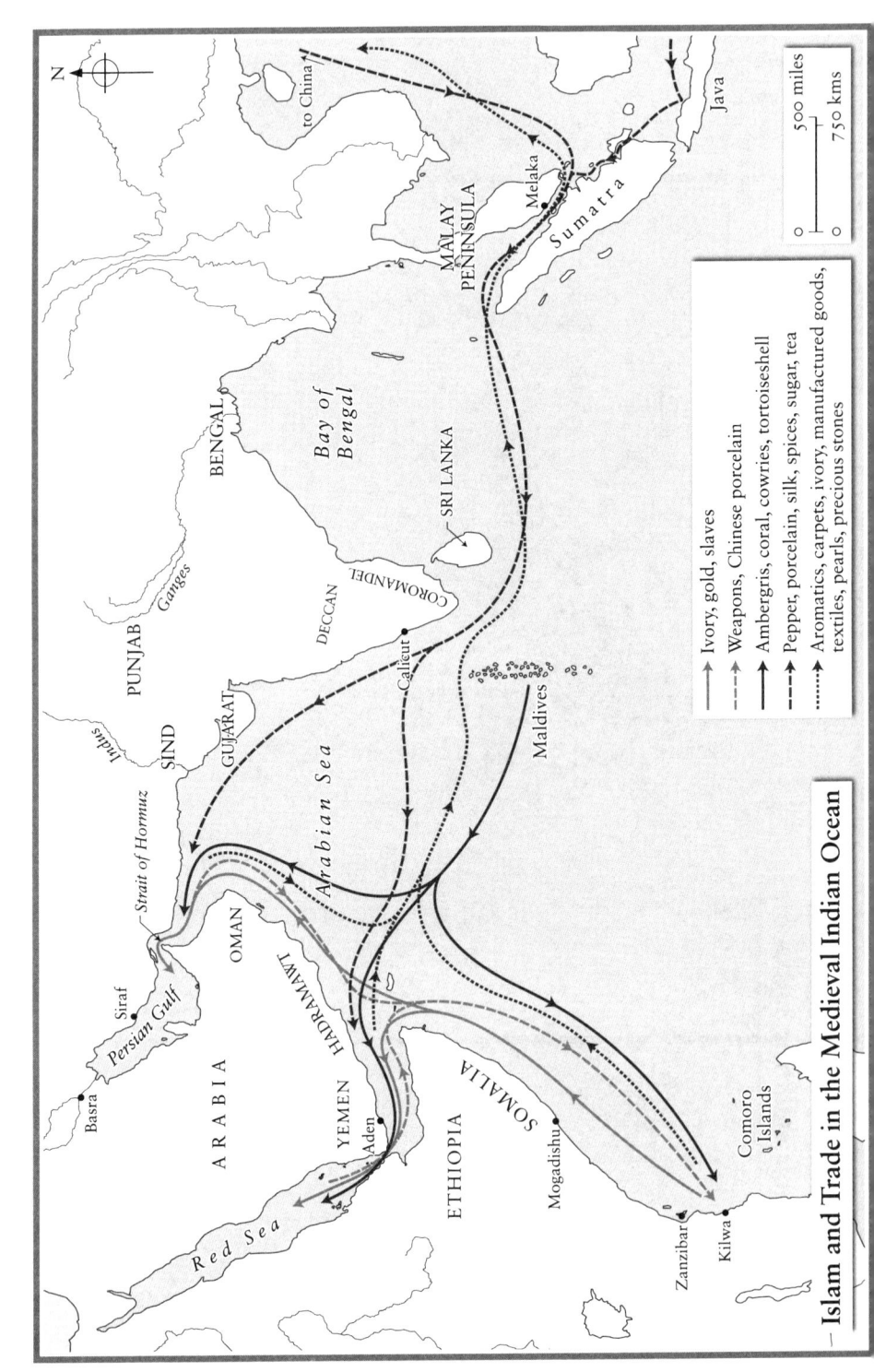

Islam and Trade in the Medieval Indian Ocean

N

500 miles
750 kms

→ Ivory, gold, slaves
→ Weapons, Chinese porcelain
→ Ambergris, coral, cowries, tortoiseshell
→ Pepper, porcelain, silk, spices, sugar, tea
→ Aromatics, carpets, ivory, manufactured goods, textiles, pearls, precious stones

to China
Java
MALAY PENINSULA
Melaka
Sumatra
BENGAL
Bay of Bengal
SRI LANKA
COROMANDEL
Ganges
PUNJAB
DECCAN
Calicut
Maldives
Indus
SIND
GUJARAT
Strait of Hormuz
Arabian Sea
OMAN
Siraf
Persian Gulf
HADRAMAWT
Basra
ARABIA
YEMEN
Aden
Red Sea
ETHIOPIA
SOMALIA
Mogadishu
Comoro Islands
Zanzibar
Kilwa

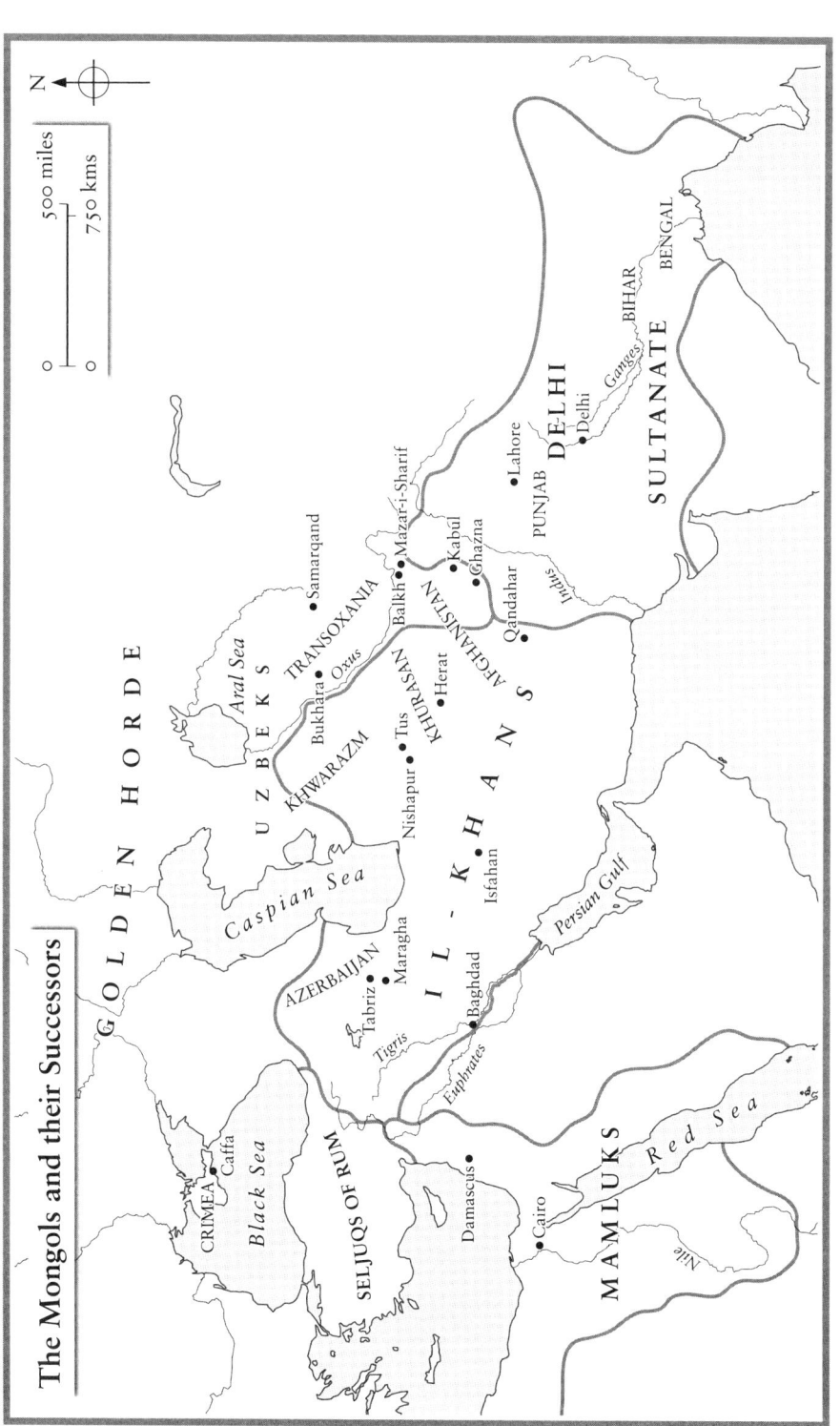

The Mongols and their Successors

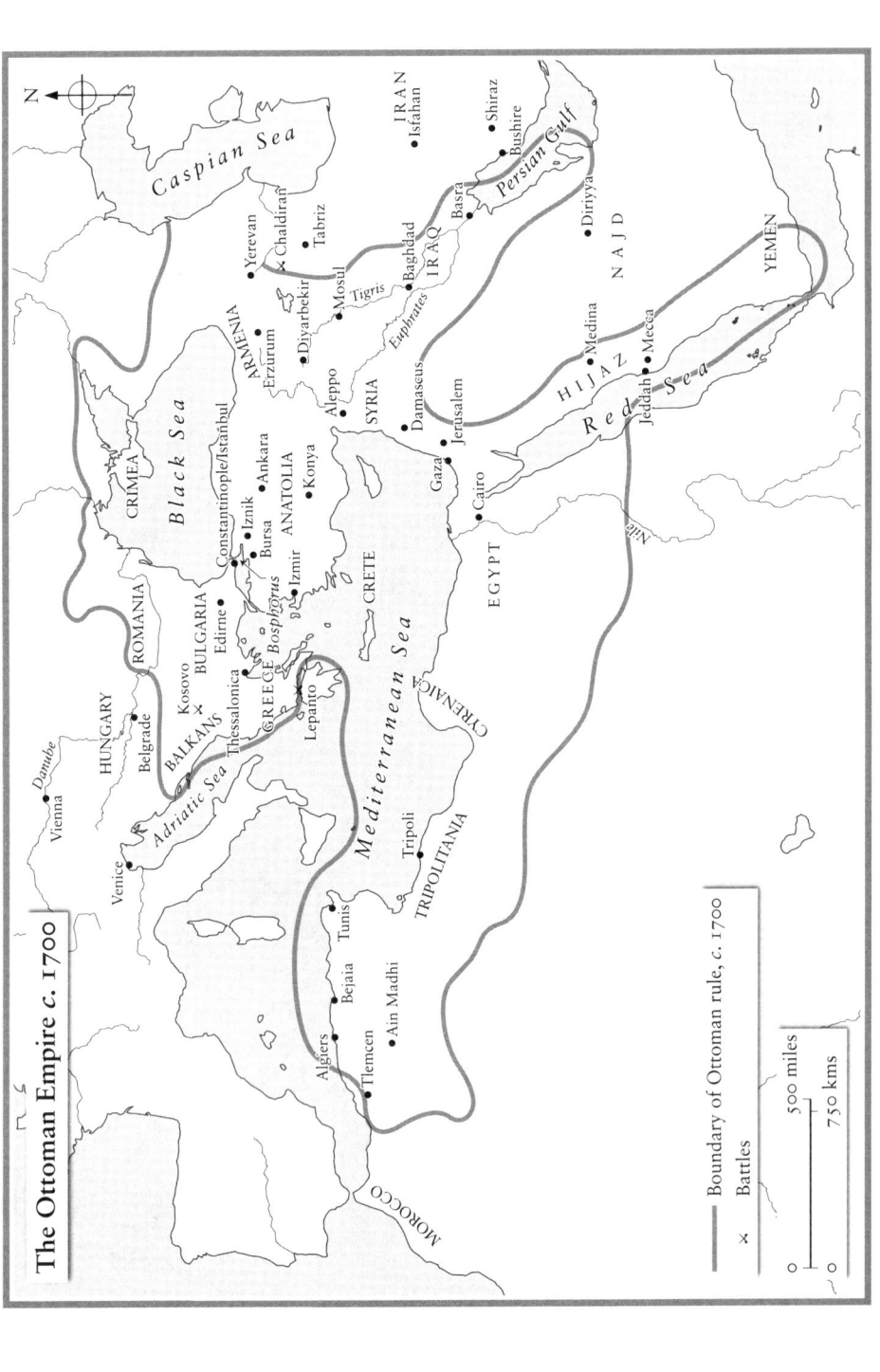

The Ottoman Empire *c.* 1700

Boundary of Ottoman rule, *c.* 1700

× Battles

500 miles

750 kms

N

Caspian Sea

IRAN
• Isfahan
• Shiraz
• Bushire

Persian Gulf
• Basra
• Diriyya

NAJD

YEMEN

• Yerevan
× Chaldiran
• Tabriz
• Mosul
Tigris
IRAQ
• Baghdad
Euphrates
• Medina
• Mecca
HIJAZ
• Jeddah
Red Sea

ARMENIA
• Erzurum
• Diyarbekir
• Aleppo
SYRIA
• Damascus
• Jerusalem
• Gaza
• Cairo

CRIMEA

Black Sea

Constantinople/Istanbul
• Iznik
• Bursa
• Izmir
• Ankara
• Konya
ANATOLIA

EGYPT

Nile

ROMANIA

BULGARIA
• Edirne
GREECE
Bosphorus
• Thessalonica
× Lepanto
BALKANS
• Kosovo
CRETE

HUNGARY
• Belgrade
• Vienna
Danube

• Venice
Adriatic Sea

Mediterranean Sea

CYRENAICA

• Tripoli
TRIPOLITANIA

• Tunis
• Bejaia
• Ain Madhi
• Algiers
• Tlemcen

MOROCCO

India in the Age of the Mughals

N

Hindu Kush

- Kabul
- Ghazna

KASHMIR

Peshawar

Himalayas

PUNJAB SIKHS

Qandahar

Lahore • • Amritsar

Indus

Pakpattan •

• Deoband

Panipat × • Meerut

Delhi •

• Aligarh

Fatehpur Sikri • • Agra

• Ajmer

Lucknow

Ganges

S I N D

R A J P U T S

Palashi ×

BENGAL

Calcutta •

GUJARAT

• Surat

DECCAN

Bombay •

MARATHAS

HYDERABAD

*Arabian
Sea*

Bay of Bengal

MYSORE

• Srirangapatna

• Calicut

| 0 | | 300 miles |
| 0 | | 400 kms |

- - - - - Extent of conquests by Babur

——— Extent of Mughal rule
under Aurangzeb

× Battles

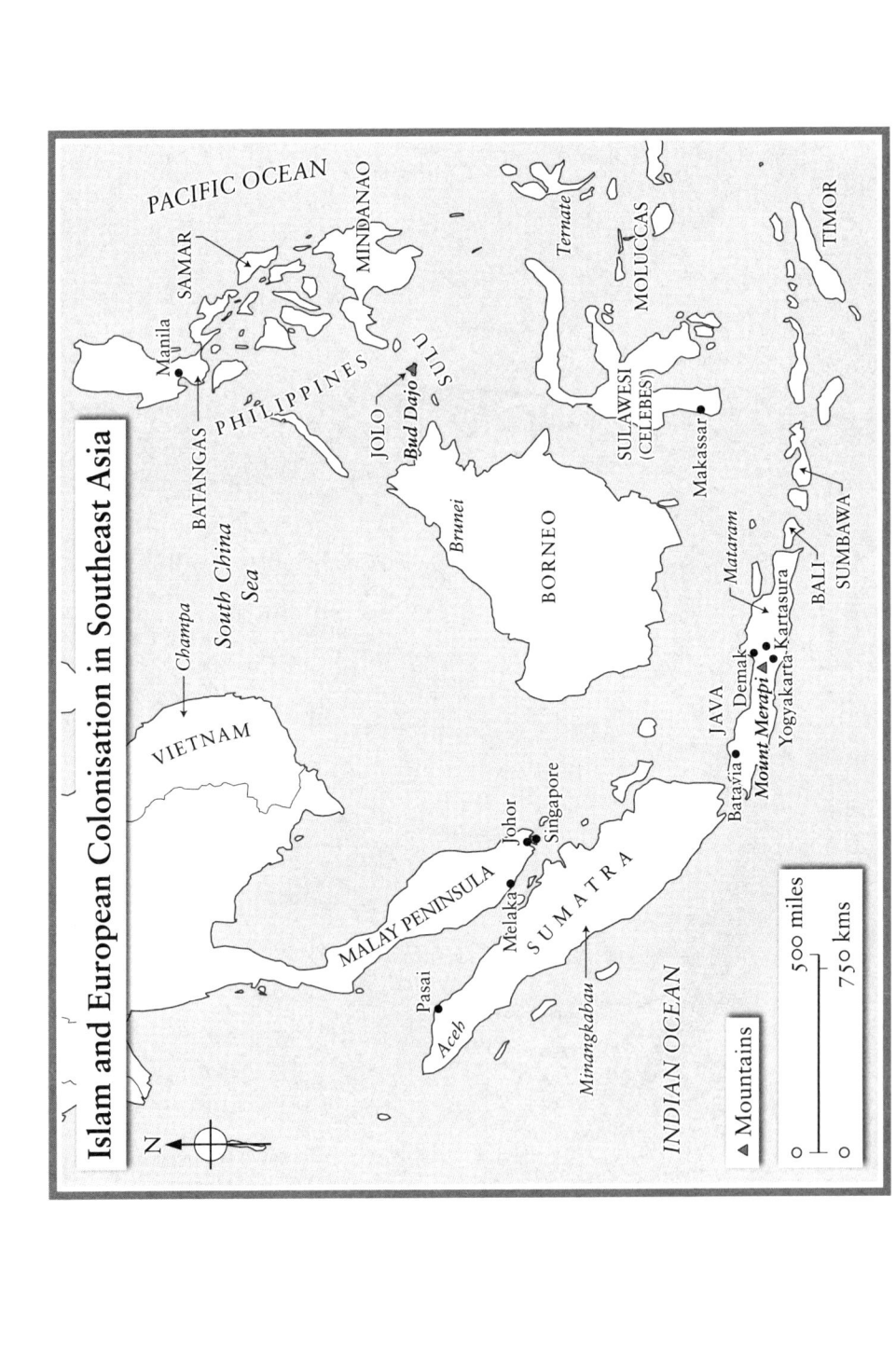

Islam and European Colonisation in Southeast Asia

PACIFIC OCEAN

SAMAR

MINDANAO

Manila

BATANGAS

PHILIPPINES

JOLO

Bud Dajo

SULU

Ternate

MOLUCCAS

SULAWESI
(CELEBES)

Makassar

TIMOR

Champa

South China
Sea

Brunei

BORNEO

Mataram

Mount Merapi

Demak

JAVA

Yogyakarta

Kartasura

BALI

SUMBAWA

VIETNAM

Batavia

Johor

Singapore

MALAY PENINSULA

Melaka

S U M A T R A

Minangkabau

Pasai

Aceh

INDIAN OCEAN

N

▲ Mountains

500 miles

750 kms

0

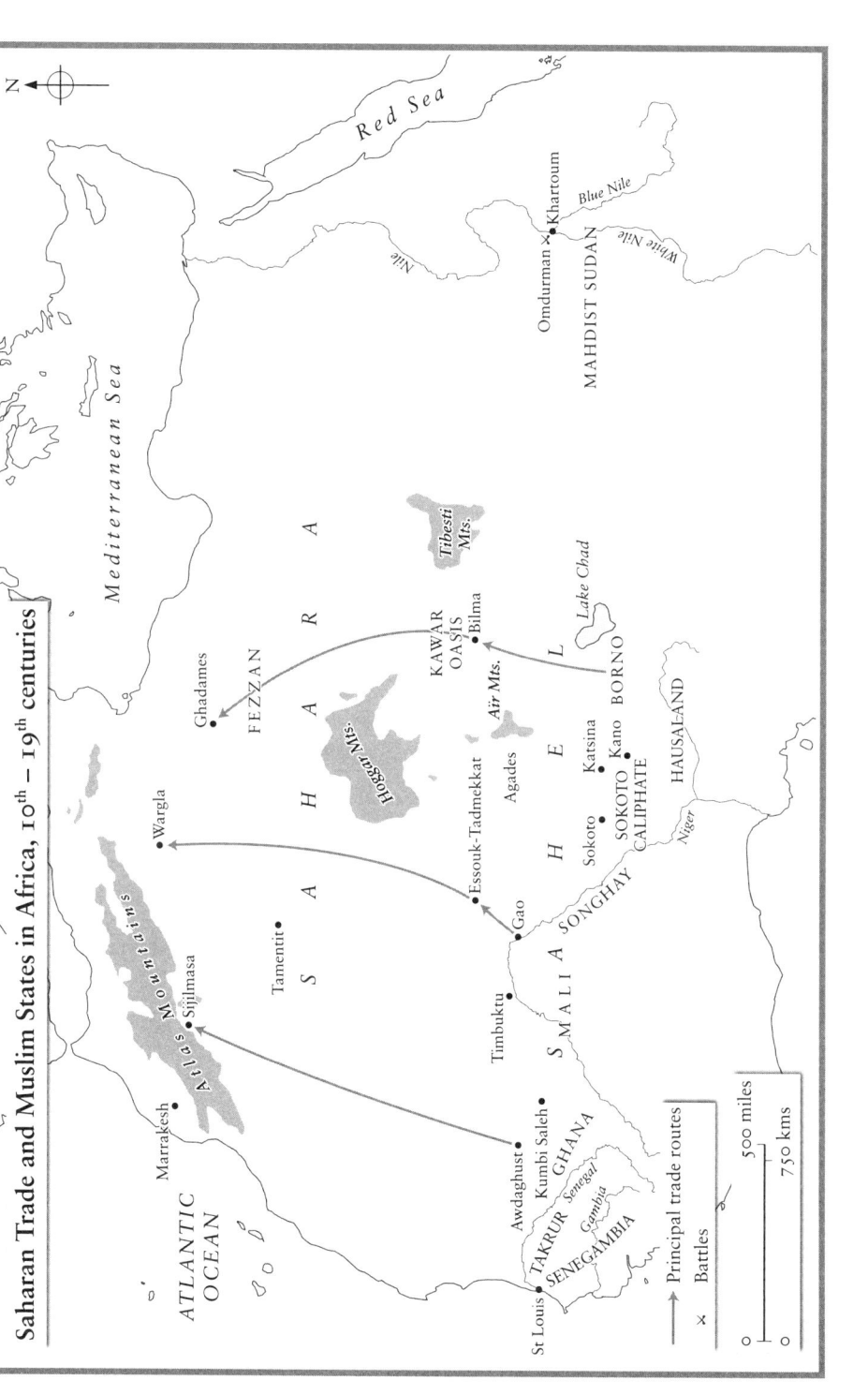

Saharan Trade and Muslim States in Africa, 10th – 19th centuries

N

Mediterranean Sea

Red Sea

S A H A R A

Nile

Blue Nile

White Nile

Khartoum
Omdurman ✗
MAHDIST SUDAN

Tibesti Mts.

Ghadames

FEZZAN

Hoggar Mts.

KAWAR OASIS
Bilma

Lake Chad

Air Mts.

BORNO

Wargla

Essouk-Tadmekkat

Agades

Katsina

Kano
HAUSALAND

Tamentit

Gao

Sokoto
SOKOTO
CALIPHATE

Niger

Marrakesh

Atlas Mountains

Sijilmasa

Timbuktu

SONGHAY
S M A L I A

St Louis

Awdaghust

Kumbi Saleh
GHANA

TAKRUR

Senegal

Gambia

SENEGAMBIA

ATLANTIC
OCEAN

→ Principal trade routes

✗ Battles

0
500 miles

0
750 kms

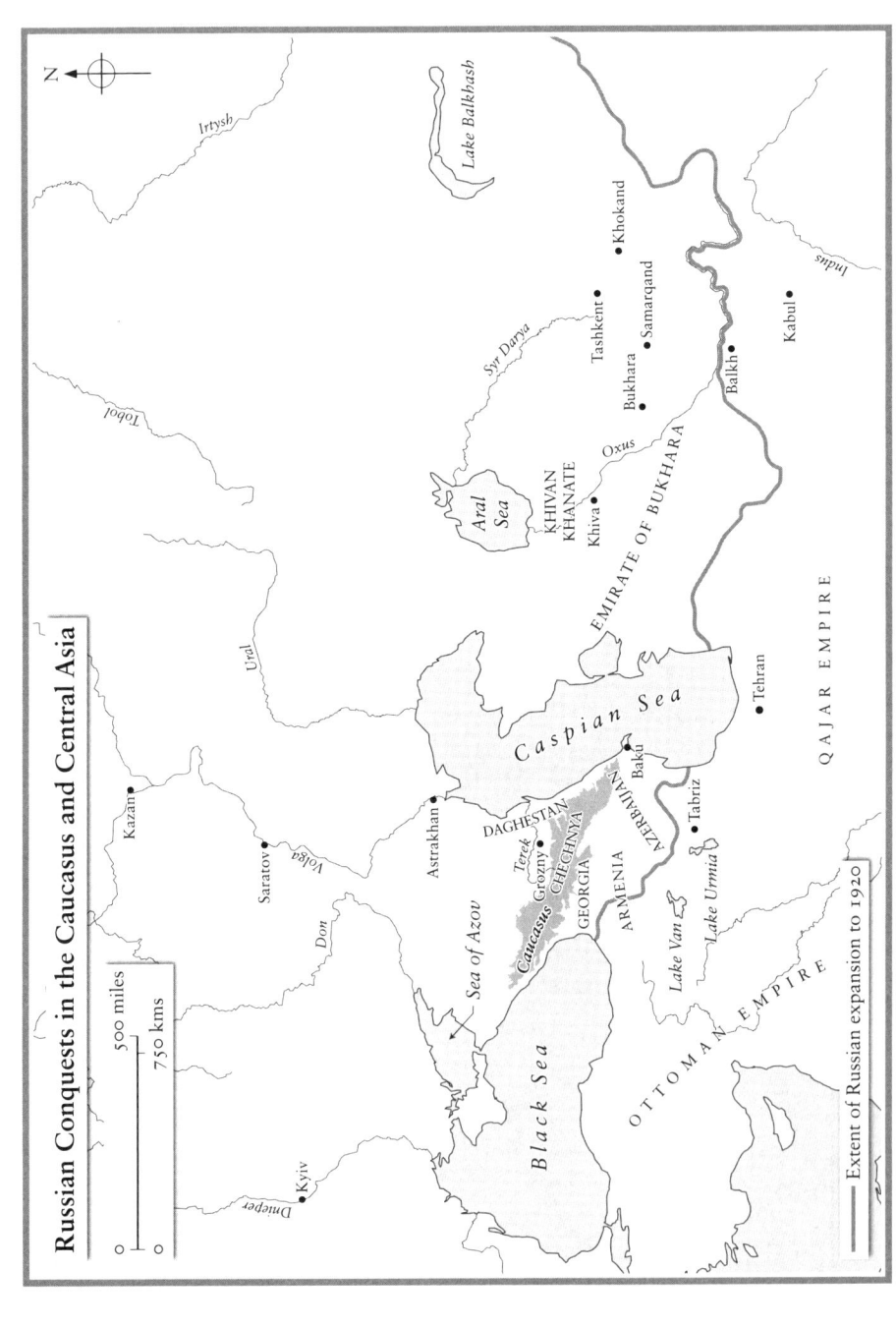

Russian Conquests in the Caucasus and Central Asia

Extent of Russian expansion to 1920

Israel and the Occupied Palestinian Territories, *c.* 2003

Israeli settlements*
Areas under Israeli jurisdiction
--- Armistice line (1949/1950 ceasefire line)
— West Bank separation wall

0	20 miles
0	30 kms

LEBANON

N

GOLAN

Haifa
Sea of Galilee

Mediterranean Sea

Natanya

•Jenin

Jordan Valley

•Nablus

Tel Aviv

WEST BANK

Ramallah•

Jericho•

Jerusalem•

•Bethlehem

Dead Sea

ISRAEL

JORDAN

GAZA STRIP
•Gaza

•Hebron

•Khan Yunus
Rafah

•Beersheba

Negev Desert

* Gaza Strip settlements dismantled 2005

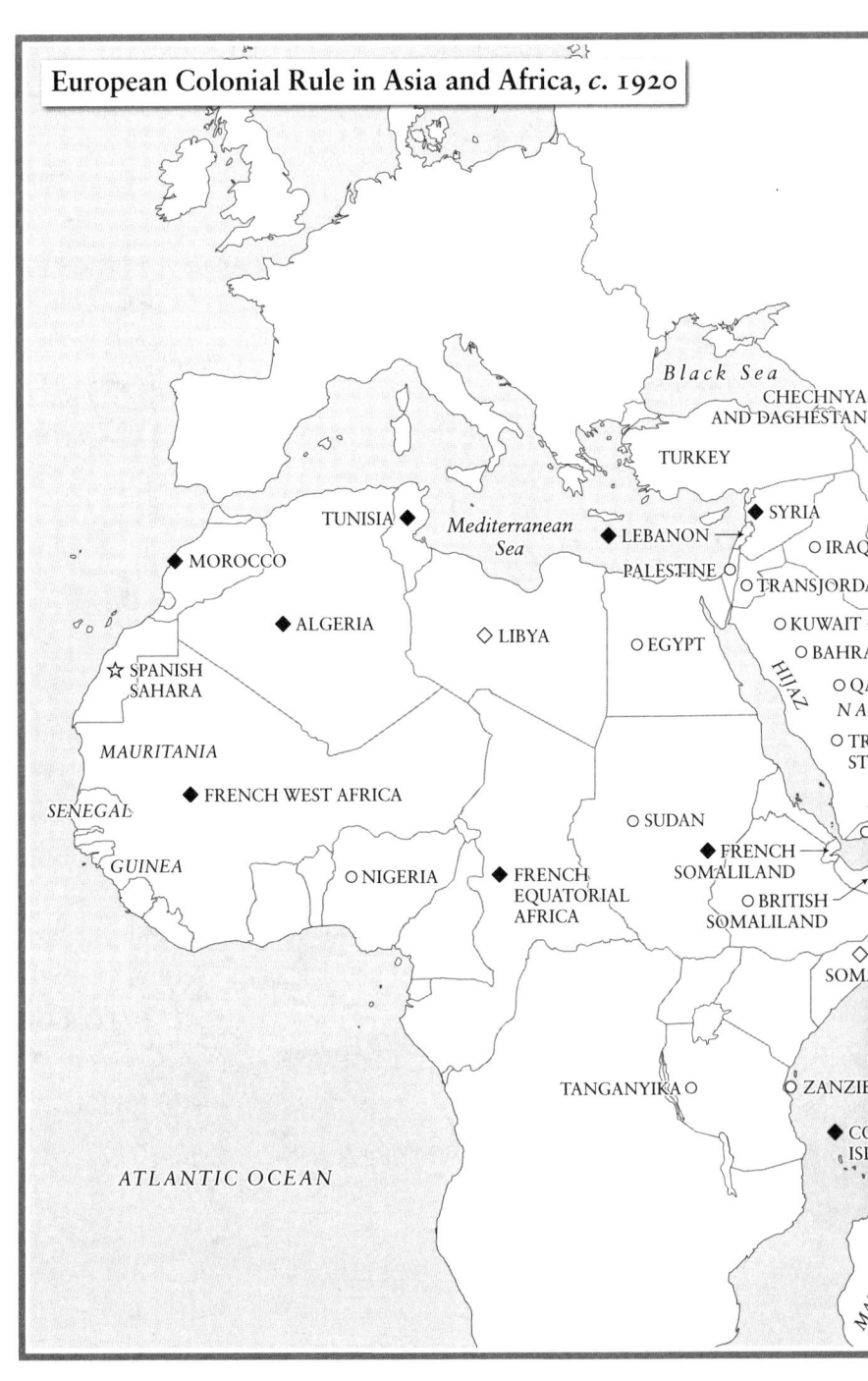

European Colonial Rule in Asia and Africa, *c.* 1920

Black Sea

CHECHNYA
AND DAGHESTAN

TURKEY

TUNISIA ◆ *Mediterranean*   ◆ LEBANON   ◆ SYRIA
Sea   ○ IRAQ

◆ MOROCCO   PALESTINE ○
                                    ○ TRANSJORDA

◆ ALGERIA   ◇ LIBYA   ○ EGYPT   ○ KUWAIT
                                   ○ BAHRA

☆ SPANISH   ○ QA
SAHARA   N A

                                         ○ TR
MAURITANIA   ST.

◆ FRENCH WEST AFRICA

SENEGAL   ○ SUDAN

GUINEA   ◆ FRENCH
                                   SOMALILAND
          ○ NIGERIA   ◆ FRENCH
                      EQUATORIAL   ○ BRITISH
                      AFRICA   SOMALILAND

                                        ◇
                                   SOM.

                TANGANYIKA ○   ○ ZANZIE

                                        ◆ CO
                                        ISI

ATLANTIC OCEAN

N

★ SOVIET CENTRAL ASIA

AFGHANISTAN

○ BRITISH INDIA

N

PHILIPPINES ●

South
China Sea

BRUNEI
MALAY STATES ○
SARAWAK ○

SUMATRA

BORNEO ●

JAVA

NETHERLANDS INDIES

DIAN OCEAN

● American
○ British
● Dutch
◆ French
◇ Italian
★ Russian
☆ Spanish

○   1000 miles
○   1500 kms

Nation States of Northern Africa, Middle East, Central and South Asia, 2020

TUNISIA

TU

LEBAN

ISRAEL
AND PALESTINE

MOROCCO

ALGERIA

LIBYA

EGYPT

MAURITANIA

MALI

NIGER

CHAD

SUDA

SENEGAL

BURKINA
FASO

GUINEA

GAMBIA

CÔTE
D'IVOIRE

SIERRA
LEONE

NIGERIA

CAMEROON

SOUT
SUDA

INTRODUCTION

When Uqba Ibn Nafi reached the Atlantic Ocean, it's said that he galloped straight into the sea. Uqba had been born only a few years before the death of the Prophet Muhammad, fifty years earlier. Now, in 681 CE, he led an Arab Muslim army that had set out from southern Tunisia and skirmished with Byzantine forces as far as Tangier. Facing the ocean and its distant horizon, we're told, he rode his horse into the surf, raised his hands to the sky, and called out that he had carried Islam as far as there was land: if the sea had not prevented him, he would have ridden on to the ends of the earth, defending God's religion and fighting against unbelief.

This is just one of many stories built up around Uqba's adventures, which medieval Muslim writers compared to the exploits of Alexander the Great, but it carries particular significance. For the historian Ibn al-Idhari, who recounted the story in Morocco six hundred years later, it was important to point out both the universality of Islam, its validity as a message from the one God to all the world, and the particular importance of his own country, *al-maghrib al-aqsa*—the farthest west—in the world that Islam had made. This, the land where the sun set, was as far as it was imaginable to go. The story of Sidi ("my lord") Uqba neatly illustrated both Islam's location and its limitlessness.

At the same time, the story also shows us that while Islam had its own history, to be told in its own terms and from the perspective of its believers, it was part of other histories too. Sidi Uqba rode into the Atlantic, not because it was as close as he could get to the ends of the earth, but because, having advanced as far as Tangier, he had decided against risking the crossing north into the Iberian Peninsula, where he would have overextended his supply lines and perhaps faced stronger opposition. In comparing him to Alexander the Great, Muslim writers were drawing on their own knowledge of earlier histories of legendary conquest and universal empire. The Greek and late Roman worlds into which Uqba rode embodied an ancient cultural inheritance that his chroniclers could also claim as their own. There are legendary traditions about his enemies too, especially the prophetess-queen Kahina and her son, Qusayla, leaders of the Amazigh (Berber-speaking) peoples whom Uqba encountered in North Africa. Qusayla and Kahina both anchor the early history of Islam in a broader, multireligious context. Qusayla is said to have converted from Christianity to Islam before turning against Uqba. His mother, Kahina ("the Seer"), is variously identified as Christian or Jewish: North African traditions portray her as a hero-queen who stubbornly resisted the Arab invaders but also foresaw their inevitable victory. Islam made its own world; but it was part of other worlds too. It was distinct, but it was connected.[1]

In the years after it emerged from the Arabian Peninsula in the seventh century CE, Islam became a global historical force in two ways. First, it had a geographically world-spanning reach. It arose in an ancient and interconnected world at the junction of Asia, Africa, and Europe, between the Mediterranean and the Indian Ocean. It would have a profound, transformative impact on that world, shaping it in new ways for over a thousand years to come. It would reach out from that world, across the lands and seas beyond, to all the corners of the earth. Second, culturally, it held a message believed by its adherents to be of universal significance. The preaching and leadership of the Prophet Muhammad, his followers believed, completed the revelation of the one true God (*Allah* is simply the Arabic word for God, used by Arabic-speaking Christians as well as Muslims). Their religion was the "religion of Abraham" that God had previously revealed in part to

Jews and Christians: they, Muslims thought, had misunderstood or falsified it. The community of Muhammad's followers, the Muslims— in Arabic, *muslimun*, "those who have submitted"—were those who truly submitted to the one God. They believed that Muhammad was the last of the prophets, completing a line of messengers from the Almighty that had begun with Adam and extended through Abraham and Moses to Jesus, "the Son of Mary." Like these earlier prophets, Muslims believed, Muhammad had been sent by God to warn people of His coming judgment and bring them to His mercy. They believed that the way of life preached by Muhammad was simply the one true religion: right guidance in life and hope after death for all humanity.

Sidi Uqba's story illustrates these two sides of Islam's global history. It presents Islam, like Christianity, as a missionary religion: as a revelation from beyond time, true for all time, whose believers' vocation is to bring its message to all the world. But it also shows Islam as existing in time and space: in particular places and in human history, in the Arabs' incursions into the late Roman, or Byzantine, Empire, at a meeting point of cultures and geographies, between the people who already inhabited the late ancient Mediterranean world and the incomers making their place in it, and writing themselves into its history. In 683, two years after he reached the Atlantic, Sidi Uqba was killed at the southern edge of the Aurès Mountains, in what is now eastern Algeria. He and his companions were buried nearby, and three years later a mosque was built on the site of his tomb. The mosque is one of the oldest in the world, its original structure a simple, elegant building with a beautiful, tapering white minaret and heavy cedarwood doors, its columns made of palm trunks encased in mortar. Sidi Uqba became part of the landscape. The small town that grew around the mosque is still known by his name.

◇◇◇◇◇◇◇

For most of Islam's history, most Muslims have lived in places like Sidi Uqba, where life and the landscape were shaped by the coming and the consolidation of Islam. They lived under rulers who claimed to be Muslims, in states that could be called Islamic, and in societies where practices and norms understood to be Muslim were central to social life. There was a basic minimum of these on which all Muslims agreed. Five essential practices became known as the "pillars of the faith," or of proper worship: the profession of belief, or bearing witness (*shahada*), that "there is no god but God and Muhammad is the Messenger of God"; the duty, for whoever had the means to accomplish it, of making the pilgrimage (*hajj*) to Mecca and engaging there in ritual devotions on the model established by the Prophet; performing the five daily prayers; fasting during daylight hours in the holy month (as reckoned by the lunar calendar) of Ramadan; and giving alms (*zakat*, levied in the early Muslim state as a tax on income above a certain level) to the community for the support of the poor. In principle, all Muslims would accept that anyone observing these duties, and believing in the oneness of God, the Prophethood of Muhammad, and the judgment to come on the Last Day, was a fellow believer.

Beyond these essential practices of worship lay a more detailed body of ethical and legal norms. These included some basic duties that were owed both to God and to people (fair treatment of wives, widows and orphans; dietary rules, similar to those in Jewish law, like avoiding pork or meat with blood still in it; the practice of circumcision for males) and more complex rules about how to manage social life (inheritance, marriage and divorce, commercial transactions, crime and punishment, rules of warfare, and so on). Together, all of these were held to constitute the *shari'a*, the "way" laid down by God for humanity to follow.

Sharia provided Muslim states with a rule of law, and Muslim rulers with the ability to claim they ruled legitimately. Wherever these Muslim practices and norms were upheld, there was *dar al-islam*, the "house" or "the home of Islam." Islamic lawyers and ethicists often taught that Muslims could only live well in such a Muslim space, under Muslim sovereignty. Geographically, this world of Muslims came to stretch continuously from the Atlantic coasts of West Africa and Morocco through the Middle East to central Asia and India, then across the Indian Ocean to the islands of Southeast Asia and the Pacific. It touched the edges of Europe in Spain and the Balkans, and the coasts and the far western provinces of China. In all these very different places, it shaped individuals, families, cultures, societies and states, and created a Muslim ecumene—a world of great diversity that was united by Islam.

But this Muslim space—what we usually think of as the Muslim world—was neither exclusive nor all-encompassing. Many Muslims lived in places such as the southeast European provinces of the Ottoman Empire, or in the Mughal Empire in South Asia, where Muslims were not the only, nor the largest, religious community. Even in Islam's historic heartlands in the Middle East, Muslims remained a minority for hundreds of years after the Arab conquests. Jews, Christians, Zoroastrians, Hindus and Buddhists—people of other religions and of none—lived in predominantly Muslim societies and under Muslim rulers. Among Muslims themselves, law, custom, and religious beliefs and practices were all richly varied. And perhaps above all, many other factors—ecology, economics, and politics; culture, language, and livelihood—shaped their lives, and their Islam, as much as their religion itself did. Islam—whether understood as a religion, a cultural system, a model of political order, or all of these combined— was never the single defining feature of Muslims' societies, any more than Christianity was ever the only thing that defined life in what used to be called "Christendom." Although Muslim writers on law and ethics (and, later, non-Muslim social scientists) often tried to prescribe one, there was never a single model of an Islamic state, or of a Muslim society.

On the contrary, beyond the faith's shared essentials, a variety of religious beliefs and practices, local histories and group identities were all understood as Muslim by those who held to them—although others might consider them heretical or un-Islamic. Many different rulers' claims about their right to rule, the way they should rule, and their wars against each other were made in the belief that they were the true Muslims, and that God was on their side. Even essentials such as prayer (the words used, the postures assumed) might vary in details between different communities. How to determine the prescriptions of sharia was a much more complex, and contentious, question, one on which Muslim scholars would continually disagree. As for the *dar al-islam*, it might be a mighty empire, or it might be a small community of pious believers, living apart from others and seeing themselves (whatever anyone else said) as the only true Muslims in a sea of unbelief. There was never complete agreement between Muslims about where Islam's boundaries lay; there was never a single, homogenous Muslim world.

Fourteen hundred years after it first came into the world, Islam today is a global force in other ways, and Muslims' worlds have grown and diversified even further. In 2010, the world's Muslim population stood at 1.6 billion, or just under a quarter of its people. It was projected to grow to 2.8 billion by 2050: almost 30 per cent of the global population. In 2010, more than 60 per cent of the world's Muslims lived in Asia. Indonesia was the most populous Muslim country, and the three major countries of the Indian subcontinent (India, Pakistan, and Bangladesh) between them accounted for almost a third of all the world's Muslims. Only one-fifth of all Muslims lived in the faith's historic "central lands" in the Middle East and North Africa. About the same number, another fifth of all Muslims or some three hundred million people, lived in countries where Islam was not the majority religion. By 2050, the most significant proportional growth in Muslim populations is expected to be in Africa (which could become home to a quarter of the world's Muslims), Europe (where European Muslims may become 10 per cent of the population), and North America (where Muslim Americans might make up 2 per cent of the entire population). By the twenty-first century, the worlds of Islam—in the simple sense of places where Muslims live, and the ways they live their lives—encompassed Jakarta, Indonesia, and Toledo, Ohio; Cape Town, South Africa, and Stockholm, Sweden. They connected the corners of the globe, from Australia to Canada, from Argentina to China. Along with the movement of people, ideas, goods, money, communications, and technology, they have grown to encompass almost the entire geographical globe.[2]

This book is about these many worlds that Muslims have inhabited: the cultures and communities, the states and societies, in which their lives were lived, and their place in a wider, shared and connected, global history. Understanding Islam in global history means exploring what being Muslim has meant in these different times and places, and how those meanings have changed. This book tells that story. It explores how Islam came into being, and how being Muslim became modern.

◇◇◇◇◇◇◇◇

There is an old and well-known argument about Muslims and modern history, an argument often referred to as "Orientalism." Nineteenth-century European thinkers, and twentieth-century writers after them, divided the world and its peoples into discrete units, civilisations defined by religious or racial belonging—and often folded religious affiliation, or culture, into what was then imagined as inherent racial identity. In the nineteenth-century age of European imperialism, this reordering of humanity into racial categories, and the narration of history as a tale of the rise and fall of their associated civilisations, became enormously popular. Like many ideas manufactured in the nineteenth century, it continues to shape many people's thinking about the world today.

This view of things assumed that there was a single, monolithic Muslim world, historically distinct from the rest of the world and, especially, separate from an equally monolithic Euro-American West. In this view, modernity—the modern world, modern values, and modern life—belonged exclusively to the West, and to its separate history and civilisation (meaning, essentially, that they were European, North American, and, implicitly, "white"). Islam and modernity, in contrast, did not seem to fit: if modernity was seen as a Western property, it was also a Western "challenge," one that Muslims, allegedly, failed to meet. This idea of "the Muslim world," and the concomitant idea of a "single, pure" West, became ideologically powerful, dominating understandings of world history and Islam for much of the twentieth century.[3]

But despite its public prominence, it was largely discredited, at least among historians of Asia, Africa, and the Middle East, by newer scholarship that emerged between the 1970s and 1990s. It could, by then, be seen as just one aspect of a nineteenth-century version of history that Europeans in the age of empire had told to explain their world, and their control of it, both to themselves and to everyone else. (Importantly, it also obscured earlier, much more complex and often sympathetic, European understandings of Asia that had flourished in the eighteenth century.) By the early 2000s, such versions of the West's own history as a self-contained and superior civilisation were not taken seriously by most historians of Europe and the Americas either. Historians came to see modernity not as a simple set of wholly owned ideas and institutions, created in isolation by Western genius and exported to the rest of the world, but as a complex and contradictory global condition, emerging over a much longer timescale in the entangled webs of Europe's relations with the rest of the world, and setting the terms by which the world would be obliged to live.[4]

The "Orientalist" account of Islamic history seemed polemical and contrarian in the 1990s, when it was reasserted by more conservative scholars reviving the older vision of world history as civilisational competition and conflict. In the aftermath of the Cold War, it was Islam above all that replaced communism as the nightmare enemy of their imagined, "single, pure" West. Meanwhile, some conservative Muslims, and especially Islamists—adherents of Islam not only as a religious faith but as a political ideology—had embraced the flipside of this vision. They also believed in a world divided into opposing civilisations; they imagined their version of a separate, self-contained, "authentic" Islam as the solution to all the modern world's problems.[5]

After the terror attacks of 9/11, this belief in inevitable antagonism between Islam and the West gained a much wider public. In the years that followed, it became even more insistent and more mainstream.

To neoconservative commentators, it is a bluntly realistic view, an honest way of "looking the world in the eye." Some make a virtue of proclaiming it, believing themselves to be courageous warriors for free speech by doing so, and seeing themselves as defenders of an embattled Western civilisation under attack from both Islamic aggression and liberal self-criticism. This may be more self-promoting paranoid fantasy than historically informed, judicious realism, but that has not prevented it from selling well. The volume of talk and writing in the news, politics, and punditry pushing myths and stereotypes about Islam is immense. Much of it must practically write itself, so easy has it become for what the historian Mahmood Mamdani calls "culture talk" about Islam—the belief that the West creatively and diversely makes culture, but that Muslims are trapped in and defined by Islam as a single, unchanging culture—to replicate itself.[6]

Orientalism has thus become part of the conflict that it claims to explain: the more people believe its claims, the more it makes its own predictions come true. Rather than a statement of hard facts, it has in fact become one of the modern world's most tenacious myths. Like other myths, it is a fiction that has real effects. It has been able to make its own predictions come true, in part, by demonising already vulnerable minorities and contributing to a climate of violence across the world, influencing disaffected young Muslims, opportunistic politicians, and a wide range of opinion in the United States and Europe, from secularist leftists through mainstream conservatives to the extremes of the alt-right. It also finds echoes in similar anti-Muslim rhetoric in other parts of the world, notably in communist China and Hindu-nationalist India. We will have to return to it, and to its effects on Muslim lives from border control in the United States to "re-education" camps in Xinjiang and street violence in Delhi, at the end of our story.

This book makes a different argument. Modernity, as a shared and profoundly unequal condition, was made in a shifting pattern of relationships in the world economy and global politics, linking the Atlantic world, Africa, Asia, and the Pacific. Muslims did not stand outside this process. On the contrary, Islam's place in the world has been part of how the world—with all its frictions and inequalities, its struggles and aspirations—became modern. And correspondingly, Islam as it exists today—and all the different things it can mean—is a product of that modern world, a product of the uneven, connected global history of states and societies, trade and empire, war and capitalism, technology and mobility, that made the world modern. This book, then, is about how Islam, as a set of ideas, practices and laws, a vision of history and of the future, a way of living one's life and of defining one's place in the world, has been bound up with the other great world-historical forces with which it has interacted, shaping them and being reshaped by them, over the whole of its history.

◇◇◇◇◇◇◇

From the perspective of its believers Islam is a timeless truth. Historical understanding, though, looks to what changes over time. Islam has always existed in particular times and places, and in the minds and actions of particular people. As the Islamic scholar Shahab Ahmed has written, Muslims have always, both at any one time and across time, "made Islam, thought Islam, and lived Islam in quite contrary ways." Indeed, as he puts it, Islam has been "a human and historical phenomenon characterized and constituted, not merely by immense variety and diversity, but by the prodigious presence of outright contradiction." The fact that some Muslims, and some interpretations of what Islam means, have created al-Qaʿida or Daesh (Islamic State), while others resolutely oppose them, does not mean that any of their actions and beliefs show what Islam really is. What they do show is what Islam, for particular people in particular circumstances in the modern world, has come to mean. What we need to understand is how that has happened.[7]

Being Muslim became modern not only in diverse but in contradictory ways. From its emergence in the seventh century to its consolidation across Eurasia in the twelfth century, Islam made its own world, but it was always part of other worlds too. It became a new religion, but it claimed to be the only true religion there had ever been. Muslims absorbed scientific and philosophical learning, economic and social institutions (like enslaved labour and veiled women) and cultural and political values (like the enjoyment of wine and the near-divinity of an emperor) from Greek, Latin, and Persian antiquity; and they created their own, new ways of learning and living, sometimes claiming that nothing was legitimate besides the exact way of life followed by the Prophet Muhammad and his companions in seventh-century Arabia. They began as a persecuted community bound together for mutual defence; they built powerful, conservatively monarchical states whose rulers claimed to be God's shadow on earth; they believed in the end of tyranny and the coming of justice and they repeatedly became revolutionaries.

From the thirteenth century to the eighteenth, Islam reached out across oceans and deserts to create its own new worlds—much more peacefully, on the whole, than how Europeans created theirs—and while the world of Islam thus expanded, it also fragmented. Through trade routes, navigation, migration, and cultural exchange, it created a network of early modern globalisation across Eurasia; and it broke apart into warring empires even before Europeans entered that network and began to capture it. While Islam was still expanding geographically, across West Africa and Southeast Asia, in the eighteenth century, many of its thinkers began to worry that Muslims had lost their way, and needed radical reform if they and their societies were to be saved. Just as more people in more places than ever before were becoming Muslim, some reformers and revivalists began to claim that most Muslims were not really Muslim at all.

In the nineteenth and twentieth centuries, Muslims' worlds became disordered and reordered as never before. Europe's comparative advantages in accumulating wealth, science, and organised violence radically unbalanced older, less uneven relations across the world, and those on the wrong side of the new, global imbalance of power found themselves subject to European guns and money—and excised from Europe's own narrative of itself as the sole agent of modern history.

Capitalism and the global market, the modern state and mechanised war, imperialism and colonial rule, nationalism and revolution, scientific knowledge and religious revival, commodities and consumerism, communication and migration all interacted with Islam through the ways Muslims experienced and participated in them, sometimes embracing their promises and possibilities, sometimes suffering their effects of dispossession, displacement, and destruction.

Islam, and its interaction with these other world-historical forces, has shaped what being modern looks like for many people across the globe, from Bangladesh and Afghanistan to Britain and America. In telling this story, this book aims to bridge the very wide gap—which in recent years has become wider—between the rich and detailed specialist scholarship on Islam and global history, and the white noise of public debate, news and commentary about Islam and what it means in the world. As the faith or the cultural identity, the heritage of the past or the guide to the future, of a quarter of humanity, Islam matters in crucial ways to all of us, Muslim or non-Muslim, today. This book explores worlds that have been part of making the wider world in which we all live, and the troubled present in which we are all, together, concerned.

Part 1

ISLAM IN THE WORLD
600–1200 CE

1

A WORLD AMONG OTHERS, A WORLD IN ITSELF

Outside the city of Mecca, in what today is Saudi Arabia, at the very top of the bare, rounded rock of Mount Hira, also called Jabal al-Nour, the "Mountain of Light," there is a narrow cave a few metres deep. Here, Muslim tradition tells us, the archangel Gabriel revealed the first words of the Qur'an (the "Recitation"), a message direct from God, to a man named Muhammad. A merchant from Mecca, about forty years old, Muhammad (whose name means "the praised one") had taken to seeking solitude and reflection in the mountains around his hometown. It was here that angelic messengers began to speak to him. The first revelation was an alarming injunction to "recite," which at first Muhammad himself did not understand:

> Recite! In the name of your Lord who created
> Created humankind from a clot of blood
> Recite! For your Lord is the Most Bountiful
> Who taught by the pen
> Taught humankind what it did not know.[1]

Such short, fragmentary, and poetic revelations would multiply. They were joined by exhortations to social justice and fair dealing, scathing criticism of the abuse of power by the strong over the weak, reminders of God's grace and compassion, evocations of God's blessings and the paradise that awaited believers, and warnings to Muhammad's people, the polytheist Arabs of Mecca and its surroundings, that they should abandon their idols and worship only the one true God, or else face a terrible doom on the coming Day of Judgment. Soon, Muhammad's preaching of this message would gain followers, first among his own family and then in the wider community of Mecca. Muhammad would become the Prophet of Islam.

In Islamic accounts of universal history, the beginning of God's revelation to Muhammad was a moment in which divine truth touched the world, in a small place from which God's great message went out to humanity. If we see it as an event in human history, rather than as an act of divine intervention, though, Islam—the religion that would grow from Muhammad's message and that would define his followers as Muslims—did not come into the world fully formed. Nor did it arise in an empty space. It was shaped by dramatic, world-shaking events, by conquest and conversion, by poets and princes and the stories they wanted told, as well as by the original message of the Prophet. It emerged in the world of late antiquity: in Southwest Asia and the eastern Mediterranean, between the third and the eighth centuries CE. This was a world shaped by religious and political plurality and competition, but where the competition was played out through claims to universal sovereignty and beliefs in one supreme creator God. It was dominated by the Roman and Persian Empires, competing claimants to rule over what they both thought of as all the known world.

Mecca was a place out on the edge of this world, far from its capital cities and distant from its concerns—but what happened there, in the early decades of the seventh century, would transform it. And if we want to understand how Islam came into the world, we need to begin with the world into which it came.[2]

◇◇◇◇◇◇◇

The late Roman, or Byzantine, Empire had been ruled since the fourth century from the great city of Constantinople, modern Istanbul. Founded on the Bosphorus by the Emperor Constantine, whose toleration of Christianity allowed the church to expand, Constantinople was the capital of an eastern Roman Empire that flourished while the western empire fell apart. Its rulers and inhabitants thought of their state and society as continuous with that of classical Rome, albeit redeemed from what they now considered to have been classical Rome's pagan polytheism. For all that they now mostly spoke and wrote in Greek, Aramaic, or Syriac rather than in Latin, they still had an emperor and a senate, and they still saw themselves as Romans. In Athens, at least until the sixth century, and in Alexandria for longer, they still discussed the philosophy of Plato and Aristotle, while at Nicaea (now Iznik, in Turkey) and Chalcedon (now, as Kadiköy, part of urban Istanbul) they debated the nature of Christ and the relationship between God the Father and the Son.

Long before the Great Schism that would split Christianity into separate eastern (later called Orthodox) and western (Roman Catholic) churches in the eleventh century, the faith was already divided by deep theological rifts. Confessional conflict became politically sensitive, and the imperial government began to do something Roman emperors had never done before: endorse one true, or orthodox (literally, "correctly believing"), religion, and declare that deviations from it were heresies, forbidden and punishable. Among ordinary believers, most of whom could not read the Bible, let alone doctrinal disputations, everyday religion was more about community and locality than ideology and authority. But bishops and patriarchs competed to have their own doctrines endorsed by the state and recognised among the people. The growing, centralised strength of the empire, indeed, meant that religious power was more important than ever to the emperor. Since the end of the Julio-Claudian dynasty in the first century CE, Rome's caesars had usually needed to be actively campaigning generals. But by the 400s, the eastern empire was more secure. The emperor could rule from his palace in Constantinople and, as one historian vividly put it, "proclaim his status by presiding over Christian ceremonies, like a glorious spider at the centre of a web." The Roman Empire was now an empire of faith.[3]

To the Romans' east lay the Persian Empire, stretching from the Euphrates and the Caucasus to the Oxus and the Indian Ocean. Its capital was Ctesiphon on the River Tigris, part of a network of cities on either side of the river, south of where Arab Muslims would later build Baghdad. Here, in the "black land" between the Tigris and the Euphrates, was the empire's wealthiest area, made rich by the productivity of the rivers' fertile alluvial soils. Since the early third century CE, Persia had been ruled by the Sasanian dynasty, a family claiming the inheritance of Iran's ancient rulers and the authority of divine kingship. Its mission was to reunite the peoples of Iran who had been divided between rival claimants to the throne and defeated by invading Romans, whose armies had twice sacked Ctesiphon at the end of the second century.

Once, under the Achaemenid dynasty at the end of the sixth century BCE, the Persian Empire had controlled all of the territory westward from the Iranian plateau to the eastern Mediterranean, Egypt, and Anatolia. While the Sasanians could not equal such ambitions, like the inheritors of Rome they nonetheless had their own ideas of universal empire. The Sasanian rulers took the title *shahanshah*, "king of kings," even styling themselves rulers "of Iran and non-Iran." Iran, in the ideology of its rulers and priests, was the bastion of settled civilisation, against "Turan," the nomadic world beyond. In the dynasty's religion, Zoroastrianism, the principle of order always had to struggle against the opposing principle of chaos: the sacred fire had to be kept alight to keep at bay the darkness beyond. Zoroastrianism might also, in this period, have been developing a tendency towards monotheism, with the priesthood presenting the creator god, Ahura Mazda, as supreme over lesser deities that were being reimagined as angels, intermediary beings between God and men.

Unlike Byzantine Christianity, Zoroastrianism was never made the official state religion. The Sasanian Empire was religiously plural: Jews, Christians, Buddhists, and polytheists were all to be found among its inhabitants. Sasanian shahs were commemorated for defending "good religion" and stamping out heresy, but persecutions, when they occurred, were more likely to be politically than religiously motivated: Christians were attacked when there was war with Rome. But although there was no official religion, religion was tremendously important for politics. Under the Sasanians, Zoroastrianism was closely associated with the ruling dynasty, legitimating the shahs' kingship and benefiting from their protection. Each new king's accession was marked by the kindling of a sacred fire, which would be kept alight throughout his reign. Sasanian coins illustrated the close ties between eternal and worldly power by displaying the throne of the shahs alongside the fire of the Zoroastrian priesthood.[4]

These two great cultures and states—the "world's two eyes," in the words of the Persian Emperor Khusraw II to his Byzantine counterpart, the Emperor Maurice, whose daughter he would marry—divided between them the lands of ancient, settled civilisation that stretched from the Mediterranean east across the Fertile Crescent to the Iranian plateau and beyond towards northwest India. North of both, across the Danube, the Black Sea, the Caucasus and the Caspian Sea, was another world of unsettled, roving nomads, a world that played by its own rules and that was always seen from the settled cities, by their kings and their scribes, as a threat. South was the great desert, the Sahara, and the Indian Ocean. And between the two empires, tucked in the peninsula between the Red Sea with its Roman shipping, and the Persian Gulf with its communities of Christians, was Arabia, where sometime in the late sixth century the man who would become the Prophet Muhammad was born.[5]

◇◇◇◇◇◇◇

Arabia lay south of the Fertile Crescent, which arced between the wealthy cities of Roman Syria and Palestine to the west, and the heart of the Sasanian domains to the east. Mountains ringed this area in a semicircle to the north—from the eastern Mediterranean coastline up through the Taurus and Caucasus to the Zagros in the east. More mountains and rocky coastline divided it from the Indian Ocean to the south, from Yemen, facing Africa, in the southwest through to Oman, facing India, in the southeast. The peninsula's people spoke and wrote inscriptions mostly in Arabic, and their language had a rich and poetic oral literature. Material life, though, was hard. Thinly inhabited, and mostly mountainous, rocky steppe and desert terrain, the region had fertile pockets where higher mountain rainfall, especially in Yemen, or oasis cultivation made farming and settled life possible. But within its circle of mountain and sea, the interior of Arabia was beyond the control of any state. Social and political order here was kept by the relative equality and reciprocal respect observed between tribes, and between their leaders, who held their positions by a combination of recognised merit, election, force of personality and, to a lesser extent, birth.

The tribe was an agglomeration of extended families or clans who identified themselves and their interests with each other, claiming descent from a common male ancestor, whether real or (perhaps more usually) imagined. A tribe might be quite stable over a long period of time, but clan groups might also join or disappear from tribes, or confederations of tribes, at different times. By necessity, if they followed a mostly nomadic lifestyle, they usually lived in much smaller groups. But the language and symbolism of common ancestry allowed people to claim rights and responsibilities towards each other, and to organise their relations of marriage, inheritance, and solidarity. Alliances were essential for survival. An offence against one of the group would be an insult to all, and might be avenged accordingly—tribal life was not lawless, but ruled by customary law. When violence led to death, retaliation was required unless blood money was accepted as redress. Organised violence in the form of retribution or raiding between tribal groups redistributed resources, including people who could be enslaved, and schooled men in the practices of warfare and the codes of masculinity.

The tribe's public life and culture was predominantly male and patriarchal. Healthy male children who could grow up to be herdsmen and fighters were prized; baby girls were sometimes killed. Female infanticide may not have been common, but it seems—because the

Qur'an specifically condemns it—that it occurred. Freeborn women might own property in their own right: the Muslim tradition would record that Khadija, Muhammad's wife at the time of the first revelations, had been a wealthy widow whose commercial interests Muhammad managed before he became her husband. A family's virtue and propriety rested on the protection and relative seclusion of freeborn women, and the warrior virtues of free men. Women may have been present on the battlefield, encouraging their men with drums and poetry, but it was especially when their brothers or husbands fell in battle that women gained a public voice, in elegies of ritual mourning and exhortation to blood vengeance.[6]

Arabia was named after the *arab*, the nomadic, Arabic-speaking Bedouin: one such nomadic group, the Tayyi or Banu Tayy, would give Christian writers further north the Syriac word *tayyaye*, which could mean "nomad," and by which they named both Arabic-speaking Christians and the Muslim Arab conquerors who would sweep out of the peninsula in the mid-seventh century. But most of Arabia's inhabitants were probably settled in towns and oases, at least for part of the year. Perhaps only a small proportion of the region's people were actually nomadic or semi-nomadic herders, and they lived in close connection with the sedentary population. Raising camels or, especially in the north near Syria and Palestine, sheep and goats, and moving with their flocks and herds following seasonal patterns of pasture and trade, they exchanged what they could raise or grow themselves with what they could obtain at markets from artisans, agriculturalists, and merchants settled in towns.[7]

Such markets often depended for their security on religious norms that forbade violence in the vicinity of a shrine, or within the perimeter of a sacred enclave called a *haram*. The absence of any governing authority meant that shared respect for such norms—sometimes upheld by a local religious family connected to a particular holy site and recognised as its guardians—was especially important. Mecca, in the Hijaz, or "curtain," the western edge of Arabia along the line of mountains that separates the interior desert from the Red Sea, was one such place. A market and a sanctuary, it was a town whose significance was both commercial and religious. As a trading town, its own economy seems to have included both bulk export trade in animals and animal products, especially leather that may have supplied the Byzantine army in Syria, and the mining and export of precious metals. It had come to be dominated by the Quraysh, an Arab tribe whose different clans would become key players in the developing history of Islam. It was to one of these clans, the Hashim, that in or around the year 570 CE, Muhammad was born. The Quraysh had established themselves, perhaps a few generations before Muhammad's time, as the guardians of the Ka'ba, the shrine at the centre of Mecca's holy sanctuary. It was probably thanks to the regional importance of the Ka'ba that Mecca had grown into a significant market town.[8]

The heart of one of Arabia's most sacred enclaves, the Ka'ba itself— a simple, cubic, stone-built structure—was an ancient holy place. In Muslim tradition it is associated with the biblical patriarch, Abraham, who with his son Ishmael is said to have built it as "the House of God." The idea of a single, supreme creator God clearly existed already in polytheistic Mecca: Muhammad would call on his hearers to return to the one God they already recognised, and not falsely to associate partners in divinity with Him. Before Muhammad's time, Abraham was identified in Arabia both as the progenitor of the Arabs, through his son Ishmael, and as the original monotheist. It was to Abraham that God had first revealed the true religion. It was Abraham who instituted the ritual worship of God through pilgrimage to the Ka'ba. The Qur'an, the recitation of God's revelations to Muhammad, would repeatedly refer to Abraham as "the *hanif*," meaning "one who turns." *Hanif* came to connote one who shuns evil: one who is upright, sound in faith. When Muhammad began preaching, what he preached was, he said, "the faith of Abraham, the upright (*hanif*), who was not one of the polytheists."[9]

But the Ka'ba had come to be sacred to several deities worshipped by the people of Arabia. Some of these were represented by idols kept in the sanctuary itself: in preaching a return to Abraham's religion,

Muhammad would take particular exception to the presence of these idols in God's House. The first Muslims would pray towards Jerusalem, the Holy City to the north that was already sacred to Jews and Christians, but while Muhammad was still alive the Muslims' direction of prayer, the *qibla*, would be changed to face Mecca and the Kaʿba, marking the centrality of the ancient sanctuary to the emerging faith.

The regional importance of pilgrimage to the Kaʿba, and the safety that its sanctity guaranteed, made Mecca a profitable marketplace. But the town itself had few other advantages. Set in a rocky, arid valley, its people depended on wells for their water and on trade for their food. One place food came from was the large oasis town of Yathrib to the northeast, a very ancient settlement that dated back, perhaps, to the seventh century BCE. Set among irrigated fields and date palm groves, Yathrib was inhabited by a mixed community of Jewish and polytheist families. It was from Yathrib, when Muhammad's preaching in Mecca had begun to gain him a reputation as a holy man, that a delegation came to ask him to arbitrate in a local dispute.

In Mecca, at the same time, Muhammad's message had begun to arouse hostility among his own tribe, the Quraysh, and their allies. The Kaʿba and its associated markets were important business interests, and Muhammad's preaching against the deities revered there was unwelcome. Nor did the Meccans appreciate his dire warnings of judgment from God, laced with social criticism:

You show no kindness to the orphan
And do not urge one another to feed the poor
Greedily you eat up the inheritance of others
You love wealth fervently.
But when the earth is crushed to dust upon dust
And your Lord comes with the angels, rank upon rank
And when on that day Hell is brought forth, then will human-
     kind remember
But what good will it do to remember?[10]

Fearing persecution, some of Muhammad's earliest followers had already fled from Mecca across the Red Sea, hoping to find sympathy and shelter with their fellow monotheists, the Christians of Axum in Ethiopia. In 622 CE, facing threats to his own safety, Muhammad departed for Yathrib, accompanied only by his father-in-law Abu Bakr, who had been one of his first followers and companions. This was the event that would become known as the *hijra*, Muhammad's "emigration" from a place of unbelief to a space that would be safe for true believers. There he joined other believers who had fled from Mecca, and who would be known in Yathrib as the *muhajirun*, the "emigrants." Along with the Prophet's supporters, or "helpers" (*ansar*) among the people of the town, they would become the first Muslim community.

Over the following years, Muhammad's leadership of this community, its growing strength and significance, and his death there ten years after the hijra would transform the town to which they had come. One of Muhammad's first documented acts was to declare part of Yathrib a *haram*, a sacred enclave like that of Mecca, asserting the importance of the town, and both its and Muhammad's independence from the Meccans. Soon, the town would cease to be called Yathrib. It became known instead as *madinat al-nabi*, "the Prophet's city," or simply "the city," *al-madina*: Medina.[11]

◇◇◇◇◇◇◇

Over the centuries that followed, both Mecca and Medina would come to be revered as holy places to Muslims; their historical importance would come to equal that of Constantinople or Ctesiphon. In the seventh century, though, Mecca and Medina were still on the fringe of the late ancient imperial world. Arabia was ruled by none of its neighbours; nonetheless, it by no means existed in isolation. Both the Byzantines and the Sasanians had clients among the Arab populations on the fringes of their territories: the Ghassanids, or Jafnids, in the northwest (the area that today is the kingdom of Jordan) being allied with the Byzantines, and the Lakhmids, or Nasrids (in what is now southwest Iraq), with the Persians. These groups created buffer zones between the two empires, and between each of them and the Arabian interior, but imperial ambitions sometimes intruded more directly. The Romans had sent an expedition through western Arabia to Yemen and maintained a garrison on the Farasan Islands in the Red Sea. The Persians, correspondingly, found support among Jewish and polytheist communities as far away as Yemen. The Byzantines considered the Christian kingdom of Axum in Ethiopia as an ally against Persia, but the Ethiopian kings had their own designs on southern Arabia. The rulers of Yemen, ancient Himyar, where some Arab tribes had converted to Judaism in the fourth century, launched a persecution of local Christians in 523 CE, and two years later an Ethiopian Christian army invaded across the Red Sea in response. The Ethiopian general, Abraha, set up his own kingdom in Yemen, built a great church at Sanaa, and marched northward, seeking to extend Ethiopian rule into Arabia. But under his sons, his kingdom fell apart. By 560 CE, Ethiopian rule was replaced in Yemen by Sasanian influence.

Muhammad's Arabia was thus a frontier zone between contending world empires. Trade routes between the Indian Ocean and the eastern Mediterranean skirted it and passed through it; imperial armies had never conquered it but were not unknown there. Jewish, Christian, and polytheist religions and their political associations both surrounded and inhabited it. Jewish groups, perhaps originally refugees from the Roman destruction of Jerusalem in the first century, had settled in the Hijaz. To both north and south there were Arab converts to Christianity and Judaism, apparently well integrated into Arabian tribal society alongside the predominant polytheists in the desert and its towns. The gods of Arab polytheism sometimes echoed, at least in their representation as statues, the gods and goddesses of ancient Greece and Rome: in the Syrian city of Palmyra, the Arabian goddess Allat was portrayed as Greek Athena. South of the Hijaz, the ancient Arabs' belief in many gods may have been giving way, from the fourth century—at the same time as some Arabs in Yemen became Jewish, and Ethiopians in Axum became Christian—to devotion to one supreme God, named in inscriptions as "al-Rahman," the compassionate. This would be one of the "beautiful names" of the one God proclaimed by Muhammad.[12]

In this wider world beyond Arabia, the era in which Muhammad lived was dramatic. Indeed, there seemed to be nothing less than a world crisis raging across the sixth and seventh centuries, against the backdrop of which an imminent end of time and the advent of a Day of Judgment were all too vividly imaginable. Such images were part of Muhammad's own preaching:

> *When the sky is torn asunder*
> *And when the stars are scattered*
> *And when the seas burst forth*
> *And when the graves spill out*
> *Then will each soul know what it has done and left undone.*[13]

They appear in Christian visions too. Monks and chroniclers of the seventh century saw world events as reflecting divine judgment on sinful humanity, and when a destructive superpower war was followed within a few years by the Arab conquests, and then the turmoil of civil wars between the new rulers, it seemed to them too that the end was at hand. "The end of the ages has arrived for us.... Here are famines, earthquakes and plagues," wrote the Syriac chronicler John Bar Penkaye in 687 or 688. According to an apocalyptic text that survives from a few years later:

> God shall send forth a mighty wind, the southern one, and there shall come forth from it a people.... And there shall rise up from among them a warrior and one whom they call a prophet, and they shall be brought into his hands.... And the South shall prosper, and by the hooves of the horses of its armies it shall trample down and subdue Persia and devastate Rome.[14]

Historians with more secular sensibilities, too, have often described this period in cataclysmic terms: as the fall of civilisation, the beginning of dark ages. When we look at this crisis of the late ancient world in the longer term, what is surprising is perhaps not just the degree of change that came out of it but the extent to which much also remained largely as before. Sudden changes on the surface—who ruled, and in whose name—overlaid much slower and more gradual currents of transition and adaptation in the social and religious lives of ordinary people. It is clear, nonetheless, that these were times of tribulation.

The first factor in the crisis was plague. The sixth and seventh centuries saw the world's first recorded plague pandemic. (The Black Death that began in the fourteenth century and lingered in the Mediterranean until the nineteenth was the second; the third, centred in South and Southeast Asia, occurred in the first half of the twentieth century.) It is often referred to as the "Justinianic" plague, after the Roman Emperor Justinian during whose reign, in 541, the outbreak was recorded. (The emperor himself contracted, and survived, the disease.) Cataclysmic though it might sound, the sixth-century plague was probably in fact much less destabilising overall than has sometimes been thought. Some estimates have claimed that between a third and two-thirds of the affected population, which would have stretched from the eastern Mediterranean through to southern France and Germany—anything from fifteen to one hundred million people—may have died, but these assessments seem highly exaggerated. If there was a sudden, severe mid-sixth-century death toll in the eastern provinces of the Roman Empire, cities and their populations in Anatolia, Syria and Palestine seem to have recovered, and indeed grown rapidly, shortly afterwards. Without underestimating the suffering the plague must have caused, arguments that it had a catastrophic and long-term impact seem to have overstated the extent of the pandemic, and underestimated states' and societies' capacity to adapt to it.

Other environmental factors, especially a cooling climate following a series of volcanic eruptions, again in the 530s and 540s CE, may have impacted agricultural production and the societies that depended on it (evidence in tree rings from the Alps to northern central Asia suggests that summers here became colder). It is unlikely, though, that the changing climate had a uniformly negative impact across the whole of the eastern Roman Empire. Regional microclimates across the eastern Mediterranean and southwest Asia were much too variable to have been affected in the same way by a "little Ice Age," the severity of which is in any case unclear. But after centuries of agricultural expansion and increasing prosperity in the late Roman world, between the mid-500s and the late 600s, plague and the changing climate do seem to have made life somewhat harder and livelihoods more precarious.[15]

The second, and certainly greater, crisis was a superpower war, a confrontation that pitted Persia against Rome and lasted twenty-five years. The Roman-Persian conflict from 603 to 628 was the ancient world's "last great war," the culmination of centuries of frontier warfare between the two empires. Sporadic conflict had moved back and forth from Armenia in the north to Arabia in the south, without one of the combatants ever seriously threatening the other's survival. This time was different. The war broke out in 603, a few years before the first angelic messages came to Muhammad in Mecca, when a coup d'état in Constantinople overthrew the Emperor Maurice, and the Shah Khusraw II seized the opportunity, declaring that he would reinstate a legitimate ruler over Byzantium. His troops overran the richest Roman provinces in Syria and Egypt, occupied Jerusalem, carried off the relics of the True Cross, and threatened the heart of the empire in Anatolia. By 626 Constantinople was under siege by the Persians and their allies, and it seemed as though the seven-hundred-year-old Roman Empire might be near death.[16]

To the Byzantines, Persia's offensive threatened not only the inheritance of Rome but the empire of Christ on earth. For the first time, they declared a holy war in defence of the true faith, promising the martyr's crown and direct entry into paradise for all those who fell in the struggle. Under their new emperor, Heraclius, a Roman army allied with Turkish-speaking nomads from the northeast staged a spectacular counterattack. Outflanking the Persians via the Black Sea, Heraclius's troops crossed the Caucasus Mountains and marched directly on Ctesiphon. In 628, with the enemy almost at his gates, Khusraw II was overthrown by a palace coup, and his successors negotiated peace with the Byzantines, giving up all the territory the Persians had conquered over the previous two decades. The fragments of the True Cross were returned in triumph to Jerusalem.

News of the war and of the Persians' early victories in Syria had travelled south into Arabia, and was echoed in the revelations being recounted in Mecca by Muhammad:

The Romans have been defeated
In a land close by
But after their defeat, they will triumph
Within a few years. Before and afterward, the matter rests with
  God. And on that day, the believers will rejoice
  At victory from God. He makes victorious whomever He wills.
  He is the Almighty, the Merciful.[17]

God was with the Romans, for now. But a new community of believers was coming into being, and they would come to see themselves as the inheritors of Rome, of Jerusalem, and of Persia too.

◇◇◇◇◇◇◇

The agreements made by Muhammad, his followers, and the people of Medina for the regulation of their life together survive in some of the very earliest pieces of documentary evidence in Islamic history. Yathrib and the other nearby oasis settlements had probably been under some degree of Sasanian authority in the mid-sixth century. But when Muhammad arrived, there was no longer any external authority, and Yathrib's different factions seem to have been feuding with one another from their fortified tower houses. While he may have been called upon initially to act in the customary role of an arbiter of tribal disputes, Muhammad soon went much further, instituting a political order in the town that both built on existing custom and created something dramatically new, even revolutionary.

What would become the community of Islam began as a set of alliances for mutual defence, drawn up in the recognised terms of Arabian social norms. These have become known as the "Constitution of Medina." The Qurayshi emigrants from Mecca and the inhabitants of Yathrib were to "keep to their own tribal organisation and leadership," each with their existing responsibilities to pay blood money, divided equitably between them, in case of feud, and to ransom prisoners according to custom. They were to fight together to defend themselves and each other against outside attack. This recognised the existing rights, duties, and leadership of the different groups who would now be living together in Medina.

But the Medinan agreements did something more. Muhammad also declared that the parties to the agreement, "the believers and the Muslims from the Quraysh and Yathrib, and those who follow them as clients, join them, reside with them, and strive along with them," would from now on be "a single community, apart from other people." This community's cohesion, and loyalty to it, would take precedence for its members over family or tribal affiliation. They would act together against anyone who rebelled, or who acted corruptly, unjustly, or treacherously against the community, "even if he is the son of one of them." Blood relatives from outside the community could not be avenged against anyone within it. Conversely, anyone who joined the community and left their old tribal ties behind would benefit instead from the community's protection. This was more than just the solidarity of a new kind of tribe; it was "the protection of God," guaranteed by the leadership of God's Prophet, Muhammad. And the community existed both for its own self-defence against hostile outsiders, especially the unbelieving Quraysh of Mecca, and for the purpose of offensively "fighting in the path of God." Their blood that might be shed, and that might henceforward need to be avenged, would not be the blood of kin spilled in mere tribal feuds, but blood sacrifice to a much higher purpose, one the Romans, in their holy war with Persia, would readily have recognised: "blood shed in the path of God."[18]

While Muhammad's community existed for following and fighting in God's way, it was not yet composed exclusively of Muslims. Indeed, at this point, who exactly the first Muslims were and what they believed is not entirely clear. What is clear is that both polytheists who lived in Medina and, in what was perhaps a subsequent addition to the original pact, some of Yathrib's existing Jewish community were also made part of this "single community" (*umma wahida*). In these documents, the Arabic word *umma*, "community," clearly already means a community bound together against "unbelievers" (*kuffar*), but it included polytheists (*mushrikun*) and Jews. The word *umma* would only later come to denote the community of Muslims distinct from the followers of all other religions.

The agreements made at Medina are especially important because they show how, in the first years of Muhammad's constitution of a new community, it was religiously inclusive, and the terms that would later define belonging and belief were not clearly settled and demarcated. The texts speak of *muslimun*, literally "those who submit [to God]," which gives us the English word *Muslims*, but also of *mu'minun*, literally "the faithful," or "believers." This term also later came to mean Muslims, but it originally perhaps referred to "the faithful covenanters," those who subscribed to the community's covenant (or pact), pledging their faith to God, the Prophet, and one another.[19] They were faithful, that is, to their promise of mutual protection. Being part of this community did not necessarily imply a single set of beliefs. And indeed, over time, while the boundaries of belonging to the Muslim community would become much sharper, as in any human community it would always be possible for different people to be part of the community while believing different things.

This new social organisation revolutionised the kin-based, tribal pattern of local conflict and solidarity in Arabia. It created a new community of the faithful that was bound together by common obligations and driven to struggle together "in God's path," under Muhammad's leadership, against unbelief and God's enemies. This was a movement born out of its own late ancient context, and with universal potential. Muhammad was no longer only a visionary preacher who proclaimed the truth of one God and the return to the true religion of Abraham, denouncing polytheism, female infanticide, and other tribal customs now disparaged as "ignorance." (The Arabic word for ignorance, *jahiliyya*, would come to denote the beliefs of paganism, and the era before the revelation of Islam.) He was the military leader of a community, the arbiter of disputes and dispenser of justice within that community, and the head of a revolutionary movement.

This movement was aimed especially against Muhammad's enemies among the Quraysh of Mecca and their allies. Over the next eight years, there would be sporadic warfare between Medina and Mecca. Fighting mostly took the form of raids by a few dozen fighters, but also of running battles that involved hundreds of warriors. A protracted, unsuccessful siege of Medina in 627 was followed by a truce, and the gradual strengthening of Muhammad's position while his opponents' support ebbed away. Having first established his right to perform the pilgrimage to Mecca, in 630 CE Muhammad led an expedition several thousand strong, which took the city with little resistance. Most of its inhabitants accepted the Prophet's offers of protection for their lives and livelihoods. The idols were removed from the Ka'ba. A few individuals who had left the community and returned to Mecca while it was still in polytheist hands, and outspoken poets who had openly mocked the Prophet, were executed, but most of the Meccan opposition, including its leaders, now accepted Muhammad's leadership and were welcomed into his community.

These events were important in marking both the openness of the Prophet's first community and the emerging boundary that divided it from others. Many of those among the Quraysh who had most bitterly opposed Muhammad's claims to prophecy followed him now that he was a proven military chief. Some among them would become the most celebrated leaders of the Muslims as they expanded outward from Mecca in the following years. In the last years of the Prophet's life, his community that had begun with its early adherents, the emigrants to Medina and their helpers, would be enlarged not only by their former enemies, but by whole tribes that became Muslim en masse following the conquest of Mecca and the expansion of Muhammad's message throughout Arabia. What did becoming Muslim mean to them?

It seems more than likely that by the time of the conquest of Mecca, joining the community to benefit from its protection, to share in its apparent success, and perhaps to achieve prominence within it was at least as important as what today we might think of as inner, individual religious conversion. This is not to cast aspersions on the sincerity of adherence to Islam at this time: modern ideas of religion as a system of belief, and of conversion as adherence to that belief in individual conscience, map only partly onto the realities of late ancient and early medieval life. For most people, faith was probably more about establishing right relations with the divine and with other people through practice—the ritual forms of worship, and the mutual obligations of community membership—than about what we might think of as theology or ideology.[20]

Islam, "submission," by now clearly meant submission to God, following the example of Abraham—as the Qur'an put it, "When his Lord said to him, 'Submit,' he said, 'I submit to the Lord of the Worlds.'"[21] It meant recognising the authority of Muhammad as God's Prophet, following Muhammad's instructions for community life and participation in its central devotional acts of prayer, almsgiving, fasting, and pilgrimage. But beyond these fundamentals, doctrines and beliefs were yet to develop. God's message to Muhammad had not yet been fully revealed, nor the revelations compiled into the Qur'an, as it would come to be known in the years following the Prophet's death. There was as yet no fully formed, distinct "religion of Islam" to which believers could adhere: there was an unfolding message they could heed, and a growing community they could join. Those who took the Prophet's vivid warnings of impending Judgment seriously may well have believed that the Last Day was at hand. And, like many other burgeoning social movements, the revolutionary dynamic of Muhammad's community was perhaps a compelling cause in itself.

But belonging to a community of the faithful, throughout the late ancient world, was a fragile as well as an important thing. The Christian churches to the north had spent the last century and a half roiled by anxiety over confessional disputes and the possibility that the faithful might be lost to the faith by following alternative sources of authority—in churchmen's terms, heresy. When the new faith of Islam, claiming to complete, correct, and supplant the old ones, burst into the majority-Christian world of Egypt and the eastern Mediterranean, it came into a world where religious competition, even within Christianity, was lively and fractious. Faithfulness when under pressure to change one's confessional identity was celebrated by clerical writers as heroic, pious virtue, precisely because leaving one community for another was by no means uncommon. Most of the faithful had only a slight grasp on what their faith—beyond belonging to the community and participating in its rituals—entailed.[22]

In an important way, then, and at its very beginnings, Muhammad's mission was perhaps concerned less with converting individual consciences than with building a new faithful community. Preventing defections, and making adherence permanent, was crucial. And so the penalty for apostasy—for leaving the community having once joined it—would be a heavy one. The refusal to acknowledge, and pay proper respect to, the uniqueness of Muhammad's position as God's appointed messenger would be an equally grave offence. Apart from the Meccan poets who catered to Muhammad's enemies before the city fell, those least disposed to accord such respect were the long-established Jewish groups who had been part of the original "single community" in Medina. Muhammad might be the arbiter of their disputes, even their leader against external attack, but he could not be their Prophet. The Muslim historical tradition would attribute the gradual breakdown of relations between Muhammad and the Jews of Medina to the Jews' alleged disloyalty during the war with Mecca, and to Medina's increasingly fractious politics, in which the most powerful Jewish families ended up on the wrong side of the man tasked by Muhammad with determining their fate. Whatever the truth, in the first years of the hijra, as Muhammad's authority in Medina increased on the twin basis of heavenly revelation from God and fighting in His cause on earth, the community's original religious plurality was eroded. Medina's polytheists would become Muslims, but some of the town's Jews were expelled, and, in a final crisis, the men of the most prominent remaining Jewish clan were killed, and their families enslaved.[23]

⬦⬦⬦⬦⬦⬦⬦

The Qur'an recounts human history as a story of repeated warnings sent to the peoples of the earth. They should return to the one true God, forsaking their idols and injustice, believing only in Him and His judgment to come on the Last Day. As the Qur'anic stories went, such warnings, and the divinely inspired prophets who brought them, were all too often ignored, with calamitous results for humankind. Now, in an age of holy war and intimations of the imminent end of the world, vivid apocalyptic and prophetic ideas spread anew. A few years before the superpower conflict to the north ground to a halt, Muhammad had led his group of believers out of persecution in Mecca to create a new community in Medina. A much smaller war than that between Rome and Persia had followed, pitting the unbelievers of Mecca against the pious followers in Medina; but its conclusion, in the defeat of the Meccan polytheists and the return of the Ka'ba to its status as God's "first house of worship," would be hardly less significant for world history than the peace made at Ctesiphon. Just four years after hostilities between Rome and Persia ended, Muhammad died, having united Mecca with Medina and spread his message to the peoples of Arabia. In the decade that followed, his successors and their followers would take that message victoriously out of the desert, and into the history of the world.[24]

2

BELONGING AND BELIEVING

The Prophet Muhammad died in Medina in 632 CE, only ten years into the new era he had inaugurated. Stories of his life and works would be passed down and incorporated into a universal history, the most famous version of which was written by a compiler of traditions from Medina, Ibn Ishaq. The son of a freedman whose own father had been a Jewish captive, Ibn Ishaq lived in the first half of the eighth century. He travelled for his learning around the heartlands of what by then had become the Muslim Arabs' empire, from the Hijaz to Alexandria and Baghdad. It is mostly from the accounts that he, and other traditionists like him, collected and compiled in the 700s CE that later Muslims would come to know the biography of Muhammad, and the history of Islam's emergence.

Ibn Ishaq's great work began with the creation of the world, placing Muhammad at the end of a long line of prophets stretching back through Jesus to Abraham, Noah, and Adam, the progenitor of all humanity. Much of it, especially the first part, was later lost, surviving only in fragments. Ibn Hisham, the ninth-century editor whose version of Ibn Ishaq's work we have today, cut out what he thought inappropriate. In particular, he thought, Ibn Ishaq had borrowed too many stories from Jewish sources that were not to be trusted. Later scholars would complain that Ibn Ishaq was too vague, reporting things on the authority of "some of the men of such-and-such a tribe," rather than from individually identifiable and accredited witnesses. Identifying such witnesses, and their reliability, would become the focus of a whole science for verifying reliable *hadith* (reports of what the Prophet said during his lifetime). Ibn Ishaq's own preoccupations may have been less with recording facts than with crafting an orally performed "popular epic" of God's intervention in history, one that would be intelligible and compelling to illiterate tribal audiences. It was later scholars like Ibn Hisham, in the eighth and ninth centuries, who set down in writing most of the Islamic historical tradition that survives. They had different concerns, over both confessional propriety and the factual details of the Prophet's life and teaching, reflecting later tensions both with other faith communities and among Muslims. Things had become more complicated since the time of the first Muslims in Medina and Mecca; and that would complicate things for later attempts to understand Islam's emergence, too.[1]

The first century of Islam was a tumultuous "whirlwind" of events, a whirlwind so strong that, in the words of one eminent scholar, the historical tradition that came out of it might be seen to contain only the "debris of an obliterated past" that had been "broken into splinters," its "bits and pieces combined and recombined in different patterns." Much of the Muslim community's early history must, indeed, have been lost to its own later memory. Arguments about their own immediate past were as crucial to eighth- and ninth-century Muslims as was agreed-upon knowledge of it. Medieval Muslim scholars recognised that much of what had surfaced in their own traditions as evidence from the first centuries of Islam was unreliable. Reports collected in oral tradition before being written down were often contrived much later than the times to which they apparently referred. Claimed as evidence of the earliest history of Islam, some stories about the acts and sayings of the Prophet, or about the time and places he lived, were not. Instead, they were created later, to give the support of the Prophet and the first Muslims to new arguments that preoccupied subsequent generations, or to explain things—in particular, parts of the revelation sent down to Muhammad, the Qur'an—that had become obscure to them. It would be too simple just to imagine finding a surviving "solid core" of historical fact that could be excavated from the rest of this tradition. The tradition has to be painstakingly reconstructed and re-contextualised for historians to make sense of it.[2]

The impact of Islam in world history was so great, and its emergence from so peripheral a place in world history so apparently improbable, that some historians have argued that Islam itself, as Muslims came to know it, was the product of the century after Muhammad's lifetime, not of his lifetime itself. Muhammad's name and the assertion of his Prophethood began to appear clearly in the Muslim community's own historical record, in inscriptions or on coins, only at the end of the seventh century, fifty years or so after the traditional date of Muhammad's death. The written historical tradition of the Prophet's biography and the early history of the Muslim community begin later still.

But evidence from the first half of the seventh century also exists. Christian, Syriac-language sources tell us that their writers knew about a Muhammad who was a leader of the Arabs within a few years of his death. From the earliest dated manuscripts, we know that the text of the Qur'an was in existence in the first half of the seventh century, and we know from inscriptions on stone and texts written on papyrus in Arabic that dating according to the historical era marked by the beginning of the Islamic calendar became widespread only a few years after it was instituted. In the Islamic, or as it became known, the *hijri*, calendar, 622 CE, the year of Muhammad's *hijra* to Medina, and his founding of a new community there, became the year 1. This was a new way of reckoning time, something that can only have come into use following an event whose significance was considered revolutionary, or epoch-making: an event like the founding of a new community by a Prophet and lawgiver.[3] The adoption of the hijri calendar was strikingly rapid: by contrast, it would be another hundred years before the Christianised Roman Empire, its successor states in western Europe, or their Christian scholars would begin dating history from the birth of Christ, which by then had occurred six hundred years earlier.[4]

Combining early Islam's late antique context with the careful reconstruction of elements of its later historical tradition, and combining critical scepticism with due respect, it is possible to make Islam's emergence historically comprehensible. And as in other faith traditions, how Muslims came to imagine their history—how they narrated it and used it to make sense of the world—is at least as important as the sometimes unknowable aspects of what really happened.

One feature of Ibn Ishaq's epic narrative, in particular, would have a profound impact on Arab and Muslim understandings of time and human history. In what would come to be an Islamic view of universal history, the time before the Prophet's revelation would be seen as the era of "ignorance," *jahiliyya*, a term that would come to have ethical as well as historical meaning. Later Muslim writers would laud the poetic culture and masculine virtues of honour, dignity, and hospitality attributed to pre-Islamic Arab society, but otherwise *jahiliyya* would mean not only the absence of knowledge but, as in Ibn Ishaq's writing, the opposite of *islam*. *Jahiliyya* connoted all that was barbarous, ignorant of God's word and his way.

◇◇◇◇◇◇◇

Already, in the first years after the death of the Prophet, the fear that newly Muslim people might be backsliding into *jahiliyya* was acute. Some of the Arab tribes that had accepted Muhammad's authority, made allegiance to his leadership in Medina and paid tax to his treasury there broke off their submission after the Prophet's death. Other parts of the region had not yet come wholly under the sway of Muhammad's community and his message. Compelled to continue the Prophet's work of expanding his community and "fighting in the way of God," Muhammad's successors fought to reintegrate Arabia under Muslim authority, stamping out alternative centres of power. These reportedly included that of an alternative prophet, Musaylima, who had established himself in central Arabia. Within a few years, the Muslim community had effectively conquered the peninsula and brought its whole territory and people for the first time under a single rule.

Within its own universalising worldview, the Muslim historical tradition would portray this as the triumph of faith over apostasy: the Muslims' campaigns in Arabia would become known as the *ridda* ("return," or in religious terms, "apostasy") wars. But although it would be given a religious meaning, the upheaval did not have simply religious causes. Not all of the tribal groups beyond the Hijaz had become Muslim in the first place (and so could not have apostatised). The peninsula's Christians did not unite among themselves to oppose a "Muslim" takeover; perhaps they did not see it as such. Changing tribal, territorial, and factional alliances were important in different parts of the peninsula, as, above all, was the uniquely united ethos and impetus of the Muslim community among the settled peoples of the Hijaz and their Bedouin allies. The conquest of Arabia was less the feat of tribal, nomadic peoples united by religious fervour—as it has often been portrayed—than the achievement of an urban, settled, and organised community with a single vision of cosmic order and universal sovereignty.

What that sovereignty should now look like was an important question. Even more important, of course, was the question of who should exercise it. Muhammad had died unexpectedly, and if he had made preparations for succession to his leadership, no one could agree on what they were. Among some Muslims, a strong conviction would develop that the Prophet had designated his cousin and son-in-law, Ali Ibn Abi Talib, the husband of his daughter Fatima, to lead the community after he was gone, and that Ali and his sons, the Prophet's own family, were those best suited to succeed him. Most Muslims, however, would deny that this had happened. In the immediate crisis of the community following Muhammad's passing, it was his close friend and early follower, Abu Bakr, who was chosen by the Muslims in Medina to lead them.

Abu Bakr was a Meccan from among the Quraysh, and his election marked the beginning of tensions over legitimate leadership that would from now on beset the community. The *ansar*, the Prophet's original "helpers" in Medina, reportedly sought to elect a leader of their own, considering their alliance with the Quraysh to be dissolved now that the Prophet was dead. There was no agreed-upon rule of precedence within the Muslim community, and the early divisions between Mecca and Medina, and between Muhammad's early followers among the Quraysh and those who had joined the Muslims after first fighting against them, still lay below the surface. It is often said that Muhammad founded a state as well as a religion, but he left neither a ruling dynasty nor (except for instituting regular taxation) a set of governing institutions. It is perhaps more accurate to say that he created a community of faithful people who would follow what, he believed, had always been "God's way."

By continuously expanding, the Prophet's community would bring knowledge of God's way to the rest of humanity, and in so doing would establish God's rule on earth—this was the combination of universal sovereignty and divine revelation that had characterised the late ancient world of both Rome and Persia. Muslims might agree on the essentials of God's way: the proper ritual worship, holy law, and right conduct among people laid down by God and expounded by the Prophet in the Qur'an and the Prophet's own example. But how and by whom the community should now be governed was more contentious. Older, tribal and aristocratic ideas resurfaced in the attribution of precedence to the "people of the House," *ahl al-bayt*, a term used for the leading families of tribal society and especially those claiming guardianship over sacred enclaves, and now applied to the family of the Prophet. The equally tribal combination of patriarchal and meritocratic principles lay behind the alternative idea that a leader must be designated from among deserving candidates by the consensus of his peers, through consultation (in Arabic, *shura*) and election.

What was not contentious was the nature and significance of leadership itself. No one after Muhammad would be able to claim his Prophetic authority—he had been the last of the prophets sent to humanity, the "Seal" of prophecy. Leadership of the community, following the Prophet's example, would be understood as the "imamate" (*imama*), meaning the authority of someone worthy of being imitated:

an *imam*. An imam was not a prophet (a messenger from God), nor was he a priest (an intermediary between God and people). He might be followed simply because he stood in front of the believers as they prayed, imitating his words and gestures in their own prayer: this is still one, and probably the most common, meaning of the word today. Or a great scholar, learned in the law and the sciences of religion, might be recognised as an imam: this was a title often given to medieval Muslim intellectual luminaries. But the "great imamate," the supreme authority, belonged to one properly able to guide the community in God's way, to keep it on the straight path toward salvation and to avoid error. When the succession was disputed, knowing which contender to follow was not only a matter of life and death, but of life after death too. Following the true imam was essential to gain felicity in the afterlife, and in the early centuries of Islam, the imam was often thought to be responsible for the welfare and prosperity of his people in this life, too. The imam held the keys to heaven, and, in an image derived from very ancient Middle Eastern ideas of just and virtuous rule, the imam also brought rain on earth.[5]

In this sense, the imam was kingly, following a pattern that went back through the Sasanian Empire to ancient Mesopotamia, and that shared with the Byzantine world a common, eastern Mediterranean and Hellenistic (Greek-influenced) cultural inheritance. His most common title, from the time of the second caliph, Umar, onward, would be *amir al-mu'minin*, the "prince of the believers" or "commander of the faithful." But he was not a king. Kings, as Muslim piety and political thought would see it, tended to seize power for themselves, and to govern in their own interests and those of their kin and cronies. A true imam was something else: not a king, a despot, or a Pharaoh—the Qur'an's archetypal image of the unjust ruler—but the deputy and successor of the Prophet, *khalifat rasul allah*, or even *khalifat allah*, "the deputy of God" himself. According to the Qur'an, God had placed both the first man, Adam, and the biblical King (and Qur'anic prophet) David on earth as *khalifa*s, caliphs. Medieval European kings would claim to rule by divine right in succession to Adam, the "first king." The successors to Muhammad, as they saw it, were to be caliphs after Adam and the other prophets, ruling in God's name and by God's will, upholding God's law and guiding God's people in the way of His prophets, now that prophecy was at an end. The Roman emperor in Constantinople was obeyed as *autokrator* or *imperator* (emperor, literally "sole ruler" or "commander") and exalted as the deputy (in Greek, *hyparchos*) or the image (*eikon*) of God. The caliph would similarly claim to be the true commander of the faithful and God's deputy—not in the image of God (since in Muslim theology, God could not be imagined in any human-like form) but as his "shadow" on earth. In visible and pointed competition with the neighbouring Byzantine emperor, the Caliph Abd al-Malik, at the end of the seventh century, issued bronze, silver, and gold coins carrying an image of the caliph himself: full-length, bearded, and carrying a sheathed sword and a whip, surrounded by Arabic script declaring, "There is no god but God alone, Muhammad is the messenger of God."[6]

Abu Bakr ruled as caliph for only two years before dying in 634 CE. Whether or not he designated Umar Ibn al-Khattab, a Meccan aristocrat who had helped him become caliph two years earlier, as his successor, Umar took office without serious opposition and ruled for ten years. Umar was the first caliph to adopt the title "commander of the faithful," but he may also have been seen by some as a messianic figure. His epithet *al-faruk*, which came to mean "one who distinguishes between the true and the false," may originally have been related to similar words in Syriac and other regional languages meaning "saviour" or "redeemer." A much more prosaic aspect of rule—a dispute over taxation—is said to have been the cause of Umar's death: he was stabbed by an Iranian slave and died of his wounds in 644 CE. The Muslim tradition tells us that Umar called a council to designate his successor by consultation, according to tribal practice, and so the third caliph, Uthman Ibn Affan, acceded to power peacefully, as Umar had. But in 656 CE, Uthman was assassinated in Medina by mutinous soldiers, and this time the community split. To the rebels, Uthman had become an "oppressor," transgressing accepted norms with innovatory policies and forfeiting his right to the caliphate: to their detractors (probably the great majority of Muslims), the rebels had unlawfully killed the rightful caliph and were guilty of sedition. "The imam Ibn Affan has been killed," lamented the mid-seventh-century poetess Layla Akhyaliyya: "the paths of guidance have become dispersed."[7]

The resulting conflict continued throughout the reign of the fourth caliph, Ali Ibn Abi Talib, the cousin and son-in-law of the Prophet who was proclaimed caliph by the rebels. What Islamic history would remember as the community's first *fitna*—a trial, or ordeal, through which God might be thought to be testing the faithful, but also a schism or civil war—lasted five years, from Uthman's death in 656 CE until the assassination of his successor, Ali, in 661. After Uthman's assassination, the old tribal principle of blood vengeance that Muhammad's covenants in Medina had revolutionised, but not replaced, kicked in. Uthman had belonged to the Quraysh, and other prominent members of the clan, even if they had opposed Uthman's policies, now sought to rally opposition to Ali. The Prophet's widow, Aisha, who was also the daughter of the first caliph, Abu Bakr, was among those who led troops against Ali. They were defeated. Then, Uthman's widow in Medina sent the murdered caliph's bloodstained shirt to his nearest kinsman, Mu'awiya, who had established his own power base in Syria. Mu'awiya refused to acknowledge Ali as caliph unless Ali punished the assassins. Ali, dependent on the support of men who had been complicit in the rebellion against Uthman, could not do this. In 657, the two sides met in a reluctant battle at Siffin, near Raqqa, on the Euphrates in what today is northeast Syria. But then, some of Mu'awiya's soldiers called for negotiation by raising pages of the Qur'an on their lances to signal their unwillingness to fight other Muslims, and the two leaders agreed to submit their dispute to arbitration. Mu'awiya subsequently won support among regional and tribal leaders, while Ali's support dwindled.

One group of Ali's supporters left his side after Siffin. Outraged that their caliph had effectively given up his own authority by agreeing to arbitration, and declaring that "there is no judgment except God's judgment," they formed what might be considered the first Muslim puritanical movement. Opposed to the aristocratic pretensions of the Quraysh (whose particular interests Uthman had been accused of promoting) and adopting a radically egalitarian, meritocratic principle of community leadership, they continued to insist not only that rebelling against Uthman had been right, but that they were the only true Muslims and that others had succumbed to unbelief (*kufr*). This group called themselves *Khawarij* (or "Kharijites," meaning "those who go out"), after a verse in the Qur'an: "Whoever emigrates in the path of God will find safe havens and great abundance in the earth, and whoever goes out from his house as an emigrant in the cause of God and His Messenger, and dies, shall be rewarded by God." The Kharijites saw the established caliphate itself as a "domain of unbelief." Some of their opponents, including Ali himself, believed that the Kharijites were anarchists, opposed to any form of government, but they would create their own dissident Muslim republics, first in southern Iraq and the Gulf, and then in North Africa and Oman. It was a Kharijite, not a supporter of Uthman, who would assassinate Ali, in the mosque at Kufa in southern Iraq, which Ali had made his capital, in 661 CE.[8]

The caliphate's troubles were not over, however. Mu'awiya now took the power that he had already claimed, and ruled until 680 CE from his base in Syria. But he was determined that his own son, Yazid, a proven general, should succeed him. Not only the partisans of Ali and the Prophet's family but also leading members of the Quraysh, especially those still living in Mecca and Medina, were appalled that hereditary kingship, something the Muslim community had never seen or sanctioned, was being imposed upon them. They demanded a council to elect a caliph who would be acceptable to the wider community. A second civil war broke out. The pious Abdallah Ibn al-Zubayr, said to have been the first child born to the Muslim community in Medina, set up a rival caliphate in the Hijaz. A Muslim army attacked Medina, bombarded Mecca, setting fire to the Ka'ba, and killed Ibn al-Zubayr. Yazid died in 683, after a tumultuous three years' reign. His own son, Mu'awiya II, of whom we know almost nothing except that he was perhaps twenty years old and ill, died after only a month or two, his caliphate recognised only in his capital of Damascus and the surrounding area. It was not until his successor in Damascus, Marwan Ibn al-Hakam, was himself succeeded by his son, Abd al-Malik Ibn Marwan, in 685, that peace was restored.

The conflict with Mecca and Medina was the most significant challenge to Yazid and his successors militarily and politically, but another event in the second civil war, though much less of a threat, would ultimately have far greater consequences. Ali's son Hasan had given up on the idea of restoring his family's claim to the caliphate before his death in 670, but his younger brother, Husayn, had not. When Mu'awiya I died in 680, Husayn, aged fifty-seven, and a small group of his family and friends set out from the Hijaz in response to promises of support from those who had originally backed his father, in the southern Iraqi city of Kufa. His party was met by the soldiers of Yazid's governor in Iraq, who had regained control in Kufa. These troops forced Husayn to make camp at Karbala, in the desert west of the Euphrates, fifty miles northwest of Kufa. After inconclusive negotiations, orders were given to deny Husayn and his supporters access to water, to force their surrender. On the tenth day (*ashura*) of the month of Muharram, the year 61 in the Muslim calendar (October 7, 680 CE), after a night spent in prayer and having urged his followers to escape under cover of darkness, Husayn and his seventy-two companions fought against Yazid's army and were all killed.

Husayn had posed a major symbolic challenge but not a serious military threat to Yazid Ibn Mu'awiya's caliphate, and on hearing of the battle at Karbala, Yazid reportedly regretted the blood that had been shed. Still, what was done could not be undone. The Prophet's grandson, who according to the tradition had played at Muhammad's knee—who had even been allowed to climb on Muhammad's back during prayer—had been killed, along with his own sons, and his head had been cut off, by soldiers of the Prophet's successor. There would be no forgetting Karbala. On the contrary, in the ninth century, the historian al-Tabari would relate the event at length and in detail from the many witnesses who had passed down reports of it. Husayn's sister, Zaynab, he wrote, was made to walk in captivity past the bodies of her relatives strewn on the field, and lamented: "'Here is Husayn [lying] in the open, stained with blood and with limbs torn off.... O Muhammad! Your daughters are prisoners, your progeny are killed, and the east wind blows dust over them.' By God! She made every enemy and friend weep." Al-Tabari goes on to relate how, dressed in her dirtiest clothes and sitting among her maids before the governor in Kufa, Ibn Ziyad, the Prophet's granddaughter defied Ibn Ziyad's claim that God had disgraced her and her family's claims to the caliphate:

> Zaynab replied: "Praise be to God, who has favoured us with Muhammad, and has purified us completely from sin. It is not as you say, for He only disgraces the great sinner.... God decreed death for [my family] and they went forward to their resting places. God will gather you and us together. You will plead your excuses to Him and we will be your adversaries before Him."[9]

As time went on, the day of Ashura and the martyrdom at Karbala would be commemorated in yet more vivid detail, with greater intensity and significance. The resulting split in the Prophet's original, single community, only sixty years after that community's foundation, would endure for over a thousand years, right down to the present day.

◇◇◇◇◇◇◇

If the leadership of the Muslim community was so hotly contested so soon after its establishment, this was partly because the stakes had so rapidly become so high. Already before Muhammad's death, the Muslims were no longer a small group of devoted religious exiles. They were a dynamic and expanding territorial and political community—a group bound by a common law, with mutual rights and obligations, under a single sovereignty, with a recognised leader who could declare war and make peace. They had returned in triumph to Mecca, absorbing into their own ranks those who had been their greatest opponents, and had spread their influence throughout Arabia.

Muhammad's message from God, sent, as the Qur'an said, "in clear Arabic" to the Arabs as other prophets had been sent before, each to his own people, was now to reach further still. Muhammad, we're told, had sent letters to the great emperors of the surrounding world, in Constantinople, Ctesiphon, and Axum, to announce God's message. He had dispatched raids into Roman Syria and Palestine—in some sources, he is said to have led some of these himself. His first successor, Abu Bakr, had time only to shore up Muslim authority in Arabia and to extend expeditions in southern Syria, but the reign of the Caliph Umar saw a dramatic expansion. And with expansion came unprecedented wealth, and the transformation of the Muslims from an embattled religious discipleship to a ruling ethnic elite.

Religiously motivated dissidents against the caliphate like the Kharijites saw hijra, emigrating or "going out" from under illegitimate rule to (re-)create an ideal Muslim community, as a continuing duty—and other Muslim dissidents or revolutionaries would continue to re-enact this dynamic, in many places, over the following centuries. The Prophet's successors and their followers, against whom such dissidence was aimed, for their part also saw themselves as continuing to observe the duties of *hijra*, "emigration," and *jihad*, "struggle" for the faith and fighting in the path of God. After the Prophet's death, these were seen as continuing imperatives, in obedience to Qur'anic injunctions and the furthering of the Prophet's own mission. There was also the more practical necessity of directing the community's energies, and the patriarchal, military traditions of its tribesmen, outwards into new territories, to avoid them collapsing inwards into internal conflict and renewing the tribal feuding that was now forbidden between groups who had all become Muslim. Like most newly living things—especially religious and revolutionary movements—the Muslim community had to move and grow if it was to survive.

Bedouin Arab populations to the north, along the settled frontiers of Byzantine and Persian territory, were brought under Medina's authority, and with astonishing speed, the neighbouring cities followed. Within ten years of Umar's accession in 634 CE, his small, disciplined armies had overrun Byzantine defences in Palestine and Syria, taking Jerusalem and Damascus, annexing Egypt, and defeating a large Persian force at Qadisiyya, a frontier post on the desert's edge in south-central Iraq. The Sasanian capital, Ctesiphon, with its related complex of walled towns that the Arabs would call al-Mada'in, "the cities," was occupied; the shah, Yazdgird III, and his court fled across the mountains to Isfahan on the Iranian plateau. Yazdgird's sons were sent to seek aid from China. But by the time of his death in 651 CE, Arab expeditions across northern and southern Iran had either put down resistance (especially in the southwest) or reached an accommodation with the Persian aristocracy (in the north), and the Sasanian Empire had collapsed. The Byzantine Emperor Heraclius, who had so recently defeated the Persians and ended their occupation of Egypt and Syria, withdrew Roman forces into Anatolia, where the frontier between Christian and Muslim empires would remain for the next three hundred years.

The rapidity and scale of these early conquests inspired celebratory, poetic and historical writing in the Muslims' own literary tradition; they inspired puzzlement in later, secular historians. Most of the Arab armies numbered only a few thousand men, and they seem to have been composed not of whole tribal groups, and certainly not of whole migrating populations, but of volunteers who were recruited and deployed by the caliphate in Medina, and officered by men whose seniority among the Muslim community outweighed more traditional precedence among the tribal nobility. They were not the marauding, opportunistic raiders that Sasanian and Byzantine observers might have expected to come out of the desert; nor were they whole nomadic peoples on the move in search of richer lands.

How did these small, albeit highly motivated and organised, armies capture so much territory from the mighty Roman and Persian Empires? We should probably not overemphasise the extent to which the plague and the previous war between the two superpowers had weakened their defences—the Muslims suffered from plague in Syria and Palestine too, and there is little reason to think that the men of Heraclius's armies, having just won a historic victory over the Persians, lacked the morale to face the Arabs. But the war had undoubtedly drained both empires of resources, especially the money they needed to pay large armies in the field, at a time when the effects of the plague had already reduced the central state's tax income. For the Sasanians, the war's conclusion had thrown the whole state into crisis. The people of Byzantine Syria and Egypt had just lived through a Persian occupation that had lasted over a decade, and which, on the whole, had been relatively benign. They could come to terms with the new invaders in the same way, and certainly preferred to do so than to risk large-scale destruction.

Once Roman troops were defeated in a few small but decisive encounters, then, the eastern Mediterranean cities negotiated with the Arab armies at their gates and found that an accommodation could be reached. When the Caliph Umar entered Jerusalem, bringing Islamic sovereignty to the sacred city of the Jews and the Christians, it was by agreement, not by force. It was especially in southwest Iran, where the imperial state had suddenly collapsed but the population was less inclined to accept Muslim rule, that the Arabs would face years of rebellion. When stability returned after the civil wars, a second wave of conquests spread Muslim sovereignty west and east during the early eighth century. Expeditions across North Africa reached Spain in 711 CE, and five years later had overrun the Visigothic kingdom that had succeeded Roman rule there. At the same time, expeditions from southern and northern Iran reached Sind, west of the Indus River valley, and crossed the Amu Darya (Oxus) from Merv, an Iranian Silk Road city in what is now Turkmenistan, bringing Bukhara and Samarqand into the empire. In Iran and central Asia, there was little or no Arab settlement. Instead, agreements were reached with local rulers who agreed to accept Muslim supremacy and the suzerainty of the caliph.[10]

The early conquests were thus achieved with relatively little bloodshed. Like Muhammad's first followers, the Arab conquerors were, as

Christian writers who called them *mahgre* or *mahgraye* recognised, "muhajirun"—in the Qur'an's language, emigrants who went out in the cause of God, to achieve their own salvation and to find abundance in the land. But they were not to take the land and settle it. Instead, the existing peasant populations in Egypt's Nile Delta, in southern Iraq, Palestine and Syria, were left to farm as they had done, whether on their own land or as tenants on estates that had belonged to the Sasanian crown and its aristocracy, which had been abandoned by their former lords and were now taken into the public ownership of the Muslim community. The peasants would pay tax and tribute to Medina instead of to the Persians or Romans. The veterans of the conquests were settled in new military garrison cities, built on the edges of existing settled areas, where they were to live apart from the subject population. They would be paid salaries from Medina out of the revenue accruing to the caliphate from its vastly expanded dominions. These new cities—Fustat in Egypt, on the Nile just south of modern Cairo, Kufa and Basra in Iraq—became new "places of emigration" where the Muslim community would develop as a settled, orderly society, with provincial governors appointed by and answerable to the caliph in Medina.

In Syria, Palestine and Egypt, therefore, urban and rural life went on largely as before, with new governors appointed and new taxes collected and recorded largely as the old ones had been. Still, the conquests were transformative over the longer term, both for the subject populations now living under Muslim rule and for the Muslim rulers. The wealth that flowed into the Muslims' hands from the spoils of war was extraordinary. The fall of Ctesiphon, from which the shah had supposedly removed his personal treasures, was nonetheless said to have yielded up the sum of twelve thousand silver dirhams for every man in an army sixty thousand strong—such figures, probably symbolic rather than factual, give a sense of the almost unimaginable scale of the event.

Piously minded Muslims would be displeased by the flood of wealth, and by the pleasure-seeking, poetry-reading, wine-drinking court culture that followed. They would remember the ascetic, simply dressed Caliph Umar as a paragon of Muslim virtue. Other figures of the early community whose biographies are more legendary, such as Salman "Pak" al-Farisi (Salman "the Pure," the Persian), said to be the first Persian convert to Islam, would also be approvingly cited as models of humility and simple devotion. Having travelled from Iran, fallen into captivity, and reached Medina at the time of the hijra, Salman is supposed to have recognised the Prophet by signs revealed to him by his previous Christian teachers. Named as governor at Ctesiphon after the city's capture by the Arabs, he is later depicted making his living there by basket-weaving, and his nearby tomb would become a holy sanctuary. Muhammad and his followers had created a community to bring God's message to the world, not to retire into seclusion: the model of reclusive asceticism familiar from the desert-dwelling monks of late ancient Christianity (some of whom, the "stylites," were known for living alone in contemplation on the top of pillars) was not one that Muslims were to follow. But a tension would from now on run through the Muslim community, as it had among Christians after the faith acquired an empire, between views of this-worldly prosperity and material fortune as a sign of God's blessing, or as a corrupting influence, in a religious culture that had begun by denouncing the love of wealth, emphasising duty to the poor, and identifying true piety with humble, self-denying frugality.[11]

The conquests also brought captives, slaves, and subjects, changing the makeup of Muslim society, and indeed what it meant to be a Muslim. God may have sent Muhammad a message to the world, but the Arab conquerors were at first not anxious to spread the faith of Islam to their new subject populations. "People of the Book"—Christians and Jews—and adherents of other faiths, Zoroastrians, Buddhists or others, who were the great majority of the population in the formerly Byzantine and Sasanian lands now under Muslim control, were not expected to join the Muslim community. Except in Syria—where there was already a significant Arabic-speaking population in Damascus— the conquerors were initially supposed to keep to themselves in their garrison cities, rather than settling directly alongside their subjects. And in the first century after the conquests, there was no encouragement given to subjects who tried to leave their lands, "going out" themselves to the new cities to take advantage of their opportunities and embrace the new faith. Peasants who tried to do so were sent back to farm their land and pay their taxes.

Over time, however, this separation broke down. Especially in Syria and northern Iraq (the area called the Jazira, the "arch" of the Fertile Crescent between the upper Tigris and Euphrates Rivers), Muslims settled into ancient cities and mosques were built, literally and figuratively, in the shadow of the existing churches. And once the Arabs were rubbing shoulders with non-Arabs in the street and the marketplace, it could be difficult to know who was who. In any case, religious identity, far from being wholly determining, was only one of several ways people defined themselves, lived their lives, and managed their social relations. Wealth and status, language, ancestry, education, civic pride and livelihood all mattered too, and crossed religious divides. Christian and Jewish communities were very varied groups, not single blocs in which every individual had the same legal status and social standing. Both the well-established, learned, and articulate religious traditions and the material and professional assets of their subjects clearly impressed the Arab conquerors. The ninth-century writer al-Jahiz would famously complain that Muslims thought too highly of Christians, because of their knowledge, wealth, and refinement: a Muslim doctor could get no patients, even when the plague struck, because everyone wanted a Christian physician. In this context, as the physical and social separation of conquerors and conquered decreased, anxieties arose about establishing and maintaining Muslim distinctiveness.[12]

These anxieties, among Muslim rulers and their scholars, would lead to an emphasis on the many sayings attributed to the Prophet and the first caliphs, especially Umar, enjoining Muslims to differentiate their dress, dwellings, and ritual practices from those of Jews and Christians. Islam thus became increasingly distinguishable within the religious environment it shared with late ancient Judaism and Christianity. Being Muslim had already meant drawing boundaries in time: in Medina and Mecca, Islam was the advent of a new age, directed to a new world, separated from the old tribal times of the *jahiliyya*. Now, in the ancient cities of Alexandria, Damascus, and Jerusalem, in the shadow and on the foundation of the ancient legacies that shaped them, being Muslim also meant drawing boundaries in space, between what was Islamic and what was not, and in the more complex society that lived there, between who was Muslim and who was not.

Nowhere was both the supremacy of Islam and its rootedness in earlier religious and imperial traditions proclaimed more explicitly than in the beauty and symbolism of the first great monument of Islamic art and architecture, the Dome of the Rock in Jerusalem. This was perhaps the grandest legacy of the Caliph Abd al-Malik, the first ruler of the Umayyad family (the kinsmen of Uthman and Mu'awiya who had prevailed in the civil wars) to reign securely and die peacefully. By the time of his death, aged sixty, in 705, Abd al-Malik ruled over lands and peoples that encompassed the worlds of Greek and Roman religion and philosophy, the ancient centres of Persian and Mesopotamian urban civilisation, and the spiritual heartlands of Judaism and Christianity. He had been driven from his own home in Medina during the second civil war, and he ruled as caliph, not in Medina, but in the ancient city of Damascus, where his son Walid would build a magnificent mosque—today called the Umayyad Mosque, after his family—on the site of the Christian cathedral that itself stood on the site of an earlier Roman temple of Jupiter. In the even more ancient city of Jerusalem, Abd al-Malik's own architects and craftsmen built the Dome of the Rock on the site of the ancient Jewish temple that the Romans had ruined six hundred years before. It was an explicit statement of the caliph's right to rule in the name of God, as a Muslim and the upholder of Islam.[13]

This great monument of Islam also testifies to a synthesis of late ancient influences. Built in late antique Byzantine style, it was almost certainly designed and constructed by Palestinian Christians. The unusual, octagonal mosque with its gilded dome was set in a place that the Arab conquerors of Jerusalem clearly recognised as a place of deeply ancient holiness. It was built at the edge of the old city, near the Church of the Holy Sepulchre and atop the buried foundations of what was (and is) believed to have been the site of both the original Biblical Temple of Solomon—destroyed in the sixth century BCE when the Jews were taken into exile in Babylon—and then of the Second Temple, which in turn had been destroyed in the suppression of the Jewish revolt against the Roman Empire in 70 CE. At the centre of the building, beneath the golden dome, is the large, exposed rock, jutting out at an angle from beneath the foundations, that gives the sanctuary its name. Sacred significance was clearly attributed to the rock already in the seventh century. It may have been associated with the ancient altar of the Jewish Temple, and some said it bore the physical marks of God's touch, though later Muslim belief rejected this idea. It would eventually be identified in Muslim tradition as the spot from which the Prophet Muhammad ascended to Heaven on his miraculous Night Journey from Mecca, having first met Abraham, Moses, and Jesus in Jerusalem and led them in prayer.

The arcades surrounding the rock may have been intended for pilgrims to walk around, as pilgrims walked around the Ka'ba at Mecca (and still do). But the monument's clearest message is expressed in the interior walls above the walkways. Magnificently decorated in coloured mosaic tiles, they feature images from Byzantine and Persian royal art, surmounted by a long inscription in gold. This proclaims the oneness of God, and Muhammad's status as God's Messenger. Citing verses of the Qur'an, it also warns of the error into which, according to Muslims, Christians had fallen concerning the real nature of God and the status of Jesus Christ and Mary, his mother:

> People of the Book, do not exaggerate in your religion, and say nothing about God but the truth: The Messiah, Jesus, Son of Mary was but a Messenger of God and His Word conveyed to Mary, through His

Spirit. So believe in God and His Messengers and refrain from talk of a "Trinity." Restraint will be better for you. God is One God.[14]

Arab armies had conquered Jerusalem, in 638, with the acquiescence of the city's Christian population. The head of the church in the city, the Patriarch Sophronius—who composed fond Greek poetry about Jerusalem's holy sites, and anti-Jewish poetry about its occupation by the Persians in 614, which had driven him into exile—is said to have escorted the second caliph, Umar, into the city and to have shown him the Temple Mount. Now, the Muslims' reigning dynasty proclaimed itself the guardian of a new, triumphant religious message that also declared itself to be the original and true version of all monotheism, appropriating the sacred space of Judaism and refuting the Christian doctrine of the Trinity. Islam, as expressed in Abd al-Malik's great mosque, was founded on the earlier revelations and prophetic histories of the Jews and Christians—and bluntly told them where they had gone wrong.

The Dome of the Rock thus materialised not only the consolidation of Abd al-Malik's triumph over his Muslim rivals, but his caliphate's succession to Rome and Persia, and its supersession of Jewish and Christian religion. It was "a missionary monument of victory" over other claimants to Islamic authority, and over the holy city's, and the world's, previous monotheistic faiths and their believers. The Islam that it proclaimed professed to be their historical culmination, and a return to their original truth. Islam, the final revelation and "the true religion with God," as a Qur'anic inscription above one of the doors of the Dome of the Rock would put it, was the cause—both the origin and the purpose—of the conquests. Adherence to it was what distinguished the conquerors from everyone else.[15]

⬦⬦⬦⬦⬦⬦⬦

The only way for non-Arabs to join the Muslim community in the first years after the conquest was as the freed slaves or clients of individual Muslim masters who became their patrons. A Christian or

Jewish captive who embraced Islam and was freed, as well as non-converts who managed to attach themselves, by virtue of their abilities, to an Arab patron, would become a dependent, a freedman or client (in Arabic, *mawla*). These clients (*mawali*) and their descendants soon became very numerous. Many became the administrators, sometimes effectively the governors, of the new empire's provinces, thanks to their prior bureaucratic experience and ability to ensure the continuity of taxation. Some who became Muslims would play major roles in the development of Islamic learning and culture. The biographer of the Prophet, Ibn Ishaq, was one, and like Ibn Ishaq, the great legal scholar Abu Hanifa, who lived in Kufa in the eighth century CE and whose teachings would form the basis of one of the main schools of Islamic law, was also the grandson of a freed slave. By the end of the seventh century, freedmen and their descendants had become important in the army, too. They were nonetheless often treated as second-class members of the community, and sometimes considered as no better than slaves. Islam was still, above all, the ethnic religion of the Arab conquerors. But it would not stay that way for long.[16]

It was a man who was probably a freedman's son of Persian origin who would catalyse growing opposition to the Umayyad dynasty and spark the revolution that brought them down. Asked by an emissary of the governor in Merv to identify himself, Abu Muslim Abd al-Rahman Ibn Muslim apparently replied: "I am a man from among the Muslims. I do not affiliate myself with any tribe. . . . My father perished in a country not his own. . . . Islam is my lineage, to the family of Muhammad goes my support, and I follow a correct course of action." Whether or not Abu Muslim really said any of this, it sums up how later history would see him and his cause: tribal loyalties were irrelevant; being Muslim was enough. Whoever he might originally have been, his assumed name ("Slave of [God] the Compassionate One, Son of a Muslim, Father of a Muslim") was itself an ideological statement. Plucked from obscurity in a jail in Kufa where he had been imprisoned, and sent east to organise a revolution, Abu Muslim would become the instigator of a massive uprising, for a while the effective ruler of the vast province of Khurasan (northeast Iran and central Asia), and the architect of the accession, in 750 CE, of a new dynasty, the Abbasids—who, five years later, murdered him.[17]

From the early 700s CE, the Umayyad caliphs—the successors to Abd al-Malik's unified, Arabic-speaking, Islam-proclaiming state—kept their power base firmly in Syria and relied on a Syrian army. They had won the civil wars of the seventh century, but they had not extinguished opposition. Having faced early challenges, and occasional subsequent rebellion, especially from Iraq, they excluded the other provinces from influence. The inhabitants of Iraq, which had a larger Muslim population than Syria and which, thanks to the productive lands between the lower Tigris and Euphrates, was also by far the richest province, thought themselves insulted and exploited. Resentment against the Umayyads and their claim to the caliphate grew.

Many people, especially in the city of Kufa, still believed that only someone from the Prophet's family, either a direct descendant of Ali or a member of the larger Hashemite clan, could truly lead the community and rule satisfactorily for all Muslims in the expanded empire. After a rebellion in the name of one such claimant, Muhammad Ibn al-Hanafiyya, was crushed, his son Abu Hashim became the focus of dissident sympathies, and the so-called "Hashimiyya" party organised a propaganda campaign to raise support for a new revolt against the Umayyads. This had already had some success in Khurasan, the eastern frontier province far from Damascus, when Abu Muslim arrived there in 746 CE. In the provincial capital, Merv, he took over the local Hashimiyya movement, and within a year he was ready to launch the revolution.

Abu Muslim preached retribution for the ungodly killing of Ali's son Husayn at Karbala, denounced the other impieties attributed to the ruling dynasty, and promoted an egalitarian and messianic vision of what Islam should be. He was not seeking the caliphate himself; indeed, his movement did not seek to elevate any particular candidate as imam. Abu Hashim was not proclaimed caliph (although his connection to the revolt was suspected, and he was captured and killed by the Umayyads). Unity among the disaffected was better achieved by the revolutionaries' slogan that promised "satisfaction from the Prophet's House": that a true imam from the family of Muhammad would rule in a way acceptable to all. The revolt in Khurasan was signalled by black flags—perhaps connoting mourning for the martyrs of Karbala, certainly picking up on apocalyptic ideas that associated black flags with the coming of the messiah, or *mahdi* (the "Rightly Guided One" who would herald the end of time), and an imminent age of justice. At the outset of Muhammad's mission, belief in the impending Last Day had been powerful, but a century had passed and instead of the end of the world and the judgment of God, there was a dynastic empire and, in many eyes, impiety and injustice. The messianic and eschatological ("end times"–oriented) dimension of Islam was still powerful—indeed it would remain powerful in many contexts for centuries to come.

What it faced now was a worldly regime that was already collapsing under its own factional rivalries. Disputes for prominence between early adherents to the Muslim cause and late-coming tribal leaders, power struggles between different kinship groups, and familial disagreements over succession to the caliphate had all plagued the Umayyads in Syria. In 744 CE a third civil war broke out. The eventual victor, Marwan Ibn Muhammad, had built up his own power base in the north as governor of Armenia and Azerbaijan. He was let into Damascus by a disaffected population and proclaimed caliph as Marwan II, but he moved the capital further north and faced both mutinies in Syria and rebellions in Iraq even before the revolt in Khurasan gathered speed. As if to signal the last days, plague, famine, and earthquake all struck Syria. By autumn 749 CE, the rebel army moving west from Khurasan had reached Kufa. There they proclaimed the Hashimiyya's candidate, Abu al-Abbas al-Saffah, a member of the Abbasid family (descendants of Abbas, the Prophet's uncle), as caliph. Marwan II's army was defeated and he fled to Egypt, where he was killed fighting south of Fustat. His head was sent to the new caliph in Kufa, other Umayyads were hunted down and executed, and the

Umayyad dynasty was extinguished—save for a refugee prince, Abd al-Rahman Ibn Muʻawiya, who escaped from Syria to find safe haven, and found his own caliphate, at the far western edge of the world, in Cordoba. Umayyad rule would endure in Spain for another three hundred years.

The Abbasid family had neither instigated nor directed the revolution that came to bear their name, but they were swept into power by it and moved quickly to take it in hand. Abu Muslim ably assisted the new Caliph al-Saffah and his successor, his brother Abu Jaʻfar, who on becoming caliph took the title al-Mansur ("the Victorious"), in suppressing their immediate rivals. But he was clearly a threat himself. He was invited to al-Mansur's camp and assassinated; his life wreathed in legends, he would later be seen as a saint. Those who had placed utopian or messianic hopes in the revolution were disappointed to find themselves under just another dynastic caliphate, albeit one that now based its right to rule on membership in the Prophet's family. It was also more accommodating of the different parts of the larger Muslim community, especially Persians and *mawali*. The caliph's capital was moved to Iraq, first near Kufa and then, under the Caliph al-Mansur, at the new city he founded near the ruins of al-Mada'in (Ctesiphon) on the Tigris. The new capital was to be called Medinat al-Salam, the City of Peace, and it would be the flourishing and fabled centre of the caliphate for half a millennium. Everyone called it Baghdad.[18]

From Baghdad, the Abbasid caliphs would rule over a stabilised, prosperous and immense empire stretching from the former Roman provinces of Ifriqiya and Numidia (modern Tunisia and Algeria) in the west to what is now Afghanistan and Uzbekistan in the east. Already, in the far west of Spain and North Africa, Muslims lived under other dynasties independent of the caliphate in Baghdad. But the Abbasids ruled at the hinge of the world—between the Indian Ocean and the Mediterranean, between Asia, Africa and the emerging world of post-Roman Europe. They could credibly claim to exercise universal sovereignty under God, their inheritance from the wider world in which Islam had emerged, under the aegis of the succession to the

Prophet that they specifically claimed. As a court poet wrote in praise of the Caliph Harun al-Rashid, who reigned from 786 to 809 CE:

All eyes are raised to his face, whereas all other eyes
Gazing on people have never been raised to the like of Harun.
You see all around him the rich masters of the House of Hashem
Just as the shining stars surround the full moon.
. . . .
When the people lack clouds [bringing water], there come down
Successively on them, through your two hands, clouds bearing
* rain.*
. . . .
The people are just like a man who goes down to your cisterns
* to drink,*
And who goes away from them with thirst quenched with
* water.*[19]

The next five centuries of the Abbasids' empire in the Middle East would later be seen as the golden age of Islamic history. Such conceptions always say more about the later times in which they are formulated than about the age they seek to describe. But there can be no doubt that the high medieval caliphate of the mid-700s to the mid-1200s crystallised an integrated, multiethnic, confident and articulate society, economy, state and culture. Islam had come into the world, and now Muslims had made a world of their own.

3

THE BOOK, THE LAW, AND THE SPIRIT

We don't know very much about the life of Fatima al-Fihri. We know that she was a merchant's daughter, and that she had a sister said to be her equal in wealth and piety. We know that her family moved from Qayrawan, the first Muslim city to be founded in what is now Tunisia, to Fez, a new city of artisans, merchants, and scholars in Morocco, the far west of the Muslim world, in the ninth century CE. And we know that she had enough money and imagination to create a mosque that would become the world's oldest still-existing university, the Qarawiyyin, founded in 859 CE: a centre of learning and religion, named after the people of her birthplace, and built in the city where she settled.

Five hundred years later, in 1369 (or perhaps in 1377, we can't be sure), another North African, the scholar and traveller Ibn Battuta, died three hundred miles to the south, in Marrakesh, after travels that had taken him all over the known world. His account of his journeys, by turns prosaic and fantastical, was dictated by him to his editor, at the command of the prince Abu Inan Faris, the mid-fourteenth-century ruler of Fez who was briefly recognised as "commander of the faithful" across all of North Africa. Known as much for his learning in law and letters as for his height and horsemanship, Abu Inan created the Qarawiyyin's library. He also founded several colleges (or madrasas, literally "places of study") for the accommodation and teaching of students. The most magnificent of these, known today as the Madrasa Bu Inaniyya, still stands a short walk up the hill from the Qarawiyyin in the old city of Fez. Between Fatima's time and his, law and learning like that taught at the Qarawiyyin, and carried by Ibn Battuta in his brain and his books, had become a shared culture everywhere from the Atlantic coast of Africa to the eastern edges of the Indian Ocean.

By Ibn Battuta's time, the Islamic ecumene overlaid a geographically vast, ethnically diverse, and politically fragmented map. Even within the Middle East, centralised Abbasid rule had lasted only until the mid-tenth century, and although the caliphate's prosperity would endure and the caliph's nominal authority was proclaimed more widely, there was no longer a single Islamic state in which Muslim sovereignty could be said to rest. Instead, across an immense and politically divided expanse of Asia and Africa, being Muslim meant being part of a vast network of cultural and commercial connections.

Ibn Battuta was able to send money from India to his wife in Syria via another scholar who, like him, was originally from North Africa. In almost every place he arrived, from Andalusia to the Indian Ocean, there were fellow scholars whom he knew, or with whom he shared a common culture and social standing. His qualifications and practical experience as a scholar and judge, learned in Islamic law, enabled him to move freely, to be received with respect, and to find work in Delhi, Sri Lanka, and the Maldives as easily as in Cordoba, Fez, and Damascus, even when the Muslim rulers of one area might be at war with those of another. He might not in fact have travelled as far as China (his account of Asia begins to lose precision and plausibility the farther east he goes), but he could have done, along sea-lanes plied by Muslim traders that linked Muslim communities from the Bay of Bengal all the way to Sumatra and Quanzhou, the thriving south China port that the Arabs called Zaytun. If there was now a wider world of Islam, created by the Arab conquests and then by the spread of Muslims beyond the borders of the caliphate, it was law and learning, credit and commerce, and the travelling scholars and merchants who carried them, as well as the conquests of ambitious state-builders, that shaped it.[1]

◇◇◇◇◇◇◇◇

Muslim law and learning became divergent and sometimes conflicting, but the divergences had a common basis in the sources of the tradition that all Muslims shared and recognised: first and foremost, the Qur'an itself. The Qur'an—the record of God's revelation to the Prophet, considered to have been God's own direct speech—was compiled and arranged in its written form sometime after the Prophet's death. It would continue to have its fullest embodiment in the act of its being spoken aloud, and the earliest written texts seem to have been intended to preserve it only when it was feared that not enough of the Prophet's early Companions, who were able to recite from memory what Muhammad had recited to them, were still alive to ensure the transmission of God's word to the community. This work is said to have been begun by the Caliph Abu Bakr, but what became the "authorised version," according to the Muslim tradition, was compiled under his successor, Uthman. He entrusted the task to the Prophet's own scribe, Zayd Ibn Thabit, and dispatched copies of the approved text to the mosques of the new garrison cities, to be read and taught there.

Because of the way the earliest manuscripts were written, and the reported survival of early variations that differed from Uthman's recension, uncertainties would persist about the exact reading of some verses. But all Muslims agreed on the contents of the Qur'an and its central importance. Although Muslim communities would develop the calligraphy and illustration used in manuscript production to a sublime fine art, oral recitation of the text, rather than its written or, later, printed form, would continue to have priority in its transmission. The devotional recitation of the text and the discipline of committing it to memory—and the emphasis laid, in doing so, on attentive listening to its oral transmission—would remain key aspects of Muslim education and piety. Particular significance would be laid on becoming a *hafiz*, one who has memorised, and thus internalised, the entire text by heart and become its carrier or "preserver." The individual, intimate embodiment and voicing of the sacred text would become a crucial aspect of Muslim religious experience and selfhood. As the great medieval mystic Ibn Arabi would put it, the Qur'an "is perpetually new for any of those who recite it." In daily prayer, in communal activities, and in the soundscape of Muslim-majority cultures, the living presence of the Qur'an would also become a formative part of collective life.[2]

The Qur'an uses the word "book" (in Arabic, *kitab*) frequently—indeed, 261 times—describing itself as "the Book, about which there is no doubt, a guide for those who are mindful of God." But as the enduring importance of its oral transmission suggests, it was not simply a text on pages between covers. A different Arabic word, *mushaf*, meaning "put on pages," would be (and still is) used to refer to a physical copy of the Qur'anic text in book form. The Qur'an itself would be understood as something more than this: as the living speech of God, given to humankind by the voice of the Prophet and intended to be spoken aloud and heard, down the ages, by his followers. From a historical perspective, the text gives evidence of its own human, historical context in its use of words that can be shown to have come into Arabic from other languages circulating in the late ancient world, especially Syriac. (It was almost certainly to counter accusations that Muhammad had "learned" his revelation from Jewish and Christian writings that Muslims would develop the doctrine that Muhammad had been illiterate.) But just as the Qur'an is not simply a book in our usual sense of the word, we should probably not think of it as a straightforward adoption by Muhammad of Jewish and Christian models of "scripture," as evidence of prophetic authority, either.

The Qur'anic conception of "God's writing" is clearly related to other monotheistic ideas of revelation. The Qur'an itself speaks of portions of the Book previously given to Jews and Christians (and misunderstood or falsified by them) and refers to Jews and Christians collectively as the "People of the Book." But it also has its own distinctiveness. Indeed, it can be argued that the Qur'an expresses a consciousness of the revealed text as divine scripture—as writing *by* as well as *from* God—in a way that the Jewish and Christian books of scripture, as consciously human compositions recounting God's intervention in human history, do not. The "book" in the Qur'anic sense of the word was an emanation of God's divine knowledge, authority, and commandment, in some accounts a copy of an eternal text existing in heaven in which all of history and all of revelation was preserved, and at the same time a revelation unfolding in time to Muhammad, and commenting on itself as it did so. Although it became a fixed text, a literary monument of world-historical importance, and the primary source of Islamic law, the Qur'an was also, for early scholars and later Muslims, an unparalleled model of poetic eloquence, God's own speech, eternal and inimitable: miraculous.[3]

The Qur'an, then, was and remains central to Muslim personal piety and devotional practice, and since being Muslim meant belonging to a community, it was also central to understanding how the community ought to live: that is, as with the Jewish scriptures, it was central to the law. There was some explicit legal content in the Qur'an, especially relating to gender and sexual relations—marriage and divorce, sexual behaviour, and inheritance—and serious crimes such as murder, highway robbery, and theft. Notably, what came to be considered the "limits" (*hudud*), penalties for certain crimes, would principally relate to actions prohibited in the Qur'an. These especially concerned engaging in illicit sex, false accusations of illicit sex, theft, banditry, and—although its prohibition was in fact slow, very unevenly enforced, and often ignored, especially in court culture—wine-drinking. But not all of the penalties for these were themselves Qur'anic. In the Qur'an's formulation, *hudud allah*, "God's boundaries" that people might not transgress, in fact usually occurs with reference to behaviour that is recommended rather than prohibited, especially with reference to relations between men and women. But the *hudud* came to be identified above all as a category of punishments.[4]

As penalties, the *hudud* could be thought of as setting boundaries to the violence that might be inflicted in retribution for a wrong, restricting to exemplary deterrence what might otherwise, in pre-Islamic tribal Arabia, have been unrestrained vengeance. Usually, in some sense these restrictions made the punishment "fit the crime," such as the stipulation that a thief's hand should be cut off (because it was the hand that had sinned). Given their severity, lawyers would develop especially demanding standards for establishing guilt in such cases. The particular social sensitivity attaching to sexual propriety in a patriarchal, late ancient society was indicated by both illicit sex and false or unproven accusations of illicit sex being crimes of the same kind, both subject to *hudud* penalties. However, the penalty for a false accusation—flogging—would come to be much lighter than the penalty for extramarital sex. In one Qur'anic verse, women found guilty of illicit sex are to be confined in the home, but another verse stipulates one hundred lashes for both parties to an adulterous affair. Islamic law, like ancient Jewish law, considered illicit sex a crime not only against the husband but against God and the community; the ancient Jewish ("Old Testament") penalty was death. Later Muslim jurists dispensed with both Qur'anic commands; they too applied the death penalty instead.[5]

In the late twentieth century, enforcement of so-called *hudud* penalties, such as cutting off hands for theft or flogging for alcohol consumption, would become touchstones of religious authenticity for fundamentalist interpretations of Islamic law, whether by repressive regimes or extremist insurgents. Such judicial violence has heavily influenced what sharia or "Qur'anic law" has come to mean in non-Muslim perceptions of Islam. But Islamic law was and is much more varied and complex than this. The word *shari'a*, literally meaning the "path," "way," or "road" laid down by God for humankind to follow, occurs only once in the Qur'an, when God says: "Now we have set you on the right way, so follow it, and do not follow the desires of those who do not know [the truth]." The Qur'an also uses other words for the "way" or "path" of God; the word *shari'a* was also used by medieval Jews and Christians writing in Arabic, at the same time as Islamic law was being consolidated, to denote prophetic law (the law of Moses) or the "way" taught by Jesus.

Finding out what Islam's sharia entailed was no simple matter. Making the law, Muslims generally agreed, was God's prerogative, and establishing it on earth was a prophetic function. But the law had not just been handed down to the Prophet in a long list of commandments. God ordained His way, and transmitted it to people via Muhammad's words and actions, but the community still needed scholars to do the human, interpretive work of figuring out what it was and how it was to be followed. This activity, jurisprudence (in Arabic, *fiqh*) exercised by legal scholars, was the only way to determine what was sharia, and what was not. And on this, Muslims would come to have very varied opinions.[6]

◇◇◇◇◇◇◇◇

In the eighth and early ninth centuries, different schools of thought proliferated, divided over questions of whose teaching and authority could be trusted, and how best to think about the nature of God and revelation, as well as over the more politically central questions of who should properly be caliph, and with what sort of authority. Not all such groups survived: some teachings disappeared while others coalesced into lasting doctrine. Most Muslims, though, would come to agree, in the course of the eighth to tenth centuries CE, about the basic shape of the law and what its sources were.

After (and sometimes explaining) the Qur'an, second only to it in importance as a source of law, but more difficult to ascertain, was what Muslims knew of the teaching and example, the "way" (in Arabic, the *sunna*), of the Prophet Muhammad. Before the Prophet's time, among the Arabs *sunna* simply meant the way that people had acted in the past—any precedent, but especially individual examples of behaviour that were worthy of emulation, was part of a group's *sunna*. It was passed down to them from their ancestors and carried their ancestors' authority. In the first century of Islam, Muslims thus referred to the *sunna* of their forebears, especially of the Prophet's Companions, other early Muslims, and the first caliphs, when looking for approved models of conduct. By the time of his death, or very soon afterward, Muhammad's own *sunna* was identified as one such exemplary "way" that Muslims should follow. But it was not until much later—in the late eighth and early ninth centuries—that "the sunna of the Prophet" acquired a uniquely important meaning and position, separate from and superior to the examples of the first caliphs, the Prophet's Companions, or other examples drawn from ancestral precedent, in formulating what by then was emerging as Islamic law.[7]

The emergence of a codified body of knowledge about what the Prophet had said and done came considerably later than the official recension of the Qur'an. It was in the first half of the 700s CE that narratives or reports (*hadiths*) about what Muhammad had done, or allowed to be done, began to be collected in the main Muslim cities from those who themselves had heard them from older members of the community. It would be another hundred years—the mid-ninth century—before collections of reports generally accepted as authentic would be established, and longer still after that, by the end of the 1100s, that six of these collections would become recognised, authoritative sources for most Muslims.

This very slow crystallisation of knowledge based on hadith accompanied, and also influenced, a shift in the way Muslims thought about and practised what became Islamic law. In the first years after the Arab conquests, order was kept and morality upheld among the expanded Muslim community by judges appointed to the garrison cities. Their function, though, had more to do with conflict mediation and the exercise of discretionary judgment (in Arabic, *ra'y*) in resolving disputes than with applying a law that did not yet exist in any codified form. Except in the relatively few clear cases where the Qur'an gave instructions as to what God said Muslims should do, customary practice—the *sunna* recognised among the people of Medina, Basra, or Kufa—and the judge's own reasoning were most important. Sound rulings were based on knowledge of the model behaviour of forebears, or the previous opinions of people deemed trustworthy, applied to new circumstances through the judge's own interpretation of what was appropriate. As the caliphs' state consolidated and expanded its capacities to govern, the role of the judge became more specialised and more clearly defined. Judges came to be appointed centrally, by the caliph himself, and their authority was independent of the political hierarchy of provincial and municipal governors.

At the same time, sound rulings came to be seen as needing a more consistent and reliable basis. Over the course of the eighth and ninth centuries, jurists became divided between those who emphasised the importance of *ra'y*—exercising independent reason, or following the reasoning of earlier distinguished judges—and those for whom the compilation of hadith and its authority as recording the Prophet's own sunna had primacy. Proponents of *ra'y* would later be called "rationalists." Their opponents, the "hadith people" (*ahl al-hadith*), by contrast would be identified as "traditionalists," because they claimed to rely wholly on higher authority transmitted from the past (not because their view was more traditional: in fact, it was newer). By the early ninth century, the sunna of the Prophet as known through hadith had come to the fore as the indispensable source of law, and the "hadith people" had come to call themselves *ahl al-sunna*, the "people of the sunna," indicating their claim to be the voice of orthodoxy—of true belief. The emphasis on reason associated with Abu Hanifa, a scholar of jurisprudence who lived in Kufa in the first half of the eighth century and who died in 767 CE, and the primacy accorded to the practice of the community in Medina (which was held to have been continuous since the Prophet's time) by the jurist Malik Ibn Anas, who died in 796 CE, were overtaken in the century after them by the ascendancy of Prophetic hadith as the principal source of law.

This development was codified by a third great scholar, Muhammad al-Shafi'i, a student of Malik in Medina who was born in southern Palestine and moved frequently between the Hijaz and Baghdad before settling at Fustat in Egypt, where he died in 820 CE. Now indisputably superior to, and displacing, other precedents (the multiple sunnas of the earlier period), the Prophet's sunna was established as second in authority only to the Qur'an. Reliance on hadith as a source of law was deemed decisively preferable to transmitted or independent reasoning. Independent reasoning, applied by analogy from existing cases, would remain a legitimate source of legal judgment, albeit an inferior one, for some jurists. But among the most scrupulous supporters of the authority of hadith, it was now seen as mere "opinion": flawed human reason that could never substitute for the authoritative word of God and the example of His Prophet, which must be observed to the letter, even if this seemed irrational or unreasonable.

The most prominent of the piety-minded "hadith people," and the individual who would become their figurehead, was the hadith scholar and jurist Ahmad Ibn Hanbal, who lived in Baghdad in the late eighth and first half of the ninth century, and died there in 855 CE. Descended from a family that had taken part in the conquest of Khurasan, Ibn Hanbal inherited family properties that allowed him the independent income to pursue a life of scholarship, although accounts of his life also portray him as intensely frugal and constantly short of cash. He would become one of the most influential figures of Muslim intellectual and religious history. "You could ask him about any issue," it was said, "and he would answer as if he had all the learning in the world laid out before him." Learning—determining the correct understanding of God's law, in order to live by it—was to him the central activity of the right-thinking Muslim. On seeing hadith scholars drawing near, we're told, Ibn Hanbal "pointed at the inkpots in their hands, and said, 'Those are the lamps of Islam.'" Asked whether it was better to pray and fast, or to write down hadiths, he replied that it was better to write hadiths, since anyone might pray and fast simply in imitation of others, but collecting Prophetic hadith showed particular devotion. Indeed, not only was Ibn Hanbal opposed to jurists who preferred the opinions of earlier scholars and judges to hadith reports, he went so far as to consider adherents of some other schools of thought as unbelievers, not Muslims at all. A true Muslim, for him, had scrupulously to observe tradition: anything considered an innovation that departed from the way laid down in the Prophet's own example was the opposite of *sunna*, and to be avoided at all costs.[8]

Prophetic hadith became central in part because Muslims everywhere needed a single basis of legal authority. Centuries before Ibn Battuta, scholars like al-Shafi'i already travelled widely to study with different masters and transmitters of knowledge about the community's past. The different traditions that they found preserved in different places, from Mecca and Medina to Basra, Kufa, Baghdad, Palestine, Egypt and Syria, came to need something more than their own authority to survive and to be spread elsewhere, into the new provinces to the east and west. Reliance on hadith, though, could not simply drive out all other ways of thinking about the law. For one thing, thanks to the assiduous work of the hadith scholars, there were now thousands of sayings or accounts of behaviour attributed to the Prophet in circulation, some considered more reliable than others. Ibn Hanbal's own massive compendium, the *Musnad*, contained thousands of reports (the most complete modern printed edition runs to fifty volumes), some of which contradicted each other. Interpretive work was still needed to determine what could be learned from these texts, and to decide how to apply them to contemporary Muslim life.[9]

By the end of the tenth century, a middle way or synthesis had developed between the competing "rationalist" and "traditionalist" bodies of thought. The extreme textualism of Ibn Hanbal and his followers was tempered by a modified acceptance of the necessity for interpretive reasoning, provided that such reasoning proceeded according to accepted rules, and always based itself on the firm ground of the authoritative texts of the Qur'an and hadith. Properly qualified scholars were required to exercise their own interpretive effort (*ijtihad*) in order to arrive at a legal opinion. Necessarily, such opinions might differ, but as long as the scholar was properly qualified, knew the sources of the law well, and proceeded according to correct jurisprudence, the opinion would be considered valid (though another opinion might be considered better). By about 1000 CE, older claims for the reliability of the consensus of a particular community—what the Muslims of Medina or of Kufa agreed upon as right and proper ways of doing things—were replaced by, or subsumed into, a more fully developed theory of consensus, or agreement. This meant that what the properly qualified scholars of any era agreed upon was binding on everyone. Far from being simply the application of a fixed set of rules handed down directly from God, then, Islamic law was all about systematic interpretation.[10]

In theology as well as in law, diverse opinions on central questions proliferated over these same centuries: Could the existence of evil be attributed to God or only to humans? What was the scope of human free will? When the Qur'an spoke of God sitting on a throne, or of His hand or face, must this be interpreted metaphorically (since God, being unlimited, could not be limited by an actual body) or were these real attributes that God somehow possessed? What was the relationship between God and His word, the Qur'an: had God created it, or was it eternal with Him? As in the debates over law, in theology and philosophy too, rational argument or reasoned disputation was suspect to some, especially the followers of Ibn Hanbal, even when used in defence of the faith.

Still, it was a self-professed follower of Ibn Hanbal, Abu al-Hasan al-Ash'ari, who came up with a synthesis in theology that, like that in law, combined rationalist and traditionalist ideas. A descendant of one of the Prophet's Companions, like many early scholars al-Ash'ari lived mostly in Iraq. He was born in Basra in 873 CE and died in Baghdad in 935 or 936, and the move between cities mirrored the development of his ideas. Basra was a centre of rationalist intellectual life, and al-Ash'ari's teacher there was a leader of one of the schools of thought most heavily criticised by the strictest "hadith people." As would often be the case in such life stories, al-Ash'ari's shift away from his early beliefs to what would come to be seen as an orthodox position was prompted by dreaming of the Prophet: Muhammad called the young scholar to adhere to "true tradition," but subsequently instructed him not to abandon the science of rational argument. Al-Ash'ari's works, expounding orthodoxy by means of reason, provided a foundation on which Muslim theology would build for the next millennium.

◇◇◇◇◇◇◇

The doctrines developed by these scholars and their followers from the 700s to 900s CE shaped the Islam of those who would come to call themselves *ahl al-sunna wa'l-jama'a*, "the people of the sunna and the community," those who, as they saw it, followed the way of the Prophet and the consensus of the Prophet's community. They would therefore be known as "Sunni" Muslims. Within the Sunni community, four schools of law crystallised around the memories of the four great teachers who came to be revered as exceptional interpreters of the sacred texts and who, by the mid-tenth century, were identified by their followers as founding authority figures: the Maliki school, after Malik Ibn Anas, the Hanafi, after Abu Hanifa, the Shafi'i, after Muhammad al-Shafi'i, and the Hanbali, after Ibn Hanbal.

Other schools of law had existed but died out over time. It was these four that would become known as the *madhhab*s ("routes," or schools) of jurisprudence, each with its authoritative texts and juridical preferences. After the introduction and spread of madrasa education, sponsored by ruling elites from central Asia to North Africa from the eleventh century onward, each madhhab would be taught in its own schools. Astute rulers would sometimes make a point of accommodating each of the four recognised, equally orthodox interpretive traditions: the great schools of medieval Cairo would have four teaching halls, one for the professors and students of each madhhab. But each would also become prominent in different parts of the growing world of Muslims: Maliki law would predominate in North Africa; the Hanafi school would be prominent in Iraq, Syria, Turkey, Afghanistan and India (and later became the predominant doctrine of law in the Ottoman Empire); the Shafi'i school was established in Egypt and spread to Yemen, East Africa and then to central and Southeast Asia. The Hanbali school, named for a founder who was himself so attached to unmediated Prophetic authority that he had never desired his own jurisprudence to become a model for anyone, was especially important in the Abbasid capital, Baghdad. Ibn Hanbal achieved extraordinary fame in the city. (This was something else he did not want: "I want to die," he apparently told his son, adding that being famous was worse than being flogged and jailed.) But his followers, the Hanbalis, remained a minority elsewhere, until the Wahhabi movement in eighteenth-century Arabia claimed them as its inspiration. Hanbalism is the officially established school of law in Saudi Arabia today.[11]

The importance of determining the law made the interpretive abilities and authority of its scholars central not only to law courts but to community life. Islam had preachers and prayer leaders, but no professional clergy or priesthood. It was not rituals dispensed by ordained ministers but knowledge (*'ilm*) refined through the disciplines of the religious sciences that permitted the community to live as Muslims. Learning, *'ilm*, thus guaranteed a particular social standing to the "learned" (*'ulama*), scholars of the law like Ibn Battuta. The emergence of the 'ulama as a social group was thus a crucial development in Muslim social and political, as well as intellectual and religious, life.

Generally drawn from the property-owning, notable or patrician urban elite, often also engaged in trade, and often hereditary—passing down their learning and their standing within families that became distinguished dynasties—the 'ulama were also capable of absorbing into their ranks poorer but capable students who could rise by intellect and patronage. They thus often combined religious status with other forms of social standing, and were often major figures—sometimes, *the* major figures—of urban life. Their prominence is clear in the medieval histories of cities, which were often histories written both by and about them. In at least some places, urban politics that were essentially intra-elite struggles for pre-eminence worked through competition between the different schools of law. In eleventh-century Nishapur, then a great city of eastern Iran on the trade roads to India and China, families identified with the Shafi'i and Hanafi law schools did not marry each other, and their rivalry led to open urban violence. In medieval chronicles, *madhhab*, as well as denoting a school of law, can also mean a "faction." Shafi'is and Hanafis were Nishapur's Montagues and Capulets.[12]

If the scholars came to be a significant social and political force, especially in the cities where learning, wealth, and political power were all concentrated, their significance also lay in their independence from the central state. Scholarly families might provide judges for the state's law courts, but their biographies might make a point of emphasising their reluctance to serve. Indeed, keeping one's distance from the worldly and potentially corrupting power of the prince's court would become almost a cliché of religious respectability. Ibn Hanbal, on being told by his teacher al-Shafi'i that the caliph wished to make him a judge, apparently replied: "If you ever mention this again, that's the last you'll see of me." At any rate, the scholars' position was not dependent on their appointment as agents of the state. Rather, as city notables they served as intermediaries between their own urban following and their more distant rulers. When Abbasid central control began to fragment from the mid-tenth century onward, and regional military dynasties established themselves as de facto rulers under the caliph's nominal sovereignty, the leading families of the provincial cities became even more important: to raise taxes, to move goods and troops, and to keep order, rulers depended more on the scholarly class than the scholars did on the state.[13]

Indeed, the 'ulama could clip the wings even of the caliph. In 833 CE, a few months before his death, Harun al-Rashid's son, the Caliph Abdallah al-Ma'mun, gave instructions that judges and witnesses in court should be tested on a specific doctrine—whether the Qur'an had been created, or was eternal along with God. Only those who accepted the doctrine approved by the caliph—that the Qur'an had been created by God—were to be allowed to hold office or have their testimony accepted. Dissenters would be imprisoned. The question at issue had been contentious for decades. Al-Ma'mun endorsed the view of the so-called Mu'tazili ("neutral," or "standing aside") school of theology, a so-called rationalist group that was strongest in Basra. (Their name reportedly came from their "standing aside" from an earlier debate about whether sinful Muslims should be considered as unbelievers, or else from their view of themselves as shunning sinful society.)

The opposing view, that the Qur'an was God's eternal Word, was held especially by the "hadith people," among whom Ibn Hanbal was the most prominent in Baghdad.

What became known as al-Ma'mun's "test" (*mihna*), however, was less a theological nicety than a major test of strength between the caliph and the scholarly class over who could determine religious truth. The caliphate, early on, had assumed an almost sacred character: the guidance of a true imam had been thought essential for individual salvation as well as community cohesion. Under the Abbasids, the courtly splendour and ritual of the caliphs and their imperial power had assumed something of the quasi-divine monarchy once associated with the Sasanian shahs. The prerogative of laying down the law in a centralised way, at the caliph's command, however, had escaped them. Judges were appointed by "the commander of the faithful," but their judgments were independent of him. (In Islamic law, there was no right of appeal to a higher authority: the properly qualified judge's opinion was considered correct. While another judge elsewhere might have a different view, or another judge in the same court might reach another verdict later, as long as the judge who had heard the case was still in post, all his judgments had to stand.)

The scholars' views on questions of creed, of true belief and error, had also been independent of the caliph. The "test" was an attempt to assert caliphal authority, both over the dispensation of the law and over doctrine. For al-Ma'mun, control over religious disputes between the people was a matter of public order. He complained that "the broad mass... of the ordinary people" were identifying themselves as "adherents of the sunna... people of the divine truth, religion and the community" —as defining orthodoxy—who took it upon themselves to denounce others as "people of false belief, infidelity and schism." Common people should not be making such divisive distinctions, the caliph thought: those who did so were themselves in error.[14]

The test lasted until 850 CE, when it was abandoned, having failed to impose adherence to the caliph's doctrine. Its most notorious episode was the imprisonment and flogging, on the orders of al-Ma'mun's successor, al-Muʿtasim, of the revered Ibn Hanbal. Humble, retiring, and unworldly, but intransigent in holding to what he believed to be the truth, Ibn Hanbal would become the icon of the pious Sunni scholar, as uninterested in politics as in wealth or fame, but wholly principled in his belief and in his refusal to give it up in the face of power or even persecution. Whether he did in fact give in and confess the doctrine of the created Qurʾan, or whether he was flogged to unconsciousness and released from prison only when there was a threat of popular insurrection in Baghdad, is unclear from the conflicting accounts of the event. It is clear, though, that Ibn Hanbal became a popular hero, and that the test and its agents became extremely unpopular. When the Caliph al-Muʿtasim died, a Baghdad judge who had apparently been especially zealous in applying the test was forced to flee his house while a crowd burned down his door and ransacked his property. A later caliph, al-Mutawakkil, ordered former agents of the test in Egypt to be cursed from the pulpit, and tried to lavish honours and hospitality on Ibn Hanbal. (This too caused Ibn Hanbal great distress.)[15]

For their part, once the challenge to their independence was over, most scholars were happy to preach obedience to the caliphate and exalt the dynasty. (Ibn Hanbal just wished that they would leave him alone.) The long-term effect of the test was clear: there was a separation of powers between the holders of political authority—a prince, a sultan, a military warlord, a commander or even a caliph—and the scholars. The caliph ruled in God's name, but he could not force compliance with his own rulings on God's law. He might be kingly, but he was no pope. Caliphal and judicial authority, political and scholarly authority, were distinct. The Muslim community lived under the rule of law: that law was given not by man but by God, and the people who determined what the law was were not divinely ordained rulers, but the learned.

◇◇◇◇◇◇◇

This was not everyone's view, however. For some Muslims—a minority who, al-Maʾmun worried, were being vilified by the majority as the people of "false belief...and schism"—the true imam was still a supreme spiritual, and to some, doctrinally infallible, leader of the community. But that imam was not the reigning caliph.

The slogan of the revolution that had brought the Abbasids to power, that a true imam from "the People of the House" would bring satisfaction to the Muslims, evoked the hopes of those who had always considered the Prophet's cousin, Ali Ibn Abi Talib, and his family (the Alids) as the legitimate successors to Muhammad. The imamate they believed in had been lost when the community, as they saw it, had gone against the Prophet's wishes and accepted first Abu Bakr, then Umar and Uthman, as caliph. After the Battle of Karbala, where Ali's son Husayn was killed, pro-Alid sentiment crystallised around the martyrdom of Husayn as not only a failed uprising but an almost apocalyptic event, an epic tragedy whose commemoration and mourning would define the community of true believers. A strong, affective and charismatic sense of loyalty to Ali's family persisted, especially among the Muslims of southern Iraq, and as time went on, they would come to attach an emotionally intense spirituality to the Karbala story. By the mid-ninth century, they had made Husayn's tomb at Karbala a pilgrimage site.

Pro-Alid opinion opposed the Umayyads, the dynasty that was seen as having seized power from Ali and abused it from the beginning. It thus supported the revolt that spread from Khurasan against the Umayyads in the 740s. The Abbasids' descent from the Prophet's uncle was enough for some, but others considered them no less usurpers of the caliphate than the Umayyads had been. Muhammad Ibn Abdallah, the great-grandson of Ali's son Hasan, wrote to the Abbasid Caliph al-Mansur reminding him of what the Qur'an had to say about Pharaoh, the archetypal tyrant. "Our paternal ancestor, Ali," he went on, "was the trustee [of the Prophet] and the imam, so how could you have inherited his sovereign authority when his own descendants are still alive?" Known to his supporters as al-Nafs al-Zakiyya, "the Pure Soul," Muhammad Ibn Abdallah based himself in Medina and led a revolt against the new caliphate in 762 CE. Without any of the revolutionary organisation or conducive circumstances that had prevailed twelve years earlier, he was quickly defeated—once again, a Muslim army besieged and attacked the Prophet's city, and the head of the Prophet's rebellious descendant was sent to the caliph. A larger rebellion in Basra led by Muhammad Ibn Abdallah's brother Ibrahim also failed. But loyalty to the Alid cause, and reverence for the People of the House, was growing into a distinct identity, that of *shi'at Ali*, the "partisans of Ali," or "the Shi'a," holding to distinctively Shi'i doctrines, a Shi'i account of Islam's history, distinctive patterns of prayer and ritual, and their own understanding of what being Muslim really ought to mean.[16]

The Shi'a would, almost by definition, remain a minority of Muslims. (Today, they make up something between 10 and 15 per cent of the world's Muslim population, concentrated in Iran and southern Iraq, Yemen and eastern Saudi Arabia, northern Afghanistan, Pakistan, and western and central India.) Those who by the end of the tenth century would define themselves as "the people of the Sunna and the community," or Sunnis, did so explicitly against the increasingly distinct confessional identity of the Shi'a. The Shi'a, of course, saw themselves as following the Prophet's "way" too. But while recognising the self-described "people of the Sunna" as fellow believers, they would come to see themselves as holding to a truer, or fuller, belief: in God's justice and its intelligibility to human reason, and in the continuing divine guidance sent by God to his people through the community's imams, who descended from the Prophet and who alone were capable of faultlessly interpreting God's law and properly establishing God's rule. Sunnis, on the other hand, saw themselves as avoiding the errors into which, they believed, sectarian Shi'i doctrines had fallen, particularly when these led to rejection of the legitimacy of the first three caliphs, Abu Bakr, Umar and Uthman.[17]

While there were differences over theological questions that divided them from the emerging consensus of the Sunnis, the Shi'i tradition focused especially on the nature of the imamate. They believed that during his lifetime, Muhammad had marked Ali out with particular favour: Ali had been a child in the Prophet's household and the first, or the youngest, Muslim, and he had carried the Prophet's standard to victory in battle. Above all, they believed that during his final pilgrimage to Mecca, at a marshy spot outside the city called Ghadir Khumm, Muhammad himself had invested Ali as his successor. Alongside the tragedy of Karbala, this event would become central to Shiʻi narratives of Islam's history. Its illustration in a beautiful fourteenth-century devotional painting, part of a manuscript copy of an eleventh-century book by the great polymath Muhammad al-Biruni, is a surviving example of medieval Muslim art in which the depiction of the Prophet, whose face is shown, was not yet considered unacceptable: but in the same image, the faces of the first three caliphs, standing around the figures of the Prophet and Ali, have been erased. Given pride of place in a book probably produced for an early fourteenth-century ruling dynasty that had embraced Shiʻi beliefs, and combining Persian and Chinese artistic motifs in depicting an Islamic theme by a Muslim artist, the portrait makes a historical and doctrinal as well as an aesthetic point. In its own time, it was already an expression of the divergences between Muslims. Today, the image remains highly contentious, with some Sunni Muslims considering such depictions as un-Islamic. In 2022, when the painting was shown to students in an art history class in Minnesota (with advance warning provided to Muslim students that it might be found offensive), complaints led to the instructor's dismissal, and a scandal over academic freedom and respect for religious sensibilities.[18]

There was plenty of contention, too, among the Shiʻa themselves. The revolt of "the Pure Soul" was only one of several pro-Alid uprisings in the eighth and ninth centuries, and it did not have the support of everyone who would later be associated with the Shiʻa tradition. Al-Nafs al-Zakiyya's own cousin Jaʻfar al-Sadiq—who traced his own parentage back through Ali's son Husayn and, via his mother, to Abu Bakr, and who was thus descended from two of the early caliphs as well as from the Prophet—refused to endorse the rebellion. Jaʻfar al-Sadiq, who would be recognised by later Shiʻa as the sixth legitimate

imam in the line of descent from Ali and Husayn, was a retiring, politically quiescent scholar of hadith and law who gave his name to a
fifth madhhab, the Ja'fari school of jurisprudence, recognised among
the Shi'a. Loyalty to a true imam took theological and cosmological as
well as, or instead of, political form, and Ja'far al-Sadiq's imamate focused on teaching and guidance while shunning calls for political activism. Before the accession of the Abbasids, we're told, Abu Muslim,
the leader of the revolution in Khurasan, had written to Ja'far al-Sadiq
offering him the caliphate: Ja'far's response was to burn the letter.

For other Shi'is, though, to be a true imam necessarily meant taking every opportunity to rise up against tyranny and attempt to establish a truly legitimate political order, however hopeless the prospect.
This was particularly the stance of those who identified themselves as
following in the footsteps of Husayn's grandson Zayd Ibn Ali, who
was killed by Umayyad forces in Kufa in 740 CE. Zayd's father, Ali
Zayn al-Abidin, as a young son of Husayn had been one of the few
survivors of Karbala, and along with his sister Zaynab thus became
an immensely revered figure: he would be considered the fourth
true imam, after Ali and his sons, Hasan and Husayn. (Zayd's older
brother, Muhammad al-Baqir, was recognised by pro-Alid opinion,
and later Shi'i convention, as the fifth imam.)

Zayd's revolt against the Umayyads became a prototypical example of jihad against oppression. It was supported not only by pro-Alid
activists but by other piety-minded critics of the regime, notably the
great scholar Abu Hanifa, who would later be recognised as one of the
founders of canonical Sunni law. Vengeance for Zayd's death and for
the desecration of his body (which was hidden by his supporters but
then exhumed and decapitated by Umayyad troops, the head sent to
Medina and the remains crucified in Kufa, where they were displayed
as a warning for three years) would be a rallying cry of the Abbasid
revolution. The Zaydi branch of the Shi'a went on to emphasise the
political aspects of the imamate. Yet at the same time, they accepted
the legitimacy of Abu Bakr's and Umar's caliphates, and would often be considered closer to Sunni law and theology than other Shi'a

were. Zaydi Shi'ism would become prominent in regions of northern Iran bordering the Caspian Sea, and especially in northern Yemen, where from the 890s CE there was an independent Zaydi imamate that would last a millennium, surviving into the nineteenth century.

After the failure of revolts like those of al-Nafs al-Zakiyya and Zayd, splinter groups and apocalyptic ideas spread among pro-Alid networks. Some believed that a *qa'im* ("one who rises up") would emerge from the Prophet's family to overthrow tyranny. In the meantime, he would be hidden ("in occultation"), or might appear to have died, so as to remain impervious to persecution until the time was right to establish the realm of justice. These images, of a messianic redeemer-figure, a *mahdi* (a "rightly-guided one"), who could defeat injustice in the world and usher in the end times, would keep the revolutionary dimension of Islam alive while the reality of life under the caliphate was deemed to fall short of the faith's ideals. Both Sunni and Shi'i Muslims over the centuries would return to such ideas in times of crisis. In the nineteenth century, these same beliefs would animate anticolonial rebellions against European invaders, especially across Africa, from Senegal to Sudan.

Ja'far al-Sadiq, in contrast, played down messianic ideas. The imam, his followers taught, was explicitly appointed by his predecessor and possessed special knowledge, not merely the *'ilm* of the 'ulama, the learned scholars, but *isma*, a protection from error granted by God that guaranteed the imam's interpretations of revelation and rulings in matters of law. By this means, God's guidance remained accessible to the community after the death of Muhammad had brought the line of God's prophets to an end. The community would always have an imam, whether he held political power or not, and thus true Muslims would always have right guidance on earth and assurance for the hereafter. By this means, too, the Shi'a would have a distinct spiritual and legal identity, even if the caliphate remained beyond the reach of the People of the House; even, indeed, if the caliphs persecuted and killed them. Another doctrine emphasised by Ja'far, *taqiyya*, or "dissimulation," permitted true believers to conceal and even outwardly act against their faith as a precaution against persecution: by this means, under the increasingly hostile Abbasids, Shi'i belief, and the lives of their imams, could be preserved.

When Ja'far al-Sadiq died in 765 CE, his followers became divided over the identity of the next imam. Some gave their allegiance to his son Isma'il, who had already died but was thought to have been the designated successor. They believed either that Isma'il's descendants were now the true imams (this view would eventually become predominant) or that Isma'il's son Muhammad had entered occultation and would return as the mahdi (the view that initially gained the most adherents, but later lost out). The followers of Isma'il—the Isma'ilis—would become a second major branch of the Shi'a, operating a far-flung clandestine missionary effort to propagate belief in the "hidden imam" and prepare for his revolutionary return. One group would establish themselves, in the late eleventh century, in northern Iran, in a network of fortresses centred on the mountain castle of Alamut near the Caspian Sea. From here, they carried out targeted killings of political enemies deemed guilty of tyranny. This gave the group a simultaneously colourful and grim reputation, and a name attached to them by their enemies, *al-hashishiyya* ("hashish-eaters"), gave European languages the word *assassins*. (There is, unsurprisingly, no evidence that Isma'ili assassinations ever involved the use of hashish, but the image was one of many to nourish vivid European imaginations.) The Isma'ili state based at Alamut would survive until the arrival of the Mongols in the mid-1200s.[19]

At the end of the ninth century, an Isma'ili leader in Syria claimed that he was the imam, and became known as Abdallah al-Mahdi. (Sunni sources would use a slightly condescending diminutive, and call him Ubayd Allah, "little Abdallah," instead.) Fleeing from Syria, he settled at the far edge of the Muslim world, in the Saharan caravan town of Sijilmasa in southeast Morocco. Isma'ili missionary activity (or *da'wa*, the "call" to Islam) was intense in North Africa. In 909 CE, the Berber-speaking Kutama people in the mountains of what is now northeastern Algeria, who had converted to the mahdi's cause, rose in rebellion. Their revolt overthrew the dynasty that had reigned in what is now Tunisia and eastern Algeria, and installed Abdallah al-Mahdi as imam in Qayrawan, in southern Tunisia. Claiming to rule by right of descent from the Prophet through his son-in-law Ali and his daughter Fatima, Abdallah's new dynasty would be known as the Fatimids. In 969 CE they moved east from Tunisia, conquered Egypt, and built a new capital north of the original Muslim garrison city of Fustat. It would be called al-Qahira, "the Victorious," or in English, Cairo. The great mosque the Fatimids built there, begun in 970 and inaugurated two years later, was named al-Azhar ("the Radiant"). Situated in what, until the mid-1800s, remained the heart of the city, al-Azhar would become one of the Muslim world's foremost centres of learning. The Fatimids' ambition to overthrow the Abbasids in Baghdad remained unfulfilled, but they would rule in Egypt until the end of the twelfth century.

The followers of Ja'far al-Sadiq who did not recognise Isma'il eventually settled on Musa al-Kazim, the imam's third son, as the seventh true imam. Constituting the largest Shi'i group overall, they would continue to give allegiance to imams who for their part would generally follow Ja'far's example of disengagement from open politics. Even the one striking exception—Ali al-Rida Ibn Musa, son of Musa al-Kazim and eighth imam, who was brought to the imperial court from Medina and named as heir to the caliphate by al-Ma'mun in 816 CE—was, we're told, very unwilling to accept this position. Known, like Ja'far, for his learning and piety, Ali al-Rida died two years later in northeastern Iran while accompanying the caliph on a journey from Merv to Baghdad. (It was rumoured that a courtier put poison in his grapes, or perhaps his pomegranate juice.) Ali al-Rida was buried next to the tomb of Harun al-Rashid, who had died nearby nine years earlier. Ibn Battuta, visiting five hundred years later, would tell of Shi'i pilgrims who venerated Ali's tomb and kicked Harun's. It was the resting place of Ali al-Rida that would make the place famous as Mashhad, "the martyr's tomb." Today, Mashhad, in Iran, is one of the world's major pilgrimage cities, with millions of visitors each year, and the sanctuary over the tomb of the imam Ali al-Rida (in Persian, Imam Reza) is one of the world's largest and most magnificent mosques.[20]

If nomination to the caliphate did not keep an imam safe, nor did political quietism prevent later Abbasid caliphs from keeping Ja'far's descendants under suspicion and sometimes under arrest. In the mid-ninth century, the Caliph al-Mutawakkil had the tomb of Husayn at Karbala demolished, to prevent Shi'i pilgrims from congregating there. It was al-Mutawakkil who put an end to the failed "testing" campaign and accepted what was by now established Sunni orthodoxy (belief in the createdness of the Qur'an, which the test had sought to impose, was a Shi'i doctrine too). He also had the tenth imam, Ali al-Hadi, brought to the new Abbasid capital—the city of Samarra, north of Baghdad—where he lived closely watched and guarded until his death. Ali al-Hadi's son, Hasan al-Askari, who was kept in Samarra with him, held the imamate for only five years, remaining effectively under house arrest, before he died in 873 CE. (Later accounts would tell of how he, too, was poisoned at court.)

At this point, no one knew who the next legitimate imam was. The tenth-century historian al-Mas'udi would claim that twenty different sects arose among the Shi'a, each with a different view. Eventually, news spread that Hasan al-Askari had a son, Muhammad, who had been kept in hiding from the Abbasids and who now, as the twelfth imam, had gone into occultation. For a while, agents of the imam were thought to be in touch with him, but after 941 CE it was believed that no further contact was possible: the twelfth imam was the last in his line. The largest of the Shi'i communities would henceforward be referred to as the *ithna'ashari* or "Twelver" Shi'a. The "hidden imam," they believed, had entered the "greater occultation," from where he would one day re-emerge, as the mahdi or *qa'im*, to re-establish justice on earth and usher in the end of days.

In the meantime, interpreting the law in the imam's absence would be up to the senior Shi'i scholars, trained in the seminaries of the holy cities in Iraq and Iran: Karbala and Kufa, the latter later swallowed up in the city of Najaf, built at the site believed to be the burial place of Ali Ibn Abi Talib; Qom, which grew up in north-central Iran around the tomb of Ali al-Rida's sister Fatima; and Mashhad. Carrying titles like *hujjat allah*, a "proof of God," or *ayat allah*—in Persian, *ayatollah*—a "sign of God," Shiʻi interpreters of the law thus came to occupy a role very similar to that of the Sunni scholars. God's law could only be known and lived out in the community through the efforts of the learned.[21]

◇◇◇◇◇◇◇

As both the emotional commitment of Shiʻi devotion and the moral strength of Sunni piety indicate, though, there was more to living as an observant Muslim than technicalities of jurisprudence or conflicts over rulership. Observing the outward, formal requirements of the law was one thing, but the deeper, mystical truths of life, God, and the universe were something else. The search for a deeper spiritual life, an experience of God often expressed in terms of love, and of knowledge (*maʻrifa*) understood as something more profound than the technical learning of the scholars, began early in Islamic history. As the institutions of Islam as a system of civil law, political authority, and community identity took shape, a deep and elaborate tradition of mystical, or esoteric, culture emerged too, among both Sunnis and Shiʻa. It would come to be called Sufism.

In the late eighth century, the female Muslim mystic and poet Rabiʻa al-Adawiyya taught a total love of God for His own sake, beyond the fear of judgment or the promise of paradise. Rejecting marriage and embracing poverty, she expressed religious devotion as a yearning for God as the Beloved, a wholehearted desire so total that even veneration of the Prophet, or enmity for the devil, was transcended. "My love to God has so possessed me," she is said to have explained, "that no place remains for loving or hating any save Him."

Rabiʻa, who lived in Basra and died in 801 CE, would become one of the most famous and revered saintly figures in Islam, a "woman on fire with love and ardent desire...consumed with her passion [for

God]," according to a thirteenth-century Persian writer of the lives of the saints. Her life story became legendary, and in the 1960s and 1970s she was the subject of popular Egyptian and Turkish films. Some of the mystical poetry attributed to her in fact originates in an older, secular tradition of Arabic love poetry, and many of the miracle tales told about her would echo themes commonly found in other, and later, stories: how food was brought miraculously to her when in need, how wild animals would gather calmly around her, or how she would outclass other revered saints and scholars with both her mystical powers and her humility. In one anecdote, she outperforms the famed Sufi preacher Hasan al-Basri (who in fact died when she would have been a child). Hasan, having laid out his prayer mat on the surface of the water, invites Rabi'a to pray with him while floating there. Rabi'a instead flies into the air on her own prayer mat, and then rebukes Hasan for showing off, saying that a fish could do what he did, while she had done no more than a fly might, and both of them should be above such things.[22]

Both the poetry and the legends surrounding the figure of Rabi'a illustrate personal devotion to God as an all-encompassing way of life. She, and later Sufis, advocated renouncing the material world and pursuing a knowledge of the divine in which the corruptible human self would finally be transcended, or obliterated, in the full vision and presence of God. In the words of the great twelfth-century Andalusi and North African mystic Abu Madyan, "Eternal permanence [with God] is in your annihilation of your self." Some of these themes are clearly related to other ideas and practices of the late ancient and early medieval religious world, especially those of Christian monks. Perhaps it was from Syrian monks that the practice of wearing woollen (*suf*) clothing, characteristic of those who would, as a result, come to be called Sufis, derived. Practices similar to those of Christian ascetics, aiming to purify the soul through the suffering of the body, were found among some Sufis. One tenth-century saint's life tells of how the skin dried and blackened on his bones through constant, devoted repetition of the names of God, and of how he went for seven years without eating bread.[23]

Such extreme devotion sometimes sat uneasily with pious scholars of the law, and some Sufis faced public condemnation, especially when they crossed a line in saying—or were understood to have said—that knowing the inner secrets of God meant no longer having to follow the outward observances of religion. This seemed to place the authenticity of individual spirituality above the authority of the law binding on the whole community. The tenth-century mystic al-Hallaj, who travelled from his home in Iraq to India and central Asia, and made the pilgrimage to Mecca three times, preached worldly poverty and the individual's search for union with God. "The calling of love calls us to desire," he wrote, "the calling of desire to rapture, and the calling of rapture calls us to God." Al-Hallaj was spectacularly executed in Baghdad in 922, partly because of court intrigues. Officially, though, he was killed for having emphasised devotion in "the Ka'ba of the heart" over the actual observance of Muslim ritual, and for having declared, of his own rapturous union with the divine, "I am the Truth!"[24]

Those who came to be called *awliya allah*, those "near to God," or the "friends of God," Islam's saints, were, however, not completely distinct from the scholars, the 'ulama. On the contrary, the pursuit of higher, mystical or philosophical truths often went hand in hand with scholarly erudition in the more regular religious sciences. Between the ninth and the twelfth centuries, both the schools of law and the first Sufi brotherhoods or spiritual "paths" (*tariqas*—groups of disciples passing down teaching from a founding *shaykh*, a master) emerged. Among the great intellectuals of the age, perhaps the most significant to have combined juridical learning with the Sufi path was the great theologian, judge and ethicist Abu Hamid al-Ghazali, who lived in the second half of the eleventh century. Born in 1058 CE near Mashhad, al-Ghazali was orphaned as a child and studied in Nishapur under the great legal scholar Abd al-Malik al-Juwayni, who was renowned as *imam al-haramayn*, the "imam of the two Holy Places," because of his teaching at both Mecca and Medina. In his early thirties, al-Ghazali was appointed to a professorship in Baghdad, at one of the new madrasas founded by the vizier (in Arabic, *wazir*, "minister") Nizam al-Mulk, who at the time was the ruler in all but name.

In Baghdad, al-Ghazali became famous, one of the city's leading figures. But he came to see his own worldly success as an impediment to living the best life. Teaching sciences that were "unimportant and useless in this pilgrimage to the hereafter," he realised that he was motivated only by the shallow "quest for fame and widespread prestige." He made up his mind to escape from the "pull of worldly desires" and seek instead "knowledge of the true meaning of things." Giving up his professorship, al-Ghazali embarked on ten years of travel and contemplation. In 1096, as the first crusaders left Europe, heading for Anatolia on their own "armed pilgrimage," al-Ghazali made the pilgrimage to Mecca. For the next ten years, he lived as a poor Sufi in Damascus, Mecca, Medina, and Iran. When he returned to teaching law in Nishapur, where he founded a retreat and gathered new students, it was with a newfound knowledge, putting worldly things in their place and opening the way to the true life of the soul. This, for al-Ghazali, entailed both the necessary discipline of everyday ritual and social obligations in conformity with sharia, through which the ordinary believer might combat bodily and worldly evils, and then—and only then—the inward, mystical purification of the heart, through which true dependence on God and knowledge of the truth might be reached.[25]

Al-Ghazali was not considered a saint, but a great scholar who combined Sufi enlightenment with the rational and orthodox interpretation of the law and its application to daily life. Most Muslims could not be dedicated Sufis, but by right living they might experience the most fleeting moments of total acceptance of God and confidence in Him: a state in which, in a famous image, the believer would be "in the hands of God as a corpse in the hands of the washer," moved only by God's agency and wholly unresistant to His will. In this way, the true potential inherent in human nature (*fitra*, an innate predisposition that, if not prevented or corrupted, will lead humans to act as they were created to: to know and love God) might be achieved. The Sufis might be the most ardent of believers, but for al-Ghazali they were to be a part of, not stand apart from, the community that lived together under the sharia. The role of the true lovers and "knowers" of God was not to lose themselves in their own esoteric experience, but to testify to the truth of the community's common belief.

This combination of sharia-minded piety with Sufi-inspired inward devotion would set the pattern for Sunni Muslim religious life for centuries to come. Al-Ghazali's works, especially his great treatise *Ihya ulum al-din* (The Revival of the Religious Sciences), are still taught in centres of classical Islamic scholarship like the *pesantren*s (Islamic religious colleges) of Indonesia today. The model he represented was that of a reviver or "renewer" (*mujaddid*) of religion. According to tradition, such a "renewer" would appear once in every century. The timing of al-Ghazali's own return to teaching, in 1106 CE, the year 499 of the Islamic calendar, was thus particularly significant. The idea of a renewer, come to revive Islam every hundred years, would play a role in many later reformist or revivalist movements up to the twentieth century.

Al-Ghazali died in northeast Iran in 1111 CE. Half a century later, in 1165, another figure whose significance would be equally great, but quite different, was born at the opposite end of the Muslim world, in the thriving city of Murcia in southeastern Spain. Muhyi al-Din Ibn al-Arabi (in English, often simply called Ibn Arabi) grew up in Seville and travelled across North Africa to Mecca and then Anatolia before settling in Damascus, where he would die in 1240. Ibn Arabi is thought to have written over four hundred books, and became known as *al-shaykh al-akbar*, "the great master."

Ibn Arabi's ideas would be condemned by many scholars and attracted ongoing controversy for centuries after his death. One of his most famous works, the *Meccan Revelations*, was briefly banned from sale in Egypt in 1979. But he would also be recognised as among the world's greatest spiritual writers. He related his inspirations as coming from visions or dreams and claimed to be directly inspired by God. But he also identified the earlier twelfth-century Spanish saint Abu

Madyan as his own master and was explicit about the centrality of scripture to his writing and teaching. "Everything of which we speak," he wrote, "comes from the Qur'an and its treasures." Ibn Arabi's work can be seen as the culmination of medieval Sufi thought, and the inspiration for most subsequent mystical thinking.[26]

Among Ibn Arabi's most influential ideas was that of "the perfect man" (*al-insan al-kamil*), the ideal saint who would be the "pole" (*qutb*) around whom God's creation revolves. Only in such a person could the purpose of God's creation—that He should be known—be realised. Often used to summarise Ibn Arabi's thought (especially by his detractors), but not in fact a phrase used by him, is the equally influential idea that came to be called the "unity of being" or "oneness of existence" (*wahdat al-wujud*): God is the Real, and all reality is manifested from Him, through humanity down to the lowliest of His creatures. Life is the journey of the spirit that first travels away from God, to be incorporated in the body, and must seek its way back to Him. Later denounced as a heretical belief that God and creation were identical (or the pantheistic idea that "everything is God"), in Ibn Arabi's own thought the idea might be related to a particular state or "stopping place" (*mawqif*) on the Sufi journey, in which awareness of God as the one, absolute Real obliterates lesser realities.

Irrespective of the disputes that would arise over Ibn Arabi's teachings and their subsequent interpretations, he and other Sufi masters inspired popular respect, even veneration. His ideas were difficult enough to understand that major efforts would be needed by his followers to explain them. But they were very popular, too, especially in abbreviated or simplified forms that circulated widely among ordinary people. More straightlaced scholars worried about ordinary believers being led astray by such simplified versions of complex ideas. Saints, they fretted, claimed a closeness to God through devotion to the spiritual path more than by proper observance of the law. But by the twelfth century, as in popular Christianity at the same time, such saintliness was perhaps the most recognisable form of religious life to most people from central Asia to North Africa.

The poor Sufi devotee who dispensed guidance and wisdom, to whom wonders and miracles might be attributed, who travelled in search of learning and enlightenment, became the saint of popular religion. A saint would be distinguished by his or her devotion and closeness to God, by the blessing (*baraka*) that such closeness conferred, and that he or she (or his or her remains, once in the tomb) might therefore transmit to others. Saints and their disciples formed a vast network spread across the Muslim world, connected by paths of pilgrimage between great mosques in major cities and tombs or retreats scattered across the countryside. The mausoleum of a revered *wali allah*, a saint or "friend of God," might grow into a Sunni *zawiya* or *khanqah*, a spiritual centre not unlike the tombs of the Shi'i imams, with a mosque, a manuscript library and a hospice for itinerant students and pilgrims. Here, learning was dispensed and spiritual exercises were performed, and a shaykh, a spiritual master, might initiate followers into the mysteries of a particular Sufi path (*tariqa*). As in medieval Christianity, saints might be thought capable of interceding with God on behalf of believers too humble to address the Almighty directly. Such beliefs—again as in Christianity—would often give rise to the accusation that the veneration of saints was in fact a form of idolatry, associating mere mortals with the divinity of the one God. Such forms of ordinary, popular religion would nonetheless endure into the twentieth and twenty-first centuries, despite periodically coming under attack as improper, even un-Islamic.

One of the most remarkable characters of this period, and a leading example of Muslim sainthood, Sayyida ("Lady") Aisha al-Mannubiyya, illustrates the rootedness, longevity, and, in more recent times, vulnerability of this way of being Muslim. Born near Tunis in 1199 CE, she followed the path of Rabi'a al-Adawiyya in refusing to marry, bearing no children, and devoting herself to the love of God. Like other saintly figures, she is credited with various miraculous exploits. She is also said to have studied and prayed among the male students of the city, and to have been a disciple not only of Rabi'a but also of several of the greatest male saints. These included her own contemporary, Abu al-Hasan al-Shadhili, who settled and taught in southern Tunisia and was said to be the *qutb* or "pole" of the age, and Abd al-Qadir al-Jilani of Baghdad, who had died in 1166, a Hanbali theologian as well as the greatest Sufi preacher and teacher of his time. The teachings of both emphasised observance of sharia alongside mystical initiation.

Aisha al-Mannubiyya thus combined learning, law, and the spiritual path. According to accounts of her miraculous life, she kept company with the rural poor and the disreputable urban lower classes as easily as with the erudite and powerful. The two shrines erected to her after her death, one in the village where she was born, the other near the centre of Tunis, became focal points of ritual in subsequent centuries. In October 2012, in an atmosphere of religious and political conflict in Tunisia following the revolution of 2011, Sayyida Aisha's mausoleum in La Manouba, now a suburb of the city, was burned down in an attack attributed to young Islamist extremists. "Our memory and our heritage are really threatened," one of Tunisia's most distinguished historians told French radio: "A crime against culture is a crime against the community, against the whole society." Tensions between different understandings of Islam's revelation, its law, and its spirituality were nothing new: in the twenty-first century as in the eighth or the twelfth, being Muslim could mean contradictory, and sometimes conflicting, things.[27]

4

ONE GOD, MANY PEOPLES

Huai Sheng Si, the "Flourishing of the Sage Mosque," today
stands near the old centre of Guangzhou, the southeast Chinese port city on the Pearl River long known to Europeans as Can-
ton. Today's mosque, with its famous *guang ta*, the "lighthouse"
minaret, dates from the fourteenth century, but there was probably
an earlier mosque here during the Tang dynasty, between the seventh and the tenth centuries. By the mid-ninth century, there was a
large Muslim community in Guangzhou, living under the jurisdiction of their own Muslim judge, and in the twelfth century, a Muslim merchant whose house may have been adjacent to the mosque,
and who served as the head of the city's foreign community, was said
to be one of the wealthiest men in the region. The local historical
tradition of the Hui (Chinese Muslim) community long held that
the first mosque on the site was founded by one of the very first
Muslims, the Prophet's own uncle Sa'd Ibn Abi Waqqas, in the first
decade of Islam. One of the origin stories of Islam in China tells of
how Sa'd, who distinguished himself in early Islamic history as the
conqueror of Ctesiphon and founder of Kufa, came to the court of
Taizong, the second Tang emperor, discussed Confucius and Muhammad, and demonstrated the reading of the Qur'an.[1]

Over Islam's first two centuries, the idea of one God whose message was revealed by Muhammad had slowly developed into a new religion, a way of life, a social order, a worldview, and an empire. And slowly, non-Arab peoples and those from other faith communities, especially former Christians in the eastern Mediterranean, came to identify themselves with it. Muslim identity initially marked the solidarity of a conquering Arab ethnic group, and of the early converts who joined them, in Middle Eastern societies that until the twelfth century were mostly still Christian. But it also came to enfold other peoples, and to be carried beyond the caliphate, as far away as China. As Muslims spread into the wider world and began to incorporate new peoples, languages, and cultures, so they had to incorporate, or translate, Islam into other places, languages, and cultures too. And, as we have seen, as the community expanded, it was also split between different contenders vying for the community's leadership, and between different understandings of what being Muslim truly meant.

By the time Muslims reached southern Europe, central Asia, north India, and Africa across the Sahara and down the Indian Ocean coast, Islam was a universal message of salvation for all humanity that reached well beyond the Arabs to whom, and in whose language, it had originally been sent. It was also a means of gaining social status, asserting power and sovereignty, and building new states and dynasties. These fought each other over the territory and the truth of Islam at least as much as they waged war against non-Muslims. By the time of the Crusades at the end of the eleventh century, Islam gave peoples from the Mediterranean to the South China Sea a shared sense of history and of themselves. But just like their Christian counterparts, medieval Muslim states and peoples fought each other—sometimes allying with unbelievers against each other—as often as they fought unbelievers in defence of their faith.

◇◇◇◇◇◇◇

As their presence in Guangzhou suggests, the world that Muslims had made was tied together by worldly interests and material goods, by merchants, money, and trade winds, at least as much as by religious teaching and spiritual values, itinerant scholars and wandering Sufis. The Abbasids' Baghdad was a glittering city of world-historical importance not only because of its caliphs and viziers, its scholars and storytellers, but because it was a magnet for trade, a hub of the medieval world economy. At the centre of Baghdad was the original, planned "round city," at the hub of which the caliph's palace and the great mosque sat in splendid isolation, with residential districts radiating out from them in concentric circles, cut through by straight avenues that led to the city's gates and the commercial and manufacturing districts in the suburbs. This was a deliberate, symbolic display of imperial majesty, as were the sprawling riverside palace complexes at Samarra, north of Baghdad, and near Raqqa, an old Roman fortress town in northern Syria, where later caliphs lived to separate themselves (and their troublemaking soldiers) from the urban population.

But the material as well as the symbolic power of the caliphate was centred on the city, too. Abbasid Baghdad at its height may have been home to up to half a million people, a city of silk traders, jewellers, and shipping magnates, of fine textiles, glassware and ceramics, while the populations of Kufa and Basra, on the road to the Persian Gulf south of Baghdad, made them ten times the size of modest, wool-exporting London. A powerful system of economic growth was built by the urbanisation that followed the early Arab conquests and the commercial demands the new cities generated. This system was fed, literally, at the local level, by the development of extensive agricultural estates in the cities' hinterlands, and figuratively, at a larger scale, by the connections forged between the Muslim world's distinct regional economic zones: the western and eastern Mediterranean, from Spain to Egypt; Iraq, the Persian Gulf and the Indian Ocean; and the roads east across the Iranian plateau and Khurasan to Balkh, Samarqand, and China.

In the late seventh century, ancient towns in Byzantine Anatolia contracted into fortified camps and the money supply dwindled (and in distant Anglo-Saxon Britain, the entire economy struggled to recover from its almost total post-Roman collapse). But in the world under Muslim rule, currency, manufacturing, and exchange all expanded. By the ninth century, the small-scale, artisanal production of manufactured goods (glass, pottery, leather, textiles and so on) that in late antique towns had been dispersed in individual workers' homes was replaced by larger, integrated workshops and a growing specialisation of tasks in manufacturing and retail. From the time of the Caliph Abd al-Malik and his sons in the early eighth century, caliphs and their governors patronised the building or renovation of urban marketplaces in towns whose populations were still mainly Christian and Jewish. This was a means of demonstrating, now on the part of the caliphal dynasty, the sort of civic beneficence that had once marked the urban notability of Roman provincial towns, as well as giving practical encouragement to commercial activity. It also reminded the citizens of who was now in charge. Mosques, especially congregational mosques where the community would gather for the Friday prayer and sermon, were often built in marketplaces, or commercial areas were established around newly built mosques. Sometimes, rents from commercial property were assigned to a mosque's upkeep as well as being ploughed back into commercial investment.[2]

The mosque thus succeeded the church that, in late ancient Roman towns, had been responsible for guaranteeing weights, measures, and honest trade. Open and well-regulated markets were seen as essential not only for stability and prosperity but also for proper morality. Muslims' responsibilities to others in society were deemed second only to their responsibilities before God, and fair dealing between individuals was central to the ethics of personal behaviour. This was perhaps partly a survival of ancient Arabian codes of honourable conduct, but it was also emphasised in the Islamic law that emerged in the eighth and ninth centuries. Hadith collections had plenty to say about commercial transactions, and the Qur'an had dire warnings for those who ignored its injunctions to "give fair weight and measure." Market regulators were appointed early on, and under the Abbasids they came to hold an important urban function: the *muhtasib*, a government official charged with market inspection and the prevention of fraud, also had responsibility for public morality and good order in the city.[3]

Rather than constituting a single massive economic bloc with a single centre—like the districts of Baghdad, pointedly laid out around the palace—the caliph's domains tied together a series of more discrete and relatively independent regional markets. These were networks of short-distance trade, carried on by island-hopping and coastal shipping around the Mediterranean, from Spain through the Balearic Islands to Sardinia and Sicily, Tunisia and Egypt, or by road traffic from the towns of Syria and Palestine, northeast around the Fertile Crescent into the valleys and canal system of the Tigris and Euphrates. Once connected, though, these regional trade systems allowed enterprising merchant families to form networks and engage in long-distance business. Sometimes an investor, or a group of investors, would advance money to finance trade by an agent, who would acquire goods and trade with them on their own account, returning the capital plus a share of the profits (thereby avoiding the addition of interest, on which sharia frowned, while still providing a return on investment). But individual merchants, too, sometimes travelled widely; in some cases, the same individuals could be found one year in Andalusia, another year in India.[4]

The sort of person who could do this was, from the ninth century onwards, a member of a newly distinctive group: an entrepreneurial class of merchants. Investing in land, manufacturing, and long-distance trade, or in industries with high levels of capital outlay like pearl fishing or shipbuilding, enterprising merchants often operated in partnership and formed a distinct social grouping. They had their own patterns of increasingly luxurious residence, where they socialised with each other in refined and exclusive company, ate and drank, patronised the arts and culture, listened to music, read poetry, and discussed literature. Under the Abbasids they came to be visible and powerful, enjoying social and cultural prestige, capable of defending their own interests in times of instability or crisis, and exerting political influence at court. They might be involved with taxation, by handling the sale of agricultural produce to convert it into cash, and sometimes provided loans to the state treasury.

Merchants were noted, too, for their displays of piety through charitable works and frequent pilgrimage (also, often, an opportunity for business). In keeping with both a concern for the ethical propriety of trade and the open, community-oriented nature of religious learning, many merchant families combined accumulating wealth with gaining distinction in hadith collection and legal scholarship. In the absence of a separate clergy or professional priesthood, many legal scholars up to the eleventh century either came from merchant families, or engaged in trade themselves. The great jurist Abu Hanifa apparently dealt in silks, and the Sufi theologian al-Junayd, who died in the early tenth century and whose father manufactured or sold wine glasses, himself owned a shop in Baghdad. As lawyers, occasionally tax administrators and judges, leading citizens and philanthropists, as well as landlords, investors, and employers, the merchant elite came close to being an early commercial capitalist class, surpassing the older, landholding post-conquest aristocracy in both economic and political importance. It has even been argued that it was their economic dynamism and inventiveness that, via their connections with northern Italian port city-states, stimulated Europe's later twelfth-century economic and cultural revival.[5]

Members of this commercial class, along with refugees from periodic political instability in the Middle East, established the Muslim merchant settlements in places like Guangzhou, and in the stopover ports all the way from the Persian Gulf along the northwest coast of India to the islands of Southeast Asia. Direct trade by sea with China was interrupted at the end of the ninth century by the extraordinary destruction of the Huang Chao rebellion. Rebel armies sacked Guangzhou, reportedly killing 120,000 foreigners, and occupied the Tang capital, Chang'an, in 880 CE, causing the collapse not only of external trade but of China's own aristocracy. But regional trade continued, with Muslim shipping meeting Chinese merchants in Southeast Asia. Curiosity about the peoples of South and East Asia, and demand for the goods that could be obtained from them, were undiminished. In the early tenth century, the sailors' stories collected as *Reports of China and India* by Abu Zayd al-Sirafi (whose name refers to Siraf, then a major port on the Iranian coast of the Persian Gulf) celebrated the marvels of the Indian Ocean and South China Sea, "in whose depths are pearls and ambergris, in whose rocky isles are gems and mines of gold, in the mouths of whose beasts is ivory, in whose forests grow ebony,...aloewood, camphor, nutmeg, cloves, sandalwood...and all the rest that no one could enumerate." This was the world that produced the legendary voyages of Sindbad the Sailor, but its riches and adventurers were perfectly real.[6]

Merchants headed northeast from Baghdad, too, to colder and less inviting lands, for both trade and diplomacy. The most famous account of such travels is that of the diplomatic mission sent in 921 CE to the "king of the Slavs" at Bolghar on the Volga, north of the Caspian Sea. The king had reportedly embraced Islam and wished to recognise the suzerainty of the caliph, and thus to be recognised by him as a ruler in his own right: he asked for instruction in the sharia, a mosque with a pulpit from which the caliph's name could be proclaimed, and "a fort to protect him against the kings who opposed him." Ahmad Ibn Fadlan, a member of the delegation, recounts the arduous journey, the river so thick with ice that pack animals and carts "used it like a road and...it did not even creak," the cold so intense that "we thought the country...was an 'infernally cold' portal to the depths of hell."

At Bolghar, Ibn Fadlan and his companions found a king uninstructed in Islam but well able to debate with his visitors, seated on "a throne bedecked with Byzantine silk" in a yurt large enough to "hold more than a thousand people...carpeted with Armenian rugs," and with a tailor who, somehow, had also come there from Baghdad. "I lost count," Ibn Fadlan wrote, "of the number of marvels I witnessed in his realm." For the Volga Bulgars, conversion had a strategic, geopolitical value, at least in propaganda terms, as Ibn Fadlan relates the king proclaiming to his neighbours: "Almighty God has given me the gift of Islam and granted me membership in the kingdom of the Commander of the Faithful. I am his bondsman. He has made me his emir. I will wage war on those who oppose me." It was no less significant, in humbler terms, at a personal and familial level, as Ibn Fadlan also relates:

> A man named Saul converted under my supervision.... His wife, mother and children also converted. They all took the name Muhammad. I taught him the suras "Praise be to God" and "He is God, One." He took greater delight in these... than if he had been made king.[7]

◇◇◇◇◇◇◇◇

The Volga River (then known to the region's Turkic peoples as the Itil) was important, despite the distance and discomfort, because it too was a conduit for long-distance trade in furs and, above all, slaves. At the junction of the Muslim, Turkic, and Scandinavian worlds, what is now southern Russia was then a major slave market. *Saqaliba*, Slavic captives, especially young women, were sold there for domestic service in Iraq, Iran and central Asia, in exchange for silver currency that travelled in the opposite direction, ending up in Russia and Ukraine, and around the Baltic Sea. A second market further west, in what is now Prague, supplied demand in Muslim Spain, where both men and women captured in modern Poland and western Ukraine were employed in the army and administration as well as in households. Venice and the Carolingian Empire in western Europe also supplied slaves south and east, into Muslim Spain and across the Mediterranean to North Africa and Syria, as well as into the Byzantine Empire. The trade was stimulated by the growing economy of the Muslim-ruled southern and eastern Mediterranean, but was also a factor in Europe's medieval economic development. The growing financial power of the Italian cities of Venice and Genoa, both heavily involved in the medieval slave trade, would be crucial to the emergence of commercial

capitalism. Enslavement and the trade in slaves across the Mediterranean and around the Black Sea would remain important into the
seventeenth and eighteenth centuries.[8]

Islamic law accepted slavery as a fact of life in the late ancient
and medieval Mediterranean world. The Islamic ethics expressed in
the Qur'an and hadith enjoined masters to treat slaves decently and
made the freeing of slaves (manumission) an act of piety, but there
was no specifically "Islamic" form of slavery any more than there was
a "Christian" one in western Europe or, later, in the Atlantic world.
Not only Muslims but Christians and Jews too owned slaves in the
medieval Middle East. Up to the fifteenth century, Italian and Egyptian merchants alike were involved in shipping Black Sea captives,
with the Byzantine emperor's permission, into Mediterranean markets. European abolitionists in the nineteenth century would often
combine their own moral antislavery with anti-Muslim and anti-Arab
prejudices when discussing the Arab slave trade or "Muslim slavery,"
especially in Africa. Such perceptions linger on today, but historians
of slavery have long discarded them. Forms and experiences of enslavement, in societies under Muslim rule as throughout world history, varied more with social and economic conditions than according
to religious belief or norms laid down in law.

Slaves were legally considered to be persons, not chattels—not
merely property—and children born to slave mothers and master
fathers were born free. Their mothers could not be sold and, as the
mothers of free children, should also be freed. Muslims could not be
enslaved, and once converted, European captives in Muslim households, especially elite ones, might marry into their former masters'
families and enjoy spectacular careers, often ending up as slaveowners
themselves. But this tendency towards restricting slavery (the opposite of what later happened in the Atlantic world) did not make all
people equal, in either servitude or freedom. Notably, while "white"
slaves from eastern or southern Europe who converted could then enjoy great social mobility, Black African slaves traded across the Sahara
also became Muslim but did not therefore become free.

Rather than a simple dichotomy between slaves and free people, in Africa and the Middle East under the caliphates and later, social status and individual rights varied along a spectrum of degrees of freedom or unfreedom. Slaves and ex-slaves were found in all kinds of situations and statuses. Slave concubines became the mothers of ruling caliphs, and male slaves in the service of elite households could hold high administrative office. From the ninth century onward, the caliphs' armies were largely composed of slave manpower, made up of Turkmen (from central Asia) and Circassians (from the Çerkes people of the Caucasus, east of the Black Sea). Soldiers of slave origin would often play a major role in politics, even becoming rulers and founding dynasties. This was most famously the case of the Mamluks (the term *mamluk* means "owned")—Turkic and Circassian slaves traded as boys, brought up in military barracks, and manumitted on completion of their training—who took power in Egypt and Syria in the thirteenth century.

In the mid-eighth-century Abbasid caliphate, imported slaves partly compensated for a loss of labourers killed by the plague. They also met a need for servile workers in manufacturing that the Arabs had inherited from the Roman world, though perhaps on a smaller scale, as well as in the domestic slavery that employed most unfree labour in the households of the elite and the moderately wealthy. Slaves endured the harshest working conditions in oasis cultivation, in mines and, most notoriously, in large-scale land clearance for agriculture. This last area of slave labour, found in southern Iraq from the late seventh to the late ninth centuries, was exceptional in the Muslim-ruled world in its scale and severity. In the marshes upriver from Basra, thousands of Black African slaves worked in gangs of hundreds, with minimal food and shelter. They were known as *zanj*, after the Arabic name for the coastal region of East Africa from which some of them came (though more may in fact have come from Ethiopia, and from central and West Africa). Here, enslaved labourers were made to work in dreadful conditions, removing the natron left on the topsoil by evaporation. Natron, a mixture of salt and soda ash, was then used as a cleaning and drying agent, and in glassmaking; the ground, once cleared, could be farmed.

At the end of the seventh century, there were two Zanj rebellions, both brutally suppressed. These were followed, over 150 years later, in the late ninth century, by possibly the largest slave revolt in world history. Its leader was not a slave but an Arab revolutionary named Muhammad Ibn Ali. Born in Iran, he claimed to be a member of the Alid family and took the title of Mahdi. Using a familiar Islamic language of justice against tyranny to make his own bid for power, he rallied the support of the slaves, whose treatment was so clearly at odds with the injunctions to humane treatment and encouragement of manumission repeatedly made in the Qur'an and hadith. Preaching the overthrow of the slave masters, Muhammad Ibn Ali turned the slaves into a guerrilla army. For fourteen years, from 869 to 883 CE, they controlled much of southern Iraq, conquering major towns and establishing an independent capital near Basra, before an Abbasid army destroyed them.

The Zanj uprising and its suppression are thought to have resulted in tens of thousands of deaths and the long-term economic decline of southern Iraq. But it was perhaps most significant for the challenge it posed to the existing social order. As the historian al-Mas'udi relates, "the insolence of the army of the Zanj was such" that the former slaves themselves became masters of women from "the noblest families of the Arabs" who "served the Blacks as concubines and performed the tasks of the very humblest slaves for their wives." The revolt's suppression restored "order" against this reversal of circumstances: the rebels were massacred and their leaders executed. But the uprising had put an end to the large-scale, heavily exploitative use of slave labour in agriculture. Not until the nineteenth century, when plantation slavery developed in Zanzibar to supply the world market for cloves, did labour-gang exploitation comparable to Atlantic plantation slavery occur again in an area under Muslim rule.[9]

Mas'udi's distaste at Black ex-slaves lording over the women of noble Arab families expressed something about racialised as well as aristocratic values. Such racial categorisation was not self-evident or straightforward. It rested on social conventions that developed over time, on economic and cultural power more than on biological difference, and on habits of perception more than on innate physical appearance. Medieval perceptions of difference, and especially beliefs about degrees of "barbarousness" or the potential to become "civilised," were informed by ideas about the different climatic zones (hot, cold, humid, or temperate) from which different people came, and by stereotypes about the aptitude of different peoples for different kinds of work. Medieval slave-buyers' guides told the informed customer what to look for: a Slav eunuch would be much cleverer than his uncastrated brother; Ethiopians and Nubians from the Nile Valley could take care of people and money; East Africans were good for manual labour. This hierarchy of statuses within the enslaved population, as well as between the free and the less free, can be seen in medieval painting as well as in written texts. In general, it placed darker-skinned South Asians or Africans below paler-complexioned people from the Mediterranean or further north.[10]

◇◇◇◇◇◇◇◇

Non-Arab peoples who became Muslims nonetheless soon wrote themselves into an Islamic view of history and found ways of asserting themselves as Muslims. In late antique times, the church in Roman North Africa had been large and powerful, producing both major religious controversies and great luminaries, most notably Saint Augustine. But after the Arab conquest of North Africa, there were no social or political movements inspired by Christianity. Instead, adherence to Islam spread rapidly among the region's majority, Amazigh (Berber-speaking) communities, as well as being carried by incoming Arabic-speaking groups who migrated westward from Egypt during the medieval period. Arabic would not become the dominant spoken language in North Africa until much later—in some areas, not until the twentieth century. But as the language of revelation, it very quickly became the language of learning and literacy, even in Berber-speaking, mountainous or desert areas well beyond the major cities.

As rapidly as Amazigh groups adopted Islam, they began to claim an equal belonging in the community alongside Arabs. The so-called Berber Revolt, a Khariji-inspired uprising against the distant and faltering Umayyad caliphate, broke out in the 740s. The Fatimid movement that would conquer Tunisia and Egypt began among Amazigh tribes (*qaba'il*, the probable origin of the term Kabyles, the Berber-speaking people of the mountainous region east of Algiers) in the tenth century. In the course of their emergence in central North Africa, in 909 CE the Fatimids destroyed another North African dynasty, the independent principality of Tahert, in the mountains of what is now central Algeria. Tahert had been founded, in 778, by another group of Amazigh Muslim dissidents against caliphal authority under the leadership of their imam, Abd al-Rahman Ibn Rustam, who was of Persian origin. Ibn Rustam and his followers had embraced Ibadism, a school of thought that had emerged in eighth-century Basra and quickly spread to North Africa. Rather than following the caliph, Ibadis believed that the community should be led by a pious imam, combining statesmanship with scholarship, alongside the learned scholars who elected him: he could be deposed if he fell into sinfulness. Ibadis considered other Muslims to have gone astray and saw themselves as the true inheritors of the Prophet's message. After the fall of Tahert, its population and their scholarly leadership fled south and built trading towns on the northern rim of the Sahara, where their descendants remain today, part of an Ibadi community that also survives in Oman and Zanzibar. They were the first Muslims to carry trade across the desert, bringing West African gold and slaves into the Mediterranean.

The impulse to lay claim to godly sovereignty in the name of true belief against reigning impiety would recur in subsequent generations. In the eleventh and twelfth centuries, Amazigh peoples launched two successive revolutions that began as missionary movements for the restoration of "true" Islam. The Almoravids (*al-murabitun*, ascetic warriors mustered in fortresses—*ribats*—for the defence of the faith), and then the Almohads (*al-muwahhidun*, "those who defend the oneness of God"), who eventually overthrew them, each created an empire that stretched from the Sahara and southern Morocco across the whole of North Africa and Spain. By later medieval times, North African origin stories had reimagined Amazigh lineages as stemming from Arab genealogies, claims that the fourteenth-century historian Ibn Khaldun, himself born in Tunis in 1332 to an Arab family that had first settled in Seville, would spend pages patiently refuting. Medieval writers of texts like the anonymous *Mafakhir al-barbar* (The Boasts of the Berbers) would emphasise Amazigh peoples' initiative in implanting Islam in local history and space, especially through the building of mosques and the foundation of cities like Marrakesh, built by the Almoravids in the eleventh century.[11]

At the other end of the caliphate's lands were the Persian-speaking inhabitants of Iran. They did not all consider themselves ethnically Persian, but they identified with an ancient Persian imperial past and with the pre-Islamic Persian, or Pahlavi, language and literature. Iranians converted over the course of the eighth to the eleventh centuries, probably first, and rapidly, in the cities, and then more slowly across the countryside. In Iran, the wholesale collapse of the Sasanian Empire and the adoption of Islam, despite a series of rebellions following the Arab conquest in the seventh century, led by the end of the ninth century to reimaginings of ancient Persian history. These told of how the Persians descended from Noah or Abraham, or associated sites of the ancient Persian Empire like the ruins of Persepolis and the nearby Sasanian city of Istakhr with the biblical and Qur'anic figure of Solomon. Local histories of particular cities either passed over pre-Islamic times altogether, or found creative ways of fitting pre-Islamic Persians and their own earlier myths and histories into a new, wider worldview and universal, prophetic history. This could both accommodate the conquest and lament its violence, depicting Islam as a predestined force of salvation while also casting particular Arab Muslim conquerors in the role of devils. As a Persian-language history of the region of Sistan (today's eastern Iran and southern Afghanistan), written in the eleventh century, put it, when the conquerors arrived, local leaders already knew what the conquest meant:

We are not powerless to wage war, for this is a land of brave men and warriors.... But [for all that], we cannot fight against the Almighty, and yours is the army of God. We have read in our books about your appearance and that of Muhammad and...we know that this reign of yours will endure for a long time. So the proper thing to do is to make peace.[12]

The older written tradition of Iranian history was all but lost, except for what was preserved in Arabic translations, or through the coins and inscriptions of the preceding dynasties. As Persians became Muslims, Zoroastrian religion dwindled and those the Arabs called *majus* (from the same words in Old Persian, Syriac and Greek that would give English "magi"), the priestly caste who guarded the fire temples, began to emigrate. From the tenth century, they settled in Gujarat in northwest India, where they became known as Parsis, from the name of the southwest Iranian province, Fars, which had been the centre of the ancient religion. Zoroastrianism remained as a small minority faith in Iran. Its echoes survived in popular celebrations such as the festival of the spring equinox, still celebrated today all over the world as *nowruz*, the Persian New Year.

After the Abbasid revolution, which had been widely supported across the caliphate's eastern provinces, Persian courtiers and influences became more prominent. As the caliphal administration became more sophisticated, a bureaucratic class of secretaries emerged at court. With their own outlook and interests, and skilled in Sasanian-era administrative practices, they soon came to rival the commanders of the Abbasids' army at the centre of imperial power. By the late eighth century, the most influential among them could make and unmake caliphs. The old courtly language of Sasanian Iran, first spoken as the dialect of the province of Fars, also re-emerged in the ninth century as New Persian, written in a modified Arabic script. Literary works on religious topics, histories, and poetry began to be written in this New Persian in northeast Iran and central Asia, in the scholarly cities of Nishapur and Merv. At the court of Baghdad, some saw this revival of Persian culture and bureaucracy as the reassertion of a pre-Islamic aristocratic sensibility that denigrated the Arabs as unsophisticated desert-dwellers. In reaction, they wrote polemics against so-called *shu'ubis*, meaning those (especially Persians) who were thought to be unduly favouring the non-Arab "peoples" (*shu'ub*) of the Muslim community.[13]

The Qur'an told humanity, "We have created you from a male and a female, and made you into peoples and tribes [*shu'uban wa qaba'ilan*] that you may get to know one another. Surely the most noble of you in the sight of God is the most mindful of Him." Ever since the emergence of the community in Medina, though, Muslims had vied with one another not only in righteousness but in other things too: nobility of family or early conversion, closeness to the Prophet or his family, and distinction in the earliest conquests had all been used to make claims to precedence. As the community expanded, more people found ways to imagine their own belonging within a world of Islam, and at the same time, to express their own distinctiveness as particular "peoples and tribes," alongside others, under one God.[14]

◇◇◇◇◇◇◇

In part, this was a consequence of the empire's enormous overextension. At the dynasty's height, the Abbasids and their bureaucracy ran an extraordinarily effective administration, facilitated by the efficient postal service that moved information quickly across the caliph's territories. By the mid-ninth century, formal authority was centralised in the hands of the small military and administrative circles of the court. But truly centralised rule under the caliphate was impossible. Provincial governors and municipal judges and notables necessarily had considerable autonomy, and factional rivalries between and within bureaucratic and military elites at court came to be more powerful than the notionally absolute rule of the caliph. The vast, regionally distinct provinces of the caliphate, and their diverse, often mobile and militarised populations, not only escaped central control but began to make their own bids for power.

To the west, as we have seen, independent dynasties had been created early on—the Umayyads at Cordoba and the Idrisids (a family
claiming descent from the Prophet through his daughter Fatima) at
Fez, followed by the Shi'i Fatimids, and the revolutionary Almoravids
and Almohads. To the east as well, effectively autonomous governors
began to rule in partnership with Baghdad, rather than under its control. As early as the 820s CE, the Tahirids, an old family of Persian
aristocrats who also claimed Arab ancestry, became hereditary rulers
in Khurasan. They sent taxes (indeed, perhaps more than before) to
the central government and were also influential in the city politics of
Baghdad; they were more like trusted auxiliaries of the Abbasids than
rebels against them. But in the second half of the ninth century, the
Tahirids were overthrown by a new, and more independently minded,
provincial dynasty, the Saffarids.

Founded by Yaqub Ibn al-Layth "al-Saffar" (the Coppersmith)—a
working man, as his name suggests—who rose to prominence as a
vigilante leader in the frontier province of Sistan, the Saffarids led an
insurgent army that conquered much of the caliphate's eastern edge,
capturing Herat, Nishapur, and Kabul, before turning west to Iraq.
Yaqub's army was defeated only when it came within fifty miles of
Baghdad, in 876 CE. The Abbasids feared a Saffarid linkup with the
Zanj rebellion, then at its height, but this failed to materialise. Although their attempt on Baghdad failed, and they soon lost control of
most of their other territories, the Saffarids would remain as rulers of
Sistan until the eleventh century. Further north and east, in Transoxania and Khurasan, was another independent dynasty, the Samanid
family. Claiming descent from a Sasanian warrior hero, they ruled
first as governors under the Tahirids, and then in their own right,
from the early ninth century to the beginning of the eleventh.

The increasing independence of these provincial rulers and insurgents, and occasionally even their ability to threaten Baghdad, was encouraged by instability at the centre of the caliphate itself. A major civil
war rocked the Abbasids after the death of Harun al-Rashid, when his
two sons Amin and Ma'mun, between whom Harun had divided the

succession, fought each other. Amin, reigning as caliph in Baghdad, sent a huge army east, towards Khurasan, which had been given to Ma'mun to govern, but was defeated by Ma'mun's general Tahir Ibn Husayn. (Tahir was later rewarded with the governorship of Khurasan, where the Tahirid dynasty was named after him.) The brothers' rivalry ended with a terrible, yearlong siege of Baghdad in 812–813 and the killing of Amin, who was pulled out of an upturned boat on the Tigris while trying to surrender and summarily killed by Tahir's soldiers. Unrest provoked by the war continued for another six years.

Ma'mun's brother al-Mu'tasim, who succeeded him as caliph in 833 CE, took the decisive—and, in the longer term, fateful—step of creating a new army. Made up of young men of mostly Turkic origin, it was recruited from the slave markets of the north and east. The intention was that these soldiers, forerunners of the Mamluks of Egypt, removed from family and regional ties and inculcated from youth with loyalty only to the caliph and the army, would prove both reliable to the dynasty and dependent upon it. The effect, though, was to produce a powerful group, divided from the society over which they held sway and with their own interests centred on the court, often in opposition to the civilian bureaucratic class, and jealous of the reigning caliph's patronage. In 861 CE, the Caliph al-Mutawakkil was assassinated in his palace by his Turkish soldiers, and despite a dynastic revival in the late ninth century, in the tenth century the army commanders (*amirs*) became the caliphate's real power brokers.

Outside Baghdad, soldiers—some Turkish slaves, but others volunteer recruits from among the Kurdish and northern Iranian peoples around the Caspian Sea—gained both military and fiscal control over the provinces. Increasingly, they tended to their own power base, on which they spent the money raised from their own taxes. They sent less and less revenue to the central government, which by the 930s was facing bankruptcy. Increasingly, it was the army that made or removed the caliph; he ceased to have any real authority outside his own palace. Real power lay in the hands of whoever rose to the position of *amir al-umara*, commander in chief of the army in Baghdad. In

945 CE, that title was taken by Ahmad Ibn Buya, one of three militarily enterprising brothers from south of the Caspian Sea who had already established themselves as rulers over most of Iran. Inspired by the inheritance of Persian monarchy, the Buyids revived the title *shahanshah*, king of kings. They also took titles for themselves that symbolised their new role as *sultan*s (power-holders, rulers), the necessary upholders of the caliph's now merely nominal sovereignty: Imad al-Dawla ("The Support of the State"), Rukn al-Dawla ("The Pillar of the State") and Mu'izz al-Dawla ("The Glorifier of the State").

Shi'i doctrines were widespread in the Buyids' home region, and they may have been Shi'a themselves. They were certainly at least sympathetic to Shi'ism, and encouraged Shi'i scholarship. They had no interest in installing one of Ali's descendants as caliph—perhaps conveniently for them, the last of the most widely recognised Shi'i imams had disappeared into occultation shortly before they took power. It was a striking turn of events that half a century earlier, an Abbasid caliph had kept the Shi'i imam locked up in a gilded cage, and that now it was a Shi'i-inclined military dynasty that kept the caliph effectively under house arrest. But more significant was the fact that, in political practice if not in theory, this did not really matter. Doctrinal differences had become decidedly secondary to more material issues: who controlled the money, and who commanded the men.

The Buyids' ascendancy over the caliphate lasted a hundred years. In the early eleventh century, nomadic Turkmen peoples from the steppe north and east of the caliph's domains began to move westward, across the northern rim of Iran and Iraq. While living on the edges of Muslim domains in central Asia, one such Turkic group under the leadership of the Seljuq family was converted to Sunni Islam, perhaps by wandering Sufi preachers. They came into Khurasan and Iran as hired soldiers and pastoralist settlers; soon they were the region's rulers. In 1055, the Seljuq chief Tughril Bey (*bey* or *beg* being a Turkish noble title) entered Baghdad and put an end to the Buyid dynasty, becoming the new sultan, king of kings and "Right Hand of the Commander of the Faithful."

Less than twenty years later, in August 1071, Tughril's nephew, Alp Arslan, defeated the Byzantine army at Malazgirt, or Manzikert, north of Lake Van in eastern Anatolia, capturing the emperor himself, Romanos IV Diogenes. A treaty was agreed in customary terms (a ransom was paid, some frontier forts changed hands), and the Emperor Romanos, having been released, was treated much worse by his own people than by the Muslim Turks: he had been deposed while in capitivity, and was blinded and killed on the orders of his successor a year later. But the Seljuq victory at Manzikert had opened the way for Turkish settlement in Anatolia. Over eight hundred years later, when Anatolia had become the core territory of modern Turkey, this would become a founding moment for Turkish nationalist history. At the time, it was the spark that ignited the Crusades.

◇◇◇◇◇◇◇

The ethnic diversification and political fragmentation of the Muslim community, from the tenth through the twelfth centuries, caused anxiety for scholars preoccupied with law and the legitimacy of rule, but it turned out that they could live with it. There were now several sectarian variants of Islam, more or less willing to accept each other as more or less Muslim, but each believing itself to be the community of truest believers, whether they were living under their own imam or in expectation of his return. For the majority, the Sunni community, there was still a single Muslim *umma*—one community in which to live according to God's way (*din*)—but there were many Muslim *dawlas*: dynasties, states, kingdoms on earth.

Not only did these different claimants to rule compete among themselves; even within the Abbasid caliphate itself, since the tenth century effective power had not lain with the nominal head of the community, the caliph. By the time of the Seljuqs, it was necessary to codify the difference between sovereignty as it was supposed to be and real life. The great scholars of the age, notably Abu Hamid al-Ghazali, came up with a political theory that was practical as well as principled: the community needed an imam, but the imam needed a strongman.

Just as later European theorists of monarchy would conclude that while a sword without justice was tyrannical, justice without a sword was impotent, so Islamic doctrines of government in the Seljuq era concluded that authority, in practice, "follows nothing but military power." The caliph was he to whom the sultan gave allegiance, and the sultan's exercise of power was legitimate if it served to defend the community, protect true religion, and uphold the caliph's moral authority. As the Seljuq minister, Nizam al-Mulk, wrote of the ideal ruler in his treatise on the *Rules for Kings*, what really mattered was not perfect righteousness, but good government:

> In every age . . . , God chooses one member of the human race and, having endowed him with goodly and kingly virtues, entrusts him with the interests of the world and the well-being of His servants.... A kingdom which is blessed by its people will endure and increase,... while its king will enjoy power and prosperity; in this world he will acquire good fame, in the next world salvation.... "A kingdom may last while there is irreligion, but it will not endure when there is oppression."[15]

The proliferation of Muslim states also meant the spread of cultural and intellectual life. Courtly and merchant cities from Cordoba and Fez through Cairo to Nishapur and Bukhara supported the scholarly class and the production and circulation of literary, scientific, artistic, and architectural work as rulers sought to establish their credentials as rivals to Baghdad. Nizam al-Mulk stressed the need for a successful king to respect "devout and pious men," and to be a patron of learning and wisdom. In the hierarchy of learning, religious sciences came first, but seeking for the truth of things in the physical as well as the metaphysical world was hardly less important. The cultivation of Arabic grammar, rhetoric, and style, in prose and poetry, was a mark of the properly cultured person. It was also a practical tool for both the exposition of true religion and the investigation of other kinds of truth through philosophy, geography, mathematics, medicine, astronomy, alchemy, and applied sciences, from engineering and optics to botany and beekeeping.

The scientific achievements of Abbasid Baghdad are justly famous, but despite political instability, scientific inquiry and learning of all kinds flourished from central Asia to Morocco. In Bukhara, the philosopher and physician Ibn Sina (known to Europeans as Avicenna), who was born in 980 CE and is said to have mastered all known sciences by the age of eighteen, studied in a vast library created by the region's Samanid rulers. Two centuries later, Ibn Rushd, the Andalusi philosopher known to Europe as Averroes, the great commentator on Aristotle, worked as physician to the Almohad caliph in Marrakesh, where he died in 1198. Umayyad Cordoba was said to have seventy libraries. The palace library of Fatimid Cairo held perhaps two million books.[16]

The vision of a good life that the hadith scholar Ibn Hanbal and his followers had was unremittingly serious and unbendingly moralistic. To be Muslim, for them, meant striving to live exactly as (they believed) the Prophet and his first followers had done, constantly seeking after knowledge of God and with as little attention as possible to the distractions of the world. Interrupted during the dawn prayer by a friend's joke, the Caliph Harun al-Rashid reportedly laughed, adding that his friend should "take care not to joke about the Qur'an and religion, but apart from those two topics, you can say what you like." For the piety-minded, in contrast, it was better not to laugh at all. One of Ibn Hanbal's associates is said to have reprimanded his disciples for laughing in the imam's presence. The son of another told how he had never seen his father laughing, only smiling, and that when his father once saw him laughing with his mother, he had asked, "Does a master of the Qur'an laugh in this manner?" Seeking knowledge and living by it was a serious business.[17]

But there were many other kinds of knowledge to be sought, and other ways of living as a learned and cultured Muslim, not all of them so arduous or so sober. Court poets celebrated love and wine as much as scholars under courtly patronage disputed points of religious doctrine and philosophy. *Adab*, meaning both cultured manners and refined literature, was highly appreciated in the caliphs' courts and in wider, sophisticated society. Its complex wordplay made for demanding reading, but it could be put to use in telling funny folktales and trickster stories, like those of the *Maqamat* (the Book of Impostures) by the twelfth-century Basran writer al-Hariri, which enjoyed extraordinary popularity in its own time and retains its status as a treasure of classical Arabic literature today. Its ostensible comedic content and verbal pyrotechnics served the more practical purpose of inculcating advanced literacy in Arabic, and an appreciation of linguistic dexterity.[18]

Popular literary storytelling, poetic sophistication, and spiritual devotion all came together in Sufi literature, nowhere more dramatically than in the Persian poetry of the mystic Jalal al-Din Rumi, whose family emigrated from Balkh, in today's northern Afghanistan, in the early thirteenth century, and settled in Konya, the Seljuq capital in south-central Anatolia. His immense *Masnavi*, an epic work in rhyming couplets that ranges from outrageously scurrilous stories with a gentle moral message to exposition of Qur'anic verses and Prophetic history, expresses love for God, and *walaya*—nearness to, or friendship with God—as achievable by even the lowliest believer.

Unlike al-Ghazali and others, who saw mystical initiation as appropriate only to a select few, and who worried about proper conformity to the law, Rumi illustrates his point through a famous story of a simpleton shepherd, who loves God in his own way. Rebuked by Moses for his ignorance, the shepherd nonetheless becomes a Friend of God through his purity of heart. As God chides Moses at the end of the story: "I don't look at what men articulate, / But at their spirit and their inner state / . . . / Beyond all the religions stands love's nation / God's their sole dogma and denomination." Rumi's universalism would make him enormously popular in the twentieth century, especially among non-Muslim readers eager for a liberal, love-centred spirituality. His verses are often read today at wholly secular American weddings, and his relationship to the larger Islamic tradition has sometimes been questioned. But in his own time, his popular, accessible exploration of the Sufi search for union with God was no less fully part of being Muslim than the legal and theological orthodoxy that had itself only just emerged in the previous century.[19]

Rumi's trek with his family from central Asia to central Anatolia, like his spiritual journeying, was characteristic of the Muslim world he lived in. Just as trade and migration routes were linked across the politically divided landscape of Eurasia and Africa, so languages, cultures, and ideas spread, combined, and coexisted too. Through the connected world from Cordoba to Guangzhou, ancient Persian, Syriac, Greek, and Sanskrit learning was rendered into Arabic, and Arabic learning was in turn translated into Latin and Chinese. "Dialectical theology," or the reasoned disputation of religious precepts that became known as *kalam*, was an Arabic and Muslim genre of thought and writing directly derived from sixth- and seventh-century Christian confessional arguments that flourished in Syria at the time of the Arab conquests and afterward, evidence of the multi-confessional social and intellectual world in which Islamic learning developed. Centuries later, in the 1600s and 1700s, and at the opposite end of Asia, as Muslims became more integrated into the Chinese communities in which they lived, an Islamic intellectual tradition written in Chinese, the *han kitab*, would give expression to specific, and varied, Muslim sensibilities in a distinctly Chinese context. Its authors were both transmitters and creators of canonical Islamic knowledge and self-identifying Chinese literati who, despite their "barbarian" ethnic origin, could be accepted as fully *Hua*, Chinese, in cultural sophistication.[20]

Nowhere, perhaps, has become more emblematic of the culturally diverse spirit of these centuries than Muslim-ruled Spain, al-Andalus. Its exquisite artistic and architectural achievements, most famously the Umayyad great mosque of Cordoba, founded at the inception of Muslim rule in the eighth century, and the Alhambra (*al-hamra*, "the red") palace built by the Nasrid dynasty in thirteenth-century Granada during its twilight, have justly become monuments of world heritage. No less significant, though less completely surviving, are its works of courtly literature, written by both men and women. The twelfth-century poet Hafsa Bint al-Hajj al-Rukuniyya of Granada wrote love poetry to her admirers, while her eleventh-century predecessor Ibn Hazm, author of the *Ring of the Dove*, explored the codes and sufferings of courtly romance. Andalusi music, too, bequeathed a major artistic inheritance: composed and performed across religious community lines (especially by both Muslims and Jews), its distinctive forms remained part of sophisticated urban culture in North Africa, where its performers fled from the Catholic conquest of Spain, down to the twentieth century. Andalus produced the philosopher Ibn Rushd (Averroes) and the mystic Ibn Arabi; it was also in twelfth-century Cordoba that Moses Maimonides, the great Jewish philosopher, theologian and physician, was born.

In later, especially liberal European, imaginations, and in more recent political and cultural attempts to bridge so-called civilisational divides, the *convivencia*, "living together" of religious and cultural communities in the glory days of Muslim Seville, Cordoba, and Granada has been a powerful, if perhaps wishful, corrective to cultural essentialism and antipathy. Andalus was certainly a multiconfessional and mostly tolerant society, but not always: Maimonides's family had to flee their home in Cordoba in the twelfth century, when the new Almohad rulers launched an unusually violent persecution of religious minorities. (They settled in the more welcoming environment of Egypt, where Maimonides died in 1204, and Maimonides had some harsh words for Muslim treatment of Jews in both Spain and Yemen, where persecutions also occurred in his time.) And if the monuments of Andalus today convey the image of a perhaps nostalgic Mediterranean cosmopolitanism, in their own time they were already part of a culture that, in the tenth century, idealised the lost Umayyad caliphate in Syria, from which the first Andalusi princes had been exiled. After the breakup of the second Umayyad caliphate, in Cordoba, in the eleventh century, its glories were sweetly remembered in the literature composed at the courts of the fractious principalities that followed. The yearning love poetry of Ibn Hazm, in the eleventh century, can be read as an evocation of the already-vanished world of

Umayyad Cordoba. Before there was nostalgia for Andalus, Andalus was already all about nostalgia.[21]

Like the lands further east, Andalus was also politically turbulent. Jihad against Christian kingdoms to the north, and Christian raiding against Muslims to the south, became part of the ideological legitimation of sovereigns on both sides. But politics and war were by no means defined simply along religious divides. After the height of the Cordoba caliphate in the tenth century, smaller and mutually hostile Muslim states proliferated. When their rulers called on the Almoravids to rescue them from Christian attack in the eleventh century, the Almoravids, having stopped the Christian advance, then reunited Muslim Spain by conquering the other Muslim kingdoms.

For their part, Christian rulers in northern Spain were also motivated by material considerations (in their case, population pressure and competition to extract wealth as tribute) as much as, or more than, by ideological fervour. They accordingly made alliances with Muslim neighbours and fought alongside them against their own rivals, as well as pursuing what would become known as the Reconquista, the somewhat oddly named "reconquest" for Christianity of a land that, by the 1200s, had been Muslim for five centuries. The most famous Christian warrior of the age, celebrated both in thirteenth-century Spanish poetry and in 1960s Hollywood film, Rodrigo Díaz de Vivar, known as "El Cid" (*al-sayyid*, the Lord), was unusual in his later legendary status but not untypical in his own time. An ambitious and enterprising mercenary soldier in a multi-confessional world, over the course of his career he fought for opportunity and advancement more than religion, serving the Muslim kingdom of Saragossa as well as the Christian kingdom of Castile before carving out his own principality in Valencia.[22]

◇◇◇◇◇◇◇◇

Cultural and religious coexistence was normal but not untroubled. Living side by side as Muslims and non-Muslims did not mean living in equality, and it sometimes seemed necessary to insist on difference.

Indeed, attention to religious difference, especially in legal terms, was important in protecting the boundaries of the community. This was more, not less, important in a context where cross-community relations, whether in business, learning, marriage, or professional life, were frequent and statuses could become blurred, where Christians and Jews might be rich and influential and get what Muslims might consider to be ideas above their station. Some might rise almost to rule, like Samuel Ibn Naghrila, the powerful Jewish chief minister of the Amazigh Zirid principality of Granada, who began building what would become the site of the Alhambra. After his son Joseph attempted a takeover, in alliance with a neighbouring Muslim king, in 1066, a violent pogrom killed Joseph and many of the city's Jewish inhabitants.

Defining community boundaries was important to Muslim rulers in demonstrating their dominance: for example, by enforcing different codes of dress for Muslim and Jewish men and women, as occurred in Mamluk Egypt, or more drastically, ordering houses belonging to non-Muslims that were built higher than those of neighbouring Muslims to be pulled down, as happened in Seljuq Baghdad. Maintaining difference was important, too, for the community leaders of subject populations anxious to maintain their own faith communities, like the Jewish rabbis of Iraq whose judgments were sought as far away as Spain, who disliked it when Jews used Islamic courts (as they often did), and who worried about conversions to Islam. For all that, though, religious identities were not fixed: al-Andalus, above all, was perhaps most vividly a world of mobility and boundary-crossing. Umayyad-era judges in Spain had to deal with problems like the legal status of a Muslim who had travelled to Christian territory, became a Christian and fought against Muslims, but once captured in Muslim territory, declared himself to be a Muslim once more.[23]

The story of relations between religious communities and of conversion to Islam in the medieval period has often, in the past two hundred years, been told more polemically than precisely. Whether later writers stress coexistence or persecution often has more to do with the politics of their own time than the mixed and messy realities of the past they relate. When Jewish historians in the nineteenth century stressed how much better life had been for Jews under medieval Muslim than Christian rule, and especially in al-Andalus (which on the whole was undeniably true), they were doing so within the context of arguments for Jewish emancipation in a Europe that was becoming more liberal, but where antisemitism was also becoming a political force. When in the second half of the twentieth century, other Jewish historians created a "countermyth" of unrelenting persecutions and Muslim, rather than European and Christian, antisemitism, they were responding to growing Muslim, and especially Arab, hostility to Jews in the context of the Arab-Israeli conflict, especially after the 1967 Arab-Israeli War.[24]

The terms *dhimmi* and *ahl al-dhimma* ("protected person" and "the people under protection") have become especially notorious, in some Islamophobic commentary, as denoting the second-class, subjugated and *un*protected status of non-Muslims under Islamic rule and in Islamic law. In its earliest formulation, in the seventh century, the term "the protection of God and of His Prophet" (*dhimmat allah wa rasulihi*) was not related to religious minorities. In fact, it derived from much older Arabian practices of negotiating sanctuary and safety. Being under "God's protection" applied at first to Muslims, and in the seventh century also to non-Muslims who now lived under Muslim rule. It was only much later, in the ninth century, when religious and political authorities felt the need to enforce community boundaries in a society that was increasingly multi-confessional, that rules around the status of non-Muslim (*dhimmi*) subjects emerged—clearly differentiated taxes, indignities like wearing a metal tag in the bathhouse, or distinctively coloured dress in the streets. The periods when such rules were actually enforced indicate times of unusual political stress, rather than giving an image of everyday normality.[25]

Forced conversion, or the killing of non-Muslims who refused conversion, was very rare. Times of persecution did occur; faced with demands for conversion, some Jewish religious authorities prescribed death rather than apostasy. (Maimonides, refuting them, pointed out that confessing Muhammad's Prophethood "out of fear of the sword" was not the same as doing so willingly, and therefore no great sin.) Very occasionally, as in Cordoba in the 850s, non-Muslims would deliberately make a stand for their religion and provoke their own martyrdom by publicly blaspheming against Islam and the Prophet. Up to the ninth century, Christian writers would record such martyrs' lives and deaths as exemplary acts of witness, recalling their own imagined golden age of an early church standing against pagan Roman oppression, and encouraging their community to remain faithful at a time when conversion to Islam was becoming more frequent.

Persecution against Christians occurred most notably at the end of the eighth century, when the first Abbasid caliphs ramped up their confrontation with Byzantium, and again under the Fatimid Caliph al-Hakim bi-Amr Allah, who ordered the destruction of the Church of the Holy Sepulchre in Jerusalem in 1009. After the Abbasids took power, and being Muslim ceased to be so closely associated with being Arab, there were inducements to convert too. One Coptic (Egyptian Christian) chronicler lamented that in mid-eighth-century Egypt, on the promise of exemption from the often-heavy tax (*jizya*) levied on non-Muslim subjects, "many of the wealthy and poor denied the religion of Christ and followed [the caliph]."[26]

Fears of violence and aspirations to social mobility, ambition and emotion, the powerful attraction of the Prophet's message itself and the powerful spectacle of flourishing Muslim power, the advantages to gain and impositions or vulnerabilities to escape through conversion must all have played parts in the increasing numbers of converts to Islam across North Africa and the Middle East up through the twelfth century. It was over this period that, in the lands of the Arab conquests, societies gradually became mostly Muslim. Learned or wealthy Christian and Jewish families increasingly found that to maintain their social status, they needed to join the dominant community. Merchants might find that it was more advantageous to be a Muslim partner alongside other Muslims in business than to remain a Christian or a Jew. Ordinary people might escape taxes levied on non-Muslims, or might simply find (in the case of some Christians in Syria and Iraq) that a confession of whose doctrinal complexities they had little understanding, and whose authorities had in the past persecuted them in its own doctrinal disputes, could be relatively painlessly replaced by another.

It was, of course, possible to remain a non-Muslim under Muslim rule, and Muslims found, too, that they could live as a minority under the rule of others. When the Normans conquered Sicily in the mid-eleventh century, after two hundred years of Muslim rule there, many of the island's inhabitants went into exile, in Spain or North Africa. But some stayed, finding ways not only to remain but to enjoy the new rulers' patronage. While some Muslim writers urged jihad to reconquer the lost land, or warned their coreligionists against the temptations of falling in with unbelievers, the new sovereign, Roger II, won praise from others as a Christian king who followed his Muslim predecessors' example of encouraging multi-confessional coexistence.

The great geographical compendium that Roger commissioned from the scholar Muhammad al-Idrisi, a descendant of the Prophet whose Andalusi family settled in Sicily in the twelfth century, is one of the most remarkable creations of medieval Islamic scholarship. It is also a monument to the Islamic norms of good government that, by this time, could be held up as examples to Christian rulers, too. When al-Idrisi wrote of Roger II that, being "empowered by God, . . . leader of the Roman empire, victor of the Christians," he "rules with justice over all his subjects, providing equal protection and welfare," he was offering conventional praise. But he was also drawing a compelling picture of a just ruler, a picture he hoped his patron would fit. As time went on, as northern Italian Lombards immigrated in greater numbers, life probably became harder for Sicily's Muslims: *convivencia* was never conflict-free. But in this part of the Muslims' world, their presence and influence remained strong enough to shape court culture and social life, even after their rule had passed away.[27]

✧✧✧✧✧

Twelfth-century Sicily and Spain were parts of a changing Mediterranean world. In antiquity, the Roman Empire had united the Mediterranean as a single political and commercial space: the western empire's fragmentation, from the mid-fifth century, meant the collapse of long-distance Mediterranean trade, which by the seventh and eighth centuries was almost nonexistent. Into the vacuum, though, had come Muslim soldiers and sailors. Written accounts from the caliphate, from the ninth century onwards, see the Mediterranean—still called "the Romans' Sea," in contrast to the Indian Ocean, which was "the Arabs' Sea"—above all as a frontier against a hostile Roman (Byzantine) state. In the first centuries of Islam, the Mediterranean as seen by Muslims, at least those who wrote about it, was both less important and more hostile than the richer seas to the south and east. Maritime activity meant defending the frontier and raiding the caliph's enemies across it. As early as the mid-seventh century, Muslim fleets raided Cyprus and defeated a Byzantine naval force off the coast of Anatolia. The Arabic historical tradition would celebrate those who gained distinction in the pursuit of holy war at sea.

But commercial profits, as well as warfare, were as important to Muslims as they were to Christians in the Mediterranean. While the northern, Latin Mediterranean would take half a millennium to recover from its post-Roman commercial collapse, the southern and eastern Mediterranean now under Muslim rule became a westward extension of the cosmopolitan trade routes centred on Baghdad and the Persian Gulf. Merchants and shipping from the Italian city states, Portugal, and Catalonia began to seize control of trade in the eleventh and twelfth centuries, and would keep hold until the sixteenth century. But through the ninth and tenth centuries, the Mediterranean was a Muslim-dominated sea. The Umayyads of Cordoba, the Almohads, and the Fatimids have been called "Mediterranean caliphates." In the tenth century, albeit only briefly, growing Cordoba may have been a larger city than Constantinople; at the same time, Tunisian glazed pottery was finding its way into Italy. As late as the 1220s, the Almohad caliphate in North Africa and Spain could hold off Latin naval threats with its own sea power while also welcoming Latin merchants in its markets.

Although it was divided between often mutually hostile states—and throughout the medieval period, local and regional production and trade were much more significant than long-distance exchange—the Muslim Mediterranean was a connected economic space. The records of Jewish merchants preserved from the Cairo Geniza (a vast storehouse of fragmentary writings) show us trading networks in the tenth and eleventh centuries based in Fustat and Cairo that connected the Indian Ocean with the Mediterranean and Sahara, shipping luxury goods like gold and pearls, indigo, spices and sugar, and bulkier commodities like copper, lead, animal hides, wax and olive oil, between North Africa, Sicily, and Alexandria. Amalfi, Naples, and more northern Mediterranean ports began to be drawn into these same networks. We have already seen the role that Venice played in the Mediterranean slave trade. Religious competition played out, too, across mercantile connections, perhaps most dramatically when Venetians stole the remains of Saint Mark from Alexandria in the mid-ninth century and took him home to be their patron saint.[28]

It was into this competitive and connected Mediterranean world that the Seljuq Turks, as the new power from the east, came in the mid-eleventh century. Like earlier caliphs and their generals, the Seljuq emirs made a propaganda point of campaigning on their northwest frontiers with Christian Armenia, Georgia, and Byzantium. But their momentous victory over the Byzantines at Manzikert was important to them at least as much for opening Anatolia to settlement by their still-nomadic Turkic followers as it was for the ideological purpose of pursuing jihad. Their most serious conflicts were with rival Muslim sovereigns, especially the Fatimid caliphs in Cairo. After conquering Egypt, the Fatimids had been unable to achieve their grandiose ambition of supplanting the Abbasid caliph in Baghdad, and fighting between Fatimid and Abbasid forces had ground to a halt in Palestine and Syria.

The Seljuqs inherited the Abbasid cause, and Seljuq princes were installed in Damascus and Jerusalem while others, further north, pressed on after Manzikert to establish a Seljuq sultanate in Anatolia (the "sultanate of Rum," that is, in Roman territory). Reaching as far north and west as Nicaea (Iznik) and the Bosphorus, they threatened the survival of the Byzantines in Constantinople and prompted the Emperor Alexius to appeal for aid to the pope and western Christendom. In the course of their expansion westward from central Asia, the Seljuqs had generally maintained the Turkic political model of decentralised rule: even, or especially, after they became sultans over the vast Abbasid caliphate, their empire from Afghanistan to the Mediterranean was more like a loose confederation of family businesses than a single enterprise. It was held together by powerful central personalities like the Sultan Alp Arslan, the victor of Manzikert; his son and successor Malik-Shah; and their famous minister Nizam al-Mulk. Constantly on the move, they were able to impose their will over subordinates from Iran to Anatolia. In 1092, however, both Nizam al-Mulk and Malik-Shah died (Nizam al-Mulk was probably assassinated by the Isma'ilis), and the Seljuq princes became embroiled in a war for succession.

When the first crusaders appeared in western Anatolia, in the autumn of 1096, therefore, they entered a turbulent, fragmented political landscape in which both the rival caliphates and the Muslim statelets of Anatolia, Syria and Palestine were far more concerned with fighting one another than with any serious threat from Christian Europe. And the first crusaders to appear in Anatolia were not a serious threat, at least not to Muslims. Their religious zeal to avenge "dishonour" against God had led to the massacre of Jews in Germany, and it was probably their lack of provisions that led them to sack the city of Belgrade on their way east, but they were quickly and easily wiped out by the Seljuqs almost as soon as they crossed the Bosphorus from Constantinople. The First Crusade's second wave, however, was another matter. In 1097 the crusader army took Nicaea, marched through Anatolia and besieged Antioch (the ancient city, modern

Antakya in southeast Turkey, settled since the fourth century BCE and destroyed in the devastating earthquake of 2023).

While the Fatimids were busy seizing Jerusalem from its Seljuq governor the following year, further north the crusaders took Antioch and Edessa, where they set up the first of the crusader kingdoms. Their capture of the northwest Syrian town of Maʿarrat al-Nuʿman in December 1098 was significant, despite its strategic unimportance, because it was the site of a wholesale massacre of the inhabitants that in Latin sources—though not Arabic ones—is compounded by reports of half-starved crusaders eating the flesh of the town's dead defenders. Whether or not torture and cannibalism really occurred, the actual atrocities were such that fear of their repetition certainly spread, and local rulers began to negotiate with the advancing crusaders rather than holding out against them, as Maʿarrat had done. Jerusalem, however, resisted. After a monthlong siege, it fell to the crusaders in July 1099. In the words of one chronicler, "The inhabitants became prey for the sword." Both Muslims and Jews were massacred: according to another account, the synagogue where the city's Jewish inhabitants had sought shelter was "burned…down on their heads."[29]

The Latin kingdoms established by the First Crusade—Edessa, Antioch, Tripoli and Jerusalem—created a sudden, intrusive swath of Frankish (European) Christian states along the eastern Mediterranean coastline. Two centuries of sporadic warfare, diplomacy, conquest and reconquest followed in which Muslim and Frankish states vied with one another, made alliances with each other against common enemies, traded across their indistinct frontiers, and viewed each other's inhabitants with curiosity, suspicion, and (especially when it came to Muslims' views of Frankish hygiene, medicine, and sexual ethics) some measure of disgust. The imposition of Christian rule over Muslims and Muslim territory, especially the holy city of Jerusalem, was undoubtedly shocking to Muslim opinion. And, at least for later chroniclers who had an expansive view of the world, the wars in Syria and Palestine were part of a larger pattern of Christian aggression in the

Mediterranean that had begun with the capture of Toledo in central Spain in 1068, and that would lead to the fall of Seville in 1248.[30]

At the same time, to a great extent the crusaders were just an exotic part of the larger, fractured religious and political picture: small and embattled statelets that happened to be ruled by Christians from Europe existing alongside the small and embattled Muslim statelets spun off from the fragmentation of Abbasid sovereignty. The piously minded scholars who would be the period's Muslim historians, and the poets whose verses they recorded, lamented the disunity and disarray of the Muslim community that had allowed such evils to befall them, and urged unity of faith and purpose in waging jihad against the Christians' own barbarous holy war. Correspondingly, they celebrated a triumph of the faith when Salah al-Din Ibn Ayyub, a Kurdish general from Armenia whose family had risen to prominence in Seljuq service, first wrested control of Egypt from the Fatimids and then, in October 1187, retook Jerusalem from the crusaders.

Salah al-Din (whom Europeans would call Saladin) confined the crusaders' presence to a strip of coastline, from which the Third Crusade under Richard I "Lionheart" of England could not break free. The truce Salah al-Din made in September 1192, a few months before his death, secured peace for three years and safe passage for unarmed Christian pilgrims to Jerusalem. Apart from some mostly fruitless attacks on Egypt, the crusaders' campaigns would not threaten Muslim rule again. The Fourth Crusade gave up on retaking Jerusalem, and in 1204, infamously, its Venetian and French forces pillaged Christian Constantinople instead. Warfare in these years was certainly religiously motivated, and replete with religious language and symbolism. But hostilities did not simply run along religious lines, either for Muslims or for Christians.

The last of the Latin crusaders were finally expelled from the Syrian coast in 1291. Crusading was a European phenomenon and would remain a European obsession: the Crusades themselves would continue in campaigns against non-Christians around the Baltic Sea and against Christian "heretics" in southern France, and the idea of the Crusades would have a long afterlife in European imaginations and Romantic literature. For the inhabitants of Syria and Palestine that were once more securely under Muslim rule, the Frankish wars had been merely part of a wider world of political breakup and sporadic conflict, albeit one that stretched across the Muslim Mediterranean to North Africa and Spain. There would be no Arabic term for "the Crusades" as a distinct historical event until the nineteenth century, when Arab authors would borrow the term from European historians and write of *al-hurub al-salibiyya*, "the Cross Wars." They would gain significance in Muslim imaginations, correspondingly, only in the nineteenth and twentieth centuries, as Europeans invoked them in their own historical imagination and as Muslim-majority lands fell under the increasing pressure of modern European colonialism. At the time—and for a long time afterwards—they had no such importance.

Muslims had, in any case, defeated the crusaders in the end. By the middle of the thirteenth century they had other things to worry about. An invasion of far more calamitous proportions, and of much greater world-historical significance, was coming from the east.

Part 2

ISLAM'S NEW WORLDS
1200–1800 CE

5

HEIRS OF THE WORLD-CONQUERORS

In January 1258, Hülegü, Genghis Khan's grandson, laid siege to Baghdad. The brother of Genghis's successor, the Great Khan Möngke, and of Kubilai, the conqueror of China, he was one of the three most powerful men in the world. A few weeks later, his armies sacked the city and executed the caliph, the last in the Abbasid line that had reigned for five hundred years.

One story, later popular in Europe thanks to its retelling by the Venetian traveller Marco Polo, has the caliph being brought before the khan. Why, Hülegü asks the caliph, has he amassed so much gold and silver in his palace, instead of using it to buy arms and men to defend his city? What use would it be to him now? Telling him that he had better eat his treasure, since he had so much of it, in this version of events the khan leaves the caliph locked in a tower, surrounded by golden cups and plates, until he starves to death. Another story (usually considered more likely) has the caliph being rolled up in a carpet, or sewn in a sack, and kicked or trampled to death, to avoid the possibly sacrilegious spilling of his blood onto the ground—this, Mongol superstition feared, might cause an earthquake. Yet another version, in some Georgian sources (there were Christian Georgian troops in the Mongol army), has Hülegü slaying the caliph with his own hands.

The caliph's ministers and family members were called out and killed, and the city's districts were divided among the Mongol commanders and given over to systematic looting and massacre. In the words of an anonymous Baghdadi chronicler:

> The inhabitants of Baghdad were put under the sword... and were subjected to forty days of continuous killing, pillaging, enslavement.... They killed men, women, youth and children.... A great part of the city, including the caliph's mosque... [was] burnt, and the city was laid in ruins. The dead lay as mounds in the streets and the markets. Rain fell on them, horses trampled down upon them, their faces were disfigured, and they became an example to anyone who saw them. Then, peace was proclaimed and those that were left came out from hiding. Their colour had changed, their minds shocked by sight of the horror that no words can describe. They were like the dead emerging from their graves on the day of resurrection, fearful, hungry, and cold.[1]

Contemporary accounts, whether hostile to the Mongols or written under their patronage, agree on the horrific scale of slaughter and pillage inflicted on the city, although the duration of the massacre varies from three to seven days rather than forty—these numbers all, perhaps, having symbolic rather than literal significance.

And yet they also tell another story, in which Safi al-Din al-Urmawi, a distinguished calligrapher and poet, the caliph's court musician and tutor to his son, lavishly buys off the Mongol commander sent to plunder his district and negotiates the safety of his friends and neighbours. To demonstrate that he can take what he likes, the Mongol emir rapes a singer, an enslaved woman in Urmawi's household, in front of everyone. But no one is killed. Then, in an allegory of the ability of civilisation to tame savagery, when Urmawi is brought before the terrible Hülegü Khan, he plays him a lullaby and sings him to sleep.

Within Islamic history, the capture of Baghdad by the Mongols certainly seemed like an apocalypse. Arabic literature would add the ruins of Abbasid Baghdad to its long, poetic list of sites of memory and nostalgia that had begun with pre-Islamic Arabian camping grounds and continued through Ctesiphon remembered from Baghdad, Umayyad Syria remembered from Cordoba, and Cordoba remembered from Granada. Although it would be eclipsed by the greater devastation of the Black Death a century later, the plague that seems to have struck Baghdad along with the Mongol armies was understood at the time as indicative of the scale of the slaughter: a pestilence that arose from the mountains of corpses, corrupting the air as far away as Tunis. For later Western Orientalist writers, and for twentieth-century Arab nationalists too, the Mongol conquest would be the first disastrous episode in a long story of decline for the whole Muslim world. Genghis Khan's own invasion, thirty years earlier, of Transoxania and Khwarazm, the central Asian regions on the far northeast frontier of the caliphate, had been described as so terrible that only a thousand years of peace would repair the damage.[2]

The Mongols themselves seem to have promoted their image as bringers of terror: it all added to the intended effect. And for pious Muslim chroniclers, the story of the starving caliph surrounded by useless treasure painted a useful moral about the corruption of kingship. In fact, after 1258, Baghdad quickly recovered, its trade flourishing, its culture undimmed. Officials were appointed immediately after the conquest to begin the city's reconstruction. Its chief judge, appointed by the last caliph in 1257, was restored to his post, which he held until he died in 1269. Urmawi, the calligrapher and musician, went on to pursue his musical career in Baghdad as well as becoming chief secretary and supervisor of religious endowments (that is, properties whose revenue was endowed to pious good works like the upkeep of mosques, schools, and charitable welfare). His annual stipend under the khan was twice what it had been under the caliphs. He eventually fell out of favour and died aged eighty under arrest and in debt, but two of his sons are known to have followed in his footsteps, holding honoured posts as government secretaries.[3]

The Mongols' policy was certainly to rape, kill, pillage, and destroy without mercy whomever and whatever would not immediately submit to them. That did not prevent them from becoming generous patrons of the arts and sciences once they had established who was in charge. While they were on their way to Baghdad, talented Muslim men of learning and letters had already won their favour. The astronomer, mathematician and philosopher Nasir al-Din al-Tusi, who had been working for the Isma'ilis when the Mongol army arrived at their fortress at Alamut, passed directly into the khan's service, where he remained until his death in Baghdad in 1274. Hülegü had an observatory built for him outside his new capital city at Maragha in Azerbaijan, complete with a school and library, which is said to have attracted astronomers from as far away as China. Al-Tusi was one of the greatest scientists of his age, ranked by biographers as a successor to Aristotle and called "the teacher of mankind." While he became most famous as an astronomer (and served as court astrologer), al-Tusi's work also established trigonometry as a distinct mathematical discipline. His observatory would serve as a model for others, built centuries later and as far away as Samarqand, Istanbul, and Jaipur.[4]

One of al-Tusi's employees gives us a striking account of the continuity of urban life, science and culture after the Mongol conquest. The biographer and genealogist Kamal al-Din Ibn al-Fuwati had been born in Baghdad and was captured, aged fourteen, when the city fell. After serving as the librarian of al-Tusi's observatory at Maragha, he travelled between Baghdad and Azerbaijan and wrote a great compilation of the lives of the scholars of his time. He describes how, in the aftermath of the catastrophe, "mosques and colleges...shrines and hospices" were rebuilt, salaries for "scholars, lawyers, and Sufis" were restored, "and the glory of Islam came back to the city of peace." The Mongols were, indeed, steppe nomads who, half a century earlier, had cared only that their subjects should submit and fear them, and who despised agriculture almost on principle and depopulated whole cities. Some of the greatest cities of Transoxania and Khurasan were wholly devastated in 1219–21 by Genghis Khan's hordes. (The word *horde* would itself come into English from the Mongolian and Turkic word for a ruler's encampment, which in Ottoman Turkish came to mean "army.") Balkh, the birthplace of Jalal al-Din Rumi, ancient already in the time of Alexander the Great and called "the mother of cities" by medieval Arab geographers, was destroyed and never recovered. The scholarly and agricultural centre of Nishapur, where al-Ghazali had taught, was similarly wrecked.

But even in these cases, Mongol destruction did not simply raze cities from the map. Balkh was partially rebuilt. It declined because it was superseded in importance by the newer, nearby shrine city of Mazar-i Sharif, which was identified in the fifteenth century as the site of the grave of Ali Ibn Abi Talib. Nishapur had already suffered from civil strife and earthquake before Genghis Khan arrived, and by the fourteenth century was again a flourishing centre of scholarship before declining slowly in subsequent centuries. Archaeological evidence from elsewhere in central Asia shows that the Mongol armies did not always destroy the towns they conquered; cities fell into ruin, rather, because their citizens were removed and resettled elsewhere. Hülegü's successor was celebrated in Baghdad as "a just ruler who cherished the building of cities." By the early fourteenth century, when the conquerors had taken the Iranian city of Tabriz for their capital, Ibn al-Fuwati could describe Baghdad, where he died in 1323, as "heaven upon earth."[5]

Baghdad had lost its claim to be the centre of a universal world empire—it had also long ceased to be the unrivalled centre of the Muslims' world. It became a provincial city on the western, Arabic-speaking edge of a Persian-speaking world that looked mostly east, one centre among many in a Muslim world that had already expanded its reach far beyond the Arab world of southwest Asia, and that would only grow as time went on. Genghis Khan himself, after his destructive campaign west of the Oxus, took back east with him a Turkic Muslim called Mahmud "Yalawach" (Mahmud "the Envoy") who became governor of Zhongdu, the former capital of the Jin Empire that the Mongols had conquered at the other end of Asia, in north China. Less than fifty years after the Mongols' sack of Baghdad, its new Mongol ruler would be a Muslim too.

The late medieval growth of communications and exchange across Mongol Eurasia was certainly a double-edged sword. Under the Mongols, the Muslims' world grew. As part of the world's largest-ever land empire, it became a conduit for transcontinental flows of ideas and culture, of people and goods. It was also, in the fourteenth century, subject to dreadful warfare under Genghis Khan's even more terrible successor, Tamerlane, and to the devastating epidemic of the Black Death. But in the longer term, beyond the immediate cataclysm and these later catastrophes, the result of the Mongol conquests was a continental shift in power and trade, and a major acceleration of the globalisation of Islam beyond its original Middle Eastern heartlands.

Between the thirteenth and fifteenth centuries, in the wake of the Mongols' conquests and the subsequent fragmenting of their empire, new dynasties and expanding successor states from the Mongol-Turkic world grew east into China, west into the Arab and Byzantine lands, and south into India. The end of the classical caliphates paved the way for the rise of new regional powers: the Mamluks of Egypt and Syria who stopped the Mongol advance in northern Palestine, the Mongol dynasties of central Asia and China, and the Timurid descendants of the Mongol conquerors in Iran and South Asia. In succession to the vast, world-conquering Mongol Empire, the early modern, regional "gunpowder empires" of the Safavids in Iran, the Mughals in India, and the Ottomans in the eastern Mediterranean would emerge. From the small, dispersed trading communities of earlier times, the centuries after the fall of Baghdad also witnessed the more permanent growth of Muslim life in the islands of Southeast Asia and on the Atlantic coast of West Africa.

A "classical" Islamic world might have ended, but Muslim life multiplied, diversified, and spread. The caliphate had claimed a single, universal sovereignty over Muslims everywhere but had not truly exercised it since the eighth century. Now, claims to rule over new as well as old Muslim lands and peoples proliferated, and new peoples became both Muslims and rulers. From the fall of Baghdad in 1258 to the capture of the "Red Apple" of Rome—Constantinople, an older, and still the greatest, symbol of world empire—in 1453, the Muslim world was the theatre, and Islam the expression, of world-conquering ambitions.

◇◇◇◇◇◇◇◇

In the khan's retinue with the Mongol army when it arrived outside Baghdad was another eminent Muslim scholar, the Persian historian Ala al-Din Juvaini. His family, from Khurasan, had a long history of government service. One ancestor had been chamberlain to the Caliph Harun al-Rashid, and, before serving at the Mongol court, his father had been in the service of the Persian rulers of Khwarazm (the plains north of Khurasan and south of the Aral Sea, now in Kazakhstan). Ala al-Din apparently travelled through the new Mongol Empire, to Mongolia and China. He wrote a major history of Genghis Khan and his successors entitled *Tarikh-i Jahan-Gusha* (History of the World-Conqueror) and became a committed supporter of the dynasty established by Hülegü in Iran, the Il-Khans. Appointed governor of Baghdad in 1259, he was an energetic improver of agricultural life and productivity in Iraq. His brother Shams al-Din would be Hülegü's chief minister and supervisor of the Il-Khanate's finances. Together, the Juvaini brothers were effectively the rulers of Iran and Iraq under the Il-Khans. The khans still adhered to their mix of Buddhist and ancestral shamanistic religion, with its belief in a supreme sky god, Tengri, and elaborate, secretive burial rites for rulers that, at the time of Hülegü, still involved human sacrifice. But the Juvainis could see themselves—being Muslims who embodied the deep traditions of Persian and Abbasid court culture—as exercising good government according to Islamic norms even if their masters were unbelievers.

Living comfortably with the Mongols' conquest—as, until their fall from favour in court intrigue, and the subsequent execution of Shams al-Din in 1284, the Juvaini brothers certainly did—required some intellectual justification. Ala al-Din Juvaini (who himself fell from his horse in 1283 and died, before he could fall from grace) found it easily enough, in seeing the advent of "the world-conqueror" and his successors as part of God's great plan in universal history. After the fall of Bukhara, "when from the reflection of the sun the plain seemed to be a tray filled with blood," and the Mongol soldiers, entering the mosque, had scattered leaves of the Qur'an in the courtyard and trampled them underfoot, Juvaini writes that Genghis Khan ascended the pulpit and spoke to the assembled people: "I am the punishment of God," Juvaini has the Khan announce. "If you had not committed great sins, God would not have sent a punishment like me upon you." For other Muslim observers outside the Mongols' domains, like the Arab chronicler Ibn al-Athir in Mamluk-ruled Damascus, the Mongols were just a plague: a calamity like nothing seen before in history, and unlikely to be surpassed before the end of the world. But accounting for the advent of the Mongols as akin to the great flood in Noah's day, or the other chastisements sent by divine justice as an admonition to sinful mankind, allowed Juvaini both to acknowledge the scale of the calamity, and to square it with a reassuring higher purpose: the Mongols were God's secret weapon.[6]

Juvaini's justifications, no doubt, meant little to the mass of the rural population. Muslim Iranian peasants were being squeezed by his tax collectors, while much of their agricultural land was also turned over to pasture for the incoming nomads' flocks, herds, and horses. They had nothing to gain from the Persian literary and cultural renaissance that flowered in the thirteenth and fourteenth centuries, its monumental architecture, its elaborate forms of poetry, or the painting that, within the cultural world connected by the Mongols, combined Persian and Chinese styles. It was the urban Muslim scholarly class, and in particular the professional, Persian-speaking elite, who inherited the Mongol conquests, by writing them into a Muslim vision of history. The Mongol rulers were also astute enough to annex such visions to their own purposes. Gold coins minted by Hülegü after the fall of Baghdad carried a Qur'anic formula: "Say, O God, sovereignty is Yours. You give sovereignty to whom You please, and You wrest sovereignty from whom You please!"[7]

Appropriating Islam and adopting it were not quite the same thing, but conversion to Islam among the Mongols occurred relatively rapidly, within a few generations. It seems to have been well established already, especially through patronage of Sufi teachers and their communities, before the accession of Hülegü's great-grandson, Ghazan Khan. The reign of Ghazan, who came to the throne in 1295 and took the Muslim name Mahmud, is usually taken to mark the definitive absorption of the Mongols into the Islamic faith and culture of the lands and peoples they had conquered. As his Persian minister and court historian, Rashid al-Din "Tabib" ("the Doctor"), put it:

> Inasmuch as during the completion of his task of world conquest his hosts encountered Islamic urban areas, divine wisdom ordained that, as a balm to that wound, the peoples who had inflicted those very wounds would become Muslim in order that the perfection of divine power be clear and obvious to all people in the world.

Rashid al-Din became one of Mahmud Ghazan Khan's chief ministers. For twenty years, he enjoyed an illustrious, powerful, and wealthy position. He was himself a convert to Islam. Born into an Iranian Jewish family, his medical profession allowed him access to the court and his conversion to Islam, at the age of about thirty, allowed him access to higher office. His chronicle of the Mongols is also an ambitious world history, placing the dynasty he served in a universal context that runs from Adam, the first man, through the patriarchs, prophets, and ancient kings of Persia to Muhammad and the caliphs, and in relation to the neighbouring worlds of China, Europe, and India. He calls his patron Ghazan Khan "the Padishah," Supreme King, "of Islam, Emperor of Mankind, Shadow of God, Supporter of God's Religion...the pearl of the ocean of Genghis Khan's offspring and sun of the sky of the imperial dynasty for all to see." When Ghazan made war on the Muslim Mamluks in Syria in 1299, according to Rashid al-Din it was "out of zealousness for the religion of Islam" that he swore "to repel the evil of these rebels...from the Muslim lands held by the Padishah of Islam."[8]

As in the time of the Abbasids and Fatimids, such claims to rule and fight in the name of God, and of God's sovereignty on earth, were made principally against other Muslims, and sometimes in alliance with non-Muslims against fellow Muslims. The Muslim Il-Khans fought alongside Christian Armenians and Georgians from the Caucasus against a rival Mongol state, the Qipchak Khanate or "Golden Horde." The Golden Horde had taken the lands to the north of the Il-Khans, in the steppe across what is now southern Russia and Crimea, and at their greatest extent their conquests reached as far west as modern Poland, Hungary and Bulgaria. As early as 1257, their ruler, Berke Khan, was a Muslim. His successors varied their religious affiliations, but from the early fourteenth century the central Asian peoples who descended from the Golden Horde—Tatars, Uzbeks and Kazakhs—increasingly became Muslims.

To the west and south, the Muslim Mamluk dynasty that now ruled in Egypt and Syria was the Il-Khans' principal enemy. In 1260, a Mamluk army had stopped the Mongols' westward expansion at Ayn Jalut (Goliath's Well) in Palestine. Hülegü himself had proposed an alliance with the Christian King Louis IX of France against the Mamluks, and an alliance of the Mongols with the crusader states in Syria was negotiated, though never realised. The Mongols' conversion to Islam disappointed Christian expectations that their coming to Christ might lead to the recovery of Jerusalem, but did not change their willingness to seek allies in Europe. Against the Il-Khans, for their part, the Mamluks allied themselves with the Mongol Golden Horde, an alliance that also guaranteed the Mamluk sultanate's access to the Black Sea slave trade. In 1261, a refugee member of the Abbasid family made it to Cairo and was welcomed by the Mamluk sultan. The Mamluks could now claim to be the protectors of the legitimate caliph of Islam, and the true defenders of the faith.

The Mongol rulers' own approach to religion was more pragmatic than pious: their general tolerance of different religious practices and communities was less a matter of principle than practicality for the rulers of highly diverse subject populations. They also appreciated the benefits to be derived from patronising able scholars, artists, and administrators, and leaving them to their own faiths. They accordingly adapted their relations to different faiths and customs according to circumstance. On the one hand, Buddhism virtually disappeared from Iran after the Mongols' conversion to Islam. On the other, in central Asia and China, Muslim practices that conflicted with Mongol customs, such as ritual washing before prayer and the ritual slaughter of animals, were sometimes suppressed. Nonetheless, adherence to Islam gradually spread among the Mongols themselves, across Iran and the Eurasian steppe, not simply as a mass shift of allegiance following the formal conversion of a ruler, but as a slower, and deeper, society-wide change. When, a century after the fall of Baghdad, in the 1360s, the Turkish-speaking Mongol warlord Temür-i Lang (Temür "the Lame," because of an arrow wound to his knee), known to Europe as Tamerlane, emerged into the unstable, fragmented central Asia that followed the breakup of the Mongol Empire, he was a Muslim.[9]

To Temür, who carried a portable mosque with him on his constant campaigns, being Muslim was perhaps an internalisation of the way the Persian chroniclers had rationalised the conquests of his predecessor and model, Genghis Khan: taking to heart the idea that he was God's vengeance on backsliding Muslims and unbelievers alike. We can't know what he himself believed, except perhaps that he was destined to rule the world. Like the Il-Khans whose successors he conquered, being Muslim did not prevent him from allying, temporarily at least, with Christians against other Muslims, in his case with the Byzantines against the emerging Ottoman Turkish sultanate in Anatolia. But his apparently serious profession of Sunni Islam added ideological, legal, and cultural dimensions to what was otherwise a return to the purely Mongol precedents of nomadic life and spectacularly violent warfare—the latter being taken to notorious extremes, symbolised in the towers of heads constructed by his soldiers in the wake of massacres in Iran and elsewhere. When he took Delhi in 1398, it was said, "some streets were rendered impassable by the heaps of dead... and a scene of horror ensued easier to be imagined than described."[10]

In the same way, when Temür's armies conquered Mamluk Syria, they "committed there more shameful atrocities than had ever been heard of before." But when Temür met the renowned North African historian and legal scholar Ibn Khaldun outside Damascus in 1401, Ibn Khaldun was impressed. Some, he wrote, said that Temür was a heretic (meaning that he had Shi'i inclinations), and "still others attribute to him the employment of magic and sorcery, but in all this there is nothing: it is simply that he is highly intelligent and very perspicacious, addicted to debate and argumentation about what he knows and...does not know." While his soldiers were bombarding the citadel of Damascus with siege engines and naphtha bombs, pillaging the town and setting the roof of the Great Mosque on fire, Temür himself questioned Ibn Khaldun about the geography of the far west and brought scholars before him to discuss claims to the caliphate and questions of Islamic law. His interest in learning and his sparing skilled artisans from slaughter, since both could be useful, were typical of Mongol rulers. His pragmatic encouragement of secure trade, insistence on Qur'anic strictures when it came to "fair" prices and market practices, and zero tolerance for popular urban protest all made him an attractive despot to the merchant bourgeoisie and scholarly classes, who—once their ransoms were paid and the massacre was over—on the whole welcomed both the return of strong, centralised rule after decades of unstable local military regimes and the suppression of the popular revolts that had broken out episodically ever since the Abbasids.[11]

Temür's attempt to reconstruct the Mongol world empire was the last such bid for universal sovereignty. After his time, no empire-builder would aspire to subjugate all the known world. From his capital at Samarqand, for thirty years following his first major campaigns in the mid-1370s, Temür's armies repeatedly ravaged territories across central Eurasia, as far apart as Anatolia and northern India. When he died in 1405, he was marching on China. His empire was one of personal ambition, a sudden, violent concentration of wealth and power on an extraordinary scale that did not outlive him. His glorious architecture at Samarqand, the riches of which were unscrupulously pillaged from the cities his armies sacked—and where he himself spent hardly any time—was damaged by earthquake within his lifetime and subsequently fell into ruin.

His successors, the Timurids, though, inherited many small parcels of sovereignty left over from his conquests, from Iran to central and South Asia, and as political power fragmented once again, cultural life multiplied. In each court and urban centre, Timurid rulers sought to patronise the style and sophistication thought necessary to the prestige of an heir to the world-conquerors. At Samarqand, under the rule of Temür's grandson Ulugh Bey in the first half of the fifteenth century, mathematicians made advances in astronomical observation, in calculating the value of π, and in the use of decimal fractions, while a great madrasa, which still stands today, was built on the city's Registan plaza. In the wake of their ancestors' depredations and destruction, the Muslim successors to the Mongols would leave to posterity a cosmopolitan culture of richly expressive music, books, and painting, and of advances in science and architecture.[12]

◇◇◇◇◇◇◇

When Temür's army pillaged Delhi, in December 1398, it had been the capital of a Muslim sultanate for almost two hundred years. Arab Muslim armies had first reached the Indus Valley in the early eighth century. In the tenth and eleventh centuries, Muslim Turkish warrior dynasties based in what is now eastern Iran and Afghanistan raided north India. By the late twelfth century, they began conquering territory and setting up their own states. Other Muslims had settled in port towns around the coasts of South Asia, all the way from the coasts of Sind and Gujarat in the northwest down to the Coromandel coast in southeast India, in Sri Lanka, and in Bengal, along the seaways that led ultimately to China. When he landed at the city of Calicut (Kozhikode) on the southwest coast of India in 1498, guided by a Muslim from Gujarat, the Portuguese admiral Vasco da Gama was met by Muslim traders from Tunis. They spoke Genoese and Castilian and congratulated him on the "lucky venture" that had brought Europeans "to a country where there are such riches"—and where Muslim trade networks had long been established.[13]

In the tenth century, the historian and geographer Masʿudi tells us, there was already a community of ten thousand Muslims just south of today's Mumbai. Originating with migrant traders and sailors from the south of the Arabian Peninsula and the Persian Gulf, these communities often saw themselves as distinct from (and perhaps as rather superior to) the Turkish Muslim slave-soldiers whose power later intruded from the north. As the Abbasid caliphate disintegrated, they came to include refugees from political instability as well as local converts. Distinct Indian Muslim communities in coastal areas were formed by local people whose conversion, between the eleventh and fifteenth centuries, was the work of Ismaʿili missionaries, and who became known as Bohras and Khojas. Small and widely dispersed confessional groups like these began to add to the enormous diversity of Indian religious and cultural life.[14]

Unlike in the Middle East, where by the end of the twelfth century a Muslim-majority society had developed in the lands conquered by the Arabs, the peoples of northern India who came under Muslim rule did not become Muslims in large numbers. The adoption of Islam was an extremely slow process, stretching from the thirteenth century to the eighteenth, and was associated with gradual changes in social life and lifestyle among the peoples of the Indus Valley and Punjab in the northwest and Bengal in the east, most of whose inhabitants eventually became Muslim, and where South Asia's majority-Muslim populations, in Pakistan and Bangladesh, are found today. In Bengal, forest-dwelling peoples became cultivators as wet rice farming was encouraged under the Mughal Empire, from the sixteenth century onwards, and came to settle in villages around mosques built by Muslim pioneers who cleared the land to make paddy fields. In Punjab, livestock-herding clans settled and became farmers and landholders around Sufi shrines that were often closely associated with Muslim rulers. In both areas, most people had fallen outside of the hierarchical caste society of Brahmanical Hinduism and came to see themselves as Muslims only over the course of many generations. Even areas that would eventually, in the nineteenth century, be almost entirely Muslim had not been so until quite recently.[15]

But by the mid-thirteenth century already, more people may have lived under Muslim rule in India than in central Asia, North Africa, and the Middle East combined. By then, Muslim rule extended eastward across the north Indian plains and down the heavily populated Jumna and Ganges River valleys, into Bihar and Bengal. The Muslim regimes established in north India by the Turkish and Persian-speaking warriors who came with their mounted archers out of Afghanistan were usually unstable and relatively short-lived. Delhi became the centre of an independent Muslim state in 1206, but in the following three centuries, five different dynasties held power there. The numerically very small and ethnically separate Muslim military elite established in the north Indian cities ruled their subjects distantly and mostly indirectly, and made no attempt to make them into Muslims.

Primarily preoccupied by the security of their borders and the insecurity of their own factional politics, they had neither the capacity to intervene significantly in the life of the countryside, nor any interest in doing so. Here, as among the first Arab conquerors in the garrison cities of Iraq and Egypt, Islam was the identity and ideology of a community of rulers. Their rule gradually expanded, into the Deccan in central India, and further south by the mid-1300s. Hindu kingdoms, once defeated, were not destroyed but made into vassal states, their kings being received with honour at Delhi and strategic marriage alliances being made between Muslim princes and the women of Indian ruling families. This did not stop subjugated Indian states from rebelling on occasion when a new king took power, leading to cycles of conquest, revolt, and reconquest, but the overall trend was toward the extension of Muslim paramountcy and influence across the subcontinent.

Also unlike the Middle East, India was able to withstand the rise of the Mongols. Temür's incursion ruined Delhi and carried off its wealth: silver, gold and jewels, "particularly rubies and diamonds" in such quantities, one historian wrote in the sixteenth century, that earlier writers' estimation of their value "so far exceeds all belief, that I have refrained from mentioning it"—though he did mention that Temür also "seized for himself one hundred and twenty elephants, twelve rhinoceroses, and a number of curious animals." But after the sack of Delhi, Temür immediately withdrew. There was no large-scale Mongol settlement in India, where throughout the thirteenth century, Mongol incursions had been frequent but temporary, and were effectively resisted by the sultans at Delhi. Those Mongols who stayed did so as soldiers hired by the sultans themselves.[16]

Like Syria, which the Mongols had repeatedly conquered and then left, India was not the extensive pastureland that large numbers of Mongol horse-breeders and their families needed to sustain their lifestyle. Another chronicler explained that it was just too hot for them—although at times, Mongol armies did come into India as they had come into Iran, with their families, horses, and flocks, perhaps for winter grazing. Throughout the thirteenth century, the Delhi sultanate's military expansion and its plundering of defeated Hindu kingdoms further south was primarily intended to finance the defence of its northwest frontier against the Mongols, who now raided the sultanate's domains from Iran and Afghanistan much as the sultanate's forebears themselves had done two hundred years earlier. From the 1290s, more effective revenue-raising—based on a systematically applied land tax rather than extraction of tribute—allowed Delhi both to extend its rule more effectively and permanently, and to raise armies large enough to fend off Mongol attacks. Temür's later invasion, which happened to coincide with a civil war between claimants to the sultanate, faced a much smaller army than Delhi had previously been able to field.[17]

Although ultimately crippling, the Delhi sultanate's unstable dynastic politics also, occasionally, provided surprising opportunities. The third independent Sultan of Delhi, Iltutmish, came to the throne in 1211 from slavery in central Asia, through military service in Baghdad and Afghanistan. In Delhi he was sold as a slave-soldier to the founder of the sultanate, Qutb al-Din Aybeg, whose son-in-law he became and whose fledgling state in north India, separate from its parent dynasty in Afghanistan, he consolidated. Iltutmish, celebrated as a pious and effective ruler, named his daughter Radiyya as his successor, in preference to any of his sons. They, he reportedly said, "gave themselves up to wine and every other excess, so that he thought the government too weighty for their shoulders; but [Radiyya], though a woman, had a man's head and heart, and was better than twenty such sons." In this highly patriarchal and masculine world of slave-soldiers, it was exceptional but not unimaginable that a woman, if appropriately pious and capable, should rule.

In the Turkish and Mongol societies of the central and East Asian steppes, like the Qara-Khitai people (called the Liao in Chinese), who were originally from the northern edges of China and from whom Iltutmish had come, women in fact often played overt and important political roles, socialising with men and receiving foreign ambassadors at court. During Iltutmish's reign, Radiyya "employed herself frequently in the affairs of the government, a disposition which he rather encouraged." Indeed, she was left to govern Delhi while her father was away campaigning. But when he died in 1236, the Turkish army commanders, the provincial nobility, and, perhaps most importantly, Shah Turkan, the mother of Radiyya's younger brother who was briefly enthroned in her place, opposed her succession, and she had to fight for it. By effective diplomatic and military manoeuvring, Radiyya broke up the coalition against her and defeated its separate armies.

Overthrown after three and a half years' reign by another rebellion and ensuing civil war, Radiyya was said to have been undone, not because she was a queen, but because of the offence taken by the sultanate's nobility at the favour she bestowed on an Ethiopian slave whom she raised to high rank and who was apparently her intimate favourite: a moral tale of a princess undone by her attachment to an unworthy man. More recent historians see Radiyya's fall as resulting from a conflict between Turkish and non-Turkish court factions, and popular disapproval of her quitting the veil, assuming male dress, and commanding armies in person. Writing much later, around 1600, the historian Firishta considered that she

> possessed . . . every good quality which usually adorns the ablest princes; and those who scrutinise her actions most severely will find in her no fault but that she was a woman. She read the Qur'an with correct pronunciation . . . [and] on her accession, changed her apparel, assumed the imperial robes, and every day gave public audience from the throne, revising and confirming the laws of her father, . . . and dispensing justice with impartiality.[18]

It was Radiyya's successors' allegedly excessive impartiality towards their non-Muslim subjects that Temür considered justification for invading the sultanate sixty years later. The rulers of Delhi, he claimed, were insufficiently serious about Muslim supremacy, and too soft on Hindus. In fact, Muslim rulers in India already had their own claims to legitimately Islamic sovereignty. From the 1350s, the Delhi sultans' own legitimacy as Muslim rulers was bolstered, if only symbolically, by recognition from the Abbasid caliph who now resided under Mamluk protection in Cairo. Trade from India now passed via the Red Sea and through Mamluk Egypt into the Mediterranean, and however politically powerless the caliph might be, his embassies still counted for something in cementing commercial and diplomatic relations. His investiture of the Delhi sultans as the sole authorised Muslim rulers in South Asia—well beyond their actual domains, and as far eastward as Java and Sumatra—allowed them, much like the caliph, to claim a sovereignty that far exceeded their real influence. These things did matter, in the observed principles if not in the effective practices of power: Temür himself, for all his ambition, conscientiously limited his own titles, and never claimed for himself the Mongol khanate, let alone the Muslim caliphate.

Religious authority also had a more material role in medieval Indian political life. Hindu temples and the statues of deities that resided there were often associated with a king and his territory. A kingdom's existence, and its king's rule, were tied to the *rashtra-devata*, "lord of the state," the land's presiding deity. From the sixth century onward, warfare between Indian states often involved the removal and relocation of statues of Hindu gods, or of the Buddha, from the territories of defeated kings whose sovereignty was seen to rest under divine protection, and to be tied to the preservation and patronage of temple sites. Breaking the connection between a king and the godly images and places associated with him was an essential part of breaking his sovereign power. The model for such behaviour among Muslims, in the Indian historical tradition, was Sultan Mahmud of Ghazna, an eleventh-century ruler of eastern Afghanistan whose predatory raiding of north India caused much destruction to sacred sites, and who would be celebrated in later Indo-Persian court poetry as an exemplary, pious ruler: an enlightened patron of learning within his own court and an energetic proponent of jihad on the frontiers of Islam.

Historic instances of the desecration of temples under Muslim rule would come to be seen by twentieth-century Hindu nationalists as part of a history of continuous Hindu-Muslim conflict, evidence of the oppression of Hinduism by ideologically zealous Muslim persecutors, of whom Mahmud was the first and worst. But Mahmud never ruled in India; he was interested only in extracting its wealth to pay his army in Afghanistan and eastern Iran. When, later, Indian Muslim sultans destroyed temples, they were not acting on Mahmud's model but rather adopting the Indian political norms that had existed before Islam arrived in India. They plundered and destroyed temples associated with the sovereign claims of an enemy, whether a rival kingdom or a rebellious subject, just as Hindu rajas had. Sometimes they built a mosque on the site, or incorporated plundered material into their own mosques, to drive home the point of their victorious and divinely sanctioned rule. But temples within their own territory, or within formerly hostile territory that had become part of a Muslim-ruled state, were considered as being under their protection. They were maintained, rebuilt, and treated as the property of the state.

From the fourteenth century onward, Islamic law in India considered Hindus, like Jewish and Christian monotheists, as *ahl al-dhimma*, protected people whose religious belief and practice should be tolerated and whose persons and property were secure as long as they knew their place and paid their taxes (the *jizya* levied on non-Muslims, though in fact its imposition in India was probably very limited outside urban areas). Ibn Battuta, who travelled through India in the 1330s and served as a judge in Delhi, tells us that the Sultan Muhammad Ibn Tughluq, whose rule extended southward deep into peninsular India, considered the building of temples by *dhimmi*s in Muslim territory as permissible under Islamic law. This interpretation would endure under his successors. The same sultan, while strenuously promoting Sunni orthodoxy and proving his defence of the faith by beating back the Mongols, employed non-Muslims in high office and adopted the ancient Indian imperial practice of having water from the Ganges brought to his court—a journey of forty days—for his personal use.[19]

A Muslim ruler's power in India was bound up in more specifically Islamic spiritual authority, too, especially that of the Sufi masters. Unlike temples in Hindu kingdoms, a mosque or a Sufi teacher's *khanqah* was not the property of the state, or a guarantor of its sovereignty. It could sometimes be a refuge from the sultan, and even a counterweight to his power, a place where dissenters could seek sanctuary, and where rebellions might take hold. A Sufi master who tied his turban onto the head of a prince was understood by all concerned to be giving a sure sign of who would next accede to power. (The same gesture was used to transmit a master's spiritual authority to his own designated successors.) Prominent Sufis were both sought after as spiritual preceptors to rulers who hoped to bolster their authority by association, and celebrated for their principled aversion to worldly power. In the fifteenth century, the descendants of Shah Ni'matallah Wali al-Kirmani, who was a renowned Sufi and descendant of the Prophet and who had travelled from his birthplace in Aleppo through Egypt to central Asia before settling in Iran, moved to the Deccan at the sultan's invitation. They were received with honour, married into the ruling family, and remained associated with the dynasty for several generations. Shah Ni'matallah himself, by contrast, was famous for finding spiritual value in farm labour as well as for his exposition of Ibn Arabi. He had spurned the patronage of no less a personage than Temür himself, allegedly dismissing the conqueror's overtures with a poetic (and, if true, reckless): "Off with you, my prince! / Don't flaunt gold and silver before me. / While your domain stretches / From China to Shiraz / Mine is a realm / That has no frontier."[20]

If Sufis could stand up to world-conquerors, they and their sanctuaries were all the more important in demonstrating a ruler's patronage and piety. The greatest sanctuaries attached to the most prestigious Sufi shaykhs and fraternities became major centres, not only of pilgrimage, learning, and devotion but of wealth, influence, and imperial display. After the great teacher Farid al-Din Ganj-i Shakar, known as Baba Farid, died in 1265, his mausoleum at Pakpattan, southwest of Lahore in Punjab, became (and remains today) one of the region's most important holy places. It attracted both poor pilgrims who came to seek Baba Farid's saintly blessing—his *baraka*—as they had during his lifetime, and powerful rulers who endowed the shrine after his death with the riches he was said to have refused from them while he was alive. Muhammad Ibn Tughluq added to the *khanqah*'s buildings, and even Temür, on his way to sack Delhi, visited it.

Over time, the shrine also became a centre of spiritual power and prestige for people of humbler origins, especially the Jat clans of Punjab who had migrated into the region from the Indus Valley since the thirteenth century. As they shifted their lifestyle from that of cattle-keeping pastoralists to being farmers and landholders, they participated in the seasonal rituals centred on the shrine and married the daughters of their leading families to the sons of its hereditary custodians. Through their relationship to the shrine, and its economic and social as well as its cultural and spiritual importance, the local population very slowly, from the fifteenth century to the eighteenth, came to see themselves as Muslim, giving Muslim names to their male children. Eventually, they would narrate their conversion "by Baba Farid" as a central part of their own local and genealogical history—even though the saint himself had died long before their ancestors arrived in the area where his blessing endured.[21]

Baba Farid was one of the exponents of the Chishti order, a Sufi way that originated near Herat, in western Afghanistan. It became particularly popular across India after the shaykh Khawaja Mu'in al-Din Chishti brought it there in the twelfth century, having been instructed to do so, we're told, by the Prophet in a dream. The Chishtis, like many mystical groups, favoured worldly renunciation and tried, as best they could, to keep their distance from the state. "Sit in solitude; do not ask for food from anyone," advised Yusuf Gada, a Chishti shaykh in the 1300s: "Know that contentment is a kingdom, a mansion full of pearls and jewels. Do not yourself go near the Sultan.... When you long for the Sultan, there will be fear and danger for you." At the same time, the shaykh recognised that ignoring earthly powers was also unwise: "Do not go to Kings uncalled—but if they summon you, go instantly."

The Chishtis' generally cautious distance from power was hard to maintain: in the fifteenth century, they allowed themselves a "calculated defiance" of the sultans who, with their own demands for spiritual legitimation, kept insistently knocking at their door. But by the sixteenth century, the Chishtis' spiritual prestige had become part and parcel of worldly Muslim sovereignty in India. The Mughal Emperor Akbar made no fewer than fourteen pilgrimages to the shrine of Mu'in al-Din Chishti at Ajmer, sometimes covering the distance from Agra (over two hundred miles) on foot, and making a point of doing so to give thanks for success in major campaigns of conquest.[22]

Akbar ascended to the throne in 1556, the third ruler of a new dynasty that would unify India under Muslim rule. The Mughals, who made much of their descent from both Genghis Khan and Temür, would reassemble an Islamic sovereignty that had grown to cover almost the whole subcontinent in the mid-1300s before being shattered when their ancestor Temür sacked Delhi. Temür left the Delhi sultanate as merely one, much reduced statelet in a patchwork of successor kingdoms. One of its later rulers was lampooned for glorying in the name Alam Shah, "world-king," when he ruled over little more than the immediate surroundings of his city. By Akbar's time, though, Islam in India had come to rest more firmly on a synthesis of conquest and adoption. Turkish, Afghan and Persian state-builders had settled across north and central India, establishing themselves as ruling elites in the cities. They recalled and celebrated their central Asian ancestry and proclaimed their connection to the universal caliphate, but they had become part of Indian history and culture.

Much like the Chinese historians who wrote the Mongols into Chinese dynastic history, Sanskrit histories—while they might disparage the conquests of *mlecchas*, "barbarians"—also integrated the incomers into their own chronicles of successive ruling houses. Some Muslims learned Sanskrit and engaged in popular Hindu festivals, while Hindu priests and scribes learned Persian and became secretaries to Muslim courts. Muslim sultans made allies of warrior caste and princely Hindu lineages who, by recognising Muslim imperial suzerainty, maintained their social superiority over other Hindus and their economic and political dominance over the countryside. In the countryside, both esoteric enlightenment and popular devotion were nourished by saintly Sufis and their successors and disciples, and ordinary people, especially those outside the hierarchical structures of Hindu society whose lifestyles were shifting from forest-dwelling or nomadic pastoralism towards settled agriculture, came very slowly, over half a millennium, to identify themselves as Muslims.

◇◇◇◇◇◇◇◇

Muslim India fought off the Mongols, but over these same centuries it remained continuously connected to the Mongol Empire's commercial network. From China to the Mediterranean via central Asia, the axis of world trade and power had become the vector of Islam's own Eurasian expansion. Indian textiles were carried by caravan into the Timurid states of Afghanistan, Khurasan, and Iran, as were Chinese silks and porcelain and Southeast Asian spices. Some of these made their way further west to Europe, but central Asia and the Middle East were primary destinations, as well as transit points, for South and East Asian trade. In the fifteenth century, after the breakup of Temür's personal empire, urban elites were sufficiently wealthy and the urban economy sufficiently buoyant that they could pay for such commodities, which combined with scholarly, artistic, and architectural creativity to make up the Persian courtly cultural renaissance. This flowering of commercial vitality and cultural sophistication was all the more impressive in that it succeeded not only the destructive waves of war unleashed between 1200 and 1400 by Genghis and Temür but also the cross-continental devastation of the Black Death.

The course of the Black Death through Europe, westward from the Black Sea and the eastern Mediterranean, is a familiar story. In a sudden, apocalyptic tide, in 1347–49 the disease wiped out between one-fifth and two-thirds, in different locations, of the populations of western Eurasia. It killed perhaps 40 per cent of the people of Europe as a whole. In the Middle East and Asia, overall mortality has been impossible to gauge, beyond the general, similar estimate that between a third and a half of the population may have died. Contemporary sources give stark illustrations of the impact where it was most dramatic. In Asyut, in Egypt, where there had been six thousand taxpayers, the Mamluks' tax collectors could find only 116 in the plague year. In the Palestinian town of Jenin, we're told, "no one survived except an old woman who fled." After the initial upheaval had subsided, aftershocks would be felt for the next half millennium, in episodic outbreaks that lingered in Europe into the mid-eighteenth century, and in the southern and eastern Mediterranean for a hundred years after that.[23]

But despite (or because of) its world-altering significance, the origins and consequences of the world's second bubonic plague pandemic remain disputed. When told from a European perspective, the story of the Black Death conventionally begins on the Black Sea. In 1346, a Mongol army besieged the Genoese port of Caffa (Feodosya) in the

Crimea. Stricken by the disease, the Mongols notoriously catapulted corpses over the walls to demoralise the defenders, thereby (although they could not have known it) inventing biological warfare. It now seems, contrary to an older consensus, that there was an outbreak of bubonic plague in north China in the early thirteenth century, over a hundred years earlier, coinciding with the outset of Mongol expansion both east and west. Plague bacilli, carried by fleas and the fleas' hosts who carried them along the Mongols' invasion and trade routes, from Jin fortresses in northern China to the Genoese trading post in Crimea, came in the footsteps of the world-conquerors too.

Combined with other factors, northwest Europe's particular path of recovery from the Black Death would be a major force in shaping the diverging fortunes of different world regions in the following centuries. It would help lay the foundations for the creation of a new global economy centred on the Atlantic world that would durably disadvantage the older world into which the Mongols had come and that they had made theirs. It has been conventional to contrast Europe's dynamism after the plague with the decline imputed to Muslim Asia in the wake of its medieval "golden age." But, again contrary to long-held assumptions, it may be that the catastrophic depopulation that the plague caused in the southern and eastern Mediterranean, on a scale similar to that experienced in Europe, did not simply result in a generalised urban and economic decline.

Instead, as in parts of western Europe, the plague paradoxically opened the way to economic and political expansion in the Muslim-ruled Mediterranean and Indian Ocean, and to increased prosperity, as the survivors' share of available wealth increased. The incomes of lower-skilled workers, women, and peasants, in particular, increased until around 1500, to levels that would not be reached again until the end of the eighteenth century. The initial effect of depopulation was certainly stark, and in some places, the longer-term consequences were dramatic. In Egypt, where agriculture and economic prosperity depended on the labour-intensive maintenance of irrigation works in the Nile Delta, the sudden loss of population had a crippling impact.

But Egypt was exceptional in this respect. Further east, cities like Isfahan and Herat, both sacked by Temür in the 1380s, thrived in the fifteenth century despite repeated visitations of the plague. India, defended by the Delhi sultans against the Mongols in the thirteenth century, was spared the plague as well, until what seems to have been its first appearance there in the seventeenth century.[24]

Calamitous as was the suffering they caused, neither the Mongols nor the plague had condemned the Muslims' world to anything like generalised devastation, despair, and decay. Poets told of the awful ravages of the epidemic of 1348, as the disease, "this spiked and hated thing," ripped through households and cities: "He preyed upon every house. / If one spat blood, / All spat blood / And in two nights / Maybe three / Were put underground." Ibn Hajar al-Asqalani, who lived in Cairo in the first half of the fifteenth century and was renowned as far as Iran and India as the greatest hadith scholar of his age, well knew how bad the plague could be. He contracted it and survived; three of his children died. But he found solace in the Islamic tradition's models of response to such disasters. Like "an enemy entering Muslim lands," he wrote, the plague was both "a calamity" and an occasion for martyrdom and mercy. Believers who succumbed were assured of God's grace. Inhabitants of cities afflicted by the disease should remain, not flee, and care for the sick.[25]

While Ibn Hajar was writing in Mamluk Cairo, further north in Anatolia, the dynasty that would eventually unseat the Mamluks was experiencing its own dramatic expansion. In 1402, after he had burned Damascus and before he turned his attention to China, Temür had defeated the fledgling Ottoman Turkish state in Anatolia, captured its sultan, Bayezit, and forced it into subservience. But only half a century later, in 1453, an Ottoman army under Bayezit's successor, Mehmet II "Fatih" (the Conqueror), would do what no caliph or khan had achieved, taking Constantinople and ending the thousand-year history of the Byzantine Empire. Proclaiming himself *qaysar*, Caesar, the Ottoman sultan claimed for Islam an inheritance of world conquest that went all the way back to Rome.

6

SHADOWS OF GOD

When the Persian poet Firdawsi composed the *Shahnameh* (Book of Kings), in the late tenth century, its stories were already old. An epic retelling of the ancient history of Persia and its kings, Firdawsi's story went all the way back to mythical times and down to the Arab conquest of the Sasanian Empire in the seventh century. It was rooted in a long tradition of heroic royal chronicles that dated from the pre-Islamic *Xwadaynamag*, a Pahlavi "Book of Kings" that was known in medieval times but that, along with the Arabic translations we know were made of it, has since been lost. Firdawsi's poem was the most monumental, and successful, of several such works composed in the new Persian cultural revival that began under the Abbasids and flourished through Mongol and Timurid times.

Like many scholars and writers of his age, Firdawsi was from the region of Tus, in what is now the northeast corner of Iran. Today a small locality outside the city of Mashhad, Tus lost out over time to its neighbour's greater significance. Its other misfortune was to have a governor who, in 1389, was unwise enough to declare independence from Temür, with the result that the population was massacred and towers of skulls were set outside its gates. But in Firdawsi's time, Tus was an ancient city in its own right, old enough to have been conquered by Alexander the Great. The Seljuq minister Nizam al-Mulk was from Tus; the Caliph Harun al-Rashid and the learned al-Ghazali were both buried there. Firdawsi was born there to a family descended from Sasanian-era landowning nobility, and died there too, in 1020. Over nine hundred years later, in 1934, a new Shah of Iran, the soldier-turned-autocrat Reza Shah Pahlavi, would preside over the completion of a monumental new tomb for the poet, a modern nationalist statement in ancient Achaemenid style, as part of his agenda to root his own authoritarian nation-building in the deep pre-Islamic history of Persian monarchy.

For most of his life, Firdawsi himself had tried to avoid getting too close to kings. But, in his sixties and short of cash, he dedicated his poem to the warrior Sultan Mahmud of Ghazna, at the time the most illustrious ruler in Muslim Asia. Having spent thirty-five years composing the *Shahnameh*, when at last he completed it he travelled to Mahmud's court in Afghanistan to present the finished work to him. Mahmud, we're told, was unimpressed, paying the poet only pennies instead of the handsome reward he'd been promised. Firdawsi went home and composed satirical verses about kings who were only interested in poets who sang their praises. The *Shahnameh* was about more than adulation. But—perhaps inevitably, if a little ironically, given Firdawsi's own unhappy experience with his ruler patron—the book became a valuable instrument of dynastic prestige. The most famous copy surviving today was made for the Safavid shahs of Iran, Ismail I and his son Tahmasp I, in the early 1500s. In 1566, Tahmasp made a princely gift of it to the Ottoman Sultan Selim II. The poem and the exquisite miniature paintings that illustrated it had become high-art expressions of royal power and regal good taste, the stuff of refined courtly manners and high-stakes diplomacy.

State-building and sovereignty in the age of the early modern empires of the Ottomans, Safavids, and Mughals, from the fifteenth through the eighteenth centuries, were never only about power and gunpowder. The nimble painters, composers, poets, and architects of

Istanbul, Isfahan, and Agra were just as crucial in shaping the language of dynastic splendour, and their rulers' relations and rivalries, as were the armies that so often fought each other. Just as important were the languages of justice and good government proclaimed by imperial ideology, and appealed to by the many distant and humble petitioners who sought redress and favour from the emperors in their palaces. This was a time of flourishing cross-continental connection and cosmopolitanism, as well as geopolitical ambition and rivalry; of sophisticated urban and court cultures, a rich diversity of literature, music, art, and architecture; and of a far-flung, flexible and—for a long time—effective system of rule. In these centuries when Europe was wracked by religious warfare, the *padishah*s, "royal kings," of the Ottoman, Persian, and Mughal domains ruled over Muslim states with multireligious societies whose wealth and industry was second only to, and for a time even surpassed, that of China. They considered themselves as sovereign, not because they incarnated the state by anointed divine right, as European monarchs did, but because they inherited an ancient tradition of semi-divine kingship, reimagined in Islamic terms as the "Shadow of God on Earth."

◇◇◇◇◇◇◇

Osman, founder of the Ottoman dynasty that would become one of the world's longest-lived imperial houses, started out in the 1280s as just one local Turkic chieftain among many others in northwest Anatolia. In this unsettled region, the Byzantine Empire's eastern border had shifted back and forth for six centuries. It was a patchwork of principalities, home to Greek and Armenian Christians, Persian- and Arabic-speaking Muslims, and Turkic nomads, some of whom had become more or less consciously Muslim, some of whom had not.

In late medieval Anatolia as in Spain, Muslim and Christian chiefs fought against each other, or together against a common enemy, irrespective of religion, as occasion dictated. Coalitions were pragmatic, cross-confessional, and short-lived. In the first Mongol incursions of the thirteenth century and again in the early 1400s, when Temür invaded Anatolia, Turkic Muslim armies fought against each other. In the 1340s, Osman's son Orhan allied with a Byzantine faction against a rival Turkic emirate that had its own Byzantine allies. In 1346, the Ottomans' importance as allies for one faction in a Byzantine civil war was demonstrated by no less an event than the marriage of Orhan to Theodora, the daughter of John VI Kantakouzenos, a claimant to the Byzantine throne who became emperor with Orhan's help the following year. Orhan's grandson, Bayezit I, lost the Battle of Ankara against Temür, in 1402, in part because his Muslim vassals and allies abandoned him or defected to Temür's side, leaving him with a smaller army made up in part of Christian troops from the Balkans. Temür's incursion into Anatolia was itself at least partly a response to appeals from other Muslim emirates that sought the Mongol warlord's aid against Ottoman expansion. As in Spain, ideas of a religious frontier war, defined as Islamic jihad or Christian Reconquista, were ideological spins on reality more than explanations of it.

Ideology did matter, though, for particular practical purposes. The earliest Ottoman written documents, from the early fourteenth century, show their emerging principality using Persian, and give Osman and Orhan the Muslim princely titles of *shuja-ud-din* and *fakhr-ud-din*, "champion" and "glory of the faith." Like other frontier warrior-nomads with state-building ambitions, the earliest Ottomans combined Turkic and Mongol military traditions of raiding, slave-taking, and wealth extraction with a more specifically Islamic vision of *ghazwa*, the virtuous expansion of the frontiers of Islam by waging war on unbelievers. Such unbelievers, though, were often other people who called themselves Muslims rather than Christians, Jews, or pagans. As ever, the claim to champion Islam was a claim made in competition with others. Later Ottoman court historians, writing in the fifteenth century in the service not of a motley warrior band but of an established Muslim dynasty, would centre the prestige of the empire's founders as *gazi*s, frontier warriors of the faith.

This required some tidying up of the Ottomans' earlier religious history. By the late fifteenth century, the empire and its advocates stood as the embodiment of what legally minded urban scholars understood as Sunni orthodoxy. Two hundred years earlier, understandings of what Islam meant in the nomadic borderlands had been, if not as unsettled as the frontier zone itself, a good deal looser than they would later become, or than they had been in Abbasid Baghdad. Osman's own later mythologising as the predestined forebear of greatness was famously symbolised in a dream he was said to have experienced, while staying in the home of an Anatolian Sufi mystic. As he slept, Osman saw the moon rise from the shaykh's chest and enter his own, from where a tree grew up to shadow the whole world; in the shade of the tree were mountains, from which streams flowed, giving drink to the thirsty, watering gardens, and feeding fountains. The divinely ordained king as provider of rain or of mountain streams was an ancient Middle Eastern idea. The mountain, tree, and streams were Mongol shamanistic images, while the blessing from the mystically initiated Sufi tapped into popular Muslim beliefs in the saintly embodiment and transmission of God's grace.

None of these were exactly orthodox claims to Islamic sovereignty. But then, being Muslim on the medieval Anatolian frontier often took forms that might shock the more straitlaced scholarly class. Wandering Sufi "friends of God" in the borderlands sometimes espoused deliberately nonconformist lifestyles, taking more conventional Sufi ideas to extremes. Not only did they live as "dervishes"—mendicants who, being devoted to God, embraced poverty and sought alms from door to door, a renunciation of the world that went back to the earliest Sufis. They also emphasised their quest for the inmost truth by refusing the basic outward observances of prayer or fasting in Ramadan. They wore ragged or revealing clothing and shaved their heads and facial hair so as to be vulnerably before God "without need of veils," sported tattoos and body piercings, engaged in tumultuous musical celebrations, and demonstrated their renunciation of the flesh by self-harming. Some used narcotics to enter ecstatic states and behaved in overtly antisocial ways in their quest to be radically outside the world.

Such radical practices were often condemned by the more orthodox and urban Sufi fraternities in Anatolia, like the Mevlevis who followed the teachings of *mawlana* (in Turkish, *mevlana*, "our master") Jalal al-Din Rumi, the mystical poet whose works we met earlier. The Mevlevis emerged around the same time as the beginnings of Osman's career, after the death of Rumi in Konya in 1273. Some other dervishes' more eccentric practices alarmed the Mevlevis, who called them heretics. (Some Mevlevi rituals, too, especially the intense *sema*, "listening," in which adult male disciples turn in circles to music, giving the English cliché of "whirling dervishes," would themselves later be considered heretical by anti-Sufi reformers.)

Accusations of unorthodoxy expressed social as well as doctrinal conflicts. The Mevlevis were an urban fraternity with aristocratic associations. More radical groups, like the Bektashis—followers of Hajji Bektash Vali, a thirteenth-century saint from Khurasan—which would become closely associated with the Ottoman army, had a more popular, and sometimes revolutionary, following. Leading Sufis were credited with the ability to bestow God's favour directly on worthy claimants to earthly power. In his accession ceremony, the Ottoman Sultan Murad II was invested with the symbols of power (a sword, or a cloak) of a Sufi shaykh. Both the respectable religion of the urban well-to-do and the popular charisma of the wilder Sufis were important in building support. For the early Ottomans, consolidating their following in the restless borderlands meant gaining the spiritual approval of eccentric mystics as well as issuing decrees in good Persian and making pragmatic alliances with Christian princes.[1]

The Ottomans' transition from nomadic raiders to settled state-builders began in earnest in the 1320s. In 1326, Orhan conquered the Byzantine fortress town of Bursa near the Sea of Marmara and made it his capital, striking his own coins there. In 1331, he signalled his religious credentials by building a school for the study of Islamic law in Iznik (Nicaea), where a millennium earlier, Christian doctrine had been debated under the Roman Emperor Constantine. In 1389, Ottoman forces defeated the Serbs at the Battle of Kosovo, an event that would become central to later Serb national mythology. Bayezit I, the victor of Kosovo, was the first Ottoman ruler to declare himself Sultan of Rum, over "the Romans." His defeat and his capture by Temür in 1402 touched off a succession crisis and civil war among Ottoman princes, followed by widespread peasant and Sufi-inspired rebellions. But by 1444, under Sultan Murad II the Ottomans were strong enough once more to face down a Hungarian crusader army. When Murad II died in 1451, his son, Mehmed II, aged only twenty, was ready to turn on Constantinople. The ancient "second Rome" was partly depopulated, and a shadow of its former self, but its massive fortifications were still formidable. In May 1453, the city was taken and plundered, its surviving population murdered, raped, or enslaved.

The Ottomans' fragile principality had become a transcontinental empire, straddling the Bosphorus and extending eastward across Anatolia and west into the Balkans. Other such frontier states tended to fragment, as local warrior-dynasties spun off their own sovereignty from former overlords. The Mongol tradition of splitting the inheritance of conquest, followed since Genghis Khan's own division of his empire between his sons, made for territorial breakup and dynastic civil war at each ruler's death. Ambitious princes with their own power bases and independently minded, landholding nobles were always a threat to the cohesion of a newborn state. The Ottoman dynasty neutralised these threats in two ingenious ways, and with a calculated exercise of deliberate violence.

Beginning in the second half of the fourteenth century, the sultans instituted new and ruthlessly efficient policies to bolster their centralised monarchy. Potential rivals to the throne were murdered: however regrettable, legal authorities opined, such targeted killing "for the sake of the good order of the world" was preferable to the greater harm of civil strife. If a designated successor could not have his brothers quietly strangled on acceding to the throne, he would have to defeat them in open warfare, in a contest between claimants to *devlet*, a word meaning both the turn of dynastic fortune and sovereignty over the state. The policy of princely fratricide would be followed until the early seventeenth century, when succession by a deceased sultan's senior male relative became the norm: instead of being killed, other princes would now be kept imprisoned in the palace.

Reliance on nobles with their own interests and ambitions, meanwhile, was remedied by the *devshirme* (collection). In each Christian tax district, from the fourteenth century until the mid-seventeenth, when the system was gradually discontinued, a number of boys or unmarried young men would be forcibly taken from their families, enslaved, and brought up as Muslims. The most promising were trained at elite schools for service in the army and administration. Owing no allegiance to anyone but the dynasty, and having (in theory) no interests of their own save their advancement within the system, they would staff an exceptionally efficient early modern bureaucracy. The most able or ambitious would go on to become the highest officers of state and even marry into the imperial family. The *devshirme* thus created an upwardly mobile, meritocratic class of "slaves of the sultan," reminiscent of the Mamluk slave-soldier model that had existed in the Middle East and central Asia since Abbasid times, but now bureaucratised and systematised in a wholly unprecedented way.

Systematically enslaving and converting the children of Christian subjects was also unprecedented—and illegal—in Islamic law. Ever since the first Arab conquests, as "protected people" Christians and Jews were supposed to gain security of person and property, and the freedom to practice their own religion, in exchange for their acceptance of Muslim supremacy. The legal status of the "sultan's slaves" once they were educated as Muslims was also questionable. As with the justification for dynastic fratricide, the dynasty's lawyers had to perform interpretive acrobatics to find a justification for Ottoman policy's divergence from Islamic legal norms. The fact that we have no definitive legal treatise reconciling the *devshirme* with the sharia suggests that the scholars' best efforts could never quite solve the problem. It was easier just to overlook it; sharia was a means to the end of imperial rule more than the foundation of it, whatever imperial ideology might say. As long as the state and the Muslim community were both expanded, some authors concluded, why worry?[2]

All the same, there was a rule of law in the Ottoman state. It some-times took a mischievously daring lawyer to insist on it, but when he did, it could not be ignored. In the early sixteenth century, Ibn Fenari, a distinguished judge in Istanbul, refused to accept legal testimony from no less a person than Sultan Sulayman I's favourite and pow-erful chief minister, Ibrahim Pasha, on the grounds that he was "an un-manumitted slave." According to Islamic law, only free persons could give evidence in court, and like other state dignitaries, Ibra-him had been taken in the *devshirme* as a boy and raised as a *kapi kulu*, a slave of the sultan's household, before rising to high office. The minister, "dishonoured and disgraced," appealed in distress to the sul-tan, only to be told that the law was the law, and the sultan himself stood "in awe of it." Sulayman then formally freed his minister, but the judge demanded a written decree of manumission, which he made a point of drawing up himself and presenting to Ibrahim, before ac-cepting his evidence as admissible in court.

It was clearly indelicate to point out the technically servile status of so great a personage as the sultan's grand vizier, and a less prominent (or less impertinent) judge might have avoided doing what Ibn Fenari did. Most slaves in the Ottoman Empire, whether white Circassians or Black Africans, were domestic servants at the bottom of the social order. Those who, as boys, were castrated and became eunuchs had endured not only a humiliation but a traumatic bodily mutilation that killed many of them—the fact that some, such as the Black eunuchs who controlled access to the palace women's quarters, could become politically power-ful can hardly have been much consolation. But the legal unfreedom of palace slaves was more often quietly ignored, and there was nothing hu-miliating about it. The sultan's slaves were firmly part of the ruling class. Ibrahim Pasha, born in Greece and enslaved as a child, was the same age as his master Sulayman, who became sultan in 1520. He was the sultan's intimate companion and close friend from boyhood. In the first years of Sulayman's reign, Ibrahim commanded major military campaigns, lived in a palace near the sultan's own, married into the Istanbul elite, and reputedly continued to share the sultan's bed—until, in a dramatic fall from grace in 1536, he was strangled in his sleep. In the mid-seventeenth century, the English ambassador Paul Rycaut noted that "the title of *Kul*, which is, [the sultan's] *Slave*...is more honourable than the condition and name of *Subject*...[and] the *Subject* cannot offer the least injury to the *Slave* without danger of severe punishment."[3]

Another Ottoman innovation that would prove crucial in the empire's expansion also relied, at least initially, on captive manpower. The sultan's corps of janissaries—in Turkish, *yeni cheri*, "new troops"— was a standing army of infantry, originally recruited from Christian prisoners of war, and then from the *devshirme*. From a small, elite palace guard in the 1300s, the janissaries' number would grow over the fifteenth and sixteenth centuries to tens of thousands. Recruitment to the janissaries meant silver wages from the treasury, an enviable social status, and, eventually, membership in a powerful commercial and political pressure group. Over time, it became open to Muslim and Christian volunteers and to janissaries' own sons. Janissaries would play a major role in Ottoman campaigns in southeastern Europe and as garrison troops all over the empire. By the time of the Battle of Kosovo, around the same time as gunpowder artillery started to appear in northern Europe, the Ottomans were using light field guns, and over the fifteenth century both cannon and arquebuses (early muskets) were integrated into their arsenals, for use especially by the janissaries. The siege of Constantinople in 1453 saw the use of the largest cannon yet constructed, firing explosive shells to destroy the city walls, and Ottoman gunboats were used in river warfare as well as on the Mediterranean and the Red Sea. The Ottomans still lived in a world of religious crusade and of Mongol-style world conquest, but they also, already, lived in a more modern world of gunpowder armies and bureaucratic state-building.

With their combined army of Turkish cavalry, Christian vassals, janissary infantry and artillery, between the 1440s and the 1520s the Ottomans swept northwest, to the River Danube and the Adriatic Sea, and southeast, into Iraq and Egypt. In 1521, they took Belgrade, and five years later the Hungarian monarchy, whose kings had led Crusades against the Ottomans in the previous century, accepted Ottoman suzerainty. In 1529, Ottoman armies besieged Vienna for the first time. After 1453, the sultan was "Caesar of the Romans" in Constantinople, the "Second Rome," and had ambitions to conquer further west, as far as the original Rome. He considered himself the rightful heir of Alexander the Great and Caesar Augustus. After 1517, with the conquest of Syria, Egypt, and the Hijaz from the Mamluks, he was also "Servant of the Two Holy Places," Mecca and Medina, and ruler of the ancient Muslim centres of Jerusalem, Damascus, and Cairo. The last of the nominal Abbasid caliphs, still living at the Mamluk court in Cairo and wheeled out by the Mamluks in 1517 to rally their troops in battle against the Ottomans, would later be said to have transferred his authority to the new Muslim conqueror, but the sultan felt no need to call himself caliph. The caliph, who bore the venerable Abbasid name of al-Mutawakkil, was dispatched to Istanbul along with a treasure trove of other holy relics: the robe, standard, and sword of the Prophet along with some of his hair and a tooth, the prayer mat of his daughter Fatima, swords said to have belonged to the Prophet's companions, and items associated with the biblical and Qur'anic prophets Abraham, Moses, Joseph and David. Encased in gold and silver, these items (today displayed in Istanbul's Topkapi Palace museum) would become part of the empire's ceremonial and symbolic power.

In 1534, Baghdad was captured and Ottoman forces moved into the Persian Gulf and the Indian Ocean. Here, it was becoming necessary to counter the Portuguese, who had begun to intrude from around the Cape of Good Hope. Deploying Ottoman naval power to the Indian Ocean, though, was challenging. In the Mediterranean, Ottoman galleys and, later, galleons were formidable. There, both the Ottoman navy and, further west, its privateering corsair subcontractors operating out of North African port cities challenged the Venetians and the Spanish and Austrian Habsburgs for control of the sea. Even after a European coalition defeated the Ottomans off the Greek coast at Lepanto, in 1571, and celebrated a great victory for Christendom over "the Turk," the Ottomans quickly rebuilt their fleet. Only three years after Lepanto they took control of Tunis from its Habsburg-backed local Muslim rulers. But putting heavy, gun-carrying ships to sea from coastlines on the Red Sea or the Arabian Peninsula that had little or no timber was much harder than doing so from the eastern Mediterranean or North Africa, and not the same as fitting out the light merchant vessels that had sailed from Basra or Siraf to China in Abbasid times.

Nonetheless, the Ottomans established footholds in Yemen and the Horn of Africa, distributed firearms across the Indian Ocean, and until the end of the 1500s were a significant imperial presence as far east as Sumatra. Ottoman trade and taste in new commodities, from textiles and tulips to ceramics and coffee, boomed, and transferred both fashions and fantasies of luxurious living to Europe. Rather than being outdone by the beginnings of European seagoing and Atlantic empire-building, the Ottomans' military, political, and commercial achievement was arguably one of their causes. It was Ottoman expansionism in the Mediterranean that forced Europeans to turn south, around Africa, and west into the Atlantic, in search of direct access to Asia. Ferdinand and Isabella, the "most Catholic" rulers of Spain, backed Christopher Columbus's first voyage, not to find an Atlantic New World that they did not yet know existed, but to finance a new Crusade to conquer Jerusalem and establish a Christian world empire, a continuation of the Reconquista and a riposte to the Ottomans. Europeans sailed west only because they were still looking east.[4]

By the end of the fifteenth century, most of the people of Anatolia had become Muslim. Greek-speaking Christian populations remained, especially in towns around the coast, and a large, Armenian Christian population also lived in eastern Anatolia. But both the slow conversion of Anatolia, and the rapid conquest of Syria and Egypt, meant that from the early 1500s, the Ottomans ruled a Muslim-majority empire. As had happened in Iraq, Syria and Palestine centuries earlier, Christian noble, merchant, or military families in Anatolia and the Balkans would sometimes decide that their status would best be preserved by assimilating to the ruling society. But in its Christian-majority provinces, Ottoman rule worked by incorporating Christian princes, nobilities, and church authorities into the imperial system, delegating tax collection, policing powers, and the management of religious affairs and family law to them in exchange for their subservience to imperial sovereignty: neither they nor their peasant taxpayers were expected to become Muslims.

Immediately after the sack of Constantinople in 1453, Mehmed II had converted the great Byzantine Church of the Holy Wisdom, Hagia Sophia, then the largest building in the world, into a mosque. Ottoman propagandists would call their new capital "Islambul," the city "full of Islam," and imagined it as a place of religious piety and fervour. Its more common name, already, was Istanbul, which came from the local Greek expression *eis ten polin*, "in the city," and that name would stick. On Ottoman coins and documents it would remain formally *Kustantiniyya*, Constantinople. The sultan deliberately repopulated the city with a mixed population—including by forcibly deporting the Jewish community of Greek Thessalonica and relocating them in the capital—where Christian and Jewish community authorities and institutions were established. Like most Ottoman towns, Constantinople would not be a purely Muslim city, but a multi-confessional cosmopolis.[5]

From time to time, especially zealous sultans or puritanical social movements would highlight their own piety, call on other Muslims to be more pious, and encourage or even coerce conversion. The policy of tolerance did not prevent everyday prejudice and occasional persecution, especially at moments of insecurity. But it did provide imperial officials and local religious leaders with a normative model of community relations that could be invoked and enforced in a crisis. Diversity was considered an unavoidable reality and even a strength of the empire. Unlike other monarchies in Europe, the Ottomans had no interest in enforcing conformity of belief. The commoners could follow their own "ancient usages" in religion, however misguided, as long as they did not disturb the good order of the state.[6]

◇◇◇◇◇◇◇

The Ottomans nonetheless understood their multireligious empire to be a Muslim state; it is worth pausing to ask what this now meant. It had been a long time since the Muslim community of believers had been synonymous, even in theory, with an egalitarian Islamic political community. Now, ordinary freeborn Muslims were mostly taxable commoners alongside, if marginally privileged by law over, other non-Muslim peasants, artisans, workers, and traders, under a ruling class of tax-exempt landholders, soldiers, administrators, and religious dignitaries, many of whom came from non-Muslim, slave backgrounds and who were themselves subject to the sultan and the highest officials and palace politics that surrounded him. Following medieval Persian precedents, a genre of "advice for princes" and political theory laid down what being a responsible ruler should involve. Up to the eighteenth century, this was often summed up in the ancient image of the "circle of equity." Justice and equity were upheld by sharia, God's law; the law was enforced by the state; the state depended on armed force; armed forces were fed by taxes and produce; taxes and produce flowed when the commoners were secure and content; the commoners' security and contentment depended on the ruler's justice and equity.

This did not mean that peasants were never overtaxed, subjected to forced labour, unwillingly conscripted into militia, or abused by landlords and soldiers. But it did provide a language of ethical good government that ordinary people could, and did, use to petition the imperial centre against local abuses of power, and that discontented soldiers could even occasionally use to justify rebellion. Villagers complained to court of oppression by self-enriching tax collectors, the hired thugs of heavy-handed governors, or judges who protected robbers. When, in 1676, the janissary regiments in Cairo deposed the governor of Egypt, they did not rely on force alone: they went to court to get a ruling about how government business should be conducted in the future, to protect their own interests and uphold what they saw as the legal limits on a governor's power.[7]

The idea that laws could be made by men in their interests, as well as by God in His wisdom, might have been disputed by Islamic scholars but was routine Muslim practice. In the Ottoman Empire, the notional supremacy of God's law, the sharia, was complemented and sometimes outbid by the sultan's law, the *qanun* (another word that entered Turkish from Greek, like the equivalent English word "canon"). This was a secular code of law derived from customary practice, precedent, and the expedient decrees of the sovereign. It was especially in the reign of Sultan Sulayman I, known in Europe as Sulayman "the Magnificent" but in his own language as Sulayman *Qanuni*, "the Lawgiver," that sultanic and religious law were most systematically aligned by the imperial religious and civil bureaucracy. When needed, religious rulings could be found that would declare necessary policies or established practices, like the *devshirme*, to be sharia-compliant, however un-Islamic most legal opinion might consider them to be.

Despite what Europeans might imagine, the sultan was not a despot ruling by arbitrary whim. He could not simply dictate doctrine any more than the caliphs had. He could, though, find religious authorities who could make the required arguments in the appropriate legal form. This became the office of the *shaykh-ül-islam*, the empire's chief religious judge, who was also Istanbul's mufti (a judge able to deliver *fatwa*s, religious rulings). As the head of the empire's religious scholars, responsible for appointing judges and for issuing definitive legal opinions, the shaykhülislam was the senior partner of the grand vizier, the chief minister of the imperial bureaucracy, in running the empire. Still, neither the sultan nor his shaykhülislam ever completely monopolised religious authority. Religious scholars, the 'ulama, still had their own interests and autonomy to defend. Charismatic Sufi teachers often followed God and the law in their own way, whatever the sultan or anyone else might say.[8]

Sulayman I's reign from 1520 to 1566 saw the Ottoman Empire reach its greatest territorial extent. He came to power at a moment of heightened apocalyptic expectation across Europe. Among Christians, proponents of the Reformation and their enemies alike talked of a coming Judgment, sometimes seeing the Ottomans as earlier Muslims had seen the Mongols: as God's punishment sent to destroy sinful humanity. Among Muslims, some believed that the year 1000 of the Muslim era (1591–92 CE) would signal the coming of the mahdi and the end of time. A different tradition held that a renewer of religion would come at the beginning of every century. Born in November 1494, in the year 900 of the Muslim calendar, Sulayman I came into the world at the start of the tenth century and became the tenth sultan of the dynasty; this too could be seen as significant. With astrology held in high regard in courtly circles, *sahib qiran*, "Lord of the Auspicious Conjunction," was a title claimed by the Ottoman and Mughal emperors alike. Sulayman, who also claimed, against the Habsburg Emperor Charles V, to be Holy Roman emperor (and had a crown made to fit the title), sought to span Eurasia in the symbolism of his universal rule as well as in his actual territories.

The sultan's spectacular prestige, first as a conquering *gazi*, then as sovereign over what had been Byzantium as well as Islam's historic heartlands and holiest cities, was a terrifying threat to the monarchies of central and Mediterranean Europe. As far away as England, popular songs printed into the seventeenth and eighteenth centuries decried the "terrible challenge" of "the Great Turk who would devour / Each Christian kingdom by his power." But it was just as much a challenge to other Muslim rulers. The titles claimed by Sultan Sulayman I were a panoply of every possible Islamic symbolism. He was the "khan" of Turco-Mongol tradition, the "invincible hero" of holy war, the "renewer" of the scholars' religion, the "pole of the universe" and the "perfect man" of Sufi mysticism, the redeeming messiah of both Sunni and Shi'i expectation. He compared himself to his namesake, the biblical King Solomon. He also called himself caliph, the first Ottoman ruler to adopt the title. But even he did not rule alone. There were always other centres and forms of power at play in the Ottoman Empire.[9]

Ibrahim Pasha was not the only enslaved convert to be close to Sultan Sulayman and to exert his own power at the centre of his master's empire. A few years before the murder of Ibrahim Pasha, and possibly not unrelated to that event, the Sultan had married his favourite concubine, Hürrem Sultan, in an unprecedented move that caused considerable scandal. Neither Islamic law nor Ottoman custom saw anything untoward in the sultan keeping a consort. Convention dictated, though, that once a concubine bore a son, she would be removed from the palace, with her child, to tutor and train him for the day when he would compete to succeed his father, and another consort would take her place. No two sons of the sultan should have the same mother. Sulayman and Hürrem had already broken this rule; between 1521 and 1525 the couple had four sons and one daughter. Most scandalously, they *were* a couple. Hürrem, wrote one European ambassador, was "so loved by His Majesty that there has never been in the Ottoman house a woman who enjoyed greater authority." Earlier sultans had married to forge dynastic alliances, but by Sulayman's time no Ottoman ruler needed support from another ruling house. On the contrary, meddling by the families of royal wives was unwelcome: to prevent this, sultans had first stopped having children by their legal wives, and then simply stopped marrying altogether, until in 1533 or 1534 Sulayman made his favourite mistress his legal wife. Tongues wagged. Janissaries mutinied. She must be a witch, people said, ensnaring the sultan with spells.[10]

Hürrem Sultan—approvingly described by ambassadors to Istanbul as "graceful and petite," "agreeable and modest"—was another, albeit an exceptional, example of an enslaved Christian who, once raised as a Muslim, rose to prominence in the Ottoman world. Her traumatic path to power began when she was captured in what is now western Ukraine, then part of the Polish-Lithuanian commonwealth, by Crimean slave-raiders. According to Polish tradition she was born Alexandra Lisowska; she became known to Europeans as Roxelana (the Ruthenian). After her marriage, she became a close advisor to the sultan and exerted an unusual degree of direct political influence. Hürrem's prominence was not unique, however, especially in the sixteenth and seventeenth centuries. The dynasty's reproductive politics, and the central role it reserved for the mothers of princes, meant that sexual and familial relationships, and the factional politics around them, were crucial for men and women alike. As Ottoman rulers ceased to be mobile campaigners and settled instead in the capital of a consolidated empire, the gender-segregated spaces of the palace and the personal networks of the sultan's entourage, both male and female, became more important.

Medieval and early modern Muslim cultures were generally more relaxed about sex and sexual mores than European Christian ones, whose associations of sex with original sin were not shared by Muslims. Lurid images of sexual licence and libidinous sultans would become stock images of European imaginings of "the East," with the harem, the palace women's quarters, a particular object of fascination and fantasy. (Puritanical Islamic movements, conversely, considered more strictly policed gender relations as an index of the moral propriety they sought to enforce: according to one popular sixteenth-century Turkish manual of correct behaviour, a man should never speak to an unrelated female, not even to say "Bless you" to her if she should sneeze.)[11]

In fact, life in the palace women's quarters was highly disciplined by a strict hierarchy of gender, rank, and age, and space was cramped and shared. Most women were servants or attendants rather than concubines. The harem was above all a school where enslaved girls were taught to be good Muslims and equipped with appropriately feminine skills in etiquette, music, reading and needlework, a complement to the palace school for pages, where the *devshirme* boys were trained for imperial service. It was a powerful place, not because it exuded sensuality but because it was where personal intimacy and political influence were organised. Senior women, especially the sultan's mother, who controlled life in the harem, often played major roles beyond it, in the palace and in imperial politics. In 1651, a palace coup engineered by Hatice Turhan, the mother of the sultan, culminated in the murder of Mahpeyker Kösem, mother of the two previous sultans. Gendered and sexual jealousies were inevitably wrapped up with political resentment. In his own lifetime, Ibrahim Pasha was called the sultan's "whore." Misogynistic commentators on seventeenth-century

Ottoman politics derided what they called the "sultanate of women," and began to blame weak-willed sultans ruled by their lovers and mothers for the problems that would begin to beset a state that had reached the limits of its expansive capacity.[12]

Misogynist detractors imagined palace women as having secretive, emotional and even magical powers over the empire's leading men. But women's influence was most effectively exercised in very material and visible ways, above all in charitable endowments that supported building projects: mosques, schools, public kitchens or baths, especially those catering to the needs of less-privileged urban women. The empire's power, its piety, and its social responsibilities were all expressed in its monumental architecture, most famously in the work of yet another slave-convert, Sulayman I's chief architect, Mimar Sinan. A Greek Christian pressed into imperial service through the *devshirme*, Sinan learned engineering as a soldier in the 1520s and 1530s. Then, in a fifty-year career until his death in 1588, he became the most celebrated of all Ottoman architects, notionally responsible for far more buildings (477 by one count) than he can possibly have worked on personally, ranging from congregational mosques and royal mausoleums to infant schools, bridges, and soup kitchens.

Sinan's most famous and most prestigious work, the great Sulaymaniyye Mosque and its surrounding complex of buildings constructed in the 1550s, still dominates the Istanbul skyline today. The heart of the complex is the great mosque and the mausoleums constructed for Sulayman and Hürrem Sultan, with their imposing central domes and many windows, and the marble courtyard, with its tall and slender arcades. Decorated inside with ceramic tiles evoking the gardens of paradise, the mosque and mausoleums were surrounded, outside their enclosure, by a medical school and hospital, a Qur'an school for children, a hadith school, a hospice, a public kitchen, a bathhouse, and four madrasa buildings, one for each of the four Sunni law schools.

Towards the end of his life, like many powerful men who lived fast in their youth, the magnificent Sulayman turned to an ascetic piety.

The law schools had a major administrative function, as their endowment deed stated: "to elevate matters of religion and religious sciences in order to strengthen the mechanisms of worldly sovereignty and to reach happiness in the afterworld." The whole site also had a symbolic and spiritual purpose, stamping the dynasty's authority on the city and on its patronage of true religion, and seeking the blessing of religion on the dynasty and its capital. In the mosque, no fewer than 120 readers of the Qur'an were appointed, who every morning would recite portions of the Holy Book in groups of thirty, "to assure the place of the sultan in heaven and on earth."[13]

◇◇◇◇◇◇◇◇

The Ottomans' claim to be champions of Islam was accentuated in the sixteenth century, after the conquest of Jerusalem, Mecca, and Medina. But they were not ideologically strict. While legally Sunni, the Ottoman ruling classes, like many ordinary people across the empire, shared some of the emotional and symbolic features of Shi'i belief. They venerated Ali and his sons, Hasan and Husayn, and mourned Husayn's martyrdom at Karbala. The Anatolian Bektashi Sufis, the order to which janissary soldiers often belonged, began by considering their founder Hajji Bektash Vali to have been the reincarnation of Ali. Rather than conflicting across a clear sectarian divide, Shi'i and Sunni elements of Islam often coexisted in this period, especially in the everyday, nonliterate religion of the steppe peoples who had become Muslims since the first Turkic migrations into Iran and Anatolia in the tenth and eleventh centuries.

To the Ottoman authorities, what mattered most was not "sound doctrine" or orthodoxy but loyalty, or at least acquiescence, to their rule. They sometimes wrote scathingly of the Shi'is, calling them *rafidis*, "rejectionists" who did not recognise the legitimacy of the first three caliphs, Abu Bakr, Umar, and Uthman, or who ritually cursed them as usurpers. They persecuted them as heretics when it was politically expedient to do so. But having a monopoly on the right to rule in Islam's name became especially important only once the Ottomans' chief rivals as Muslim rulers, the Safavid dynasty in Iran, took a very different line to the Ottomans on religious politics and made Shi'i Islam their state's official, and only, authorised religion.[14]

The Safavid movement began as a Sunni, Turkic, Sufi fraternity in Azerbaijan and eastern Anatolia, but it became a Shi'i, Persian social revolution that built a new empire in Iran. The founder of the order, Shaykh Safi al-Din, a Kurdish mystical dreamer from Ardabil on the southwest coast of the Caspian Sea, lived in the late thirteenth and early fourteenth centuries. Under his descendants, the fraternity became wealthy and influential, one of the many eccentric Sufi movements that flourished in Anatolia and further east in the uncertain world that followed the breakup of the Mongol Il-Khanate. Many Sufis at this time, as we have seen, practised "deviant" or unorthodox versions of Islamic truth-seeking. But the Safavids went further: by the late fifteenth century, they had come to believe that their leader, the "perfect spiritual guide," was nothing less than the restorer of justice, "the Living One," the divine presence of God on earth, and the long-awaited hidden imam of Shi'i tradition. Wearing red caps made of twelve pieces of fabric, representing the twelve Shi'i imams, they were called *qizilbash* (redheads). Under their charismatic leader Ismail, they became a revolutionary movement. Aged barely fourteen, in 1501 Ismail entered the old Il-Khanate capital of Tabriz in northwest Iran and became Shah Ismail I, the founder of a new dynasty and, to his followers, a God-king.

In the sixteenth century of apocalyptic imaginings, the Qizilbash saw things a little differently. For them, time was not rushing in a straight line toward its predetermined end, but cycling through seasons of justice and oppression, through which the mysteries of the universe would slowly be unfurled. Firdawsi, in his *Shahnameh*, had seen Persian history in similar terms. During their own lifetime, the Qizilbash believed, they would encounter God on earth and live in the perfect society. Life under the consolidated and bureaucratised Ottoman state was increasingly restrictive for Turkic nomads. Their mobility had once served the Ottomans' own expansion, but settled

Ottoman rule now curtailed it, making them vulnerable to outbreaks of plague and famine. They sought an alternative, and Ismail I encouraged them. The Ottomans saw the Safavids as a major threat and denounced their Qizilbash followers, many of whom lived in central and eastern Anatolia, as a dangerous, heretical sect. They first deported Qizilbash to southern Greece and then, after uprisings in 1511 and 1512, massacred them.

The Ottomans claimed no Prophetic ancestry. Their right to rule had originally been based on their pre-eminence as frontier warriors; it now rested on their upholding the law as embodied in the Sunni legal tradition. Ismail I saw himself as a descendant of the Prophet through Ali, as the reincarnation of the prophets, and even as God Himself on earth. In his own poetic self-presentation, he declared: "Adam has put on new clothes! God has come!" Ismail's own pretensions to divine kingship were as alien to Shi'i legal scholars as to Sunni ones. But Shi'ism carried the emotive as well as the political dynamic of early Islam's revolutionary impulse to remake the world in justice, and Ismail declared it the true faith. After conquering Tabriz, he ordered the mass conversion of the inhabitants of his territories, declaring that he would put to the sword any who resisted. Turning south, Ismail captured Baghdad in 1508 and then moved east. In 1510, he defeated the Uzbeks (descendants of the Golden Horde Mongols) at Merv and entered Herat. The following year his troops reached Samarqand. All of ancient Persia and the former central and eastern lands of the classical caliphate were in his hands: the Safavid Empire stretched from Yerevan in Armenia and Diyarbekir in eastern Anatolia all the way to the Oxus River and to Qandahar in Afghanistan.[15]

Political, dynastic competition was now tied to confessional legitimacy. The Ottoman Sultan Selim I wrote to Shah Ismail that as the "defender of the faith" he would wipe out the Safavids' "evil innovation." Ten years later, Selim's son, Sulayman I, wrote to Ismail's successor, Shah Tahmasp, on the latter's accession in 1524, encouraging the shah to put on the plain Sufi habit of his ancestors and, like a poor dervish, "come and beg a crust of bread at my door for the love of God." If, instead, the Safavid ruler continued "to act with the pride of Pharaoh," the sultan would "rid the world of your poisonous presence." This was not the first time sectarian difference between Sunni and Shi'i Islam would both shape and express political rivalry, and it would not be the last. But it was a significant moment in the sharpening of the division between the two. From the time of the Safavids, Iran would be a Shi'i-majority country, and its cultural and religious specificity would be set off, from this time on, against neighbouring, self-proclaimed Sunni states.

In 1514, before his campaign into Syria and Egypt, Sultan Selim I led an Ottoman army into eastern Anatolia, where there was considerable support for the Safavids. At Chaldiran, east of Lake Van, the Ottomans outnumbered, outgunned, and defeated the Safavids. It seems that, despite having used siege cannon in the past, the Safavids at Chaldiran had no battlefield firearms, and the Ottomans' "mobile fortress" of chained-up cannon and carts, behind which janissaries could fire and reload their arquebuses, could not be broken by the Safavids' Mongol-style mounted archers. Selim briefly occupied Tabriz, and the frontier between Ottoman and Safavid territory was now fixed, more or less where it would remain—along today's border between Iran and Turkey. The Safavid capital had to be moved to safer territory further east; at the end of the 1500s, it was established at Isfahan, on the central Iranian plateau.

If Ismail's belief in himself as both Shi'i imam and Persian Godking was dented by defeat at Chaldiran, it did not curtail his reign or undermine his dynasty, though it did halt Safavid expansion. It is said that he never smiled again—but also that he retired to palace life, wine, and "rosy-cheeked" young men. Under his successor, Shah Tahmasp, Ismail's messianism was toned down, and he was celebrated instead as a warrior for justice and restorer of true religion. Tahmasp himself cultivated the peaceable image of a wise ruler upholding the law and preserving his flock from harm. How could he, he wrote to his Ottoman antagonist Sulayman I, pursue war between two Muslim armies, "and thus expose these Muslims to such danger," when his opponent had ten times his own strength in numbers? When his father's army had faced the Ottomans at Chaldiran, Tahmasp protested, the Safavid troops had been drunk. The new shah himself cultivated gentler arts. Inheriting the refinements of Timurid courtly culture, he patronised poets and was himself a master painter and calligrapher.

Tahmasp was only ten years old when he came to the throne in 1524. Despite civil war and repeated invasions, he asserted himself forcefully enough to reign for fifty-two years. In the latter part of his reign, even more than his counterpart Sultan Sulayman, Shah Tahmasp turned to a stricter piety. Prompted by a dream he had during a pilgrimage to Mashhad, he embarked on a morality campaign. He prohibited wine, which along with the rest of the court he had drunk freely in his youth, and which had been central to Qizilbash religious ritual. The tribal armed force of the Qizilbash, once the Safavids' revolutionary vanguard, had become a threat to the dynasty's stability. (Ironically, by 1534, Qizilbash rebels in Iran were working with their own old oppressors, the Ottomans, against the Safavids.) Tahmasp had to face them down. He also suppressed prostitution, which had been tolerated and taxed, and gambling: "My army and my realm have given up on wine, vice, and all that is illicit," the shah wrote, so that they would be victorious against the Ottoman invader.

But the political was also personal, and spiritual. Tahmasp made a break with his father's warrior masculinity, not only by peacemaking but also in rejecting his style of imperial virility, expressed in the lavish banquets, drinking, and luxury of palace life. Instead of spectacular Mongol-style royal hunts, in which animals were systematically herded together to be killed in the largest possible numbers, Tahmasp preferred fishing. Along with wine and narcotics, he banned the painting that he had loved. Obsessed with cleanliness and ritual purity, he eventually even gave up the quintessentially male and kingly pursuit of riding. His court historian wrote that "he abstained from all the pleasure of life, and for nearly twenty years he did not mount a horse."[16]

A different tone again was struck by Tahmasp's grandson, Shah Abbas I, who came to the throne aged sixteen and in the midst of civil war, with Safavid territory occupied by both the Uzbeks in the east and the Ottomans to the west. In the 1590s, Abbas retook Khurasan and Afghanistan from the Uzbeks and, in a long war (1602–23) against the Ottomans, was successful enough to retake Baghdad and push the Ottomans back into Anatolia. He also fought against the Mughals, who had expanded into their own ancestral territory in Afghanistan, taking Qandahar in 1622. In the same year, with the help of an English fleet, Safavid forces took the strategic trading island of Hormuz, in the Persian Gulf, from the Portuguese.

Under Abbas, the revolutionary dimension of the Safavid project was finally cut loose. The Qizilbash tribes were supplemented, and partly supplanted, by an Ottoman-style standing army of slave recruits from the Christian Caucasus—Armenians, Georgians and Circassians. The new army was paid directly by the shah's treasury, which was enriched with lands transferred to the crown domain from the Turkic princes who had held them as grants. As in the Ottoman Empire, a centralised monarchy emerged, freed from dependence on regional aristocrats. At the same time, the monarch's worldly power increased as his religious standing—as the Sufi head of the Safavid movement—became less central. His being seen to rule in justice was no longer about bringing heaven to earth, but rested more mundanely on a system of secular law courts, run by provincial governors, and the patronage of religious scholars. Many of these were brought in by the state, especially from the Shi'i community of southern Lebanon, to make Iran more firmly Shi'i.

Also brought to Iran in Abbas's time were Europeans, especially English, Dutch and German emissaries seeking access to South and East Asian trade around the monopoly that the Portuguese had seized in the Indian Ocean. In the city Abbas had made his capital, Isfahan, they could meet merchants from the Ottoman lands, the Caucasus, central Asia and China. When the French-Protestant-turned-English-knight and jewel merchant John Chardin arrived in Isfahan in 1672, he "met with a bag full of letters . . . , which were directed to me from almost all parts of the world." Isfahan was already a great city—it had been a capital under the Seljuqs. But Abbas built a new, imperial city adjacent to the old and made it a centre of court culture, religious patronage, and commerce.

Like the Ottomans, Abbas deliberately resettled economically useful minority populations, moving Armenians into Isfahan, and laid out its spaces on a grand scale and with deliberate planning. Its great open square, the Maydan, was laid out as a polo ground with marble goalposts, adjacent to the royal palace and flanked by the great market to the north and the Masjid-i Shah, the Royal Mosque, with its long arcades, reflecting pools, and spectacular blue-and-turquoise-tiled gateways, minarets and dome, to the south. West and south of the Maydan was a broad public boulevard lined with trees and gardens, the Chaharbagh, four kilometres long, connecting the old city to a great royal park.

These were not just imperial power statements. They became vibrant urban spaces, especially through the coffeehouses that were established in the Maydan and along the Chaharbagh, sometimes along with officially sanctioned wine shops, in the seventeenth century. They were not quite the popular, sometimes rowdy public spaces created in Cairo and Istanbul by coffee consumption, which spread in the sixteenth century across the Ottoman and Safavid lands, initially among Sufis, before reaching Europe. They were places of class distinction. Here, tobacco and coffee were served, music and dancing might be laid on, and Isfahan's elite and middle classes—both men and women, on different days—could gather, socialise, discuss, tell stories, listen to Sufi preachers or ignore them, and do business. Shah Abbas even received ambassadors there. According to Chardin, at the same time, "It is there that news is communicated and where those interested in politics criticize the government in all freedom."[17] Isfahan was an imperial city, but it had the beginnings of a public sphere.

◇◇◇◇◇◇◇◇

Personalities clearly mattered in early modern Muslim empires, especially where a personality was powerful enough to be taken for God's shadow, or even God Himself, acting on earth. The chronicles, court records, and cities of these times loudly proclaimed the centrality of the sultan or the shah. But the notionally absolute sovereign hand of God was able to act only through the agents of the state, its tax collectors, judges, administrators and soldiers, and these were all more than capable of pursuing their own interests, too. The sultan's word or the shah's decree might be law, but so were the rulings of religious scholars, who had their own claims to authority as the custodians of Sunni jurisprudence, or as the deputies of the Shi'i hidden imam. Even the *devshirme* boys, who supposedly owed no loyalty to anyone but their master, the sultan, often remembered the families and communities from which they had come, and did their best for them when they came to power. Theoretically slaves in the sultan's extended household, the Ottoman Empire's bureaucrats—its pashas and viziers—came to include many freeborn Muslims, whose sons followed them into official careers. These men also created their own households, dependents, and networks of patronage and influence, which became centres of power in their own right. Kingdom-building under God, whoever the builder, depended greatly on its worldly context. Its ideological claims often covered untidier realities.[18]

Nowhere was this more obvious than in India. There, an Islamic empire was built in a mostly non-Muslim society by a dynasty whose descent from medieval world-conquerors gave them the grandest claims of all. Their own territories afforded them the greatest wealth of all, too, and yet their fortunes, to begin with, were the most fragile. The Mughals, as they would become known—though they never used this name, from the Persian word for "Mongol," for themselves—began as one among the many Timurid families contending for pre-eminence in fifteenth-century central Asia. Zahir al-Din Muhammad Babur, descended directly from Genghis Khan on his mother's side, and from Temür on his father's, had correspondingly grandiose ambition but very modest beginnings. In 1498, aged fifteen, he was a wandering prince without a throne in the Ferghana Valley in today's Uzbekistan. In 1501, the year Ismail I became Safavid shah in Tabriz, Babur was defeated and forced to flee from Samarqand by the Uzbeks. Seeking refuge in Kabul, Babur ruled there for the next twenty years in a sophisticated Persian style while still looking north, hoping to regain Temür's old capital, which he saw as his rightful inheritance. Only after trying and failing three times to conquer and hold Samarqand did he turn his attention southward, to the Indus Valley and Hindustan, the land of India, beyond. But once he did so, in 1519, his fortunes changed.

Since he could not make good on his claim to be Temür's successor in Samarqand, Babur pursued the opportunity of expanding his rule in northern India, which his ancestor had ravaged more than a century earlier. In 1526, at Panipat, north of Delhi, he defeated the Afghans who now ruled there and occupied their capital at Agra. Babur was not much taken with India or its people. The exclusiveness of caste society meant that there was no "convivial...social intercourse" of the kind he so prized in Persian court culture. The fact (as he saw it) that "in the skilled arts there is no symmetry, order, straightness" meant that there were none of the geometrically laid out gardens with neat waterways, familiar in Samarqand and Kabul, where such refined and courtly conviviality could take place. But, on the other hand, India was, he wrote, "vast, populous, and productive."

Babur saw India as a source of wealth and prestige for his personal and familial ambition. Unlike Temür, he stayed there after his victory, until his death in 1530. The family's travails were not yet over: like Babur, his son, Humayun, would spend years as a throneless refugee when the Afghan princes and Rajputs—north Indian Hindu military clans—threw off Mughal sovereignty in 1540. For fifteen years, Humayun sought refuge and allies in Afghanistan and Iran, before beginning the reconquest of his father's territories, with the help of Safavid troops, in 1546. A decade later, he had retaken Delhi, but within the year, he tripped and fell on the steps of his library, perhaps fracturing his skull, and died. It would be his twelve-year-old son and successor, Akbar, who would reclaim and consolidate the Indian empire his grandfather had first imagined. He would reign for fifty years. By the time of his death in 1605, the Mughals were the greatest power in South Asia.[19]

When, in his own writing, Babur referred to God, he used the Turkic word *Tengri*, the name of the Mongol steppe sky-deity, as well as the Arabic *Allah*. In Kabul, he wrote a lengthy work in verse on Islamic law. He observed daily prayer and was clearly, consciously, a Sunni Muslim. But he felt no great need to legitimise himself, as the early Ottomans did, as a warrior for the faith. Still less, though he was aided by Shah Ismail in his attempts to recapture Samarqand from their mutual enemy, the Uzbeks, did he subscribe to the Safavids' millenarian Shi'ism. (He did briefly endorse Shi'ism while in Samarqand, almost certainly as a condition of Ismail's backing, but this lost him support in the city, and did not last.) His conquest was motivated and pursued, not as holy war to expand the frontiers of Islam, but as dynastic aggrandisement. As he himself put it, his vocation was *mulkgirliq*, "kingdom-seizing," the proper pursuit of a princely family descended from the world-conquering Turkic-Mongol khans. The Delhi sultans in the thirteenth century had seen their state as a safe haven for Muslims fleeing the Mongols, and their Persian court historians wrote some of the most damning accounts of Mongol barbarism. Babur also had some harsh words for the disorderly and "treacherous" Mongols of his own time. But, especially in the context of competition with the Uzbeks, Safavids and Ottomans, the dynasty he founded would stress their Timurid lineage. They continued to do so down to the eighteenth and nineteenth centuries.[20]

Mughal rulers also preserved the Mongol custom of sending their sons to rule provinces, from where they might attempt to seize their father's power either at his death or during his lifetime. The Ottomans had stabilised their dynasty when they replaced this practice, first by princely fratricide and then by succession of the most senior male relative. Maintaining it, for the Mughals, meant recurrent succession crises in the family, and a series of civil wars. The Emperor

Akbar's son Jahangir, "the World-Seizer," rebelled against him, and Jahangir's son Shah Jahan, builder of the iconic Taj Mahal as a tomb for his wife Mumtaz Mahal, did likewise. This did not prevent Jahangir using Akbar's great prestige as a ruler of celebrated wisdom and ability to bolster his own image, while Shah Jahan liked to present himself as inheriting his crown from Temür via Akbar, bypassing his father. Mughal rule was a fractious family business, and a masculine exercise of personal power.[21]

But despite the invocations of Temür and conquest, Mughal rule under Akbar and his successors did not rely on the force of their heavy cavalry, musketeers, and artillery alone. By the seventeenth century, the Mughals had established an imperial paramountcy across India by integrating high-ranking non-Muslim families into the ruling class. They recruited north Indian Rajputs for their military and financial expertise and subordinated existing Hindu kingdoms to their overrule, sometimes marrying Rajput princesses to seal the deal. They systematically surveyed the land and distributed it to their supporters, allowing Hindu princes to keep their estates in their families. (Muslim aristocrats, on the other hand, were awarded grants of land on a temporary basis, and were moved around to prevent them from becoming an entrenched provincial nobility.) Mughal sovereignty was one among several, especially in central and southern India. Sanskrit histories show us a patchwork of kingships and would-be kingships among both Muslim and *kshatriya* (warrior-caste Hindu) dynasties, sometimes aligned with the Mughals, sometimes fighting against them, depending on circumstance rather than religious affiliation. In some cases, it is even unclear what a ruler's religious affiliation was.

Indeed, what we think of today as clear distinctions between Muslims and Hindus were much less clear in the sixteenth and seventeenth centuries. Not only did Mughal rulers have no single policy towards Hindus as a group: Hindus did not consider themselves as a single group. "Hindu" itself is originally a Persian, not a Sanskrit, word. Its use, in India and around the world, to denote a single religious identity came into being after the Mughals. In Mughal times, writers in Persian, Sanskrit and other languages certainly compared and contrasted the kings and the religious practices of people they called "Hindus" and "Turks," but they were not mainly concerned with differences between people we would today call Hindus and Muslims. They were more interested in celebrating kingly prestige, or social superiority, and with the difference between lower-status people and their betters, whatever their ethnic origins or religious practices.[22]

As Babur recognised, India's "vast, populous and productive" potential made it the richest of Muslim imperial domains. By the seventeenth century, the Mughals ruled over one hundred million people—more than in all of Europe. Their empire rivalled the size of Ming China, and they were richer than any other sovereigns of their day. Taxes on agriculture and a flourishing trade surplus, with fine textiles leaving and silver (and central Asian horses, the Mughals' only major import) entering, made the Mughal elite spectacularly wealthy. Trading and banking families, especially members of the commercial *khatri* caste from northwest India, settled as a merchant diaspora through central Asia and as far away as Moscow. And despite Babur's complaints about India's unpromising environment and charmless society, the Mughals' courts at Agra, Lahore, and Fatehpur Sikri, the city Akbar built in the 1570s, splendidly re-created the conviviality—the courtly culture and conversation, the refined enjoyment of food and wine, poetry, painting and music—that he had so missed. Describing Fatehpur Sikri, Akbar's red sandstone "city of victory," his son Jahangir wrote of how "those mountains and jungles filled with wild beasts became a city replete with buildings, gardens, pleasure spots, and delightful places."[23]

Through cultured conversation, and his own intellectual and spiritual curiosity, Akbar also fostered a religious and cultural pluralism that, to doctrinally stricter minds, pushed the boundaries of what being Muslim or non-Muslim might mean. Akbar, "the Great," the most celebrated of Mughal rulers, is often thought to have been illiterate, or perhaps dyslexic. Unlike both his grandfather Babur and his son Jahangir, Akbar wrote no memoir of his own, relying instead on his family and close companions to record their own recollections of his and his father's time. This disability, though, did not limit his interests or his expansive view of himself and his sovereignty, and their place in the cosmos. Akbar encouraged open religious debate between representatives of various faith traditions in his "House of Worship" at Fatehpur Sikri. He saw himself, perhaps less fervently than the Safavid Shah Ismail, but more firmly than the Ottoman Sulayman I— or indeed, any caliph since the ninth century—as the arbiter of both religion and the rule of law. In 1579, his courtier scholars declared that, as *sultan-i adil*, "the just sultan," Akbar would himself be the final authority on disputed questions of Islamic law, provided only that his decisions respected the Qur'an. In 1582, Akbar went further, instituting as religious policy and dynastic law the principle of *sulh-i kull*, "universal peace," or "peace for all," meaning official respect of all religions and their believers.

Sulh-i kull prohibited religious violence. In a remarkable departure from the sixteenth-century norm anywhere in the world, Akbar declared that he would—and, that as a condition of good government, his successors must—"regard all conditions of humanity, and all sects of religion with the single eye of favour." The Mongols had been generally permissive about religion, but no state anywhere in the world had ever before gone so far in formally legislating the equality of different religions and faith communities. As long as everyone recognised the divine light, in whichever of its many manifestations they found it, Akbar's decree protected them. Even apostasy from Islam, breaking one's personal testimony of faith in God and leaving the Muslim community, was apparently permitted. Akbar's son Jahangir explicitly said so.

This was more than an edict of toleration. It was a decree of the sultan's supremacy, and a departure from the supremacy of Islam. According to the Qur'an, Islam was sent by God to Muhammad as "the religion of truth, to make it prevail over all religion." Ever since Abd al-Malik built the Dome of the Rock, Muslim sovereigns had based their right to rule on the claim that, whether by right of descent, election, or conquest, they were the ones to make Islam prevail. But Akbar's "universal peace" placed the sultan himself "over all religion," including Islam. This was not what we, in the twenty-first century, mean by secularism. Peace for all religions excluded atheism. And it was guaranteed, not by a state that was itself religiously neutral, but by the divine sovereignty inhering in Akbar as God's Shadow on Earth, "His Excellency the Greater Light," the "Manifestation of Truth." Akbar's religious liberalism was also a shocking executive power grab: a violation of what Muslim scholars had always understood to be the rule of God's law, which limited the sovereignty of any man.[24]

Akbar, whose own religious ideas changed several times over the course of his life, was at least partly motivated by the practical considerations of ruling over mostly non-Muslim subjects. Crucially, Akbar's Hindu subjects believed in many gods. They were not the non-Muslim monotheists, Christians and Jews, who had become subjects of the caliphs after the first expansion of Islam in the Middle East, and whom early Islamic law had had to accommodate. This caused legal difficulties. According to conventional legal opinion, Muslim men should not marry unconverted women from non-monotheistic communities, like the Rajput princesses who became Akbar's wives, and whom he allowed to build temples for their own religious devotions. Muslims should not eat meat slaughtered by non-monotheists. Muslim kings could not make peace treaties with them, since their oaths, sworn on deities other than the one God of Abraham, were not to be trusted. "Peace for all," validating any belief in the divine, solved such practical problems simply by overruling the scholars' understanding of the law.[25]

But Akbar's rule was not only pragmatic. It may have been an enlightened absolutism ahead of its time, but it was also in the messianic spirit of the sixteenth century. It drew on the signs and wonders of the age, especially the astrological "auspicious conjunction" of Jupiter and Saturn that occurred in 1582, presaging the year 1000 of the Muslim calendar (1591–92). It came out of the utopian dimensions of Muslim, Mongol, and ancient Persian and Indian beliefs: Ibn Arabi's idea of the many manifestations of a singular God, the Sufi ideal of the spiritual guide and "perfect man," the Islamic revolutionary hope for a "just imam," the Persian and Indian veneration of a divine king and the heavenly light that would radiate from him. For Akbar, as for any early modern ruler, religion was about personality and prestige as well as policy. The two greatest world-historical events of the previous thousand years had been the rise of Islam and the rise of the Mongols, and Akbar was the legitimate inheritor of both, at the moment when, many believed, a new cosmic dispensation was at hand. It was as such that he could declare universal peace.[26]

Always suspicious of sultans, some Islamic scholars were outraged by Akbar's religious policy, the veneration of which he was himself the object, and his usurpation of their own authority to interpret God's law. They accused him of supplanting Islam with his own religion and supported rebels against him. But until the reign of Aurangzeb, who came to the throne in 1658 and who, as a token of his own sincere piety, reintroduced the *jizya*, the tax on non-Muslims that Akbar had cancelled, Akbar's "universal peace" remained in place. Indeed, it survived into the nineteenth century, not as the law, but as a "mannerly" way of living that accorded equal respect and value to all believers. As an ethics of Mughal courtliness, it remained part of the gentlemanly behaviour of north Indian Muslims, even as British colonial historians were rewriting early modern Indian history as a tale of Mughal tyranny.[27]

Later views of Mughal emperors have tended to judge their religious policy according to twentieth-century preoccupations. Akbar is often seen as both especially enlightened, and as not "really" Muslim at all; his successor Aurangzeb is seen as a "truly" pious Muslim, and as a persecutor of Hindus. Both views are equally mistaken. Akbar consolidated his family's empire, while Aurangzeb enlarged it to its greatest territorial extent. Both continuously sought, in different ways, to achieve what they thought of as just rule under God over their diverse subjects. As Aurangzeb wrote to a Rajput king in 1654, "Men of various dispositions and different religions should live in the vale of peace and...prosperity, and no one should meddle in the affairs of another." Aurangzeb did try, and fail, to enforce Muslim morality, notably by forbidding alcohol (from which he himself abstained), but so had his predecessors. Akbar's son Jahangir had prohibited alcohol, as he himself admitted, "despite the fact that I myself commit the sin of drinking wine and have constantly persisted in doing so from the age of eighteen."[28]

Shadows of God were fallible people too, after all, and capable of recognising it. Aurangzeb wrote of his despair at his own failings, as a ruler and as a Muslim. Being Muslim mattered to the Mughal family, and not only as an ideology of rule that justified their immense power and wealth. For Akbar it was the best of many ways to the Truth, whose light on earth came through his own person. For the women of his court, it was also a way of finding themselves in a wider world, as shown by the remarkable pilgrimage made by several of them, led by Gulbadan Begam, Babur's youngest daughter and Akbar's aunt, in 1575. The women, travelling on Portuguese ships, made the pilgrimage four times while in the Hijaz, were shipwrecked on their way home, and altogether spent seven years abroad.

Being Muslim could also mean simple devotion, striking in its humility even, or especially, when evoked by a princess like Jahanara, Aurangzeb's sister, a daughter of the emperor Shah Jahan who built the Taj Mahal. Visiting the shrine of the Sufi shaykh Muin al-Din Chishti, about whom she wrote a devotional biography, in 1640, Jahanara describes how

> I went to the holy sanctuary and rubbed my pale face on the dust of that threshold. From the doorway to the blessed tomb I went barefoot, kissing the ground....I went around the light-filled tomb of my master seven times, sweeping it with my eyelashes, and making the sweet-smelling dust of that place the mascara of my eyes. At that moment, a marvellous spiritual state and mystical experience befell this annihilated one, which cannot rightly be written. From extreme longing I became astonished, and I do not know what I said or did.

Jahanara was a well-educated and practical Mughal woman: the eldest child of Shah Jahan, she was the first lady of the court and her father's confidante and agent, especially after he was deposed and imprisoned by her brother, Aurangzeb. She certainly knew plenty about law and politics. (In this, she was not exceptional among Mughal women: Nur Jahan, the favourite wife of the Emperor Jahangir, who used to ride out hunting to shoot lions with her husband, had been actively involved in government alongside him, even issuing coinage and decrees in her own name. Babur's advisors included the royal family's women, especially his grandmother.) But for her, God's presence on earth was tangible most of all, not in the men of her family, but in the sacred spaces of saintliness where the love of God could overwhelm her own consciousness. It was saints and teachers, after all, as well as conquerors and kings, who had brought Islam to India. They were equally central to what it meant in the farther-flung corners of Islam's new worlds.[29]

7

SHORES OF THE DESERT, ISLANDS IN THE SEA

Sometime in the late 1400s, Muhammad al-Maghili, an itinerant and intolerant North African scholar, left city life and settled in the Sahara. He made his home in Tamentit, a red-walled oasis town in what is now southern Algeria. Thriving on long-distance trade across the desert, Tamentit was also under pressure from an influx of refugees fleeing the persecution of Jews and Muslims in Spain. Al-Maghili wrote dozens of books and would be credited with bringing Islam to much of West Africa south of the desert. Preaching an uncompromising Muslim supremacy and separation from "unbelievers," he also sparked a vicious antisemitic campaign that destroyed the previously peaceful and prosperous Jewish community of the oasis.

At around the same time, and at the other end of the world, tradition says that the *wali sanga* (nine saints) brought Islam to the coasts of Java, then ruled by a Hindu-Buddhist dynasty. The celebrated tombs of these legendary holy men are still major pilgrimage sites in today's Indonesia. Among the nine saints, Sunan (Lord) Kalijaga was the only one of Javanese origin. The others, each associated with a holy place in different parts of the island, are said to have come from all over the Muslims' known world: from North Africa, Iran, Vietnam, and China. It is Sunan Kalijaga who is supposed to have invented one of the forms of *wayang*, the characteristic Javanese form of shadow-puppet theatre whose stories are Hindu epics. Music for the *gamelan*, the island's distinctive bell-like percussion ensemble, is attributed to another of the saints, Sunan Drajat. Sunan Ampel is said to have made a special, large ritual drum (*bedug*) one metre long, still used today to mark prayer times at the mosque dedicated to him in Surabaya, in East Java. In some accounts, the saints used *gamelan* and *wayang* to attract local people to Muslim festivities, and to explain the true religion.

Like other faiths and the people who carry them, Islam could be rigid and exclusive, like al-Maghili, or flexible and accommodating, like the saints of Java. Stereotypes about regional styles or traditions—an unbending, puritanical Islam in northwest Africa, or a malleable, syncretic Islam in Southeast Asia—emphasise aspects of the tradition that in fact can be found everywhere. Al-Maghili's extreme views were defeated in debate at the sultan's court in Morocco, where other scholars had no time for them, and where Jewish communities would thrive for centuries. The "soft" syncretism attributed to the *wali sanga* airbrushes over the tougher edges of north Java port city-states run by Muslim strongmen, and the doctrinal disputes at Muslim courts that occasionally saw books burned and "heretics" executed.[1]

Islam did not travel only, or even mainly, with conquering armies. Between 1200 and 1800, trading and credit networks and everyday social relations, followed by ambitious state-formation and religiously inspired social reform, brought Islam into the Sahara and savannah of West Africa, and across the Indian Ocean to what today are Malaysia, Indonesia, Brunei, and the Philippines. Islam came with different people into different cultures. It came to look different as a result. Muslim travellers in the medieval period and Muslim reformers in modern times would often disparage local customs that seemed to them to be holdovers of ignorance from before the arrival of Islam, and that did not belong in their own ideas of a pure religion. But people had always become Muslim in particular times and places, whether they were Arabs and Persians in the seventh century or Africans and Malays seven centuries later. Islam spread so far because it offered a single, coherent, and compelling model of living a good life within both cosmic and social order. It did so, too, because being Muslim allowed people in many places to make a new kind of sense of their own, already familiar worlds.

◇◇◇◇◇◇◇◇

In the tenth and eleventh centuries, traders and envoys with Muslim names were already arriving at the imperial Chinese court from ports in Vietnam, Sumatra, and Brunei, as well as from "the Arab lands" of the caliphate. The mainland and islands of Southeast Asia were both a stopover and a refuge for medieval Muslims. Early Muslim settlers may have been pro-Alid refugees from the Abbasid Middle East. By the twelfth century, when there was upheaval in southern China, Muslim traders living there would move to Sumatra for safety.

Islam thus reached Southeast Asia both from the northwest, from Arabia and India, and from the northeast, from Vietnam and China. Around 960 CE, a ship was wrecked north of Java carrying moulds for jewellery-making with pious inscriptions in Arabic, showing that small consumer items by this time were being tailored to Muslim customers. One of the earliest Muslim gravestones to have been found in Southeast Asia, marking the resting place of a Muslim man in Brunei and dated to 1264, is also the oldest known gravestone in the region inscribed in Chinese.

Muslims were also crossing the seas *from* Southeast Asia *to* the Middle East. In the thirteenth century, a revered Sufi master known as Masud "al-Jawi" is known to have lived and taught, and probably died, in Yemen. He may not have been ethnically Javanese, but he was clearly identified with the island region of Southeast Asia, from where sweet-scented aloes, sandalwood, pepper and spices (nutmeg, cloves, mace) were exported to the Red Sea.[2]

The Mongol conquest of China in the thirteenth century pushed Muslim merchant families to flee from south China's coastal cities. But, once the Mongols became established as the Yuan dynasty, they encouraged the migration of Muslims into China from Mongol-ruled central Asia and the Middle East. At the same time, rulers of port cities on the northern tip of Sumatra, where the shipping route to China from the Indian Ocean runs between the island and the Malay Peninsula, began to become Muslims. By 1407, soon after the Ming dynasty came to power, Muslims were numerous and important enough in China for the emperor to issue a decree forbidding violence against them. In the late fourteenth and early fifteenth centuries, Ming China set out to bring oceanic trade under its control and to project its power for the first (and last) time south and west by sea. It may well have been because of the existing Muslim presence along the trade routes through Southeast Asia to India and East Africa that the Ming naval expeditions from 1405 to the 1430s, with what were then the largest ships in the world, were led by a Muslim admiral, Zheng He. There were also Muslims among the officers and soldiers in his fleet.[3]

Zheng He is a national hero in China today, his exploits celebrated as evidence of a long history of open and peaceful engagement between China and the Indian Ocean world as far away as East Africa. His achievements at the time were short-lived: court politics and continental pressures shifted Ming priorities away from the ocean, back to China's northern and western frontiers. The late medieval Muslim pre-eminence in maritime Asia would also end soon. By the mid-seventeenth century, Chinese trade in Southeast Asia was mostly in non-Muslim hands, and shipping was dominated by Europeans. Even the pilgrimage route to Mecca from Southeast Asia and India was partly operated by European shipping, as it was for North African pilgrims who made the journey from the western Mediterranean through Alexandria. Gulbadan Begam and her companions from the Mughal court travelled to Mecca via Yemen in Portuguese ships. A century after the brief Ming foray into maritime empire-building, the Portuguese had arrived, more violently, with the express aim of displacing Muslim merchants and rerouting trade into their own hands.

When the Portuguese captured Melaka (Malacca), the port commanding the straits on the southwest coast of the Malay Peninsula, in 1511, it was part of a network of independent, cosmopolitan city-states. The Portuguese apothecary Tomé Pires, who stayed in Melaka in 1512–15, wrote of how the port's trade had grown thanks to the Muslim community that had settled there. From the Muslim-ruled port of Pasai in northeast Sumatra, Persian, Arab, and Indian Muslims who "were very rich, with large businesses and fortunes" had crossed the strait to trade, bringing with them "mollahs and priests learned in [Islam]," especially "Arabs, who are esteemed in these parts for their knowledge." The ruler of Melaka, being "very pleased" with these Muslim traders, whom Pires calls *moros* (Moors),

> did them honour; he gave them places to live in, and a place for their mosques, and...they built beautiful houses after the fashion of the land and town. Trade began to grow greatly—chiefly because the said Moors were rich—and [the] king of Malacca derived great profit and satisfaction from it, and he gave them jurisdiction over themselves; and the Moors were great favourites with the said king, and obtained whatever they wanted.[4]

Muslims like those of Melaka enjoyed the protection of local rulers, but their livelihoods depended on being part of a community that operated across jurisdictions, without either the hindrance or the support of state authorities. Islam for them was defined not by sultans and supremacy over other faiths, but by a "cosmopolitan frame of mind." Coming from different birthplaces, cultures, and language communities, their common faith and code of law tied them together. It created connections with brothers and sisters in the faith who shared acceptable food when they met in person, and the respect of contracts and credit when they corresponded over vast distances and the long timescales needed to travel them. Belonging to the transoceanic community of Islam meant both social propriety and security of property.[5]

Indian Ocean communities' own narratives of their conversion reflect more ancient, local beliefs. They also convey a sense of Islam as having come from across the sea, bringing not only trade but a new and better kind of social and moral order. Ibn Battuta considered the Maldives, the archipelago of over one thousand islands on the monsoon trade route from southern Arabia to India and Sri Lanka, "one of the wonders of the world." All the islands' inhabitants, he wrote, "are Muslims—religious and upright people." They had been so for perhaps two hundred years when he arrived there in the 1340s. Buddhism had previously been dominant, but the islanders' narrative of the coming of Islam blended maritime folktale with popular Muslim belief. Every month, in the old days, they said, a *jinn* (a spirit, "genie") had come out of the ocean, in the form of "a ship full of lamps," demanding the sacrifice of a young girl, who would be chosen by lot, left by a Buddhist temple on the seashore, and invariably found the next morning to have been raped and killed. Then a Muslim came from faraway North Africa, named Abu al-Barakat al-Barbari ("The Berber Blessings Man"). Hearing of the violent and violating spirit, he himself took the place of the next girl due to be sacrificed. The holy man sat by the seashore reciting the Qur'an all night long, thus banishing the *jinn* and saving the people from its depredations. When he repeated the same miracle the following month, the king and all his people embraced Islam. A seventeenth-century mosque that still stands in the islands' capital is said to be Abu al-Barakat's tomb.[6]

Similar stories, tying particular localities to distant centres of Islam through local women, local kings, and miraculous power, can be found at the opposite end of oceanic Asia. In Java, Sunan Ampel, one of the "nine saints," is remembered as the son of a missionary from Samarqand. His father had married into the royal family of the kingdom of Champa, in Vietnam, and brought its people to Islam. Sunan Ampel, before becoming known by this name in Java, was originally called Makhdum Rahmat ("the Gracious one who is Served"). He is believed to have travelled from Vietnam to Java, where his aunt had married the King of Majapahit, the Hindu-Buddhist state held to embody a Javanese golden age of pre-Islamic power and refinement. Welcomed by his uncle, Sunan Ampel married a local noblewoman—who happened to be the sister of another future saint, Sunan Kalijaga—and received a gift of land. There he built a mosque and a school and peacefully spread Islamic teaching. Islam is similarly said to have come to Sulu, in the southwest Philippines, with one Karim al-Makhdum ("the Noble one who is Served"), who "crossed the sea in a vase or a pot of iron and was called Sarip" (from Arabic *sharif*, "noble," descended from the Prophet). "The people flocked from all directions" to hear his teaching, we're told, and he "built a house of religious worship."

Also in the Philippines, the traditional genealogy of the ruling dynasty in Mindanao tells of how Sarip Kabungsuwan, a descendant of the Prophet through Ali and the Shiʻi imams, sailed from Johor, at the southern tip of the Malay Peninsula. He married Putri Tumina, a princess born from a bamboo stalk, and converted the local people. In another account, paradise itself was originally placed in Mindanao by "angels from the west," before "the angels took paradise and carried it to Mecca," leaving a fragment of it in Mindanao. One Sharif Awliya ("the Noble of the Saints"), knowing of this remnant of paradise, came to find it: seeing a column of smoke on the island, he came towards it, found that it was a woman, married her, and had a daughter named Paramisuli, "whom he left in the blessed land." Later, the stories say, other sharifs came to Mindanao from Johor. One of them, Sarip Maraja, arrives and sees Buraq—the fabulous animal, by this time often imagined as a winged horse, on which the Prophet Muhammad is said to have made his miraculous Night Journey from Mecca to Jerusalem before ascending to heaven. As Sarip Maraja watches, Buraq alights on a bamboo tree, slips, and drops his rider: none other than "the lady, Paramisuli." Sarip Maraja dives into the river to rescue Paramisuli, and later marries her: the royal lineage of Mindanao is said to descend from these ancestors.[7]

Such stories, which were still being told in the late nineteenth century, tie local places, their people, and their rulers into universal Muslim history. Islam here is seen to complete existing cultures and beliefs rather than supplant them. Like the fragment of heaven left by the angels in Mindanao, existing beliefs in spirit propitiation, ideas of divine kingship, or belief in ascending grades of being that were common in Indic-influenced Southeast Asian cultures could be seen as anticipating Islam, and could be reimagined in Islamic terms. Local spirits, good or evil, were *jinn*, the spiritual beings whose existence was attested in the Qur'an. As we have seen, sacred kingship had become attached to Islam as early as the Umayyads, and was strengthened in the political cultures that adopted Islam across South and Southeast Asia. Hindu and Buddhist understandings of society and spirituality as ascending through successive stages of purity or enlightenment were receptive to Sufi conceptions of progressing from outward observance, through a series of mystical stages, to inner realisation of the Truth.

But while these conversion stories suggest Islam's universality, they also accord pre-eminence to particular ruling families. High status was attached to Islam in societies where the first Muslims were coastal merchants accumulating cultural prestige and political contacts as well as material wealth. Becoming Muslim often meant becoming "Malay": adopting the dress, social distinction, and language of the merchant elites in port cities that made them both part of a cosmopolitan network and members of a local nobility. Proper Muslim behaviour here meant observing social boundaries. Poorer women might go about buying and selling at market, but Muslim women indicated their superiority as well as, or more than, their piety (or their husbands' control over them) by remaining indoors and unseen by strangers. A sixteenth-century Muslim text from Java admonished: "A free woman who does not stay in her house is like a slave."[8]

◇◇◇◇◇◇◇

After foreign merchants and their local wives, it was indigenous rulers who next adopted Islam. The earliest evidence of Javanese becoming Muslims is in gravestones from the 1360s and 1370s, in the cemeteries of what was then the royal capital of Majapahit. Inscribed with dates in both the Islamic and the Old Javanese calendars, some of these stones are also engraved with the sunburst emblem of the royal family. This was at a time when the Hindu-Buddhist King of Majapahit was described in praise poetry as "Shiva and Buddha, . . . lord of the lords of the world, . . . the deity of deities." Accepting Islam would mean fusing such older ideas into Muslim forms. In later royal imagery, the Prophet Muhammad would be described as wearing the golden royal crown of Majapahit. The actual crown, in the shape of two intertwined golden dragons set with pearls and diamonds, survived as part of a Muslim dynasty's royal regalia into the eighteenth century.[9]

Such spiritually powerful material objects—like the swords and banners associated with Prophetic history that the conquering Ottomans took from Mamluk Cairo—were central to the symbolism of rule in Java. Supernatural powers of kingship were thought to be held in royal heirlooms, especially weapons like the lances, swords, and *kris*es (long, perfectly balanced Javanese daggers) whose fine workmanship and gold inlay impressed visitors to Majapahit. Muslims settling on the northern coast evidently much admired and emulated the aesthetic elegance and regal symbolism, the "courtesy and civility" as Tomé Pires put it, that already characterised inland Javanese court culture. Conversely, Javanese aristocrats and royalty who accepted Islam found ways to make being properly Muslim equate with being nobly Javanese. An undated Javanese text, written sometime between the 1300s and the 1700s, insists on a sharp distinction between "the religion of Islam" and "the religion of Java" and denounces as an unbeliever anyone who would doubt Islam's separateness and superiority. But in all likelihood, such insistence in the text was only so strident because the boundaries in life were actually so blurred. By the eighteenth century it was possible for no less a text than one attributed to the king, *The Teachings of Pakubuwana II*, to present the Arabic and Javanese languages as analogous to a person's left and right eyes: one to see "the order of life" and the truth of God, the other to see one's own material self. The same writer who described Muhammad as wearing Majapahit's golden crown also explained that the prophet Jesus could speak both Arabic and Javanese.[10]

For merchant households and princely families, becoming Muslim thus fused with existing codes of social distinction. As Islam spread into the countryside, customary cultural practices among ordinary people also had to be squared with being Muslim. In many ways, this was unproblematic. Existing beliefs and practices around women's dress and behaviour, for example, might mesh with Islamic norms. Highborn city women may have been expected to keep indoors, or to go outside only when suitably covered and hidden from prying eyes, to distinguish themselves from "slaves." But peasant women did not wear veils or live in seclusion in Java and the Philippines any more than they did in Syria and Egypt. Female fertility and menstrual blood were often associated with especially powerful magic in indigenous Southeast Asian religious cultures, but taboos around them coincided with, and could be folded into, Islamic rules about women's ritual purity. Women also had a central role in communicating with spirits and in healing practices, especially around childbirth and protecting newborns. These translated into popular Muslim practices in Southeast Asia as they did in North and West Africa, where similar rituals involving music, dance, and trance states can still be found today.

The Qur'anic (and biblical) story of Joseph, the upright youth who is sold into slavery and resists the seductions of his master's wife, provided a familiar model of morality that was especially widely adopted in both elite and popular culture. Elaborate versions commissioned by Javanese royalty found Joseph, the "noble angel," a congenial exemplar of older Javanese courtly values of male beauty, refinement, and duty. The tale of Joseph would also be told by villagers during ceremonies to mark young people's rites of passage and at weddings. Sufi sayings describing the relationship between God and the believer as analogous to that between husband and wife, and Qur'anic exhortations to fair treatment and faithfulness between spouses, reinforced existing beliefs in the importance of marriage.[11]

Some other Southeast Asian customs, though, were less widely shared with other societies that had become Muslim. In the Philippines and elsewhere, sexual experience with several partners prior to marriage was not uncommon among young women (much to the horror of Spanish Catholic observers). Once married, women could also separate themselves from husbands they no longer wanted. Neither practice was easily reconciled with Islamic precepts, but nor did they die out when villagers became Muslims. The existence of third-gender individuals, *bissu*, in the Bugis society of south Sulawesi was not obviously amenable to conventional Muslim expectations around sex and gender roles either. In ancestral Bugis belief, *bissu* were the offspring of an androgynous moon goddess, part of a creation myth that accorded great power to beings who combined male and female characteristics. Accounts refer to both women and men becoming *bissu*, though since the nineteenth century, at least, *bissu* have been male-born individuals who adopt aspects of women's dress and gesture. Socially recognised as neither men nor women, androgynous *bissu* were said to be able to harness and re-enact the primal magic of chaos and creation. It was believed that they could heal the sick and bless crops. They were maintained at court by royal families, living in the women's quarters and protecting both the purity of the rulers' "white blood" and their sacred regalia.

In the seventeenth century, when Sulawesi's rulers began to convert to Islam, attempts were made to abolish the *bissu*'s status. As with the communities of transgender women, *hijras*, in northern India, varying forms of sexuality and gender existing in society began to be codified as the power of the state (and, subsequently, social and medical sciences) came into contact with them and sought to define and regulate them. They would also become targets of religious violence. In the mid-1960s, *bissu* were attacked and sometimes killed by Islamist militia in south Sulawesi, alongside others—especially communists—who were considered "non-Muslims." But even where attempts were made to eliminate them altogether, as the British colonial state tried to eliminate hijras in nineteenth-century India, they survived. Most *bissu* in Indonesia today affirm that they are Muslims.[12]

◇◇◇◇◇◇◇

The legends of Java's "nine saints" cannot be linked to historically identifiable individuals. What they convey is the importance of Sufi teachers and Sufi forms of spirituality in bringing Islam to Southeast Asia. By the fifteenth and sixteenth centuries, being a Sufi usually meant being inducted into, and remaining affiliated to, one or more of the fraternities (*tariqa*s, "ways") that preserved the mystical teachings of a founding saint and that were named after him. Unlike the eccentric or messianic mystics we have met elsewhere, most such Sufis were perfectly orthodox, in that they emphasised the basic precepts of religion: right belief in God and His prophets, prayer, and observance of the law. No one could seek deeper, mystical knowledge of God without constant adherence to this more basic piety. Accommodation to local contexts did not do away with such essentials. There were definite obligations and prohibitions upon becoming Muslim. The dead had to be buried, not cremated as in Hindu and Buddhist practice. Pork could not be eaten. Men had to be circumcised (and should grow beards, if they could).

At the same time, there were tolerable limits on what could practically be expected. It was hard to ban gambling, and even when Muslim rulers did so, they tended to have to make exceptions for the Southeast Asian masculine social ritual of the cockfight. There were other ways, too, of smoothing the transition to being Muslim. The earliest Islamic texts in Java use a Javanese term for God (*pangeran*, "Lord," rather than the Arabic *allah*), and do the same for "prayer," "soul," and "paradise," words that named concepts that were already familiar to Javanese who were not yet Muslims. Ascetic holy men were apparently very numerous in Java in the early sixteenth century, and revered by Muslims on the coast as well as by the majority non-Muslim society inland. They may have provided a familiar model for the ascetic Sufi teachers who came later.[13]

Some Sufi teachers carried sophisticated understandings of Islamic philosophy and mystical thought as well as the orthodox rulebook. In particular, in the fifteenth and early sixteenth centuries, they were influenced by the visions of Ibn Arabi and his quest to know God as the ultimate and only true Reality. One of the earliest Islamic literary works from Southeast Asia, the poetry of Hamzah Fansuri, expresses this way of being Muslim. Hamzah was from west Sumatra and taught in what became the sultanate of Aceh, at the island's northern tip, but died and was buried in Mecca in 1527. His work was one of the first to be written down in the Malay language (in Arabic script), for the benefit of local Muslims who could not read Arabic or Persian.

Hamzah's poems emphasise the necessity of the outward observances of religion: prayer, law, reciting the Qur'an. But he also encourages ordinary people, not only the select few, to strive for the hidden knowledge of God accessible only through the Sufi way. The creator God is everlasting and everywhere, but "created forms are mere shadows." In a frequently repeated metaphor, God is the ocean and humanity is the waves on its surface, or the fish that swim in its waters. The aim of the mystic is to disappear into the eternal, as the waves are swallowed in the infinity of the sea:

> *Our Lord is comparable to the fathomless ocean*
> *The waves of which are rolling on all sides*
> ⋯⋯⋯⋯⋯⋯⋯⋯⋯⋯⋯⋯⋯⋯⋯⋯⋯⋯ .
> *Vacate your heart*
> *So as to become the Sublime Ocean*
> *When the wind dies down, the waves disappear*
> *You return to the sea of the Living One, the Eternal.*[14]

As in al-Ghazali's time, not everyone thought that deep Sufi spirituality was appropriate for the masses. Indeed, most scholars thought it absolutely was not. In a society where most people were not yet Muslim, they were more concerned about the proper outward behaviour of those who were. In one tale of the nine saints, the popular Sufi teacher Siti Jenar is asked by the saints' leader, Sunan Giri, why he and his followers do not come to the mosque to join the congregation for Friday prayer. "He answered saying that in truth there was no such thing as

Friday, there was no mosque, only God exists." The exasperated saints, the story goes on, concluded that Siti Jenar must be put to death, and Sunan Kalijaga beheaded him with his sword. This was not for heresy: Siti Jenar's fault lay in leading his followers away from their essential religious duties, by teaching "the secrets of esoteric knowledge to the uninitiated public" rather than keeping his insights to himself.[15]

In another story, preserved in nineteenth-century manuscripts but seemingly recounting events thought to have occurred in Java in the 1730s, a Sufi named Haji Amad Mutamakin is similarly taken to task for democratising what should be hidden knowledge. Mutamakin, from a village called Cabolek on the east Java coast, is said to have brought back books, knowledge, and enlightenment from his own teachers in Yemen. He is accused of "disclosing the essence of the mystical science of Reality" without having due regard for the law. Brought before the king to account for his actions, Mutamakin is defeated in disputation by other scholars who demonstrate the error of teaching mystical truths to ordinary people. Unlike Siti Jenar, he is not killed but pardoned and sent home. And surprisingly, the other Muslim scholars who are his enemies at court prove him wrong, not with superior knowledge of doctrines from the Middle East, but by referring to Hindu-Buddhist books of Javanese mysticism that were part of the island's religious culture before Muslims arrived. In competent hands, they show, these books too are in fact Islamic, and all Haji Amad's knowledge from Arabia can't help him get Islam right if he doesn't understand them. Javanese culture, this story's writer is telling his audience, is already truly Muslim if properly understood. And no less importantly, Islam means the good order of society under the monarchy, which irresponsible religious leaders ought not to disturb:

Do not repudiate the law,
For this is treason against the King.
Truly the King has authority to punish
Since he is the representative [of the Prophet].

By the time this story was being told, Islam was both knowledge from elsewhere *and* wholly indigenous, both authoritative *and* rebellious. Even when condemning him as reckless and possibly heretical, the writer describes Mutamakin as "resolute" and "courageous." His grave is still a place of veneration today; he is remembered locally as a saint with supernatural powers.[16]

Such disputes over religious authority, and the enforcement of orthodoxy by royal command, certainly occurred in fact as well as in cautionary tales. In the late 1630s, a reforming scholar from Gujarat named Nur al-Din al-Raniri rose to prominence at the court of Aceh. From a family of south Arabian origin whose members had settled in India and spent time in Southeast Asia, Raniri was a typical example of Indian Ocean Muslim cosmopolitanism. He wrote in Malay but his thought-world was the whole Muslim ecumene. Among other things, he provided rulings on whether it was acceptable to eat camel and giraffe, neither of which was to be found on tables in Sumatra. This expansiveness, though, did not make him any less inflexible in his attitude to what he thought of as improper belief.

On Raniri's watch, pork-eating Chinese merchants were excluded from Aceh, and Hamzah Fansuri's works were burned as heretical. Hamzah's followers, having repeatedly refused the king's command that they should "repent of their wrong belief," were executed. A subsequent legal opinion sought by an opponent of Raniri, the Sufi teacher Sayf al-Rijal, from scholars in Medina ruled that it had been quite wrong to carry out these killings: the condemned persons had argued that their beliefs had been misunderstood by Raniri, and if another interpretation was possible, their statements of faith could not be considered heretical. Raniri returned to Gujarat, and the king's successor adopted a very different policy. Being Muslim in Southeast Asia might entail creative synthesis with existing cultures, and tolerance of a wide range of belief and practice. But this was not peculiar to Southeast Asia, nor was it always the case there. Like everywhere else, it depended on who was in charge.[17]

◇◇◇◇◇◇◇

Large-scale adherence to Islam among ordinary people in Southeast Asia came only slowly, in and after the sixteenth century. This must have happened in part through the peaceful spread of teaching and example, which is mostly how the tales of the nine saints remembered things. At the same time, those same tales remembered other sides of the story. Adopted by kings and their courts, Islam had become a language of power. It meant the use of force as well as the force of argument.

We previously met Sunan Ampel, one of the great saints, as he moved from Vietnam, settled in east-central Java, married into the local nobility, and set about preaching and conversion. But at least one story about him continues differently. One of Sunan Ampel's disciples was himself a king, Raden Patah, the ruler of Demak, Java's first Muslim state and site of one its earliest mosques. Once it became a Muslim principality, Demak could no longer be a vassal of the non-Muslim kingdom of Majapahit, whose king—Raden Patah's father and Sunan Ampel's uncle—had not accepted the faith. Eventually, Sunan Ampel and the other saints sided with Demak and its king in overthrowing Majapahit, ending the rule of the island's last and greatest Hindu-Buddhist kingdom. This account of Majapahit's fall taps into mythical motifs, also found in other conversion stories, of sons who become more powerful than their fathers, and of older royal and spiritual lineages finding their culmination and truest expression in Islam. The story also acknowledges the role played by armed force and warfare in expanding Muslim rule in the islands.[18]

States were not central to Islam in Southeast Asia before the 1500s, but they rapidly became so. It was no coincidence that, at the same time, European commercial companies and their armed forces were playing an increasingly muscular role in the region. Seeking control of the lucrative spice trade, the Portuguese seized control of Melaka from its Muslim rulers and merchant community in 1511. Coming from the opposite direction, across the Pacific, in 1571 the Spanish took Manila, also an emerging Muslim port, as their capital in the Philippines. In 1578 they sacked Brunei. In 1619, the Dutch East India

Company (the *Vereenigde Oostindische Compagnie*, VOC) established what would become its own capital on Java at Batavia, today's Jakarta. Within a century, Europeans went from marginal intruders to prominent powers in Southeast Asia.

European dominance was not established by a sudden conquest. Nor, as ever, was this a simple matter of European Christians on one side against Muslims on the other, despite the crusading zeal introduced by the Portuguese, and the calls to defensive holy war (*perang sabil*, "fighting on God's path") that their aggression provoked. It was a slow, messy process, shaped by interactions between Europeans and Muslim traders, rulers, and rebels more than by imperial design or religious antagonism. Europeans were initially welcomed as new customers who would push up prices. For much of the seventeenth century, one Muslim state in the southern Philippines was able to resist the Spanish partly through maintaining trade with their rivals, the Dutch. And just as the process of European encroachment was shaped by Muslims' actions, so the European presence would also shape what Islam would come to mean.[19]

After the fall of Melaka, Muslim traders found a new protector in the emerging sultanate of Aceh. Aceh became the most important, and at times the most militant, of the Muslim states. Responding to Portuguese aggression with an expansionism of its own, Aceh swallowed up smaller neighbouring statelets. In 1521, the Acehnese defeated a Portuguese fleet in the straits, and by 1537, they were strong enough to mount their own attack on Melaka. They had also re-established Muslim-controlled trade, via the Maldives, to the Red Sea, making Aceh itself *serambi Mekkah*, "the porch of Mecca." As both the port of embarkation for pilgrims to Arabia and the outpost of Islamic rule in Sumatra, Aceh was linked directly to the centres of Islamic learning and Muslim rule in the Middle East.

Indian Ocean rulers had already sent petitions to their trading partners, the Mamluk sultans in Cairo, for assistance against the Portuguese. After the Ottomans defeated the Mamluks in 1517, it was to the sultan in Istanbul that requests for aid went. Acehnese envoys may have reached Istanbul as early as the 1540s. Certainly, by 1567, shortly after the death of the Ottoman Sultan Sulayman I, when his successor Selim II wrote to Aceh promising to send a fleet "to crush your enemies and to conquer the fortresses from the infidels," direct relations were already established. By this time, some Ottoman gunners had already been sent out to Sumatra. Seeking to overcome the logistical difficulties of deploying an Ottoman navy outside the Mediterranean, Selim II ordered investigations to be made into the possibility of cutting a canal through to the Red Sea at Suez.

The promised fleet was diverted to put down a rebellion in Yemen, and never reached Aceh; the Suez Canal would have to wait for nineteenth-century engineering and European finance. The guns locally called "Ottoman" cannon at Aceh were actually cast in Gujarat. Some soldiers did arrive, at this time and later, and though they were more motley Mediterranean adventurers than janissaries, the Portuguese reported that the Ottomans had sent Aceh "men, weapons, blacksmiths, sailors, and cannoneers." The recognition and assistance obtained from Istanbul by emerging Muslim states like Aceh, through expressions of transoceanic Muslim solidarity, strengthened their local expansion against non-Muslim neighbours. It also boosted resistance to the Europeans, all the way from southern India to the Moluccas, the tiny "spice islands" east of Java, where in 1575 the Muslim Sultan of Ternate was able to expel the Portuguese.[20]

For all that Aceh's rulers began to see themselves as Ottoman-style *gazis* waging jihad against unbelievers, however, their international relations were more pragmatic than ideological. When the Dutch emerged as the principal European opposition to the Portuguese, Aceh and Batavia exchanged emissaries and planned joint military operations against their common Portuguese enemy. The Dutch also worked against the Portuguese with Aceh's enemy, the Muslim state of Johor on the Malay Peninsula. In the seventeenth century, rulers of Aceh maintained relations with both the English and the Dutch. Both nations had trading privileges and a commercial presence in Aceh. One sultan had diamonds cut and set for him in the Netherlands. The sultanate's rulers allowed a Franciscan mission to minister to resident Christians, sent elaborate, beautifully illustrated diplomatic letters to the English kings James I and Charles II, and hedged their alliances—with the Dutch against the Portuguese, then with the English against the VOC.[21]

Similarly, although the Middle East was an important point of reference, Aceh was a centre in itself. Its inhabitants called it *dar al-salam*, "the abode of peace," the title of Abbasid Baghdad. Its ruler proclaimed himself *khalifa* (caliph) and "God's Shadow on Earth," like an Ottoman or Mughal emperor. When enemy troops threatened, appeals to legitimate authority were made to the more senior caliph at Istanbul. When religious disputes broke out, appeal was made to the authoritative "belief of the people of Mecca and Medina": this was how the Sufi shaykh Sayf al-Rijal, whose arguments ultimately won out over Raniri's inquisition at Aceh, defended his own doctrine. But being Muslim retained its distinctively local expression, too. Aceh's royal gardens, laid out in the seventeenth century under forcefully Islamising sultans, contain the Gunongan, an elaborate, whitewashed "artificial mountain" that may have been intended to represent Mount Meru, seen in Hindu and Buddhist cosmology as the sacred mountain at the centre of the universe. As the Ganges is said to descend from Mount Meru, so a river called *dar al-ishq* (the House of Love) flowed through the Gunongan garden, the whole space radiating both Sufi and Hindu-Buddhist symbolism.[22]

Seventeenth-century Aceh was also unusual among Muslim states in being ruled for more than half a century by women. Women could be influential in many Muslim monarchies, and exceptionally came to rule in some—Radiyya Begam in the Delhi sultanate, and a ruler of the Mamluk sultanate in Egypt, Shajar al-Durr. A slave concubine who became the wife of the ruler, Shajar al-Durr was elected by the army in Cairo to succeed her husband on his death. She ruled briefly in her own name in 1250, then jointly with her second husband until 1257. In Aceh, though, queenship was more stably established, with an unbroken succession of four women ruling between 1641 and 1699.

There does not seem to have been any debate as to the legality or appropriateness of a woman acceding to the throne when Safiyat al-Din Shah, the first of Aceh's queens, was crowned following the sudden death of her husband in 1641. Female rulers had been known elsewhere in Southeast Asia, and in the absence of a male heir, a woman of impeccable Acehnese royal lineage (a royal widow who was also the daughter of royal parents on both sides) seems to have been preferred to any of the available foreign princes who were allied to the dynasty only by marriage.

It may be that the merchant nobility at court preferred a queen to any one of the leaders of their own factions. They may also have believed that royal absolutism would be constrained under a woman, saving them from the arbitrary cruelties for which her husband and father had made themselves known. Although she might be a pious patron of religion, a queen's own religious authority would also be limited. This would wisely avoid the sovereign's involvement in doctrinal disputes such as those that had led to Raniri's inquisition and the killing of "heretics" in the late 1630s. Religious zealotry, after all, was bad for business. So was an over-mighty sultan monopolising foreign trade. Whatever the considerations behind her enthronement, Safiyat al-Din went on to rule capably for thirty-four years and was succeeded by three more queens in turn. She received foreign envoys behind a gilded curtain, and seems skilfully to have managed foreign diplomacy, factional politics, religious controversy, and the administration of criminal justice according to sharia norms. She even made Dutch envoys dance for her, to their considerable discomfiture and the entertainment of her male courtiers.[23]

If effective Muslim rule by the queens of Aceh could be achieved by managing factions and foreigners from behind a curtain, a very different pattern was followed in Islam's spread to inland Java. In 1641, the same year that Safiyat al-Din took the throne of Aceh, the ruler of Mataram, at Kartasura in south-central Java, received assent from Mecca to his assuming the title of "sultan." He styled himself Sultan Agung (Great Sultan), by which name he would be known to history.

Agung had first come to power in 1613 and established his rule by conquering neighbouring lords. Facing Muslim opposition centred on the saintly grave site of Tembayat, he first crushed the rebels, and then adopted and co-opted Islam, making a pilgrimage to Tembayat himself. Here, tradition says, the king met the spirit of a saint and "was taught the secret mystical science" that would give him supernatural powers. Agung sought to make himself the centre of religious authority, fusing Islamic and indigenous forms of spirituality. He proclaimed himself a pious Muslim, and at the same time was said to be mystically married to the Javanese deity Ratu Kidul, "the Goddess of the Southern Ocean."[24]

Agung's distinctive appropriation of Islam set the tone for subsequent generations. As the Mataram dynasty spread its rule through inland central Java, Islam became both an expression of ruling power and an ideology of opposition. When later kings came to rely more and more on trade with the Dutch, and then on the VOC's troops to secure their rule, being Muslim increasingly came to mean opposing the monarchy and its foreign allies, and pursuing "holy war" against them. The dynasty's own creative adoption of Islam, though, continued. Ratu Pakubuwana, the wife of a usurping sultan in 1704, mother and grandmother of his successors, was a constantly powerful presence in Javanese politics and religious life for three decades. By 1726, when her sixteen-year-old grandson, Pakubuwana II, took the throne of Mataram, she was aged over sixty and completely blind. But she was also a pious Muslim, learned in Sufism, and determined to shape her grandson to be a powerful Sufi king, harnessing the supernatural force of Islam to secure his rule.

Shortly before her death in 1732, Ratu Pakubuwana commissioned the composition of three monumental magic books, retelling the Qur'anic stories of Alexander the Great and Joseph, and relating a meeting between Muhammad and Jesus in a work entitled *Kitab Usul-biyah* (the title, derived from Arabic, *kitab usul al-anbiya*, means "the Book of the Origins of the Prophets"). While their content provided edifying lessons to the new king, the books themselves were claimed to possess supernatural potency. Copying the *Usulbiyah* was said to be an act equivalent to making the pilgrimage to Mecca "a thousand times in a day," or reciting the Qur'an a thousand times in one day and one night. The book itself contained "what is truly the teaching of religion.... Those who disbelieve it are infidels. Those who hold firm [to it] are true Muslims." An unbeliever who read it would become a true Muslim; an ignorant person would find in it "the mystical science of perfection." If taken into battle, the book would guarantee victory: "If it is taken along, great citadels will fall."[25]

Ratu Pakubuwana's miraculous scripture, it was hoped, would strengthen Islam at the Javanese court and bring both worldly supremacy and blessings in Heaven. In the event, her grandson's attempt to embody the role of Sufi warrior went badly awry. After siding with an anti-Dutch war party, he was decisively defeated, faced a rebellion of his Muslim and Chinese subjects, and ended up switching sides. He sought spiritual relief from non-Islamic Javanese deities and was restored to his greatly diminished throne by VOC troops. By the time he died in 1749, being Muslim in Java was identified more than ever with opposition to the growing influence of European power. The events of the next century would work to strengthen this even further.

◇◇◇◇◇◇◇

According to Muslim tradition, Islam came to Africa at its very beginnings, with the first Muslim emigrants. Even before the Prophet Muhammad's hijra to Medina, some of his early followers had sought refuge from persecution in Mecca with their fellow monotheists, the Christians of Ethiopia. Later, the Arab conquests brought Islam across Mediterranean Africa to the Atlantic, and Arab traders brought it down Africa's east coast. By the fifteenth century, Coptic Christians were a minority in Egypt, the Amazigh (Berber-speaking) population of North Africa had been entirely Muslim for several centuries, and Arabic-speaking Muslim herders had migrated west and south, through what is now Mauritania, toward the Senegal River. Muslims were a tolerated minority in the Christian kingdom of Ethiopia, and

Islam was the pre-eminent religion of East African coastal peoples as well as of Arab, Persian, and Indian merchants scattered through East Africa as far south as the Comoro Islands and Madagascar.

Two African "coastlines" provided havens where Muslims settled, did business, and spread their faith. The southern shore (in Arabic, *sahel*) of the Sahara was already part of regional networks producing and selling copper, salt, gold, and perhaps slaves before Muslims arrived. Trade and towns had an ancient history in the region. An Amazigh queen's tomb from the fourth century CE, in the Saharan Hoggar Mountains in today's southern Algeria, contained Roman oil lamps, and the Roman Mediterranean may have imported African slaves, wild animals, and perhaps gold across the desert. By the tenth century, Muslim traders from North Africa had established themselves on both sides of the desert. What we today call the Sahel, the region south of the Sahara and north of the West African forests, known to Arab geographers as *bilad al-sudan*, "the country of Black people," connected the Mediterranean to African kingdoms further south.

The shores—in Arabic, *sawahil*—of the Indian Ocean, meanwhile, were similarly an interface between African and Asian commercial networks navigated by Arabs, Armenians and Jews before the arrival of Islam. By the time of the Abbasids, there was a thriving trade taking slaves, gold, ivory, and foodstuffs out of East Africa, and bringing in spices and manufactured goods like porcelain from China, and cotton textiles from India. By the time Portuguese ships rounded the Cape of Good Hope, and the Ottomans took control of the Red Sea, what we now call the Swahili coast, the Swahili people, and their language were all clearly identifiable, and being Muslim was central to being Swahili. In the Horn of Africa, where small Muslim trading states sprang up along the southern edge of the Ethiopian Empire, nomadic peoples further inland like the Somalis had become Muslim, too.

State-building followed commerce. Seeking control of trade routes, the Ethiopians expanded southwards, and the fourteenth and fifteenth centuries saw sporadic warfare in northeast Africa between Ethiopia and coalitions of Muslim cities. This conflict reached its height in the

1530s, when an ambitious Muslim ruler, Ahmad Ibn Ibrahim, known to the Ethiopians as Ahmad Grañ ("the Left-Handed") conquered much of Ethiopia. Ahmad had become ruler of the merchant city of Harar, today in eastern Ethiopia, with a revolutionary agenda that included redistributing the alms tax, which had been appropriated by the ruler, to the poor. Taking the titles of imam and *gazi*, Ahmad presented himself as a restorer of true Islam. In 1529, he won a major victory over the Ethiopians. His troops occupied one region after another—at enormous cost both in lives and to Ethiopia's medieval cultural heritage, much of which was plundered or ruined. Here, as across the Indian Ocean, emerging world powers were beginning to intervene in local conflicts. Ahmad's army included Ottoman troops and firearms sent from the Hijaz. He met his death in 1543 while fighting against Portuguese troops who had been sent, under the command of Vasco da Gama's son Cristóvão, to aid the emperor of Ethiopia. (Cristóvão da Gama himself had been captured and killed by Ahmad's forces the previous year.)

Muslim rule in Ethiopia collapsed after Ahmad's death, and his short-lived principality broke up. But the legacy of these years would be significant. In Ethiopia, the Muslim war of conquest would be remembered as a terrible trauma, while among Muslims, Imam Ahmad would be celebrated as a great unifier and conqueror. Although his own ethnic origins are obscure, he would eventually be seen as a forerunner of Somali nationalism. As has so often been the case—as with Serbian history and the Battle of Kosovo, or Turkish history and the capture of Constantinople—the sixteenth-century jihad would later be seen as the origin of long-standing tensions between Ethiopian Christians and neighbouring Muslims, occasionally re-emphasised at moments of regional stress. But at the same time, another legacy of the war was the increased presence of Islam in Ethiopia itself. While many Ethiopian peasants and townspeople must have become Muslim under duress during the wars, many of them remained Muslim thereafter. Perhaps a third of Ethiopia's population was still Muslim one hundred years later, and the same is true today.[26]

Far to the west of the fertile Ethiopian Highlands, the Sahara too saw the emergence of states on the back of trade. Here too, both trade and state-formation were vehicles for the spread of Islam, as a code of conduct creating trust, and a code of law legitimising rule. By the tenth century, a mixed population of North African, Saharan, and West African origins was established at a settlement called Essouk, in a valley at the desert's edge in what are now the remote reaches of northern Mali. Essouk ("the market") became a centre for trade in gold, with its own standardised gold coinage. This was exchanged for imports from the north: glassware, silver, brass, textiles and glazed ceramics, some of which came from as far away as southern China. The town was also a centre for metalworking, including steelmaking, and other trades.

In this apparently most remote of places, Islam was also a set of coordinates enabling people to locate themselves and their homes in a new understanding of space and time. In the early eleventh century, the first known, dateable writing in West Africa was being inscribed here, on rocks and tombstones, in Arabic and Tifinagh (Amazigh-language) letters. These announce local knowledge of the date "in the era of the Prophet," instruct visitors to say the Muslim profession of faith, and advertise the town's Islamic credentials, declaring that it has "a market in conformity to Mecca, and the Book [the Qur'an]." The Amazigh name for the settlement, Tadmekkat, announced the place as "this very one, Mecca," identifying the Saharan town in its own barren valley with the original "mother of cities" in Arabia. The eleventh-century Arab geographer Abu Ubayd al-Bakri, thousands of miles away in Cordoba, knew of the town and endorsed its grandiose claim. He wrote that "of all the towns in the world," it "resembles Mecca the most." After the fourteenth century, it seems to have declined as Muslim inhabitants moved away, but it had flourished for five hundred years.[27]

Still further west, Awdaghust, in what today is southern Mauritania, was a flourishing town from the ninth to the eleventh centuries, based on the salt trade. The southern terminus of trade across the

Sahara from Sijilmasa on the desert's edge in Morocco, Awdaghust was also the northern point of trade from the kingdom known to medieval Arab geographers as Ghana, only ten days' travel further south. The site of Kumbi Saleh on the Mauritanian desert's edge, identified by early twentieth-century archaeologists as Ghana's principal city, had a mosque and a large Muslim cemetery in the eleventh century, with a mausoleum whose design echoed princely or saintly tombs found as far away as Bukhara. In Ghana, according to medieval Arab authors, the ruler was not Muslim, but he welcomed Muslim merchants who traded under his protection.[28]

The rulers of Ghana and Awdaghust are said to have raided neighbouring populations for slaves, who at first were not traded north but employed domestically within the region: their own trade was in salt, metals, and gold. Trade in African slaves was most significant from Central Africa across the eastern Sahara, especially from the Lake Chad region to Libya, and from Darfur (in what today is western Sudan) into Egypt. But over time, it expanded across the western Sahara too, to Morocco and to what by the sixteenth century were the Ottoman regencies (*beyliks*) of Algiers and Tunis. It is impossible to know exactly how many people were enslaved, trekked across the desert, and sold in the Saharan trade, just as it is impossible to quantify the suffering endured by its victims—young boys mutilated to become eunuchs, young women separated from their families to become domestic servants and concubines. Best estimates suggest that perhaps five thousand slaves were trafficked each year between the eleventh and the fifteenth centuries, and between six and eight thousand per year from 1500 to the end of the nineteenth century: all told, between six and seven million people over the more than one thousand years of the trade's existence.[29]

For men engaged in trade, being Muslim in Saharan Africa, as in Southeast Asia, meant a relationship of equality and trust with business partners far away, and with one another in a local society where they were a minority. More than in Southeast Asia, though, over time, as Saharan and West African rulers first employed literate Muslim secretaries, then adopted Islam themselves, and, following them, more people became Muslims, sharp social hierarchies also developed. Racial and gender identities founded on slavery, dependence, and clientship would endure well into the twentieth century. Medieval Arab writers fantasised about the sexual attributes of Black African women and worried about the sexual potency of Black African men, creating early racial stereotypes that would endure for centuries. By the fifteenth century, the people of the Sahel and western Sahara were a mutually dependent mix of urban, scholarly, and commercial families; freeborn or "noble" nomadic warrior lords and property owners; and their servile or freed-slave cultivators, artisans, domestic servants and salt-miners. Nobles identified themselves as "white" (*bidan*) in contrast to their "black" (*suwadin*) dependents.

These ethnic distinctions, originating in histories of enslavement and emancipation, endure today, especially in the region now covering southern Algeria and Morocco, Mauritania and Mali. Here, being one of the *haratin* or *gnawa* (both terms of very uncertain origin but connoting blackness, "mixed" ancestry, or subordinate status) is a social and also a cultural identity. Specific musical, religious and therapeutic practices are associated, in particular, with the *gnawa* of Morocco and Algeria. Nor have forms of slavery and servitude wholly disappeared from Saharan societies. In principle, all Muslims—or at least, all Muslim men—were equal, at least before God and the law, and religious otherness was the most important form of difference. But as in other communities, social, cultural, and gender distinctions, especially differences of wealth and status, all of which often intersected with racialised or ethnic identities, mattered among Muslims too.[30]

◇◇◇◇◇◇◇

Like the port cities of Southeast Asia, Saharan trading towns that became centres of commerce and religion also became hubs of political power, controlling trade and the people involved in it. By the late eleventh century, Ghana had become a Muslim state, like the kingdom of Takrur further southwest in the region of today's Senegal. It also

became a more militarised place, enslaving non-Muslim subject populations and less inclined to accommodate the ancestral religions that
its rulers had discarded. Weapons, armour, and above all horses were
traded from the Mediterranean for gold and slaves. Horses were symbols of power, distinguishing the elite from commoners and illustrat-
ing a sharpening of hierarchy between rulers and ruled. Horses also,
more basically and brutally, were instruments of power. They brought
speed and mobility, giving slavers greater predatory power. One good
horse might cost between ten and thirty enslaved people—a price that
suggests both a sizeable investment, and a significant anticipated return. Slaving meant a sharper distinction between who was a Muslim
(and therefore, at least in principle, safe from slave raiding) and who
was not. More zealous ideas of "true" Islam both spread northward
into Morocco from the western Sahara, with the founders of the revolutionary Almoravid movement that began there in the eleventh century, and came south with preachers and jurists like al-Maghili, tying
West Africa more closely into the world of the Arab Middle East. In
the twelfth century, the Sicilian geographer al-Idrisi wrote that Ghana's king was said to be descended from the Prophet through Ali Ibn
Abi Talib, and that he recognised the ultimate authority of the Abbasid caliph. Such claims to legitimacy signalled an awareness of Islam's central political symbols, and their local adoption to create new
centres of power in Africa.[31]

But more distinctively West African cultures did not disappear.
Arabic texts written by literate Muslims concerned themselves with
who was, and who was not yet, properly Muslim. But other texts told
stories that combined the presence of Islam with older and still reso-
nant ideas of both worldly and spiritual power. In the 1200s, Ghana
was eclipsed by a greater empire centred further east, on the upper
reaches of the Niger River, where it flows northeast towards the desert
before turning in its great bend southwards. This was the empire of
Mali, whose founder is said to have been the legendary hunter, warrior, and magician Sundiata (or Sunjata) Keita. Sundiata's story is told
in epic poems, passed down to this day in the Mande-language oral

traditions of the *jeliw*, the praise-singers or "griots" in what today are Mali, Senegal, and the Gambia.

The Sundiata epic tells of a breakdown of order in society, and the rise of Sumaoro Kante, a tyrannical, ironworking sorcerer-king, who robs merchants and abducts young women, and whom Sundiata ultimately defeats. The characters of the epic may be symbolic rather than historical. That is, rather than preserving a literary version of a dynasty's political history, they set out lessons for kingship by dramatising a struggle for power between the magic of the blacksmith (Sumaoro) and that of the hunter (Sundiata), two figures endowed with deep significance in ancient West African understandings of the relationship between humans, animals, and the earth. But the figure of Sumaoro might also represent the effects of intensified slaving, both in the thirteenth century when the events of the poem are usually thought to be set, and in the nineteenth century, when the versions we have today were circulating. By the time the poem was being sung, perhaps in what were originally masked ceremonies at the court of Mali, in the fourteenth century, the state's rulers were officially Muslim, and the West African story was tied in to universalising Islamic history.

Sundiata is sometimes seen as a Muslim, whose "real name was Mohammed," battling an occult enemy. Much of the story's content in fact concerns the symbolic centrality of women, especially Sundiata's mother, a "wild" princess from the bush. But paternity is also emphasised, and Sundiata's family, the Keita, are said to be descendants of "Bilali Bounama," or Bilal Ibn Rabah. The historic Bilal was an Ethiopian slave in Mecca at the time of Muhammad; one of the first to accept Islam, he was an early and close Companion of the Prophet. Bilal is celebrated in Islamic tradition as the first muezzin, who made the call to prayer for the first Muslim community. Integrating Bilal into the long list of Sundiata's ancestors ties a distinctive, indigenous West African cosmology and culture into the wider world and normative history of Islam.[32]

A striking illustration of the connections between the Sahel and its wider worlds can be seen, too, in the life and writings of the man who became early modern Europe's best-known guide to the region. Hassan al-Wazzan, known in Europe as Leo Africanus, was born in Granada in 1498, shortly after Muslim rule in Spain ended, as Muslims and Jews were emigrating to North Africa and only a few years after the massacre of the Jews of Tamentit. He grew up in Fez, where he and his father both served the Moroccan sultan. He visited Timbuktu on a diplomatic mission, was captured and enslaved in the Mediterranean by Spanish corsairs, entered the service of the pope, was freed, and converted to Christianity. Under his new name of Leo "the African," he became the acknowledged authority on what to Europeans were still fabulous and mythical lands beyond the Sahara. The inhabitants of Mali, Leo wrote, were "rich, and have plenty of wares." There were, he said, many "temples, priests and professors" in the kingdom, whose people excelled "in wit, civility, and industry." They were also (he thought) the first in the region to embrace Islam. In Timbuktu, which boasted "a princely palace... built by a most excellent workman of Granada," there was also "great store of doctors, judges, priests, and other learned men, that are bountifully maintained at the King's cost and charges. And hither are brought [many] manuscripts or written books [from North Africa], which are sold for more money than any other merchandise."[33]

Mali flourished into the fifteenth century by aggregating smaller states under the sovereignty of a single ruler (*mansa*) who controlled, above all, the booming gold trade. By this time, West African gold, mined further south and traded northward via the kingdoms of the Sahel, was a crucial component of the Mediterranean and Middle Eastern economy. It drew in Europeans, too. In the 1490s, Mamluk, then Ottoman, control of Indian Ocean trade from China and Southeast Asia pushed the Portuguese and Spanish into maritime adventures to gain their own direct access to silks, spices, and porcelain, incentivising what would become Europe's "voyages of discovery." Only a few decades earlier, it was West Africa's command of the flow of gold across the Sahara that first drew Portuguese navigators into the Atlantic. When Abraham Cresques, a Jewish manuscript illuminator from Majorca, made the world map known as the "Catalan Atlas" in the 1370s, he knew of "the King of Mali," whom he drew as a prominent, regal figure on a throne, holding a giant nugget of gold. (He also knew enough about Southeast Asia to portray a queen, holding a sword, on the "isle of Java.")

The African king Cresques likely had in mind was the best-known of Mali's rulers, Mansa Musa, whose stopover in Cairo during his pilgrimage to Mecca in 1324 was notable for the gold he spent there in gifts to the Mamluks. The "Easterners" who saw him there, according to a later West African chronicler, "were astonished at how mighty a ruler he was." On his return from Mecca, Musa is credited with adding the territory of Songhay, around the eastern arm of the Niger bend, to his empire. He extended Mali's rule over the cities of Timbuktu, where he had a palace built, and Gao, where "he built a mosque and a prayer niche." Gao, on the east bank of the Niger, and Timbuktu, north of the bend in the river, were already long-established trading centres. They would become important regional capitals and centres of Islamic learning, too.[34]

From Gao and other towns, a Mande-speaking trading diaspora spread south into forest regions like the Akan goldfields, in today's northern Ghana, seeking commercial opportunity and taking Islam with them. They came to be known collectively as the *dyula* (or juula) people: an occupation, "trader," that became an ethnicity. Welcomed as immigrants in non-Muslim societies, the dyula espoused a personally pious and socially pluralistic understanding of being Muslim. They reconciled living as Muslims with living under non-Muslim rulers, and in daily contact with non-Muslim neighbours. The Malian teacher Hajj Salim Suware (also called Mbemba Laye Suware), whose biography is very uncertain—he seems to have lived sometime between the thirteenth and the fifteenth centuries—formalised this way of living a properly Muslim life outside of an Islamic state. Suware was part of a West African scholarly tradition and social group that set itself apart from ruling families even within the Muslim Mali Empire. These learned scholarly lineages differentiated themselves from the "aristocratic" warrior castes. They sometimes lived in distinct set-tlements, "cities of God" that secular kings could not enter except to perform religious duties on festival days. And they eschewed the use of worldly power, whether for themselves or as a means of spreading the faith.

Unlike the uncompromising al-Maghili, Suware did not insist on Muslim supremacy and the "abasement" of non-Muslims. He held that God would bring all people out of ignorance in His own good time, and that seeking to convert nonbelievers, whether by preaching or by conquest, was inappropriate. Jihad as armed struggle was per-missible only in self-defence, when Muslims' own survival was threat-ened. Instead, believers should peacefully keep their own faith and obey those in authority wherever they found themselves, providing a model of virtue that would set a good example to others. Suware's teachings, which remain influential in much of West Africa today, anticipated questions that would arise for many more Muslims living outside of Muslim-ruled states in the centuries to come.[35]

Barely a century after Mansa Musa's fabled pilgrimage, Mali's con-stituent principalities began to break apart. Rivalries for succession within the empire and nomadic pressure from Tuareg confederations to the north weakened the empire's cohesion. The Tuareg—Berber-speaking Saharan camel nomads whose own, sharply hierarchical warrior society was also Muslim, but politically independent of any regional state—captured Timbuktu in 1433. Mali's most powerful successor was the Songhay Empire, centred on Gao and Timbuktu. Songhay, in its turn, would become a major centre of trans-Saharan commerce, Islamic learning, and Muslim rule. The scholars of Tim-buktu, in the words of the town's seventeenth-century historian al-Sa'di, were "righteous folk...equalled in their righteousness only by the Companions of the Messenger of God." They studied literature (*adab*, or belles lettres) and law, lexicography, grammar and hadith, and composed poetry in praise of the Prophet. Some were said to work miracles, in demonstration of God's blessings upon them; some (like the scholars of caliphal Baghdad) gained great wealth through trade, while others (like the first Sufis) abjured it. Of one of the most famous, Ahmad Baba, who lived in the second half of the sixteenth century, it was said that he was "unique in his time, and…excelled in all branches of learning." His judicial opinions were sought throughout northwest Africa: "He stood up boldly for the truth, even if it came from one of the humblest of men, and would not temporize, even for *amir*s [princes] and sultans."[36]

As for Muslim rule, it still had to balance upholding Islamic law to the satisfaction of commercial and court elites with respect for the ancestral beliefs and rituals of the larger, still mostly non-Muslim, population. This balance was delicate and could be dangerous. Sonni Ali, the founder of the Songhay state, was an effective military leader who recaptured Timbuktu from the Tuareg, but was judged not to be a true Muslim. Al-Sa'di condemned him for tyranny and impiety, as a "great oppressor and notorious evil-doer" who killed and insulted the scholars and holy men and was wont "to make a mockery of his religion." In 1493, a few months after Sonni Ali's death, his son was overthrown by a more pious general, Askia Muhammad Turé. He and his successors sought to rule with more unambiguously Muslim credentials.[37]

Askia Muhammad made the pilgrimage to Mecca; passing through Cairo, he managed to get the nominal Abbasid caliph to approve his seizure of power in Timbuktu. He sought guidance from Muhammad al-Maghili, who had a better reception in Gao than he had received in Fez, and who issued lengthy advice on governance, taxation, property, and proper conduct. Unlike Suware, al-Maghili had no patience for Muslims living under non-Muslim rule (they should be compelled to acknowledge a proper Muslim prince, he wrote, on pain of death if need be). Nor did he make allowances, as other authorities did, for folk religious practices like charms and amulets (anyone using them was like a sorcerer or enchantress, and anyone persisting in doing so should be killed). And in a region where Islam was spreading precisely through creative accommodation to mostly non-Muslim societies, al-Maghili insisted that Muslims could have nothing to do with unbelievers: jihad, he wrote, should be waged against them, and against Muslims who were their friends, as well.[38]

◇◇◇◇◇◇◇◇

In 1591, a Moroccan expeditionary force armed with muskets crossed the desert and crushed Songhay's defenders at Tondibi, north of Gao. From its capital in Marrakesh, Morocco's own empire was ascendant. It had defeated a Portuguese invasion at Ksar al-Kabir in the north, in 1578, at the so-called Battle of Three Kings. (The three being a recently deposed Sultan of Morocco, his Portuguese ally to whom he had turned to regain his throne, and his successor, who drew on Ottoman support against the Portuguese: as so often, pragmatic alliances crossed religious affiliations as well as mobilising them.) Now the Moroccans turned south, to capture the southern side of a caravan traffic that was still flourishing despite Portugal's incursions into the gold trade, and the beginnings of a new, more intense slave trade on the Atlantic coast.

The resulting flow of gold to Morocco was such that the sultan, Ahmad al-Mansur, was known as *al-dhahabi*, "the golden." But in 1603, civil war broke out in Morocco following the sultan's death, and the ambitious empire lost control of its distant provinces. Financial controllers at Timbuktu were appointed from Marrakesh for another thirty years, but in 1612 the Moroccan garrison became effectively independent, when the soldiers elected their own pasha to govern them. Moroccan sovereignty was formally recognised as late as the eighteenth century, and in the twentieth century Moroccan nationalism would make vast territorial claims on the basis of historic pledges of allegiance to the sultanate by the peoples of what, following French and Spanish colonial rule, would become Mauritania, Western Sahara, and southwestern Algeria. But Morocco's trans-Saharan empire had been short-lived.

Within West Africa, other consequences of the fall of Songhay were more significant. Scholars fled from Timbuktu, or were taken into exile in Morocco. While Timbuktu itself never really recovered as a centre of learning, the dispersal of its scholars led to a great increase in the spread of Islam, across the southern Sahel and into the regions of the Senegal and Gambia Rivers. At the same time, a protracted war of resistance against the new rulers of Timbuktu both sapped the invaders' strength and led to the founding of new, non-Muslim states south of the Niger bend, where Muslim traders and teachers would settle. Trade was reoriented away from the western Sahara towards the rival Muslim state of Borno, near Lake Chad, in today's northeast Nigeria. To counterbalance Moroccan empire-building, the rulers of Borno made their own alliance with the Ottomans, who controlled Borno's trade outlet on the Mediterranean, at Tripoli in Libya. Ottoman instructors brought firearms to strengthen Borno. The strength of the sultanate there, and its claim to exercise its own Islamic sovereignty, would endure through the nineteenth and twentieth centuries, down to the present-day politics of Nigeria.

In these ways, the Moroccan capture of Timbuktu touched off a chain of reactions that would influence West African history for centuries. The region's great medieval empires had broken up, but its mobile Muslim scholars had spread throughout the region, west along the Senegal and Gambia to the Atlantic, south along the Niger and into the forests of present-day Burkina Faso, Ghana, Côte d'Ivoire, and Nigeria. Trade across the Sahara shifted but did not die out. Indeed, it continued, although much diminished in significance, into the nineteenth and twentieth centuries. Muslim ideas and symbols of just rule as well as of community belonging proliferated, and when there was no longer a single ruler to appropriate them, claims to them proliferated too.

But as more West Africans became Muslims, Muslims also found themselves caught up in a new, and terrifying, chapter of West Africa's history. For each individual captured, enslaved, perhaps tortured, and transported into servitude—whether within Africa, across the Sahara or the Red Sea, or across the Atlantic to the Americas—the experience may have been equally horrifying, and its effect equally incalculable. But the scale, intensity, and impact of the Atlantic slave trade, from the sixteenth century through the early 1800s, was unlike anything seen before. Islamic law (though not always Muslims' practice) protected Muslims from enslavement by other Muslims. But Muslim Africans were just as much at risk as African non-Muslims from the rapidly expanding slaving that began to feed the growing demand of the Europeans' slave-ships and their Atlantic plantations, as a new and voracious slave trade began to accelerate along the coasts, from Senegambia down to Benin and beyond.

Enslaved African Muslims thus found themselves in the Caribbean, in Spanish America, and in what would become the southern United States. They could sometimes maintain their sense of community: in 1620, a Catholic priest in Colombia noted that a number of Africans in Cartagena, despite their different languages and ethnicities, "communicated well with one another" because they were all Muslims. Their literacy in Arabic could mark them out, for good or ill: in 1805, the *Charleston Courier* described an enslaved man who had escaped, noting that he "writes the Arabic language." An early and remarkable Arabic-language contribution to American literature exists in the laconic autobiography of Omar Ibn Said, a Muslim from western Senegal, born around 1770 and enslaved in 1807, who lived out his life in North Carolina. "I cannot write my life," he began his account, written in 1831, "for I have forgotten much of my talk as well as the talk of the Arabs." But he had memorised passages of the Qur'an. Among those he wrote out, and which survive in his hand, is the *sura* (chapter) that he used to preface his account, *surat al-Mulk* ("Possession," or "Authority"): "Blessed is He Whose hands hold all authority...Who created death and life in order to test which of you is best in deeds."[39]

Perhaps these happened to be the verses he best remembered. Or perhaps he was making a point. With the forced mobility of the Atlantic trade, Muslims like Omar had come into another New World, beyond even the farthest lands of Islam, and it would be an understatement to say that the experience was a testing one. It was a sign of more testing times to come.

8

VOICES OF RENEWAL

In the 1670s, an Amazigh West African religious leader and revolutionary named Awbik al-Lamtuni led an uprising on the banks of the River Senegal. Preaching against pillage and enslavement, he took the Arabic name Nasir al-Din, "the Protector of the Faith," and the title *amir al-mu'minin*, "Commander of the Faithful," and overthrew the region's aristocratic rulers. Nasir al-Din and his movement were eventually defeated, partly because French traders on the coast supplied firearms to his slave-catching enemies. But his was the first in a long series of socially reforming, religiously inspired state-building movements that would recur across West Africa over the next two centuries. Statesmen and courtiers in the self-proclaimed centres of the Muslim world, in Agra, Istanbul, and Isfahan, where dynastic empires seemed to have passed their peak, were fretting about decline. But in other places—in West Africa, South Asia, and the Arabian Peninsula—expansion and reinvention were underway. Across a long eighteenth century stretching from the late 1600s to the first decades of the 1800s, thinkers and social reformers across the Muslim world recognised the challenges facing their societies. They found innovative ways to address them in their own time within the frameworks they inherited from their past.[1]

By the mid-1800s, these preceding centuries would come to be seen as times of stagnation and decay that had paved the way for the inevitable decline of the Muslim world in the face of European imperial expansion. "Islamic decline," twinned with the corresponding "rise of the West," would become a favourite theme in European-centred histories of a world that Europeans, increasingly, saw only in their own terms. Many nineteenth-century Muslims would adopt this vision too, and came to criticise their own recent forebears as having been led astray by unthinking traditionalism, despotism, or ignorance of the true faith. They would demand reform and revival as antidotes to what they thought of as merely blind imitation of past tradition in religious matters, and for societies that they thought had lost their capacity for self-direction. But these were perceptions born of a nineteenth-century world that was being suddenly and dramatically transformed. They could not see how their own swiftly changing present really related to its recent past, in Europe itself (where rational scientists had also pursued alchemy, and where mesmerism, spiritualism, and religious revivalism too flourished alongside revolution, evolution, and electricity), let alone in the rest of the world.

Far from being in decline, in the seventeenth and eighteenth centuries Islam had expanded further than ever before across Africa and Asia. The Muslim community, if measured by the number of people in the world who called themselves Muslims, would continue to expand dramatically into the nineteenth century, even as Muslim sovereignty was eroded. These were times of creative, confident reimaginings of what Islam and Muslim life should be. In West Africa, a series of reformist campaigns against the enslavement of Muslims and for the moral improvement of what reformers saw as only "nominally" Muslim societies led to a new wave of empire-building. In India, the defeat of the Mughals in Delhi by their rival, the Iranian ruler Nadir Shah, stimulated reflections on social and spiritual revival. The ideas that emerged were both deeply philosophical and very much oriented towards the practical issues of Muslim life in the world.

In pursuing internal self-criticism, moral regeneration, and the "rectification" of the faith, thinkers in these times evoked a theme recurring throughout Muslim history: the necessity of reform and the questioning of tradition in order to return to the truth. The same theme would return with even greater urgency in the centuries to come. In the twentieth century, this theme of reform, or rectification—in Arabic, *islah*, "putting things right"—would often hark back to the eccentric and controversial jurist Ibn Taymiyya, who lived in Damascus around the turn of the fourteenth century. From time to time throughout Muslim history, some scholars invoked what they believed was the true and original faith and practice of earlier authorities, or their earliest forebears—the *salaf*, "those who went before," or the first generations of Muslims—against whatever it was that they disapproved of in the society of their own time. Some, like Ibn Taymiyya, prescribed a purely *salafi* way, in the image (as they imagined it) of those pious ancestors, as the antidote to the ills of a later, corrupted age.

But calls for reform never belonged to a single school of thought. Nor did they always prioritise the first Muslims, those of the generation of the Prophet's own Companions, as models of authoritative behaviour. Indeed, a striking feature of seventeenth- and eighteenth-century writers, as historian Khaled El-Rouayheb has shown, is the extent to which they affirmed "the value of the present and its legitimacy." The Moroccan logician Hasan al-Yusi, who died in 1691 and whose influence spread to Egypt and the Ottoman Empire, had little time for people who denigrated their own times in comparison to an idealised past: "The world has always been thus," he wrote, "and people have been people since they were created. It would be better for a person to acquiesce and even to be content with his own time." Rather than the later, nineteenth- and twentieth-century emphasis on *islah*, the "putting right" of a truth that had allegedly been forgotten or corrupted, earlier reformists in the seventeenth and eighteenth centuries were concerned with *tahqiq*, the "verification" or "actualisation" of a truth that was known but not yet fully realised. Far from being a single movement, such impulses to reform produced contradictory tendencies: the Sufi writings of Shah Wali Allah al-Dihlawi of Delhi, as well as the puritanical, anti-Sufi preaching of Muhammad Ibn Abd al-Wahhab in Arabia in the mid-1700s; the anti-slavery state-building jihads in Senegambia in the 1670s, as well as the jihad that created the Sokoto caliphate, which would become one of Africa's largest slave-holding states, in what is now northern Nigeria, in 1804.[2]

One thing, though, these thinkers and activists did have in common. For them, Muslim societies' problems came mostly from within, from division and intolerance, from injustice, from misunderstanding and deviation from God's "straight path." The outside world was not yet a threat.

Europe's intrusions and the effects of emerging global capitalism, in the flow of money and commodities, the spice trade and the slave trade, could certainly be felt already in India, Southeast Asia, and West Africa. But for Islam's reformers in the long eighteenth century, Europe was not yet their problem. Muhammad Ibn Abd al-Wahhab, who in the 1740s forged a lasting alliance with the ambitious Al-Saud family in the out-of-the-way province of Najd, on the fringes of Ottoman sovereignty in central Arabia, was only one, and by no means the most important, of the voices of renewal in his own time. He saw himself as a lone voice of renewal in a wilderness of error and unbelief. In his own time and for more than a century afterward, his teachings were mostly refuted, and his movement was generally considered as heretical and schismatic. Elsewhere, at the same time, other Muslim thinkers were working, as another historian of this period, Ahmad Dallal, has put it, with "an originality and radicalism...that was hardly equalled in any other period." Indeed, the eighteenth century has been called "one of the most lively and creative periods" in Islamic intellectual history, one whose "erudition and depth" was unparalleled in the reformist and revivalist thinking of the late nineteenth and early twentieth centuries. Its ideas, and their diversity, show the extent to which Muslim intellectual culture was in fact still full of energy, and capable of its own regeneration.[3]

◇◇◇◇◇◇◇

The seventeenth-century Ottoman Empire, once thought to have slipped into intellectual decline and religious zealotry, saw philosophical and rationalist as well as spiritual revivals. There were, indeed, ecstatic religious movements, especially the widespread excitement caused by a Jewish mystic from Izmir, Sabbatai Zvi, who in 1665 went to Gaza, in Palestine, and proclaimed himself to be the messiah, and puritanical ones, most notably the Kadizadelis, followers of a Turkish preacher, Mehmed Kadizade. They pursued a noisy campaign of morality policing: denouncing music, dancing and drink; demanding the conversion of non-Muslims to Islam; attacking Sufis; and "putting women in their place." But for all the noise they made, the Kadizadelis were a minority, and quieter, deeper currents of reformist thinking also existed that had perhaps greater significance. Thinkers whose influence extended from Morocco to Sulawesi argued with each other over the inheritance of Ibn Arabi and the necessity of rational proofs for faith. They shared a common culture of emphasising the need for "verification" of the truth.[4]

"Verification," in Arabic *tahqiq*, can also mean "making real" or "actualisation": this could be pursued through the deep reading of texts, the application of formal logic, or the mystical experience of "witnessing" God's truth. All three modes of engaging with the Islamic tradition flourished in the seventeenth century, through both textual scholarship and Sufi spiritual experience. Critical textual study was reinvigorated in this period in the Ottoman lands by traditions of learning that were brought westward by Kurdish and Persian scholars, and eastward by North African ones. Sufi thought and practice, at the same time, showed a renewed interest in Ibn Arabi, and especially in the idea of *wahdat al-wujud* (the unity of being, or "monism") that his disciples had derived from his work. This was sometimes understood to imply that there was no difference between God and His Creation, since God was to be found in everything, and this idea had long been denounced as heretical. (It was, for example, on these grounds that Hamzah Fansuri's poetry had been burned and his followers executed at Aceh in 1637.) Even Ibn Arabi's defenders were wary of it. But in the seventeenth century, it was also openly adopted by Sufis who, far from advocating spiritual experience over the observance of sharia, were also experts in the study of the Qur'an and hadith, theology and the law, and who served as leading religious scholars in Syria and the Hijaz.[5]

The significance of this intellectual preoccupation with fully "realising" Islam reached beyond elite circles. Indeed, one of the defining features of eighteenth-century Islamic thought was its encouragement, as Ahmad Dallal has pointed out, of "the active participation of all Muslims in the definition of Islam." Influential scholars insisted that, rather than it being enough to observe the basics of correct ritual practice, ordinary Muslims must rationally understand what they believed. In some cases, as in the desert trade town of Sijilmasa in southern Morocco in the 1660s, local followers of such doctrines took them to extremes, saying—to the exasperation of the scholars—that anyone unable to answer abstruse theological questions was in fact an unbeliever. Such misunderstandings among "the commoners" only emphasised the need for clear, accessible explanations of the faith aimed at ordinary people. North African scholars disseminated the work of the fifteenth-century theologian Muhammad al-Sanusi, from Tlemcen in today's western Algeria, who wrote such popular creeds. These circulated widely across Muslim Africa and beyond: they were translated not only into North and West African languages (Tamazight and Fulfulde) and Turkish, but also into Malay and Javanese.[6]

Individual believers were thus called upon to know and interpret the truths of religion for themselves. At the same time, reformers sought to unite the community by transcending the divisions that had grown up between schools of law in which, sometimes, jurists in one school would consider those of another legal tradition as being outside the faith entirely. They equally had to transcend the divisions between the many different Sufi fraternities, whose shaykhs sometimes claimed a monopoly of truth for themselves, promising immunity from hellfire to their followers, and to their followers alone. The participatory impulse of these times was thus a reaction against the hierarchies of knowledge that had tended, since the medieval period, to invest both scholars of the law and charismatic saints with particular authority. Both scholars and saints (and often the same man—less often the same woman— was both saint and scholar) had thus become intermediary authorities between God and His believers; not only puritans like the Kadizadelis but also more moderate reformers thought this was a problem.

At the same time, reformers were not about to give up their own authority, or say that just anyone could define Islam however they liked. (The trouble caused at Sijilmasa by overzealous Bedouin who went about accusing others of unbelief was just one example of why this would be a bad idea.) And the main way that ordinary people participated in Islam, experienced its realisation in their own lives, and gained learning in it was through the presence and the practices of Sufism. Reformers, in the seventeenth and eighteenth centuries and also later, disliked the idea of disciples giving blind allegiance to supposedly infallible Sufi masters. They were suspicious that shaykhs could be seen as granting blessings to their followers themselves rather than simply seeking such blessings for them from God, and they sometimes protested about claims to miracle-working and predicting the future. They vigorously objected whenever they thought that venerated teachers and spiritual guides were themselves being revered, thus taking the place of God as the sole object of worship. But for most of them—Ibn Abd al-Wahhab would be the exception—Sufism itself was perfectly legitimate. Many reformers were themselves active and learned Sufis.[7]

Sufism itself, like the world of which it was part, was becoming both more diversified and more connected. Medieval Sufism (like the Christian monasticism that was widespread in the late ancient Middle East) may have had its origins in renunciation of the world, voluntary poverty and withdrawal, but Sufism now was often about social engagement, preaching and improvement. Saintliness did not just mean venerating the pious dead of ages past but was an active presence in Muslims' lives and an active agent in the ongoing spread of Islam. In the eighteenth century, widely dispersed Sufi teachers and disciples who had carried Islam into local communities, and whose shrines had become the centres of popular devotion, became increasingly integrated into networks. Organised around affiliation to the major *tariqa*s, the "paths," "ways," or fraternities that passed down the teaching of saintly founders, Sufi students would travel far and wide to gain initiation, sometimes into several different tariqas, before becoming recognised as a shaykh and settling in their own centres to dispense teaching and blessing in their turn. Sometimes, such shaykhs, as masters of their own disciples, could create a new offshoot of an existing tariqa, which might then have its own disciples and its own new centres of learning. From North and West Africa to Afghanistan, India, and Java, the everyday presence of Islam for ordinary Muslims was, more often than not, rooted in the local landscape and in local society by the presence of such teachers and students gathered around saints' tombs.

The localised spiritual authority and prestige of individual learned and saintly families, in sometimes very small rural centres, could thus be enhanced by their connection to larger social networks and spiritual lineages, and to more distant, historic centres of learning and spiritual power. Cities like Fez, Damascus, Baghdad, and Bukhara, where famous saints were buried and where their tombs were focal points of pilgrimage, were meeting places for disciples from across the world. In this way, for example, the apparently remote Sufi centre of al-Hamil, at the southern edge of the Atlas Mountains that divide the steppe grasslands from the northern Sahara in today's Algeria, became a major centre of the Rahmaniyya tariqa. The Rahmaniyya way, founded in Algiers in the 1700s, was an offshoot of the older Khalwatiyya tariqa, a popular fraternity that had originated in western Iran and Anatolia in the fourteenth century. By linking their local leadership with such larger networks, the Qasimi family, custodians of the shrine at al-Hamil, were able to mobilise the support and prestige that enabled them to resist the incursions of French colonial authorities in the mid-1800s. Similarly, by the beginning of the nineteenth century, saints' tombs could be found strung out along the roads crossing the Kyzylkum Desert in central Asia, and their authority was invoked from Tibet, through East Turkestan (now Xinjiang in western China), to southern Siberia.[8]

◇◇◇◇◇◇◇

The effects of globally networked Sufism spread far and wide, from the Atlantic to the Indian Ocean, but it was especially important and dynamic in northwest Africa. Both reforming and revolutionary Islamic movements spread through thousands of miles of territory, across the vast area that today stretches from Morocco and Libya to the Gambia and northern Cameroon. North African Islamic revivalism in the 1700s, expressed through Sufism and oriented to individual "verification" of the experience of God and living in accordance with His will, also had major social and political legacies. New fraternities like the Rahmaniyya were being founded here with a new energy in the eighteenth century by a new generation of teachers. Two of the most influential such teachers were Sidi Ahmad al-Tijani, founder of the Tijaniyya fraternity that would become one of the largest in Africa, and Sidi Muhammad Ibn Ali al-Sanusi, founder of the Sanusiyya order and one of the eighteenth century's most important Islamic thinkers.

Like many other figures in Islamic history, Ahmad al-Tijani came, not from a major courtly city, but from an out-of-the-way place, the fortified little oasis town of Ain Madhi on the northern edge of the Algerian Sahara, where he was born in 1737. He travelled and studied across North Africa, and in Cairo, Medina and Mecca, becoming initiated into several different Sufi ways, including the Khalwatiyya. For al-Tijani, like other reformers of his time and like Sufis down the ages, "verification" was essential. Sufism was the "way of verification" of Muslim belief, the path to both outward and inward conformity to the will of God that alone could allow the full "realisation of the human condition." In 1782, back in North Africa and on retreat in the desert, "when he had fled from contact with people, . . . not yet daring to claim shaykhship," according to the account left by his closest disciple, he is said to have experienced, while fully awake, a direct encounter with the Prophet Muhammad. The Prophet told Sidi Ahmad to leave the other ways that he had already learned, and instructed him in the special litany that he was himself now to transmit to others. The Tijaniyya path, its founder believed, was singled out as the "seal" of sainthood, the consummation of all the different Sufi ways that had preceded it, and the one "verified" way, stemming directly from the Prophet himself, that transcended and surpassed all others. Sidi Ahmad settled in Fez, where he was received with honour by the Moroccan sultan and where he died in 1815.[9]

Spreading first across Morocco and into today's Mauritania, Mali, Senegal and Nigeria, al-Tijani's teachings reached the Americas, Malaysia and Indonesia in the 1900s. In mid-nineteenth-century West Africa, the Tijaniyya became a force, not only for religious revival but for armed jihad and state-building, under the leadership of al-Hajj Umar Tall. Born in 1796, al-Hajj Umar mobilised his Tijani followers in campaigns against non-Muslim states on the middle Niger, and then against rival Muslim rulers, from 1852 until his death twelve years later. For him, Tijani discipleship was both a learned, mystical calling, and a means of creating a disciplined and motivated community of his own for the purposes of waging war in a world where true belief had to be imposed by force against ignorance and injustice.

He was not above working with unbelievers where necessary—ironically, whereas his predecessor Nasir al-Din in the 1670s had been defeated in part by European-supplied weapons, al-Hajj Umar's forces were equipped with French and British artillery and ammunition—or fighting a long and ruinous campaign against other Muslims when he thought them guilty of deviation. At the same time, he preached avoidance of "friendship" with nonbelievers (especially Europeans) and promoted emigration from areas under non-Muslim rule, especially the parts of western Senegal that were already under French colonial control. Sidi Ahmad's legacy, like so much else in Islam's history, was very different in different places. By the mid-twentieth century, the Tijaniyya would be seen as having survived and spread by accommodation and adaptation, preaching obedience to established political rulers, whoever they were. Especially in Algeria and Morocco, this meant working with rather than against French colonial authorities. But in West Africa, they would be remembered as having opposed ignorance and paganism, and as having spearheaded resistance to European imperialism.[10]

A similar set of preoccupations marked the teaching and legacy of Muhammad Ibn Ali al-Sanusi. He was born fifty years after al-Tijani, in 1787, and a few hundred miles to the northwest, on the Mediterranean coast in Mostaghanem, a provincial port town of Ottoman Algeria. He travelled on pilgrimage to Mecca, where in 1838 he founded his own Sufi centre, but local opposition forced him to leave. Eventually, only three years before his death in 1859, he settled in an oasis in the far southeast of today's Libya, seeking to avoid worldly authority and to propagate Islam by building a truly Muslim community on the Saharan frontiers of the faith. The order named after him, the Sanusiyya, spread on the routes of desert trade across a great swath of the central Sahara, the territories of today's Libya, Chad, and Niger.

For al-Sanusi, observance of the law was absolutely central, but he sought, as some anti-Sufi reformers also would, to "return" from the authority of the legal schools to direct knowledge of the Qur'an and the example of the Prophet. At the same time, he said, denying that "the friends of God," or saints, had supernatural abilities (which saints claimed to have been given by the Prophet) was tantamount to denying the powers of the Prophet himself. "Ignorance," he wrote, "is better than a rationality which denies the traits that belong to the friends of God." Al-Sanusi wrote an encyclopaedic compendium of forty different Sufi litanies, all of which, he said—in a claim to unifying different traditions that echoed al-Tijani—were fulfilled by his own way. His way, above all, stressed the importance of mercy, an inclusive conception of the law against the "zealotry" shown by partisans of one school over another, and an insistence on individual responsibility and rationally following (not merely blindly "imitating") the community's best-informed guides, both friends of God and scholars of hadith. While the "zealotry" of the masses, he wrote, was in following fallible men, that of the Sufis was their "scorn for the law," and that of the scholars their "claim of monopoly over the truth." All such zealotries must be resisted, he taught. Above all, Muslims must be extremely cautious in their accusations of unbelief against other Muslims. Against those who threw around judgments of *takfir* (anathema, or labelling someone an infidel), al-Sanusi insisted that only someone who openly espoused unbelief "as his religion" in place of Islam, leaving the faith and the community entirely, could be labelled an unbeliever.[11]

Al-Sanusi himself was concerned to avoid involvement in politics—his relocation into the deep Libyan Sahara was probably intended as an escape from the Ottoman authorities—and even by his death in the mid-1800s, European imperialism was still a very distant concern. His followers, though, could not avoid being dragged into the increasingly hostile world that surrounded them. As the French military encroached across the Sahel and southern Sahara in the late nineteenth century, its officers and "native affairs" experts saw the Sanusis as a fanatical sect standing in their way that would need to be eliminated. By the late 1800s, French authorities considered other Sufi movements popular among African (as opposed to Berber or Arab) ethnic groups as relatively peaceable and pliable. But their view of the Sanusis was a "black legend." By the eve of the First World War, the Sanusi movement further north was also the main force of opposition to the Italian invasion of eastern Libya, begun in 1911. In the 1920s and 1930s, under its leader Omar al-Mukhtar, it was a guerilla movement engaged in an anticolonial revolt. When the Italians were ejected from Libya after the Second World War, it was the hereditary leader of the fraternity, Idriss al-Sanusi, whom the British brought out of exile in Egypt to be the first king of a newly independent Libya. The contrast with his ancestor's attempts to escape from political entanglements was striking; it was a measure of how much the world had changed.[12]

Perhaps the best known, and most lastingly significant, of the eighteenth-century reform movements in Africa, though, was that which also gave rise to the region's most overtly revolutionary Islamic state-building movement. This was the movement begun and led by Shehu Usuman Dan Fodio (in Arabic, shaykh Uthman Ibn Fudi) in Hausaland, in today's northern Nigeria. Shehu Usuman was born in 1754. His people, the Fula or Fulbe, speakers of the Fulfulde language, had migrated from south of the River Senegal, in the ancient territory of the Mali Empire, to the eastern side of the Niger bend around the 1400s. They claimed that their real origin went back to the first Muslim conqueror in Africa, Sidi Uqba Ibn Nafi, and a Berber princess. They were mostly cattle pastoralists, but some families, like Usuman's, had become religious specialists and, over time, intellectually distinguished Muslim clerical lineages. Shehu Usuman, like other revivalists of his time, belonged to a Sufi fraternity, in his case the Qadiriyya order that traced its origin to the great medieval saint Sidi Abd al-Qadir al-Jilani of Baghdad. Usuman studied the works of Ibn Arabi and al-Ghazali and experienced mystical visions in which, he believed, he encountered both Sidi Abd al-Qadir and the Prophet himself. His own tomb would, in time, become a centre for pilgrimage. But Usuman himself never claimed to be a saint.

Following the breakup of the Songhay Empire, the Hausa-speaking region where the Dan Fodio clan settled had been divided between small city-states based on cotton textile production, artisanal crafts, and trade. As elsewhere in West Africa, rulers had adopted Islam as a form of power and prestige, calling themselves emirs or sultans, and employing Muslims literate in Arabic as advisors. But they also respected the religious practices, oriented around spirits, that continued to inform the life and worldview of most of their people. Many such spirits, and the practices associated with them (called *bori* in Hausa) had acquired Muslim names, and were considered *jinn*, the spirits spoken of in the Qur'an and recognised as causing both good and ill fortune in daily life and popular healing practices across northwest Africa.

Nonetheless, *bori* practices as well as other social and religious customs, including social mixing between men and women and the influence exercised by women at court, were increasingly criticised by scholars like Usuman. He objected, not only to those who called themselves Muslims paying respect to "magicians and soothsayers," and to general "moral laxity," but to the kinds of social injustice and oppression specifically condemned in the Qur'an, and which he now saw in his own society: men taking more than the four wives allowed by law and treating them unequally, the strong taking the rightful inheritance of the weak, traders in the marketplace taking more than a fair price for fair measure. To Usuman, it seemed that such social ills were the result of non-Muslim rule, rather than of individual unbelief. He himself taught members of the royal family of Gobir, where he lived, and exhorted the local sultan to mend his ways. But in 1804, after a confrontation in which some of Usuman's followers were captured and enslaved by his opponents at court, he moved away, founded a new and purely Muslim community, and declared war on unbelief. To create a righteous society, he thought, Muslims must take power.[13]

In this, as in his condemnations of society's "ignorance" of God's way, Usuman was consciously re-enacting the Prophet's own career. He was called the *mujaddid*, the "renewer" of the faith. He saw his work, not as converting unbelievers, but as bringing those who already claimed to be Muslims to the truth of the faith. For him, such a renewal was the re-actualisation in his own time and place of the founding dynamic of Islam. His removal from the jurisdiction of an "unbelieving" ruler was a hijra like the Prophet's from Mecca; his jihad followed shortly after his emigration, "keeping the pattern" that the Prophet first established.

Having fought and defeated the larger Gobir army in 1804, Usuman's forces then moved against other rulers, capturing the regional centres of Kano and Katsina in 1807 and establishing a new capital of their own, Sokoto, in 1809. When Shehu Usuman died in 1817, his son and lieutenant Muhammad Bello succeeded him, taking the title of *khalifa*. Sokoto became a caliphate, ruling over a confederation of subordinate Muslim states and waging war not only against non-Muslim African communities but against the neighbouring Muslim state of Borno. (Borno's own Muslim scholars refuted the legitimacy of Sokoto's jihad, claiming that it furthered Fula, not Muslim, rule, and had no business taking up the sword against other Muslims, sinful though they might be.)

In seeking to re-create the idealised Muslim community of the Prophet in his own time and place, Shehu Usuman at first drew followers from among escaped slaves who had fled non-Muslim masters: becoming Muslim in a Muslim settlement, they also became free. But Usuman's jihad, especially as it expanded beyond its first conquests, fit into an existing pattern of West African warfare and state-building.

Prisoners of war were enslaved, and as the war expanded, non-Muslims who resisted the Fula conquest either became slaves or, where they kept their independence, exchanged slaves with the caliphate or sent them as tribute to it. As the Atlantic slave trade left West Africa in the early 1800s, moving southward to the routes that linked Angola and Mozambique with Cuba and Brazil, slavery expanded within the region. The agricultural production that supported aristocratic elites and rulers—and Muslim scholarly families—had long relied on servile labour. Now, the cotton textile industries of Kano and Sokoto were fed by plantations worked by slaves, who in many parts of the caliphate's territories constituted as much as half of the total population.

The sharp differentiations in social status, between Muslim and non-Muslim, slave, dependent, and free, and the legacies of Shehu Usuman, as a moralising social reformer against injustice and as a zealous holy warrior against unbelief, would all remain significant in the Sahel, and especially in what would become northern Nigeria, down to the present. His movement would have other consequences too. Literacy in vernacular languages, Hausa and Fulfulde, had been the preserve of a small number of scholarly families who also read Arabic, but literacy would be spread by the poetry and the teachings of Shehu Usuman and his followers, and especially through the work of his daughter, Nana Asma'u.

Asma'u was highly educated, herself a Qadiriyya Sufi adept, and a major supporter of her father and brothers in the course of their jihad and state-building. She was also a poet and a promoter of Islamic revival in her own right. Her verses celebrated the example of Sufi women down the ages, urged obedience even to unjust rulers while exhorting rulers to be just, expressed anguish at her own faults and her yearning for grace, related the story of her father's life, called down destruction on the caliphate's enemies, and lamented the deaths of friends and relatives. Her network of *yan taru*, "associates" sent as missionaries to further religious instruction among rural women, sought to replace *bori* practices common among women with reformed Muslim practice, good works, and personal virtue. It became a major conduit for Muslim women's education and has resurfaced as a model for Muslim women organisers today, both in West Africa and among African American communities in the United States.[14]

◇◇◇◇◇◇◇

If Muslim thinkers and teachers were especially concerned with re-uniting the community of faith across its legal and spiritual divisions, this was partly because they were increasingly concerned about the political state of the world in which they lived. The fragmentation of Muslim sovereignty was nothing new: it had begun within a century of the caliphate itself being established. Criticism of rulers and how they ruled was also as old as the first caliphs. Across the three great empires that had dominated the Muslim world in the wake of the Mongols, though, the 1700s marked a time of trouble and transition as momentous as that from which those empires had emerged, five hundred years earlier.

In Iran and India, the first years of the eighteenth century saw political turmoil at the centres of the Safavid and Mughal Empires. In Iran, a series of young and inexperienced shahs proved unable to assert themselves. Religious scholars with their own agenda to create an exclusively Shiʻi society became influential at court, alienating Sunni Muslims as well as Jews and Christians, and provoking opposition on the edges of the Safavids' territories, in Sunni-majority Afghanistan to the east as well as in Christian Georgia and the northwest. Iranian territory in the west was occupied by Russian and Ottoman troops, but it was an Afghan revolt that precipitated the fall of the Safavid dynasty.

In 1721, Mahmud Ghilzai, an Afghan prince from an already independent ruling family in Qandahar, marched with a small army on Isfahan, put a much larger Safavid force to flight, and besieged the imperial capital. The siege lasted seven months and brought plague and famine to the city before, in October 1722, the last Safavid shah abdicated in favour of the invader. Mahmud faced revolts elsewhere in the country and was killed in a coup d'état organised within his own family three years later. His successor, too, was assassinated in 1730, after a civil war that saw the murder of almost all of the notables of

Isfahan, turning the formerly glittering and sociable Safavid capital into a "dead and devastated city."[15]

The victor in this first war of succession after the Safavids was Nadir Shah Afshah, a Turkish-speaking Sunni Muslim, albeit from a Qizilbash tribal background, who saw himself as a new conquering Temür. He had risen to prominence as an army commander who ostensibly supported the restoration of the Safavids against the Afghan invaders. But in 1736 he had himself declared shah instead. He pushed the Ottomans out of western Iran, besieged Ottoman Baghdad, took Bukhara from the Uzbeks, and reconquered Kabul, Qandahar, and Peshawar from the Afghans. In 1739, like Temür, he marched on Delhi. And like Temür, he sacked it, massacred its inhabitants, plundered its riches, and went home, leaving the Muslim state that had ruled there as a tattered remnant of its former self.

Nadir's grandiose conquests culminated in the subjugation of Transoxania, but far from re-establishing a Persian empire across Iran and central Asia, he too faced constant revolts. The new Temür became less capable and more paranoid. In 1747, he ordered that a group of his own commanders, whom he distrusted, should be killed: instead, they murdered him. Control over his territories fragmented. One of Nadir's generals, Ahmad Khan Dorrani, established a new dynasty in Afghanistan that would rule there until 1928. But Iran was fought over until 1796, when Aqa Muhammad Khan, the leader of the Qajar clan and himself a victim of the civil wars—as a six-year-old child, he had been castrated while imprisoned by a rival family—won out. Aqa Muhammad had himself crowned in Tehran, which he made his capital. He too was murdered, in 1797, but he was succeeded by his nephew, Fath Ali Shah, who reigned for the next thirty-four years. His dynasty, the Qajars, would endure until 1925.

Nadir Shah had briefly tried to turn Iran back towards Sunni Islam, by having Shiʻi jurisprudence recognised as a fifth school of law alongside the Sunni ones. This was unsuccessful. But over the course of the eighteenth century, while the empire was fought over by competing claimants to worldly power, and its cities, from Tiflis to Isfahan, were ransacked, other new forms of religious power developed. One was the popularisation of *ta'ziyeh*, the "passion play" cycle remembering and mourning the martyrdom of the imam Husayn at Karbala. This became a centrepiece of popular religious devotion and of distinctively Iranian Shi'i culture. *Ta'ziyeh* was staged during the first days of the month of Muharram (the first month of the Islamic calendar year). The story cycle culminated in the re-enactment of the Battle of Karbala on Ashura, the tenth day of Muharram: the killing of Husayn by the tyrant Yazid, and the subsequent heroic sufferings of Husayn's sister, Sayyida ("Lady") Zaynab. Ashura was also marked by popular processions, in which the faithful would beat their breasts and cut themselves to shed blood in visually dramatic (but not dangerous) symbolic identification with the suffering of the martyrs. *Ta'ziyeh* dramatized the early history of Islam as a potent ethical narrative for the present. Alongside such public mourning, it brought the people out onto the streets in a powerful demonstration of community belonging.

Shi'i scholars were suspicious of such popular religious culture, which escaped their control. But they were also busy with power struggles of their own. The original Safavid movement had fused messianic religious promise with empire-building ambition. Inevitably, once a state was established and the end of time did not come, the messianism had to be toned down. But the Safavid shahs had still claimed descent from Ali and the Shi'i imams, and the religious status that went with it. By the late 1700s, Shi'i religious scholars and ordinary believers alike had adapted to a new situation. Following the civil wars, not only was there no dynasty with a monopoly of religious authority, there was not much of a stable functioning state at all. The Qajars, whose genealogy stemmed from Turkmen tribal origins, had no religious legitimacy to claim: they revived the ancient Iranian title of *shahanshah*, (king of kings), as well as the Mongol *khakhan* (khan of khans). But they needed the support of the scholars if their rule was to be accepted as legitimate, and to last.

A new relationship was thus worked out between the king and the clerics, in which the religious establishment gained considerable independence in exchange for its support of the new regime. At the same time, another development within Shi'i thought, which in some respects echoed reformist trends among Sunnis, gave the scholars greater individual authority and greater scope to exercise it. The dominant, more conservative school of thought among Shi'i clerics had held that, in the absence of the hidden Twelfth Imam, legal rulings should rely on tradition—the sayings and doings of the Prophet (*hadith*, just as the Sunni scholars argued), and of the medieval Shi'i imams. A more flexible view now developed, according to which it was permissible, indeed necessary, for properly qualified scholars to exercise their own independent judgment to reach rulings on matters related to their own times. As long as their reasoning was justified by knowledge of the sources of the law, the opinions of living jurists should be preferred to those of dead ones, however distinguished they had been.

This second, less tradition-bound school held that rulings by such qualified interpreters (*mujtahids*) could then be followed, or emulated, by other scholars and ordinary people. A scholar of particularly great authority would be recognised as *marja-e taqlid*, a "source of emulation" whose rulings would be definitive in his own generation. This second school won the argument, and from the late eighteenth century onward, it became dominant among Iranian Shi'i clerics and in their seminaries at Najaf and Karbala in southern Iraq. (Although they lay in Ottoman territory, these were the cities where devotion to the cause of Ali and his family had begun, and they were still centres of Shi'i scholarship.) Both the scholars' spiritual authority, and their capacity for practical innovation and activism in contemporary political and social life, were greatly expanded. Together with their increased independence from the state, this would prove tremendously significant for the later course of Iranian history.[16]

◇◇◇◇◇◇◇

Mughal India, too, was wracked by succession crisis in the early 1700s—though the problem was that rulers were too old, not too young, to rule effectively. Aurangzeb, who had extended Mughal power to its greatest territorial extent, was ninety years old when he died in 1707, and his successor came to the throne aged sixty-five. Mughal succession had always been fought over, in Mongol dynastic style, but now a rapid turnover of struggles involving strongman courtiers and short-lived claimants to the throne turned the succession into a crisis of the empire itself. Mughal power had always worked by binding local princes into an overarching imperial sovereignty, but provincial rulers and governors now looked to their own security and turned both their attention and their provinces' tax revenues away from their increasingly nominal overlords. The imperial centre had already faced increasing breakaway pressures from Sikhs in the northwest and Marathas to the south. Now these pressures combined with the instability of the court itself to fragment the Mughal Empire into a jostling set of successor states.

The Sikhs had emerged as a distinct faith community among the commercial and small landowning middle classes in the sixteenth-century Punjab. They borrowed from both Islamic and Hindu traditions while rejecting both Muslim rule and caste distinctions as oppressive. Their leaders, the divine gurus who began as disciples of the faith's founder, Guru Nanak, came to be seen as threats to the emperors: in 1605 and again in 1675, gurus were executed. Sikhs increasingly armed themselves in opposition to the Mughal dynasty, and by the late 1600s they constituted a "state within a state" in Punjab, the empire's wealthiest province.

The Marathas emerged as a cross-caste coalition and a political force in the seventeenth century. Their social base was among lower-caste peasants and artisans who, for part of the year, hired themselves out as soldiers to local rulers, who might be aligned with or opposed to the Mughals in the turbulent politics of west-central India. Under their military leader, a self-reinventing and charismatic organiser named Shivaji, the Marathas established themselves in the mountainous area around Bombay (Mumbai). Twice, in 1664 and 1679, Shivaji occupied Surat, the Mughals' crucial trading port on the Arabian Sea, and from the 1670s onward, he and his heirs claimed an empire of their own. Aurangzeb spent the last twenty years of his reign constantly campaigning against them.[17]

Aurangzeb's successors already ruled over a much reduced and divided empire when Nadir Shah sacked Delhi in 1739. Mughal sovereignty still existed—it would endure, at least formally, down to 1857—but real power lay elsewhere. The Mughals' opulent style was adopted by regional rulers who had done well out of the Mughal system and now became independent princes. Tax collectors kept cash flowing to them. Banking families supplied both rulers and revenue collectors with credit against anticipated tax returns in an increasingly monetized and, in some areas, expanding economy. Cash crops like salt, indigo, and opium became state monopolies, traded abroad for the rulers' profit. Landholders now looked to secure their own interests rather than seek favour from distant suzerains, and sought to maximise their own income from the peasantry. Military contractors hired out mercenary soldiers to support ambitious rulers' expansion, or to defend them from their rivals.

It was in this competition over regional politics, tax revenue, and economic opportunity that French and British chartered trading companies and their mercenaries became players. India had long been part of a transcontinental trading system, but now it was also part of an emerging global division of power dominated by emerging European empires. French and British traders had established commercial footholds on the Indian coasts in the 1600s. In the eighteenth century, their respective states fought a series of global wars for predominance. The Seven Years' War (1756–63) was centred on Europe and North America but was also fought in West Africa, Southeast Asia, and India.

In 1757, thanks to a secret agreement with their Muslim Indian allies who defected from the other side, the British East India Company's army defeated the ruler of Bengal, Siraj al-Dawla, and his French allies at Palashi (which the British called Plassey). Eight years later, the company gained a formal grant from the Mughal emperor to collect taxes and administer the law in Bengal. In 1789, the French Revolution began, and Britain's rivalry with France in India became a counterrevolutionary war as well as an imperial one. In 1799, alleging a dangerous alliance between the revolutionary French and Tipu Sultan, the Muslim ruler of Mysore in south India, the British, allied with the Marathas and the Muslim ruler of Hyderabad, besieged Tipu's capital at Sriran-gapatna (Seringapatam), and killed him. A full-fledged colonial state would not emerge until the 1820s and 1830s. But by insinuating them-selves into the late Mughal struggle for succession, the British had be-gun to gain their own territorial, as well as commercial, empire across India. The Dutch, as we have seen, had already begun to be military as well as commercial players in Southeast Asia. A new European imperi-alism had begun to encroach on the old Muslim empires.[18]

But the problems preoccupying Muslim reformers did not yet in-clude, let alone centre on, Europe. The foremost revivalist thinker in India at this time, indeed, was much more concerned with his own community. Shah Wali Allah al-Dihlawi was born in 1703 and died in 1762, five years after Palashi, aged only fifty-nine. Growing up in a scholarly family, he attended a school founded and run by his father and was inducted into several Sufi orders, including both the Chish-tiyya and the Qadiriyya. He made the pilgrimage to Mecca in 1730, staying and studying in the Hijaz for two years. He was thirty-six, and already engaged in a career of teaching, reflection, and writing, when Nadir Shah sacked his city nine years later.

Both his participation in larger networks of revivalism, via his stud-ies in Arabia and his Sufi affiliations, and the instability that he saw around him in late Mughal India gave him a sense of the necessity and urgency of religious reform. Rather than building a new Sufi fraternity, or seizing power to create a revived Muslim state, though, Wali Allah focused on the principles that, he thought, could revitalise the living presence of the Islamic tradition. By both renewing knowl-edge and observance of the law and enabling a deeper realisation of Islam in the lives of believers, he sought to reunite the community and strengthen it against adversity. Shah Wali Allah felt—as later gen-erations of Muslims would more acutely feel—that the problems his community faced were fundamentally caused by its own disunity.

Much of Wali Allah's work was preoccupied with reconciliation—with allowing for legitimate differences of opinion between dif-ferent schools of law and Sufi orders while seeking to overcome the divergences and disputes that, in the hands of overly zealous and partisan scholars down the ages, such differences had created. Public ills and political turbulence might be the result of deficiency in the "outward caliphate" of the political realm, but the remedy for them was not to be found in politics. Instead, Wali Allah looked to the "inward caliphate" of social order that ought to have been properly regulated by the 'ulama, the learned scholars of Islam and the enlightened Sufi masters, but which they had too often neglected in favour of scoring points against each other, claiming a monopoly over the truth, or engaging in unnecessarily abstruse intellectualism.

If the scholars—and, indeed, suitably educated Muslim laypeople—could correct such errors, Wali Allah thought, then Islam would be more truly understood and lived, and the divisions within the Muslim community could be healed. His work on Sufism sought to rescue core ideas like the "unity of being" from the sometimes-violent disputes in which they had become enmeshed. He stressed the necessity of interpreting the law on the basis of its original sources rather than in imitation of the traditional legal schools. In arguing for the exercise of such interpretation by a larger number of sufficiently educated laypeople, rather than just by professional jurists, he advocated what has been called "a measure of democratization of knowledge." Islam, Wali Allah reminded people, is God's way for humanity to live its fullest and truest life: not simply a set of regulations to be imposed upon people by clerics, but "the religion of nature," in accordance with humanity's true inmost nature (*fitra*). Properly knowing the law, then, meant Muslims using reason to interpret the Qur'an and the Prophet's example in order to decide "what they think is best for their well-being,... in harmony with and in the interest of their natural dispositions."[19]

Such ideas would be revived over the following centuries—even as Shah Wali Allah's own significance, the meaning of his work, his affiliations, and his views would themselves become objects of some-times bitter dispute between rival claimants to his legacy in India. The desire for reconciliation and revival would endure. But the divergences and disputes would not go away.

◇◇◇◇◇◇◇◇

The story of the Ottoman Empire after its sixteenth-century apogee has often been told as one of inevitable decline and disintegration. But unlike the Safavids and the Mughals, the Ottomans did not lose their empire in the eighteenth century: they would hold onto it until it was broken by nineteenth-century nationalism and the First World War. What happened after the end of the sixteenth century was a shift in the relationship between the Ottoman state and Ottoman society, a shift that changed the nature of the empire itself.

At its height in the long reign of Sulayman I, the old "patrimonial" empire had been imagined and run as a vastly extended household. Power was personalised in the sultan himself and exercised by his household slaves. But this (despite what Europeans thought) was not a static system, with obsequious courtiers revolving unthinkingly around a single centre of gravity like satellites around the sun. There were motive forces of change within the system. High-ranking bureaucrats' own households had their own interests and formed their own networks of influence. Jurists and scholars still claimed their own authority as *mevali*, "lords of the law," the interpretation of which rested with them, not the throne. Muslim-born commoners, whose wealth and social status were rising, increasingly demanded inclusion in a hierarchy that, as we have seen, placed elite slaves over freeborn subjects. Leading families, the so-called notables of provincial cities, and military entrepreneurs in rural areas that the central state could not effectively police all carved out their own local portions of sovereignty as intermediaries between Istanbul and its distant dependencies.

Europeans theorised about the despotic absolutism of the sultan—a useful tool, in Enlightenment Europe, for criticising their own absolute monarchs, with their expensive armies and the expanding tax burdens and credit flows needed to fund them. But Ottoman government was limited, both in practice, by the enormous and fragmented territory of the empire, its long distances and often mountainous terrain, and in principle. Even the mighty Sulayman "the Lawgiver," as we have seen, occasionally had to admit that he "stood in awe" of the rule of the sharia. After Sulayman's time, the multiple centres of power in the Ottoman state and society grew stronger. An understanding emerged of the "state" itself—in Turkish, *devlet*—as an institution, rather than as the personal "fortune" (also *devlet*) and ruling power embodied in the person of the sultan.

In 1622, jurists and janissaries combined to overthrow and kill Sultan Osman II, the first time Ottoman subjects had shown such assertiveness against the throne. In 1703, another uprising in Istanbul put an end to attempts to reassert the sultan's unchallenged primacy. A modus vivendi was worked out between the dynasty and the larger social and institutional forces with which it was obliged to negotiate its rule. Some European observers of the empire in the eighteenth century, like the Italian scholar and Habsburg statesman Count Luigi Marsigli or the British diplomat Sir James Porter, began to characterise the Ottomans as exercising "a species of limited monarchy." Its subjects' liberties, they thought, were in fact relatively extensive in comparison with those of European sovereigns.[20]

In geopolitical and military terms, however, the Ottomans faced a series of setbacks against those European sovereigns and their new, drill-disciplined and expensively equipped armies. A second, abortive siege of Vienna in 1683 began a territorial rollback in southeast Europe, and the end of the pretensions to universal rule that had been the dynasty's early boast and sixteenth-century expectation. Thereafter, like their European neighbours, the Ottomans were one dynastic state among others. For a century after 1750, they were constantly on the defensive, especially against Russia, and then against nascent nationalisms among their mostly Christian subjects in Romania, Bulgaria, Greece, and the Balkans. By the 1830s, they faced not only their first permanent loss of Muslim-majority territory, when the French invaded their outlying Regency of Algiers, but also a rebellious Muslim vassal threatening the dynasty itself. Mehmed Ali Pasha, the governor of Egypt, was an Ottoman success story who had begun his career as a soldier in imperial service. But having taken power in Egypt in 1811, he began building an empire of his own. From Cairo, he invaded

Palestine and Syria, threatened Istanbul, and could only be brought into line with the aid of the British.

The empire's problems really began, perhaps, in its 1768–74 war against Russia, which had a serious economic as well as territorial impact, or else in another war with Russia in 1806–12, when provincial lords' autonomy risked the integrity of the empire: in Iraq, they flatly refused the imperial centre's demands for troops and taxes. But foreign wars did not become a really severe crisis, deeply affecting the internal sovereignty of the empire and the nature of its regime, until the Greek war of independence in 1820–21. This, as we shall see, would signal a reassertion of centralised power, the curbing of autonomous groups like the janissaries and provincial notables, and the beginning of a new, more bureaucratic and top-down attempt to increase the capacities of the state to mobilise its people and defend itself. Before that point, reforming the state had instead meant expanding what Europeans would call the "political nation," those capable of participation in the affairs of governance.

The fullest expression of this was the *Sened-i Ittifak*, the "Deed of Agreement," signed at Edirne in 1808 between the new sultan, Mahmud II, and a coalition of Balkan, Anatolian and Istanbul power brokers led by the grand vizier, Alemdar Mustafa Pasha. The Deed sought to put the government of the empire on a firmer footing, ensuring both the provincial lords' solidarity with the sultan, and the sultan's respect of his subordinates, who for the first time were now to be partners in rule, not simply the sovereign's "slaves." The agreement asserted the necessity of "the union and mutual agreement of all and...their joint guarantee and pledge for each other," binding the sultan into a contractual government with the notables.

This constitutional monarchy was never implemented. Within months, Alemdar Mustafa was killed in a janissary revolt, his coalition was ejected from power, and the sultanate took a different, more autocratic tack. But the story of Ottoman state and society in the long eighteenth century is one, not of despotism in decline, but of an opening of the formal political realm to diverse constituencies well beyond the palace walls: artisans' guilds and soldiers, religious scholars and

1. The Dome of the Rock in east Jerusalem, viewed from the Mount of Olives. Built in the 690s CE within the *haram al-sharif*—the "noble sanctuary" that also includes the Al-Aqsa Mosque—it proclaimed the Caliph Abd al-Malik's right to rule as the upholder of Islam and rooted Islam into Jerusalem's older religious histories.

3. Abd al-Malik, with sheathed sword and simple, flowing robes, depicted on a "standing caliph" coin. A gold dinar struck in Damascus between 693 and 697 CE, this is an early and unusual figural representation on Islamic coinage.

2. The interior of the Dome of the Rock: Byzantine and Persian royal motifs combine with Qur'anic inscriptions to proclaim the new dynasty and its faith as superseding the Roman and Persian Empires while also "completing" the revelations of both Judaism and Christianity.

4. Folio from an elaborately ornamented copy of the Qur'an made in eastern Iran or Afghanistan, ca. 1180. The text is from *surat al-ma'ida* ("The Table"): the end of Q 5: 20 and Q 5: 21, in which Moses instructs his people to enter the Holy Land.

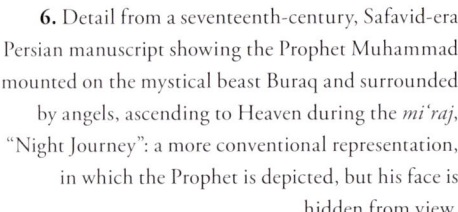

5. A fourteenth-century manuscript illustration of the investiture of Ali Ibn Abi Talib at Ghadir Khumm, according to Shi'i tradition. This is an example of Islamic devotional art in which the face of the Prophet Muhammad is depicted.

6. Detail from a seventeenth-century, Safavid-era Persian manuscript showing the Prophet Muhammad mounted on the mystical beast Buraq and surrounded by angels, ascending to Heaven during the *mi'raj*, "Night Journey": a more conventional representation, in which the Prophet is depicted, but his face is hidden from view.

7. Mecca photographed in the 1880s, showing the city in its valley, the courtyard of the Great Mosque, and the Ka'ba in the left foreground.

8, 9. In the medieval Arab Mediterranean, great mosques showcased dynastic power as well as fostering learning and piety. (*Above*) The great courtyard of al-Azhar in Cairo. Built in the tenth–eleventh centuries by the Shi'i Fatimid caliphs, it would later become a centre of Sunni scholarship. (*Below*) Interior of the great mosque *(mezquita)*, after 1236 the cathedral, of Cordoba. Built in the eighth–tenth centuries by the Umayyads in the capital of their new Andalusian caliphate, it was reckoned a wonder of the world and was largely preserved despite major Christianising alterations in the sixteenth century.

10, 11. From Anatolia to central Asia, distinctive architectural forms expressed piety and power in the early modern Turkic and Timurid empires that succeeded the Mongol conquests. (*Above*) The monumental gate of the 15th century madrasa of Ulugh Bey, Samarqand. (*Below*) The Suleymaniyye Mosque in Istanbul, built for the Ottoman Sultan Sulayman I in the sixteenth century.

12. A Venetian portrait of Sultan Sulayman I "Qanuni" ("the Lawgiver"), known in Europe as "the Magnificent," as a young man, ca. 1520.

13. A sixteenth century Italian portrait of Hürrem Sultan, known as "Roxelana," consort and wife of Sulayman I.

14. An eighteenth-century illustration from a Persian book of poetry showing Alexander the Great conversing with the philosophers Socrates, Plato, and Aristotle. Classical Islamic cultures readily absorbed the themes, figures, and learning of Greek antiquity as part of their own inheritance . . .

15. . . . while also preserving elements of pre-Islamic Asian cultures. In this illustration from the Safavid Shah Tahmasp's 1530 copy of the *Shahnameh* of Firdawsi, the Sasanian emperor, Shah Khusraw II Parviz "the Victorious" (r. 590–628 CE), is rescued by an angel. Composed in the tenth century, the *Shahnameh* retold classical Persian tales of kings back to mythic times and would become Iran's national epic.

16. Imperial splendour: A gold coin depicting the Mughal Emperor Jahangir (r. 1605–1627), seated on a throne and holding a goblet, 1614. Medallions like this were given to courtiers to be worn as marks of particular favour.

17. Diplomatic elegance: An illuminated letter from Iskandar Muda, Sultan of Aceh in Sumatra, to King James I of England, 1615. This is the earliest known and most elaborate surviving example of such a letter in the Malay language.

18. View over the roofs of Timbuktu towards the Sankoré Mosque, sketched in the 1890s. The mosque, a celebrated example of West African Islamic architecture, has been continuously rebuilt since the eleventh century.

19. The miracle of Shaykh Amadu Bamba (ca. 1853–1927) praying at sea while being deported into exile by French colonial authorities in 1895. A scene frequently depicted with the Senegalese technique of reverse-glass painting: here, by Mor Gueye, 1998.

20–23. Resisting and reasserting empire in the nineteenth century: (*Above L*) Imam Shamil (1797–1871), Sufi and social reformer who opposed Russia's conquest of Chechnya from 1834 to 1859. (*Above R*) Prince Dipanagara (1785–1855), leader of resistance to the Dutch during the Java War, 1825–1830. (*Below L*) Emir Abd al-Qadir (1808–1883), who tried to build an independent state in opposition to the French conquest of Algeria between 1832 and 1847. (*Below R*) An Ottoman emperor in the Victorian age: Sultan Abdülhamid II (r. 1876–1909). Inheriting an empire in crisis, Abdülhamid at first issued a constitution and convened a parliament but came to rule through secret police, spies, censorship and pogroms.

24–27. Muslim modernists: (*Above L*) itinerant anti-imperialist Jamal al-Din al-Afghani (1838–1897). (*Above R*) Egyptian reformist Muhammad Abduh (1849–1905). (*Below L*) Indian educationalist Sir Sayyid Ahmad Khan (1817–1898). (*Below R*) Liberal Egyptian jurist Ali Abd al-Raziq (1888–1966).

28, 29. 1919: Confrontation and negotiation at the height of European imperialism. (*Above*) Egyptian women at a nationalist demonstration demanding an end to the British occupation, May 1919. (*Below*) Emir Faysal Ibn Husayn, leader of the Arab Revolt in WWI (*centre*), with his advisors and an attendant at the Paris Peace Conference. Third from right is Colonel T. E. Lawrence, Faysal's British liaison officer and Britain's "Lawrence of Arabia." Second from left is Nuri Said: formerly an Ottoman army officer, he joined the revolt and became a central figure in Iraqi politics, closely identified with British influence, until the monarchy's overthrow in 1958.

30–35. Alternative visions of community: nationalism or Islamism? (*Top L*) Algerian liberal Ferhat Abbas (1899–1985), who tried to achieve multiracial equality in French Algeria. (*Top R*) Shakib Arslan (1869–1946), Lebanese writer who advocated pan-Islamic unity. (*Centre L*) Muhammad Ali Jinnah (1876–1948), Indian lawyer who hoped for Hindu-Muslim unity but became the founder of a separate Pakistan. (*Centre R*) Syrian journalist Rashid Rida (1865–1935), who hoped for a restoration of the caliphate and advocated for religious revival. (*Below L*) Hassan al-Banna (1906–1949), Egyptian schoolteacher and Islamist activist, founder of the Muslim Brotherhood. (*Below R*) Abu'l-A'la Mawdudi (1903–1979), Indian journalist and Islamist ideologue who founded the Pakistani Jamaat-i Islami Party.

36, 37. Authoritarian modernisation could take republican or royalist guise. (*Left*) Mustafa Kemal Atatürk (1881–1938), architect of the post-Ottoman Turkish republic, teaching the new Latin alphabet that replaced Arabic script for writing Turkish in 1928. (*Below*) The marriage of Mohammed Reza Shah Pahlavi (1919–1980), then crown prince and the future shah of Iran (r. 1941–1979), to Princess Fawzia of Egypt in Cairo, 1939.

38. A French sailor checks a Senegalese rifleman's life jacket during an exercise on board a troopship carrying soldiers to France, 1940. The Second World War, like the First, mobilised and impacted Muslims from across European colonial empires...

39. …but also ushered in a new world, dominated by nuclear superpowers and oil states. President Franklin D. Roosevelt (right) meets with Ibn Saud, king of Saudi Arabia, on board USS *Quincy* in the Great Bitter Lake, Egypt, 14 February 1945. Roosevelt had declared in 1943 that Saudi Arabia was "vital" to American security.

40, 41. As the Cold War reshaped Great Power rivalries, decolonisation and national sovereignty were hard-fought gains in the Global South. (*Right*) Mohammed Mossadegh (1882–1967), the liberal constitutionalist prime minister of Iran, makes a speech outside parliament in Tehran, 1951. Mossadegh would be overthrown in an American- and British-backed coup in 1953. (*Below*) Soldiers of the Algerian National Liberation Army, ca. 1961. When non-violent demands for equal rights in Algeria failed, more radical revolutionaries began an armed struggle. Algeria's war of independence (1954–1962) became a centrepiece of Third Worldist aspiration.

42. Civil rights, decolonisation, and racialised politics combined with images of Islam in novel ways in the United States. Malcolm X (1925–1965), whose own faith and politics shifted from the NOI to mainstream Sunni Islam, is seen here at a halal restaurant for Black Muslims in Harlem, New York, in August 1963.

43, 44. Struggles for national sovereignty also meant civil war and the partition of homelands. (*Left*) Palestinian refugees flee from the West Bank across the demolished Allenby Bridge into Jordan during the Six Day War, June 1967. Some 750,000 Palestinians had already been made refugees in 1948, at the creation of the State of Israel. (*Below*) Refugees from Bangladesh flee across the border into India during Bangladesh's War of Independence from Pakistan, August 1971. "It was the peak of the monsoon season," photographer Raghu Rai remembered, and the family on their cart appeared "as if they had emerged from a bygone century." But their experience was repeated many times in the twentieth century.

45. Ayatollah Ruhollah Khomeini (1900–1989) giving a press conference on his return to Iran from exile in France, February 1979. Khomeini's theory of government was a radical reworking of the Shi'i tradition of clerical authority; it would sideline and repress other elements of the Iranian revolution to make a new Islamic republic.

46. Afghanistan, 1996. The Taliban, who took control of Kabul in September 1996, rose to power in a country devastated by seventeen years of war.

47. A young Syrian man films the destruction in Raqqa, northern Syria, October 2017. After three years as the capital of the self-proclaimed Islamic State's caliphate, and a four-month offensive by mainly Kurdish forces and international airpower, the city lay in ruins.

48. French Muslim women wearing headscarves and the tricolour demonstrate against the "law on ostensible religious symbols," with slogans against exclusion and for individual religious freedom, in Paris, 17 January 2004. French law on the *laïcité*, "secular status," of public space formally mandates the religious neutrality of the state and its agents, but it has increasingly been invoked to limit private citizens' wearing visibly Muslim dress in schools or on beaches.

49. Mecca in 2022: the Kaʻba within the Great Mosque. The Abraj al-Bait complex and clock tower that now dominates the skyline appear in the background. Built between 2002 and 2012, the seven towers principally house hotels and a shopping centre catering to pilgrims.

50. A child holds a lantern to welcome the beginning of Ramadan in the old city of Mosul, Iraq, 28 February 2025. In June 2014, Daesh (Islamic State) captured Mosul and proclaimed their "caliphate" there; the largely ruined city was liberated in July 2017 and a multi-billion-dollar program was launched for its reconstruction.

jurists, the notable families of provincial cities, and regional strong-men. This opening was stymied, and ultimately reversed, in the nine-teenth century by the military threats the empire faced both on its frontiers and within them.[21]

While the 1808 Deed of Agreement bore little fruit, it expressed a sentiment that would become a recurring refrain in the following de-cades. It was self-evident, the Deed began, that the empire's earlier glo-ries had all been achieved through "union, unity, and the removal of selfishness and strife" among Muslims under their legitimate ruler, the Ottoman sultan. But now, it seemed, "the passage of time has caused the elements of order to deteriorate," bringing about "weakness and dis-order in the entire Muslim community." Echoing the concerns of reli-gious reformers, the empire's statesmen sought more materially to turn "disorderliness into unity" through "the reinvigoration of the religion and the state," acting "as a single body and in union and concord."[22]

On the farthest fringes of Ottoman sovereignty, a different response to the perceived disorder of the Muslim community had emerged. Its author, though, was entirely uninterested in social and political ques-tions. He saw salvation for the community strictly in terms of right belief and the correct practice of religion. What would eventually be-come the most significant movement of revivalism to emerge from the eighteenth century began far from the imperial courts of Istanbul and Edirne, in Najd, the steppe and desert plateau region of the central Ara-bian Peninsula. It was here, in 1703, the same year that Shah Wali Al-lah was born in India, that Muhammad Ibn Abd al-Wahhab was born.

Ibn Abd al-Wahhab came from a family of judges settled in the oasis towns of Najd, and travelled for study to the Hijaz and Basra, where he began preaching, and from where he may (according to some accounts) have been expelled early in his career. Unlike most of the other revivalist thinkers of his time, he had no Sufi affiliations: indeed, any kind of respect, let alone reverence, for the mystical tradition was anathema to him. He may have been taught in Medina by teachers who had Sufi connections, and who taught other revivalists like Shah Wali Allah, but some of those teachers would later refute Ibn Abd al-Wahhab's doctrines. His own followers would claim (somewhat ironically, like some saintly figures had) that his "rediscovery" of the true faith had come to him directly by divine inspiration.

His works were mainly short, polemical tracts sent as letters to individuals or localities, and brief commentaries focused on his core argument. In sum, this was that polytheism (*shirk*), the worship of beings other than the one God, was in fact rampant among Muslims, who were therefore not truly Muslims at all. Veneration of saints at their tombs or shrines, raising mausoleums over the graves of pious ancestors, seeking intercession with God from those believed to have been His "friends," all of this was unbelief, no better than the pagan worship of stones or trees. The pre-Islamic polytheists of Mecca had been guilty of such things in the Prophet's time, and the Prophet had denounced their idols, *taghut*s, a term used in the Qur'an. Ibn Abd al-Wahhab now said that the "Friends of God" whom Muslims revered were themselves guilty of allowing themselves to become objects of worship: they too were nothing more than *taghut*s.

Ibn Abd al-Wahhab, like Usuman Dan Fodio in West Africa, saw himself as renewing the Prophet's mission in his own time. But Shehu Usuman recognised Sufi practice as legitimate Islamic piety (his daughter Nana Asma'u explicitly allowed the popular use of talismans and amulets, so long as they were disassociated from un-Islamic spirit beliefs) and opposed what he considered unjust rule, seeking to establish his just society by political means. Ibn Abd al-Wahhab was very different on both counts. For him, following what had often been the position of conflict-averse Sunni scholars, an unjust ruler was to be gently advised to change his ways, but should be obeyed however unjust he might remain. More serious than "the oppression of wealth" (socio-economic or political injustice) was "the oppression of polytheism" that removed believers from truly professing the oneness of God (*tawhid*). Only by such profession, as Ibn Abd al-Wahhab understood it, could one be truly Muslim: and such profession also mandated avoidance of and enmity towards anyone who failed to follow. Ibn Abd al-Wahhab's detractors recognised the radical implications of his extreme position, which was, as one wrote, tantamount to declaring "that Muslims have ceased to be Muslims for six hundred years." His own claim to have truly understood and to be truly propounding Islam was dismissed by another of his opponents as the baseless posturing of a "pretender-prophet."[23]

In 1744 or 1745, Ibn Abd al-Wahhab settled in Diriyya, a town in Najd ruled by the Al-Saud family. The preacher and the prince made an alliance: Ibn Abd al-Wahhab's controversial teachings would be protected and promoted, if he would agree to remain in Diriyya and not settle elsewhere. At the same time, the Al-Saud began their own expansionist campaign to bring neighbouring towns under their authority. For those who became their subjects, acceptance of Wahhabi doctrine went with recognition of their political hegemony. Ibn Abd al-Wahhab justified the campaign as legitimate jihad, a holy war in the path of God. From demanding the repudiation of what he called unbelief, and his own followers' dissociation from unbelievers, he now supported armed violence against them. In what would become a recurring pattern of emirate-building in Arabia, the Al-Saud's territorial ambition combined with the Wahhabi claim to be re-enacting the Prophet's mission. In 1773, their forces conquered the rival neighbouring centre of Riyadh, which became their capital. Ibn Abd al-Wahhab himself retired into study and contemplation and died in 1787, but Saudi-Wahhabi expansion continued. In 1808, they conquered Mecca and Medina.

This, for the first time, brought Wahhabism to the full attention of the Ottoman sultan and his nominal vassal, the viceroy of Egypt, Mehmed Ali. Revolts in Istanbul and Mehmed Ali's own priorities in Cairo delayed a response, but in 1812–13, an Egyptian army under Mehmed Ali's eldest son, Tusun, ejected the Wahhabis from Medina and Mecca. Mecca's religious scholars wrote to Cairo to thank Mehmed Ali for removing the "heretic, violent, belligerent" Wahhabis from their city. In 1818, after Tusun's death in Cairo from plague, a further campaign under Tusun's brother, Ibrahim Pasha, destroyed the Saudis' central Arabian emirate. The family's leader, Abdallah Ibn Saud, was sent in chains to Istanbul, where he was executed. The

Al-Saud survived as one among several rival princely families competing for primacy in central and eastern Arabia, and Wahhabism survived too. But it would be almost a century before they found an opportunity to renew their partnership and return to power.[24]

◇◇◇◇◇◇◇◇

In some important ways, Ibn Abd al-Wahhab's zealous revivalism took an opposite tack to that of his contemporaries. They were concerned with reconciliation and unity, but he starkly divided Muslims between "true" believers and those who in truth, as he saw it, were unbelievers, exhorting his own followers to "hatred and enmity" against them. Other reformers were almost unanimous in being careful to restrict the grounds on which one could pronounce *takfir* (anathema), declaring someone to be a non-Muslim, but Ibn Abd al-Wahhab made such pronouncement the centre of his doctrine. They drew on and sought to synthesise a rich and diverse inheritance of Sufi and scholarly traditions, but he produced what has been called "a grim and narrow theory of unbelief."[25]

Ironically, Wahhabism would gain an unprecedented prominence only once these other currents of reform and revival, and other ways of responding to a changing world, were extinguished or subjugated by the sudden rise of European imperial power. Wahhabism had begun in a place, both geographical and intellectual, entirely undisturbed by Europe; the unbelief it sought to fight was within the Muslim community. It would come to be seen by some Muslims as the Muslim world's remedy against European imperialism—and, ultimately, by some Europeans and Americans as the great threat to Western civilisation. But it would largely owe its re-emergence to the new circumstances that, over the next two centuries, European imperialism and global capitalism would impose on the worlds of Islam.

Part 3

DISORDERED WORLDS
1800–1950 CE

9

THE COUNSEL OF THE SAINTS

Ahmad Ibn Tuwayr al-Janna (his name means "Ahmad, Son of the Little Bird of Paradise") came home from his pilgrimage at a bad time. He set out for Mecca in November 1829 from the caravan town of Tishit, on the western edge of the Sahara in today's Mauritania. He was away only a year, but by the time he returned to North Africa at the end of 1831, his world had changed. In Tunis, he heard news of the French conquest of the neighbouring Ottoman Regency of Algiers. His mind ran over prophecies of the Last Day, when, it was said, the Christians would capture Constantinople. The sun would reverse its course in the sky to announce the hour of repentance, and the *mahdi*, the Messiah sent by God to save humanity, would wage war on the Anti-Christ until, with the aid of Jesus, evil would be destroyed.

Driven by the winds to put in at the port of Bejaia, east of Algiers, Ahmad met a holy ascetic who recounted to him how an assembly of the saints had resolved to bring about the fall of Algiers. Its people, he said, had "oppressed and...transgressed the limits of God's law." The city's own patron saint, consulted by the Prophet, had apparently given his assent. While in Tunis, Ahmad himself had heard tell, he wrote, of terrible immoralities, such as rape and infanticide, being committed in Algiers. "Due to that," Ahmad wrote, "and other abominable acts, Algiers was taken."

When Ahmad arrived in Algiers en route to Tangier, with his numerous companions and large collection of books, the French authorities took him for a Saharan prince. He was accordingly accommodated and entertained by the usually violent-tempered and authoritarian French military governor, the Duke of Rovigo. The French were keen to learn about Ahmad's home region of Shinqit, its population, products and commerce, part of the imagined fabulous interior of an Africa whose edges they barely occupied but whose resources they already sought to acquire. Only a year earlier, in 1830, the same year that French troops had occupied Algiers, the traveller René Caillié had published his account of explorations from central Africa to Timbuktu and across the Sahara to Morocco. His journey struck Europeans as an almost unimaginably epic adventure; the fantasy of a Saharan El Dorado was in the air, and even the impatient Rovigo must have sensed a longer-term opportunity.

For Ahmad, Caillié's exotic narrative was a description of home, a region that Muslim traders and pilgrims had regularly traversed for centuries. He was very careful about what he told his hosts, massively exaggerating the size of the Mauritanian population. The cause of his lavish reception, he thought, was not simply the material interests of the French; it was "without a doubt…due to the blessing of the Messenger of God." The conquerors' friendliness to him was evidence, too, of the protection afforded by the "two or three saints" who, according to the holy man in Bejaia, had accompanied Ahmad in spirit all the way from Mecca. They would continue to watch over him until he safely reached his own country.[1]

Ahmad's written account of his experiences would lie for a hundred years in a library in the Mauritanian desert before it was published by a British scholar and made accessible to the rest of the world. It captures the calamity of European colonialism as it intruded into the Muslim-majority world. But it also illustrates the containment of European power by a world, and a worldview, in which the ultimate sovereignty of God over human affairs was unquestionable. Ahmad wove the news of dramatic current affairs into a deep, and no less dramatic, imagination of cosmic history, making sense of things through stories of human sinfulness, divine judgment, and saintly mediation. Stories like these attributed victories over Muslims to the Muslims' own unfaithfulness.

The French had invaded Algiers in June 1830, to rally domestic support for the monarchy that had been restored to power after the fall of Napoleon. Facing popular opposition and the threat of renewed revolution, King Charles X and his right-wing government hoped that attacking a Muslim enemy would win over patriotic and Catholic opinion. (They failed: the July 1830 revolution overthrew them anyway just weeks later.) They also coveted the piles of cash stored in the Casbah's treasuries. (Here, they were more successful.) For Ahmad, though, the invasion could only take place because Algiers's saints had withdrawn protection from the city's people after they themselves had deserted the saints. All was the slow working-out of God's great plan.

Over the next four decades, France's expanding war of conquest would devastate Algeria, killing perhaps one-third of the pre-conquest population in a combined maelstrom of war, famine, and disease. After the army's officers pillaged the Casbah's palaces, the country's best agricultural land was seized and parcelled out to European colonists. The saints, vivid figures in popular piety and constant companions in Ahmad's journey, would remain but give different lessons as time went on. They could be imagined as sanctioning the judgment on Ottoman injustice that permitted the Christian conquest, but also as inspiring revolt against the conquerors and promising an apocalyptic "realm of justice" on earth that would put an end to all the suffering. They might counsel acceptance, accommodation, and a path of least resistance; or they might spearhead the resistance.

A century after the conquest, in line with the rethinking of the past that occurred across the Muslim world in the late 1800s and early 1900s (and reconstructing the ideas of Muhammad Ibn Abd al-Wahhab), a new generation of Muslim scholars and community leaders would come to see things differently. They would castigate the people's attachment to saints, their shrines, their descendants, and their intercession in human affairs as irrational and irreligious superstition, itself an indicator of unfaithfulness. This, they thought, was what had allowed Muslims to become "colonisable" in the first place.[2]

∞∞∞∞∞∞

Another Ahmad, also in Algiers in the 1830s, already saw things very differently. Ahmad Bu Darba was a businessman, the son of a merchant who, like many of Algiers's commercial families, claimed Andalusian Arab ancestry. His cosmopolitan roots went back to the Muslim refugees who had been forced out of Spain in the late 1400s. They had settled in North Africa, bringing their architectural, musical, and culinary sophistication with them, and had got right back down to business, trading across the Mediterranean with the Christians who had expelled them, often with the help of Jewish intermediaries who had been expelled too. Ahmad Bu Darba had a French wife, and his son Ismail had been born in Marseille.

If for Ahmad the Mauritanian pilgrim, the French invasion stirred anxieties about the end times, for Ahmad the Algerian businessman, it was at the same time both a profound shock and a moment of opportunity. It was Bu Darba, alongside the English consul and two Ottoman officials, who went out from the besieged city of Algiers on July 4, 1830, to negotiate terms of surrender with the French generals. Like most of the city's notables, he could see that the war was lost and that resistance would be not only useless but ruinous to lives and property. And after all, he knew these people. He spoke their language. He was married to one of them. He was well placed to make a deal. Or so he thought.

Algiers's capitulation, and the evacuation of its ruler, his janissaries, and the remaining Ottoman establishment, was supposed to guarantee the lives, property, and religious freedoms of the city's inhabitants. It did not. But for a few years, while the new French regime brought in by the revolution of July 1830 debated what to do with the conquest, it seemed that there were openings for something more progressive. Bu Darba and others like him thought of themselves as citizens of a cosmopolitan, urban and urbane Mediterranean where, for centuries, trade and mobility had blurred and crossed religious lines. They saw the end of the Ottoman regime as their chance to play a larger role in the city's government, to spread liberal, improving ideas, and to expand the possibilities of commerce.

Bu Darba was briefly president of a new municipal council in Algiers, set up by the French army to manage the day-to-day civil administration. He proposed proportional representation on the council for each of the city's ethnic and religious communities, and that the council should be made permanent. Going beyond municipal government, he suggested that a "grand council" should be set up, which would receive delegates from the country's inland tribes and send its own deputy to Paris. A newspaper should be published to "spread civilisation and commercial relations." There should be a separation of powers between the police and judiciary, and mixed courts with Muslim, Jewish, and French representatives to manage legal disputes between members of the different communities.

Others made similar proposals. One of Bu Darba's associates, Hamdan Khoja, was a professor of Islamic jurisprudence from a leading Ottoman family in Algiers. He had sent his son to a school near London and had met the English philosopher Jeremy Bentham there. Hamdan went to Paris to argue the Algerians' case. He did so in distinctly post-revolutionary terms, evoking "the time of the emancipation of peoples" in which "all men . . . should be considered as belonging to one and the same family." Fair dealing between peoples, he wrote, meant that Europeans should respect "the law of nations" that had emerged in the eighteenth century—an early iteration of what would become international law—in respect of Muslim countries as much as Christian ones. "Algerians too," he wrote, "have the right to enjoy liberty and every other advantage enjoyed by the nations of Europe."

Hamdan was adept at mobilising the emerging norms of liberal society for a Parisian audience. But more than this, he creatively fused them with his own understanding of classical Islamic principles. Good government, he said, should uphold "universal morality, seeing justice done to the weak as to the strong . . . , contributing to the welfare of humanity . . . for the pursuance of what is good and the avoidance of evil." These were surely ideas on which all liberal-minded men of law and business, whether Algerian Muslims or French Catholics (even atheists), should be able to agree. But such pleas were quickly swamped by the onset of colonial settlement and a war of total conquest.[3]

There had been a moment, forty years earlier, when French revolutionaries themselves had imagined that Muslims might be citizens of a free and fraternal new world too. But then, in 1798, they had invaded Egypt and provoked a war with the Ottoman sultan. That war brought brief glory for the rising star of France's army, General Napoleon Bonaparte, but otherwise ended dismally. Instead of liberating Egypt from its tyrants and going on to knock Britain out of India, Bonaparte headed back to Paris to seize power there and make himself emperor. His army in Egypt, facing local insurrections and counterattacked by the Ottomans and the British, was evacuated in 1801. European liberals increasingly became imperialists, seeing "civilisation" as belonging to them alone and its progress as their own world-historical vocation. The few voices from the other side of the Mediterranean who still spoke the language of universal rights, fraternity, and justice as one that belonged to Muslims too were silenced.[4]

Bu Darba and his family members were arrested and deported. He eventually resettled in Marseille; his son became an interpreter for the French army and a noted "explorer" of the Sahara. Hamdan escaped arrest by fleeing from Paris under the protection of the Ottoman ambassador and settled in Istanbul, where he helped plan the empire's introduction of quarantine restrictions to combat recurring bouts of plague. It would be nearly a hundred years before a politically re-emerging commercial and intellectual middle class, in the Arab world, Turkey, Iran, and India, began to speak the language of universal liberalism again, and by then it would be harder to fuse it so seamlessly with the language of Islamic principle. To many Muslims as well as to Europeans, it would come to seem as if such ideas had always belonged to quintessentially different worlds.

◇◇◇◇◇◇◇

The two Ahmads illustrate two very different Muslim responses to the sudden shock of colonial conquest, an experience that was to spread across almost all Muslim lands in the next ninety years. But personal piety, saintly authority, and belief in the overarching sovereignty of God were not incompatible with rational state-building along the lines now needed to maintain one's place in the world.

Further west in Algeria, hard times and rural unrest in the early 1800s had already led to rebellion against an Ottoman regime seen as oppressive and corrupt. Saintly religious families had led and legitimated the revolt. At one point, Ottoman troops besieged the Tijaniyya order's fortress at Ain Madhi, and Tijani forces attacked Ottoman government centres. Now, central Ottoman authority had collapsed. It would be decades before French armies could effectively occupy the country's vast plains and mountains, but a French general ruled in Algiers and the imposition of foreign, non-Muslim rule was a real threat.

In 1832, the twenty-four-year-old son of a saintly family, Abd al-Qadir Ibn Muhyi al-Din, was proclaimed "commander of the believers" by the tribes of western Algeria and invested with the responsibility of defending the community against foreign invasion and internal strife. Abd al-Qadir's family claimed descent from the Prophet through Ali Ibn Abi Talib and the Idrisid dynasty that had founded the great city of Fez further west. His father was the regional head of the Qadiriyya fraternity, one of the largest of the Sufi orders; the family's small but influential centre of religious learning, near the provincial garrison town of Mascara, was one of those local nodes in cross-continental networks that had become so powerful in the eighteenth century. Its spiritual connections to larger holy places and revered holy ancestors, above all the saint for whom the order was named, Sidi Abd al-Qadir al-Jilani of Baghdad, were made more tangible when Abd al-Qadir and his father made the pilgrimage to Mecca, visiting Cairo, Damascus, and Baghdad, in 1826. It was said that Sidi Abd al-Qadir himself, in a dream, had revealed to the old man the choice of the young Abd al-Qadir as leader of the community in its time of need. The charisma and authority that the family enjoyed were now to be employed to create a new state, with Abd al-Qadir at its head.

For seven years, until 1839, Abd al-Qadir adroitly balanced the competing pressures of the Moroccan sultan to the west, the French in the coastal cities to the north, his own coalition of supporters, and other claimants to power who rejected his sovereignty. He built an emirate (a principality) covering most of the west and centre of today's Algeria, set up industries in arms and munitions, made an uneasy peace with the French that gave him control over foreign trade, and, initially with French assistance, trained and equipped a "new model" army of riflemen and artillery. Having first thought to make Abd al-Qadir a vassal prince, subcontracting their sovereignty over the interior tribes, however, French policy gradually shifted to one of "total conquest." Total conquest meant total war. The French commander, Marshal Thomas-Robert Bugeaud, declared that since in Africa the enemy had no capital city, no seat of power to seize, the target must be the population's means of subsistence. Refusing all negotiation and accepting only unconditional surrender, his flying columns began a systematic devastation of the countryside, burning crops and cutting down orchards, destroying grain stores, slaughtering livestock and razing villages. Alexis de Tocqueville, the commentator on democracy in America, wrote that "such methods...are unfortunate, but anyone wishing to make war on the Arabs will be obliged to adopt them."[5]

Beginning in 1839, and facing overwhelming numbers and firepower, Abd al-Qadir fought an eight-year guerilla struggle. Evading pitched battles that he could not win, the emir operated first from a mobile headquarters on the Algerian steppe, and then from the mountains of northern Morocco. With Abd al-Qadir being hailed within

Moroccan territory as a hero and *mujahid*, a fighter for the faith, the Moroccan sultan found himself obliged to join the war. But in 1844 the Moroccan army was defeated in pitched battle by the French, the country's coastal ports were bombarded by French gunboats, and the Moroccans sued for peace. Abd al-Qadir's continuing struggle became a threat to the sultan's own dynastic security. The Algerian emir's popularity rivalled the sultan's status as "commander of the faithful" within his own domain and undermined his own prerogative to declare war or suspend hostilities. Abd al-Qadir was now declared to be, not a *mujahid*, but a *mufassid*, a spreader of corruption and disorder. In 1847, he was forced out of Moroccan territory. Expressing his "wish to rest from the weariness of war," he surrendered to the French.

Imprisoned for four years despite a promise of safe-conduct to Egypt or Syria, in 1852 Abd al-Qadir was at last released. He settled in Damascus, where he devoted himself to study, contemplation, and teaching. He corresponded with French intellectuals and learned societies and wrote a refutation of critiques of Islam, a treatise on revealed and rational knowledge, and a work on Arabian horses. Above all, he produced the *Kitab al-Mawaqif* (The Book of Stopping Places), a great Sufi commentary on the Qur'an and hadith that was much influenced by the work of Ibn Arabi. Like Ibn Arabi's work, the *Kitab al-Mawaqif* was said to be the result of divine inspiration. Already a respected religious authority and urban dignitary in Syria, Abd al-Qadir also became an international celebrity when, in 1860, sectarian rioting broke out in Damascus. The city's Christian population and its European residents were attacked; Abd al-Qadir offered them shelter, protected them with his own armed entourage, and reprimanded the Muslim crowd for going against God's law, which guaranteed the Christians' protection. The French gave him the medal of the Legion of Honour. Abraham Lincoln sent him a pair of pistols.

After Abd al-Qadir's death in 1883, French propagandists would claim that his heroism in Damascus demonstrated the effect of their own "civilising" influence on a man who had started out as a Muslim "fanatic." He would later be seen as an anticolonial nationalist, and as Algeria's foremost national hero. But his life and career most clearly demonstrate other things. His own writing and his charismatic authority show the continuing vitality of the saintly and Sufi traditions, both for ordinary believers and for the leaders of their community. His unhappy relationship with the Sultan of Morocco exemplified the struggles over religious and political power that had always existed within the lands of Islam, but that were now brought into crisis by the destabilising impact of European invasion. His own diplomacy, as well as the Moroccan pressure that ended his fight, illustrated the competing imperatives of taking up arms to fight off foreign aggression, or seeking peace to avoid further harm befalling Muslims.[6]

Other charismatic leaders would see the conquest, and resistance to it, less as a matter of sovereignty and state-building than as an apocalypse. Like Ahmad Ibn Tuwayr al-Janna, rural communities and the inspired holy rebels who emerged from them were well versed in traditional Muslim expectations of the end times. When disorder came to rule the earth, it was widely believed, a "lord of the hour" would appear as the herald of the mahdi, the messiah, and the realm of justice. Especially after the collapse of Abd al-Qadir's attempt to rebuild a centralised Muslim sovereignty, from the 1840s to the 1880s several such figures emerged in the mountains and oases of Algeria, mobilising Sufi networks and inspiring popular rural insurrections. To the French, such movements only gave repeated proof of their growing belief that "Muslim fanaticism" was an irrational and dangerous force to be stamped out, and that their colonial subjects understood only the rule of force, not the rule of law. Some of the worst atrocities of the war of conquest were committed in suppression of such revolts: whole communities asphyxiated while they took shelter in caves, entire oases and villages destroyed and their populations massacred. To their victims, such cataclysmic violence made colonial conquest look very much like the end of the world.

◇◇◇◇◇◇◇

The emir Abd al-Qadir combined spiritual authority with military prowess and statesmanship to create a Muslim state in resistance to European invasion, ending his days as a distinguished Ottoman notable. Further east in Africa, in the territory that would become the modern country of Sudan, it was "the Turks" themselves, and the Egyptians who were formally subject to Ottoman suzerainty, who would be the targets of resistance. Here, a state-building movement would emerge that combined apocalyptic revolt with religious revivalism, political ambition and Sufi spiritualism: a powerful fusion of the kind of reforming zeal that had motivated Shehu Usuman Dan Fodio with the messianic energy of the popular "lords of the hour."

This was the movement led in the 1880s by Muhammad Ahmad Ibn Abdallah. His name echoing that of the Prophet Muhammad (who in mystical works is also called Ahmad), Muhammad Ahmad was a preacher and ascetic from a boatbuilding family north of Khartoum. Devoted to Sufi mysticism and a rigorous piety, he preached, gained followers, and in 1881 declared that he himself was none other than the long-awaited mahdi, the redeemer sent by God at the end of time. There had been many claimants to the title over the centuries, but it was Muhammad Ahmad who would impress himself upon European imaginations as "the Mahdi."

In the upper Nile Valley, south of Egypt, Islam had spread gradually from the sixteenth century onward. The medieval Mamluks had conquered Nubia from Cairo, but it was local dynasties, built on the gold, slave, and ivory trades, that adopted Islam at their courts and spread it, slowly, among their people. These were the sultanate of Funj, based around the confluence of the Blue and White Nile Rivers (where Khartoum is located today) from the 1500s to the 1700s, and the sultanate of Darfur (the "house," or land, of the Fur people) further west that succeeded it. Holy men who combined practical Arabic literacy and knowledge of the law with the charisma of mystical Sufism and magical practices were attracted to the sultans' courts and became teachers and preachers. This was an area that had long been a source of Black African slaves, captured and trafficked north for a thousand miles along the terrible Forty Days' Road to Egypt, or east to the Red Sea ports. As in both Muslim and non-Muslim societies of West Africa, slavery was also part and parcel of local society and business, and for elite families in particular, slaveholding was an important factor of both their material wealth and their social status.

Sudan had long been considered by the rulers of Egypt as a natural dependency of their own territories. In the 1820s, the ruler of Egypt was Mehmed Ali Pasha, the soldier who had seized power in Cairo in 1811, after the French occupiers had gone and he had massacred his local rivals. Mehmed Ali spoke Turkish, but he had been born in northern Greece into a family that may originally have been Kurdish, and he never learned Arabic. Egyptian national history would know him as Muhammad Ali and celebrate him as the founder of the modern Egyptian state. Formally speaking, he was a vassal of the sultan in Istanbul, but in practice he was an autonomous ruler with dynastic, empire-building ambitions of his own. It was his soldiers who drove the Al-Saud family and the Wahhabis out of Mecca and Medina in 1818, and it was his army that occupied Syria and threatened to topple the Ottomans themselves in the 1830s. In the 1820s, Mehmed Ali extended his rule south into Sudan. Over the next sixty years, he and his successors established a new kind of centralising, bureaucratic state with a greater reach than had previously been seen in this region: Sudanese Arabic speakers would call this the *turkiyya*, or "Turkish" rule.

Few if any of the people involved would have called themselves Turks, though some, like Uthman Bey Cerkes, the military governor and founder of Khartoum, were Turco-Circassians, descendants of the Mamluks brought from the Caucasus who had been Egypt's governors and aristocrats since before the rise of the Ottomans. Others, like the later provincial governor-general Charles Gordon, were Europeans in Egyptian service. Gordon was a British soldier, nicknamed "Chinese" Gordon because of his time spent in the Chinese army, fighting for the Qing dynasty against the Taiping Rebellion—a Chinese version of apocalyptic, revolutionary and "heavenly" state-building—in the 1850s. In Sudan, men like him ran a state that had put local populations under an unprecedented tax burden and curbed the autonomy of local leading families. State-appointed Muslim judges replaced, or threatened to replace, the authority and standing of local holy families, like that from which Muhammad Ahmad came. Mehmed Ali's state-building in Egypt generated an immense demand for labour and soldiers. Part of this was met by forcibly conscripting Egyptian peasants, but it also meant a drive to import slaves from Sudan. By 1838, ten to twelve thousand enslaved Africans reached Egypt each year.[7]

Such drastic and rapid changes created powerful new interests, especially among those who profited from enslavement, as well as threatening older ones. In the 1860s and 1870s, under pressure from their European, and especially British, creditors, the Egyptians tried to suppress the slave trade that they had done so much to expand in the previous decades. This meant yet more coercive action by the rulers against the economic interests of Sudanese. The British liked to present their antislavery pressure as a moral crusade, although they had pragmatically bought off their own Caribbean slaveowners in the late 1830s by paying them compensation for loss of property when slavery was abolished in Britain's colonies. Egyptian or Sudanese slavers could expect not compensation, but imprisonment. To Sudanese Muslims, though, it was not Europe's selective morality that was at issue: it was more simply that a supposedly Muslim government was seen to be oppressing the people and, what was worse, employing non-Muslims to do it for them. The man who became known, to his followers and Europeans alike, as the Mahdi thus came to his mission in a context ripe for a religiously inspired revolution.

Muhammad al-Mahdi was rapidly successful. After proclaiming his mission in 1881, he made his own hijra, modelling his career, like Shehu Usuman had, on the Prophet's own. In Sudan, that meant moving from the Nile Valley into mountainous territory where government forces could not easily operate. From there, he gained support from Sufi networks and nomadic communities, displaced peasants and disgruntled notables. He announced that he would restore the true

Islam, establishing justice according to the Qur'an and the sunna, and the instructions he received directly from the Prophet. He had been deeply imbued with the Sufi tradition, but when he sought support from the Sanusi order to the west, he was rebuffed. Although he was a revivalist, his own understanding of his mission went well beyond anything imagined by the eighteenth-century reformers.

He declared that the Prophet Muhammad himself had appointed him as his successor and as the "Seal of the Caliphate" (as Muhammad himself had been the "Seal of the Prophets"). "I am created from the light of the core of the Prophet's heart," he wrote, referring to the Sufi doctrine of Prophetic light, created by God and passed down to Muhammad and his true successors, and "my Companions are as his Companions." His own closest disciples were named as successors to the first caliphs of Islam. He named his followers *al-ansar*, "the helpers," after those who had first supported the Prophet in creating his new community at Medina. (Europeans, adopting an exotic-sounding Persian and Turkish term for Sufi disciples, called them "dervishes.") He imposed Qur'anic penalties against immorality: this, inevitably, meant a stream of pronouncements focusing on sexual propriety and the behaviour of women. He sought to uphold but also reform the social order: this, while affirming the legality of slavery, included injunctions to be kind to slaves, not to overburden them, and to feed and clothe them with the same food and clothes as their owners had. ("God has vested the ownership of the slaves in your hands," he reminded his followers: "Had He so wished, he would have vested the ownership of your person in their hands.") His struggle was a jihad against unbelievers. Muslims who opposed him, he said, were counted by the Prophet himself not as Muslims but as unbelievers.[8]

In 1885, the Mahdist forces besieged the Egyptians' provincial capital at Khartoum and captured it. General Gordon, who had stayed behind in the city, was killed, his already existing celebrity becoming Victorian martyrdom. Muhammad al-Mahdi himself died a few months later. He had overthrown what he had denounced as the "Turkish" tyranny while claiming for himself a wholly disinterested mission: "I have no need of the sultanate," he wrote, "nor of the wealth of this world and its vanity. I am but the slave of God, guiding unto God and to what is with him."

The Mahdi's movement had begun as an apocalyptic revolt against the encroachments of an "iniquitous" state. But he had conquered a kingdom comparable in extent to the area from the East Coast of the United States to the Mississippi. His successor, Abdullahi, who took the title of caliph, had to stabilise and institutionalise rule over this territory. This meant further state-building and centralisation, and that provoked renewed rebellion. A war with Ethiopia and campaigns against internal revolts were successful. But eventually, a British and Egyptian army under General Herbert Kitchener—later to be the face of British valour on the recruiting posters of the First World War—was sent to reconquer Sudan, avenge the death of Gordon, and (above all) preempt French imperial expansion into the upper Nile region.

In September 1898, Kitchener's army arrived before the Mahdists' capital at Omdurman, just north of Khartoum, with railway tracks and machine guns. Two-thirds of its soldiers were themselves Sudanese, many of them the same enslaved soldiers who had been taken north over the previous decades. This included men who, "freed" from slave traders during the attempted suppression of the trade, then found themselves conscripted for lifetime service into the army for which the traffickers had in any case intended them. These Sudanese troops, who suffered the most casualties on the Anglo-Egyptian side at Omdurman, were essential to the victory that would make a national hero of Kitchener and that would be breathlessly narrated, to his own emerging fame, by a junior officer and war correspondent named Winston Churchill. The gap in military technology that had only recently been opened up by long-range, rapid-firing guns and expanding "dumdum" bullets (which spread out on impact, causing massive internal damage) was starkly translated into the arithmetic of bodies on the battlefield, and the catastrophic injuries inflicted on them. The enormous death toll—eleven thousand killed, sixteen thousand wounded, in the Mahdist army, against forty-eight killed and fewer than five hundred wounded on the Anglo-Egyptian side—would become an iconic statement of the asymmetries of late Victorian colonial war.[9]

Muhammad Ahmad had said that his armies would be preceded by the angel of death; Winston Churchill wrote of the victory of science over superstition. The carnage inflicted on the Sudanese did not go unnoticed in England. *The Saturday Review* mused that "the awful destructiveness of new weapons has...received a lasting and blood-curdling proof." Its writer worried about the implications for the next European war: new military technology had evidently created an "appalling prospect which stares civilisation in the face." But far from deploring the new means of violence, the *Review* told its readers that "it is in the very magnitude and hideousness of the danger that the greatest safeguard lies." It was the newly unimaginable destructiveness of war, as weapons "still more diabolical in their power of destroying human life" came into being, that would ensure peace in the future. Omdurman announced the onset of the twentieth century's lethal technology—and of some of its most dangerous delusions.[10]

◇◇◇◇◇◇◇

In Muslim Africa, the new European imperialism brought new kinds of violence and a new sense of crisis. In Southeast Asia, the Europeans had been around for much longer, and their encroachment on indigenous Muslim sovereignty came more haltingly. But the 1820s and 1830s were a watershed here, too.

Europe's revolutionary upheaval had been felt as far away as Java. In 1799, the Dutch East India Company collapsed, and its Southeast Asian army, territory, and interests were taken over by the Dutch state, which in 1795 had become a "sister republic" of revolutionary France. In their global war against the French Revolution and the Napoleonic empire that succeeded it, British forces occupied Dutch-controlled territory in Java, Sumatra, and the spice islands. In 1812 they sacked the Javanese royal capital at Yogyakarta. When the wars ended, the British and Dutch governments redrew their respective spheres of influence around the Strait of Malacca, where trade between East Asia and the Indian Ocean was now firmly in European, and to some extent American, hands.

By treaties signed in 1814 and 1824, Dutch pre-eminence was recognised south of the strait, in Sumatra, with the British taking control in the Malay Peninsula to the north. (The British also gained Dutch recognition of their control over an island in the strait: Singapore. Notionally subject to the sultanate of Johor in southern Malaysia, it was becoming an entrepreneurial city-state and trading centre, as Muslim Melaka had been centuries before.) Each European power guaranteed free trading rights to the other in its own sphere, while also promising not to make treaties with "any native prince, chief, or state" in the sphere of the other. Within ports under the British East India Company's control, commercial law courts were already being used to disregard the sovereignty of local princes, who were treated simply as private merchants. The Strait of Malacca might have been the first place where European diplomats divided up between themselves, not yet control of, but controlling influence over, the geography of Muslim states with largely Muslim populations; it would not be the last.[11]

At the same time, the effects of eighteenth-century Islamic revivalism were also felt across the Indian Ocean. Sufi influences, as we have seen, had long been important in Southeast Asia, and in the seventeenth and eighteenth centuries, sometimes through their own journeys of pilgrimage and study to Yemen and the Hijaz, Southeast Asian religious teachers became affiliated to the networked Sufi fraternities. Some of these, like the Naqshbandiyya, which originated in medieval central Asia and whose teachings spread through Arabia and India, became identified with connections to the Ottoman world, and with a reforming pietism that became prominent in the first decade of the nineteenth century. Critics of these reformers, particularly in west Sumatra, associated them with the Wahhabis. Some may indeed have been influenced by the Wahhabis, and may even have been present in the Hijaz during the Wahhabi occupation of the holy cities. But rivalries within and between local Sufi affiliations were also part of the story. Claims to better or truer Islam invoked both connections to Mecca (not necessarily to the Wahhabis), and prestigious saintly heritage of which the Wahhabis would not have approved. One early nineteenth-century account of the reformist struggle in Sumatra explained that instructions for the island's conversion had been given by none other than the saint of Baghdad, Abd al-Qadir al-Jilani, and that his own teacher had inherited this mission.

Competition between revivalists—who attempted, notably, to ban alcohol, cock-fighting and gambling—and their opponents became what one of them called a "war of religion." Open civil war broke out in west Sumatra from 1803 and lasted for almost twenty years. The more "traditionalist" establishment—the aristocrats of Minangkabau— dismissively called their reformist opponents *padris* (from the Spanish and Portuguese word for a priest, *padre*). But by 1821 the padris had gained the upper hand, and only Dutch intervention, and a further war lasting until 1837, defeated them. Once drawn into the religious politics of Sumatra, the Dutch would not be leaving in a hurry. They imposed formal colonial rule, and began to build a more expansive colonial state.[12]

The basis of that state had been laid in Java thirty years earlier. In 1807, Napoleon's brother, Louis Bonaparte, whom the emperor of the French had made King of the Netherlands, appointed a forceful new governor-general of the Dutch "possessions" in the East Indies. Under Marshal Herman Daendels, the new Dutch administration was determined to impose a more aggressive and effective sovereignty than the Dutch East India Company had exercised in the territories its trading interests had led it to conquer. Their position had to be defended against the British, and independent local sovereigns were a liability.

Changes in the etiquette of European representatives at the court of Yogyakarta were a small but telling sign of the changing balance of power. Javanese rulers had considered the Dutch East India Company with respect, seeking to adopt the Dutch into the island's own political order. In this view of things, the company and the sultans could be seen almost as equals in their respective domains, the Dutch in west

Java, the Javanese Muslim rulers in the centre and east. Dutch emissaries had been treated as the "servants" of both the company and the sultan. They showed due deference to the sultan by bowing to him, removing their hats, and receiving his advice on Dutch affairs as they gave advice themselves (and poured the wine). Now the emissaries, decked out in splendid new uniforms, referred to as "ministers," and provided with their own cavalry escorts, would not remove their hats; nor would they bow and serve. Instead, the ruler was expected to rise to meet them, and seat them beside him on the same level as himself.

This was deliberately offensive diplomacy (and part of a pattern: similar changes occurred elsewhere, for example at the court of the Bey, the hereditary Ottoman viceroy of Tunis in North Africa, where Europeans would soon abolish the protocol of kissing the Bey's hand, and other customary signs of deference). The versifying court chroniclers knew what it meant: "The sultan was disturbed at heart / ... [that] the Dutch would rule / Push aside his royal dignity / And break his authority." More tangible pressures followed: annexation of productive territory where pepper, indigo and linen were to be had, and the co-option of rival princes who sided with the Dutch in hopes of their own preferment, and perhaps in recognition of the balance of military forces. The interlude of British occupation and the British assault on Yogyakarta in 1812 did nothing to ease the tensions. On the contrary, when Dutch rule returned after the fall of Napoleon in Europe, its brash assertiveness only increased.[13]

To one Javanese prince, all this portended "the ruin of the land of Java," a coming chastisement in which it had been foretold that he would have a great part to play. This was Prince Dipanagara, who would come to play a role in Southeast Asia similar to that of Abd al-Qadir in Algeria, or Muhammad al-Mahdi in Sudan: soldier of virtue, commander of the faithful, and in the twentieth century, hero of national resistance. Dipanagara was born in 1785, the year 1200 of the Islamic calendar. In some accounts of the "Jayabaya" prophecies, attributed to the medieval Javanese king of that name, this was the year when the *ratu adil*, the "just king," would arise.

Dipanagara had a religious upbringing from an early age. He inherited a Sufi charisma, and his reforming piety was combined with a mystical sensibility. His mother claimed descent from Sunan Ampel, one of Java's "nine saints." He had a Sufi tutor, and during his spiritually formative pilgrimage to the south coast of Java as a young man, he first visited religious schools (*pesantren*) but then took to solitary meditation in caves. Here, he recorded both visions of the Javanese saint Sunan Kalijaga, and—like his predecessor Sultan Agung—a mystical meeting with the Javanese spirit deity, Ratu Kidul, the "goddess of the Southern Ocean." Ratu Kidul appeared to Dipanagara, we're told, offering him her power to rid Java of the Dutch, if only he would intercede with God so that she might be returned to human form. (In Javanese mythology, Ratu Kidul was a human princess who had become a spirit.) Dipanagara, though, mindful of the oneness of God, replied: "I do not ask your help / Against my equals [fellow humans] / For in religion there is only the assistance of the Almighty."[14]

Dipanagara's childhood and adolescence were spent mostly away from the court, on the estate of his formidable great-grandmother, Ratu Ageng, the mother of the reigning sultan, in whose charge he was from the age of seven until her death in 1803. Ratu Ageng was descended from the royal family of a Muslim principality on Sumbawa (one of the Sunda Islands lying east of Java) and was closely related to the Javanese Muslim scholarly class. As a younger woman she had accompanied her husband on campaign against the Dutch, given birth to her son in an army camp on a mountainside, and commanded a troop of female bodyguards. Known for her piety, her religious learning, and her observance of traditional Javanese court culture, she was also by all accounts frugal, preferring a simple life among the farmers and pious ascetics of the countryside to the luxuries and intrigues of the palace. Similar qualities were passed on to Dipanagara. Javanese manners, Europeans observed, "are always extremely exalted and distant in their dealings between superiors and inferiors," but Dipanagara "consorts as easily with the common man as with the great ones. Because of this he has made himself much loved everywhere."

Because of this—plus an apocalyptic, prophetic vision of his destiny, and an inheritance of the Javanese ideal of the Sufi king—the prince became an unlikely revolutionary.[15]

When he came of age, Dipanagara could not avoid becoming involved in the affairs of the court, which was increasingly polarised by pro- and anti-Dutch factions. But he maintained his closeness to the peasantry, whose situation reached crisis point in the early 1820s. Land taxes, internal customs duties at tollgates (which were often run by Chinese clients of the Dutch administration, adding an element of ethnic conflict to the perceived injustice and indignity of goods being searched and taxed on the road), rural insecurity and European encroachment on land all combined with poor harvests. In 1821, famine and a cholera epidemic struck too. A contemporary court poet in the neighbouring principality of Surakarta lamented the corruption of the times:

The law . . . was not enforced
Nor was the administration of justice upheld
Often foodstuffs were scarce and there were epidemics
Many common people fled to other villages
. . . .
Much of their attachment for the state and their king was lost.

In a biting comment on the proliferation of the common and unworthy at court, and the absence of royal leadership, the poet went on: "The ricinus tree [castor oil plant] sprang up / But the teak tree died." In 1822, Mount Merapi, a volcano in central Java whose guardian spirit was traditionally identified as one of the island's most important spiritual forces, erupted, destroying nearby villages. Rivers were blocked and overflowed, flooding rice and tobacco fields. More than the physical damage, all of this looked like signs of cosmic anger and coming judgment.[16]

A series of millenarian revolts had already broken out in the countryside but lacked effective leadership. In 1825, Dipanagara, by now convinced that he was the promised "just king," declared a *perang sabil*, holy war. For five years, he waged a campaign that was part military confrontation, with troops equipped with firearms, and part rural guerilla uprising, with farmers fixing *kris* daggers to bamboo poles as improvised lances. He drew support from the peasantry and the more religiously active Javanese (learned "people of religion" or *santris*, including Islamic scholars and students, and those who referred to themselves as *putihan*, pious "white ones"), and from other princely families. This included women who could have matched his great-grandmother in piety and fortitude. One, Raden Ayu Serang, a descendant of Sunan Kalijaga, had held a position at court and like Dipanagara, spent time in meditation on the south coast. She commanded a cavalry force five hundred strong, survived the war, and lived on into her eighties. Finally defeated in 1830, Dipanagara went into exile in Makassar, the formerly independent Muslim sultanate in the south of the island of Sulawesi, northeast of Java. He died there in 1855.[17]

The Java War of 1825–30 is thought to have killed two hundred thousand Javanese people, along with some eight thousand Europeans and seven thousand Javanese soldiers on the Dutch side. Its defeat marked the consolidation of Dutch rule, but not the end of resistance to it, in what was becoming the Dutch East Indies (or Netherlands Indies, today's Indonesia). In Sumatra to the west, the status of Aceh as an independent state and self-consciously Muslim society had not dissipated. Long open to the Indian Ocean and the cosmopolitan, connected world of which it had been part, Aceh now found its place in the world reconfigured. From being a centre in its own right, Aceh was increasingly seen as the remote and refractory edge of the new Netherlands Indies state being built far to the east. In 1871, the British abandoned their previous stance of supporting the sultanate's independence. In 1873, the Dutch invaded, and war broke out. The war would drag on, at devastating cost, until organised resistance was finally crushed on the eve of the First World War. It was followed by sporadic anticolonial violence into the 1920s and 1930s, leaving a legacy of Muslim resistance to outside, non-Muslim rule that would be reactivated later in the twentieth century.

The Dutch-Acehnese war was seen by the Dutch in terms of what they, like other colonial powers, considered as innate and irrational Muslim "fanaticism." It was understood in Aceh as a defensive war for the preservation of life and religious freedom from foreign violence and violation. But unlike the war in Java, in Aceh the struggle was not mobilised by a princely "just king." Long before the Dutch declared it abolished in 1874, Aceh's sultanate had fragmented, losing much of the centralised state power it had possessed in the seventeenth century. By the 1820s, the region was producing half of the world's pepper crop, for which there was an expanding global market. But it was divided by new imperial borders from the Malay coast with which it had long interacted, and split internally between the locally dominant chiefs of newly cultivated pepper-growing areas. Their trade relations bypassed the sultan, who had little effective control over their territories.

When the Dutch invasion came, Acehnese leadership was devolved and distributed among aristocrats, local chiefs, individuals who had made the pilgrimage to Mecca and thus bore the dignity of being a *hajji*, and rural religious scholars and preachers, often affiliated to Sufi orders. The aristocratic elite increasingly came to favour settlement with the Dutch. The scholars and local chiefs, on the other hand, became the organisers of resistance defined in religious terms as a duty of all Muslims to save Aceh from the fate that had already befallen other areas under Dutch occupation. Since the eighteenth century, Muslim belief and practice in Aceh had come to be defined less by following religious authorities than as an ethical responsibility of the individual before God. As in Java, though, local politics and patronage, factionalism and opportunity, as much as communal solidarity and moral duty, decided whether individuals and groups would join the resistance or seek an accommodation with the invaders. Participation in the war could be a matter of family loyalty as well as individual piety, as in the case of Cut Nyak Dien, a woman who took command of her fallen husband's armies after his death and became one of Aceh's most celebrated war captains in her own right.[18]

The Dutch response, facing an entrenched guerilla struggle and enormous losses of their own, was to resort to a scorched-earth strategy, burning villages and destroying livestock, orchards, and rice fields. Refugees fled into the mountains, where they died of starvation and disease. Over its dreadful course, the war may have taken one hundred thousand lives. For decades afterwards, individual acts of resistance, or vengeance, against the Dutch occurred. Usually leading to the perpetrator's death, such individual acts, understood by Acehnese as a deliberate seeking of martyrdom, would become known in Dutch as *atjeh-moord*, an "Aceh murder," which the emerging language of colonial psychiatry considered to be the result of a racially "deviant mental condition." In the Netherlands itself, other voices, more critical of both the conduct of the war and the assumptions of imperial superiority, had already accused the Dutch themselves of *volkerenmoord*, "the murder of a people." Half a century later, the same word would be used in Dutch for the newly defined crime of genocide.[19]

A similarly slow colonial encroachment, beginning in the sixteenth century, was followed by a similarly sudden, cataclysmic storm of Victorian-era violence further north, in the Philippines. The Spanish Empire had never completely conquered the Muslim-majority southern Philippines—the Sulu Archipelago stretching eastward from Borneo, and the principal southern island of Mindanao. While large-scale conversion to Christianity occurred in the north, Spanish governors in Manila settled for policing the southern islands' coasts and such indirect control as they could exercise from time to time through local Muslim rulers, who remained effectively independent until the mid-nineteenth century. Economic connections that included both slaving and piracy, but also more modest trades in dried fish and other goods, joined the southern Philippines to the rest of Southeast Asia and remained important into the early 1800s. The sultanate of Jolo, in the Sulu Islands, formally recognised Spanish sovereignty only in 1878, in the face of gunboats and occupying soldiers. The tenuous Spanish hold on coastal enclaves was resisted by sporadic attacks, similar to those the Dutch in Sumatra would call *atjeh-moord*, by Muslim warriors whom the Spanish would call *juramentados* ("oath-takers," since before embarking on their action they were believed to swear an oath that they would "vanquish or die," killing as many unbelievers as they could before being cut down themselves).

In 1898, the conclusion of the Spanish-American War ceded control of the Philippines to a new imperial power in the Pacific, the United States. When the Spanish garrisons in the south gave way to American troops in 1899, the new occupiers initially negotiated with what came to be called "Moro" (Muslim) rulers. The Americans were preoccupied with a counterinsurgency war against Filipino nationalists in the northern islands that would become notoriously destructive, especially in the Batangas province and on the island of Samar, where in 1900–1902 massacres and forced population resettlements killed tens of thousands, and torture became routine. But as the war in the north wound down, the US army turned its attention to the south. In 1903, military rule was established over the "Moro Province" with a view to integrating the region (as northern Filipino nationalists also demanded) into the reformed colonial state and its "benevolent assimilation" to an American vision of progress.

The new government's agenda was dramatically transformational. In imposing its agenda, it saw the people it sought to govern as requiring only discipline, and understanding only force. Sporadic, insurgent *juramentado* attacks occurred in response, which the Americans, borrowing an older Dutch and British expression, called "running amok" ("running mad" or "in a fury"). Like the British and Dutch, the Americans began to think of such actions as both the result of a racial mental instability and an unpredictable violence innate to "fanatical" Muslims. Deliberately degrading, ritually polluting and spectacular reprisals were adopted by the Americans in imitation of what they believed to be British practice in Singapore and India. In 1903, when three *juramentados* killed on the island of Jolo were buried, the gravediggers were forced to throw a wild pig into the grave with the bodies.

Such acts only increased both resentment and resistance. What the American governor, Leonard Wood, thought of as the necessary "pacification" of the Moro population was a campaign of indiscriminate violence that reached its peak in March 1906, on the slopes of Bud Dajo, a volcanic mountain on Jolo, where some six hundred unarmed Muslim men, women and children were massacred. This was a war crime that outdid much better-known atrocities at Wounded Knee and My Lai in numbers killed, and at the time it provoked scandalised outrage in the United States (including especially biting comment from Mark Twain). But, along with the rest of America's war in the Philippines, it would be mostly forgotten by the American public—until the emergence of a new American controversy over counterinsurgency and torture, a century later.[20]

◇◇◇◇◇◇◇

While an American empire was fledging in the Pacific, at the opposite, northwestern end of Muslim Asia, an older empire was dramatically expanding. In the 1300s, the lands of Muscovy had been part of the empire of the Mongol Golden Horde, and its princes were vassals of a Muslim khan. Russian historians would write of the chafing "Tatar yoke." But by the sixteenth century, with the conquest of Kazan, east of Moscow on the Volga, an emerging Russian state was ruling over Muslim subjects. By the end of the 1500s, Russian rule crossed the Urals. Empress Catherine the Great annexed formerly Ottoman Crimea in 1783, but Russian imperial expansion to the south was fitful until the early nineteenth century.

Then, in a century of rapid conquest, the tsars' empire pushed its boundaries across the central Asian steppe towards Afghanistan and the western edge of China, and into the Caucasus between the Black Sea and the Caspian Sea towards the borders of Iran and Anatolia. Russian imperialism aimed to emulate the British and other European empire-builders, asserting Russia's claim to be part of the new post-Napoleonic world order of "civilised" nations. Imperial expansion would burnish the Romanov dynasty's conquering credentials, expand the Orthodox church, and bring improving "Aryan" rule to "savage" Turkic peoples. Beginning in the 1830s, Russian campaigns pushed south. They seized Tashkent in 1865, occupied Samarqand in 1868, and reduced the independent emirate of Bukhara to the status of a Russian protectorate in 1873. Some of the greatest centres of medieval Muslim life and learning, cities that had flourished despite the devastations of repeated conquest and plague from Abbasid to Timurid times, came to be Russia's subordinate periphery.[21]

Russian wars against Iran between 1796 and 1828 transferred much of the western and southern Caucasus, including the ancient Christian kingdom of Georgia and the khanates of Azerbaijan, to Russian sovereignty. But the more imposing mountains in the northeast Caucasus, the regions of Daghestan and Chechnya, remained outside Russian control, as they had remained effectively independent of Ottoman or Iranian rule before. This region's scattered Sunni Muslim communities were governed by local assemblies of adult men, who elected a *qadi*, a judge, to arbitrate conflicts and give rulings. As in some other rural regions encountered by nineteenth-century Europeans, notably the mountains of Kabylia in northern Algeria, where similar village self-government existed, Russian writers and others after them would see such villages as little "republics" or primitive "democracies." They saw the Caucasus through romantic eyes: as a wild, austere fastness of blood feuds, violence, and savage nobility. The landscape, and its people's attachment to their independence, would inspire work by the poets Pushkin and Lermontov, and the Muslim resistance to Russia's conquest would be dramatized in the late novella *Hadji Murat* by Leo Tolstoy, who fought in the region as a young man. But there was nothing romantic about the region's incorporation into Russia's empire.

In 1819, the Russian army built a fortress, nicknamed *groznaia*, "menacing," an appropriately named foundation for what would become Grozny, the capital of Chechnya. Russian policy under the military governor, General Alexei Ermolov, was summed up in his own words: "Gentleness," he wrote, "in the eyes of Asiatics, is a sign of weakness, and out of pure humanity I am inexorably severe." This was a view that could well have been found among colonial officers in Algeria or Aceh, in the Philippines or Sudan. The belief that the peoples being subjected to European power were innately violent, and that European violence against them was therefore justifiable, even "humane," and necessary for their ultimate betterment, was fast emerging as a central conceit of the new imperial world. In the Caucasus, this meant collective reprisals and out-of-hand executions of suspects, the massacre of whole villages and the enslavement of women, or their distribution as "native wives" for officers. And as in other places, rather than terrorising the population into submission, such violence provoked their most desperate resistance.[22]

A current of Islamic reform and revival had come into the Caucasus, too, in the late eighteenth century, organised around the Naqshbandiyya Sufi fraternity that emphasised both mystical piety and rigorous social morality. The Naqshbandi *murshid*s ("guides"), though they preached against social ills and for a puritanical style of social morality, were not political actors. But their students, *murid*s, could be. In 1828, Ghazi Muhammad, a Naqshbandi whom the Russians called "Kazi-Mullah," was recognised by local leaders and religious scholars as the "imam" of Daghestan. He was already an activist for the reform of what he considered un-Islamic behaviour, seeking to bring the community to a truer observance of God's law. Now he also declared war on the Russians and their supporters among the local nobility. Ghazi Muhammad waged a three-year guerilla struggle before being trapped and killed in 1832. After his successor was assassinated in 1834, the banner was taken up by Imam Shamil, a Naqshbandi Sufi and fighter who had been Ghazi Muhammad's student, friend, and lieutenant, and one of the two survivors of the fight in which Ghazi Muhammad had been killed.

Shamil, as he became known in Europe, had been born to a freedman's family in Daghestan as a sickly child named Ali. It was said that he was renamed Shamuyil (Samuel), or Shamil, in infancy to ward off infirmity. He grew to a towering stature in every sense. Over six feet tall, he was a respected horseman and marksman, and a man learned in Islamic law and devout in its observance. He was also a revered Sufi disciple endowed with spiritual insight who was believed to communicate directly with the Prophet, and to have powers akin to telepathy and foresight. With appropriate modesty, Shamil is said to have refused the office of imam repeatedly, until the assembled people and scholars obliged him to acquiesce. Once elected, however, he held tenaciously to his position as "commander of the faithful" for the next twenty-five years, against both local rivals and the increasing weight of numbers and firepower thrown into the mountains by the Russian Empire.

Shamil's rule built on the campaign for a reformed social order that had preceded the *ghazavat*, the holy war. Observance of the law here meant adherence to a strict, sober Muslim morality. Music and dancing were banned, as were smoking and drinking alcohol. But the reforming impulse applied to the state too. Penalties were corrective rather than punitive: offenders were publicly shamed by being seated backwards on a donkey and paraded around the village. Imprisonment and fines rather than corporal punishment were imposed for crimes like theft. The revenues of religious endowments like mosques were appropriated by the central treasury, with religious officials being paid salaries rather than controlling their own finances. A social trend of expensive dowries had made marriage unaffordable for young men, which in turn raised pious fears about sexual immorality, so maximum sums were set for dowries to encourage marriage. Deputies were appointed, taxes collected, a consultative council set up, and complaints heard. Pragmatically, Shamil allowed Russian money to circulate rather than minting his own coinage, so as not to throttle trade with the lowlands. Also pragmatically, in 1835 he made an agreement with the local allies of the Russians that left him with effective sovereignty in the mountains, in exchange for his purely nominal recognition of Russian suzerainty.

With his leadership established and a functioning state in place, Shamil put his people on a war footing. All men between fifteen and fifty were expected to be armed and available for mobilisation. A group of ten families would combine their resources to support a single permanently equipped cavalryman. A standing army of followers, who like Sufi disciples were called *murids*, was established. Shamil's attempt to create a "new model" infantry along the lines that Egyptian and Ottoman armies had adopted from Dutch and Prussian practice was a failure (when it was deployed in 1851, it was destroyed), but his guerilla forces were formidable. At its peak, Shamil's army could field more than ten thousand soldiers and manoeuvre artillery rapidly and accurately across the mountains. Like his predecessor Ghazi Muhammad, who had told the Russians that a settlement could be reached "if you do not oppress our law by your taxes," Shamil engaged in constant cat-and-mouse diplomacy with his adversaries. The Russians, though, refused to countenance his independence, and in 1836 they launched a major campaign against his emirate. Telling his people that the Russians were "as poisonous as the snakes that crawl in the desert," Shamil called on them to "be strong and hold fast together like the tops of the mountains above your heads."[23]

After a series of protracted campaigns, Shamil eventually surrendered in 1859. His appeals to the Ottomans came to nothing, even during the Crimean War that pitted the Ottomans with their French and British allies against Russia, and that war's end in 1856 released Russian forces to complete their forcible "pacification" of Chechnya and Daghestan. He was exiled, settled south of Moscow where the tsarist police could keep an eye on him, before moving to Kyiv in 1866 and making the pilgrimage to Mecca in 1868. In 1871, he died in Medina, where he was buried. One of his sons became an Ottoman general and fought against Russia in 1877–78; another son became a Russian general. Such migrations, in different directions, were repeated on a larger scale in the mountains: between 1861 and 1864 almost half a million people were forcibly deported from the Caucasus by the Russian army. Only by removing their people, it seemed, could such places be secured.[24]

◇◇◇◇◇◇◇

The Russians called the movement led by Shamil *miuridizm* ("murid-ism"), after his followers. *Murid*s, though, were not everywhere engaged in armed anti-imperialist struggle. Far to the west in Senegal, the fraternity that would become known by the same name, *muridi-yya*, the Murids, or in French, *mourides*, found a very different place in the emerging colonial world. "The country at this moment is in a very confused state," Amadu Bamba Mbacké's father reportedly advised him: "The only way in which you can aid others and yourself is to flee from the things of this world."[25]

Shaykh Amadu Bamba, the founder of the Senegalese Murid movement, was born in about 1853 (the precise date is uncertain), in the kingdom of Bawol in the fertile agricultural area of today's central Senegal, and died there in 1927. Stretching down the Atlantic coast between the old French slave-trade town of Saint-Louis at the mouth of the Senegal River to the north, and what would become the steamship port and colonial capital of Dakar to the south, the region where Bamba was born was divided between Bawol and the neighbouring kingdom of Kajoor. These kingdoms, and their sharply divided caste societies of freeborn nobles, artisans, peasants, and slaves, were dominated by Wolof-speaking rulers and their military retainers (in Wolof, *ceddo*).

The *ceddo*, whether aristocrats or soldiers of slave origin, lived by a martial culture that prized provision for dependents, the consumption of alcohol, and the singing of epic poetry by their bards in praise of manly honour. Such worldly power was often seen as diametrically opposed to the spiritual power represented both at court and in wider society by the presence of Sufi-affiliated Muslim preachers and teachers. So it would seem to Bamba. Retiring from court, where his father had been an advisor, he spent time in study and meditation, followed several Sufi masters, was inducted into several different fraternities, and wrote prayerful poetry. In 1887, he founded a religious and agricultural settlement, Touba, not far from his birthplace. Here he sought to build a faithful community of *murid*s, disciples or "seekers," who might live faithfully in God's way in the troubled times that had come upon the world.

In the 1870s and 1880s, as they extended their control inland, the French built a railway from north to south through Kajoor territory. They sought to expand the production of cash crops (rice and especially peanuts), restrict traditional grain-growing, and forge a partnership with the Wolof commercial aristocracy against the King of Kajoor, Lat Joor Joop (sometimes written Lat Dior Diop), who opposed French expansion and was killed in 1886. A protectorate was established over Kajoor, and over the following years, more assertive French control would be imposed, through chiefs who became colonial auxiliaries in the countryside, and through direct administration by colonial officials and municipal government in the growing towns. All of these were suspicious of the influence of Sufi leaders whom the French called *marabouts* (from Arabic *mrabtin*, the same word that had given the name of the militant Almoravid movement in eleventh-century North Africa and Spain).

For their part, the Muslim leaders and their disciples saw both the French and the secular chiefs as guilty of worldly vice, corruption, and the exploitation of slaves and peasants. The *murids*' slogan, "God alone is king!," was a repudiation of their worldly authority. It expressed a growing popular disdain for the chiefs as oppressive allies of the new colonial administration, compared with the growing popular authority of Bamba and the *murids*. Unlike an earlier generation of revivalists, though—and unlike other contemporary ones, in the as-yet-unconquered Sahara or the deserts and mountains of Mauritania and Morocco further north—Bamba chose not to preach armed resistance.

Despite his quietism, Bamba was accused of plotting an insurrection, and in 1895 he was exiled to Gabon, in central Africa, where he remained for seven years. This experience, which Bamba referred to as having to wear a "robe of misery," proved nonetheless to be spiritually powerful. A story quickly spread that, since he was forbidden to pray on-board the ship taking him from Dakar to Libreville, he had unrolled his prayer mat over the side of the ship and prayed while afloat on the surface of the ocean, to the great astonishment of the watching French sailors and their priest. Echoing a motif common in the stories of Sufi saints all the way back to ninth-century Basra, this story remains popular today, and is often illustrated on the glass paintings used to depict Bamba's life and miraculous resistance. He would be exiled again in 1903, only a year after returning to Senegal, and then held under house arrest. In 1910, he made a declaration opposing the pursuit of jihad against the French and counselling acceptance of their rule—which in any case, as he had evidently concluded, could not be resisted by force without unconscionable losses, and would not for the foreseeable future be removed.

In Bamba's prolonged absences, his principal disciples continued to lead the *murid* community and expand its following. One of them, Shaykh Ibra Fall, had his own disciples who formed a movement of their own, the Baye Fall. The Baye Fall today have a distinct identity within the Murid community, characterised by colourful patched or striped clothing, dreadlocks, and sometimes ecstatic ritual practices. At least in their appearance, his followers evoked the older tradition of Sufi mendicants. But Ibra Fall, an ex-*ceddo*, was an example of a fervent *murid* who also gained great material prosperity through the growing success of the order. He lived an aristocratic lifestyle and invested in businesses and property. In 1913, his annual gift to Amadu Bamba was equal to the salary of the governor-general of French West Africa. Fleeing from the world meant avoiding the corrupting influence of politics, but piety could go with prosperity. Thanks to Ibra Fall, it was said, "thousands of scoundrels" from the old, disreputable society of the royal courts became good Muslims, following *lamp Fall* ("Fall's way"), joining the *murid*s and devoting themselves to the labour of cultivation in the community's agricultural settlements.[26]

Indeed, while some *murid*s were capable of disciplined study and spiritual reflection, and directed to teachers suited to their abilities, the discipline the fraternity prescribed for everyone was hard work, whether mental or physical, or both. The order valued, and provided, education, but it also promoted a work ethic by which personal moral improvement could be experienced, and God's grace obtained. This put an indigenous and Islamic spin on the developing colonial economy, which had encouraged farming cash crops since the 1860s. The movement's followers were often young men and women who fled slavery, or rural poverty and dependence, for the *murid* settlements. There, their agricultural labour fed both the fraternity's financial independence, and the growth of colonial exports.

Critics of the *marabouts'* influence thought them merely a new class of exploiters, replacing the old aristocracy. *Murids* themselves were more likely to see membership in the community, as a free cultivator and a Muslim, as a way of finding a personal dignity that had been denied to the slaves and "powerless" peasants of earlier times. According to one story, a *murid* once offered his slave as a gift to Amadu Bamba, to which Bamba replied: "If you own him, then you own me, because he and I have the same Master." The shaykh might have accepted the inevitability of the foreigners' empire, but like other Muslims throughout the long, calamitous nineteenth century, he had not stopped believing in the sovereignty of God.[27]

10

THE EMPIRE OF MISRULE

On the evening of June 15, 1858, twenty-two people were murdered in the Arabian port town of Jeddah. They were Ottoman, British, French, Russian and Greek, most of them Christians and either citizens or protégés of European states. In the British House of Lords, swift retribution was demanded against "the relentless fury of the fanatics." The previous year's Indian Mutiny was fresh in British imaginations, and rumours ran wild of anti-Christian plots uniting Muslims across the Indian Ocean in a threat to order, empire, and the march of progress.[1]

In fact, the riot had been sparked by a dispute between two British Indian Muslims who were both firmly part of the world that European empire and global capitalism were creating. One of them, Faraj Yusr, was the Hijaz's foremost banker. Thought to be the richest man in Jeddah, he had sometimes served as Britain's vice-consul. He also worked as the representative of a Greek trading company based in Cairo that had branches and partnerships across the British Empire, from Liverpool to Bombay. The other was Salih Jawhar, the business agent of a Jeddah-based Indian Muslim family, born in the Ottoman Balkans but now also a British Indian subject of Queen Victoria.

Jawhar and Yusr had found themselves on opposing sides in a business dispute in which Jawhar sought to escape legal action by taking advantage of the several imperial jurisdictions he now lived in. Invoking his Ottoman nationality, he tried to have a ship of which he was part-owner, the *Irani*, registered under the Ottoman instead of the British flag. The local authorities allowed the change. The British objected; British sailors seized the ship, allegedly trampling on its Ottoman flag in a show of contempt. Infuriated local officials, already resentful of both British and Ottoman government attempts to stop the Red Sea slave trade, incited locals, who had their own grievances against foreign interference and competition, to riot. They hoped the British would back off. Instead, a British gunboat shelled Jeddah, killing seven people and causing the townspeople to flee towards Mecca. Eleven men—shopkeepers, artisans, sailors—who may or may not have been involved in rioting and murder were publicly beheaded by the Ottoman governor to appease British demands for retributive justice. The captain of the British gunboat made sure all the Indians in town were watching.

The British put the Jeddah riot, like the Indian uprising, down to religious fanaticism. But its causes were more material: economic and social stresses created by rapidly expanded trade, and the wealth and influence it brought to a small town's very visible expatriate community, which enjoyed preferential access to capital and credit; local people's resulting fears for their own livelihoods; and local authorities' resentment at outsiders' interference in local affairs. Jeddah's Muslims did resent non-Muslim influence in their town, the port of Mecca and the gateway of pilgrims from across the world to the holiest cities of Islam. But their outbreak of violence was not primarily religious; even less was it, as European observers believed, an expression of backward fanaticism. It was a symptom of their disorienting, headlong rush into a world of imperial globalisation.[2]

◇◇◇◇◇◇◇

Between 1820 and 1920, the worlds in which Muslims lived were overturned and reordered—or, from Muslim perspectives, thrown into deep disorder. By the end of the nineteenth century, the world's largest Muslim empire, with some sixty-three million subjects, was that of British India. Tsarist Russia extended its rule over some four-teen million Muslims in central Asia—almost as many as lived in the Ottoman Empire. Afghanistan and Iran, which for half a millennium had been imperial centres of the world in their own right, were now caught between these rival imperialisms from outside. British in-fluence expanded from India eastward to the Malay Peninsula, and westward to the Indian Ocean, the Persian Gulf, and East Africa. The French had spanned the Sahara, from Tunisia to Senegal, and ruled, albeit very unevenly, all of northwest Africa except for a few Spanish enclaves. The Dutch, early arrivals in the new imperial competition, had their own Muslim-majority empire, with some thirty million sub-jects, in Southeast Asia. The late-coming United States had fought its first sustained counterinsurgency war against Muslims in the Philip-pines. Everywhere, it seemed, Muslims had suddenly lost control over their lands and lives.

European rule often arrived as a sudden shock from outside, but the march of colonial empire was erratic. It proceeded in bursts of ter-ror but also by grinding attrition. Gradual encroachments on Muslim communities had begun in West Africa, the lower Volga, India, and Southeast Asia in the 1600s. They grew through North Africa, the Persian Gulf, and the Caucasus from the 1820s to the 1850s. Then, in a rush, the new imperialism swept over almost all of Africa, central Asia, and finally the Middle East, in only forty years, between the 1880s and the aftermath of the First World War.

The growth of European empire was never the work of Europeans alone. Indeed, most of the actual work was done by Asians and Afri-cans, many of them Muslims: dockers, railway workers, conscripted labourers, soldiers, porters, interpreters, clerks, traders, and many oth-ers. Dutch rule in Indonesia had grown slowly for two centuries be-fore the conflagration of the Java and Aceh Wars, and by the time the Dutch army invaded Aceh, in the 1870s, it included many Javanese soldiers whose own independent states had been extinguished fifty years earlier. The Berber-speaking Muslims in the mountains of Morocco were forced into submission by France's colonial army only in the mid-1920s, seventy years after the Berber-speaking Muslims of neighbouring Algeria, some of whom were by now serving in that colonial army after the long and desperate defence of their own independence had to be given up. When the British invaded Iraq, during the First World War, they did so with an Indian army. When the French invaded Syria, in 1921, to put an end to an independent Syrian Arab government, many of their soldiers were North Africans. There were Muslims on both sides, as we have seen, even at Omdurman.

If armed resistance against the now nearly ubiquitous colonial empires was unsustainable, then Muslims would have to find ways of living with them. The accommodation worked out by the Murids in Senegal was one example. Restating the kinds of claims that had been made, in 1830, by Ahmad Bu Darba in Algiers would be another: using the imperialists' own language of rights, improvement, and good government to demand that Muslims too, or at least the more educated and "civilised" (in European terms) among them, should have a greater say in how their countries, while still under European supervision, should be run. Perhaps nowhere was this argument made so strongly, and with such lasting effects, as in India, in the immediate aftermath of one of the imperial world's most dramatic moments of revolt, the Indian uprising (later known in Britain as the "Mutiny") of 1857.

In mid-nineteenth-century India, the British Empire was still the business of the East India Company, not of the British crown. The company had been continually attacked in Britain for its corruption and misrule, and in 1813 it lost its monopoly on trade in everything except tea. In 1833, its stockholders were persuaded (by payment of a generous, government-backed annuity) to give up their commercial interests, and the company's business was restricted to governing, collecting taxes, and running its army. Official proclamations in Indian towns still expressed the formal situation in Mughal political language: "Creation is God's, Sovereignty is the Emperor's, Government is the Company's." In each of the empire's provinces, formally speaking, the company was just another subcontractor of the Mughal *padishah*, the local agent of the legitimate emperor, albeit an unusually powerful and corporate one, whose soldiers wore red coats and carried the latest rifles.

Those soldiers were often recruited from the same north Indian, Muslim and high-caste Hindu warrior clans who had served Mughal princes and governors before. They were not conscripted peasants, nor penniless young men joining up for want of better prospects. They had a strong sense of their worth and dignity; they could see their service less as expanding "British" rule than as pursuing local traditions of martial professionalism and valorous conquest. As in other aspects of company rule, like tax collection or law courts, the complexity of Indian society and its institutions necessitated some sort of partnership. But from the 1830s onward, just as a new and more liberal language of improving government became more insistent in Britain itself, the conviction spread that only a firmer, centralised, authoritarian rule would do for India.

Liberals, who had often attacked the company for its "despotism," became imperialists, but imperial rule did not become liberal. As Thomas Macaulay, the liberal intellectual, historian and poet, explained in 1834 as he set out for India to rewrite its law code, its "conquered race" were people "to whom the blessings of our constitution cannot as yet be safely extended." Macaulay's vision of India chimed with that of James Mill, his philosophical antagonist back home— and, perhaps more surprisingly, with the disparaging picture that Babur, founder of the Mughal Empire, had painted of Hindu society centuries before. Babur had lamented the lack of order, geometry, regularity and civilised discourse to be had in India. Mill wrote that "in the writings of the Hindus" there was "no coherence, wisdom, or beauty.... All is disorder, caprice, passion... violence, and deformity."[3]

Faced with such a lack of "order," as they saw it, British rulers set out to impose one that they could understand. Uniformity and clarity would mean honesty and procedural propriety, putting an end to corruptions of all kinds and smoothing the way for progress. In practice, this meant assessing tax burdens with no regard for customary arrangements that were seen as rights, disregarding, humiliating and dispossessing local lords, and pressing a newly intrusive and unresponsive kind of state directly onto merchants, religious notables, small landholders, livestock-farmers and peasants. They had generally done well out of the breakup of Mughal power and the relative local autonomy it had allowed them. Now that autonomy was being trampled on.

The problem was not, as the British would later claim, that imposing "order" meant overcoming Indian resistance to beneficent liberal reforms: such reforms were talked about more than they were enacted. The complex landscape of Hindu and Muslim law frustrated would-be rational reformers, but the new criminal law code devised by Macaulay and his colleagues in 1837 was left unimplemented for more than twenty years. The famous outlawing of *sati*, the patriarchal cruelty of high-caste Hindu widows being immolated on their husbands' funeral pyres, in 1829 was an exceptional intervention. Sati was outlawed only when the British were convinced that it was not properly Hindu practice anyway. (And the argument over it—as would often be the case—was more a struggle of competing patriarchies than a struggle for women's rights.)[4] On the whole, British rule had not yet interfered much with religion and law.

Instead, the East India Company and its agents had become more intrusive and arrogant. They had exercised the rights of rulers—collecting revenue, controlling markets, demanding obedience—without accepting their responsibilities. When harvests failed in Bengal, in 1768 and 1769, the British lamented the resulting famine as a natural disaster. But the crisis had been greatly exacerbated by their own demands for tax, hoarding of grain, and destruction of older safety nets for provision in hard times. Between three and four million people may have died as a result. The new rulers seemed to disregard the basic elements of what, to Indians, in fact made for good order: the social distinctions and practices, the recognition of rights and responsibilities that gave people status, self-respect, and protection.

Now, Indian soldiers worried that they would all be made to eat the same food, without regard for the dietary distinctions that were so essential to status and cleanliness. Having conquered all of India, they worried that they would be made to serve abroad to conquer other countries. They found that they were expected to submit to increasingly harsh discipline; expression of their grievances was punished as insubordination. In 1857, they heard rumours that they would be expected to use new rifle cartridges greased with cow or pig fat, polluting to Hindus and Muslims, respectively. The fear was that the British were out to make everyone into a Christian. In fact, no such cartridges were ever issued, no Indian troops would be deployed outside India until the First World War, and there was no project of mass evangelisation. But underlying discontent was ignited by the soldiers' revolt and became an insurrection that spread across north India. The insurgents took Delhi and called for the ageing and effectively powerless Mughal emperor, Bahadur Shah Zafar, to exercise his right to rule over "the Hindus and Musulmans [Muslims] of Hindustan."[5]

The revolt was put down by the deployment of forty thousand soldiers, and then the British wreaked vengeance, expelling the whole population of Delhi and shooting captured rebels to pieces from the mouths of cannon. (This spectacular form of Mughal execution was deliberately religiously offensive, since bodies could not be recovered for proper burial or cremation; its adoption gave the lie to British claims that their rule was a moralising improvement on Mughal violence.) The cultural life of music, dance, and literature that had flourished in the old capital was wiped out. The destruction was compared to Nadir Shah's depredations over a hundred years earlier. Company rule and the formality of Mughal sovereignty were both abolished. Nineteen years later, Queen Victoria would become empress of India.

The revolt had been precipitated and followed largely by Hindus, but the Muslim Mughal emperor had become its figurehead. Muslims in Meerut, at the insurgency's outbreak, had celebrated, crying "Ali, Ali, our religion has revived." For years afterwards, anxious British governors asked whether India's millions of Muslims were "bound in conscience to rebel against the Queen," as an influential book by William Wilson Hunter, a government statistician and prolific writer on Indian affairs, put it in 1871. They were troubled by currents of Muslim revivalism, and by the growing legend of Sayyid Ahmad Barelwi, a revivalist preacher and descendant of the Prophet who had led a five-year campaign to re-establish Muslim sovereignty against the Sikhs in northwest India before being killed in battle in 1831. Hunter wrote that, while India's Muslims might for now have accepted subjection to British rule, they nonetheless constituted "a source of chronic danger." A "religious war," he warned, might at any time be provoked by "fanatics" on the northwest frontier and spread among the "seditious masses" of Muslims at the heart of the empire.[6]

After British control was extended over Delhi in 1803, Ahmad Barelwi's teacher, Abd al-Aziz Shah, the son of Sufi revivalist Shah Wali Allah al-Dihlawi, had issued a judgment that India was now a "domain of war," *dar al-harb*, since Muslim sovereignty was no longer effective and government had passed to non-believers. British alarm grew at the influence of "Wahhabis," as they almost invariably called pious and revivalist Muslims, irrespective of whether they really followed Ibn Abd al-Wahhab's teachings. In fact, Abd al-Aziz Shah's ruling had more to do with sorting out the practicalities of life under an un-Islamic empire than fomenting rebellion against it, and his advice was generally liberal. Was it permissible in their new circumstances, Muslim businessmen seeking Abd al-Aziz's opinion wanted to know, to earn interest on investments? (It was.) Did Muslims now living under non-Muslim rule have to emigrate to the jurisdiction of a Muslim sovereign, even if the new rulers allowed unimpeded public prayer? (They did not.) Could Muslims wear European dress, as long as they did so for their own comfort, not to impress unbelievers? (They could.) And could they take government jobs, if the government was not inimical to Islam? (Again, they could.)[7]

An even stronger position in favour of accommodating to the new order of things was espoused by Sayyid Ahmad Khan, who believed the old Indian ruling class needed to accept the reality of its defeat, embrace the new rulers' institutions, and work within them. For his loyalism, he was knighted and became known as Sir Sayyid—but he was no obsequious imperial servant. Sayyid Ahmad was an educator and social reformer, a poet and historian. Born to an Afghan Mughal family, he grew up close to the Mughal court. Having worked in the colonial judicial system, and having lived through the uprising in rebel-held territory, after 1857 he sought to convince the British that India's Muslims would be loyal subjects, if given the chance.

"The evils that now exist" in India, he wrote in the 1870s, "owe their origin greatly to the want of union and sympathy between the rulers and the ruled." Obsessing about "fanatics" and sedition, as the British did, only made things worse. What was needed was the political culture cultivated by the Emperor Babur and his successors, namely "cordial intercourse" between properly educated gentlemen, the courtly art of conversation through which divergent interests could be understood and conflicts resolved. But the British now tended to keep aloof from their Indian subjects and increasingly thought of the differences between them in racialised terms. There was little space for "cordial intercourse": Indians did not "have a voice in Government's councils." Sayyid Ahmad did not think the fault lay all on one side: he thought his own community needed to recover its self-esteem and work on "the refinement of morals" (*tahzib ul-akhlaq*), the title he gave to his Urdu-language educational periodical in the 1870s. The problem with the British was that they did not listen.

Muslim and Hindu upper-class gentlemen and upwardly mobile men of capital alike maintained that, if only the British could be made to listen and grant them their due share in the government of their country, both colonial misrule and ruinous insurrection could be avoided. This was the basic position of the Indian National Congress when it was created in 1885—although Sayyid Ahmad himself would disparage the Congress, seeing it as a vehicle through which "power… over the whole country will be in the hands of Bengalis or of Hindus of the Bengali type," leaving Muslims to "fall into a condition of utmost degradation." Having previously declared that Hindus and Muslims in India formed one *qaum*, one community of purpose—one people, one nation—he came to see that political participation, as now envisaged in an era of mass politics and electoral democracy, would slip from the grasp of true aristocratic gentlemen. It was already being claimed by Bengali businessmen and bureaucrats. Soon it would divide the masses, by number, into majority and minority communities, and Muslims would count among the latter.[8]

The British, for their part, while fretting about Muslim sedition, also came to imagine Muslims as a potential source of strength. It was not lost on British politicians that the size of India's Muslim population made Britain, in a phrase often repeated from the 1870s to the 1920s, "the greatest Mohammedan power in the world." Imperial policy, it was often said, had to take account of Muslim opinion, especially in India. Britain's support of the Ottoman Empire against Russian expansion in southeast Europe, and its facilitation of the pilgrimage to Mecca across the empire's steamship and railway routes, offered grounds for claiming that the British Empire was a protector, not an oppressor, of Muslims. By enshrining what they thought of as the forms of Islamic law in use in India into a fixed civil legal code, "Anglo-Muhammadan law," in the 1860s, the British thought they were protecting religious sensibilities in the regulation of family law while also rationalising the legal process. (Criminal, commercial, and other branches of the law had been removed from the purview of Islamic judges.) They acceded to Muslim demands in establishing a separate electorate, in which Muslim voters would vote for Muslim candidates, when Indian representatives were first allowed a small role on government councils in 1909. But by enshrining the law in a fixed code, and taking it out of the hands of Muslim judges whose expertise lay in its interpretation, the British were making law around marriage, inheritance and divorce less flexible, and putting it under the authority of the state. By recognising Muslims as a separate political community, they began to institutionalise Indian politics along communal lines. All of this would have dramatic, unintended consequences.[9]

◇◇◇◇◇◇◇

In the new world of European imperialism, many Muslims began to look again to the institution of the caliphate. The Ottoman sultan still held that title, though for centuries it had lain somewhat hollow and mostly unused. Much like their unfriendly neighbours, the Habsburgs and Romanovs, the sultans still ruled over an older kind of empire: sprawling, dynastic, multiethnic and decentralised. After the Napoleonic wars ended, the Ottomans found themselves excluded from Europe's new, international society of self-declared civilised nations. To Europeans, increasingly, Muslims seemed to stand outside of History as they understood it, as enemies of progress. Medieval European religious prejudices that had seen Muhammad as an impostor and Islam as a false sect were being replaced, somewhat ironically, by the more modern belief that Muhammad had been (in the philosopher Jean-Jacques Rousseau's words) a great "lawgiver" and political genius, but that contemporary Muslims were irrational and their Islam impervious to change.

The early Ottomans had seen themselves as rightful heirs of the caesars, and for centuries the empire and its rulers had been part of Europe. Early modern statesmen from England and Italy had praised the good order of the "Grand Signior's" state. But perceptions had changed. The "Turks," according to the German philosopher Gottfried Herder, writing at the end of the 1700s, were a "foreign nation in Europe," their empire "one vast prison" ruled over by "Asiatic barbarians." There was never a uniform antipathy to the Ottomans in Europe: in nineteenth-century Britain, figures as influential as the poet Lord Byron and the Prime Minister Benjamin Disraeli wrote appreciatively of the "Turkish" world. But these were colourful highlights in an increasingly dark picture. In the 1820s, Greek rebels against Ottoman rule gained sympathy in France and Britain: they were fellow Christians who belonged to European civilisation, suffering under an Eastern despotism. By 1876, the Ottomans' repression of Bulgarian nationalists, deplored in the British parliament by the liberal leader William Gladstone, could be used to drum up popular support in an election campaign. The equation of Ottoman rule with misgovernment came to seem self-evident.[10]

The Ottomans themselves, of course, did not see things this way, but they knew they had to do something to cope with the seismic changes of the new age of revolutions. After the upheavals of the turn of the century, which saw four sultans in quick succession on the throne between 1798 and 1808, the 1808 Deed of Agreement was meant to put an end to the instability. Istanbul had been rocked repeatedly as the different centres of power in the Ottoman state—the palace, provincial strongmen, the religious scholars, the bureaucracy, the janissaries and the crowd in the street—struggled to expand their prerogatives or defend their interests. The Deed formalised an alliance between the dynasty and the provincial lords, aimed against the janissaries and their allies in the capital who more than once had been able to impose their will on a reigning sultan. It also, not for the first time, envisaged a new provincial standing army that the janissaries correctly saw as a threat to themselves.

The sultan who signed the Deed, Mahmud II, had been on the throne for barely a month. Two months later he faced a janissary revolt that killed many of the other signatories; thousands of people were killed in Istanbul, and the navy shelled the janissary barracks, but the sultan had to compromise. The Deed was a dead letter. A further showdown between the palace and the janissaries was inevitable. It finally came in 1826: this time, Mahmud II sent loyal troops against the six thousand or so janissaries in Istanbul, massacred them, and abolished the corps altogether. A wholesale purge followed. More than a military force, the janissaries had been a social institution. They were still closely associated with the popular Bektashi Sufi order. They had their own quartermasters, families of Jewish bankers who were among the empire's chief credit brokers, and they owned a third of Istanbul's coffeehouses. The Bektashis' lodges were closed, their shaykhs executed, and their assets transferred to other Sufi groups more supportive of the dynasty, especially the more traditionally aristocratic Mevlevis, with whom members of the imperial family were affiliated. The corps's three leading Jewish quartermasters were murdered, and their wealth confiscated.[11]

Mahmud II's ruthless action was part of a pattern of autocratic assertiveness around the Muslim Mediterranean, as the long eighteenth century ended by burning up the old order of things. Ottoman history would remember the suppression of the janissaries as *vaqa-i hayriye*, the "auspicious incident," a decisive moment in the refoundation of the dynasty's authority. It was the last in a series of similar moves that had begun elsewhere. In 1811, the hereditary Ottoman ruler of Tunis had faced down a janissary revolt of his own and suppressed the janissary corps there. In that same year, Mehmed Ali Pasha, the ambitious Ottoman soldier who had risen to power in Egypt, massacred the Mamluks, the local Egyptian military class inherited from the medieval period, in the citadel of Cairo. In 1817, the Ottoman viceroy in Algiers recruited his own new militia, decamped with the treasury from his palace in the lower town to the fortress atop the city, destroyed the janissaries who had threatened his rule and, as his chronicler put it, disturbed the peace. Moves to consolidate and centralise power were frequent in the troubled years of revolutionary war in and beyond Europe.

In the European parts of the sultan's empire, too, local magnates had built their own positions of power. But some of them were Christians, and although Christian lords and princes had always had their place in the Ottoman regime, now they came to see themselves as belonging elsewhere, in a Slavic world championed by Russia, or a European world inspired by Romantic and revolutionary ideas. They saw themselves as destined, not for a greater portion of power within the empire, as had been the aim of almost every assertive provincial lord for three centuries, but for their own sovereignty outside it. The American and French Revolutions had proclaimed the sovereignty of the "nation" in place of the sovereignty of the dynast on the throne; first Greeks, then Serbs, and later others identifying themselves as patriots seeking liberty for their people and homeland—Bulgarians, Macedonians, Armenians—began to organise revolutions of their own.[12]

The Greek uprising, beginning in 1820, rapidly threw off Ottoman rule in much of the peninsula, killing both Muslims and Jews in the process. In the mid-1820s, Ottoman forces regained control thanks to an invasion force sent from Egypt via Crete by Mehmed Ali, under the command of his son, Ibrahim Pasha. Their brutal reprisals included massacring the men of insurgent towns and enslaving their women and children. Europeans, who generally thought of their own empires as benevolent, and violence against their own empires' disorderly, non-white subjects as necessary and justified, saw Ottoman violence against that empire's white, Christian, European subjects as unspeakable. The Ottomans' massacre of Greek insurgents on the island of Chios was dramatized by the French Romantic painter Eugène Delacroix, introducing a burgeoning European public opinion to what, ninety years later, the British historian Arnold Toynbee would call "the murderous tyranny of the Turks." In 1827, the European powers sent a combined British, French and Russian fleet that destroyed Mehmed Ali's navy at the Battle of Navarino off the Greek coast. Combined with a Russian invasion, this European intervention saved the Greek revolt and obliged the sultan to accept autonomy for Greece and then Serbia in 1830, followed soon after by independence. The Orthodox Greeks were provided with a Bavarian Catholic king, who would later be succeeded by a Danish prince.[13]

In contrast to its Christian-majority provinces in southeast Europe, nationalism and revolutionary politics would emerge as mass movements among the mostly Muslim—Arab and Turkish—parts of the empire only at the end of the 1800s and around, and in response to, the First World War. Local patriotisms—identification with a particular homeland, its people, and its distinct language, lifestyle and culture, in Anatolia, Palestine, Lebanon, or Egypt—could still sit within the frame of the empire as a focus of political loyalty. There was not yet any revolutionary or nationalist threat to Ottoman sovereignty from the south and east. The threat here came from another product of the revolutionary era: the self-made military empire-builder with no religious mission, but a ferocious belief in himself and his own dynasty-founding destiny. Napoleon Bonaparte had not stayed long in Egypt, but he left a model to follow. Mehmed Ali's troops may have sailed to the sultan's rescue in Greece, as they had earlier put down the Saudi and Wahhabi movement in Arabia. But as we have seen, Mehmed Ali himself had empire-building ideas of his own. By 1830, his was the most serious of all the challenges to the Ottomans.

Mehmed Ali Pasha liked to tell people that he had been born in 1769, the same year as both Napoleon and Napoleon's nemesis, Arthur Wellesley, the Duke of Wellington, who had helped overthrow Tipu Sultan in India (and briefly ruled over Mysore from Tipu's former palace at Srirangapatna) before becoming the victor of Waterloo. In fact, Mehmed Ali seems to have been born a year later. But the association clearly mattered to him. He came from a Turkish-speaking Sunni Muslim family in Kevala, a tobacco-growing port town east of Thessalonica (Salonica, Ottoman Selanik) in northern Greece. He arrived in Egypt in 1801, aged thirty-one, as the second-in-command of a roughneck Albanian force of irregular soldiers. In the political disorder that followed the evacuation of the French occupiers, Mehmed Ali manoeuvred with astute ruthlessness, becoming the most powerful man in Cairo and the arbiter of factional conflict to whom the city's lawyers, businessmen, and artisans all turned. In 1805, the sultan accepted a situation he could not control, by withdrawing his own appointee as governor from Cairo's citadel and investing Mehmed Ali as governor in his place, recognising that "the religious scholars and subjects approved of that." It was another six years before the new governor was strong enough to eliminate his last rivals, the remaining Mamluk princes: they were invited to a ceremony at the Cairo citadel, then trapped and massacred as they left. The survivors were systematically hunted down and murdered.[14]

The new ruler of Egypt had a mission to "arouse" the country, as he put it, "from the sleep of ages and mould it to a new existence." The way forward was through technology, industry, military power, and a new role in the new world economy. He despatched students to France and brought in French doctors and engineers to establish a hospital and medical school, and to supervise public works projects. Food crops were displaced by a new and high-quality strain of cotton, grown for export on the booming world market and for processing in new textile mills to make uniforms and caps for the new army. State monopolies on cereal crops, rice, and sugar increased the pasha's revenue and immiserated the peasantry, who were drafted into the army and mercilessly conscripted as labourers. One hundred thousand men, women and children, or a third of the workforce, were said to have died digging a canal between Alexandria and the Nile. Egypt had little available wood or coal, so machinery in the new factories set up to mill cotton, refine sugar, process gunpowder and manufacture guns was often powered by animal or, where necessary, human muscle. Peasants were forbidden from leaving the land, and those who fled and were caught were "chained by the neck, put into boats and sent to the Pasha's farms." Conditions in cotton mills were so bad, according to one of Mehmed Ali's Armenian technical advisors, that workers preferred "to put an end to their miserable existence by throwing themselves out of the windows, and attempting to hang themselves."[15]

It may not have been Mehmed Ali's intention to overthrow the Ottoman Empire to which he nominally owed allegiance, but he aspired to expand his own rule as far as he could, and to secure his independence and his family's dynastic rule after him. With this aim in mind, an Egyptian army under his son, Ibrahim Pasha, invaded Syria in 1831. After a series of unanticipated successes, Ibrahim found himself with the empire at his feet, having defeated Ottoman forces at Konya, in southeast Anatolia, and with the empire's chief minister as his prisoner of war. Another round of hostilities in 1839 persuaded a new Ottoman sultan, the seventeen-year-old Abdülmecid I, to accept the fact of Mehmed Ali's independence from Istanbul. But by threatening to topple the Ottomans altogether, potentially opening the way to Russian control of the eastern Mediterranean, Egypt's autocrat pulled the western European powers into the struggle. Facing both British troops landing at Beirut and an uprising against his rule in Syria, Mehmed Ali was obliged to accept European terms. In 1840, he removed his army from Syria in exchange for the sultan's, and the Europeans', guarantee of his hereditary sovereignty in Egypt.

The push and pull of independent, dynastic state-building and entanglement with European interests continued under Mehmed Ali's successors after his death in 1849. Increasingly exposed to European creditors on whom their ambitious financing depended, Egypt's rulers also began to figure more centrally in Europe's strategic calculations after the opening of the Suez Canal in 1869. In 1873, European bankers and their debtors were all hit by the first great depression of global capitalism, and three years later Egypt defaulted on its public debt. (The same fate had already befallen the central Ottoman treasury in 1875.) European controllers brought in to supervise the budget and guarantee repayments to foreign lenders imposed swingeing cuts, including to the army.

Foreign control thus combined with a threat to the livelihoods of Egyptian-born army officers who already chafed under the social superiority of the Turkish and Circassian ruling class of aristocrats, landlords, and senior commanders whose wealth and power had consolidated around Mehmed Ali's family and hangers-on. In 1881, they rebelled, demanding an "Egypt for the Egyptians," an end to foreign interference, and a constitutional government. Rioters in Alexandria attacked foreigners and foreign-owned property. British ships shelled Alexandria. British soldiers landed and defeated the Egyptian army. A British occupation began that would last for seventy-four years.

◇◇◇◇◇◇◇◇

An autocratic, militarised state that bent society to its economic imperatives, such as that begun by Mehmed Ali and inherited by the British, was one striking model of what the new world of the nineteenth century might look like. The Ottoman Empire was too diverse and unwieldy for such a rapid, forced-march experiment in modern development. In principle, the Ottomans' "Sublime State" was still an autocracy, in which the sultan guaranteed the security and prosperity of what courtly convention called *memalik-i mahruse*, his "well-protected domains." But in practice, it was a state whose power was spread so thin, and contested by so many provincial lords, that effectively mobilising its considerable resources was impossible. It had not fallen apart as the Mughal domains had, but it was being eroded from outside.

Russia, France, and Britain competed with each other over the Ottomans' strategic territory: Russia on the Black Sea, the French in North Africa, Britain in the eastern Mediterranean. They competed, too, for rights to "protect" and influence the empire's non-Muslim communities: Russia among Orthodox Christians, France among Catholics and Maronites, Britain among Jews, Syrian Druze, and the newly emerging Protestants. The empire was also being fractured from within by Balkan nationalism, Egyptian sub-imperialism, and growing social tensions. As trade expanded and European manufactured goods flooded in, landlords and merchants profited from new opportunities while workers and peasants struggled to maintain their livelihoods. Artisanal crafts became unprofitable, and tensions between producers and owners, buyers and sellers—which sometimes overlapped with religious differences—flared up.[16]

Strengthening the empire thus meant pulling its people, its productive capacity, and its manpower together, overcoming internal divisions to face outside threats. This would be the essential aim, pursued by different methods, of everyone who came to rule in Istanbul from the aftermath of the Egyptian crisis in the 1830s until the empire's end ninety years later. The first attempt at such change was a program of legislative and administrative reform, in effect a revolution from above with the bureaucracy at its centre. In China this would be called "self-strengthening." In the Ottoman Empire it was called *tanzimat-i hayriye*, the "beneficent reorganisation" of the state. It was set in motion in November 1839, publicly announced in what became known as the Gülhane (the "Rose Room" or "Rose Garden") edict.

The decade after the showdown with the janissaries in 1826 had already seen dramatic institutional moves to give the empire's rulers a firmer grip on its territory and peoples. A "new model" (*nizam-i cedid*) army replaced the janissaries. Religious scholars were made functionaries in a state-controlled hierarchy that also controlled their material resources in a new ministry of religious foundations. The palace bureaucracy was reorganised into functionally separate ministries, court officials became a ranked, salaried civil service, and a permanent diplomatic corps was established with permanent embassies abroad. A census of the population was carried out. New schools were set up. And in a sign of how being in step with changing times (or rejecting them) would often be expressed, in 1829 the sultan ordered that men working in government offices should wear a fez instead of a turban, and jacket and trousers in the new European style. The measure was intended to remove visible distinctions of religious community belonging, making men more equal in public space—and changing dress codes over the following decades would indeed have this effect. But it also indicated that, while what Muslim men and women should or should not wear might become less a matter of religious status, it would not cease to be a matter of political concern.

The reformers' expectations, and their view of their own history, were initially imbued with a nostalgia and an optimism that were both characteristic of the nineteenth century. Ottoman statesmen had been complaining about the "dissolution of order" as early as the mid-sixteenth century, in the very era later imagined as the empire's golden age: the lament that things were better in the old days was nothing new, and not unique to the Ottomans. But in the 1830s, there was a newly powerful sense of disjuncture with the past, and a reset was needed. "All the world knows," the Gülhane edict began serenely, "that since the first days of the Ottoman state, the lofty principles of the Qur'an and the rules of the sharia were always perfectly observed." But for the past century and a half, things had gone awry. Now, it was hoped, putting things right would restore the empire's fortunes "within five or ten years." Putting things right meant harnessing both the foundational principles of Islamic good government, which had supposedly been lost, and the technological requirements of modern times, which needed to be acquired. The reformers drew both on the eighteenth century's legacy of religious revivalism, the well-established idiom of periodic "renewal" (*tajdid*, in Turkish *tecdid*) in the Muslim community and its faith, and on the practical imperatives of government that demanded more efficient taxation, and more and better soldiers.[17]

Rather than generating both revenue and manpower by brute force, as in Mehmed Ali's Egypt, however, the Ottomans sought to increase their subjects' loyalty by equalising their legal status. If a man "enjoys perfect security," they reasoned, "it is clear that he will not depart from the ways of loyalty, and all his actions will contribute to the welfare of the government and of the people." This was as true of the bureaucratic class—whose legal status as slaves of the sultan meant that their wealth and property were not safe from confiscation—as of anyone else. To some degree, they were talking about themselves. But the reformers' radical move was to declare that the sultan would now guarantee "to our subjects perfect security for life, honour, and property," equally and "without exception" to both "Muslim and non-Muslim." A second declaration in February 1856, on the eve of negotiations to end the Crimean War, was more explicit. Not only was each community guaranteed "entire freedom in the exercise of its religion," "all forms of religion" were to be "freely professed," and forced conversion was to be prohibited. There was also to be religious equality: "Every distinction or designation tending to make any class...whatever of the subjects of my empire inferior to another . . . , on account of their religion, language, or race," was to be "forever effaced."[18]

Religious equality for all, and the neutrality of a secular state relative to the religious sphere, was far from well established in Europe. Catholic emancipation had only been enacted in Britain in 1829, and confessional equality was far from being the reality in British-ruled Ireland. In Germany, a "cultural struggle" would be waged over the political life and loyalty of German Catholics in the 1870s and 1880s. The formal separation of church and state remained the most contentious of all struggles in France until it was enshrined in law in 1905. Russia made the loudest noises about the need to protect its Christian cousins from Ottoman depredations, but Russia's Jews were the target of pogroms, and Muslims were forcibly deported in the thousands from Crimea and the Caucasus. Religious equality in the Ottoman lands, then, was not about catching up with a more enlightened Europe. It was about avoiding the splintering of the empire as its non-Muslim communities were used as proxies for the competing interests of European imperial rivals, and countering the pervasive European claim that Ottoman Muslim despotism necessitated European intervention to save its Christians from persecution.

The timing of the 1856 decree as the empire emerged from the horrors of the Crimean War was no accident. The war had broken out in 1853, with Britain and France as allies of the Ottomans against Russia. It was sparked by competing claims to precedence and protection over the Christian holy sites of Jerusalem and Bethlehem. Rival European powers saw themselves as patrons of different Eastern Christian churches (France for the Catholics, Russia for the Orthodox) and were prepared to go to war to defend their respective protégés' prerogatives. The *casus belli* may have been absurd, but it was the Victorian combination of artillery, food shortages, and cholera that made the war especially atrocious. Alongside the American Civil War in the following decade, and the carnage at Omdurman at the century's end, it gave an indication of what modern industrial warfare would be. Its conclusion, with the Treaty of Paris in 1856, marked the Europeans' re-admission of the Ottoman state to the diplomatic top table, at least in principle. The guarantee of protection to the empire's religious minorities was a particular concern of British policy; to some degree, the 1856 Reform Decree was a mark of Ottoman acquiescence to the Europeans' view of things, as the text had the sultan describe it: "with a view to establishing a state of things conformable with the dignity of my empire and the position which it occupies among civilized nations."[19]

But the Ottomans also had their own reasons for seeking to consolidate their people into a single, newly imagined Ottoman nationality. To be Ottoman, *osmanli*, had been a marker of status: a superior, literate, urban identity mostly held by the imperial elite. (To be a "Turk," by contrast, from that elite's perspective, was to be an illiterate and unrefined Anatolian peasant or, worse, nomad.) Now, everyone, whether

Turk, Albanian, Armenian, Greek, Kurd, or Arab, Christian, Muslim, or Jew, was to be given, if not citizenship—sovereignty in the empire was still the sultan's, not the people's—at least an equal subjecthood and membership in the political community. Thomas Macaulay may have considered the blessings of constitutionalism inappropriate for Britain's Indian subjects in the 1830s, but by the 1850s it was exactly what Ottoman reformers thought their own empire needed.

The central provisions of the 1856 decree were taken up, in 1861, in a constitution for the effectively autonomous Ottoman Regency of Tunis, where the reformist statesman, Islamic scholar and historian Ahmad Ibn Abi Diyaf would celebrate the triumph of "rule bound by law." In 1876 the *tanzimat* effort reached its culmination with the promulgation of an Ottoman constitution. It declared the sultan to be absolute, and Islam to be the religion of the state, but established elected assemblies, protected "the free exercise of faiths," and guaranteed personal liberty. It declared that "all subjects of the empire are... Ottomans, without distinction whatever faith they profess.... All Ottomans are equal in the eyes of the law. They have the same rights, and owe the same duties towards their country, without prejudice to religion."[20]

But as was true in other empires, the Ottoman rulers' actions did not have the intended effects. There were contradictory impulses even within the constitutional program. While the 1876 constitution borrowed its more liberal aspects from the Belgian constitution of 1831, it also took more autocratic provisions from the Prussian constitution of 1850. And if reform cut both ways in its conception, it did so more strongly in its application. The expansion of the state was led by, and greatly increased the power of, the bureaucrats of the central government service (known to Europeans, from the name of its headquarters building in Istanbul, Bab-i Ali, "the most high gate," by the somewhat florid term the "Sublime Porte"). Bureaucratic centralism was opposed by many, including more liberal constitutionalists and religious scholars. The imperial integration of territory, its extension of control into what had been relatively autonomous borderlands and rural areas, was resented and resisted. The census and land registration, to peasants in Syria and Palestine, could only portend more taxation and the conscription of their sons, and they avoided it as much as possible. (In the process, urban notable families registered lands in their own names instead of in those of the peasant communities who worked them, creating a class of absentee landlords. From the 1880s onwards, this was crucial to the buying up of land in Ottoman Palestine by the emerging Zionist program to settle Jewish "pioneers" from Europe in what they considered to be their ancestral homeland.)

Equality could produce conflicting and destabilising results. For many Muslims, expanded formal rights did not make up for the loss of real privilege. For non-Muslims, a promised (but as yet only theoretical) legal equality was not necessarily preferable to practical ways of negotiating their interests that were bound up in older notions of justice and equity. Universal liability to military service was not universally welcome. In Tunisia, the reform program was identified with foreign influence, the government's foreign loans, and the radically increased taxation being levied to pay for them: in 1864, a widespread peasant insurrection forced the suspension of the constitution only three years after it was announced. A few years earlier, in Lebanon, on the other hand, peasants rose up against their landlords using the language of rights and equality proclaimed in the Gülhane edict to legitimise their protest against taxation and oppression.

To Ottoman bureaucrats, rural revolts and urban rioting in Syria and Lebanon from the 1840s to the 1860s were evidence of backwardness and disorder, proving the case for strengthening the state. In fact, like the murders in Jeddah in 1858, these outbreaks of violence were exacerbated, or actually created, by the local impact of European economic dominance and the politics of Ottoman reform: newly acute social stress between rich and poor, new languages of rights and representation. In establishing religious communities as formally equal, and their representatives as interlocutors with the state, the reformers did not abolish religious distinctions between their subjects. Instead, they made religious communities into political ones.[21]

Some communities worked hard to become the Ottomans they were told they could be. Jewish inhabitants of cities like Thessalonica (Selanik) and Izmir (Smyrna) thought of themselves as a "model community" and identified themselves fully with the empire. Others, especially the Christian Armenians, whose communities were especially concentrated in Istanbul and in eastern Anatolia, were less sure. They had formally gained constitutional government earlier than the rest of the empire—in 1863, the Armenian community's internal affairs were vested in an elected assembly, rather than in the church's patriarch. But they increasingly emigrated, especially to France and the United States, evading the Ottoman state's ban on Armenian emigration, or formally giving up their Ottoman nationality and any right to return to their homeland when they did so.

In the 1890s, the Armenians became the target of vicious persecutions, carried out especially by Kurdish militia. These Kurdish troops themselves were made up of rural populations that previously had often lived outside effective imperial control: on the empire's margins, more closely integrating some of its subjects worked by turning them against others. In the case of the Kurds and Armenians, the conflict ran along economic and ecological lines—between generally impoverished Kurdish mountain villagers and somewhat better-off, commercially connected Armenian townspeople—that were also ethnic and linguistic boundaries. Fatefully, these were also divisions of religious community between Kurdish Muslims and Armenian Christians. Declaring everyone to be Ottoman, and all Ottomans to be equal, irrespective of such dividing lines, was not enough to erase them. As mass politics and new ideas of nationhood took hold within the old empire, they were, on the contrary, becoming more politically relevant than before, sometimes with disastrous consequences.[22]

◇◇◇◇◇◇◇◇

While they generally denigrated Ottoman rule, European observers often thought that what the "Turkish" empire really needed was a more enlightened despot. When Ottoman rule did take a more decisively authoritarian turn, it would be in the person of a sultan who, to European ambassadors, at first looked promising. Like a cultured European gentleman of his age, Abdülhamid II liked champagne, spoke French, and enjoyed comic opera—none of which prevented him from being a piously believing Muslim in his own estimation. He came to the throne in 1876 promising to enact constitutional rule; he was involved in drafting the constitution itself. But he soon determined that saving the empire meant pursuing technocratic power and efficiency without concern for liberal inclusivity or European sensibilities.

Almost immediately, in 1877, Abdülhamid faced the crisis of a renewed war with Russia that resulted in the most severe territorial losses the empire had yet sustained. In 1878, Romania, Serbia, and Montenegro became independent, Bulgaria became an autonomous principality, the Austrians occupied Bosnia-Herzegovina, and the British (in exchange for promising to defend the Ottomans next time) occupied Cyprus. The war also gave the sultan a pretext for suspending the constitution, dissolving parliament, and removing leading reform-minded bureaucrats, who were subsequently murdered. The constitution would remain suspended for the next thirty years.[23]

Over that time, what became known in Europe as the "Hamidian despotism" instituted a regime of police spies, press censorship, and political repression, combined with a renewed drive to integrate the empire's territory by telegraph lines, railways, and clock-towers, to increase its military power with conscription, equipment, and training, and to expand its reach. While the empire was losing productive land and taxable subjects in southeast Europe, it attempted to grow its influence elsewhere, both geographically in areas like Kurdistan, Transjordan, the Arabian Peninsula, Libya, and the eastern Sahara, and symbolically throughout the wider world of Muslims. Reviving the title of caliph, and claiming a particular interest in, and responsibility for, Muslims everywhere, was Abdülhamid's riposte to European imperial claims of protection over his own non-Muslim subjects.

The Ottomans lacked the capacity to turn such claims into real influence. Nonetheless, both the Ottoman imperial rhetoric and the

European imperial phobia of "pan-Islamism"—a unifying solidarity, or networked conspiracy, connecting all Muslims across the world—became prominent ideological forces by the end of the century. They combined with the reality of massively increased numbers of pilgrims making the hajj by steamship to Mecca, and the growing rapidity with which news and ideas could spread across old networks from West Africa through to the Indian Ocean. Ottoman connections with faraway places like Aceh were re-established; Muslims in India began to take note of British promises to protect Ottoman sovereignty, and to judge how well they were kept.

The claim to be caliph did not, however, blunt opposition to Abdül-hamid's regime among other Muslims within his empire. Some had their own objections to what they saw as Ottoman misrule. In Damascus, a burgeoning Islamic reformist movement criticised the state's appropriation of the authority that properly belonged to religious scholars. In the 1890s, one such scholar, the Syrian intellectual and newspaper editor Abd al-Rahman al-Kawakibi, envisioned an Arab revival of Islam freed from what he too called Ottoman "despotism." Al-Kawakibi worked for the Ottoman government but ended up dying in exile in Cairo—it was suspected that the sultan's agents had poisoned him. Among the Ottomans' many misdeeds, he wrote, was the fact that their administration was "methodical in name but arbitrary in practice." The Ottomans, although Muslims and rulers of Arab lands, had failed to assimilate to "the characteristics of the Arabs" in the way the other Turkic conquerors, the Timurids, had become Persianised or Indianised in their respective domains. Instead, they were becoming more like the French or Germans and had an "intense hatred toward the Arabs." Their government was tyrannical because it was unaccountable. "Despotism," al-Kawakibi wrote, "is the characteristic of an absolute, unbridled government...which administers the affairs of its subjects just as it wishes, without fear of having to render an account, or of the impediment of those who would hold it to the truth."[24]

A different set of opposition movements developed elsewhere in the empire and among political activists exiled in Europe. The European label "Young Turks" covered a wide range of political programs, from interconfessional liberal constitutionalists to Armenian revolutionaries to exclusive, and increasingly racialist, Turkish nationalists. A "Congress of Ottoman Liberals" brought them together in Paris in 1902, but all they agreed on was the aim of overthrowing the sultan and his autocracy. In 1908, a conspiracy of army officers affiliated to a Turkish nationalist secret society, the "Committee of Union and Progress" (CUP), fearing an imminent police crackdown, began an insurrection that quickly escalated into a popular revolution. The constitution was restored, and Ottomans of all religious and ethnic communities gathered in the streets to celebrate. "There are no Greeks, Jews, or Bulgarians," one Jewish enthusiast for the revolution declared in Thessalonica, "there are only Ottomans."[25]

The enthusiasm would not last. An attempted counterrevolution to restore the sultan's clipped powers was defeated by CUP troops marching on Istanbul, Italy invaded Ottoman Libya, war broke out again in the Balkans, Muslim refugees flooded into Anatolia, and the empire was in crisis again. In 1913, a coup d'état ended the constitutional experiment and brought a faction of CUP radicals to power. Their "Young Turk" government was made up mostly of men who identified with pan-Islamism, both as an effective, practical policy that could capitalise on the caliphate's symbolic importance to Muslims everywhere, and as an affective, felt solidarity. They were also influenced by late nineteenth-century European ideas of science, progress, Freemasonry, atheism, racialism, social Darwinism ("survival of the fittest" applied to human life) and militarism. As nineteenth-century Europeans had begun to do, they saw religious and ethnic belonging, "civilisational spirit" and "racial character," as entwined. Turkish-speaking Muslims from the Balkans were fellow Turks. Non-Turkish Muslims, such as Arabs or Kurds, were at best "noble savages" to be protected and civilised, at worst "blacks" and inferiors to be kept in line. Non-Muslims in Turkish-ruled lands, like Greeks and especially Armenians, were at best suspected of disloyalty, at worst "the enemy within," traitors to the state, "a load of harmful microbes" that would need to be wiped out—or turned into Muslims, which might make them loyal.[26]

When the Ottomans entered the First World War on the side of the Central Powers (Germany and Austria-Hungary), in October 1914, they and their allies hoped to appeal to a global Muslim solidarity against the British, French and Russians. On November 14, a call to jihad against the sultan's enemies was proclaimed in Istanbul. But within the empire, "saving the state" also meant keeping its own majority-Muslim "colonial" fringe in the Arab provinces under strict discipline. "What do you expect?," the brutal governor of Syria, Cemal Pasha, asked a new subordinate, shocked at his peremptory exiling of whole families from Palestine in 1915. "Here, one has to behave this way!" Cemal would become notorious for a reign of terror that saw the mass hangings of suspected Arab nationalists in Damascus and Beirut. Worse was to come: the army's requisitioning, a British naval blockade, and the destruction of crops by locusts combined to cause horrific famine in Syria, Lebanon and Palestine in 1916. Half a million people may have died.[27]

The worst was to strike the empire's Armenians. Saving the state also meant taking drastic measures against those who, the empire's rulers believed, were its inveterate internal enemies. Armenians in Istanbul did show open support for the Allies, anticipating in early 1915 that British ships would sail up the Bosphorus and "liberate" them. Some Armenians supported revolutionary organisations pursuing an armed struggle against Ottoman rule. Some hoped for a Russian victory that would give them independence: an uprising in the city of Van, in eastern Anatolia, in 1915, briefly linked up with a Russian advance and seemed to promise just that. At the same time, many Armenians also served in Ottoman uniform on the horrendous eastern front, where in the winter of 1914 they had taken part in a disastrous Ottoman offensive against the Russians. Leading personalities in the Armenian community were also public figures and members of the Ottoman parliament; many had been prominent supporters of the 1908 revolution.

But the truth of loyalty or resistance to the empire did not matter much. The Armenians had become an existential threat in their enemies' imaginations, at a moment when the empire faced what seemed like a struggle for survival. In early 1915, the CUP leadership took the decision to destroy the Armenian population: first, the community's leaders in Istanbul were imprisoned. Many were moved east and murdered. Then, Armenians were to be removed entirely from regions in the east of Anatolia. Men and boys over twelve years of age were murdered; women and children were sent on death marches into the Syrian Desert. Perhaps six hundred thousand, perhaps one million people were killed. Orphaned children who survived were forcibly converted to Islam and brought up as Turkish in Turkish families, or in orphanages where they were beaten for speaking Armenian or using their Armenian names. Before the war's end, up to 90 per cent of the pre-war Armenian population was gone.[28]

The Armenian genocide had not come out of an "age-old" clash between Christians and Muslims, but out of the breakdown of the project to make the empire's peoples into one community of equals, and out of the ruthless calculations and racialised fears of military imperialists. And the genocide did not save the empire. By 1920, its Arab provinces were under British and French military occupation. An Arab revolt against the empire, led by the family of the Ottoman-appointed chief religious dignitary of Mecca, had put an Arab nationalist government in Damascus. Anatolia's coast was invaded by Greek and Italian troops, portions of its territory were promised to Armenian and Kurdish autonomy or independence, and the Ottoman Empire was no more.

The Ottoman sultanate would not survive its acceptance of a disastrous peace agreement with the Allies. The 1920 Treaty of Sèvres looked set to partition the entire empire and reduce Turkish self-rule to a restricted part of the Anatolian plateau. The CUP's wartime leadership had fled to Germany and the Caucasus. But their inheritors in the Ottoman army, with a former CUP officer, Mustafa Kemal Pasha, at their head, refused the armistice terms, and fought their own war of independence to create a Turkish republic in Anatolia, which was now declared a Turkish homeland. In 1922, they deposed the sultan, Mehmed VI, and abolished the monarchy. The caliphate remained— once more a residual, symbolic title, as it had been when the Ottomans took it from Mamluk Cairo half a millennium earlier. Its end came in 1924, by a peremptory decree of the new Turkey's national assembly, which simply declared it, too, abolished. A new kind of sovereignty, the will of the national community, had come to rule instead.

11

THE SCIENCE OF THE AGE

Abdürreşid Ibrahim was a journalist, an intellectual, and a traveller—perhaps one of the most widely travelled men of his day. A Tatar Muslim and a subject of the Russian Empire, he studied in Mecca, Medina, and Istanbul. From his exile in Turkey in the 1890s, he published political pamphlets calling for opposition to the tsarist regime. He participated in Russia's constitutional revolution of 1905, promoted autonomy for Russia's Muslims, and helped organise the first All-Russian Congress of Muslims. Believing in the potency and necessity of an Asia-wide solidarity against European imperialism, he visited Japan for the first time in 1902. In 1909 he crossed central and East Asia, travelling through Mongolia, China and Korea, and reached Japan again, four years after that country announced its arrival on the global stage of imperial competition with its victory in the Russo-Japanese War. He is credited with converting the first Japanese Muslim to make the pilgrimage to Mecca: Omar Yamaoka Kotaro, a Russian-speaking member of the ultranationalist Kokuryukai (the "Black Dragon Society") who worked for Japanese intelligence in Manchuria.

When Italy invaded Libya in 1911, Ibrahim was among the pan-Islamist activists who joined the Ottoman resistance on this latest colonial front. Like others involved in that struggle, he apparently joined the Ottoman "special services," the *teshkilat-i mahsuse*, one of the agencies that would later be most heavily implicated in the Armenian genocide. By then, his son Ahmed Münir had also travelled from Turkey to Tokyo, one of three young Turkish Muslims invited to Japan as an official Ottoman student delegation. Ahmed enrolled at a Japanese university and lived there for several years, possibly all through the First World War, and for some time afterwards. He worked at a Japanese bank in Vladivostok. He may have been in Berlin after the Russian Revolution. In 1924, he found himself in Turkey, now a republic and no longer an empire, working for the Japanese embassy. His father, soon afterward, was back in Tokyo, and worked for the Japanese during the Second World War, producing propaganda aimed at Southeast Asian Muslims. Abdürreşid Ibrahim died in his nineties, in August 1944, still in Japan, shortly after the landing of US marines on Guam, and almost exactly a year before the dropping of the world's first atomic bomb.[1]

Both the intensified global connections of the nineteenth and early twentieth centuries, and the increasingly destructive, worldwide conflicts they brought, shaped the lives of people like Abdürreşid Ibrahim and his son. Muslims' political and economic worlds were transformed by global capitalism, empire, technology and war; their intellectual, cultural, and religious worlds were transformed too. New knowledge took new forms, and was transmitted in new ways: the telegraph, the newspaper, the radio, the printed book or pamphlet, the state-run primary school. These enabled new kinds of connection and solidarity across a global Muslim community.

Students from the Ibadi community that had preserved its distinctive pious society in the Sahara since the tenth century travelled to Tunis and Cairo. They published newspapers, made contact with other Ibadis in Oman and Zanzibar, and mostly settled their doctrinal differences with mainstream Sunni law and ritual. Dar al-Ulum, "the house of sciences," set up in 1867 at Deoband in India, trained frugal students from all over South Asia to preserve the Muslim community by spreading knowledge of the law and Prophetic tradition. In Cairo, another school with the same name, Dar al-Ulum, founded in 1872, trained teachers for state-run schools in a modern curriculum grounded in Islamic knowledge. Egyptian teachers became a new class of religious intellectuals, not classical legal scholars but lay advocates for a remoralising of society. They were often also proponents of a progressive education, like that being promoted at the same time by pedagogues in Britain and America, that would free children's individual psychological development and creativity. Ottoman propaganda devised by North Africans in Istanbul was spread as far as Singapore. After experiencing a century of rebellion and revolt, as the westward-pushing Qing Empire conquered East Turkestan (Xinjiang) and defeated a major uprising in 1856–73, Chinese Muslims re-established connections with the Middle East. Muslim students from Java and Sumatra studied in the Hijaz and printed newspapers in Cairo.[2]

But the rapidity and reach of communication, as well as the content of the knowledge being spread, had ambivalent effects. News came to far-flung places more quickly than before, evading colonial states' attempts to suppress and censor it. It interacted unpredictably with older forms of communication—songs, rumours, manuscripts, and folktales—rather than simply replacing them. But it could seem to push people and places apart as much as it brought them together. When it reached old places of learning and spirituality in mountains and deserts that had long been confident of their own authority and status as centres of knowledge, it could make them feel backward, peripheral, even ignorant. "The science of the age has arrived," wrote a Berber poet in the mountains of Algeria in the 1930s, celebrating a new kind of authority figure: the teacher, journalist, and social activist who, "wearing trousers and a shirt" instead of a turban and prayer beads, would both revive religion and increase local literacy. He would bring tensions, too. New movements for social reform and religious revitalisation became sharply critical of how the previous generation had come to terms with colonial rule, blaming them for the "backwardness" their societies now suffered. They would start to see local, still lively forms of Muslim life as ignorant and inauthentic—and even as not truly Muslim at all. Sufis, in particular, who had often brought Muslim culture and learning to rural societies and preserved it there under colonialism, were now accused of having divided the community by their "sectarian partisanship." Instead of promoting learning, they were said to have caused "stultification and moral degradation."[3]

Navigating this fraught and changing landscape was a generation of Muslim thinkers, writers and activists born, like Abdürreşid Ibrahim, in the middle decades of the nineteenth century, as the new imperial world was coming into being. Their lives spanned the height and the crisis of that world, from the mid-1800s through the first decades of the twentieth century. They could not avoid being part of that world: its language of newness and progress, its objects and its images, were all around them. Its telegraph, railway, and steamship lines carried their news and shaped their travels, which were determined by its opportunities as well as by its police, censorship, and deportation orders. They sought to redefine a way of being Muslim that might escape the subjugation to other people's interests that being on the wrong side of the new global imbalance of power entailed. But they recognised that they could not get out of their age and its new ways of doing things; one way or another, they had to reckon with, and by, them.

◇◇◇◇◇◇◇

The Mughal aristocrat Sir Sayyid Ahmad Khan, who had lived through the 1857 uprising and seen its dreadful consequences, advocated working with and through the British Raj as the path to revival and reform. Over the course of his long life (he died in 1898, aged eighty) Sayyid Ahmad pursued a mission to reconcile rulers and ruled, and to "improve" his own community. He valued faith above all: for him, simple believers who had no need of rational proofs of their faith were models to admire. But on the other hand, the world needed technical sciences for the improvement of everything from agriculture to engineering, and it was apparent that scientific knowledge made unquestioning faith harder to sustain.

Centuries earlier, Muslims had engaged with Greek philosophy to expound the truths of both faith and the universe, and in the process they had mixed the fundamentals of belief with other ideas now known to be scientifically untrue. Now, it would be necessary to find new ways of reconciling the undoubted truth of God's religion with modern understandings of God's creation, the natural world and its discoverable laws. Islam was true, Sayyid Ahmad told an audience in 1884, echoing Shah Wali Allah, because it was demonstrably "in correspondence with the natural disposition of humankind, or with nature." Being Muslim (as the Sufis had always taught) was to be fully human, to live as the Creator intended for His Creation. God's work, the natural world, must similarly be in harmony with God's word—miraculous events in the Qur'an, for example, must have rational explanations, and on the other hand, if current scientific theories seemed to run counter to God's word, they must be refuted (or they would eventually turn out, like the ancient Greeks' understanding of matter, to be wrong).[4]

Sayyid Ahmad was a controversial figure, frequently attacked in his own lifetime, particularly by other Muslims who labelled him a "materialist" and an unbeliever. Later in life he considered his own life's work to have been a failure. But by the 1880s, he was widely seen as a leader of India's Muslims, and his legacy was significant. In 1864, he moved to Aligarh, southeast of Delhi, and in 1875 he founded the Mohammedan Anglo-Oriental College, later Aligarh Muslim University, there. In 1869, Sayyid Ahmad had travelled to England, an experience that seems to have been a profound shock. In a man accustomed to emphasising the martial nobility and superior manners of his Mughal background, the confrontation with mid-Victorian England's technology, literacy, and rising well-being (even, by this time and before the slump of the 1870s, for the new working class) produced an alarming sense of humiliation.

The remedy for this, he rapidly decided, was educational improvement. Indians must return to the levels of intellectual distinction their forebears had enjoyed. Education must be generalised to the public,

Sayyid Ahmad thought. It must embrace science and technology, alongside religious instruction, history, and languages. Somewhat ironically, the model he chose as his inspiration was the English public school and the colleges of Oxford and Cambridge, which at the time were bastions of conservative thought and teaching, and by no means beacons of education in technology, engineering, and the natural sciences. But they were religiously disciplined schools for the inculcation of "character" and the training of a ruling class, and in this, they were exactly what Sayyid Ahmad wanted. At Aligarh, young Muslim men would be taught a modern scientific and liberal arts curriculum in English, while also following religious instruction. They would be equipped for higher study in literature, the religious sciences, the law, or the natural sciences, and they would be able to disseminate "useful knowledge" to wider society. What was needed, he wrote, in educational if not yet in political terms, was "equality of rights with our European fellow subjects" of the British Empire.[5]

Two hundred miles north of Aligarh, and eight years before Sayyid Ahmad and his colleagues opened their school there, a different group of Muslims founded a different school in the small provincial town of Deoband, northeast of Delhi. Formerly a well-to-do Mughal market town, with several mosques and palaces dating back to the time of the Emperor Akbar, Deoband had suffered during and after 1857. But it was said to have an "odour of learning" about it, and several of the scholars who would be founders of the school had dreams about it, associating the place with the Ka'ba and the Prophet. In 1867, they began teaching there, in a mosque under a pomegranate tree. But if they took inspiration from dreams, as saints and Sufis often did, they were intent on teaching an Islam in which saints and their shrines, often central to local religion and personal piety in India as elsewhere in earlier centuries, would not have the authority that popular devotion often gave them. And if their teaching began, as had often been the case, in a mosque under a tree, their intention was to create something very different.

Three of the founders were deputy inspectors of education for the government, and they envisioned a new kind of school. Their Dar al-Ulum, "house of sciences," would have a fixed curriculum, professional teachers, and rigorous examinations. There would be desks, chairs, and a timetable. Like Sayyid Ahmad, in fact, in some respects they modelled the education they sought to promote on nineteenth-century English models. But in other ways they were very different. Rather than seeking a place for Muslim gentlemen in the colonial system, the Deobandis' response to the violence of 1857 was to preserve Muslim life and morality within the Muslim community and in the individuals that made it up. Instead of engaging with the state, they sought to shelter from it within their own community institutions. Instead of seeking recognition from the British or, as under the Mughals, patronage from princely families, Deoband would be financed by the community. It would shun endowments and wealth in favour of austerity and even "a sort of deprivation." It was run by a self-governing council, not by a single leading personality. And rather than training judges and officials for state service, the Deobandis would above all seek to propagate and renew the faith among the community, issuing legal opinions (*fatwas*) and sending their graduates to open new, similar schools elsewhere—over time, many more Deobandi schools would be created across India and, later, Pakistan. Instruction for all students, who came from all over South Asia, in the emerging vernacular language, Urdu, rather than in literary Persian, played an important role in generalising the use of Urdu as a common language among Muslims in the subcontinent.

Deoband thus combined the forms and methods of nineteenth-century education with the frugality and devotion of Sufi tradition (many of its early leaders were members of the Chishti fraternity) and the community-building of other contemporary reformers. Where it differed from some of them, and especially from the Aligarh movement, was in emphasising classical Islamic religious studies, especially hadith and jurisprudence (*fiqh*), and excluding "rational" sciences. As one of the leading founders, Muhammad Qasim, a printer who had been involved in the 1857 uprising, argued, the "new" sciences and philosophy could be learned elsewhere, in government schools: the purpose of Deoband was to preserve Indian Muslims' knowledge of their own tradition to guide individual believers and community life. Initially, even the Islamic classics of logic and philosophy were not to be taught. Focusing on correct ritual practice, direct knowledge of Prophetic hadith, and individual moral character, Deoband became one of the most important centres of Muslim learning in the world, and an influential model of what being Muslim, in a world that seemed hostile to the preservation of a Muslim way of life, should mean.[6]

◇◇◇◇◇◇◇

The itinerant, anti-imperialist activist Sayyid Jamal al-Din al-Afghani, on the other hand, took a very different view of how to relate the "new" science to the preservation of Islam. Al-Afghani died a year before Sayyid Ahmad Khan, but much younger, aged only fifty-eight. In that relatively short life he became perhaps the most celebrated and the most controversial Muslim intellectual and activist of his time. Later identified as a forerunner of both anticolonial nationalism and political Islamism, as well as the foremost pan-Islamist activist of his age, his subsequent legendary stature has sometimes obscured his real significance. He was more influential after his death than during his lifetime; both he and his disciples regularly inflated his importance. Some of the most basic details of his life were disputed. He claimed to have been born in Afghanistan, and to have been raised in Sunni Islam (hence the name al-Afghani, which he adopted in his thirties), but in fact he was born in the Shi'i environment of western Iran. He worked, more than anything, for Muslim unity, but sectarian sensitivities affected his account of his own origins. He believed, above all, in the necessity of Muslim strength and solidarity to free Muslims from both foreign dominance and the despotism of their own rulers, but his career was an itinerary across the British Empire and through the courts of Qajar and Ottoman autocrats. He lived between India, Iran, Russia, and London and spent his final years in gilded confinement as a distrusted guest of the sultan in Istanbul, where he died in 1897.

Such contradictions marked his whole life. He complained that Muslims had lost themselves "in the corners of...dervish convents," but he was heavily influenced by Sufism. He criticised Muslim rulers' "despotism" and was believed to have inspired the assassination of the Qajar Shah of Iran, but he offered to work for the autocratic Ottoman Sultan Abdülhamid II. He would become famous as a campaigner against Europe's imperialism, but he also sought influence at the centres of imperial power. In Afghanistan in the 1860s, he was believed to be a Russian agent. He supported the Mahdist movement in Sudan, but in 1884 he proposed to the British that he might be able to mediate between them and the Mahdists. In 1885, he tried to persuade Randolph Churchill, the British secretary of state for India, that if Britain re-established independent Muslim rule in Egypt, Muslims would join with Britain in a jihad against Russia in central Asia; and in 1887, he told the Russians that an uprising of Indian Muslims would come to their aid if only they would declare war on the British.

Like Sayyid Ahmad and the scholars of Deoband, al-Afghani was influenced by the brutal British repression that followed the Indian uprising of 1857. He was probably in India at the time of the revolt and seems to have spent some time there in its aftermath, having travelled to India from Iran after studying in the Shi'i holy cities of southern Iraq. It was in India that he encountered both European styles of learning and the violence of British rule. From India, al-Afghani moved on to Mecca, Iraq, Iran, and Afghanistan. In 1870, he appeared in Istanbul as a proponent of educational reform, condemning Muslims for falling under foreign domination through their own "lack of vigilance, laziness, working too little, and stupidity." For the rest of the 1870s, he was in Egypt, then back in India, before moving to Paris, where he published *Al-Urwa al-Wuthqa* (The Firmest Bond). A pan-Islamic, Arabic-language newspaper, *Al-Urwa al-Wuthqa* ran only eighteen issues, between March and October 1884, but had a wide circulation and a significant impact despite its short life. It offered its readers both analysis of Great Power imperialism (especially regarding Britain's recent occupation of Egypt and expansion into Sudan) and a diagnosis of the internal weaknesses of Islam, calling for pan-Islamic renewal and unity in the face of European aggression.

Al-Afghani was wholly a man of the late 1800s, an anti-imperialist whose globe-trotting career was possible because of the globalising reach of empire, a religious activist whose understanding of religion was transformed by the philosophy of the times in which he lived, a proponent of Muslim unity whose concept of a single "Muslim world" was forged across disparate and historically distinct countries, cultures, and communities. He became a proponent of Muslim solidarity and religious reform, but like many intellectually inquisitive and politically engaged men in the late 1800s, he was also a Freemason, and in his early life he seems not to have been especially pious. Like Sayyid Ahmad—whom he denounced in *Al-Urwa al-Wuthqa* as a "materialist" who had sold out to the British—he too was attacked for unorthodoxy and even irreligion. He was not, as some claimed, an atheist, but he does seem to have been more interested in religion than religiously committed. In India in the 1880s, he was taken for "a freethinker of the French type, and a socialist." He adopted a more religious image as time went on, but he appealed to religion for political ends, not to politics for the sake of religion.[7]

Above all, for al-Afghani as for an increasing number of Muslim thinkers, being Muslim meant belonging to a "civilisation" rather than to a community of believers. Muslim intellectuals were adopting an understanding of "civilisation" in the sense that word had only recently acquired in nineteenth-century European thinking: a total social system, with its own distinct history, that could be ranked on a universal scale of historical progress, as more or less "primitive" or "advanced." This was an idea gaining traction in the 1830s, when the Egyptian scholar Rifaʿa al-Tahtawi used it in his account of his stay in Paris, and the French statesman and historian François Guizot was publishing his *History of Civilisation in France*, which was translated into Arabic in the 1870s.

Islam was coming to be seen as one such civilisation. In the past, according to the new accounts of world history being produced by

Europeans, it had been a great one. The racist, imperialist, and antisemitic writer Gustave Le Bon argued as much in his book *La Civilisation des Arabes*, published in 1884. (The problem, he thought, was that since their medieval golden age the Arabs had become "racially mixed" and thus "degenerate.") Adopting this powerful new way of thinking—which would dominate European worldviews for the next century—Muslims argued that, if Islam had once been a great civilisation, then despite what Europeans said, it could become an advanced one again. The task for the defenders of Islam was thus quite unlike what the reformists of the eighteenth century, or earlier, had thought they were doing. It was less to restore "true religion" than to recover Islam's civilisational status. The task was not to restore the Islamic tradition but to rescue Islam, and its civilisational potential, from what was now seen as stagnant "traditionalism," bringing it "up to date" with Europe.[8]

Al-Afghani agreed with Sayyid Ahmad and the Deobandis that education was key to this recovery. For him, scientific knowledge and true faith needed to be embraced together, rather than viewed as incompatible. Conservative Muslim scholars, defending their own traditions of learning and their social authority to define both what was true and what was permissible, had sometimes sought to resist Europe's encroachments on their societies by declaring anything foreign to be illicit. They "have divided science into two parts," al-Afghani told an audience in India in 1882: "One they call Muslim science, and one European science." But there was no such thing as either. Science, he went on, "has no connection with any nation, and is not distinguished by anything but itself." In the new age of empire and industry, as throughout history, he said, "science rules the world." European dominance was only the result of European states' having harnessed the power that came from science, and Muslims needed only to overcome their own ignorance to do so too.

Moreover, doing so would mean simply reclaiming their own birthright as Muslims. All the different branches of knowledge, al-Afghani maintained, were united by philosophy, "the comprehensive soul for all the sciences." Philosophy "shows the sciences what is necessary [and] employs each of [them] in its proper place," relating each science to the others and determining the ends to which they should be put. It was the "philosophic spirit" of a community that enabled people to acquire and advance scientific knowledge. And it was the "philosophic spirit" of Muslims, kindled by Islam, that had allowed the progress of science in the medieval caliphate, and that needed to be recovered in the nineteenth century. Natural laws and scientific demonstration were "self-evident truths," he said, and true religion could only be in conformity with such truths. Of all religions, al-Afghani maintained, Islam "is the closest... to science and knowledge, and there is no in-compatibility between science and knowledge and the foundation of the Islamic faith."[9]

Al-Afghani's leading disciple and successor, the Egyptian scholar and jurist Muhammad Abduh, heartily agreed. Ten years younger than his mentor, Abduh was born to a modest farming family in the Nile Delta in 1849. Having, in his youth, fled from what he later de-scribed as the stultifying religious education intended for him by his father, he found inspiration in Sufi teaching before meeting al-Afghani in Cairo in 1870. By the late 1870s he was himself teaching at Cairo's great university-mosque, al-Azhar. As a student and tutor in logic, the-ology, ethics, history, and politics, Abduh combined readings in Ar-abic classics with the philosophical history of the fourteenth-century North African scholar Ibn Khaldun and Guizot's civilisational histo-ries of Europe and France. Ibn Khaldun's theory of the cyclical rise and decline of societies, between primitive but dynamic tribalism and civilised but ultimately decadent urban life, had become popular in Ottoman circles in the previous century before being rediscovered and translated by French scholars in the mid-1800s, just as Guizot's works were being published. Both Ibn Khaldun and Guizot offered univer-sal histories that seemed to explain the past brilliance of Muslims' societies and their present state of subordination. Abduh himself was working on a "philosophy of history and society" and seems to have been thinking along the same lines.

For Abduh too, it was education that was crucial to the task facing all Muslim societies. Muslims, he said, were ignorant of the truth of their religion, suffered under despotism, and had lost sight of the way to learning and progress because of a "blind, exclusive attachment to things inherited from their fathers." Religious education followed by scientific training would allow all Muslims, irrespective of their background, to achieve their individual potential and collective good. His writings emphasised a natural affinity between Islam and innate human reason, and the need for Muslims to apply reasoning, rather than what he saw as unthinking "imitation" of past practice, to the understanding of religion. Like other reformers, while he had taken inspiration from Sufism, he decried what he thought of as excessive popular devotion to saints. In response to the ideas of French secularists, he argued that the separation of religious and civil life might be necessary for Christianity, whose history showed it to be intolerant and obscurantist, but not for Islam, which taught tolerance and "was the first religion to address the rational mind." It was quite wrong, he thought, for Muslims "to espouse the view of some in other nations who [have] alleged an enmity between knowledge and faith."[10]

Abduh worked with al-Afghani in Paris in the 1880s and travelled in Europe and North Africa. In 1889 he accepted a position as chief judge (mufti) of Egypt, which he held until his death in 1905. Despite his anti-imperialism, as Egypt's most senior Muslim legal authority he worked with the British and became friends with Lord Cromer, the man who was effectively the British ruler of Egypt (and who considered Egyptians, like Indians, to be a naturally "subject race"). The apogee of Victorian empire made for strange bedfellows. Some Muslims considered Abduh himself to be an unbeliever and an apostate— Cromer thought him an "agnostic." His disciples hailed him as the "renewer" of Islam for his age. His work was widely read and admired; his best-known treatise, *Risalat al-Tawhid* (The Theology of Unity), appeared in Chinese in 1935. Within the Middle East, he became an important figure in the constellation of Arab intellectuals and cultural figures, both Christian and Muslim, whose works in these decades would be seen as constituting the *nahda* ("revival") of Arabic language, literature, and cultural life. In the following decades, this revival would be looked to as part of a new consciousness among Arabs that, whether Christian or Muslim (or, indeed, for some, Jewish), they constituted one people, one nation, and that escaping from ignorance and "despotism" meant escaping both European domination and the Ottoman Empire.[11]

◇◇◇◇◇◇◇

While there was still an Ottoman Empire to look to, reformers and pan-Islamist activists could nonetheless still imagine a revival of the caliphate as a counterweight to European power that might rebalance the disordered state of the Muslims' world. Some Arab critics of Ottoman rule had called for a resumption of the caliphate by an Arab descendant of the Prophet, and the Arab *nahda* and Arab nationalism amplified such ideas. Later, mid-twentieth-century Arab nationalists would consider the Ottoman period as a dark age in Arab history: the Ottoman "occupation" of Arab lands, as they would see it, had finished the Mongols' work of extinguishing the golden age of the classical caliphates and paved the way for European colonialism. But before 1914, Arab nationalism was mostly confined to urban literary circles in Cairo, Beirut, and Damascus. Arab activists who mobilised to oppose European rule in the Middle East during the 1920s, leading revolts in Syria and Palestine, had often fought in World War I for the Ottoman Empire, not against it: the first generation of Arab nationalists was also the last generation of Ottomans.[12]

But the First World War ended the Ottomans. Colonialism came late to the historic heartlands of Islam, but by the end of 1921, the holy city of Jerusalem, the historic caliphal capitals of Baghdad and Damascus, and old provincial cities across the Middle East from Beirut to Basra were all under European rule. For the first time since the Arab conquests in the late seventh century, there was no state under Muslim rule that could call itself a Muslim empire, except for Iran; and Iran, which had gone through its own protests against European commercial imperialism in the 1890s and its own constitutional revolution in 1906, was wracked by famine and revolt at the end of the war.

The fate of the Middle East as it emerged from the First World War would weigh, perhaps more than any other factor, on Muslim sympathies, aspirations, and anxieties around the world for the rest of the twentieth century. The greatest horrors of the war in the Middle East were surely the Armenian genocide and the Syrian famine. But its best-known aspects are probably the Gallipoli campaign, in which Ottoman defenders held off the Allied attempt to capture the Bosphorus and Istanbul, and the Arab Revolt against the Ottomans in the Hijaz, whose British liaison officer was T. E. Lawrence. Later famous in literature and film as Lawrence "of Arabia," he was perhaps the last Romantic hero of British imperial imagination. But Lawrence did not make the revolt. It was led by an Arab prince brought up in Istanbul, Emir Faysal Ibn Husayn al-Hashemi, following negotiations between his father, Husayn Ibn Ali, a provincial ruler increasingly at odds with the Ottomans, and the British authorities in Egypt, where Lawrence worked in army intelligence. Husayn Ibn Ali held the office of Sharif of Mecca, a religious title indicating descent from the Prophet, and the nobility that this descent conferred. It was also an Ottoman political appointment, traditionally held by members of the Hashemite family. With responsibility over the holy cities and the pilgrimage, the office was a sensitive and significant one, and carried a symbolic power second only to the caliph's.

In a series of letters exchanged between the summer of 1915 and spring of 1916, Britain's representative in Cairo, Sir Henry McMahon, appeared to promise Husayn and his family a sovereign Arab kingdom in the Arabian Peninsula, and most of Iraq and Syria—the core territories, minus Egypt, of the original Arab Muslim caliphate—after the war. After the fall of the Ottomans, Sharif Husayn would also be a contender for the title of caliph. With British and French support, in 1916 the Sharif's forces began an uprising in Mecca. The Ottoman garrison shelled the town. Not for the first time in a war between Muslims, they set fire to the Great Mosque, damaging the Ka'ba, but were driven out after a few weeks. Faysal's army went on to capture the port of Aqaba on the Red Sea, then pushed north into Palestine and Transjordan in tandem with British imperial troops from Egypt. They entered Damascus on horseback as liberators in October 1918, just under a year after the British General Allenby had entered Jerusalem, ending four centuries of Ottoman rule there, in December 1917.

After the war, British promises of independent sovereignty to Husayn and his family inevitably clashed both with Britain's own strategic priorities—above all, securing territory, oil, and air routes between the Mediterranean and the Indian Ocean—and with other wartime agreements with other allies, especially France. The formerly Ottoman Arab provinces were partitioned. Faysal and his fledgling Arab government were ejected from Damascus by a French army that occupied Syria and Lebanon. Faysal became King of Iraq, under British protection, while his brother Abdallah became emir of a new principality, Transjordan, later the Kingdom of Jordan, on the east bank of the Jordan River between Palestine and Iraq. Their father, Husayn, had declared himself King of the Arab Lands, but was recognised by Britain only as King of the Hijaz. In 1924, he lost that kingdom to a new rival, the revived Saudi dynasty and their Wahhabi followers from central Arabia, who went on to unite most of the Arabian Peninsula and create a new, independent kingdom of their own. By the mid-1920s, the ambition of building a unified, post-Ottoman, Arab nationalist kingdom had been snuffed out, and the post-Ottoman territorial states of the Middle East had come into being. The aspiration to unite the Arabs would endure, but so would the territorial and political divisions between them.

The First World War involved and affected Muslims in other ways, too, far beyond the Ottoman Empire's battlefronts. Tens of thousands of Muslims found themselves facing the Ottoman Empire and its allies as soldiers in French uniform from Algeria, Tunisia, Morocco, Guinea, and Senegal, or in British uniform from India and East Africa, as labourers in logistics from India and Egypt behind British lines and workers from North Africa in French munitions factories. As well as serving in the trenches on the western front in Europe, West

African Muslims were in the French army at Gallipoli, and North African Muslims were in the French army that defeated Emir Faysal's attempt to keep his Syrian kingdom. From French Algeria, twenty-two thousand "European" French citizens, and twenty-five thousand "French Muslim" subjects, were killed. Casualty rates in French West African regiments were especially high. An Egyptian Labour Corps of half a million contracted or conscripted young men was put to work in the British war effort in France, Italy, Iraq, Sinai, Sudan, and Palestine: many were killed, and some were effectively forced labourers. For Muslims, being on the side of the war's victors did not mean that the conflict would have a better outcome.[13]

Egypt was still formally under the suzerainty of the Ottoman Empire when war broke out in 1914. Mindful, at least in appearances, of international law, the British declared a protectorate over the country, formalising what had been de facto reality since 1882. Egypt was a crucial British imperial base of operations, a hinge of imperial communications, and a source of labour and money, both of which were drained to serve Britain's war effort. In 1919, Egyptians demanded some recognition of their contribution to victory. A movement emerged in favour of Egyptian representation at the Versailles conference that would determine the new, postwar shape of the still-imperial world order. It was led by Saad Zaghlul, a village headman's son from the Nile Delta who studied under al-Afghani and Abduh, became a lawyer, and in 1906 was appointed minister of education. There was a mass petitioning campaign, followed by peasant uprisings across the countryside and huge demonstrations in cities in which women protestors were prominent.

The British response was, first, to crack down, before realising that they would have to negotiate. Zaghlul and his colleagues were arrested and deported; some three thousand Egyptians were killed. What Egyptians came to call the 1919 revolution would lead to a British declaration of Egyptian independence in 1922, and to the consolidation of a new sense of Egyptian political community. Zaghlul, like Abduh, took pride in his origins, which were not in the landowning urban aristocracy of Cairo but in the agricultural village society of Lower Egypt. The plight of young men who had been taken from that same society into the Egyptian Labour Corps was seen by Egyptian nationalists as a new kind of slavery. Such "slavery" was all the more odious in that, especially since the 1800s, Egyptians tended to consider themselves as naturally superior to the enslaved Africans brought north from Sudan as soldiers, domestic workers, or labourers. The coercive conditions under which the wartime Labour Corps had been recruited and made to work, combined with the violent repression of peasant insurgency in 1919, emphasised an image of the suffering "sons of the land" as the embodiment of oppressed Egyptian nationhood.

Such ideas were increasingly seen through Europe's supposedly scientific lens of biological racism, which also coloured beliefs in civilisation and progress. Together, these ideas provided a new way of seeing both the community and its history. Being Muslim was still important. But so was the common Egyptian-ness shared, across lines of both religion and class, by Muslims and Coptic Christians. Egyptians, the nationalist leader and newspaper editor Ahmad Lutfi al-Sayyid wrote, "have a majority religion, and ways of performing our activities, and a blood which is nearly one blood flowing through our veins." The idea of a single pan-Islamic community that would connect Muslims politically across territorial boundaries was to him only a "myth." He saw Egyptians as a race of people moulded by their land and their deep history of civilisation that long predated the arrival of Islam. Egypt, as he wrote elsewhere, was "that good country that established civilisation in the most ancient of ages."[14]

In India, too, an emerging mass nationalist politics stressed the ancient pedigree of South Asian civilisation. But that civilisation was most often seen to embody the religious, cultural, and linguistic heritage that over the nineteenth century had come to be identified as Hinduism, rather than the inheritance of the Muslim dynasties that had ruled most of India for the last half-millennium. India's "Hindus and Musulmans" had united, in 1857, in a shared defence of their differences—to demand respect for their distinctive, and coexisting, ways of life and belief. In the 1880s and 1890s, mass politics and local protests increased, and in the absence of any representative political forum in which community tensions could be negotiated (because the British did not allow participation in any), they happened on the streets and sometimes resulted in violence. At the end of the war, it was unclear whether a common Indian nationhood could still bring Hindus and Muslims together politically. But leading figures considered Muslim concerns as Indian ones: "As a Hindu," the lawyer and emerging activist leader Mohandas K. Gandhi told the British in 1918, "I cannot be indifferent to their cause. Their sorrows must be our sorrows."[15]

India's blood and money, like Egypt's, had been crucial to the British Empire's war effort. Some 1,700 Indian soldiers were killed at Gallipoli, and it was Indian troops who captured Baghdad from the Ottomans. At the end of the war, a quarter of a million Indian soldiers were occupying Iraq, where they and their supplies were transported on railways that had been torn up from India and shipped to the Persian Gulf. Indian taxpayers "gifted" the British government one hundred million pounds. Like Egyptians, Indians reasonably wanted compensation at the war's end. Like Egyptians, what they got instead was repression. Not the only, but certainly the most infamous, incident was the massacre at the Jallianwala Bagh in Amritsar, in April 1919, when soldiers opened fire without warning on an unarmed and peaceful crowd of protestors and bystanders. According to the official account, 379 people were killed. Nationalist estimates put the figure at over one thousand.[16]

Unrest in India had been growing since the early 1900s. In 1919, Gandhi's nonviolent protest movement against the extension of repressive wartime legislation was joined by Muslim anxiety over the imminent dismemberment of the Ottoman Empire and the fate of the caliphate. Muslim community leaders themselves were divided over the issue, and how far it might be in their own interests to press the British on it—the Deobandi scholars, for example, stayed away from the question. Nonetheless, between 1918 and the final disappearance of the caliphate in 1924, there were mass demonstrations in India in support of what became known as the Khilafat (caliphate) movement. Protestors demanded that Britain should defend both the Muslim Holy Places in Arabia and the continued security and sovereignty of the caliph. A delegation of Indian Muslims facilitated by Sir Sultan Muhammad Shah, the Aga Khan (a title held since the early 1800s by the Isma'ili Shi'i imams, who in the 1860s moved from Iran to India), presented Indian Muslim grievances to the postwar Paris Peace Conference, to no avail.

In 1920, tens of thousands of Indian Muslims followed a call to emigrate to Afghanistan, making a hijra out of British India and into Muslim-ruled territory to preserve their faith and pursue a nonviolent struggle in defence of the caliphate. Many died on the way, and many more faced destitution and starvation in Afghanistan, which could not deal with the influx of migrants. Most eventually returned, having lost their properties and livelihoods. Only a few went on to aid Turkish nationalists in the Caucasus or to join up with Bolshevik revolutionaries in central Asia. British fears of greater instability in India weighed on outcomes in Anatolia: in the end, Britain favoured a less punitive peace for the new Turkey than had at first been imposed on the remnants of the old empire at Sèvres in 1920, and negotiated more favourable terms with Mustafa Kemal's Turkish nationalists at Lausanne in 1923. But India's Muslims, like others around the world, would be disappointed that the Turkish nationalists cared a great deal less for the caliphate than did their supporters elsewhere.[17]

◇◇◇◇◇◇◇

The collapse of the Ottoman state was momentous, but other changes in the makeup of the imperial world were equally so. In 1917, both America's entry into the war and Russia's exit from it, following the revolutions in February and October, announced major changes in the lineup of the Great Powers. Two new ideas were now in the air: a new international order under a new kind of international law, and a socialist internationalism working for world revolution.

In the radical world revolution of which the Russian Bolsheviks thought they were the vanguard, imperialism and capitalism would both be overthrown. The inevitable crisis of the capitalist world order would bring opportunity for the working class to seize power, and a new age of fraternity and peace would dawn in which illusions—like religion—would pass away. But the failure of international socialism to stop the world's workers going to war with each other, whether they joined up enthusiastically in London and Berlin or were dejectedly conscripted in Istanbul and Baghdad, had already dented expectations. And the uprisings that broke out in 1919 and the 1920s across North Africa, the Middle East, and India were only "Bolshevism" in the minds of panicked European colonial officers and American newspaper editors. Only a very few Indian Muslims who joined the hijra movement to Afghanistan in 1920 made it as far as training with the Bolsheviks in Tashkent, and although some joined the fledgling Communist Party of India there, they were mostly caught and arrested when they returned to India.[18]

On the other hand, ever since the time of the Prophet, Islam had carried a revolutionary social energy as often as it had justified a conservative social order. New, anti-imperialist republics were declared in 1919 in the Egyptian countryside and in 1920 in the Rif Mountains of northern Morocco. Socialism and communism offered new ways of articulating old themes of justice, freedom, and solidarity. These often worked in tandem, rather than being in conflict, with ideas of religious reform. They would be powerful forces in many Muslim-majority countries, from Morocco to Indonesia, over the next sixty years. In much of the Middle East, in particular—in Egypt, Iraq, Algeria, Morocco, and even, for a time, in Palestine—socialist and communist movements would provide spaces for political organising and social struggle that united Muslim and Jewish activists in a common, radical aspiration for social justice and equal citizenship against both colonial control and global capitalism.

In the liberal international order proposed by US President Woodrow Wilson, at the same time, sovereign self-determining nation-states would in principle be equal (as long as their self-determining citizens were sufficiently "civilised," and, implicitly, white), and would find their freedom from imperial oppression within the liberal capitalist world. The victorious powers—Britain, France, Italy, America, and Japan—would henceforward, at least on paper, treat their own imperial rule as "a sacred trust of civilization." They would rule, not in their own interests, but for the benefit and improvement of their subjects, until the latter were "able to stand by themselves under the strenuous conditions of the modern world," as the Covenant of the League of Nations put it.

Such declarations did not make colonial rule any more accountable or any less coercive for those subjected to it. Egyptian protestors in 1919 were singularly unimpressed by Wilson, and the few attempts by Muslim spokesmen to appeal directly to the new, liberal international order were studiously ignored. The leaders of the would-be Egyptian delegation to the peace conference at Versailles were arrested and exiled, while peasant protestors in the Egyptian countryside were shot and flogged. The Algerian activist Emir Khaled, a grandson of the nineteenth-century resistance leader Abd al-Qadir, wrote to Wilson in 1919, describing the oppressed and disenfranchised plight of Algerian Muslims under French rule, and pleading for "law and justice." Khaled had been brought up as an Ottoman gentleman in Damascus, but trained at the French military academy at Saint-Cyr and served in the French army as a cavalry captain during the war. His letter went unanswered. He had more success finding a hearing among his fellow Algerian Muslims, but his victory in the Algiers municipal election of 1919, where Muslims were allowed a limited representation, was unbearable to the French authorities. He was soon hounded out of Algeria; he died in Syria in 1936.[19]

Still, Muslims did not abandon the idioms or the ideas of liberalism and improvement, constitutional rule and national self-determination, social justice and revolution. These languages had already expressed Muslim ideas and aspirations long before 1914. In 1905, the Tunisian religious scholar Abd al-Aziz al-Tha'alibi published a book entitled

L'esprit libéral du Coran (The Liberal Spirit of the Qur'an) in Paris. A journalist, a religious reformist whose antiestablishment views had led to his being tried for blasphemy in Tunis, and an advocate for constitutional rule, al-Tha'alibi argued that "the Qur'an is a marvellous instrument of progress and civilization, because it affirms, proclaims and imposes every principle of truest liberalism." In 1912, an Indian barrister, Mushir Hussein Kidwai, published *Islam and Socialism* in London. Kidwai, who was educated at Lucknow in north India, scene of some of the worst violence in 1857, had founded a Pan-Islamic Society in London in 1903 and spent time in the Ottoman Empire. In *Islam and Socialism*, he explained that the Prophet and the early caliphate had pioneered egalitarian social order, representative politics, a citizen army, and accountable government. Pointing out how unrepresentative of their people Europe's politicians really were—for example, that the unelected British House of Lords had, until 1911, exercised a veto over the elected House of Commons—he observed acerbically that "the natives of the West have not yet evolved a fully democratic constitution for their states." In contrast, he wrote, the early Islamic community was an "ethical" socialism, "almost to perfection."

Writing at a time when the "new liberalism" of British politics was often associated with reforming socialism, Kidwai identified Sufism as the truest expression of "Islam's liberal spirit," and as "suited for an advanced age and progressive nations." For al-Tha'alibi, however, the true principles of Islam were also the truest "principles of the French revolution," and it was the fault of the Sufi brotherhoods that "the Muslim religion is no longer the Muslim religion, but a kind of idolatry." Both writers were engaged in reforming and reviving Islam in their own societies, with radical political agendas for their futures, and with divergent views of what being truly Muslim should mean. Both found ways to address the imperial world they lived in, through its own languages, for their own purposes.[20]

These same ostensibly universal principles, and the idioms used to express them, would be seized upon by Muslims across the world that, after 1920, was almost entirely divided between the European empires. In the older colonised territories, in India, Africa, and South-east Asia, demands for constitutional rule, equal civil rights, or the return of effective indigenous sovereignty had already come from mostly small, elite groups. Such demands now rapidly grew into mass movements. In 1920, Abd al-Aziz al-Tha'alibi founded the Liberal Constitutional Party (or Destour Party, from the word *dustur*, "constitution"): the first Tunisian nationalist party, its program centred on its demand to re-establish Tunisia's own 1861 constitution. Mushir Hussein Kidwai played a major part in the Khilafat movement, was a member of the All-India Muslim League's committee on a new Indian constitution, and led the socialist group in the new Indian legislature in the 1920s. In the territories newly acquired from the defeated Central Powers, the new League of Nations delivered "mandates," internationally sanctioned legal jurisdiction, for the imperial powers to govern in the expectation that they did so to prepare those territories and their inhabitants for self-determination and independence. France in Syria and Lebanon, and Britain in Iraq, Transjordan, and Palestine, faced demands from a burgeoning nationalist mass politics that both should come at once. Even those who favoured working through the colonial state, and with its foreign rulers, rather than fighting against them to achieve independence, thought that independence needed to come quickly.

Some imperialists thought so too, if only to avoid the popular uprisings that the British faced in Egypt in 1919 and in Iraq in 1921, where an insurrection centred on the Shi'i shrine cities of Najaf and Karbala could only be put down by deploying thousands of soldiers, and the newly established Royal Air Force was used to bomb and strafe villages. Egypt was declared formally independent in 1922. Iraq became a member of the League of Nations in 1932. But formal independence came with continued control: British troops remained in Egypt and Iraq, and British officials continued to lean on their Arab governments, for another thirty years. Revolutions in Egypt in 1952, and in Iraq in 1958, would be led by a new generation of more radical nationalist army officers against what they saw as upper-class collaborators with colonialism. They would create authoritarian military governments that dispensed with the formally liberal, constitutional politics of the interwar generation of nationalists, as well as finally dislodging the imperial powers that those politics had been unable to remove.

◇◇◇◇◇◇◇◇

From the 1860s to the 1930s, Muslim scholars and activists across the imperial world thus insisted on the fusion of revelation and science to recover a true Muslim civilisation, or looked to liberalism or socialism as ways to emancipate both religion and society from superstition and foreign domination. By the 1940s and 1950s, their states were barely independent of colonial rule, their societies mostly impoverished, largely illiterate and overwhelmingly rural, with little industry and only fledgling centres of scientific higher education and research. But it was still possible to fuse understandings of being Muslim inherited from the Islamic tradition with the most avant-garde understandings of selfhood emanating from the new sciences in Europe. Freud, for example, was already being widely read in Egypt by the 1930s; in 1945 a term borrowed from the mysticism of Ibn Arabi was repurposed to denote the "unconscious" in an Egyptian psychology journal. Psychoanalysis and Islam were by no means mutually exclusive ways of understanding the *nafs*, the Arabic term for "self" or "soul," related in Muslim belief to the original life-imparting breath of God and long familiar to Muslim philosophers and Sufis, that could now also mean "psyche."[21]

Others sought to harness the power of science, which they saw the colonial empires wielding so effectively, in the service of their own equally forceful programs of reclaiming their states and rebuilding their societies. They sometimes saw Islam, its cultural heritage and social norms, and the scholars who proclaimed it (and whose authority, sometimes threatening to rulers, was based on it), as backward and anti-scientific. They sometimes saw religion, not as a creative nexus of belief, behaviour, law, culture and belonging, but simply as an ideological dogma and a set of ritual practices. While "religion," indeed, was coming to be seen by some as a total way of life, for others it was a distinct and disposable thing, separable from other domains of life, and preferably discarded, or at least kept in its place: the home, the private conscience, and the dutiful minds of women and children. Especially in Iran and Turkey, new, autocratically inclined state-builders would seek to marginalise Islam entirely, embracing European ideas of being modern that saw being Muslim, very often, as getting in their way.

Iran was not a belligerent state in the First World War, but it was a battlefield. The Ottomans in the west, Russian armies in the north, and British troops intent on securing access to oil fields in the south all fought on Iranian soil and ruined the country. The Qajar monarchy had lost power, in the late 1800s, both to foreign intrusions and to growing demands for more constitutional and democratic rule. In 1890, the shah granted a monopoly on the production, export and sale of tobacco (which was widely grown and consumed in Iran) to a British company. Two years of mass protests and a boycott of tobacco products, encouraged by Jamal al-Din al-Afghani and uniting popular protestors with Iran's Shi'i clerics, followed. In 1906, further protest bringing the street, the market, and the mosque together became a constitutional revolution, and an elected assembly, the *majles* ("council"), met in Iran for the first time. But the war wrecked the country and threatened to partition it between Britain and Russia. In 1917, the revolution took Russian armies out of Iran; over the next two years, the British fought nationalist uprisings, and a terrible famine killed up to a quarter of the population in the north of the country. Iran was on the brink of being subjected to a British protectorate in all but name before an ambitious soldier from a modest background, Reza Khan, with Cossack troops and British acquiescence, seized power in February 1921. In 1925, he adopted the surname Pahlavi, evoking the ancient Iranian language and monarchy, removed the last Qajar ruler, and set himself up as a new shah.

Reza Shah Pahlavi, as he was now known, was an ambitious nationalist who intended to build up his country to withstand foreign domination. He was also a centralising, dictatorial ruler who suppressed dissent, jailed or killed opponents, and saw progress as achievable through the top-down transformation and re-education of society. He favoured a pre-Islamic, racialised vision of Iranian nationhood—which also, in the late 1930s, made Iran popular with the German racial nationalists of the Nazi Party, who saw Iran as a pure Aryan nation. He favoured a secularisation that meant, not the freedom of religion from politics, but the government of religion by politics. He was an anti-socialist, which won him support from the British and American governments. He was also an "étatist," believing in the essential power of the state, in a country with little of its own capital to invest and, as yet, little foreign investment outside the oil fields, to drive economic development and modernise society.

As in the nineteenth century, expanding the state's capacity meant that the army and the bureaucracy grew; government became less negotiated and more coercive. An urban working class grew as industry developed, but unions and strikes were banned, as were socialist and communist parties. An educated middle class grew too and found jobs in the expanding bureaucracy, but while the *majles* still met, it was powerless. Nomadic tribes whose lifestyle had generally assured them a better standard of living—in particular, better nutrition and health—than that of peasants, but whose independence was a threat to state control, were forcibly settled. New laws secured property rights for landlords at the expense of peasants and tenants, and expanded the jurisdiction of the civil courts and the new bureaucracy at the expense of the religious clerics. High taxes on products like tea and sugar weighed most heavily on the poor to pay for infrastructure, especially railway-building.

Seeing modern life as embodied in European middle-class manners and behaviour as much as in styles of architecture or military power, Reza Shah legislated in the 1920s on what both men and women should wear: professional religious clerics (necessarily men) were exempt, and could still wear their traditional robes and turbans, but everyone else had to wear "European" dress—jackets and trousers, neckties, dresses and skirts. Women, who even in the cities generally still wore a full-length covering (chador) and face veil, were to be unveiled by law, and if necessary by force—policemen in the streets enforced the ban on veiling, which was experienced both by women and by the men of their families as a humiliating violation. Middle- and upper-class city women increasingly gained access to education and jobs like teaching and nursing, but girls from more religiously conservative families lost the educational opportunities they had had when their families took them out of mixed schools, where they could no longer dress with what was felt to be respectable modesty. A cultural gulf began to open up between the lifestyles and worldviews of urban, better-off classes and the great majority of the population in the countryside and provincial towns.[22]

When he looked around for ways to catch up with the times, Reza Shah looked especially to Turkey. Anatolia had become an overwhelmingly Turkish and Muslim country, since the Armenian genocide and postwar "population exchanges" with Greece, in which Greek-speaking Christian communities were deported from their ancient homes in Anatolia to Greece, and Turkish-speaking Muslims were similarly moved from their homes in the Balkans to Turkey. The war had turned the multi-confessional, multilingual heartland of the Ottoman Empire into a much more ethnically homogenous place. That suited its new leaders' vision of becoming modern. The Ottoman soldier Mustafa Kemal Pasha had been celebrated across the Middle East and South Asia as the "Lion of Islam," or a new Saladin, when he defeated European attempts to partition Anatolia. But having come to power, he forcefully turned post-Ottoman Turkey in a new direction. He took a new surname, Atatürk, "Father of the Turks": the reform, by law, of personal names, like the abolition of old titles such as "Pasha" or "Khan," the introduction of birth certificates, and other forms of registering personal identity, were all ways of moulding individual citizens into a new national body through the power of the bureaucratic state.

Being modern, Atatürk thought, meant being like Europeans. Modern Turks would write their language in Latin letters, not the Arabic script that had always been used for Ottoman Turkish. They would dress and behave as middle-class Europeans did. Men should wear hats, not the fez (a move updating the nineteenth-century order that men should wear the fez, not the turban). They should use machines, and believe in progress. Women should wear skirts and dresses, and not cover their hair. They should be educated, raise patriotic children, and serve tea to guests. Beyond the level of individual urban lifestyle and family life, becoming modern was the larger transformative effort of applying to government and society, to manufacturing, economic organisation, and education, the technology and bureaucracy that had developed over the previous century in Europe. No less impatient than the Islamic reformers with the alleged ignorance and degradation of the old Sufi orders, he closed down the fraternities. But not only that: he believed, as the French had decided (though only recently, in 1905, and after a bitterly divisive, century-long struggle), that religion should be stripped out of education and public life entirely.

Europeans, at the same time, were caught up in their own, equally ideological visions of progress that equated being modern with technology and secularism—although religious revivals had happened in their societies, especially in North America, very recently too. Religion and politics for them were now formally separate domains, especially in the United States, where the constitution had made a point of protecting religion from political interference. But religion was hardly irrelevant to political life or to prevailing ideas of community. While religious authorities, on the whole, exercised less public power in Europe and the United States than they once had, Europeans and Americans firmly believed that their societies and their global power rested on what they thought of as "Christian civilisation." At the same time, being modern, to Europeans, could also mean being technically efficient, authoritarian, and racially "hygienic." Democracy and liberalism, although only recently extended to the European working class and barely at all to European women, already seemed tired and inadequate to some, and still seemed dangerously unstable to others. By the 1930s, many Europeans, especially in the conservative ruling classes, thought something more muscular was needed to keep progress in their hands, and prevent the masses from being seduced by socialism. Some were caught up with an enthusiasm for strongman dictators, and applauded them when they appeared in Muslim countries, too. Nazi Germany looked for an ally in "Aryan" Iran, but Britain and the United States also supported the Pahlavi autocracy. When Atatürk died in 1938, the right-wing British press likened his legacy to the "accomplishments" of other architects of national regeneration: Mussolini and Hitler.[23]

Without the enthusiasm for fascism, many other Western commentators saw in the Turkish and Iranian modernisers the future of the whole Muslim world, and approved of their authoritarian regimes' material achievements. Twenty years after his death, as Turkey was slowly becoming more democratic, millions of American TV viewers heard from respected anchorman Walter Cronkite, on the popular documentary series *The Twentieth Century*, how this "strong man... led Turkey out of the Middle Ages and into the twentieth century." A pattern had been set of Western democracies seeing the tolerance of autocracy, and even enthusiasm for it, as justifiable in Muslim countries. After 1940, this argument could no longer respectably be made about Europe. But it could be made about "backward" countries that were still (despite—or because of—decades of imperial tutelage) not deemed ready for constitutional liberties. Authoritarian rule had always characterised colonial states. It would still be seen as a regrettable necessity in ensuring "stability" long after the colonial states became nationalist ones.[24]

12

THE COMMUNITY OF FAITH

Shakib Arslan was a Druze, a member of the minority religious community created in Egypt and Syria in the early eleventh century, and he lived in Geneva. Born into an aristocratic family in Lebanon, he supported the Ottomans during the First World War. Living in exile until shortly before his death in 1946, from his home in Switzerland in the 1920s and 1930s he came to be one of the most prolific and influential exponents of a global, anticolonial Islamic revivalism. He wrote up to a hundred newspaper articles a year in Arabic, published a political magazine in French, lobbied the League of Nations, received visitors and corresponded with Muslim intellectuals and activists from across the world. He was banned from entering his home country but travelled to Detroit, where Syrian Christians accused him of being a "Muslim supremacist," and to Moscow, where British diplomats thought him a Soviet agent. He was a personal guest of Abd al-Aziz Ibn Saud, the founder of Saudi Arabia, and was visited by David Ben-Gurion, who would be one of the founders of the state of Israel.

In 1930, Arslan published a book, *Why Have Muslims Lagged Behind and Why Have Others Progressed?* Castigating both conservative traditionalists and "ultra-moderns" who had abandoned religion, and declaring that Muslims had given in to "ignorance" and "cowardice," he saw the path to progress in a conception of civilisation and nationhood drawn directly from right-wing European nationalisms. "Every nation adheres rigorously to its religion and clings steadfastly to its religious heritage, traditions and national characteristics and peculiarities," he wrote. "The Muslims alone seem not to understand their value." Having previously maintained that the survival of the Ottoman Empire was the only way the Muslim community could avoid dismemberment at the hands of the European powers, he now diagnosed the "decline" of Islam as a whole and prescribed one great remedy: a single community of faith, the *umma*, the Muslim nation, united across the world.[1]

Ferhat Abbas, who lived at the same time near an ancient city in eastern Algeria that was named after the Roman Emperor Constantine, was a member of a different kind of minority. He was an Arab Muslim pharmacist, one of the very few Algerians of his generation who not only entered the French school system but also studied at university. Born the son of what the French called a "caïd" (Arabic *qa'id*), an assistant rural administrator, Abbas grew up revolted by the harsh treatment meted out to local peasants by the colonial authorities. He was no less dismayed by the discrimination that he and other educated—or as the French called them, *évolués*, "evolved"—Muslims experienced every day under a regime that oppressed and excluded them from equal rights while claiming to "assimilate" them into liberty and equality. In 1936, he wrote a newspaper column entitled "I am France!," advocating a single, equal, and multicultural citizenship for all inhabitants of French Algeria. Ten years later, disillusioned by the intransigence and racism of Algeria's European settler community, he would call for the "abolition of colonialism," which he referred to as a new form of slavery, and the creation of a separate Algerian republic. Another ten years after that, in April 1956, he reluctantly gave up the nonviolent political fight for civil rights and threw his support behind the armed struggle of Algeria's National Liberation Front. In 1958, he became the first president of revolutionary Algeria's Provisional Government in exile.

Mohammad Ali Jinnah was from both kinds of minority background, religious and professional. Born to a modest merchant family with Isma'ili Shi'i heritage, in Karachi, a booming trade town on the coast of Sindh, in northwest India, he trained as a barrister in London, returning to India in 1896. He began his political career as a supporter of Indian unity across religious lines. Seen as an "ambassador of Hindu-Muslim unity," Jinnah did not join the All-India Muslim League, which had been set up in 1906 by the Muslim middle and upper classes, until 1913. In 1919, he walked out of a conference in protest at what he saw as the irresponsible radicalism of the Khilafat movement. He opposed "agitation" and violence, and hoped to gain independence for India with a constitution that would guarantee each community some form of proportional representation. But in 1940 he told his audience in Lahore, in the north of British India, that a single citizenship for Indians of different communities was impossible. Muslims, he said, "are a nation according to any definition of a nation." When he died in 1948, he had become the founder of a new nation, Pakistan, that had been divided from India in dreadful violence and an abiding enmity.[2]

Arslan, Abbas, and Jinnah were from different backgrounds, and from different religious communities within the broader world of Islam. For all three, unity among Muslims of all the faith's communities was important. And all three were seeking to solve the same problems: what would the community of Muslims become in a world that had been remade by European imperial rule, the end of the caliphate, the abiding reality of Western dominance, and the principle, supposedly now respected by everyone but evidently so hard to achieve, of self-determination? Above all, what did the community of faith, already so hard to unite, mean for that other kind of community (also, in Arabic, called an *umma*)—the nation? Because for everyone, to have self-determination or indeed any rights at all, it was belonging to a nation that mattered now.

◇◇◇◇◇◇◇

Both Ferhat Abbas and Mohammad Ali Jinnah were well versed in the language, culture, and professed values of the European powers. After the First World War, while Arslan became a globe-trotting polemicist, espousing Muslim unity across territorial boundaries and seeking a counterweight to the imperial powers, Abbas and Jinnah both became nationalist politicians, negotiating with those powers for their people's self-determination within the territorial boundaries that colonial state-building had drawn. By the 1940s, both Abbas and Jinnah were national leaders, defining their respective political communities—the Muslims of Algeria, and the Muslims of India—by their religious and cultural identity, and envisioning their liberation in a secular, constitutional, and democratic nation-state. Neither believed that their countries' politics should be defined by Islam, as a state religion or as a code of law. Both had begun their careers seeking liberation through a common, equal citizenship across their countries' religious and racialised communities. But both had been forced to adapt their ideas: Abbas, because the French republic refused to grant equal citizenship to the Muslim majority in minority-ruled North Africa, and Jinnah, because he feared for a Muslim minority in a Hindu-dominated India. Both came to believe that being Muslim defined their nations.

Shakib Arslan believed both in one transnational Muslim solidarity, and in one transregional "Arab nation." He fulminated against what he called the "childish and theatrical" Westernisation of republican Turkey. But he too was wholly at home with the European view of history that had emerged in the nineteenth century, as the linear progress of modern civilisation out of dark ages. He saw his own community as deserving its own place in that history. As his French-language monthly review, *La Nation Arabe*, declared in 1930, Arab demands for independence were those of "a nation that shone its civilising light on the shadows of the Middle Ages, and on the ruins of the Greek and Roman world, and was thus one of the principal makers of the modern world." Like others in the twentieth century, he found both inspiration for a revival of Arab glories and evidence of past civilisational coexistence in medieval Muslim Spain, about which he wrote extensively. The Arab nation "is worthy," he wrote "of entering into the concert of civilised nations": its doing so, indeed, would "strengthen the spirit of peace and solidarity between East and West."[3]

Arslan, Abbas, and Jinnah, and the meanings of being Muslim that they all defended, were all products of the late nineteenth century: the age of the steamship, the telegraph, printing and electricity; belief in civilisation and progress, nations and nationalism; and intertwined, globalised politics. Arslan's audience was in Jeddah and Cairo, but also in Budapest, Warsaw, Berlin, Geneva, Detroit, and New York. More people than ever made the pilgrimage to Mecca from as far away as Africa and Southeast Asia, more people than ever read or heard printed and broadcast news from further afield, and more than ever, Europeans had come to fear the networks of news, rumour, and conspiracy that, they imagined, tied Muslims together around their imperialised world.

Pan-Islamic solidarity was an imaginary imperialist bogeyman, but also a real Muslim aspiration, especially as Muslims everywhere struggled to reimagine the meaning of both their global community and the homelands to which they more immediately belonged. Arslan was influenced by the late nineteenth-century revivalists al-Afghani and, especially, Abduh, but their world had vanished into the shell-storm in 1914. Now that a notionally global focus of loyalty, the caliphate, was no more, the *umma* grew in importance. If there was no caliph to exercise even symbolic Muslim sovereignty, how was the Muslim *umma* to re-create legitimately Islamic rule? And within the various national frontiers into which Muslims had now been divided, where most of them were struggling for their own liberation from colonial rule, what sort of national communities would they be? How did being Muslim relate to being a nationalist, and a citizen?[4]

Some thought that the solution was to find a new caliph, a figure to symbolise and embody the continuity of an overarching Muslim sovereignty in a world of separate nation-states. Rival dynastic rulers in the Middle East, each seeking to marry a more global significance to their struggling national sovereignties, each thought they might best fit the bill: most notably Egypt's King Fuad, and Husayn Ibn Ali, the ex-Sharif of Mecca who had rebelled against the Ottomans in 1916 and become King of the Hijaz. Arslan, detesting Husayn for his wartime alliance with the British against the Ottomans, at first promoted the Egyptian monarchy as the worthiest candidate for the caliphate. Later, he became an admirer of Abd al-Aziz Ibn Saud, whose sudden rise to prominence in the 1920s gave a striking new example of expansive and explicitly Islamic sovereignty.

Others argued that there was no need for a caliphate at all. In 1925, Ali Abd al-Raziq, a judge and professor at al-Azhar in Cairo, a supporter of Egypt's Liberal Constitutional Party and no admirer of the Egyptian monarchy, published an eloquent and forceful essay on *Islam and the Foundations of Government*. The book caused a storm in public opinion and lost him his job. Accused by his detractors of importing European secularism into Islam, Abd al-Raziq in fact had constructed a traditionally Islamic scholarly argument, based heavily on interpretation of the Qur'an. He emphasised the uniquely higher calling of Muhammad's Prophetic mission, distinguishing sharply between Prophetic and political authority. As originally established by the Prophet, Abd al-Raziq maintained, Islam was "a message, not a government; a religion, not a state." There was nothing in the Qur'an, the hadith, or Islamic law that made the caliphate necessary; Muslims could adopt different forms of government if they chose. In Abd al-Raziq's view, the historically existing caliphate had not been the ideal imagined by both medieval scholars and modern activists. It was a worldly institution, one that had rarely served the true interests of the Muslim community. When the last of the Abbasids left Mamluk Cairo in 1517, he wrote with a poetic flourish, the caliphs "departed, and the world wept not for their ruin."[5]

Abd al-Raziq was very much in the minority. He argued that on the whole, the caliphs had been despots misusing a power that, like European absolutists, they claimed to derive from God. He also considered that it was for the community to choose whatever form of government would best serve its interests. Both arguments were seen as illegitimate.

By arguing that Muslims could choose any form of government for themselves, his colleagues at al-Azhar said, he was opening the door to communism. His opponents restated the orthodox argument that the caliph, far from being above the law like a European absolutist, was in fact bound by it. The caliphate, they maintained, was essential to Muslims, mandated by the sharia. Muslims were already disunited, under foreign domination in a disordered world: the last thing they needed was to lose what had, until recently, seemed to be one of the last institutions of both worldly power and spiritual authority holding them together.

In less febrile conditions, this debate might have sparked a creative synthesis of views, but instead it produced only angry controversy. Almost everyone fell into line in concurring that the caliphate was necessary, but no one could agree on who should be caliph. Three pan-Islamic congresses, in Cairo and Mecca in 1926, and in Jerusalem in 1931, failed to resolve the question. Of the three, only the Cairo congress was primarily concerned with it anyway, and that was sparsely attended and widely seen as a manoeuvre to drum up support for Egypt's King Fuad. The threat to the caliphate had mobilised mass opinion, especially in India, but once the caliphate was gone, it mattered much less to ordinary Muslim workers and peasants than to religious scholars and commentators. Sidelined by more urgent anti-colonial issues, the caliphate faded from significance in the 1930s and 1940s. It appeared in no major Islamic movement's political program and retained only a symbolic and sometimes nostalgic importance. But it remained unresolved, and available to be reactivated, both as a potent fear among non-Muslims, and as an aspiration to a different kind of sovereignty for Muslims, in a world where national liberation would prove less liberating than at first was hoped.[6]

◇◇◇◇◇◇◇

Also writing about the caliphate in Egypt in the 1920s was Rashid Rida, a Syrian intellectual, journalist, and religious reformer. Rida was a close, if occasionally exasperated, friend of Shakib Arslan. Like Arslan, he was also a follower of al-Afghani, and a disciple of al-Afghani's student and colleague, Muhammad Abduh. After a broad education in Lebanon that had included French, Turkish, mathematics, and natural sciences, as well as Islamic studies, in 1897 Rida moved to Cairo to escape Sultan Abdülhamid II's press censorship and to gain Abduh's support for his own publishing enterprise. He eventually became Abduh's foremost disciple, his biographer, and the self-appointed guardian of his legacy. In 1898, Rida launched a monthly journal, *Al-Manar* (The Lighthouse), which until his death in 1935 would be widely read and influential across the Arab world and beyond.

Rida belonged to the generation of religious and political activists who looked to the Ottoman caliphate as a rallying point for Muslims across the world, but opposed the autocracy of Sultan Abdülhamid II, and hoped for an Arab emancipation fed by cultural revival and religious renewal. He had celebrated the Ottoman constitutional revolution in 1908 at an Armenian church in Cairo. Unlike his friend Arslan, he supported the Arab Revolt against the Ottomans. After the war and the collapse of Ottoman rule, he at first tried to help create a new government for his own country. In Damascus in 1920, rival claims on Syria's future were being made by popular crowds in the street and their grassroots political organisers, the aristocratic Emir Faysal, Faysal's British patrons, their French allies, and a newly constituted Syrian Arab Congress, of which Rida became president. The congress saw itself as the embryo of a democratic, representative government. Rida himself insisted both that there should be an Islamic dimension to the new state, with sharia as "the main source" of legislation, and that the congress should act as a democratic constituent assembly representing the nation. He hoped that it would assert itself against the dynastic ambitions of Faysal—who, he said, was made king by the congress, not by himself—as well as against the threat of partition by the imperial powers. The fear of a split in the congress and popular unrest being stirred up by more conservative factions seems to have prevented him from supporting votes for women, but he endorsed constitutional equality for citizens of all faiths, and a democratically elected government.[7]

After a French army threw out the Syrian Arab kingdom and its hopes of immediate independence, Rida returned to Cairo and turned to the fate of the caliphate, publishing a book on *The Caliphate, or the Supreme Imamate* in 1922. He favoured the re-establishment of the caliph as a supreme spiritual, legal, and political authority over all Muslims everywhere, elected by a properly qualified body of experts. Using a classical formula, he called these experts "the people who loosen and bind," meaning the legal scholars who, for Rida, must also be fully abreast of the modern world and its sciences. They would themselves be the representatives of the community as a whole. Such experts would, in Rida's scheme, be properly qualified to develop legislation, on the basis of sharia and in the public interest, that would then be endorsed by the caliph for implementation by governments in each Muslim state.[8]

Rida himself was a new kind of Muslim intellectual. As a *sayyid*, a descendant of the Prophet, he had an inherited religious prestige. But it was his chosen professional standing as a journalist that mattered most to him. Although he provided legal opinions, he did not see himself as one of the traditional scholars, the ʿulama, whom he caricatured as thoughtless imitators of the past. Nor was he one of the so-called "Westernised" bourgeoisie, who (like his Syrian Christian competitors in the Egyptian Arabic press) wore clipped moustaches and three-piece suits, and whom he lampooned as "Frenchified" imitators of Europe. He saw himself as an influencer of public opinion, a man who worked in the public domain and for the public interest. His professed vocation was "guiding the faithful to the ways of progress and civilisation." In the interwar world where Muslim sovereignty had collapsed almost everywhere, new ideas and lifestyles were all around, and society seemed—as it did to religious conservatives elsewhere— increasingly alienated from religious values. Remaining "faithful" while following the "ways of progress" to him meant reconnecting with the original truth of Islam.[9]

That original truth was to be found in the way of the *salaf,* the "pious forebears" of the time of the Prophet and the first generations of

Muslims. Rida, like the late nineteenth-century reformers, thought that their true Islam had long been abandoned by Muslims. That abandonment, rather than the power asymmetries of capitalism and empire, was, he thought, the real cause of Muslims' present troubles. Quite unlike the eighteenth-century revivalists whom he cited as his models, though, Rida was imagining Islam in a world that capitalism and European empire had transformed, and in which the nation-state had become the model for social cohesion as well as the vehicle for freedom from colonial rule. In imagining a new kind of Islamic state that might function in the absence of the caliphate, Rida espoused an understanding of Islamic tradition that in fact was profoundly new. He saw Muslims' social relations, as well as ritual duties, as being regulated by religious law, rather than by the discretion of a temporal ruler, in ways that earlier scholars had not. In adapting Islamic law to the demands of the bureaucratic nation-state, which sought to govern every aspect of citizens' lives in ways earlier Muslim rulers could never have imagined, he reimagined Islam as a total way of life. In doing so, he advocated a fusion of religion and politics that would define later twentieth-century Islamism.[10]

Rida would later be seen as the exponent of *salafi* Islam, or *salafiyya*. "Salafism" or Muslim "fundamentalism" (a term borrowed by English-language writers from late nineteenth-century American Protestantism) would later be seen, especially in Europe and America, as a single trend or movement within Islam. Muslims who called themselves salafis claimed that their understanding of the faith was simply "true Islam"—anything not "salafi" would necessarily be a deviation from the true faith. Salafism was never a distinct school or movement, but a claim to authenticity. Increasingly, it was a claim to a monopoly on the truth.

In the twentieth century, this claim would be made by many different teachers and social movements. They would often have in common a claimed intellectual ancestry, going back through the fourteenth-century Syrian theologian Ibn Taymiyya to the ninth-century hadith scholar Ahmad Ibn Hanbal. But they would take different and sometimes conflicting positions on many issues. Some would be militant activist organisations whose programs would veer between seeking revolutionary change through political violence, and pursuing grassroots social reform through peaceful preaching, education, and welfare work. Others would profess to avoid politics altogether: or rather, their politics would be conservative and quietist, disavowing dissent, aligning themselves with incumbent regimes, focusing on social morality and personal piety, and teaching obedience to authority and the avoidance of "strife."

Both of these tendencies were already coming to prominence in the 1920s. The foremost activist social movement, throughout the Arab world and far beyond through the twentieth century, would be the Society of Muslim Brothers. Better known as the Muslim Brotherhood, the society was founded in Egypt in 1928 by a charismatic schoolteacher, Hassan al-Banna. Al-Banna began his religious life as a devotee of a Sufi fraternity. But as a student at Cairo's teacher training college, Dar al-Ulum, he was also a frequent visitor to salafi discussion circles, and to the Salafiyya Bookshop that was run by another Syrian journalist and activist, Rashid Rida's associate Muhibb al-Din al-Khatib. Al-Banna had seen the 1919 revolution and its repression firsthand as a child, growing up in the Nile Delta northwest of Cairo, and was intensely conscious of the ongoing British military occupation in the Suez Canal zone, where he taught in a primary school after graduating in 1927. He saw the struggle against colonialism as bound up with a larger and longer struggle to re-Islamise a society whose faith, he believed, had been "corrupted" by foreign domination and Muslims' own immorality. In a long statement of the Brotherhood's program, sent to Egypt's new King Faruq in 1936 and later published as a tract entitled *Towards the Light*, he emphasised both "the liberation of the nation from its political bonds so that it may…regain its lost independence and sovereignty," and the nation's "reconstruction, so that it may take its own way among the nations and compete…in its progress towards social perfection."[11]

In finding its "way," according to al-Banna, the nation had to choose between two stark alternatives. In moving from the countryside to

Cairo as a young man, he had been shocked by urban life. What he saw as a "frivolous world, reeking with sin and redolent with vice,... doubt and heresy" seemed to him the effect of European intrusion into what he imagined as having been a purer, more perfect Egypt of the past, devoted to "its dear and precious Islam." Adopting the polarised view of European versus Islamic "civilisation" that had emerged, first among European scholars and politicians, and then among Muslim intellectuals, since the mid-1800s, and seeing the conflict between them materialised in British-occupied Egypt, he could imagine his country's future only as following "the way of the West" or that of Islam. "The West," he said, was now "bankrupt and in decline." Observing the crises of the mid-1930s, the Great Depression, Stalinist purges in the Soviet Union, and the ascent of fascism, he saw Europe's "political foundations... destroyed by dictatorships.... The millions of its wretched unemployed and hungry offer their testimony against it." "All of humanity," he wrote, "is tormented, wretched, worried, and confused, having been scorched by the fires of greed and materialism. They are in dire need of some sweet portion of the waters of True Islam to wash from them the filth of misery and lead them to happiness." Any Christian revivalist might have said something very similar. But al-Banna saw True Islam as something more than personal redemption and public morality: his tract went on to affirm that Islam was the solution to organising both the state and social life.[12]

A new kind of state, in a new kind of international order, had emerged from the demands of the First World War and the crises of the interwar years. Central economic planning, the mobilisation of people and resources, and legislating every area of life had suddenly become not only possible but, for some, desirable. Everything that now came under the remit of the "renascent" nation-state, devoted to the goal of "national greatness," was imagined by al-Banna as being properly regulated by Islam. The government, he said, should close dancehalls and bars, censor books, films, and radio broadcasts, prohibit alcohol and prostitution, enforce gender segregation and police personal morality. Islamic precepts should also guide the state in regulating everything from the economy and the military to healthcare and education, international relations and minority rights. The Brotherhood's aim was to realise such a goal, first within Egypt, then in other Muslim countries, and ultimately—Islam being God's universal message for all humanity—in the entire world.[13]

If this sounded like a totalitarian program, the Brotherhood lacked (and would continue to lack) not only the means but any practical agenda to achieve it. To convince its readers, *Towards the Light* relied simply on the words of God as transmitted in the Qur'an, not on any novel intellectual paradigm or political manifesto. For the Brotherhood, personal rectitude and organisational discipline, leading to the remoralisation of society, would mostly remain a sufficient program; they believed that divine aid would in due time come to empower the faithful in achieving all their divinely ordained goals. This did not prevent members of the movement, at different times, from either participating in elections and standing for office, or stockpiling arms and ammunition, forming paramilitary groups, assassinating their enemies, and planning for revolution. In the mid-1940s, their involvement in both armed struggle against the British in the canal zone, and in political violence against the Egyptian establishment—and, it was widely believed, against Egypt's Jewish community—led to al-Banna's assassination in 1949. Three years later, in July 1952, the Brotherhood would support the coup d'état by a group of young army officers, led by Colonel Gamal Abd al-Nasir (known in English as Nasser), who overthrew the monarchy.

But Nasser and his allies would turn out to have their own, mostly secular nationalist, ideas about national renewal. The Brotherhood would be brutally repressed in Egypt in 1954. But it and its offshoots, not only in the Arab world but as far away as Nigeria and Indonesia, too, would become the main exponents of Islamism—Islam repurposed as a political ideology, believing that the life of the political nation was identical with that of the moral community of faith—for many years to come.[14]

◇◇◇◇◇◇◇◇

The other "fundamentalist" tendency gaining prominence in the 1920s was to be found in the only Arab territory that had escaped colonial over-rule, the Arabian Peninsula. It would ultimately clash both with the Brotherhood and with more secular, revolutionary Arab nationalists like Nasser. In the Hijaz, in western Arabia, where the Hashemite Sharifs of Mecca had held sway and where they had allied with the British to launch the Arab Revolt, everything was changing. Abandoned by his imperial patrons after the war, not only did Sharif Husayn not become caliph, or king of the Arabs: he lost his kingdom of the Hijaz, too, to the rival and also British-sponsored dynastic ambitions of the Al-Saud and their Wahhabi supporters.

The Al-Saud family had lost their emirate in the early 1800s, and by the end of the nineteenth century they were driven out of their original power base in Najd by a rival local dynasty, the Al-Rashid. But having been reduced to the status of refugees in exile, after 1900 both the Al-Saud and Wahhabism, the reforming, militant brand of Islam that they had made their ally in the 1740s, made an extraordinary comeback. In 1900, Abd al-Aziz Al-Saud, who would become known more simply as Ibn Saud, left his exile in Kuwait to rebuild his family's principality in Najd. In 1902, aged twenty-seven, he captured Riyadh. From this small beginning, he would go on, until his abdication in 1953, to create and consolidate what would become one of the world's most significant states. Since the Al-Rashid, his main regional rivals, had gained recognition from the Ottomans, Ibn Saud sought support from the British. Initially hesitant to involve themselves in central Arabia, where (unlike on the Gulf coast) they had no strategic interests, the British changed their minds after the outbreak of the First World War. In 1915, they recognised Ibn Saud as the ruler of eastern and central Arabia and began to supply him with money and guns.

Over the next decade, Ibn Saud's individual dynamism and dynastic ambition combined with the opportunities created by regional and global conflict to enable his rapid rise. For Ibn Saud and especially for his followers, though, it was also the result of a divinely ordained mission to "return" the original heartlands of both Arabs and Islam to the true faith that, like other revivalists, they believed had been corrupted or forsaken. The legacy of Ibn Abd al-Wahhab had been preserved in Najd by his own descendants, the Al-Shaykh ("family of the shaykh"), and by large numbers of preachers committed to spreading and enforcing what, following Ibn Abd al-Wahhab, they considered to be proper Muslim ritual and behaviour. These focused on the strict regulation of personal and social life, with meticulous stipulations for correct ritual prayer and fasting, dress, wearing of facial hair (for men) and covering (for women), public gender segregation and strict personal morality. A central mission of these preachers was to bring the region's nomadic populations to follow this true Islam, settling them in agricultural communities that they called *hujjar*, "hijra places." The name and the nature of these settlements alike indicated that, like the Prophet's first followers and like many revivalist communities since, they had left their previous lifestyles and become a pious community of the faithful.

These settled Bedouin groups became known as *ikhwan*, "Brothers" (the same word used by al-Banna's Muslim Brothers, *al-ikhwan al-muslimun*; the term had also been used for centuries by Sufi fraternities). Beyond their tight regulation of individual and social life, their preachers emphasised three crucial duties. The first of these was obedience and payment of legitimate tax (as *zakat*, alms) to a properly established imam, the leader of the community. The second was strict adherence to the community and avoidance of those outside it, meaning, in particular, other Muslims who were not Wahhabis, especially the Shi'i communities of eastern Arabia and the non-Wahhabi, "cosmopolitan" populations of the Hijaz. The third, following from the first two, was readiness to wage jihad in the way of God against those who did not follow the true faith, to spread Islam under the imam's command.

From 1902, when Ibn Saud took Riyadh, he was accepted by the Wahhabi clerics as imam, renewing the historic alliance between his family and the Wahhabi movement. He embarked on a campaign to unify Arabia under his rule, a campaign that was also, for the Wahhabi clerics, one to put an end to division in the community and unite Arabia's peoples, as the Prophet had done, under true monotheism. The Ikhwan became *jund al-tawhid*, "the army of the unity of God." Eastern and central Arabia were gradually brought into the Saudi principality. The west, the Hijaz, remained independent for longer. But in 1924, hostilities with the Hashemite dynasty broke out. Ibn Saud refused to recognise Sharif Husayn's claim to the caliphate and, more prosaically, looked for the revenue to be gained from the pilgrimage to replace the subsidy that Britain, in 1924, had ceased to pay him. The Hijaz was rapidly overrun. In December 1924, Ibn Saud's troops entered Mecca, and in 1925, after a yearlong siege, they also took Jeddah. Having declared that he had invaded the Hijaz, not out of dynastic rivalry with the Hashemites but to "guarantee the liberty of pilgrimage and . . . settle the [Holy Places'] destiny in a manner satisfactory to the Islamic world," in 1926 Ibn Saud was proclaimed King of the Hijaz and Sultan of Najd. In 1932, the territories he had unified became the kingdom of Saudi Arabia. The following year, the Standard Oil Company of California successfully negotiated oil exploration rights in the new, and geologically promising, kingdom.[15]

The Saudis' kingdom-building ambition rode on the Ikhwan's zealous mission, but Wahhabism was never meant to be a revolutionary movement: quite the reverse. Political conservatism and the maintenance of order were just as important, for the Wahhabi clerics, as correct belief and correct ritual practice. They held Ibn Saud to account for his own religious propriety (it was said that on one occasion, when his shirt was longer than ritually prescribed, they cut it shorter while he was still wearing it), but they also emphasised obedience to the imam for everyone else. From 1921 onwards, Ibn Saud reached agreement with the British, delimiting the frontiers of his kingdom with those of the British-controlled territories in Iraq and Transjordan, and with the British-protected state of Kuwait. The Ikhwan, deprived of the material gains, the personal prestige, and the pious vocation they had come to enjoy as warriors for the faith, were not pleased. In 1927, rumbles of protest came to a head: the king shouldn't be dealing with the British, the Ikhwan's leaders said. He levied taxes that were not properly Islamic, and his lifestyle was becoming too luxurious. They objected to his series of marriages with the daughters of leading tribal families (by which strategic alliances were made and the dynasty expanded), and to his limiting the Wahhabi mission, which they wanted to expand to enforce "true Islam" on the Shi'i population, on pilgrims from Egypt and Syria, and on the tribes of neighbouring Iraq, Kuwait and Transjordan.

In response, Ibn Saud convened a council of clerics. Their rulings accepted some of the Ikhwan's points on popular rituals associated with the pilgrimage, and on the legality of taxes. But they asserted, above all, the imam's discretion in decision-making and his sole prerogative to declare or suspend jihad, and forbade rebellion against him even if he failed to apply the law in every respect (notably, regarding taxation). The Ikhwan rejected the ruling, and rebelled. Between 1927 and 1930, aided by the British Royal Air Force and backed by the Wahhabi religious establishment, Ibn Saud crushed them. Practical state-building had taken over from zealous revivalism. The Wahhabi clerics (quite unlike the Muslim Brothers) accepted the restriction of their own role to ruling on ritual matters and the acceptability of innovations like the telegraph: as had been the case ever since Ibn Hanbal, the king could not dictate religion himself any more than the caliph could, but religious authority, while separate from temporal power, was also subordinate to it. Its role was to support political order, not to contest it.[16]

Nonetheless, there was a radicalism to the Wahhabis' enforcing the "fundamentals" of faith. The Ikhwan became known for their violent enforcement of Wahhabi norms, which were alien to other Muslim communities in Arabia. Their campaigns had involved plunder and sometimes massacre in towns that resisted them; the Saudi conquests may have killed between ten and twenty-five thousand people. The clerics' response to the Ikhwan, in 1927, ordered among other things the destruction of mosques, including one historically associated with the Prophet's uncle, Hamza. The Wahhabis' puritanical interpretation of Islam sought, as they saw it, to purify the land and rid the community of idolatrous deviations from the true faith—historic graves that commemorated the sites where early Muslims had lived, or that marked their resting places, were to them monuments that led the ignorant to venerate people instead of God. The Wahhabi conquest of the Hijaz was marked by the destruction of "idolatrous" monuments like the early Muslim tombs in the cemetery of Medina, including the tombs of Companions of the Prophet, and the house of Khadija, the wife of the Prophet, in Mecca. Their destruction shocked other Muslims, who saw the Ikhwan's "purification" as appalling acts of desecration.[17]

At the same time, influential voices began to see the Saudis' independent sovereignty, standing almost alone in a world carved up by the Europeans, as emblematic of what Islam might be if properly applied to social and political life. Shakib Arslan wrote enthusiastically of Ibn Saud that "rarely do we see among contemporary rulers anyone whose successes have been so rapid and so significant, and whose undertakings have met with such success." Ibn Saud, he affirmed, was a "good democrat" whose religious advisors were open to progress (they had, after all, allowed use of the telegraph) while preserving religion. In a series of articles, published in 1925 as a book entitled *The Wahhabis and the Hijaz*, Rashid Rida defended the Najdi doctrine and its preachers as truly orthodox and deserving of support. "Wahhabism" had been a term of abuse, denoting an extremist sectarianism. It was a label that Ibn Saud himself sought to downplay, preferring his religious scholars to refer to themselves as Salafis. Nonetheless, they adopted it themselves; one wrote defiantly in a religious poem: "Indeed, we are Wahhabis, the true monotheists, who make our enemies suffer!" From the mid-1920s, with the Saudis bolstering their credentials as well as their finances through control of the pilgrimage and the Holy Places of Mecca and Medina, Wahhabism began to be identified as acceptable, mainstream Sunnism, and even—as its proponents themselves claimed—as simply the "true Islam."[18]

◇◇◇◇◇◇◇

As Rashid Rida got older, he became more conservative. The constitutional reformer, who in 1920 was hailed by the progressive middle-class women of Beirut as one of their most promising champions, by 1931 was fulminating against "a time that is threatened by women's revolution, the violation of marital vows, the disintegration of the family," a time when "nothing remains stable to raise our youths and teach them respect." Preoccupations with being modern, remaining authentic, and achieving national liberation all meant a concern with the family and gender roles as well as—and often much more than—with geopolitics.[19]

Conservative men saw women as the vulnerable site of their own and their community's honour. This became a major anxiety, especially in societies that found themselves under scrutiny and surveillance by intrusive colonial rulers, and exposed to the freer—because dominant, privileged, and wealthier—social norms of middle-class, expatriate or settler-colonial European society, and what Rida called "their half-naked women." Masculinity was threatened by colonial rule and by the "abandonment" of religion: Hassan al-Banna thought Muslims had become "servile" and subservient, losing their manhood and their honour as well as their virtue and their sovereignty. Masculinity was imagined and embodied in new ways, in education, dress, physical health, psychology, and social manners. The Muslim Brothers were, among other things, an athletic association, practising martial arts and prizing a manliness that affirmed bodily as well as spiritual integrity. For Wahhabis, the proper length of a man's beard, the proper shortness of his trousers and shirt, were signs of his proper masculinity and membership of the patriarchal, male community of true Muslims, among whose duties one of the most important was the proper protection, guardianship and guidance of truly Muslim wives and sisters.

Religious authorities and ordinary male heads of households alike anxiously defended the intimate spheres of sex, motherhood, and what they saw as traditional morality and the protection of women by strict norms of modesty. In contrast, others in more confident, more liberal—usually, more urban and wealthier—circles advocated for what they called the "new woman": an educated, emancipated (and implicitly, urban and middle-class) woman, freed from seclusion, ignorance, and the veil, who would herself contribute to social progress and the welfare of the community, and who—above all—would raise and educate the rational male citizens of the future. An associate of Muhammad Abduh, the Egyptian intellectual, lawyer, and social reformer Qasim Amin, caused a stir with two books published in Cairo, in Arabic, in 1899 and 1900, on *The New Woman* and *The Liberation of Women*. Amin asserted that the status of women best indicated a society's level of development, and that an end to seclusion and the provision of proper education for women were the surest ways to advance civilisation, progress, and national renewal.[20]

Practices like domestic seclusion in separate women's apartments and veiling when out in public were, as they always had been, mostly restricted to the wealthier, "respectable" urban upper classes. Amin's argument for bringing women out of the harem applied only to households large and aristocratic enough to have such things in the first place. Norms of dress and behaviour, and the ways they changed, depended more on social and economic circumstances than on piety or progressiveness alone. Above all, the rapid twentieth-century increase in urban population saw city-dwellers in all Muslim-majority countries become a much greater proportion of the population than before, as they did everywhere in the world. The greater numbers, and proportion, of women living in towns and cities simultaneously both afforded greater opportunities for their education and for different kinds of work—though women's freedom of choice over both would remain very limited—and increased men's anxiety around their status, behaviour, and protection.

By the early 1900s, upper- and middle-class women in Ottoman cities often wore hats trimmed with lace veils just as upper- and middle-class women in Paris and New York did. Full veiling for women, however, was still common in upper-class and conservative circles in urban Egypt, as it was among nomadic Bedouin in the Egyptian countryside. In French North Africa, cities were partly segregated between European and Muslim populations, but the proximity and dominance of European colonial society accentuated anxiety about women's safety and social respectability, and a generalised impoverishment made the emergence of middle-class consumption and dress impossible beyond a very few families before the 1950s. Upper-class women demonstrators in Cairo in 1919 indicated their impeccable social status by wearing the long black headscarves and robes, and long white veils below their eyes, that any elite woman would be expected to don in the street—and they demonstrated separately from lower-class women. Peasant women in the fields and women workers in factories and workshops, on the other hand, everywhere covered their hair just as peasant women and workers everywhere in Europe did, but they did not go about veiled, except perhaps in marketplaces and on the road where strangers might be met. When working-class Egyptian women took to the street in 1919, they sometimes did so alongside men, instead of marching among the veiled "ladies" of the urban elite.[21]

Across all social classes, a generally recognised culture of respectability, rather than any straightforward rule of veiling or seclusion, dictated how men and women should behave both in the household and in public space. Mothers and daughters would serve male guests but not eat with them; fathers would socialise with the men but not with the women of other households. Men and women all celebrated marriages, attended public prayer, and participated in religious festivals like the birthday of the Prophet or local saint's days, but did so separately. Women might be segregated but they were not inactive. The Muslim Brothers, recognising the necessity of mobilising the whole of society for the change they sought to achieve, created a separate, parallel organisation, the Muslim Sisters, to involve women in their movement. More generally, mass politics, nationalist mobilisation, and burgeoning urban culture involved women as active participants, not only as symbols of national purity. Women attended concerts, plays, cinema screenings and public lectures, vocalised their approval of male speakers at rallies, and gave essential material support to striking male workers and imprisoned male activists. In Algeria, women who were domestic workers in European households by day might be actresses in satirical theatrical productions in the evening. Women's periodical publications, written by women and advocating women's rights and a "women's awakening," had been appearing in Egypt since 1892, when Hind Nawfal, the daughter of Syrian Christians who had moved to Alexandria, began editing the monthly *Al-Fatat* (The Young Woman). She assured her readers that concerns for women's "modesty...purity and good behaviour" held in common by Arab Christians and Muslims would not be compromised by "a woman who writes in a journal."[22]

Around the same time, in the 1890s, Zaynab Fawwaz penned assertive essays on women's education and aspirations. Girls should be educated, she wrote, so that they might work and achieve a measure of financial independence, not merely so that they might become good mothers to patriotic boys. Fawwaz, who had moved to Egypt from a Lebanese Shi'i background and an early life in domestic service with a family that taught her to read and write, became a novelist and playwright. In 1894, she published an extraordinary collection of biographies that constituted a kind of world history seen through women's lives, from the ancient world to the nineteenth century. Even earlier, one of Fawwaz's subjects, the poet and social commentator Aisha Taymur, had written both about girls' education and about the larger world of social change affecting women, men, the social values that governed their relationships, and their respective roles in defending the nation.[23]

Taymur was born in 1840 to an elite, Turkish-speaking family of Iraqi Kurdish origin that had moved to Egypt in Ottoman army service. Her mother was a freed Circassian slave, her father a senior court official who was several times a provincial governor under Mehmed Ali and his successors. Taught to read and write by her father, and fascinated from childhood both by "the accounts of nations" and "the nightly chats of elderly women," Aisha wrote poetry in Persian and

Turkish, and prose in Arabic. Like Rashid Rida decades later, Aisha critiqued the social mores that she already saw, in the late 1880s, as influenced by the transformative effects of capitalism and colonial society. But for her, it was the behaviour of men that was at fault, with husbands abandoning proper Islamic morality, masculinity, and the duty they owed their wives: motivated only by "greed and the possession of wealth," such a man "spends his time in bars...listening to music, gambling and drinking" until "a wife feels alienated from her husband and serves him with a broken heart."[24]

Even where women's emancipation became a national and religious duty for men, women's own struggles to change their status and expand their opportunities often achieved what they did despite men's modernising agendas more than through them. Male reformers sometimes argued that veiling was merely a cultural custom, not an Islamic requirement. Some, like the Tunisian nationalist Abd al-Aziz al-Tha'alibi, claimed that the veil had been adopted from Byzantine and Persian court custom and was not truly Muslim at all. But they were incensed when women said the same for themselves. Nazira Zain al-Din, a young Lebanese advocate of women's rights, wrote in 1927 that she found it "inconceivable that we claim to be defenders of honour when the veil is our strongest shield. We must understand as everyone else does that honour is rooted in the heart and chastity comes from within and not from a piece of transparent material lowered over the face." Reformist as well as conservative Lebanese clerics attacked her book, *Unveiling and Veiling*, claiming that she could not possibly have written it herself.[25]

In the same way, while Mustafa Kemal Atatürk would be celebrated by his admirers as the "strong man" who "freed" Turkish women from tradition and obscurantism, his modernising state sometimes disliked women's own activism in journalism, social welfare, education and literature. Nezihe Muhiddin, for example, was a campaigner for women's rights, suffrage, the integrity of the late Ottoman Empire and emerging Turkish nationalism. She ran a school during the First World War, published a women's newspaper, *Türk Kadini* (The Turkish Woman), wrote fiction, and was elected to parliament in 1935, the year after Turkish women gained the vote in national elections. In the mid-1920s, the Turkish Women's Union that she had co-founded to press for political and social rights for women faced surveillance and harassment by the regime, and Muhiddin was prosecuted on embezzlement charges. When Keriman Halis, the Turkish contestant, won the 1932 Miss Universe title at a beauty queen pageant held in Belgium, the event was celebrated as proof of the Kemalist liberation of women. But Muhiddin's novel *The Beauty Queen*, published three years later, subtly criticised Turkish men's adoption of European definitions of female beauty, and the embodiment of national progress in the visibility (to men) of women's bodies.[26]

Renewing the community and liberating it—from what was variously diagnosed as ignorance or backwardness, materialism or colonialism—was no straightforward matter. Who should be freed and how, what the community should look like and how—once foreign control was removed—it should properly be governed were questions with no clear answer. The only consensus was that the community—both the transnational *umma* of Muslims and the more immediate territorial nation, both the people and their homeland—had to be liberated. Women as well as men expressed "the feelings of disappointment that our generation experienced in the shadows of imperialism and foreign occupation," as Anbara Salam Khalidi would put it in her memoirs. A feminist and nationalist writer and activist, Khalidi was one of the first generation of Arab Muslim women to remove her veil, in 1928, to make a speech in public. Born in Lebanon in 1897, she remembered her father being arrested twice by the Ottoman authorities during the First World War, her house being ransacked by French authorities under the mandate, and her home being lost when she was forced to flee from Jerusalem, during the first Arab-Israeli war, in 1948. She had travelled, she wrote, "the thorny road travelled... by the women of my generation who sought knowledge, dignity and self-respect."[27]

<><><><><>

Through colonialism's interwar high tide, the Great Depression, and the Second World War, territorial nation-states coalesced into a new international order. Most of them, in Asia and Africa, were still under some form of colonial rule in the 1940s. Disappointed in the promises of the so-called liberal imperialists, the British and French and their American allies, a few Muslim activists would turn to the emerging Axis powers of Nazi Germany, Fascist Italy, and imperial Japan. Shakib Arslan was twice a guest of Mussolini. Rashid Ali al-Gaylani, the nationalist prime minister of Iraq, led a short-lived pro-Axis coup in Baghdad in 1941—but this lacked popular Iraqi as well as effective German support, and was quickly suppressed by the British. Hajj Amin al-Husayni, son of a notable Palestinian family who became the British-appointed "Grand Mufti" of Jerusalem (an office the British invented), supported the coup in Baghdad, where he had fled to avoid arrest by the British. In the 1930s, Hajj Amin had become an influential leader of the Palestinian national movement demanding independence from Britain. When his calls for popular support of the coup in Baghdad failed, he notoriously travelled to Berlin, met Hitler, broadcast German propaganda to the Arab world, and adopted the Nazis' antisemitic language.

Both Allied and Axis powers by 1940 assumed that "the Muslim world" was a unity, Muslims one community, and that in "the Muslim world" faith and power, religion and politics, were one and the same. These simplifying ideas, generalised since the mid-nineteenth century, were historically ill-founded but universally believed. Ironically, the ambitious goal that pan-Islamists had never been able to realise was taken to be an already existing, indeed historically unchanging reality by Europeans on both sides of the global conflict. Both Allied and Axis powers accordingly sought, as the Entente and Central Powers had twenty-six years earlier, to harness "world Muslim" opinion to their cause. From 1942, the Nazi regime assiduously sought to mobilise Muslim support against Britain, France, and Jewish populations in the Middle East, and against the Soviets in eastern Europe and the Caucasus. In the Caucasus, where Soviet rule was no less hated than the tsarist Russian imperialism it succeeded, advancing German soldiers were looked to as "liberators." Religiously legitimated revolts broke out among Muslim populations behind Soviet lines in the Caucasus, one of which lasted until 1947. By the end of the war, Muslims from Albania, Bosnia, the Caucasus and Crimea (along with equally anti-Soviet but Christian nationalist Ukrainians, Lithuanians, Georgians and Armenians) could be found in the Wehrmacht and in Waffen-SS units. Hundreds of thousands of Muslims from South Asia, central Asia, the Balkans, the Middle East and Africa fought in German, British, French, and Russian uniforms.[28]

Tactical wartime alliances between Muslim activists and the Axis were most effective and longest-lived in Southeast Asia. Japanese expansionism and the claim to be creating an anticolonial "Greater East Asian Co-Prosperity Sphere" built on pan-Asian networks and ideas already established before the First World War. From Tokyo, Abdürreşid Ibrahim claimed that Japan's "Greater East Asian war is a sacred one ... comparable to the war carried out against the infidels by the Prophet Muhammad." In the island archipelago that was coming to be seen as the single homeland of Indonesia, anticolonial nationalism was already mobilising both Islamic and secular ideas of community that would mostly function in unison. The nationalist leader, Sukarno, taught at a reformist Muslim (*Muhammadiyah*) school in the 1930s and liked to invoke the Egyptian nationalist and journalist Mustafa Kamil and the reforming Amanullah Khan of Afghanistan alongside Sun Yat-sen, Gandhi, and Mustafa Kemal Atatürk. (His more Islamist opponents objected that Atatürk was "a dictator, a *Führer*, a *duce*.")

In November 1939, the "Greater Japanese Association for Islam" (Dai-Nihon Kai-kyo Kyokai) hosted Muslim delegations in Tokyo and Osaka. After the Japanese occupation of the Dutch East Indies in 1942, sympathetic nationalists were looked to as allies while their countries' resources (rubber, tin, and other materials essential to the war effort) were extracted. In 1943, Mas Mansur, a nationalist leader from Surabaya in eastern Java who had studied in Mecca and Cairo, wrote that "for hundreds of years the peoples of Asia have lived in misery amidst the natural wealth of their homelands.... But God is truly just!... It is Dai Nippon that God has ordained to save the other people of Asia." The following month, Mansur could be seen listening to Sukarno at the founding of the Putera ("People's Power Centre") organisation, set up to work under the Japanese occupation authorities, wearing the modernist male Muslim attire of a black felt cap together with the Japanese imperial symbol, a chrysanthemum. Having taken up arms alongside other nationalists against the re-establishment of Dutch rule after the war, he died in prison in 1947 and would later be declared a national hero.[29]

In the Middle East and North Africa, in contrast, few nationalists bought into the idea that Germany might be an effective ally. In Egypt, despite the Muslim Brotherhood's quasi-totalitarian aspirations and belief that multiparty politics should give way to "channeling...the political forces of the nation into a common front and a single phalanx," fascism was mostly rejected by public opinion. By the end of the 1930s, it was seen as another threatening form of racist European imperialism. Nazism's racial ideology was well known to Algerians, who had seen far-right French nationalism up close during the 1930s and knew what it meant for them. The few radical anti-French nationalists who advocated alliance with the Germans were generally disavowed. When Tunisia was liberated from German occupation in 1943, the French deposed the monarch, Munsif Bey, on the pretext that he had collaborated. In fact, he had resisted the imposition of anti-Jewish measures in Tunisia (which French colonial officials had enthusiastically applied in Algeria); the returning French administration removed him, rather, because of his anticolonialism and popularity. Muslims were not impressed by Mussolini's declaration in Tripoli, in 1937, that he would now be the "Protector of Islam" (complete with a jewelled sword, made in Italy). The Duce's army and air force had spent the previous decade brutally repressing an insurgency in Libya led by the Sanusiyya order and its revered shaykh, Omar al-Mukhtar. Omar was hanged by the Italians in Benghazi in 1937 and became a hero in the Arab world. Many of his supporters had been crowded into concentration camps and starved.[30]

Between 1939 and 1945, the great majority of Muslims across the world instead replayed the experience of the First World War, fighting, manufacturing, and suffering famine for their imperial rulers, hoping for a better outcome at the end of the war when freedom and democracy, they were once again assured, would triumph in a new and better world order. Anticolonialism and secular politics, projects for liberal constitutions and for radical revolutions, jostled with ideas of cultural community and religious renewal. To the crisis of the old European empires was added an awareness that new superpowers, the United States and the Soviet Union, were emerging in the 1940s more powerfully than they had after 1917.

In French North Africa, socialist and communist parties and trade unions often created space for cross-community politics in the 1920s and 1930s. Everywhere, such solidarities ran into dead ends. Radical French workers, hoping for a revolution in France itself, saw themselves as making common cause with oppressed and exploited Muslim workers and peasants. But they could not countenance the idea that North African Muslims would need their own national independence, rather than becoming part of a revolutionised French republic. The conservative, landowning settlers who dominated local politics in any case believed that French rule would be permanent, and that Muslims would need to be ruled by force indefinitely to keep their inherent violence in check. Ferhat Abbas, the French-speaking Algerian liberal who began his career believing in Republican inclusivity, was jailed in May 1945 when nationalist demonstrations in his hometown, Sétif, were met with police violence, and turned into rioting, and then a rural revolt, in which Europeans were killed. The uprising was quickly repressed, but indiscriminate retaliatory massacres of Algerians—by settler militia, aerial bombardment, naval fire, and artillery—killed tens of thousands in the countryside and convinced Algerian nationalists that armed struggle was the only possible solution to their situation. Nine years later, on November 1, 1954, a small splinter group of radical nationalists launched an insurrection, announced themselves as the National Liberation Front, and began a revolution that would last for seven years.

In India, British law and methods of bureaucratic governance like the census fixed religious community as the determining factor of social identity. British imperialism largely worked on the assumption that the populations under their sway had to be ruled according to what the British thought of as essential, and essentially separate, characteristics. Often, from the nineteenth century onward, religion was conflated with race in imperial thinking, and Hindu and Muslim communities' separation became institutionalised in new ways. By the 1940s, not only were there separate Hindu and Muslim electorates; different taps at railway stations even provided separate "Hindu" and "Muslim" water. Communal divisions combined with, and were exacerbated by, the mobilisation of mass politics. They began to harden, and became violent.

Wartime sufferings were as great in India as anywhere: harvest failure, war and requisitioning killed between two and three million people in the dreadful Bengal famine of 1943. Keeping India loyal, as far as possible, meant promising independence, but the nationalist political parties—the Hindu-dominated Indian National Congress and the All-India Muslim League, which from the mid-1930s was led by Mohammad Ali Jinnah—could not agree on how the different communities of an independent India should govern themselves. By 1946, Jinnah's demand for "Pakistan," a self-governing nation for India's Muslims, was formulated as a scheme for two separate federations of provinces, one "Muslim" and the other "Hindu," depending on the majority community in each. These two federations, each with its own constituent assembly to decide on its own government, would equally belong to a single all-India federation managing foreign affairs and national defence.

Such complicated schemes were undermined by the question of how to fairly represent each province's minority communities of Hindus, Muslims, Sikhs, and others. They also ran up against the abrupt and unexpected British announcement, in February 1947, that Britain would finally, suddenly quit India no later than June 1948. Only days later, it became clear that in fact it would do so imminently, on

August 15, 1947. As late as June 1947, only two months before independence, it was announced that the country would be partitioned into two states, India and a new state of Pakistan. The latter would be formed of two territorial units, East Pakistan in Bengal and West Pakistan in the older northwestern provinces of Muslim South Asia. Their independence, and the end of Britain's Indian empire, was declared only weeks later, on August 14 and 15, 1947. The calamity that ensued was wholly unpredictable, and mostly unforeseen. As fear and insecurity ran riot, so did armed men from each community that saw itself threatened by the others. The violence was indiscriminate and appalling: women of one community were raped by members of another, or killed by their own to pre-empt such violation. Children and the elderly were murdered, whole villages massacred. As India and Pakistan were divided along rapidly drawn and largely arbitrary geographical lines, refugees crossed the new borders in both directions, fleeing violence and being subjected to it as they went. At least half a million people, perhaps one million, were killed. Some twelve million were displaced.[31]

A more predictable, if no less unforeseen, catastrophe was to occur only months later, in another contested homeland that the British Empire had ruled according to its assumptions about religion and race, and from which it would suddenly scramble to remove itself. Across the Muslim world, throughout the interwar years, attention was continuously drawn to the struggle over the homeland and the holy places of Palestine. Zionist settlements that aimed to create a safe national home for Jews fleeing persecution in eastern Europe, especially the Russian Empire, were tolerated by Ottoman authorities in Palestine, from the 1880s onward, provided that the settlers would be loyal to the Ottoman Empire. Jewish Palestinians, like their Muslim and Christian neighbours, fought in Ottoman armies in 1914–18. But on November 2, 1917, in the midst of tactical, incompatible wartime alliances, the British government agreed—in a letter from the Foreign Secretary Arthur Balfour to Lionel Rothschild, a leader of the British Jewish community—that it would view with favour the establishment in Palestine of a national home for the Jewish people...it being clearly understood that nothing shall be done which may prejudice the civil and religious rights of existing non-Jewish communities in Palestine, or the rights and political status enjoyed by Jews in any other country.

Ironically, the thinking behind what became known as the Balfour Declaration contained some of the same antisemitic ideas of global "Jewish influence" that had made Zionism seem necessary as an escape for Jews from European prejudices. The declaration, British politicians thought, would be "extremely useful propaganda" both among Russian Jewish Bolsheviks, then about to exit the war, and among American Jewish capitalists, who might prevail upon their country to commit more fully to it. When the League of Nations granted Britain a mandate to rule Palestine in 1922, the Balfour Declaration was written into it. For the next twenty-six years, successive British governments tried and hopelessly failed to develop a coherent policy for the future of Palestine, wavering between plans for a single binational state for all its citizens, or the territory's partition into two separate sovereign states.[32]

At the end of 1946, Palestine had just over six hundred thousand Jewish inhabitants, and almost 1.27 million Muslim and Christian Arab Palestinians. The Zionist movement openly intended from the outset to establish not only a "national home" within a homeland shared with the Palestinians, as the British initially conceded and as Winston Churchill, as colonial secretary, insisted was what had been promised, but a Jewish-majority state of their own under Jewish sovereignty. Palestinians refused to see their own homeland partitioned, and rejected the claim to equal sovereignty for the immigrant Jewish community that was, by the end of the mandate in 1947, one-third of the population. Violence flared repeatedly between the two communities, which rapidly became two competing national movements each seeking independence for its own national homeland in the same space. The British repressed a Palestinian nationalist revolt in 1936–39, effectively destroying the Palestinians' capacity for both attacks on Jewish settlements and armed self-defence. The British then faced a campaign of terrorism from Zionist armed groups, in 1944–46, that killed British soldiers and administrators, and that in 1946 sparked a vicious spate of antisemitic attacks, and even a brief fear of the revival of Blackshirt fascism, in Britain itself.

In 1947, despite what had only recently been considered the strategic significance of Palestine to Britain's postwar empire, the British announced their intention to withdraw. Tension in Palestine escalated into civil war. From March to early May 1948, there was fierce fighting between the Hagana, the Jewish "defence force" created in the 1930s to protect Jewish settlements, and the Zionist armed groups (Lehi and Irgun) that had been waging their insurgency against the British, on one side, and Palestinian militia and a "Salvation Army" of Arab volunteers, on the other. On April 9, Lehi and Irgun forces massacred the Palestinian population in the village of Deir Yassin, near Jerusalem, killing one hundred people, sixty-seven of whom were women, children, or elderly. News of this atrocity spread, and other villagers fled in fear. In retaliation, Arab forces murdered some seventy Jewish doctors and nurses in a medical convoy on April 13. An appalling cycle of violence had begun; it would characterise the conflict for decades to come.

On May 14, 1948, the state of Israel declared its independence in the territory allotted to it by a United Nations partition plan that Palestinians and the Arab states had rejected. Arab armies—at odds with each other over their separate, conflicting war aims, underestimating the Israelis, and more concerned with defending their own interests than Palestinians' homes—invaded the territory. Israel's armed forces saw themselves as fighting for their lives against a united coalition of larger states in an unequal, existential battle only three years after the Holocaust in Europe. But they outgunned and outnumbered their enemies on the battlefield. In the first phase of the war, in May and June, they fought them to a standstill. In the second phase, in early July, following a truce that allowed Israeli forces to rearm, the Arab states were driven back and defeated. Having captured more than the territory it had been allotted by the UN, the state of Israel was established. Three-quarters of a million Muslim and Christian Palestinians fled in terror, or were forced out, from their homes and became refugees in Lebanon and Syria, or in Palestinian territory that was occupied by the new kingdom of Jordan (the West Bank) or Egypt (the Gaza Strip). Many of the villages they had come from were quickly bulldozed to prevent their return. Independence for Israel was *nakba*, "catastrophe," for the Palestinians. Ceasefire lines were drawn, but no peace settlement was made.[33]

In Palestine as in Pakistan, by 1948 being Muslim meant having a sharply politicised identity that was in direct and unresolved conflict with others, and that was both religious and national. National identity meant being tied to a place that was sacred in a new way, not only as a landscape marked by earlier generations of believers and by the action of God in the world, but as a national homeland. As the colonial world collapsed, older, shared countries were divided, and older, porous boundaries became hard, policed frontiers. The fracture lines of twentieth-century conflicts, and the new borders they drew, were cut deeply through places, through communities, and through people's lives.

◇◇◇◇◇◇◇◇◇◇◇◇
Part 4
◇◇◇◇◇◇◇◇◇◇◇◇

MUSLIMS' MODERN WORLDS
1950–2020 CE

13

THE WRETCHED OF THE EARTH

The shrine of Fatima Masoumeh, resting place of the sister of the eighth Shi'i imam, Imam Reza (Ali al-Rida), in the city of Qom, south of Tehran, is one of Iran's holiest centres of piety and learning. Reza Shah Pahlavi, the self-made soldier who founded his own new dynasty in Iran, made concessions to shows of piety early in his reign. But in 1928 he marched in his boots, backed by armoured cars full of troops, into the shrine of Fatima Masoumeh, found the religious scholar who had dared to reproach his wife (or was it his mother?—no one was sure) for briefly uncovering her face while changing her chador from an outdoor to an indoor one the day before, and beat him up. In 1935, crowds gathered near the yet-more-venerated shrine of Fatima's brother in Mashhad, to hear preachers denounce the shah and his policies in the courtyard of the Goharshad Mosque, a magnificent place of prayer built by a fifteenth-century Timurid empress. The shah's soldiers opened fire with machine guns, killing one hundred protestors. Three soldiers who had refused to obey the order to shoot unarmed civilians were also summarily shot.[1]

In 1941, Reza Shah, whose enthusiasm for Aryan nationalism pleased the Nazis and worried the Allies, abdicated in the face of a

British and Soviet invasion and his own lack of any popular support. His son and successor, Mohamed Reza Shah, lacked his father's brutal self-confidence but shared his nationalism, his view of himself as the lynchpin of his country, and his intolerance of dissent. Reza Shah had constructed a monumental tomb to the poet Firdawsi, author of the epic *Book of Kings*, and inaugurated an ideology of kingship rooted in ancient Iranian history as the basis of national community. His son continued the policy of recasting Iranian history as embodied in the pre-Islamic Persian monarchy, of which he himself was now the incarnation.

In alliance with the USA and Britain, Mohamed Reza Shah sought to reinvent dynastic sovereignty on the basis of military power, national security, forced-march economic development, and revolution from above. In some respects, the Pahlavi shah was the most traditional kind of ruler: an autocrat who inherited power from his father. But he saw himself, and his allies in the West saw him too, as the architect of modernisation. During the Second World War, Iran served as a crucial supply corridor from the British Empire and the United States to their ally the Soviet Union. It was also an essential source of oil—drilled in the south by the British-owned Anglo-Iranian Oil Company, later British Petroleum (BP)—for the Allied war effort. In 1943, the Iranian capital, Tehran, hosted the first major wartime conference of the "Big Three" Allied leaders, when Roosevelt, Stalin, and Churchill met there to begin outlining the shape of the postwar world. Whatever their intentions, it was already shaping up to be a competition between the powers represented by the first two of the three, while the third was slowly eclipsed.

Roosevelt's advisors in 1943 already saw Iran, in their words, as an American "experiment station" for "post-war policies... to develop and stabilize backward areas." What Roosevelt himself called an "unselfish American policy" of financial and technical assistance would help the Iranians achieve their potential as a populous and mineral-rich country, offsetting the older imperial influence of the British, promoting "self-government and free enterprise," and keeping the Soviets out. For a decade after 1941, Iran saw a return to constitutional monarchy, with political parties of left and right and, despite the power of landlords to dominate parliament, relatively free elections. In 1951, one such election saw Mohammed Mossadegh, a veteran politician widely admired for his staunch nationalism and incorruptibility, become prime minister. British and American tolerance of independent self-government in Muslim countries was about to be tested.

Mossadegh had been born, in 1882, into the privileged circles of the Iranian court. His father had been a senior official in the shah's treasury, and his mother was a Qajar princess. He studied political science in Paris and law in Switzerland, wrote a somewhat idiosyncratic doctorate on Shi'i jurisprudence, and believed firmly both in liberal constitutionalist politics and in defending the integrity and interests of his country. He wanted to have Iran's case considered at the Versailles peace conference in 1919. In the 1920s he stood up to Reza Shah's seizure of power in Iran's parliament, the *majles*. He spent time in prison for opposing the Pahlavi monarchy's antidemocratic tendencies, and while out of politics in the 1930s he devoted himself to improving education and healthcare for the villagers on his estate, where he ran his own pharmacy and built a primary school.

Mossadegh's nationalism, unlike that promoted by the Pahlavi shahs, respected the centrality of Shi'i Islam as fundamental to Iranians' culture and beliefs. "Every honourable person," he once told the *majles*, ". . . must defend his country on the basis of two principles and not submit himself to any power. One of those two principles is being Muslim, the other is nationalism." Like many members of the ruling elite before him, he adopted a flexible and pragmatic understanding of Islamic law, of which, he wrote, reason as well as scripture was an acknowledged source, and public interest a legitimate consideration. (Conservative clerics would not have appreciated his assessments of their jurisprudence and did not support him politically.) The public interest demanded that Iran's oil, the country's most valuable economic resource, the territory in which it lay, and the means by which it was produced should not be controlled by foreign interests—Iran would never achieve true democracy and sovereignty under such conditions.[2]

In September 1951, Mossadegh accordingly announced the nationalisation of Iran's oil industry. Workers at the world's largest refinery, in the southern coastal town of Abadan, enthusiastically hoisted an Iranian flag. The British government, which had started working covertly to remove Mossadegh as soon as he came to office, feared not only its loss of control over a cheap and essential source of energy but an end to its influence across the Middle East. As attempts to settle the dispute dragged on for two years without resolution, American analysts became concerned that Mossadegh would not be able to control the situation. They worried about the strength on the street of the Tudeh Party ("Party of the Masses"), Iran's communist party, which had shifted its stance from opposing the aristocratic Mossadegh to tactical support for his government against their common enemies: the royalists, the right, and the British. The CIA and State Department believed that a Tudeh takeover would move Iran into the Soviet sphere of influence.

The Truman administration had publicly supported Mossadegh, hoping for a resolution to the crisis with the obstinate British, but when Dwight D. Eisenhower took office in January 1953, planning for a coup was stepped up. On August 16, 1953, the shah, working with covert British and, especially, American support, tried to oust his popular prime minister. The coup initially failed, and the shah fled the country. Three days later, in the midst of demonstrations and counter-demonstrations orchestrated by the CIA and their Iranian agents and allies, the shah was brought back, with promises of millions of US dollars in development aid. Mossadegh was put on trial and disappeared, first into prison and then under house arrest.[3]

The democratic phase of the experiment in Iran had been brought to an end, not by communist subversion but by British and American neo-imperialism. Iran returned to autocracy, and the autocracy became increasingly repressive. In 1962, a teacher and writer from a clerical family of Tehran who had briefly been a member of the Iranian

Communist Party, Jalal Al-e Ahmad, diagnosed what he thought was the real cause of the country's suffering. He called it *gharbzadegi* ("West-struck-ness" or "Euromania"), a state of being at once fascinated and "stricken," or "afflicted," by the West. Iran had never been formally colonized, but in the era of political decolonization, Al-e Ahmad thought, it was still suffering from a deeper condition of "coloniality," imprisoned by global forces on the wrong side of the global imbalance of power. The division of the world between machine-powered industrial societies, whose economies sucked resources from the Global South, and the societies of the South that they kept in subjection and onto which they foisted their products—not only material goods but mythology, ideology, and culture too—was, he wrote, the real malady from which Muslims had to recover.[4]

Al-e Ahmad was a cosmopolitan and creative thinker, heavily influenced by Third Worldist revolutionary socialism and a universalist vision of emancipation. In 1950, he married the novelist Simin Daneshvar, one of Iran's greatest writers: the first Iranian woman to publish under her own name, she was also the first to be translated from Persian into English. Their home became a meeting place for Iran's rising literary, intellectual and political stars. "Were it not for her, how much gibberish I would have published," Al-e Ahmad wrote in 1967. Daneshvar's best-known work, her novel *Suvashun* (Requiem), dramatises the sufferings of her hometown, the southern Iranian city of Shiraz, under British occupation at the end of World War II: the occupying troops' requisitioning of food supplies causes famine, a landowner who resists them is murdered, and his widow's mourning becomes a public and political revolt. The couple central to the novel's storyline have been seen as fictionalisations of Daneshvar and her husband.

Al-e Ahmad died aged only forty-six, in 1969, a few months after the publication of *Suvashun* and ten years before the revolution that would overthrow the shah's "West-stricken" regime. He certainly thought of himself as a Muslim and saw the Islam of Iran's villagers, workers and peasants as a domain of authentic life, untainted by *gharbzadegi*. He was not himself religiously devout in his personal life, and intellectually he was anything but sectarian. He criticised Iran's Shi'i clerics for their intellectual narrowness and superstition but also saw among them a source of intellectual potential that was genuinely attuned to the cultural world of Iran's people. He would later be considered one of the major ideologues of the Iranian revolution, but he could not have predicted, and would certainly not have sympathised with, the authoritarian and Islamist turn that the revolution would eventually take.[5]

The year after the publication of Al-e Ahmad's book *Gharbzadegi*, in 1963, another of the shah's antagonists would be arrested, marking the regime's final descent into a brutal dictatorship. This time the target of repression was not a democratically minded, liberal-constitutional nationalist, but a radical Shi'i cleric with revolutionary ideas: Ayatollah Ruhollah Khomeini. Since the 1940s, Khomeini had developed a political theory that expanded the prerogatives of the religious scholars, seeing properly Muslim rule as guaranteed by the "guardianship of the jurisconsult" (*vilayat-e faqih*). In the absence of the Shi'i imam, and in the absence of the Sunni caliphate, it had long been understood that the temporal power of princes should be subordinate to the law. The law was determined by the jurists, the scholars who had inherited from the Prophet the duty to transmit it from God to His people. Too often, though, sultans and kings had disregarded the clerics and the law they upheld. Now, Khomeini argued in 1970, "in order to attain the unity and freedom of the Muslim peoples, we must overthrow the oppressive governments installed by the imperialists and bring into existence an Islamic government of justice that will be in the service of the people." The clerics themselves would rule. When the shah was finally overthrown, in 1979, by a coalition of Iran's oppositional forces, it would be Khomeini's ideas, his allies, and his armed followers that would win the ensuing power struggle, throwing off the revolution's more leftist and cosmopolitan elements, and harnessing the momentum to build a new, repressive kind of Islamic republic.[6]

In his account of the covert operation that brought down Mossadegh, published in 1979, the CIA agent Kermit Roosevelt (grandson of Theodore "Teddy" Roosevelt, president of the United States in

1901–9) wrote that "we were all heroes." Writing immediately after the fall of the shah and as the revolution was unfolding in Iran, he conspicuously failed to see any connection between his own "success" twenty-six years earlier and the more recent collapse of the regime he had saved. The coup, and the client-state relationship subsequently built by the USA with the shah's dictatorship, brought to an abrupt end the progress that had been made by the different parts of Iranian society, from peasants and oil workers to middle-class intellectuals and liberal aristocrats, towards shaping participatory politics and a state whose sovereignty might work in their own interests. From 1953, and especially after 1963, despite the material successes of economic development, the shah came to rule by fear and the violence of his secret police, eroding what support he had among Iranians. He came to be seen as a puppet, and America as the malign force behind his oppressive regime. Roosevelt dedicated his book to "the longstanding friendship between the Iranian and American people." But nothing had done more to destroy it than the coup he had helped orchestrate.[7]

◇◇◇◇◇◇◇◇

Antipathy towards the West, and anti-Americanism in particular, were by no means predominant among Muslims in the years after 1945. Most Muslims around the world—farmers, artisans, workers and business-owners, artists and journalists, teachers and students, land-owners and politicians—looked to the dawn of decolonisation with hopes for less arbitrary rule, better opportunities, and more control over their own and their countries' futures.

Many, including in the Arab world, had positive views of America in the 1950s: it was a constitutional republic and a dynamic, enterprising society, such as they hoped to build; it talked of spreading freedom; and, above all, it was a counterweight to those diehard colonialists, the British and the French. American diplomacy and oil companies were supplanting British pre-eminence in the Gulf: Franklin D. Roosevelt had inaugurated a lasting US-Saudi alliance when he declared in 1943 that Saudi Arabia was "vital for the defence" of the

USA, and in 1945, with only weeks to live, he met Ibn Saud aboard an American warship. It was American diplomacy, too, that pushed the Dutch towards decolonisation in Indonesia. It was the Americans who pressured the French and British to put an end to their attempt to overthrow Nasser's regime in Egypt when, in collusion with Israel, they invaded Suez in 1956. In 1957, John F. Kennedy made a speech in the Senate in favour of Algerian independence. (It was French Algerian settlers, not Muslim Algerian nationalists, who attacked a US consulate in response.)

More religiously inclined Muslims were probably more suspicious of communism than of the United States, especially where socialist and communist influences were strong among students and workers. Not everyone believed, as another Iranian revolutionary thinker, Ali Shariati, did, that rediscovering Islam as the active principle of human agency in the world was the essential way forward. Many Muslims looked to secular nationalism and the primacy of the nation-state, and embraced the visions of modernity trumpeted by both capitalism and communism that seemed to have been so efficient elsewhere. They certainly did not oppose the freedom and democracy that America claimed to offer the world: what JFK, speaking about Algeria, called "man's eternal desire to be free and independent." On the contrary: they only came to detest America when, as in Iran, America destroyed their democracy and curtailed their freedom.[8]

The Cold War era had a profound and lasting impact on the worlds in which Muslims lived, not only through the revolutionary and counterrevolutionary politics that it fostered but through the ideologies of modernisation that both sides of the global conflict implicitly believed, and which they sought to put into practice. "Traditional society," as the emerging social sciences had begun to define it, was passing away everywhere. The Muslim-majority countries of Asia and Africa, especially those that were being changed within a generation or two from nomadic pastoral or peasant economies to urban, industrial and, above all, oil-driven ones, were the most volatile and dramatic laboratories of this epochal transformation.[9]

The political stakes attached to modernisation, especially as they were imagined in the minds of American sociologists and policymakers, were high. Would what they called the "new nations" join the "free world" or "fall" to communism? Would so-called traditional forces—above all, religious attachments and authorities—hold back or derail modernisation itself? Nineteenth-century Europeans' beliefs about Muslim irrationality and fanaticism were still alive and well among the theorists of modernisation and would be available to provide explanations when things went wrong. But as late nineteenth-century Muslim reformers had already insisted, the need to catch up and keep pace—in education, industry, organisation, and sovereignty—was the one thing that almost everyone, both Muslims themselves and those who anxiously watched them, agreed on. What was less obvious was what that should look like. After all, by the 1950s, in Africa and Asia as well as in Russia and America, modernisation was more than wearing a hat, using a telephone, and driving a car. It was a thing you believed in.

"The Muslim world" that had been imagined as a potential ally for both sides in World War II did not fall into any one camp in the new, bipolar postwar world. Nor was it possible for Muslims who now exercised the sovereignty of their nation-states to build a single bloc of their own. International organisations intended to advance Muslim-majority nations' interests on the world stage—the Arab League, founded in Cairo in 1945, or the Organisation of the Islamic Conference, subsequently renamed the Organisation of Islamic Cooperation, founded in Rabat, Morocco, in 1969—continued to articulate the need for unity but rarely spoke meaningfully with one voice. While some emerging Muslim-majority states, like Turkey, Iran, Pakistan and the monarchies of the Arab world, aligned themselves with the US, other "new nations," and popular opposition movements, embraced the revolution.

In many places, socialism was identified with the cause of the poor and disenfranchised, those whom the Qur'an called *al-mustad'afin*, "those who are made weak": "the downtrodden," "the oppressed upon the earth." Were they not the same *damnés de la terre*, "the wretched of the earth," whom the communist anthem "L'Internationale" called on to "stand up" for themselves? Despite official Soviet atheism (and American warnings about Soviet imperialism), the Soviet Union's image was often one of anti-imperial solidarity with the oppressed against both the old European empires and the new assertiveness of America. Before his death in 1953, Stalin's masculine image was widely admired and "Stalin-style" moustaches were popular with men from North Africa to Iran. Local communist movements could be natural homes, or natural allies, for Muslim activists oriented toward social reform and anti-imperialism.

It was easy enough in the mid-twentieth century to see "the oppressed," *al-mustad'afin*, not as the deserving poor who should be aided by the affluent (as more classical Islamic ethics assumed), but as the Third World's revolutionary classes. *The Wretched of the Earth*, according to the influential, incendiary 1961 book of that title by the Afro-Caribbean psychologist Frantz Fanon, needed no one's charity. They would realise their own humanity by turning the dehumanising violence of colonialism back upon it in their own armed struggle. Fanon, who quit a French psychiatric clinic to join the Algerian revolution, saw Algeria's struggle for independence in the 1950s as part of a continent-wide African self-assertion, within a larger vision of Third World revolution. Quite the reverse of a religious struggle, for Fanon decolonisation was an escape from the mystifications that, he thought, had prevented the peoples of Asia and Africa from confronting the truth of their material existence. In the revolution, he wrote, "after centuries of unreality, after having wallowed in the most outlandish phantoms, at long last the colonised man, gun in hand, faces up to the only forces that contend for his life." After independence in 1962, Algiers would be celebrated as "the Mecca of revolutionaries," a haven for American Black Panthers on the run and a hub for pan-African and internationalist anti-imperialism.[10]

Not only conservative monarchs but authoritarian military nationalists and radical Islamists alike, on the other hand, though often at odds with each other, often saw the Soviet Union as another infidel empire, and communist movements or Marxist intellectuals in their own societies as atheistic enemies and foreign agents, a corrupting fifth column, no better than the old Western imperialists. "Protestantism, capitalism, Marxism, and Fascism," wrote the Iranian thinker Ali Shariati—who himself was heavily influenced by French sociology, Jean-Paul Sartre, and Fanon as a student in Paris in the 1960s—"are brothers born of the same materialism and raised in the same household." Arab nationalist regimes in Egypt and Iraq trumpeted their anti-imperialism while repressing their own communist parties, and moved from buying Soviet arms to accepting American aid. Egypt in the 1970s, after the death of Nasser, and Iraq in the 1980s, under Saddam Hussein, aligned themselves with the US, the former to benefit from making peace with Israel, the latter to prosecute a destructive war against revolutionary Iran.[11]

Even within revolutionary movements like Algeria's National Liberation Front, which absorbed guerilla units formed and armed by the Algerian Communist Party, leftists were suspect, and there were anti-intellectual purges. After independence, in Algeria Islam was officially declared compatible with socialism, but the Communist Party was outlawed, and conservative Muslim clerics denounced land reform—the central plank of leftist programs that sought to empower the peasantry and curb the power of landowners throughout the Global South—as antithetical to Islamic law. Fanon might have theorised Algeria's struggle in terms European leftist intellectuals admired. But for many Algerian revolutionaries, their war had been sustained by the grassroots solidarity of the village and its code of Muslim community discipline. Sympathisers like Fanon were welcome to adopt Algerian nationality, but for the cultural politics of more conservative nationalists, being "authentically" Algerian really meant being more rigorously Muslim. By the late 1970s, this was a vision that independent Algeria's single-party state, like other secular nationalist regimes elsewhere, was trying to co-opt—but which threatened it, too.

◇◇◇◇◇◇◇

In April 1955, the "emerging forces" of Asia and Africa met to affirm their own priorities for the future in Indonesia's third largest city, Bandung. A mountain resort in west Java where the Dutch plantation elite had enjoyed cool air and Art Deco buildings, Bandung now became synonymous with the aspirational solidarity of an assertive, new international order in which all nations would be equally respected. The twenty-nine national delegations at the Bandung conference represented around half of the global population. The conference itself was significant for its famously fractious proceedings, the no-less-famously deft diplomacy of Chinese Premier Zhou Enlai that held proceedings together, the affective display of nationalism that inspired African American civil rights activists, and the resulting statement of principles that emphasised racial equality, sovereignty, and the respect of international law as embodied in the United Nations charter.

Most of the nation-states that now covered the territory of the old Muslim ecumene across Asia and Africa were present at Bandung, except for the West and East African countries that would still be under colonial rule until the early 1960s. A delegation from North Africa obtained the conference's recognition of the right to self-determination for Morocco and Tunisia, still under French protectorates, and for Algeria, whose revolutionary war had begun only six months earlier. There was nothing pan-Islamic about Bandung: specifically Muslim solidarity was not a theme, and specifically Islamic considerations were absent from the delegates' foreign policies. It was true that the host country, Indonesia, had gained recognition of its independence struggle from Arab countries whose statesmen evoked Islamic fraternity in their rhetoric: in 1947, Egypt's Prime Minister Mahmud Nuqrashi had said that, "as a state based on Islam," Egypt was duty-bound "to support the struggle of the Indonesian people who are also Muslim." But anticolonial rather than Islamic solidarity was what was really crucial. (Nuqrashi's domestic critics would anyway have denied that the Egyptian state was "based on Islam": the following year, he was assassinated by the Muslim Brotherhood.) Practical considerations of how best to advance meaningful national sovereignty in the international arena were uppermost. Some of the countries represented, like Pakistan, Iran, and the Philippines, were close to the US. Others, like Nasser's Egypt, were leaning towards the Soviets. Still others were anxious about their own bilateral relations between themselves. (There would be armed confrontations between India and China, and between India and Pakistan, in the early 1960s.) But that did not mean that Islam had become an irrelevance, either for the peoples represented at Bandung, or in Bandung itself.[12]

Indonesian nationalism had developed simultaneously secular and Islamic dimensions since the early twentieth century. Many of the grassroots militants of Indonesia's "national revolution" against the Dutch had understood their struggle in distinctly Islamic terms. Their struggle was "in the path of God," their deaths would be martyrdom, and their cause was defence of "the republic, religion, and the homeland." By the early 1950s, President Sukarno's secular republic was contested by militants who saw that struggle as unfinished. In 1949, while the national independence that Sukarno and his allies had proclaimed in 1945 was not yet realised, pious militants fighting against the Dutch in west Java had proclaimed a *Negara Islam Indonesia*, an "Islamic State of Indonesia." Attempts by leftist elements of the national struggle, mobilised in the large and powerful Indonesian Communist Party, to set up their own Soviet republic in eastern Java were quickly suppressed. But what became known as the "Darul Islam question," the demand for a *darul islam* or "Islamic state" in west Java and elsewhere, remained unresolved. The staging of the Afro-Asian conference in Bandung, in the west Javan territory claimed by Indonesia's movement for a more emphatically Islamic state, had domestic as well as international significance: for Sukarno's secular republic, it was an assertion of the new state's unitary sovereignty against rivals at home as well as on a world stage.[13]

In Southeast Asia as elsewhere, competing visions of Islam, sovereignty, and nationhood produced starkly contrasting alliances and outcomes in the context of decolonisation and the Cold War. Indonesia's independence had been won in the late 1940s by armed struggle and international diplomacy against a Dutch counterinsurgency campaign, by an anti-imperialist coalition that united pious Muslim militants with communists and secular nationalists. Across the straits in Malaya, independence would not be achieved until 1957. There, in contrast to the Indonesian experience, while the Bandung conference was taking place a British counterinsurgency campaign was being supported by the country's Muslim sultanates to preserve their own sovereignty against a communist uprising.

In Malaya, British colonial rule had established a single territorial state combining the lands and the subject populations of several older Muslim principalities. Anticolonial revolts associated with religious leaders in the 1800s mostly gave way to the bureaucratised management of Islam by the colonial state in the 1900s. The authority of Muslim judges was carefully circumscribed and religious affairs were supervised by the state. This meant curtailing the remit of Islamic law but also incorporating it into British colonial law: in 1938, the Mohammedan Offences Bill allowed the imposition of fines for eating during daylight hours in Ramadan, drinking alcohol, or engaging in illicit sex.

The British saw Malaya's sultanates as akin to the princely states of India and patronised their rulers, at whose courts splendid mosques were built. The sultans in turn patronised their followers, who shared in their prestige and reputation. In the first decades of the twentieth century, a new current of more liberal political thinking and activism began to criticise the conservative, hierarchical politics of the sultanates, promoting instead the education, improvement and common citizenship of the *bangsa Malayu*, a "Malay race." Being "Malay" had developed over the centuries as a social and cultural identity, tied up with particular kinds of dress, language, commercial activity, and being Muslim, but it denoted more a cultural and social style than membership of an ethnic group. Now, it became a racialised identity.

The journalist and political activist Mohamed Eunos Abdallah, founder of Malaya's first political association, the Singapore Malay Union, in the 1920s, was the foremost exponent of *bangsa Malayu*.

Having absorbed the racialising but also liberal-improving rhetoric of the British Empire, like Sayyid Ahmad Khan in India he believed that his community's improvement and emancipation would come through, not against, imperialism. A Malay's political future, he proclaimed, was to be "a happy and contented citizen of the British empire." As Malayan politics developed into the 1950s, a focus on the Malay community gained primacy over the competing claims of both the princely courts and attachment to the more universal Muslim community—the *umma*, or in Malay, *umat*—without erasing either. Alternative, nonracial and left-wing forms of politics, on the other hand, were suppressed, including those espoused by Malays but especially those associated with the large non-Malay minorities, above all the Chinese.

From 1948 to 1960, across the transition to Malaysia's independence in 1957, British and Malayan troops fought a twelve-year war against mostly ethnic-Chinese Malayan communist insurgents. While the numbers of those killed did not approach that of other long-running Cold War conflicts, up to ten thousand people at any one time were detained, more than half a million were forcibly resettled, and the war would have enduring consequences. The Chinese community had grown in the first place, to more than one-third of the Malay Peninsula's population, thanks to the British colonial economy's demand for labourers. During the Second World War, Chinese groups had been armed by the British to resist the Japanese occupation. They now fought the British for their own vision of national independence in a socialist society of racial equality. Malaya's Muslim sultans and "*bangsa*-minded" middle class wanted independence too, but an independence that would preserve both the sultanates and a pro-Western, anti-communist conception of being Malay and Muslim. Independent Malaysia became a federation of sultanates, a constitutional monarchy, a capitalist economy, and a parliamentary democracy. Being Muslim would be a dominant aspect of national identity—and the communal tensions created under colonialism would endure, along with the older politics of clientship and deference.[14]

◇◇◇◇◇◇◇◇

The only West African states represented at Bandung were Liberia and Gold Coast, the latter soon to be independent as Ghana. But Muslims across West Africa too were caught up in the politics of sovereignty and decolonisation.

In West Africa's largest emerging country, Nigeria, decolonisation seemed to proceed peacefully but was followed by more violent consequences. As in Malaya, in Nigeria British colonialism had preserved the distinctiveness of pre-colonial Muslim ruling groups and the interests of a Muslim community in what became a new, ethnically divided state. By 1914, British rule had edged north from the Niger River Delta into the domains of the Sokoto caliphate. The colonial economy's interests lay in the south, in the cultivation and export of palm oil in the Niger Delta. From the mid-1950s onwards, the country's petroleum industry would also develop there. The less economically productive but more populous north was important only because colonial security dictated that neither an independent Muslim state nor the French Empire's expansion from further west should threaten British control in the south. The Sokoto caliphate was conquered by force in 1903. Many of its leading families fled into exile, but those who remained, and who were willing to work with the British, retained considerable prestige and official positions. By 1951, the old core territories of the caliphate had come to constitute the northernmost provinces of a new Nigeria, federated with the non-Muslim provinces to the southeast and southwest, where Muslim rule had never reached.

Nigeria's western and eastern regions had long dynastic histories of their own, and newly defined ethnic politics, centred on the Yoruba peoples of the southwest and Igbo in the southeast. Missionary education among the non-Muslims of southern Nigeria had made much of society Christian. Divisions of religion and ethnicity thus overlapped with those of political geography, and Nigerian politics came to centre on distinct and powerful regional identities that were also ethnic differences. In the 1950s, each of these three regions, southwest, southeast, and north, gained its own elected assembly. Each came to be dominated by a different political party, each of which was based on an agenda of protecting its region's interests in the country as a whole, against domination by the others, under a relatively fragile central federal government.

In the north, the Northern People's Congress, a political party created in 1949, was led in the 1950s by Ahmadu Bello, a descendant of Usuman Dan Fodio and a leading member of the Sokoto aristocracy who was knighted by the British. He became the premier of the northern region in 1952. In contrast to nationalists elsewhere, the NPC was not in a hurry to claim independence. On the contrary: keeping the Muslim north from absorption into the more religiously diverse south meant slowing down demands for self-government through the 1950s, so as to avoid non-Muslim southerners coming to dominate the bureaucracy in northern regions, where British-sponsored education efforts had been more limited than in the south. When Nigeria became independent in 1960, the NPC was the largest party in the new national legislature. A Muslim former schoolteacher of modest family origins and one of the NPC's founders, Abubakar Tafawa Balewa, became the first prime minister of the new united country.

Nigeria's northern regions, though, had remained the least economically developed under British rule, and although it had a majority of the country's population, its share of trained professionals was smaller than the south's. Tafawa Balewa perhaps genuinely believed in working to build a united Nigeria for all its citizens. But under the country's first government, protecting the Muslim north's interests meant taking a greater share of development funds for northern projects, and making sure northern candidates for government jobs and northern recruits to the army were preferred over (sometimes better-qualified) southern ones. Resentment at "northernisation" was a major factor in the breakdown of Nigeria's fledgling democracy. In 1966, a military coup overthrew the government, and both Tafawa Balewa and Ahmadu Bello were murdered. A few months later, officers from the north seized power and installed one of their own as head of state in a counter-coup. Tens of thousands of people, easterners living in the north and northerners in the eastern region, were massacred. Nigeria would not see a peaceful civilian transition of power for another forty years. A succession of authoritarian military regimes, mostly dominated by northerners, would preside over the oil economy and the distribution of its riches, while suppressing dissent, wherever it came from, with spectacular brutality.

In the 1970s, a radical Muslim opposition movement emerged in the north, led by an unorthodox preacher from Cameroon, Muhammad Marwa, who came to be called "Maitatsine" (a nickname derived from part of a Hausa saying that meant roughly "May God curse the one who disagrees with his teaching"). His followers were mostly poor artisans, attracted by his condemnation of the ruling minority's wealth and the country's rampant inequality. Following a materially austere and anti-European tradition among some Hausa preachers, the corruption of "wealth" came to be associated with all material goods and technology that were seen as artefacts of Western ways. Wearing a watch, travelling by bus or car, going to the state's schools to acquire a "Western" education, or indeed reading any book but the Qur'an were all condemned as the acts of unbelievers.

Maitatsine was himself condemned by orthodox Nigerian Muslim authorities; as his title had come to suggest, he claimed that anyone outside his own movement was no true Muslim. After escalating confrontations and rioting in Kano in 1980, the movement was put down by army and air force bombardment, killing between four and ten thousand people. Further revolts attributed to the Maitatsine movement would break out into the mid-1980s. Its core teachings would later be taken up again, in the early 2000s, under a new name that focused on the alleged illegitimacy of non-Muslim education: Boko Haram (literally, "books are forbidden"). In oil-rich and impoverished Nigeria, being Muslim could mean being part of the country's ruling group, and it could mean seeing the country's rulers as a corrupt gang of unbelievers in league with the devil and the West.[15]

Elsewhere in West Africa, decolonisation happened very differently, and Islam took on a very different significance. Ahmed Sékou Touré, the nationalist hero who became a tyrant as the first president of independent Guinea, descended from a family with long-established prestige as Muslim state-builders. He was believed to be the maternal great-grandson of Samory Touré, a Muslim warrior, proselytiser and revivalist who had founded an empire and resisted the invading French on the Middle Niger before being defeated and exiled in 1898. Sékou Touré was said to resemble Samory both in his powerful physique and in his heroic spirit. The image of determined anticolonialism was certainly one he cultivated, and propaganda, aimed at Guineans who associated past greatness with the line of Muslim kings and emperors going back to ancient Mali, presented Sékou Touré as a kind of reincarnation of his heroic ancestor. The son of a peasant farmer, he began his political activism as a postal worker and labour organiser. The author of dozens of books, he was a radical philosopher who was said to have been expelled from school at the age of fifteen. He became an African icon, ruling his country from 1958 until his death in 1984 through the twists and turns of the Cold War, from the aspirational heroism of anticolonial freedom through the stagnation and repressiveness of state socialism to its exhaustion and collapse. He met Chairman Mao in the 1960s, inspired the Black Panthers in the 1970s, and shook hands with President Reagan in the 1980s.[16]

In the mid-1950s, Sékou Touré led an African nationalist party, the Democratic Party of Guinea, that was characterised by a vociferous internal democracy at a time when elsewhere in Africa, elite-led nationalist parties often had closer relations to the colonial government than to their own supporters among workers and villagers. He was responding to the leftward pressure of grassroots militants—especially trade unionists, teachers, women, and young people—when in 1958 he made his resounding declaration that Guinea would prefer "poverty in freedom to riches in slavery." Alone among the territories of French West Africa—all of which would become independent two years later as France's attempts to reinvent its empire collapsed—in September 1958 Guinea's voters demanded immediate independence, incurring the vindictive reprisals of the former coloniser. Acting on the instructions of Charles de Gaulle's government, French officials destroyed infrastructure plans and sabotaged the economy by immediately withdrawing credit, removing cash reserves, and destroying records and statistics. They diverted ships carrying food, prevented teachers on vacation from returning to their schools, stripped hospitals of medicines, burned archives, and cut telephone lines. Office workers in the colonial administration reportedly even removed the lightbulbs and smashed the crockery in government buildings before departing.[17]

Sékou Touré was more pragmatic than his image suggested, and he had in fact repeatedly sought to reopen negotiations for a more productive post-independence relationship with the French. Intent on holding the African empire together as their counterinsurgency war in Algeria escalated, the French refused: if Guineans voted for independence in the constitutional referendum that was held across French West Africa in 1958, they would have to suffer the consequences. Newly independent Guinea was pushed into the Soviet camp as much by neocolonial intransigence as by anticolonial ideology. But ideology played a crucial role in the way Guinean Muslims—around 80 per cent of the population at the time of independence—were to become modern, and make the rest of their country modern too. As an avowed Marxist and pan-Africanist, Sékou Touré based neither his own claim to rule nor his vision for his nation primarily on being Muslim. Nonetheless, religion was vital in legitimating the power of the newly independent state, and central to what the state sought to do with its power.

In the first years after independence, one of the regime's first large-scale programs was the so-called "demystification" campaign. Officials backed up by soldiers went into the remotest regions of Guinea, where minority communities followed ancestral cultural and religious practices, in an attempt to forcibly incorporate them into the national community, "the people's" state and the modern world. "Demystification" sought to extirpate what were seen as superstition, magic, and the avoidance of the state by communities that had remained on the fringes of the French administration and its colonial economy. Secret societies, into which the men of villages were traditionally initiated, were banned. Elders and ritual specialists were beaten and humiliated, ritual dances were publicly performed as folklore to rob them of their spiritual power, and the elaborate masks that were often used in ceremonies were gathered up, exposed to view by women and children (an act sometimes believed to be fatal to the onlookers), and publicly burned.

Adherence to a monotheist religion (Christianity being acceptable as well as Islam) was demanded. Citizens were encouraged to dress in white, nonconformist fashions in dress or hairstyle were reproved, and virginity tests were imposed on schoolgirls. Sufi teachers and leaders of fraternities, the principal religious figures among Guinea's Muslims, were also attacked, their property confiscated. This moralising mass mobilisation drew on Islamic reformist themes—spreading Islam and educating the people out of "ignorance," campaigning against idolatry and "immorality"—but in a wholly new way. It was part of a revolutionary, coercive politics of integrating people into the state's socially transformative project, a project in pursuit of which anywhere from ten to thirty thousand people are also thought to have been murdered.[18]

◇◇◇◇◇◇◇◇

Despite Cold War enmity between communists and anti-communists, modernisers of both kinds sometimes shared prejudices about Muslims. Like the shah's regime that pursued authoritarian modernisation with US support under the banner of a "White Revolution" in 1960s Iran, technocrats in Soviet central Asia too were implementing schemes to transform Muslim societies by developing them in ways that generally did not include consulting their people. Sometimes the architects of such schemes considered people's being Muslim (as Guinea's party cadres considered non-Muslim Guineans' attachment to ancestral religions) as a cause of their being "backward." No less than European colonial authorities in India, North Africa or the Middle East, Soviet planners in the southern USSR saw their efforts to impart progress as hindered by what they called Muslims' "primordial habits and religious fanaticism," their "wild customs and superstitions."[19]

Since the 1920s and early 1930s, Communist Party officials in central Asia had sought to break down Muslim communities and reconstruct them into a socialist society. Mosques were closed and religious endowments confiscated. The replacement of Arabic script with Latin and, later, Cyrillic alphabets limited the transmission of written Islamic learning. The Soviets saw an older generation of central Asian Muslim reformists who had promoted Islamic revival, education and social reform—called the *jadids*, for their espousal of "the new"—as bourgeois nationalists. Some were packed off to labour camps. Others died in the Stalinist Terror. As in the Arab world, in central Asia some women had begun to lay aside traditional forms of veiling by the mid-1920s, abandoning the full body- and face-covering *paranji* (a women's garment similar to the Afghan burqa) and wearing only a headscarf instead. But in 1927, claiming to emancipate and modernise Muslim women, Soviet authorities launched an anti-veiling campaign, the *hujum* ("assault"), and staged forced mass unveilings and burnings of paranjis. In a brutal backlash, the *hujum* campaign was followed by a wave of rapes and murders, by the community's outraged menfolk, of "their" women who had unveiled in public. Thousands of women are thought to have been killed. Not for the last time, Muslim women were targets of violence both from men who wanted to remove veils and from men who wanted to impose them.[20]

After World War II, as elsewhere in the Soviet Union, the intensity of repression diminished, but the pressures of modernisation persisted. Under Nikita Khrushchev, in the late 1950s and early 1960s there were mosque closures and campaigns against popular practices like local pilgrimages (demonstrating that such things had persisted, despite earlier attempts to repress them). Officials continued to report tensions over veiling and the customary payment of bride-wealth or dowries. In a crackdown on non-Russian nationalisms after 1945, Uzbek, Kyrgyz and Turkmen works of literature that took themes from Islamic history were condemned as "the poison of feudalism and reaction, breathing Muslim fanaticism." Forcible population resettlements substantially reshaped society, as Muslims from the Caucasus were deported to central Asia, and central Asian villagers were moved from the highlands to cotton-growing plains. Collective farms, *kolkhozes*, were intended to rationalise peasant production and resocialise peasants as productive Soviet citizens. Only a very few tightly supervised pilgrims were permitted by Soviet authorities to make the trip to Mecca.[21]

At the same time, the Soviet Union's constituent republics began to gain greater autonomy from Moscow. Regional party hierarchies were more stable and less fearful: people were occasionally demoted or imprisoned, but they were no longer deported or shot. Economic growth improved living standards, and local leaders began to see themselves less as functionaries of the party-state than as leaders of their own nations. They were both loyal Soviet citizens and "national communists." To a certain extent, in the 1960s and 1970s, the Soviet Union was more successful at adapting its imperial structure than its rivals, the old European empires, were at holding on to theirs. Khrushchev's years in power have even been called "a moment of decolonisation" for central Asia. At any rate, throughout the Soviet period, both official anti-religious campaigns and the survival of religious and cultural life at the local level were primarily the work of central Asian Muslims themselves. The experience of Muslims and the conflicts over what Islam should mean in society under communism were not just confrontations between local society and ideology imposed by the state. They were struggles fought by people on the ground, within local society itself.[22]

By the end of the Soviet period, it was clear that although Islamic learning had often survived only in fragmentary, discreet forms, the sense of belonging to Muslim communities had proven very resilient. Unofficial Muslim congregations continued to exist outside the small number of officially accredited mosques. Informal or "parallel" Islamic study and prayer circles generally enjoyed much greater respect than the state-sanctioned Islam governed by the Soviets' bureaus of religious affairs. They flourished within the kolkhozes, some of which became known as centres of religious teaching where formerly persecuted and imprisoned Muslim scholars could find refuge on their release from the gulag. What would become known in post-Soviet central Asia as "new" Muslim congregations (*jamaats*) were often created on the basis of older Soviet-era communities and the preachers and teachers, born in the late 1940s, who grew up in them. At the end of the Soviet period, the KGB was on the lookout for anything it thought of as dangerously "Wahhabi," and would seize documents in Arabic script. But Persian Sufi poetry still circulated orally and in manuscript among small circles of trusted initiates, expressing a kind of Muslim dissidence. One such poet, Damulla Iskandar, from the Karotegin Valley in Tajikistan, lived right through the Soviet century: born in the 1890s, he died in March 1989, only eight months before the collapse of the Iron Curtain, and the end of the Cold War.[23]

◇◇◇◇◇◇◇

Some, though, saw the problems of Muslim societies as the result, not only of Soviet and Western imperialisms, but especially of what they saw as Muslims' own abandonment of religion. This seemed all the more dangerous now that Muslim countries had their own ruling elites who, whether they called themselves revolutionaries or anti-communists, often seemed intent on seeing modernisation as becoming somehow less Muslim. Muslims, these voices declared in response, had lost sight of what Islam really was: they could not be truly free until they became "truly" Muslim again.

Such voices had never gone away. The first generation of Islamists, Rashid Rida and the Muslim Brotherhood, had been prominent in the interwar years and were present in anticolonial nationalist coalitions. Their agenda was generally marginalised in the 1950s and 1960s, as confident, secular nation-building coincided with an unprecedented global economic upswing and long-term investments in ambitious development schemes. In the 1970s and 1980s, though, ambition and growth gave way to a global economic downturn, to stagnation and disappointment, persistent poverty and indebtedness, corruption and authoritarianism. The Islamists gained more listeners. Observers from outside, and often within, Muslims' societies had mostly based their ideas of modernisation either on a Marxist ideology of historical progress, or on an equally idealised understanding of the history of capitalism in western Europe and North America. They accordingly anticipated modernisation taking a predictable route towards technical development, secularisation, and some version of political progress. In the early 1980s, they began to talk of an "Islamic resurgence" instead. They were often surprised at what seemed to be the derailment of modernisation by the aggressive return of something traditional. In fact, it was something very modern. But their own selective vision of modernisation had made it hard to see.

Many observers would see Islamism as a reckless, retrograde application of unchanging medieval theology to modern politics. But Islamism, like the ideologies of its adversaries, like its historical context, and like other forms of religious politics that promised salvation elsewhere—like evangelical Christianity in America or redemptive religious Zionism in Israel—was new. It drew on old beliefs, but in new ways. Not only did it apply old Islamic concepts—sharia, the sovereignty of God, "commanding right and forbidding wrong," jihad, consultation (*shura*) and community (*umma*)—to new social and political aims, but the meanings that those concepts carried were themselves being changed by the contexts in which they were now being used.

The most central concept of all was that of sharia, Islamic law. Sultans had always supposedly been bound by sharia, which it had been the jurists' prerogative to interpret. As a distinguished scholar in Damascus had put it back in the fourteenth century, since the scholars of the law had inherited the Prophetic duty of transmitting God's law to humanity, "the duty to obey the jurists is derived from the duty to obey the Prophet," and "the duty to obey the rulers is derived from the duty to obey the jurists." Alongside sharia, in practice sultans and princes had always ruled by their own discretion and according to codes of royal or customary law. But faced with the massive expansion of codified, positive law that was now enforced by the bureaucracy of the nation-state, sharia (and its scholars' authority) began to be reasserted in a new way. Sharia had been a flexible, interpretive practice. Now it came to be thought of as a fixed, all-encompassing code, like the state law to which it was compared. The less sharia was actually present in everyday life—since the state's law courts and officials had taken over—the more it was seen as a utopian solution to the state's failings, offering escape from the arrogance and oppressiveness of the state and its imposition of corrupting, un-Islamic ways.[24]

God's ultimate sovereignty was rarely in question for Muslims before the twentieth century: kings ruled *in* the world, often with very grandiose ideas about their importance as "God's shadow" or "world-ruler," but they did so (in principle, at least) subject to God and to His law *over* the world. But now, there was "popular sovereignty," in the name of which all kinds of jumped-up tyrants, whether revolutionaries or counterrevolutionaries, exercised oppression on earth. Islamists came up with a new word, *hakimiyya* ("judgeship" or "rulership"), for the old idea of God's sovereignty. Now it meant that because only God, and not man, could make law, the pretension of mere politicians to legislate for their societies was illegitimate—at least, wherever they did so without reference to the authority of those best placed to determine what God's law was. Traditionally, this meant the scholarly class. Now, it meant society's "more virtuous elements," the Islamists themselves. Jihad, from being restricted to self-defence, or the expansion of Islam's borders at the ruler's prerogative, became every Muslim's duty to resist subjugation and fight for a true moral order. *Shura*, the ruler's duty to consult the community, became a more authentic alternative to "Western" democracy. The *umma* became the embodiment of what Europeans called the Muslim world.

Making a state and society that would be modern, Muslim, and freed from the afflictions of the West, though, could mean a number of different things. In some respects, by the 1960s many of the older forms of divergence within Islam had never looked closer to being resolved. The aim of achieving unity among Muslims that had animated reformers since the 1880s, combined with the effects of printing and increased literacy, urbanisation and mass schooling, and the relative uniformity of religious teaching and practice under national ministries of religious affairs, had made older differences within the faith less salient than they had once been. Reformists castigated Sufi teachers for their "superstition" and exploitation of the poor and credulous but even more for their "sectarianism" that divided the faithful between different, exclusive "ways" of seeking God. Islam, after all, was all about oneness, both God's and His community's.

Even the split between Sunnis and Shi'a looked to be narrowing. In Cairo an "Organisation for the Conciliation of the Schools of Law" (*Dar taqrib al-madhahib*) had been created in 1947, and Mahmud Shaltut, the rector of al-Azhar from 1958 to 1963, was celebrated for his ecumenical outreach. In the 1960s and 1970s, Iranian Shi'is who opposed the shah became closer to the Sunni authorities in Nasser's Egypt. In 1961, Muhammad Asad, the author of a proposed constitution for Pakistan, called for a single codification of the "true sharia," which he thought could be achieved by scholars from each of the faith's different legal traditions working together to (re)unify the law for all Muslims.[25]

Asad was himself a product of the tumultuous twentieth century. Born in 1900 as Leopold Weiss, to a Jewish family in the Austro-Hungarian city of Lemberg (Lvov), he visited Palestine in 1922, became sympathetic to Palestinians and opposed to Zionism, and converted to Islam in 1926. His subsequent intellectual career took him from Europe to Morocco, Saudi Arabia, India and Pakistan. After the partition of India, he worked for the Pakistani government, becoming its ambassador to the United Nations. A pluralistic and liberal thinker as well as a Muslim revivalist, he sought to connect Islam to constitutionalism and representative democracy. Science, he wrote in 1961, could not teach people to live well: "The problems of ethics and morality" fell outside of its scope. Politics and religion, like science and religion, were distinct domains of life, but politics must be informed by religion, since a truly Muslim life could not be led outside of a truly Islamic community, which could only be guaranteed by a truly Islamic state.

For Asad, governing an Islamic state required the reconciliation of an enormous diversity of "views as to what Islam aims at and how a Muslim should behave in social and political matters." Jurists of the different Sunni schools, Shiʻis, and Sufis, "not to mention many lesser schools of thought," all had legitimate differences of opinion. Such differences, moreover, were not a weakness but (as Asad wrote, quoting a well-known saying of the Prophet) "a sign of God's grace." A parliamentary legislature elected by universal suffrage was the appropriate way, in accordance with "the exigencies of the present age," he believed, to resolve such differences and discern how Muslims should live together both as a community of faith and as a nation.[26]

In other ways, though, divisions and divergences had never been more marked, and other thinkers proposed less pluralistic ways of overcoming them. For Islamists who saw the faith as a total social system, and who sought to create what Hassan al-Banna had called a true "Islamic order," it was essential to distinguish between true believers and only "nominal" Muslims who had slipped back into "ignorance," *jahiliyya*. And for them, creating a truly Muslim order meant not conciliating different points of view, but imposing the truth on the ignorant. Asad's proposed constitution for Pakistan was never implemented. Other thinkers had less democratically minded solutions for how to create a properly Islamic state in South Asia's new Muslim homeland. For the Pakistani ideologue Abu'l-Aʻla Mawdudi, it meant enforcing a total social order defined by a moralising Islam that alone could drive wrongdoing from Muslims' lives.

Like many of the new Islamists, Mawdudi was not a classical scholar but a journalist. Born in 1903, he came from a distinguished spiritual lineage, tracing his ancestry back to the Prophet through a twelfth-century luminary of the Chishti Sufi order said to have been instrumental in bringing the Chishtiyya to India from Afghanistan. But his own activism worked through the institutions of the twentieth century. At seventeen, he was editor of a newspaper; at thirty-eight, the leader of a political party, the Jamaat-i Islami ("Congregation of Islam"). He was heavily influenced by Sufism and asceticism, though he later denounced Sufi piety as merely personal, inner devotion, at odds with Islam's political vocation. He was involved in the Khilafat movement in the 1920s, but he opposed the politics of Jinnah's Muslim League, which he accused of betraying the historical legacy of Muslim supremacy in India.

Islam's universalism, for Mawdudi, meant that all of India should eventually be converted to Islam. The communalist politics he preached had its equivalent in the Hindu nationalism that also developed in India during the 1930s, and that came to define Indian-ness by an exclusive and racialised Hinduism (Hindutva). By 1941, when he founded the Jamaat-i Islami, Mawdudi had accepted that his struggle would not be for a Muslim India, but for an Islamist Pakistan. (He also, later, endorsed the notion that Hindu India should base its laws on Hinduism, whatever the effect on India's remaining Muslim minority: as far as he was concerned, they were now in the wrong country.) The Muslim League's secular nationalism saw Muslims as a national community but did not see Islam as a political program. For Mawdudi, on the contrary, secularist politics were unbelief: the only proper way for a Muslim community to live was in a state whose politics were entirely defined by, and collapsed into, religion.

The "root of all evil," Mawdudi wrote in 1940, was "corrupt rule." All the ills afflicting the world could be explained by the simple fact that "power is wielded by wicked and evil hands." The solution was equally simple: "getting rid of all powers based on rebellion against the laws of God." Society, he believed, would never be virtuous until the virtuous controlled the levers of power and used them to abolish wrongdoing. The belief that Islam was not only the way of life laid down by God for humanity to follow but a way of being naturally in accordance with humanity's true and innermost nature was a very old one. So was the idea of God's transcendent sovereignty over all earthly powers. Mawdudi combined these beliefs with the politics of the mid-twentieth century. Mass politics and self-government for him did not lead to secular nationalism, but to the belief that God's sovereignty on earth should be vested, not in any one individual, but in the Muslim community as a whole, creating a "popular caliphate," a total, virtuous society of believers under God. In practice, though, building the moral order could not wait for the properly Islamic re-education of all Muslims (ideal as this would be). A virtuous minority, the Jamaat—a kind of vanguard party—would have to gain power, against all those who believed that man could legislate for himself rather than following what God had already ordained.[27]

Once in power, this vanguard would exercise the duty of the state to enforce its vision of sharia over all aspects of life, thus enabling the community to live truly as Muslims. "Life is a unity," one of Mawdudi's most prominent followers and interpreters wrote in 1955: "The function of religion is to direct the affairs of life. Therefore its domain is life in its entirety, and not any specific aspect of it." Accordingly, sharia should be understood to cover everything, as Mawdudi himself had written: "family relationships, social and economic affairs, administration, rights and duties of citizens, judicial systems, laws of war and peace and international relations.... The Sharia is a complete scheme of life and an all-embracing social order." For Mawdudi, not only was it necessary to collapse the separate domains of religion and politics: there was no distinction between public and private, or between crime and sin.

Mawdudi's ideal state was thus implicitly totalitarian. In his own view, it would be a force for good simply because it would enforce God's law and prohibit evil. It would enable the flourishing of a truly Muslim, and therefore fully humane, society. Like Soviet visions of building communism, Mawdudi foresaw the creation of an ideal community, from which not only want but also vice would disappear. Life under fully-realised "true" Islam, like "full communism," would be a utopia. The application of *hudud* penalties (such as cutting off hands for theft or stoning to death for fornication) were unsuited to an impoverished and "filthy" society, so could not be applied for now. They would finally be appropriate, Mawdudi explained, once no one had to steal to eat, men and women no longer mixed in public, and sexual "perversions" had disappeared—but they would hardly be required, because hardly anyone would sin.[28]

◇◇◇◇◇◇◇◇

Mawdudi died in 1979, the year of Iran's revolution, without seeing his utopia achieved. From the 1950s onwards, the Jamaat-i Islami would engage in Pakistan's multiparty politics, accepting pragmatic participation in democratic competition as a means to achieving their founder's ideals. When Pakistan's democracy was curtailed or overthrown—as occurred repeatedly, in 1958–71, and again in 1977–88—the country's military dictators saw Mawdudi's ideas and the Jamaat as a principal adversary in the first case, and as an inspiration in the second. Elsewhere, in different political contexts, similar ideas were developing with different results. In Iran, the Shi'i revolutionaries led by Khomeini, who had a similar view of God's sovereignty, the world's corruption, and the duty of a virtuous government to impose proper moral order, took power. In Egypt, a faction of the Muslim Brotherhood took the same ideas in an even more radical direction.

Between bouts of repression and imprisonment, and release and relative freedom, from the 1940s onwards the Brotherhood became Egypt's most significant opposition movement. For many, they came to incarnate Islam as a religiously principled resistance to the powers in place. At first, this meant the constitutional monarchy, which dissolved the society and arrested its leaders, and at whose government's behest Hassan al-Banna was assassinated in 1949. After 1952, it meant the military regime that overthrew the monarchy, initially with the Brotherhood's support, and that ruled the country thereafter. A male, patriotic organisation oriented first of all at the individual, and through the individual, at grassroots change that would "re-Islamise" society from the bottom up, the society focused on the "raising" or "cultivation" (in Arabic, *tarbiya*) of its individual members in personal religious devotion, activism for the group, and avoidance of dissenting opinion or argument. The parallel women's organisation, the Sisterhood, played a crucial role in mobilising support and disseminating the movement's literature, especially when its leaders were imprisoned. The Brotherhood was principally about action, not ideas. But in the 1950s, it acquired a major ideologue.

Sayyid Qutb was born in 1906, three years after Mawdudi, near Asyut in Upper (southern) Egypt. Growing up in the anticolonial atmosphere of the 1920s and 1930s, like Hassan al-Banna he trained at Dar al-Ulum, the teachers' training college in Cairo. He worked for the Ministry of Education and wrote poetry, novels, short stories, and literary criticism. In 1948, he went to the United States, arriving in New York and then studying English in Washington, DC, and education in Colorado before spending some time in California. His impressions of America seem to have confirmed his already existing belief in a sharp divide between the worlds of Islam and the West. For Qutb (as for many of his American evangelical contemporaries), America was lost in materialism, individualism, moral dissipation and spiritual emptiness. Even in the civic-minded and bucolic town of Greeley, Colorado—where in 1949, alcohol was still banned—he saw little to impress him and much to disapprove.

Despite the many churches in town, Qutb wrote, "no one is as distant as the Americans from appreciating the spirituality and sanctity of religion." A church social event where young men and women danced together was to him a disreputable spectacle "of bounding feet and seductive legs." The pre–civil rights US also impressed on him a strong sense of racial injustice. "In America," he wrote, "they talk about the white man as though he were a demi-god. On the other hand, they talk about coloured people, like the Egyptians and Arabs generally, as though they were half-human." Racism combined with material wealth, Qutb thought, characterised America's growing global power, and all of it was repugnant: "I also saw the conceit and luxury...in the people, their feeling that this was the white man's endowment. I saw the way they treat the coloured people with despicable arrogance.... Their swaggering in the face of the rest of the world is worse than that of the Nazis."[29]

In 1951, on his return to Egypt, Qutb began writing for Brotherhood publications, and two years later he joined the movement. In 1954, he was arrested in the military government's crackdown against the Brotherhood that followed a failed (some claimed, staged) assassination attempt against Nasser. He would spend most of the rest of his short life in prison. He was hanged by Nasser's regime in 1966, following something of a show trial. In the final years of his life, Qutb became the best-known and most radical theorist of Islamism, as well as an author whose commentary on the Qur'an, *In the Shade of the Qur'an*, would be widely read and admired by Muslims more generally. After his death, which was seen as a martyrdom, he would become perhaps the most influential exponent of Islamist ideas across the Arab world and beyond. His works were translated into Persian, Turkish, Malay and Urdu. Heavily influenced both by Mawdudi, whose work he read in Arabic translation, and by the context of political repression that fell heavily on the Brotherhood from 1954 onwards, Qutb had shifted, along with much of the wider Islamist movement, from prioritising social reform to advocating political revolution.

Against the advocates of secular politics and purely technical modernisation, he wrote that "humanity will see no tranquillity or accord, nor can peace, progress or material and spiritual advances be made, without total recourse to God." Having "total recourse to God" meant distancing oneself, as the Prophet himself had done, from the evils of a society that in Qutb's view had long been lost in *jahiliyya*, "ignorance" of God, His sovereignty, and His way for humanity. This meant not just non-Muslim, Western societies—though their responsibility for spreading oppression and corruption among Muslims was, he thought, severe—but more particularly among Muslims themselves. Before his move to the US, Qutb had already written a treatise on *Social Justice in Islam*, in which he declared that "Islamic society today is not Islamic in any sense of the word." He called for "a renewal of Islamic life, a life governed by the spirit and the law of Islam." Islam, for Qutb, was "a universal declaration of the freedom of man from servitude to other men and from servitude to his own desires."[30]

This true freedom—for all people to live as God intended for humanity, under the sovereignty of God alone, collectively exercising Mawdudi's "popular caliphate"—meant the abolition of the "lordship" of some men over others, and the institution of an Islamic social order. Crucially, for Qutb, the "Islamic order" was not something that needed to be theorised. It simply needed to be enacted. This, Qutb wrote in his most famous work, the 1964 tract *Signposts on the Road* (also translated as *Milestones*), was the task of "an organised and active group," a virtuous vanguard that would "separate itself from the *jahili* society." This vanguard must create a movement that would use preaching and persuasion to change people's beliefs, and where necessary also "physical power and jihad for abolishing the organisations and authorities of the *jahili* system which... forces [people] to obey their erroneous ways and... serve human lords."[31]

Jihad could (and for Qutb, did) mean first of all "inner struggle" against one's own failings. It also meant physical, if necessary armed struggle against the oppressive forces that usurped God's sovereignty and prevented Muslims from exercising their freedom of choice to be truly Muslim. If the movement to create an Islamic order were repressed by the brute force of the existing "*jahili* order," then force would be required against it. After Qutb's death, these ideas were picked up and put to work by small, radical armed movements that constituted themselves as vanguard Islamist *jamaat* ("groups"). It was one of them that, in 1981, assassinated Egypt's president, Anwar al-Sadat.

◇◇◇◇◇◇◇

In the decades after World War II, nationalist leaders and Islamist ideologues alike claimed to speak for the people and sought to mobilise them in pursuit of a fuller sovereignty, through revolution and regeneration. At the same time, conservative rulers, from Morocco to Malaysia via Saudi Arabia, sought to contain these same rhetorics and direct a sense of Muslim belonging into politically quiescent private piety or a moralising aversion to what they saw as both the disorder of radical politics and the corruption of foreign ways. Both conservative and radical visions of progress focused on harnessing the power of the state to achieve it. Power-sharing, public freedoms, and political pluralism were at best a minor part of the equation for any of them.

But by the end of the 1970s, in Africa and Asia as in Europe and America, belief in the state as the engine of making, directing, and managing large-scale social and economic progress was fading. With the onset of a global economic downturn that plunged many African and Asian countries into debt crises where before there had been optimistic, long-term development plans, the state's capacity was sharply curtailed. For the next thirty years, a changed economic consensus would restrict the state's role, seeking to empower private sectors and often, in formerly colonial and socialist countries, enriching crony capitalists and kleptocrats instead.

The radical revolutions that many anticipated and worked for in the 1950s and 1960s had failed to materialise; even those that had been most celebrated, in Egypt or Algeria, seemed not to deliver on their promises. And at the same time as state-driven development plans ran into the ground, their economic growth failing to keep pace with their growing populations, the world market price of oil, capitalism's most crucial commodity, leapt, in 1973 and again in 1979, in response to crises in the Middle East. The spectacular rise in the profitability of oil exports transformed both the financial power and the global significance of the Gulf monarchies, both among Muslim-majority states and beyond them. Another, conservative, revolution was in the making.

14

THE HOMES OF ISLAM

In September 1930, Umar Ibn Sliman Naji wrote to his "esteemed excellency," his "happy brother," to congratulate him on his conversion to Islam. Naji was an Arab scholar teaching in Java at a school founded there by a Sudanese Islamic revivalist movement. His "happy brother" in the faith was Harry St John Bridger Philby, who had just taken the name Abdallah as a sign of his becoming Muslim—and who, despite all his other names, was known to his friends as Jack. Philby was a former British colonial officer, an eccentric polymath, an explorer and a writer. He had worked for the British imperial government in India and Iraq and had been part of the British mission that struck a deal with Ibn Saud during the First World War, before resigning in protest at British policy in the Middle East. In the 1920s, he settled in Saudi Arabia.

At the time of his conversion in 1930, Philby was already both a famous English personality and a close advisor to Abd al-Aziz Ibn Saud. He would soon be helping to negotiate the first Saudi oil deal with the Americans. (Only in 1963, three years after his death, would his name also be famous because his son Kim, a senior British intelligence officer, was unmasked as a Soviet spy.) Expressing his hope that Philby would now be a leading figure in the struggle on behalf of the world's

431

oppressed Muslims, Naji also wrote of his appreciation for English achievements in science, quoting the English writer Aldous Huxley in support of his arguments about the future of Islam in the world, and the importance of reconciling science with faith.[1]

Like the Liverpool lawyer Abdullah Quilliam, who died in 1932, and the novelist Muhammad Marmaduke Pickthall, who published his English translation of the Qur'an in the same year Philby converted, Philby was unusual for his high-profile conversion (which was reported, albeit briefly, in the British press) and the use he made of it. At the height of European imperialism, while the Muslim subjects of the British Empire numbered in the millions, he was one of only a handful of people who were both Muslim and a member of the British middle and ruling classes. In Philby's case, it was often suspected that being Muslim was more a matter of convenience than of conviction. He seems to have admired Islam as an ethical way of life, and to have wanted to belong more fully to Arabian society. But he had abandoned belief in God along with Christianity when he was an undergraduate student at Cambridge in 1906–7, and according to a British diplomat who knew him in Saudi Arabia, "He made no pretence whatever that his conversion was spiritual." But inward conscience and spirituality had only ever been one dimension of any religious identity. Instead— like many other converts in many places over the centuries—Philby had good practical reasons for joining a new faith community. He hoped that being Muslim would help his business interests (he ran a company, Sharqieh Limited, and imported Ford motor cars into Saudi Arabia). A romantically minded explorer, he also valued the freedom that being Muslim gave him to travel freely around the as-yet-unsettled borders of the kingdom. Philby wanted to be a celebrity: "My ambition," he wrote when outlining his reasons for undertaking hazardous journeys across the desert, "is fame, whatever that may mean and for what it is worth."[2]

Abdullah Quilliam was rather different. Thirty years older than Philby, he was brought up in Methodism and temperance in mid-Victorian England, in a religious culture where people already tended to shop around between churches and denominations rather than feeling bound by one religious authority. After becoming a solicitor, he also became a Freemason, a common affiliation at the time for philanthropically minded professional men. In 1887, after travels in southern Spain and Morocco that made a great impression on him, and some study of the life of the Prophet and the Qur'an, Quilliam announced his conversion (which he had apparently made five years earlier). He went on to found the Liverpool Muslim Institute and to lecture on Islam, initially via temperance drives, and to have a colourful, quixotic, and controversial life. He came to the notice of the Ottoman sultan, Abdülhamid II, who evidently thought that Quilliam had some propaganda value, gave him some decorations, and invested him as "shaykhülislam" of the British Isles. Quilliam wrote articles in defence of the Ottomans and spent some time in Istanbul. He kept two households, with a legal family and a second one from a long-running affair, was implicated in various scandals that led to his being struck off as a solicitor, and from 1913 to the end of his life he lived in London, not only under an assumed name but in a different persona.

Quilliam was consistent, though, in his attempts to convince a sceptical and often highly prejudiced British public of the rationality and universality of Islam. In tune with other middle-class social campaigners of his time, he also stressed Islam's stance against drink, gambling, and prostitution. He published a newsletter and a monthly magazine to propagate the faith in Britain. The institute in Liverpool, he wrote, would "widen the sphere of our influence...remove prejudice," and promote "the spirit of enquiry." It offered lecture courses in various scientific subjects and held "services" that were open to curious non-Muslims as well as to its small number of converts. An observer of one such "service" noted in 1891 that it "was done almost exactly as an evangelistic service amongst Christians would be." Such "Muslim missionary meetings," distinct from the congregation's regular prayer, were Quilliam's attempt to foster interest in his adopted faith along lines familiar from contemporary anti-alcohol meetings or Christian revivalist missions. His mission made a small number of converts, perhaps three hundred altogether, before the institute's activity petered out after 1908, when Quilliam moved to Istanbul.

Quilliam saw himself as the exponent of a reasonable, peace-seeking way of life, embracing the universality of Islam and seeing it, above all, as a faith that made sense in a scientific world. "Those who cannot understand how 'Islam can be accepted by a European,'" he wrote, "have no proper comprehension of Western peoples. In the British Isles we are taught to be logical, and to think and reason for ourselves. Islam as a reasonable and logical faith appeals to men's reason, and therefore is likely to be adopted by those who reflect and think." He was a defender of religious freedom and a bridge-builder between faiths and cultures, a supporter of the pan-Islamic caliphate and a British citizen whose advocacy for another empire made him suspect, especially during the First World War.

A century later, his name would be revived in very different circumstances, and adopted for very different purposes. The Quilliam Foundation, a controversial "counter-extremism" think tank operating in London between 2008 and 2021, was closely associated both with the British government and with neoconservative, anti-immigrant personalities. The unrelated Abdullah Quilliam Society, in contrast, was founded in 1997 as a community heritage association in Liverpool dedicated to restoring the premises of the institute, the first mosque in England, which it reopened in 2014 as a historic landmark and educational centre. In August 2024, when far-right xenophobes incited anti-migrant, Islamophobic rioting in England, volunteers there made headlines when they gently offered food and conversation to the demonstrators outside.[3]

∞∞∞∞∞∞

Philby wanted to be at home in Arabia, and being Muslim was a means to that end. Quilliam wanted Islam to be at home in Britain and hoped that British people would feel at home in Islam. For both men's detractors—as for Qutb, Mawdudi, and other Islamists—in contrast, Islam was essentially separate from the other worlds around it, whether in India, Egypt, England or America, and as implacably hostile to them as they were to it. In medieval times, it had been possible to imagine a clear division between *dar al-islam*, the home or "abode of Islam" or lands under Muslim rule, where it was safe for Muslims to live unmolested and virtuous lives, and *dar al-harb*, "the domain of war" where the peace of Islam had not yet spread, where war was the rule and it would be necessary to fight against unbelief and the persecution of Muslims. As non-Muslim rule had spread over Muslim lands in the age of European empire, fewer and fewer places were "safe" homes of Islam, and Muslims had often emigrated—sometimes believing it to be their duty to do so—to escape the sovereignty of unbelief. Most had never been able to do this: they adapted where they were and as they had to. Islamists like Mawdudi and Qutb might insist that a true home of Islam had to be reconstructed even within Muslim-majority societies that had fallen into "ignorance" of God, but at the same time, many more Muslims were making their homes outside the old lands of Islam. They followed the flows of the globalising economy, its educational opportunities, labour markets, and political vicissitudes.

But the age of European empires had also changed what being Muslim was understood to mean. From early in its history, as different peoples had become absorbed into the community of believers in the centuries after the Arab conquests, Islam had—at least in principle—meant equality between different ethnic groups. By the time Quilliam found himself arguing as to why Islam could be accepted by "a European," being Muslim in some places had become a racial, more than a religious, category. Europeans thought of Christianity, especially Protestant Christianity, as a universal, missionary faith. Its truth was accepted by individual conscience. But they thought of Muslims not as individuals with autonomous consciences, but as a mass ruled by instinctive, inherited behaviours. Being Muslim, for colonial administrations, was an inherited identity that one could never really leave behind even by changing one's religion. This was most starkly illustrated, for example, by the apparently nonsensical fact that in French Algeria,

Algerian converts to Christianity who had not been accorded French citizenship were still legally classified as "Muslim natives": despite being Christians in conscience, in French law they were Muslims. White British women who married Muslims in interwar Liverpool or Cardiff were seen as crossing racial, not religious, boundaries: they were accused of "miscegenation" and of having "half-caste children."[4]

From the mid-nineteenth century, colonial rule had often drawn such racialised legal lines both between different groups subjected to colonial rule (for example, between Muslims and Hindus in India) and between subject populations and their rulers. In the post-imperial world, however, all citizens were supposedly equal: those lines no longer demarcated the political statuses of rulers and ruled. From the 1950s, new patterns of migration towards Europe and America from Asia and Africa also made it increasingly obvious that such lines did not, in fact, map onto a geographical separation between a homogeneous "Christian West" and a religiously exotic world beyond. No such division had ever really existed—there had been Muslims in America and France in the eighteenth century, and a community of Moroccan Muslim (and Jewish) cotton exporters in Manchester from the 1790s until 1936. From the 1970s onward, Muslims became more and more a part of European and American societies. But just as minority immigrant populations became more visible in the urban landscapes of Marseille, Detroit, or Bradford, Western perception of Muslims—perceptions that shaped policing, education, and social welfare policies as well as everyday attitudes—became more racialised than ever.[5]

On the other hand, especially in America, being Muslim could also mean embracing the dividing line of racialised difference, and turning it to one's own empowerment. Most American Muslims, by the end of the twentieth century, would be Sunni or Shi'i immigrants or the descendants of immigrants, some of whom had begun to arrive in the United States in the late 1800s from the Ottoman Empire. After 1965, when immigration restrictions imposed in the 1920s were eased, many more came from a wider range of backgrounds, and from South and Southeast Asia, central Asia and West Africa, as well as from the Middle East. Their community organisations and politics were overwhelmingly aimed at gaining recognition and improving their position within American society.

But within American society, among African Americans, Islam had also come to carry very different and more varied meanings. In the 1910s and 1920s, images of spirituality and emancipation associated with Islam were familiar in African American communities: stars and crescents, Arabic titles like "bey," wearing fezzes and sashes, ideas about Egypt as a civilisation and place of origin, or about the "Moorish" (Spanish-Arab) inheritance shared by Arabs, Africans, and Latin Americans in contrast to imperialist white "Anglos." ("Let us be Moors!," the Cuban revolutionary poet José Martí wrote in 1893.) At a time when "Negro improvement" often advocated the "return" of African Americans to resettle in Africa, especially in Liberia, identifying African and "Asiatic" origins with Islam was a way of creating a new or recovered cultural dignity for Black people in America.

This was the message of the Moorish Science Temple of America, founded in 1913 by Noble Drew Ali. Born Timothy Drew, Noble Drew Ali worked his way from North Carolina to New Jersey and Chicago, preaching "love, truth, peace, freedom and justice." He presented himself as a prophet of God sent to his community as other prophets in the Qur'an had been sent to theirs, and claimed to possess a "Holy Koran" as his scripture (though it was evidently not the Qur'an known to Muslims). He encouraged African Americans to empower themselves and their community by setting up their own small businesses, to leave behind the "slave names" imposed on them by slaveowners, and to take new names for themselves. His movement remained small but still exists: it also prefigured some of the themes that would become much more prominent in the more radical teachings of the Nation of Islam (NOI).[6]

The NOI propounded a very particular set of beliefs and practices. Like the Moorish Science Temple, it borrowed images and ideas associated with Islam and combined them with a wholly original message and vision. The Nation's founder, W. D. Fard, or Master Fard Muhammad, appeared with his redemptive message to a suffering people at a time of hardship: in the summer of 1930, among the growing Black American communities of the United States' northern industrial cities. In the midst of the deepening Depression, Fard, a door-to-door pedlar in Detroit whose own origins and ethnicity are obscure, began preaching a message that offered this-worldly salvation to Black Americans. He claimed to have come from Mecca, the holy city. Islam, he said, was the true inheritance and identity that had to be restored to Black people in America after slavery and oppression had robbed them of it. He set up his own temple in Detroit and constituted his small group of followers as the "Lost-Found Nation of Islam in the Wilderness of North America."

After three years of mission, Fard disappeared in 1934. The movement he had created was now led by Elijah Muhammad, whose personality would shape it into the 1970s. Born in Georgia, Elijah Poole was the son of an impoverished farmer who was also a Baptist minister. Like Noble Drew Ali, Elijah moved north, settling in Detroit in 1923. He was an early adherent of Fard's teachings: after Fard vanished from the scene, it became NOI doctrine that Elijah had recognised Fard as God incarnate, and that he, as Elijah Muhammad, was God's Prophet. The unorthodoxy of this belief—contrasting with the well-established Muslim understanding of Muhammad as the "Seal of the Prophets," God's final messenger on earth—does not seem to have troubled Elijah Muhammad. The significance of the NOI's Islam, in any case, was not to be found in relation to Islam as it existed historically elsewhere, but in its own particular context: as a movement for African American self-improvement, self-reliance, and separatism from "White society," a reinvention of being Muslim as a racialised identity in a highly racialised society.

God, according to Elijah Muhammad, was a Black man, and Black people were the descendants of God's original chosen people, the Meccan "tribe of Shabazz," originators of all human culture and civilisation. White people, the inferior product of genetic experiments by a Black scientist, had come out of the caves of Europe to take power in the world and had enslaved God's people: but their time was coming to an end. African Americans needed to separate themselves from evil white society and from the sovereignty of the United States. They should replace their slave names with an X, and set up their own independent economic, educational, and social organisation in anticipation of their liberation in a nation-state of their own.

By the 1970s, Elijah Muhammad presided over a nationwide movement claiming a million members, and a multimillion-dollar business empire. His followers saw him as "black America's moral, mental and spiritual reformer." The NOI had become a community whose members saw it as providing dignity, promoting personal integrity, and promising emancipation from the legacy of slavery. "Islam is the natural religion of the black man," wrote Ronnie X Shorter, an NOI brother from Chicago, in 1969: "Islam means freedom, justice, and equality. Islam is the true nature of the Black man.... The entire creation of Allah is of peace." The movement was seen by others as a dangerous, subversive cult. The US government denied its claim to be a religious movement, and during the Cold War, considered it a threat to national security. It was a constant preoccupation of the FBI.[7]

In some ways, the NOI was a mid-twentieth-century American version of the older dynamic of messianic community-formation that had recurred within Islam's history since the medieval period. In their own understanding of their mission, both Fard and Elijah Muhammad were replaying the Qur'anic theme of a messenger sent to his particular community, to bring their people to God against the unbelief and oppression around them. In other ways, their teachings and their movement were profoundly distinct. Not only was Fard "God in person" and Elijah Muhammad the "Messenger of Allah," but there was no Heaven or Hell, no day of resurrection; God was a man, not a supernatural "spook," and salvation would be had in material prosperity on earth, not in an afterlife. The NOI selectively borrowed Islamic language and symbols, and creatively combined them with science-fiction mythology, fundamentalist Christian themes, Black nationalism, and the American middle-class values of cleanliness, punctuality, smart dress (symbolised in the bow ties worn by men), and prosperity gained through abstemiousness, thrift, self-discipline and hard work.

From early on, such creative appropriations of Islamic elements had been criticised for their unorthodoxy by Muslim immigrants to America, especially from the Middle East, who were present in small but significant numbers in the East and the Midwest. In the 1960s and 1970s, Sunni Muslim commentators were anxious to disassociate Islam from the NOI. They considered it not only un-Islamic but a "hate group" whose teachings could only add more harm to the already-prejudiced view that most white Americans had of Muslims. Such challenges to the Nation's teachings prompted NOI members, from the 1950s onward, to engage more with the Qur'an and sunna, and may partly have helped, over time, to influence the movement's direction towards greater alignment with the Sunni faith.

One who began to question the movement's particularistic teachings was Elijah Muhammad's son, Wallace D. Muhammad. When Elijah Muhammad died in 1975, Wallace succeeded him as leader of the movement. Five years later, Wallace took the Arabic name Warith Deen Muhammad (meaning "inheritor of the religion of Muhammad"). Under his leadership as imam, a more conventional title for the leader of a Muslim community, the movement underwent a series of changes in its name and doctrine, abandoning its Black supremacism and Black nationalism. It became avowedly multiracial and eventually fully aligned with Sunni Islam. Imam Muhammad would explain that this had always been his father's intention. In reaction, a charismatic NOI minister from New York, Louis Farrakhan, re-emphasised Black nationalism and Elijah Muhammad's earlier teachings, and re-constituted the NOI in the 1980s as a separate movement.[8]

Even before the 1970s, the NOI itself, and disaffection with its doctrines and internal politics, had become a gateway into the Sunni faith for some of its adherents. This was most famously the case for the political activist Malcolm X. Born Malcolm Little, the son of a Baptist minister in Nebraska, he joined the NOI aged twenty-two, in 1947, and became its best-known and most vocal spokesman. But in early 1964, he left the NOI and set up a separate Muslim congregation. Partly influenced by his friend Wallace Muhammad, and also, according to his autobiography, by his sister Ella, who had herself begun studying with "Boston orthodox Muslims" and who paid for his trip, he undertook the hajj in 1964. Seeing other pilgrims "of all complexions" at Frankfurt airport on the way to Cairo, he later wrote, "The feeling hit me that there really wasn't any colour problem here. The effect was as though I had just stepped out of a prison." Meeting Crown Prince (soon to be King) Faisal of Saudi Arabia, Malcolm explained that his purpose in making the hajj was "to get an understanding of true Islam." Under his new name of El-Hajj Malik El-Shabazz, he became internationally known as a human rights activist and proponent of international Black liberation. In February 1965, almost a year after he left the NOI, he was assassinated in New York.[9]

Malcolm X became one of the best-known advocates of the radical politics of the sixties, and an icon of both Black and Muslim struggles outside the Muslim-majority world. Like other members of the NOI, and like other converts to Islam from different communities in Europe and the USA, he also embodied a particular experience of becoming and being Muslim. In his case, that experience was expressed in, and gave form to, his famous autobiography. *The Autobiography of Malcolm X* constructs a narrative of life as a series of personal transformations, from the young Malcolm Little whose family faces recurrent white violence, through the street hustler known as Detroit Red, to NOI Minister Malcolm X, and eventually El-Hajj Malik El-Shabazz. The name changes track an increasingly expansive worldview, from survival on the streets of Boston and Harlem to a vision of worldwide liberation that spanned the United States, the holy city of Mecca, and the whole African continent. They also chart a story of personal liberation, through his changing sense of himself and his own physicality: he writes of his changing perceptions of his own skin colour, his hair, his ankles, and the awkwardness he feels in learning to perform the ritual of Muslim prayer.

For twentieth-century converts to Islam or the NOI in the USA as in Europe, physicality and bodily self-respect, masculinity and femininity were important personal dimensions of being Muslim that also shaped Muslims' dress and behaviour in public, and their presence in public spaces that were often hostile to them. An especially powerful symbol of the Black Muslim masculinity promoted by the NOI—healthy, strong, and self-disciplined—was provided by the boxing champion Cassius Clay, who left his "slave name" behind to become Muhammad Ali. Famous first as a world champion, and later for being stripped of his title and imprisoned for his refusal—like other men in the NOI—to serve in the US Army in Vietnam, Muhammad Ali was befriended by Malcolm X and joined the Nation of Islam just as Malcolm was leaving the movement. When he dramatically announced his conversion in 1964, after winning the world heavyweight title, he was making the first of a series of political statements that were also highly personal. "I know where I'm going and I know the truth and I don't have to be what you want me to be," he said: "I'm free to be what I want."[10]

Being what one wanted was of course not an unlimited choice, but a choice of one set of social and personal codes over another, and these interacted as much as they conflicted. The NOI's vocal rejection of "integration" with white American society was combined with a conscious embrace of the values of middle-class American "respectability," and an emphasis on becoming "civilised." Its strict dietary rules borrowed from Islamic prohibitions (especially on pork and alcohol) but derived more from the belief that Black Americans' eating habits, along with their psychology and spirituality, had been degraded by slavery. Foods associated with older Southern diets (shrimp and catfish, trapped animals like rabbits, various kinds of beans and greens) had to be purged from Black bodies if they were to be made whole and healthy.

The political radicalism of the Nation of Islam came packaged with its patriarchal social conservatism, and its rhetoric of becoming "civilised" often also reused the common tropes of American anti-Black racism. Afro hairstyles among Black women were considered "savage," and African-style coloured "tribal" clothes unbecoming. Black men were exhorted to overcome their laziness and control their sexual desire. In contrast to mainstream and especially salafi Islam, NOI men were prohibited from wearing beards. Heterosexual marriage and procreation were encouraged. Birth control (which was especially suspect given the history of forced sterilisations of poor Black women earlier in the twentieth century) was decried as a tool of "race genocide." Proper masculine and feminine behaviour and virtues were cultivated and policed through separate organisations, the quasi-paramilitary male "Fruit of Islam" that kept order at meetings and patrolled urban neighbourhoods to put a stop to vice, and the "Muslim Girls' Training" that taught female members literacy, domestic skills, and childcare. Women in the movement, like those in Christian evangelical circles with similarly conservative ideals of womanhood, embraced their "home-focus activities" as part of a larger struggle: "We considered ourselves as soldiers in Islam," a former female member of the NOI would say, "we were nation-building." By 2000, the NOI accounted for only a fraction of the African American Muslim population, which itself made up perhaps less than one-third of America's estimated six million Muslims. But the NOI's prominence, both in the American public imagination and in the wider Muslim-majority world, remained significant despite the relatively small size of its community. The NOI's Islam was as much about a vision of the nation as it was about Islam.[11]

◇◇◇◇◇◇◇◇◇

In contrast to the racialised context, the particular doctrines, and the "nation-building" of the NOI, other missionary and revivalist movements that flourished in America and elsewhere in the mid-twentieth century stressed Islam's universalism, its "call" (da'wa) to all people, everywhere, and sought specifically to transcend the politics and the territorial boundaries of nationalism. But no less than the NOI, such movements were also the products of their own time and space, and their own particularities reflected the globalising twentieth century.

One such movement, the Ahmadiyya, was founded in northern India in the 1880s. In response to Christian missionaries in India, it was a missionary organisation focused on spreading Islam in English. Mirza Ghulam Ahmad, the community's founder, was born in 1835 and died in 1908: he thus belonged to the generation of revivalists whose lives spanned the age of Victorian imperialism and Ottoman pan-Islamism. Unlike his contemporaries al-Afghani and Abduh, however, Ghulam Ahmad did not think of himself as a modernising reformist. Instead, like many others before him, but in radically new circumstances, he claimed to be the mahdi, the awaited one who would usher in the rule of God's justice at the end of time.

Ghulam Ahmad's messianism sought to unite all existing faiths in his own conception of Islam. This included the syncretic belief that he was "the promised Messiah of Christianity and Islam, and an avatar of Krishna for the Hindus," and unorthodox beliefs about Jesus Christ. (Ahmad claimed that Jesus survived the crucifixion, travelled to India to preach to the "lost tribes of Israel," and was buried in Kashmir.) The belief that Ghulam Ahmad had claimed a status equivalent to Prophethood meant that his movement would be (and still is) considered heretical by Muslims across the world. Opposing the Ahmadis would be a core preoccupation of Mawdudi and his followers in Pakistan: in 1974, an amendment to Pakistan's constitution declared the community to be non-Muslim. The Ahmadis would nonetheless establish themselves across the world, from Indonesia to America. By the end of the 1990s, the community claimed a membership of over ten million in more than one hundred countries.[12]

The Ahmadis themselves have always claimed simply to be Muslims. In opposition to the missionaries who, maligning the Prophet Muhammad, sought to propagate Christianity in India, their vocation was to spread Islam in the same way, through the arteries of the British Empire. British rule, according to the first Ahmadi missionary to London, an Indian lawyer named Khwaja Kamal-ud-Din, was "a blessing for India," not least because it protected a community that other Muslims considered as heterodox. For Ahmad and his followers, as for other Indian Muslims, the collapse of Mughal rule and the presence of Christian missionaries had brought a crisis. But the British Empire, having caused the crisis, could also resolve it, by furthering the spread of Islam. Ahmad was said to have had a vision, seeing himself "standing on a minbar [a mosque's pulpit] in the city of London demonstrating the truth and excellence of Islam in a most cogent form in the English language." In another vision, he apparently said that the Islamic apocalyptic image of the sun rising in the west meant something other than what had commonly been believed. Instead of announcing a reversal of the natural order and the imminent end of time, it signified "that the Western countries, which, from ancient times, have been enveloped in the darkness of disbelief and error, will be illumined by the sun of truth and will partake in Islam." The Ahmadis' magazine in the USA was (and is still today) titled *The Moslem Sunrise*.[13]

Between 1912, when Khwaja Kamal-ud-Din arrived in Britain, and the 1950s, when the migration of Sunni and Shi'i Muslims from South Asia to Britain increased, Ahmadis were the most prominent exponents of Islam in England. They distributed English-language Muslim literature in Britain and elsewhere in the empire, especially in West Africa, and in America. The first Ahmadi missionaries arrived in the US and in Gold Coast (later Ghana) in the early 1920s: in the 1940s and 1950s, African American jazz musicians in Chicago and cocoa farmers in Ghana joined their community. In Britain, they picked up where Quilliam's mission had left off. In 1912, their mission was established at Britain's first purpose-built mosque, the Shah Jahan Mosque in Woking, southwest of London. The mosque had been constructed in 1889 by William Leitner, a Hungarian Jewish linguist and educator who became a prominent British government official in India, with money from Shah Jahan Begam, the female ruler of the Indian princely state of Bhopal. Intended to provide congenial surroundings and suitable amenities for Indian Muslim visitors to London, by the eve of the First World War the mosque had fallen into disuse. It became the centre of the Ahmadis' Woking Muslim

Mission, before becoming a Sunni mosque in the 1970s. The Ahmadis emphasised an essential truth inherent in all religions. Into the twenty-first century, they combined their particular reverence for Mirza Ghulam Ahmad with a stress on Islam as bringing peace and understanding across faiths, a rejection of radicalism, and, especially, opposition to political or religious violence.[14]

At the same time as the first Ahmadi missionaries were travelling beyond India, another missionary movement, also originating in South Asia, and also apolitical and emphasising nonviolence, but insistent on a much more mainstream Muslim orthodoxy, was also developing. They called themselves *dini da'wat* ("religious mission"), but others called them the Tablighi Jamaat ("Preaching Communities"), and that name stuck. The Tablighis originated in northern India in the mid-1920s as a grassroots organisation of lay preachers, sent out in small groups to teach peasant communities the essentials of Islamic faith and practice. The movement was founded by Muhammad Ilyas, a graduate of the college at Deoband who lived a devotional life in a Sufi sanctuary at Delhi, but who saw "struggle in the way of God" as the duty of every Muslim to preach God's message in the world. The *tablighis'* aim was to strengthen Islam and counter the efforts of Hindu revivalists to "reconvert" Indian Muslims to Hinduism: their mission was initially addressed not to non-Muslims, but only to "nominally" Muslim groups whose faith was seen as falling short of proper orthodoxy, and as threatened by the preaching of other religions. Tablighi preachers called them to "return" to the Islam of the "pious ancestors," the *salaf*; but unlike salafis in the Middle East, Tablighis did not oppose Sufi practices, and indeed used Sufi rituals in their mission.

The movement grew rapidly: its 1941 congress in Assam was attended by over twenty thousand people. At a time when communalist politics were also growing in India (and at the same time as Mawdudi was creating the Jamaat-i Islami), the Tablighis avoided politics altogether. Muhammad Ilyas's son and successor as leader of the movement refused to relocate to Pakistan in 1947; he also extended the mission to non-Muslims. By the 1960s, their mission extended beyond India, to Malaysia, Burma and Indonesia, Turkey, and the Arab world. In the 1970s, it reached France, Belgium, Britain, and North America. By the mid-1990s, Tablighi missionaries were preaching in English in the Gambia, on the Atlantic coast of West Africa, and in Bengali among South Asian immigrants in Japan. The movement is seen as especially egalitarian, and its emphasis on preaching as a duty for all Muslims means that while Tablighi men undertake sometimes long missionary tours away from home (lasting anything from three days to twelve months), they also stay at home to look after children while Tablighi women engage in public speaking and other mission activities of their own.

The Tablighis' global vocation was emphasised by the movement's second leader, Mawlana Muhammad Yusuf, in the mid-1960s: "The words, 'my nation,' 'my region,' and 'my people,'" he said, "all lead to disunity, and God disapproves of this more than anything else." The movement enabled its followers to have a sense of inhabiting a Muslim space, and of seeking to re-create the ideal Muslim community of the Prophet's time, anywhere in the late twentieth-century world. As a Canadian Tablighi put it in the early 1990s, "Where I am, there it is *dar-ul-islam*." At the same time, the Tablighi movement's own makeup and local significance was shaped, in different countries, by their different circumstances. In the Gambia it was principally a youth movement, whereas in South Africa it flourished among a middle-aged middle class, and in the United Arab Emirates, it appealed to poor South Asian migrant workers. In West Africa, it was identified as a "new religion," opposed to Muslims' own existing conceptions of Muslim "tradition," and in Indonesia it was initially seen as foreign, an "Indian Islam." The Tablighis' global Islamic mission was like other kinds of twentieth-century globalisation. It could be equally at home anywhere; but it did not mean the same thing everywhere.[15]

◇◇◇◇◇◇◇

Muslim universalism always insisted, as the Tablighis preached and as Malcolm X discovered, that being Muslim transcended every other affiliation, to people, home, or homeland. But at the same time, in the many diaspora communities of migrants to Europe and America, being Muslim was also an aspect of being something else, belonging to an ethnicity and a culture associated with another homeland as well as an inhabitant and a citizen of a host country that was not always hospitable. Being Pakistani or Bangladeshi in Britain, Syrian or South Asian in America, Algerian or Senegalese in France, Moroccan in Belgium or Turkish in Germany, all meant different things, determined by particular histories of colonial and international relationships, experiences of migration from villages to cities, and patterns of both opportunity and prejudice.

Movement from Muslim-majority countries to Europe, or to European settler societies in Australasia, Africa, or the Americas, after 1950 was not new. The world of Europe's colonial empires was built, in the 1800s, over older routes of Muslim movement, as well as building new ones of its own. Some twentieth-century migrants followed much older sea routes that had become globalised by the networks of capitalism and empire. Muslim dockworkers and sailors from Somalia, India, the Malay Peninsula and Yemen moved all over the British Empire and as far as the Americas. South Asian Muslims settled as merchants and business owners in East Africa, which had been connected to the Middle East and India by medieval trade long before both India and East Africa were incorporated into the British Empire. Muslim Malays from Southeast Asia had been carried as slaves by Dutch colonists to South Africa as early as the 1600s, and formed a community at the Cape of Good Hope that by the 1900s considered itself permanently South African: in 1961, they declined the offer of resettlement in Malaysia to escape apartheid. The first Muslims in North America and the Caribbean had been enslaved and transported from West Africa; twentieth-century Muslim revival movements, or messianic ideologies like the NOI, would be seen as reclaiming their lost heritage. Long before Afghan camel-drivers were recruited to transport goods across the Australian outback in 1866, later settling to form the nucleus of the country's first Muslim population, Southeast Asian fishermen may have visited the north coast, perhaps from as early as the 1500s, married Aboriginal women, and been buried in Muslim graves.[16]

What is often called the "first generation" of Muslim migrants to Europe, from the 1920s to the 1950s, was in some ways only an extension of this much older pattern. But their experience was nonetheless new, and it signalled the beginning of the permanent presence of Muslim communities in western and northern Europe. That experience was initially one of temporary labour migration by men, moving from the fringes of the colonial economy to the urban, industrial imperial metropole. Men went alone to work "in the lands of others" (in North African Arabic, fi'l-ghurba, a term that connotes strangeness and alienation), and their experience there was often one of loneliness and exile, of the smallness and powerlessness of the individual. As the Algerian sociologist Abdelmalek Sayad, himself an immigrant to France, wrote, they suffered from a "double absence": absent from their own home, and invisible in someone else's, always imagining a return. Like the hardships sung by bluesmen in Chicago and Detroit, the sufferings of migration from North Africa to France found expression in music, in popular songs (shaabi) that told of the dislocation and servitude of the precarious migrant labourer. As Abderrahmane Amrani, known by his stage name Dahmane El-Harrachi, put it: "How many crowded cities have I seen, and emptied countrysides / How much time you have lost, how much have you left to lose? / You who are absent in the lands of others, how weary you'll become / ... / So long as the days grow longer, so little time our youth endured."[17]

From the 1970s, though, families joined their menfolk, and emigrant communities became permanent. The diaspora, the opportunities it offered, and its remittances to extended families and rural economies back home became a feature of many Muslim-majority countries. At the same time, the Muslim presence in Europe and North America became a more visible part of European and American societies, and increasingly recognised as part of their own histories. By the mid-1990s, it was estimated that more than twenty million Muslims lived in Europe, the United States, and Australia. Muslims' presence in these societies would obviously become one of the most important ways in which the worlds of Islam and the worlds outside it were increasingly entwined and interdependent, their boundaries blurred. At same time, the distinctiveness of Islam and of Muslim identities would perhaps be nowhere more evident than in their negotiation and expression on the streets, and in the schools, newspapers, public opinion, and domestic politics of Europe.

From the 1920s onward, the Muslim population in France, migrating for work from France's colonial territories in North and West Africa and the Comoros Islands near Madagascar, began to grow. In the 1920s and 1930s, France was both a secular republic and an imperial "Muslim power." The secular republic was torn between right-wing Catholic nationalism and leftist inheritors of the Revolution. The "Muslim power" both portrayed itself as a patron and protector of Islamic culture and heavily restricted the legal rights of Muslims under its rule. An official mosque was built in the heart of Paris, and imams were appointed to African army units. At the same time, independent Muslim schools were closed in North Africa, and revivalist preachers—even ones who sincerely sought to advance Muslims' civil rights within the republic rather than against it—were suspected of sedition and spied on. One, Tayyib al-Oqbi, a prominent preacher and educator in Algiers, was even framed for murder.

In contrast to the United States, being Muslim in France was not supposed to be about race. According to the law, race was officially invisible, and the state was officially neutral with regard to religion: it managed all religions, and endorsed none. But the racialised policing of Muslims was commonplace in the colonial era, in France as well as in the colonies. The Paris police targeted North African Muslim "Arabs" (many of them, in fact, from the Berber-speaking, not the Arabic-speaking, community), most notoriously in October 1961, when hundreds of Algerians were killed in the repression of a peaceful nationalist demonstration. Implicitly racialised segregation became a feature of French cities, as poor migrant labourers and their families congregated in shantytowns on the edges of cities, and then in the high-density, low-income suburban housing projects built when the shantytowns were bulldozed. Polish and Portuguese immigrant families lived there too, but by the late 1980s "the suburbs" (*la banlieue*) had acquired a distinctly non-white racial connotation in the media and in public perceptions. So did the violence, often in response to heavy-handed policing, that repeatedly broke out there.[18]

The number of Muslims in France grew, especially, from the 1950s to the 1970s, as France's postwar economy boomed and its empire came apart. By the early 2000s, France was a post-imperial, multicultural society in which the descendants of immigrants were formally fully equal citizens. It was also a state becoming more neoliberal, and anxious both about its place in the world and about the place of its different inhabitants relative to each other. The nationalist right, inheriting anti-immigrant xenophobia along with the justification of colonialism and an appeal to region, locality, and implicitly Catholic "traditional values," claimed to defend Western civilisation against a Muslim "invasion." The republican left held to its vision of culturally assimilating immigrants, denying the claim that "they" were somehow essentially different and insisting that, especially through the school system, everyone in France could become equally French. But it had been unable to deliver genuine equality, whether of life chances or before the law, alongside individual liberty. And it insisted that religious freedom should mean freedom of individual belief, not the freedom to belong to a distinct community: religious belonging should be kept in private conscience, not displayed in public life. Crises of confidence in the capacity of the state to hold a diverse society together focused on the most visible symbols of such diversity in public space: above all, on Muslim women's dress. From the late 1980s onward, politicians and the media repeatedly obsessed over the sight of women and adolescent girls wearing headscarves, the minimal form of veiling that was increasingly common as modest dress for urban Muslim women across the world. In 2004, wearing such a headscarf in French schools or other public buildings, considered an "ostentatious sign of religious belonging," was prohibited by law.

At the same time, as older internationalist and antiracist leftist politics were marginalised, identity politics came to the fore to express abiding socioeconomic grievances. It was because they were Black, Arab, or Muslim, a new generation of activists in the early 2000s claimed, that they were denied good jobs, kept in poor housing, and beaten up by the police. It was only as Blacks, Arabs, or Muslims that they could organise for their rights. "The social question" in France was supposed to be about the unequal distribution of resources and opportunities, and the confinement of poor populations on the margins of society. But it was increasingly posed, in public debate and politics, as a question of race and religion. Muslim girls were the targets of discriminatory laws that showed republican France to be, not religiously neutral, but actively anti-Muslim. Issues like the headscarf law, or the provision of prayer rooms in workplaces or mosques in areas deprived of public services, identified being Muslim as a problem of educational or social policy. French Muslims were exhorted to embrace a "French Islam" endorsed by government institutions. What this would actually mean was never clear, except that it would show Muslims' "maturity," indicate distancing from "cultural and ethnic traditions," and avoid teachers and teachings imported from outside France (which, more or less explicitly, were seen as ideologically anti-French security risks).

Some Muslims saw opportunities in this agenda. Soheib Bencheikh, a liberal French Muslim intellectual descended from a distinguished family of Algerian religious scholars, was born in Jeddah in 1961 and educated both at al-Azhar and in the secular university system in Belgium and France. In his view, "Islam as it is taking root here, Islam in a French way" should be recognised by the state so as to "consolidate" the "fragile" French-ness of the country's Muslims. To many others, such "official Islam" was merely another means of controlling their lives and policing their opinions, a continuation of colonial policy long after the end of empire. Politicians and the media regularly accused French Muslims of a kind of social separatism. But when French Muslims mobilised to protest, they did not usually do so, like the NOI, to reclaim their dignity through racial distinctiveness. Nor even, as immigrant groups had in the 1980s and as entrepreneurs of identity politics in the early 2000s tried to, did they mostly assert a "right to difference" from the dominant culture. Instead, on the whole, they demanded the respect of their rights as citizens within the formally egalitarian republic. Some of the women and schoolgirls who joined marches in Lyon and Paris to protest against the 2004 law on "ostentatious religious signs" did so wrapped in the French flag as well as a hijab, or wearing red, white, and blue tricolour headscarves.[19]

British political culture was shaped more by class and deference, by pomp, property, and politeness, than by the equal rights of common citizenship, but Britain too had ruled over millions of Muslims, and as its empire unwound, Muslims too became British in Britain itself. Imperial ideology held not only that British rule was good for "subject races" not (yet) fit to govern themselves but also that "coloured" or "black Britishers" could be equally loyal subjects of the Crown and thus entitled to equal consideration within the multiracial empire. Such arguments were used, as we have seen, in the early 1900s to claim that Britain's empire might itself become a vehicle for the advancement of Islam and the achievement of political rights for Britain's Muslim subjects. This did not prevent racism and racist violence. In 1919, one of the three men killed in Cardiff, in south Wales, during the spate of race riots that swept British port cities (and American cities, too) that year was a Muslim sailor, Muhammad Abdallah, whose skull was fractured, allegedly by the police, when a white crowd attacked an "Arab" boarding house.[20]

Like those arriving from West Africa and the Caribbean, Muslim immigrants from South and Southeast Asia, East Africa or the Arab world were an increasingly integrated but still very vulnerable part of British society more than half a century later, when in the 1960s immigration and race became significant political issues. Whereas in 1919 it had been labour organisers and trade unionists—especially in the seafarers' unions—who had agitated for a "colour bar" and provoked violence against visible minorities, now it was especially Conservative politicians and xenophobic right-wing nationalist groups who identified migrants as a threat to British culture, values, and social cohesion. The number of self-identifying Muslims in Britain grew from perhaps ten thousand in 1945, and 690,000 in 1982, to almost four million (6.5 per cent of the population) in 2021. While twentieth-century racism had fastened on "colour," specifically anti-Muslim prejudice became increasingly visible and voluble in the 2000s. The migration routes followed by predominantly rural families from South Asia, especially, seeking security of housing and employment through existing village and family networks, led to the concentration of Muslim communities in the English Midlands and West Yorkshire. Their visibility in particular neighbourhoods provided a pretext for alarmist news reports alleging that whites were becoming a minority, and even, in some egregiously fanciful misreporting, that some districts of British cities were governed by Islamic law and were effective "no-go" areas for non-Muslims.[21]

Muslim community organising, in the meantime, had been focused above all on gaining parity of protection against discrimination for Muslims, often on the model of community representation pioneered earlier in the 1900s by British Jews. In Britain, the model of "race relations" that emerged in the 1960s and 1970s identified racialised groups as communities negotiating their position with majority society via the political establishment. Somewhat ironically, British governments now found themselves applying a similar logic of equal protection for minorities that, in the nineteenth century, British diplomats had castigated the Ottoman Empire for failing to ensure (and, often, being criticised for failing to ensure it themselves). Muslims, as themselves a multiethnic religious group, did not conveniently fall into the categories that shaped British governments' conceptions of race relations, and over the course of the 1980s and 1990s, Muslims often also came to identify themselves and their community more by religion than by their different countries or ethnicities of origin. They articulated demands for protection from anti-Muslim hate speech and other forms of discrimination less in terms of particular minority protections than in terms of universal human rights.[22]

Despite rising anti-Muslim sentiment, often inflamed by right-wing media, and the pervasive "securitisation" of government approaches to community relations in the early 2000s, Muslim life in Britain had become more diverse, more confident, and more visibly successful in the political mainstream. In 2016, Sadiq Khan, a social-democratic politician and Labour member of parliament, was elected mayor of London (he would convincingly win re-election in 2020 and again in 2024); in 2023, another British Muslim and child of Pakistani immigrants, Humza Yousaf, became leader of the Scottish National Party and first minister (leader of the devolved national government) of Scotland.

◇◇◇◇◇◇◇

While Muslims relocated ever more widely across the globalising world, the balance of power and influence between the regions of the old ecumene was also shifting. On the defensive in the radical 1950s and 1960s, conservative regimes in the Arab world and Southeast Asia saw their fortunes dramatically improve after the 1970s. The Muslim-majority world's centre of geopolitical and ideological as well as economic gravity shifted from the radical politics of decolonisation to the conservative monarchies of the Gulf, with their oil and gas industries and the wealth that flowed from them as they fed the world's rapidly expanding carbon capitalism. At the same time, the rightward shift of the Thatcher–Reagan era in the Atlantic world brought free-market ideology along with a rhetoric of "family values," attacks on single mothers and sexual permissiveness, and a generalised backlash against the progressivism associated with the 1960s. In geopolitics as well as in moral tone, Thatcherite and Reaganite priorities, and the politics of a conservative revolution that stemmed from them, aligned with the interests and values of the increasingly super-wealthy oil states and their rulers.

They also chimed with the politics of other countries that increasingly, in the 1990s, turned from anti-imperial revolution to free-market neoliberalism under the pressure of international financial institutions, global credit markets, and their own creaking state infrastructure and growing populations. In Egypt, as the state and its provisions were rolled back at increasing speed in the 1990s, small-and medium-sized businesses grew, and began to supply a market for "Islamic" consumer goods—leisure spaces, music, beauty salons, coffee shops, and life-style videos. Ideas about an "Islamic economy," seeking to escape both from the failures of state-driven development and the corruptions and wastefulness of unfettered capitalism, had been developing since the 1970s. Now, an Islamisation of public space and behaviours emerged that was less about preaching and politics than it was about consumer choice and commodities. By the early 2000s, from Morocco via the Gulf to Southeast Asia, the personalised, success-oriented, and politically as well as socially conservative "market Islam" of this rising, pious middle class had to a great extent supplanted older Islamist calls to overthrow "impious" rulers and capture the state. Instead, a new generation of personally pious, business-oriented Muslims sought to enact sharia in their corporate workplaces. Sharia-compliant finance, investment, regulation, and corporate social responsibility, their exponents believed, would produce both a more moral capitalism for the world and have a salutary, Islamising effect on the societies whose money, workers, and public space "corporate Islam" would ultimately reshape.[23]

Some Islamists still saw global capitalism as part of an enduring system of foreign domination over Muslims; some saw Islam as the true home of anti-capitalist resistance. But like evangelical Christianity in the United States, socially conservative forms of Islam not only coexisted with but greatly benefited from the worldwide right turn in economics and politics that followed the 1970s. Fuelled by petrodollars and expanding their ambitions on the global stage, regimes in the Gulf and Pakistan amplified the once-marginal influence of Wahhabism, welcomed the Muslim Brothers exiled from Egypt, and promoted the teachings of Mawdudi. These doctrines were more inflexible, and no less anti-Western, than those of Khomeini in Iran. But their conservative sponsors were more immediately concerned with shoring up their own rule at home, bolstering their credentials as properly Muslim regimes, containing the Iranian revolution's anti-monarchism, and countering the insurgent Islamism inspired by Sayyid Qutb. Teachings that focused on personal morality and obedience to authority, rather than on social justice and political accountability, and that played up sectarianism by denouncing Shiʻi Islam as not really Islam at all, served these purposes well. Doing business with the West, especially the United States, at the same time was not a problem.

Wahhabism had remained a relatively minor school of thought in the two hundred years since its emergence. Its scholars mostly came from family networks within Saudi Arabia, and Muslim scholars elsewhere sometimes saw it as parochial and unsophisticated. But its ideas and emphases overlapped with other salafi currents of thought that developed in the Arab world and South Asia in the twentieth century. From the 1960s to the 1990s, scholars from as far afield as Mauritania and Mali, Ethiopia, Egypt, Pakistan, and India were drawn to Saudi Arabia, where they contributed to the kingdom's agenda of building up its educational resources and strengthening its global ideological standing. In 1961, the Islamic University of Medina was founded. An all-male, fully state-funded school, its aim was to educate young, mostly foreign Muslims and send them back home as missionaries. Until the 1990s, its staff as well as its students were mostly either non-Saudis, or foreign-born scholars who settled in Saudi Arabia to live and teach. The export of Wahhabism from Saudi Arabia to the world was based as much on importing expertise and scholarship to the kingdom from elsewhere as it was on the Saudis' own lavish funding and expansionist ideological program.[24]

The kingdom also faced its own internal Islamist dissenters. In 1979, a Saudi citizen named Juhayman al-Utaybi led a group of protestors in occupying the Kaʻba and the Great Mosque in Mecca during the annual pilgrimage. Al-Utaybi, a preacher from one of the *ikhwan* settlements, castigated the monarchy's corruption and its alliance with the Americans, and claimed that another leader of the revolt, Muhammad al-Qahtani, was the mahdi. The kingdom's scholars could easily declare this claim to be a heresy, giving the green light to the authorities' military intervention. After two weeks, the rebellion was crushed and al-Qahtani had been killed. Many of the rebels had been students at the Islamic University in Medina. From the 1990s onward, especially following the Iraqi invasion of Kuwait and the ensuing Gulf War in 1990–91, the university's teaching became more explicitly apolitical. Having previously welcomed foreign Muslim activists and Muslim Brothers, from the late 1970s onward, and especially in the 1990s, the Saudi regime became increasingly hostile to them.[25]

Founded as the true home of the true Islam, the kingdom was denounced in 1989, by the Palestinian Islamist Abu Muhammad al-Maqdisi, as "a graveyard of clerics and a prison for preachers." Claiming Arabian ancestry himself, al-Maqdisi had lived in Saudi Arabia before joining the anti-Soviet war in Afghanistan and becoming an advocate of global jihad. But not all religiously minded critics of the kingdom were radical jihadis, any more than the kingdom held a monopoly over Wahhabi and salafi ideas. The Sunni revivalist *sahwa* ("awakening") movement in Saudi Arabia from the 1960s onward was more the work of grassroots social activists—youth organisers, women's groups, charities, and social work organisations—who criticised the royal family's wealth and behaviour, the kingdom's alignment with the United States and US influence within the kingdom, and the state's arms imports and authoritarianism. In the early 2000s, all such movements, along with other kinds of dissent—atheism as well as Islamism, free speech or association of any kind—were criminalised as "terrorist" and repressed by the Saudi security state, supported by its European and American allies.[26]

◇◇◇◇◇◇◇◇

Like other aspects of the "flow" of globalisation, the globalisation of Muslims' lives was not friction-free. Tensions arose within Muslim communities as well as between Muslims and the non-Muslim worlds around them. A second generation of young people, born in Europe and America to parents who had often tolerated widespread racism in resilient silence, was more educated and more socially mobile, and more insistent on proclaiming Islam as their cultural, ethnic, and religious identity, than their parents had been. Sometimes, living in cities and influenced by globalising currents of revivalist or Islamist interpretations of the faith, they became sharply critical of their own families' often originally rural cultural traditions, which they now saw as uneducated or "ignorant." Young French Muslims who adopted salafi ideas, styles of dress, and politics might do so as much to criticise their parents' "Algerian" or "Senegalese" Islam as to mark themselves out in opposition to the anti-Muslim sentiments of the wider society around them. Some young British Muslims, especially university students, were drawn to the transnational project of Hizb ut-Tahrir ("the Party of Liberation," founded in Jordan in 1949) because it presented Islam as a rational worldview rather than as a set of family rituals, and because its politics—Islam as a total and self-sufficient system, Muslim supremacy, the re-establishment of the caliphate—were combined with an attractive, "slick," and identity-affirming sociability.[27]

But the high point of late twentieth-century globalisation, after the fall of the Berlin Wall and the Soviet Union's dissolution, seemed above all to herald a worldwide victory of consumer goods over ideological contest. Conservative Muslim regimes, allied with their Atlantic world business partners and military suppliers, had apparently won both the ideological battle and the test of financial muscle with their various adversaries. They shared a suspicion of militant Islamism as well as of other kinds of antiestablishment activism. They also shared a readiness to promote and instrumentalise Sunni Islamists where they seemed to serve their goals: to claim religious legitimacy, to counter the revolution in Iran, and to fight the Soviets in Afghanistan. In the neoliberal moment of the 1990s, multicultural diversity as well as globalised finance capitalism seemed to have won the day.

And then, on the morning of September 11, 2001, nineteen young men, all but one in their twenties and almost all Saudi nationals, several of whom had been living in Germany, flew commercial airliners into the Pentagon, into a field in Pennsylvania, and into the Twin Towers of the World Trade Center in New York, killing almost three thousand people.

15

THE WAR PROCESS

Mohamed Atta, the Egyptian architecture student who led the 9/11 hijackers and who killed himself, his four co-conspirators, and more than 1,600 people when he flew American Airlines Flight 11 into the North Tower of the World Trade Center, does not seem to have had a political project. Much speculation has focused on his personal psychology and motivations. His movements and associations, from Cairo and Hamburg to Afghanistan and America, are well documented. But the will he left behind, in a rental car in an airport parking lot, written long before 9/11, says nothing about politics. Instead, it gives unsentimental, punctilious, and prudish instructions for a funeral he knew his body would never receive, revealing only his attachment to an astringent version of Islamic puritanism. The final instructions he wrote for his terrorist group before 9/11 contain no political manifesto, statement of demands, nor any list of grievances, but only a set of ritual preparations for martyrdom, emphasising personal rectitude and purity of intent. From his life before terrorism, the most significant thing we know seems to be that he thought ugly high-rise buildings had destroyed the urban fabric and authenticity of the Middle East's Arab cities, and that this was a symptom of civilisational conflict between Islam and the West.[1]

Atta was, apparently, angered by American influence in Egypt, by the gap between rich and poor, and by the absence of opportunity for ordinary lower-middle-class people like himself with professional aspirations. He complained about what he saw as an alienated ruling elite that served foreign interests and its own enrichment while its country was impoverished and exploited. He believed and voiced antisemitic clichés. But he joined no political group, espoused no political ideology, and was not a political activist. Instead, he moved in a close, and closed, group of young men who worshipped at the same mosque in Hamburg. They had little religious education but became devoutly observant. In early 1998, it seems, he travelled to Afghanistan. When he returned, he and his co-conspirators began planning a spectacular atrocity that would respond to the Saudi ideologue Osama Bin Laden's injunction, issued from Afghanistan in February 1998, to "launch the raid on the soldiers of Satan." This was not an instrumental act, aimed at achieving a real-world political goal. As Atta seems to have understood it, it was a "God-pleasing" act, "better than this world and what is in it": a moral duty undertaken for its own sake, an expression of personal purity and devotion with no purpose but to do God's will, and seek paradise.[2]

◇◇◇◇◇◇◇

Just as Islam cannot be reduced to Islamism, a further distinction needs to be drawn between political Islamism—the ideologies that emerged in twentieth-century Muslim politics following al-Banna, Mawdudi, and Khomeini—and what we might call the post-political Islamism of al-Qaʻida and its later rival, the Islamic State group (IS), or Daesh (the pronunciation of its Arabic acronym, from *al-dawla 'l-islamiyya fi'l-ʻiraq wa'l-sham*, "the Islamic State in Iraq and Syria," ISIS). In the 1980s, the global significance of Islam as a force in world politics seemed to lie somewhere among the various, often conflicting forms that political Islamism was taking in different Muslim-majority countries. But in the early 1990s, it was the failure of political Islamism that was beginning to be apparent. A different form of Islamism began to emerge, one in which men like Mohamed Atta would find meaning and purpose. It was concerned less with correcting political order in the world than with transcending the world entirely, bringing about an apocalypse, and entering the afterlife.

From the 1920s through the 1980s, political Islamists had made a political ideology out of Islam, selecting from the legal and ethical traditions of the faith the elements of a blueprint for what they imagined as a better kind of modern society. Their project could be gradualist, aimed at reforming and moralising society from the grassroots up, or revolutionary, seeking to capture the state and impose an "Islamic order" from the top down. Some movements, like the Egyptian Muslim Brotherhood, moved between these options at different times, or argued among themselves as to which they should pursue. In the aftermath of Sayyid Qutb's execution in Egypt, while militant radicals set about putting his ideas into action, the society's leadership explicitly distanced itself from them. Taking up arms against the regime, the Brotherhood's Supreme Guide, Umar al-Tilimsani, wrote, would be "a futile use of the people's strength which benefits no-one but the enemies of this country."[3]

With the collapse of the socialist and communist left, the sclerosis of authoritarian military regimes whose nationalist rhetoric increasingly rang hollow, and the consolidation of the global conservative revolution, political Islamism was ascendant in many places during the 1980s. The various forms it took, from the Iranian revolution to the Saudi "awakening" to the religious nationalists of Pakistan and Turkey, were often at odds among themselves. Much as they talked about unity among Muslims, they were not creating it—quite the reverse. After 1979, the regional geopolitical rivalry between the revolutionary, anti-monarchical, Shi'i Islamic republic of Iran and the conservative Sunni and Wahhabi kingdom of Saudi Arabia revived and exacerbated the sectarian division between Sunni and Shi'i Muslims that earlier in the twentieth century had looked like it might be bridged. At the end of the twentieth century, particularly in Iraq, in the Gulf, and in nearby Pakistan, the faith's oldest confessional split became more politically divisive than it had been since the Safavid revolution, almost five hundred years earlier.

Islamists imagined themselves as part of a global network pursuing a universal struggle. But they usually worked within the politics of their own societies, their own nation-states and territorial borders. Shaped by these national contexts, branches or offshoots of the Muslim Brotherhood and other groups developed into very different movements in different countries. In 1987, for example, the Palestinian Muslim Brotherhood found itself outflanked by other Palestinian nationalist factions when a popular uprising, the first intifada, broke out against the two-decade-old Israeli occupation of the West Bank and Gaza. Since the 1950s, the Palestinian branch of the Brotherhood had renounced armed struggle and focused on charitable and welfare activities. In January 1988, though, it established its own paramilitary organisation, the "Islamic Resistance Movement" (*harakat al-muqawama 'l-islamiyya*, or Hamas). While the intifada's leadership called on "brother workers" to join a general strike, Hamas espoused overtly antisemitic rhetoric and asserted that "only Islam can break the Jews." Hamas became increasingly uncompromising and increasingly violent over the following decades.[4]

At around the same time, another organisation with the same acronym, but a different name, emerged from the Muslim Brotherhood in Algeria. Algeria's Hamas (*haraka li-mujtama' islami*, "Movement for an Islamic Society") was a political party aiming to promote an Islamist agenda within the newly legalised multiparty politics of what, until 1989, had been a single-party state. In 1997, when the Algerian regime reintroduced multiparty elections, and as the country was embroiled in the worst violence of a civil war that had lasted five years, Hamas changed its name (without changing its Arabic acronym) to *harakat mujtama' al-silm*, "Movement for a Society of Peace." Over the following decades, it remained active in national politics and grassroots social work. Its militants ran after-school homework groups. Its leaders were ministers in coalition governments. The party's emergence and later career were largely determined by its conscious demarcation from the more uncompromising rhetoric and, in the 1990s, the armed insurgency of other Algerian Islamists.[5]

Similarly divergent examples could be seen in other places through the 1990s and early 2000s. After the Cold War, previously closed regimes allowed for limited public debate and some degree of managed political competition. In Jordan, the leading Islamist political movement became more involved in multiparty politics as a "loyal opposition" to the monarchy; it tended to moderate its ideological stance. At the same time, a similar party in Yemen, some of whose members became part of the regime's ruling coalition, showed no such moderation. Everywhere, though, from Indonesia to Morocco, Islamist political movements continued to share essentially this-worldly goals of reshaping existing states and societies in what their adherents believed to be a more truly Islamic mould.[6]

Engaging with practical politics showed both the limits of utopian formulas, and the capacity of Islamist movements, when turned into political parties, to effect more limited but practical change. In Turkey, building on the legacies of the Islamist Welfare Party and Virtue Party, in 2002 the Justice and Development Party came to power, presenting itself as a Muslim version of European "Christian democracy." Another party with the same name, and with a similar profile, won elections in Morocco in 2011, and its leader became prime minister. Having been behind the curve in the upsurge of anti-authoritarian popular protest across the Arab world in 2011, the Muslim Brotherhood also, finally, came to power in Egypt in 2011—before it was removed in a return to even more repressive military rule two years later.[7]

But while many movements—and probably most Islamists—followed these generally moderating institutional trajectories, other, less moderate Islamists grew impatient. By the early 1990s, political Islamism seemed to have failed. The Iranian revolution had not been successfully exported anywhere. Sunni Islamists—whether they were deemed radical or moderate, whether they espoused armed struggle or non-violence—were persecuted, imprisoned, and in exile. Incumbent regimes in the Middle East had shown how far they would go to repress them. Nowhere was this more dramatically clear than in Syria, where in 1982, Muslim Brotherhood–led opposition to the secular-nationalist, and brutally authoritarian, regime of Hafiz al-Assad broke into an uprising in the city of Hama. Regime forces sealed off the city and destroyed it, killing tens of thousands of civilians in a demonstrative massacre that would terrorize a whole generation of Syrians. Ten years later, when street protests in Algeria led to an opening of the one-party system and an Islamist party, the Islamic Salvation Front (Front Islamique du Salut, commonly known by its French acronym, FIS), swept the first round of legislative elections, the army stepped in to curtail the electoral process, instituted a state of emergency, and plunged the country into a decade of civil war.[8]

In the face of such repression, and the apparent impossibility of engaging effectively in the often-rigged rules of the formal political game, a different kind of Islamism emerged. It was focused neither on the practical work of social reform nor on the ambition of political revolution. Instead of a political project aimed at reorganising society, it offered a personal ethics of radical action and self-sacrifice. It used violence, not in targeted assassinations and attempted coups d'état against governments, but in indiscriminate, spectacular acts of existential self-realisation through martyrdom. Its utopianism was less about creating a proper "Islamic order" within a particular country than about pursuing a global war of good against evil, and ushering in the end of the world. This was a form of Islamism whose imagination delved deep into the past, into the millenarian, apocalyptic movements of a much older religious history. And at the same time, it was something profoundly new: the expression of all the alienation that a moralising religious imagination could feel about what seemed to be the worldwide victimisation of Muslims in a neoliberal, capitalist world that seemed to be both hoarding the world's wealth and making war on Islam.

The Islamic emirate of the Taliban that emerged from the Afghan civil war in the mid-1990s stood at the junction of these two, quite different, tendencies. It was a nationalist Afghan, and ethnic Pashtun, Islamist state-building effort whose leaders had little vision of the world beyond their own borders, and a narrow conception of the authoritarian social order that they sought to create in their own country. At the same time, they were inclined to see the world in purely moral terms, with little in the way of a political program and a conception of government simply as enforcing good and punishing evil. They were unaware, on the whole, of the thinking or experience that had been developed over the previous sixty years by Sunni Islamist ideologues and organisers in the Arab world and South Asia. They had a sectarian hostility to Shi'i Iran and its Islamic republic. At the end of the 1990s, the influence of Arab volunteers fighting in Afghanistan, and their organiser and mentor, the Saudi millionaire Osama Bin Laden, encouraged the Taliban to take a more global view, espouse a more anti-American rhetoric, and play a role in a wider-ranging war. Out of the Afghan experience, combined with the belief that other wars—in Palestine, Algeria, Bosnia and Chechnya—were all related fronts in a single global struggle for the survival of Muslims, came al-Qa'ida.[9]

Al-Qa'ida developed, but also radically departed, from the earlier revolutionary Islamists like the Egyptian armed groups of the late 1970s and 1980s. Their aim had been to use violence to precipitate the overthrow of "apostate" regimes in Muslim-majority countries, the Islamists' own "near enemy." Al-Qa'ida, instead, came to target America, a strategic shift from focusing on the overthrow of Muslims' oppressors at home to striking against the heart of the entire world order, "the far enemy" of the USA. No less significantly, this was also a move from Islamism as a political project to Islamism as an existential ethics. As a political project, Islamists' aims at some stage might become a matter of practical negotiation over this-worldly interests— something even the Taliban, seeking international recognition, were still to some extent trying to do in the late 1990s. As existential ethics, though, al-Qa'ida's Islamism stood for a universal confrontation of belief against unbelief, good against evil, humanity against inhumanity, in which there could be nothing to negotiate about. And as their initiators at least partly intended, al-Qa'ida's attacks on America on 9/11 met with a response couched in precisely these same terms.[10]

◇◇◇◇◇◇◇◇

In 1993, predicting the next phase of global politics after the fall of the Iron Curtain, an American political scientist wrote that "conflict along the fault line between Western and Islamic civilisations has been going on for 1,300 years." Escalation of this millennial clash would, he declared, be the shape of things to come. Judged against historical detail or contemporary reality, Samuel Huntington's sweeping assertion was absurd, as other scholars were quick to point out. It recycled the nineteenth-century European narrative of history as defined by separate, self-contained and competing "civilisations" (sometimes interchangeable, for earlier authors, with "races"), each imagined as having its own innate character. It repeated the old cliché of antagonism between enlightened Christian powers and irrational "Muslim rage." It was ideology masquerading as analysis. The assumptions behind its arguments had been dismantled by more careful scholars of world history and Islam thirty years earlier. But it was not meant to be a careful argument. And for its intended audience, it was rhetorically very effective. It was eagerly adopted by other ex–Cold Warriors anxious to get ahead of the next conflict curve. Embraced by policymakers and the media, it was a clear, simple argument for the integrity and supremacy of a conservative vision of the West. As a view of history it was irresponsibly oversimplifying, but as a myth it was very powerful.[11]

As Huntington himself observed, the belief that "Western and Islamic civilisations" had been at war for 1,300 years was also widespread in Muslim communities, especially among Islamists. If the global Cold War had been a European long peace, and the end of the Cold War brought expectations of a new era of global progress, for much of the Muslim-majority world the experience of the decades from the 1950s into the 1990s had been one of intermittent but always, somewhere, uninterrupted war. The reality of the string of conflicts in which Muslim-majority societies were involved easily fed the perception that "the Muslim world" as a whole, indeed Islam itself, was under sustained attack. Most such conflicts were wars between Muslims, but the frequent involvement of outside actors made it easy enough, for some, to be persuaded that "the West" had been waging war on Muslims from the very beginning—or at least since the Crusades of the eleventh century—and that it would never stop doing so. Just as the global jihad of the early 2000s developed from, but also broke away from, earlier kinds of Islamism, it was also both a response to, and a departure from, the twentieth century's longer processes of war. It was generated by the existence and experience of actual conflicts, but even more by how they were imagined and perceived.

One of the most dreadful and earliest such conflicts was a civil war within a newly established Muslim homeland. In 1971, the Liberation War between East and West Pakistan led to the independence of East Pakistan (formerly East Bengal) as Bangladesh. The Pakistan Army was supported by both the United States and China in its campaign to repress Bangladeshi nationalism; Bangladesh's independence was supported by India and the USSR. The fact that both Bengalis, in the northeast, and Pakistanis from the northwest of India were Muslims did not prevent perceptions of ethnic or racial difference—in particular, a derogatory prejudice against "black" Bengalis among traditionally higher-status and "whiter" Muslims from what had been the older, northwest provinces of Mughal India. The notion that Bengal's Islam was impure, or "Hinduised," was combined with racist and gendered ideas inherited from Mughal and British colonial times: Bengali men from the lowland Ganges Delta were seen as weak and "effeminate," "real" Muslims from the northwestern mountains as virile conquerors. Such perceptions contributed to extremes of violence, particularly sexual violence, which was widespread during the war. The initial Pakistani campaign of repression, and the guerilla war that followed, pushed millions of refugees across the border into India. Both Hindu and Muslim civilians were murdered. There was systematic rape of women in the countryside, and (though less well-documented) of men, too. Accusations of genocide were already being made during the conflict, and persisted after it. Some 1.7 million people may have been killed.[12]

Other wars broke out between Muslim states, and ratcheted up sectarian hostility among Muslims as much as they generated Muslim hostility to the West. The war between Iran and Iraq, the "last total war" of the twentieth century, began when Iraq invaded its neighbour in September 1980. Iraq's rulers hoped for a short conflict that would cement Iraq's then-rising power as a leading Arab state in the Gulf, and force recognition of Iraqi regional dominance by what seemed to be an insecure Iranian regime, following the revolution that had overthrown the shah in 1979. The war was also intended to secure Saddam Hussein's own newly established personal control of the Iraqi state. In 1979, Saddam had seized the presidency, purged the Ba'th Party, and imprisoned or executed his political opponents, including large numbers of both Sunni and Shi'i clerics. He now aimed to impose his will on the Iranians, too.

But instead of reaching a quick conclusion, the war dragged on for eight years, mobilising two million soldiers and killing several hundred thousand people on both sides. Iraq's aggression solidified popular Iranian support for the revolutionary government, which itself became more secure (and more authoritarian) in the hands of Khomeini and his allies. Iraq's invasion was halted and then beaten back. The conflict became a terrible war of attrition, in which young Iranian men died by the thousands in suicidal assaults on the fortified Iraqi border, and Iraq used chemical weapons against both Iranian soldiers and Iraqi Kurdish civilians. It also became a war for the survival of both regimes within their own countries, radicalising the politics of both. It amplified a Shi'i cult of martyrdom in Iran and accentuated tensions between the ruling Sunni minority and the Shi'i majority in Iraq. A cross-sectarian Iraqi Arab nationalism still held Iraqis together, although it was increasingly marked by religious rhetoric rather than by secular nation-building: to court Iraqi Shi'i opinion, it was even claimed that Saddam was a descendant of Ali Ibn Abi Talib. But such nationalism was fraying. In 1991, three years after the war ended, and as Iraqi troops were ejected from Kuwait by a US-led international coalition, a spontaneous, leaderless uprising against the regime would break out in the old Shi'i cities of the south: Najaf, Karbala, and Basra.

Iraq was supplied with arms by France and the Soviet Union, and with money from the Arab Gulf states. The United States did not, as is sometimes claimed, encourage Iraq's invasion. But from 1984 onwards it did provide the Iraqi regime with economic support and satellite intelligence. Air battles over oil tankers in the Persian Gulf also internationalised the war, with British and US naval forces deployed to protect Arab Gulf oil shipping, effectively aiding Iraq's war effort. In the spring of 1988, US warships directly engaged the Iranian navy and attacked oil platforms that were occupied by Iranian militia. Iraq waged a brutal campaign against Kurdish nationalists in the north of the country, which destroyed whole villages and may have killed one hundred thousand people. None of this lessened support for Saddam's regime among its Western backers, even when Kurdish civilians were attacked indiscriminately with chemical weapons, most notoriously at Halabja, near the Iranian border, in March 1988. By the end of the war, Iraq significantly outgunned both Iran and the other Arab Gulf states combined.

Iranian arms came from almost every country in Europe as well as from China and elsewhere in the world, but given the international support that Iraq increasingly enjoyed, Iran seemed to be fighting the world alone. The experience of the war accentuated anti-Western, and especially anti-American, sentiment in Iran. On July 3, 1988, the American guided-missile cruiser USS *Vincennes* sailed into Iranian territorial waters and shot down an Iranian civilian airliner carrying 290 people. No one survived. The US account was that the *Vincennes*'s commander had mistaken the airliner for a warplane. Iranians believed that he had committed a deliberate war crime. It has been claimed that the bombing by Libyan agents of Pan Am Flight 103, over Lockerbie in Scotland in December 1988, killing 270 people, was carried out in revenge, at the behest of the Iranian regime, as well as in reprisal for America's air raids on the Libyan capital, Tripoli, two years earlier.[13]

Still other conflicts took the form of wars within states, in which the fault lines between religious communities were also those between ethnic or economic groups, political factions, or regions: in Yemen, Oman, Sudan, Lebanon, the Philippines, and Indonesia. Islamist movements in northern Nigeria, the southern Philippines, and Indonesia all drew on distinctly local histories of Muslim revival, Islamic state-building, and their historic distinctiveness from neighbouring regions that had come to dominate them within new nation-states. By the 1950s, Aceh, the former sultanate that had seen itself as "the porch of Mecca" on the Indian Ocean, had become the northwestern periphery of Indonesia. It was one of several regions where activists favouring the establishment of a formally Islamic state, having played a role in achieving independence from the Dutch, were now in rebellion against the national government. In addition to the Darul-Islam movement in West Java, whose insurrection would continue until 1962, the new Indonesian republic faced guerilla movements in central Java, South Sulawesi, and Kalimantan (Borneo). In 1953, the first of a series of revolts also broke out in Aceh.

Some of these conflicts—notably, in Sulawesi and Borneo—were local rebellions by disgruntled regional strongmen who used Islamic rhetoric and moral discipline to legitimate what was sometimes little more than banditry. In Aceh, the movement went deeper. President Sukarno was supposed to have promised that Islamic law would be instituted in Aceh, in line with a provision in the preparatory texts for the national constitution. Drawn up in 1945, these had stipulated that within Indonesia's unitary, multiethnic and multi-confessional state, Muslims would follow Islamic law. This had been quietly dropped from the actual constitution at independence. Acehnese support for the wider Darul-Islam movement ended when Aceh was promised autonomy as a "special administrative district" within the new republic, but this did not happen either. As Indonesia's parliamentary system gave way, from the late 1950s, to Sukarno's "Guided Democracy," martial law, and a state of emergency, the regional revolts were crushed. Other conflicts followed, in which Muslim groups aligned themselves with the central state instead. In 1965, when General Suharto seized power in reaction to an abortive pro-communist coup, a murderous campaign against the Indonesian left followed; the death toll is unknown, but it is thought that between two hundred thousand and one million people were killed. Islamic youth groups and militia connected to Muslim organisations assisted the army in carrying out the killings to "exterminate" the Indonesian Communist Party.[14]

In the 1970s, a new movement arose in Aceh. The leaders of what became the GAM (Gerakan Aceh Merdeka, the Free Aceh Movement) reimagined the region's longer history as a distinctly Acehnese national past. Aceh, they said, was a nation in its own right, not properly part of Indonesia, and only "Javanese propaganda" and domination had made it so. Its people's mistreatment and exploitation by Indonesia, for whose liberation they had previously fought, now justified their own struggle for national liberation. The movement's initial name, the National Liberation Front of Aceh-Sumatra, staked the region's claim to be part of the late Cold War wave of independence movements across the Global South. Aceh's regional grievances were as real as, but perhaps no greater than, those of any other area in the strongly centralising, militarised state that emerged under Suharto's "New Order" regime in the mid-1960s. From the late 1970s, when substantial oil and gas fields began to be developed in the region but produced little local employment and much local friction, they became more significant.[15]

Hasan Di Tiro, a prominent anti-communist and Muslim activist who had studied and built a business career in the United States in the 1950s and 1960s, returned to Aceh in 1976. He began a new revolt on the basis of the region's earlier Darul-Islam movement. His was a small, poorly armed, and isolated insurgency, and by 1978–79 it was broken up by the Indonesian military. Di Tiro escaped to Malaysia. His message of national liberation, though, struck roots. The movement was kept alive, and became more popular as both economic disparities and the central state's repressiveness grew. When the Suharto regime collapsed in 1998, in the wake of the 1997 Asian financial crisis, the GAM emerged into the open. Amidst mass popular support for a referendum on Acehnese independence, GAM leaders mobilised crowds of thousands in meetings at mosques across the territory. While the GAM's cause gained popularity and its fighters gained control over much of rural Aceh's territory, though, it was now very different to the Darul-Islam rebellion from which it had originally sprung.

In the mid-1980s, Hasan Di Tiro was happy to espouse a rhetoric of perennial culture clash, telling an audience in London that since the sixteenth century Southeast Asia had been in "a conflict...between the predatory Western Christian civilisation and the Islamic civilisation." He also hoped that Washington would airdrop M16 rifles to his guerillas. (It did not.) By the early 2000s, his successors hoped for Western support in what they portrayed as a struggle for post–Cold War democratisation, like those of Eastern Europe. They were quick to deny any suggestions that they had anything to do with Islamism, let alone a global jihad. The GAM did not want to create an Islamic state in Aceh, let alone in all of Indonesia, and the government's institution of sharia in the region (a core demand since the 1950s) was dismissed as a distraction. Unlike Islamist groups elsewhere, the GAM did not want to "re-Islamise" Aceh, because, its leaders said, their people were "already religious." In contrast to other Indonesian insurrections, notably that of Laskar Jihad ("the Army of Jihad")—a militant, salafi internationalist group founded in 2000 that preached an overt anti-Christian war in the Maluku Islands (the Moluccas)—Aceh's revolt had become no less a Muslim but a wholly territorially focused movement.[16]

In the Philippines, another multiethnic, multireligious nation of islands, a similar story was playing out at the same time. Like Aceh's struggle for national independence, the Moro resistance movement in the southern Philippines emerged in the 1970s. Like the movement in Aceh, "Moro liberation" was imagined by its leaders, and by outside observers, as part of a single long history of Muslim resistance to Christian colonisers. It was supposed to have begun against the Spanish (who first called the islands' Muslims, like the "Moors" of Andalus, "Moros") and continued against the Americans, then after 1946 against the independent Filipino state, which was dominated by Christians from the north.

This was actually a new view of history, similar to those emerging elsewhere at the same time. In Aceh, the pre-colonial sultanate was reimagined as an Acehnese nation, whose people needed to assert independence against "Javanese colonisers" just as they had against the Dutch. In Malaya, we saw how a *bangsa Malayu*, a racialised conception of a "Malay nation," emerged in the first half of the twentieth century as European ideas, new forms of education, journalism, and mass politics reshaped older cultural inheritances. In the same way, the belief in a *bangsa Moro*, the "Moro nation" in the Philippines, emerged when young Muslims from the south, sent north to study, reappropriated the disparaging image of "Moros" for themselves, and made it a rallying cry. It was above all during American colonial rule that this occurred. When Filipino Muslims were taken to St. Louis, Missouri, for the 1904 World's Fair to be staged (as was then common) in an ethnographic exhibition, they returned with "the very latest models" of US-made revolvers and rifles. Both "Moro" ethnicity and their armament were produced, to a considerable extent, by America as well as by Islam.[17]

In the 1950s, the southern Philippines—Mindanao and the Sulu Islands—were economically disadvantaged relative to the more developed and more Christian north. The Filipino government had inherited its view of the nation's south from American colonial perceptions, attributing its people's problems to "their ignorance and their trend towards religious fanaticism." The state-sponsored migration of Christian farmers from the north had been encouraged under American rule as a "civilising" influence on the "Mohammedan and pagan" south and continued apace after independence. But instead of integrating the southern islands, Christian agricultural settlement, land registration and roadbuilding made existing disparities of wealth and welfare even sharper and more visible. Land laws and access to markets favoured the Christian settlers and further marginalised the existing Muslim peasant population, many of whom lost land they had traditionally occupied.

At the same time, prominent Muslim families, descended from the autocratic dynasties of earlier centuries, invested in Islamic symbols, building mosques and going on pilgrimage to boost their cultural credentials. More materially, they maintained their dominance of local politics by buying into the new republic's party-political machinery and buying votes. But a rising generation of educated Muslims increasingly contested both this local elite's inherited status and its complicity in the economic and political system. Tensions within the Muslim community (which was also divided into language and clan groups), as well as between Muslims and Christians, or between Muslims and the central government, would be as important in shaping subsequent violence in the region as was the separatist movement that in 1968 declared its aim of setting up an Islamic state.[18]

Violence broke out in the late 1960s and entered a new phase in 1972, when the regime of President Ferdinand Marcos declared martial law, and the Moro National Liberation Front (MNLF) was founded. The MNLF, and its later splinter faction, the Moro Islamic Liberation Front (MILF), aimed to create an independent "Bangsamoro" homeland. They maintained an armed struggle against the government beyond the collapse of the Marcos regime and the end of martial law in 1986. The MILF emerged from dissatisfaction with the Tripoli Agreement, brokered in Libya in 1976, which provided for regional autonomy for the south. More openly Islamist than its predecessor, it positioned itself as a force for "equality, purity and morality" against an existing order denounced as "feudal, immoral, and elitist," and against the corruption of MNLF leaders who took control of the autonomous regional government. Conflict continued into the 2000s—in 2014, a "comprehensive agreement" was announced as the lead-up to a peace deal and the establishment of Bangsamoro with its own legal status. By then, the MILF was widely seen as part of a global jihadi network. But its objectives remained primarily national and territorial. Its success was a result of its working through civil society as well as by violence, and its ability to work through the institutions of the state as well as against it.[19]

Each of these conflicts unfolded according to local, specific logics; each was the product of the particular circumstances of the peoples and geographies involved. At the same time, all of them were caused by the same overarching factors that caused wars elsewhere in the twentieth century: colonial legacies, nationalism, territory, and sovereignty; economic disparity, political ambition and repression, regional rivalry and competition over resources; fear and animosity between neighbouring religious or ethnic communities. None was caused by anything intrinsic to Islam, or to an imaginary "fault line" between Muslims and non-Muslims. But as news and networks of solidarity became globalised, they increasingly moved global Muslim opinion. Taken together, and out of their own contexts, they could be interpreted as separate fronts in a single process of civilisational confrontation.

By the late 1990s, conservative Western political scientists would point to what Huntington claimed were Islam's "bloody borders," theorising that there was something pathologically violent about Muslims that would need to be policed and suppressed. Osama Bin Laden agreed that there was a "clash of civilisations," telling a journalist in October 2001 that "this is a very clear matter." But he saw things the other way round: the violence was that of global "unbelief" against Muslims and "the terrorism America inflicts in the world."

The vast majority of Muslims around the world plainly did not support Bin Laden and his call for all Muslims everywhere "to kill the Americans and their allies." But it did seem to many that it was the perpetual victimisation of Muslims' societies by more powerful others, and the wider world's indifference to their suffering, that was pathological. At the end of the twentieth century, the wars that most marked imaginations in this way were those that could credibly be portrayed as pitting embattled, martyred Muslims, heroically standing up for their community and their faith, against oppression and aggression: Russia's war in Afghanistan in the 1980s; the wars in Algeria, Bosnia, and Chechnya in the 1990s; and, bleeding across the decades, the Arab-Israeli conflict over Palestine.[20]

◇◇◇◇◇◇◇◇

In the 1950s and 1960s, it seemed to Palestinians that the world had forgotten about them. The 1948 war for Palestine had left most of them as stateless refugees in a world that, despite the massive population displacements that had immediately followed the Second World War, had yet to devise an agreed legal framework for refugees' rights and protections. The United Nations' convention on the status of refugees would be agreed only in 1951. The UN resolution, adopted the day after the Universal Declaration of Human Rights, that had called for Palestinians to be allowed "to return to their homes and live at peace with their neighbours," or else receive compensation for loss and damage to property should they choose not to return, was without effect. Their homes had been destroyed, or reoccupied by other refugees: Jewish families fleeing Europe in the aftermath of the Holocaust, who arrived in Israel from displaced persons camps in Cyprus and elsewhere. These immigrants from Europe would soon be joined by some three hundred thousand more Jewish people who sought refuge in Israel from places across the Middle East and North Africa that had been their homes for many centuries, but where, as the conflict over the land of Palestine came to be identified as a conflict between Jews and Arabs, or between Jews and Muslims, they were no longer safe: Iraq, Syria, Egypt, Morocco, Yemen.[21]

The Arab states that had so loudly denounced Zionism and promised to protect the Palestinians' homeland had failed abysmally on the battlefield. They did little to protect Palestinians themselves now that they were dispossessed and impoverished residents of refugee camps in Lebanon, Syria, and Jordan, under Jordanian rule in the West Bank, or under Egyptian rule along the coastal strip around the ancient city of Gaza. For the Hashemite monarchy in Amman—disappointed in its hopes of a united Arab state after the First World War—the West Bank was the major gain of the 1948 war. The territory, incorporated into the existing emirate of Transjordan to form the kingdom of Jordan, included the old city of Jerusalem and the venerable, and venerated, towns of Bethlehem, Hebron (believed to be the burial place of the patriarchs Abraham, Isaac, and Jacob), and Nablus (supposedly the resting place of the biblical figure, and Qur'anic prophet, Joseph).

More than half a million Palestinians now lived in Jordan. Unlike the other Arab states, Jordan granted them citizenship, and Jordan's King Abdallah sought a permanent settlement on the basis of the existing partition of mandate-era Palestine between Israel and his own kingdom. Palestinians believed—not incorrectly—that before 1948, Abdallah had sought to make a deal with the Zionists to deny Palestinians their own state. In 1951, he was assassinated outside the Al-Aqsa Mosque in Jerusalem. Lebanon's prime minister had been assassinated four days earlier, and the aftershocks of the Palestine conflict would continue to contribute to upheavals across the Middle East. There were three military coups d'état in Syria in 1949. Nationalist army officers like Egypt's Gamal Abd al-Nasir (Nasser) saw their armies' defeat in 1948 as a symptom of the corruption of their states' rulers and their inability to stand up to enduring Western imperialism: they overthrew Egypt's monarchy in 1952, and that of Iraq in 1958. The regional spillover into domestic politics contributed to the outbreak of civil wars in Lebanon in 1958, in Jordan in 1971, and in Lebanon again in 1975. The liberation of Palestine became a rhetorical mainstay of both secular-left nationalism and of Islamist movements like the Muslim Brotherhood across the Middle East. The actual presence, especially in Jordan and Lebanon, of refugee Palestinians struggling to assert their own dignity and national aspirations was often seen, at the same time, as a threat to both national and regional stability.

The armistice that ended the fighting in 1949 had paused the conflict rather than resolving it. Over the next seventy years, the conflict would not be resolved but pursued, entrenched, and exacerbated. In June 1967, war broke out again. Again, this time in only six days, Israel won a dramatic victory, destroying the Arab states' air forces and routing their armies. The West Bank (which some Zionist groups referred to as Judaea and Samaria), East Jerusalem, including the historic Old City, and Gaza were occupied along with the Sinai Peninsula and the strategic Golan Heights in southwest Syria. In October 1973, a third war (this time a surprise attack on Israel on Yom Kippur, the Jewish "day of atonement") pushed Israel out of Sinai. This partial victory was enough to give Nasser's successor as president of Egypt, Anwar al-Sadat, room to make a separate peace in 1979, ending a war of attrition that his country could not afford to sustain. It was making peace with Israel, despite his much-publicised personal piety and his policy of releasing Muslim Brothers who had been jailed under Nasser, that made Sadat a target of Islamist assassins two years later.

In Israel, the partial defeat of 1973 was enough to remove the historically dominant Labour Party from power, bringing in the country's first right-wing government under the nationalist Likud Party, in 1977. Likud's uncompromising charter insisted on sole Israeli sovereignty "between the sea and the Jordan": there could never be a Palestinian state in any part of mandate-era Palestine. In defiance of international law, parts of Gaza and especially the West Bank began to be settled by religious Zionists who, rather than pursuing the secular and socialist project of early Zionism, were devoted to the idea of "redeeming" what they considered to be the whole of "the land of Israel." For the next fifty years, Israeli governments would continue to expand these settlements, fragmenting Palestinian territory, displacing and dispossessing Palestinians, and making the establishment of a viable Palestinian state, and a two-state resolution of the conflict, ever less feasible. When Yitzhak Rabin, a Labour prime minister who was a veteran of the 1948 war and the army's chief of staff in 1967, sought to concede a limited degree of sovereignty to Palestinians in Gaza and the West Bank through the peace process of the early 1990s, he was assassinated by an ultranationalist supporter of the settler movement.

After the 1967 war abruptly destroyed the illusion that Arab nationalism would defeat Israel and restore Palestinians to their homeland, Palestinians took their political fate into their own hands. The Palestine Liberation Organisation (PLO) that brought together different nationalist factions under the leadership of Yasser Arafat, head of the mostly Muslim Fatah ("Movement for the Liberation of Palestine") movement, aimed to wage a guerilla struggle for the creation of a single secular state in the whole territory of mandate-era Palestine. Some other groups, like the Popular Front for the Liberation of Palestine (PFLP), founded by George Habash, a Palestinian Christian in exile in Syria, believed that Palestinians were the vanguard of a revolutionary struggle against conservative regimes across the Arab world, which must all be overthrown before Palestine could be freed. The attempt to use Jordan as a base for such a revolution led to civil war in September 1970, when Jordanian troops shelled refugee camps and battled Palestinian guerillas. Some three thousand people were killed, and the PLO was expelled from the country.

The PLO's subsequent relocation to Beirut, and then the collapse of Lebanon into civil war, led to Israel's invasion of Lebanon in 1982. The Israeli-Palestinian struggle intersected with Lebanon's own sectarian politics. Over two days in September 1982, the Israeli army facilitated the massacre, by right-wing Lebanese Christian militia, of at least eight hundred people, mostly Palestinian women and children, in the Sabra and Shatila refugee camps south of Beirut. Israel's occupation of southern Lebanon also sparked resistance from the local Lebanese Shi'i population, and the creation of Hizballah ("the Party of God"), a Shi'i militia backed by revolutionary Iran that would become both a major force in Lebanese politics and a significant military threat to Israel.

The Palestine conflict also had international repercussions beyond the Middle East. Like other revolutionary factions in the late 1960s and 1970s—far-left groups in Germany and Italy, republican nationalists in Northern Ireland—some Palestinian groups carried out terrorist outrages that sought both to attract global attention and to make specific gains, such as the release of political prisoners. Most notoriously, during the 1972 Olympic Games in Munich, terrorists from the Black September Organisation (named after the September 1970 civil war in Jordan) attempted a hostage-taking that ended in the deaths of eleven Israeli athletes. The Palestine conflict was local, regional, and global all at once, distilling the different ideologies and forces at play across the Cold War world.

By the end of the 1980s, and the end of the Cold War, however, the PLO came to recognise the state of Israel and committed itself to a two-state solution to the conflict. The aim of reaching a two-state peace settlement that would see Palestinians recognise Israel, alongside their own sovereign state in the Occupied Territories of Gaza and the West Bank, had by now gained international consensus. But the solution that was negotiated, through the 1993 Oslo Accords, broke down. The Israeli right still refused to accept the prospect of a Palestinian state: it became more radical, more imbued with redemptive, religious Zionism and with anti-Arab racism, and more powerful within Israeli politics. The most radical Palestinian factions, above all Hamas, for their part refused to recognise Israel, seeing all of historic Palestine as a sacred Muslim trust. The Oslo process tended to turn the Palestinian National Authority, supposedly the Palestinians' state-in-waiting, into a security subcontractor to which Israel, without granting the Palestinians any substantive sovereignty and without withdrawing from the West Bank settlements, could outsource the work of continuing its occupation. By the end of the 1990s, the peace process had foundered, and the return to more, and worse, violence was on the horizon. A second intifada broke out in September 2000. More militarised than the first uprising in 1987–93, it was marked by suicide bombings, the building of a concrete "separation barrier" that effectively annexed parts of the West Bank to Israel, further fragmenting Palestinian territory, and the Israeli military reoccupation of West Bank towns. By 2006, between three and four thousand Palestinians had been killed and between twenty-two and forty-five thousand injured; around one thousand Israelis had been killed, and seven thousand injured.[22]

By 2001, when Osama Bin Laden could claim that the 9/11 attacks had been "in self-defence, defence of our brothers and sons in Palestine," the world's attention had been drawn back repeatedly to Palestine, but not usually to the plight, the voices, or the aspirations of ordinary Palestinians—who repeatedly, whenever they were asked, said their greatest worries were poverty and corruption, and that they favoured democratic government and a two-state solution. While the most militant Palestinian faction, Hamas, claimed that Palestine was "the spirit of the *umma* and its central cause," it too, by 2017, came to recognise the practical reality, if not the principle, of having to live with the existence of Israel for the foreseeable future, and declared that the aim of establishing a sovereign Palestinian state within the 1967 borders was now "a formula of national consensus." But the conflict only grew deeper, West Bank settlers more aggressive, Palestinians more disenfranchised, and further rounds of violence more inevitable.[23]

In contrast to the recurring focus of media and political attention on Israel and Palestine, the world's headlines rarely paid attention to other regional conflicts until, after 2001, they too could be claimed as connected fronts in a global jihad, and its symbiotic twin, the "global war on terror." This was true of insurgencies in the Philippines, in Aceh, and in northern Nigeria. It was true, too (except to the extent that the conflict spilled over into France), of the violence that ravaged Algeria in the 1990s. A Third World revolutionary icon of a nation to many Muslims and others across the Global South in the previous generation, by the late 1980s Algeria was a single-party state that had lost much of its popular legitimacy. Its economy, crashed by the same collapse of oil and gas prices in the mid-1980s that hastened the fall of the Soviet Union, was in crisis. A hasty political opening in 1989 led to the electoral victory of the Islamist FIS in 1991: Algeria, in the early 1990s, was one place where political Islam looked like it might win.

The Algerian army, whose generals had dominated the state and its oil and gas wealth, had other ideas. Elections were cancelled, and FIS militants were detained, to "save the republic" from the Islamist threat. The spiral of violence that followed saw the splintering and radicalisation of the Algerian Islamist movement, widespread torture and human rights abuses by security forces, and massacres of civilians attributed to insurgent groups generically known as the GIA (*Groupes islamiques armés*, "Islamic Armed Groups"). In some districts, GIA "emirs" were effectively local warlords, franchising the look and language of radical Islamism to gain control of a local war economy. In other cases, GIA groups were sometimes alleged to be "pseudo-gangs," militia controlled or manipulated by factions of the security services to spread terror and confusion in the civilian population and to discredit the jailed Islamist opposition and the insurgents who supported them. By 2007, when a successor group to the GIA, the "Salafist Group for Preaching and Combat" declared allegiance to Bin Laden and rebranded itself as "Al-Qaʻida in the Islamic Maghreb," the war was routinely, and vaguely, said to have caused anything between one hundred thousand and two hundred thousand deaths. No one could say for sure how many people had died, and controversy raged over who, in many cases, had really killed them.[24]

More global media attention was directed to Bosnia: the Balkans, after all, were in Europe. Emerging from the breakup of post-Communist Yugoslavia with a vote for independence in 1992, Bosnia had inherited its religious and linguistic mixity from the days of Ottoman rule. But now, the Balkans' communities were divided by the way that, since the 1800s, religious belonging had become fused into ethnic and national identity, such that Orthodox Christians were Serbs, Catholic Christians were Croats, and Muslims were Bosnians (or Bosniaks) or Albanians. The territories they all lived in could be disentangled only by the violence of what was coming to be called "ethnic cleansing." Serbs had been dominant in the federal Yugoslav state and demanded their own ethnic enclave within Bosnian territory, which they sought to expand and from which they intended to expel—or within which, they would annihilate—non-Serbs. The war was marked by the Serb army's prolonged siege of Sarajevo, from 1992 to 1996, and atrocities against Bosnian Muslim civilians that, notoriously, culminated in the genocidal massacre of eight thousand Muslim men and boys at Srebrenica in July 1995.[25]

The end of the Cold War and the breakup of the Soviet bloc were also the context for the war in Chechnya. As happened with the conflicts in Algeria and Bosnia (and with accounts of Sunnis and Shiʻis in Iraq, or Christians and Muslims in Lebanon), oversimplifying accounts of Chechnya in the 1990s and early 2000s often drew on superficial stereotypes. Commentators and public opinion resorted to clichés about "savage" ethnicities, saw late twentieth-century conflicts as replays of nineteenth-century struggles, or explained them away as "upsurges" of allegedly ancient hatreds. If there was a relevant historical background to the movement for Chechen independence from Russia in 1990, it was not Imam Shamil's Islamic state in the 1850s but rather the Stalinist deportation of over half a million Chechens, along with other North Caucasus people, to Kazakhstan in 1944. The deportations, which ended only when Chechens began to return from central Asia after 1957, were remembered by some as a genocide. But by the end of the Soviet period, much of Chechen society was secular and Sovietized. Chechnya's first post-Soviet president and leader of the nationalist government in the early 1990s, Dzhokhar Dudayev, had been a career officer in the Soviet air force. He was decorated for distinguished service against the mujahidin in Afghanistan, and ended his career commanding a nuclear bomber base in Estonia. Chechnya's demand for secession from the Russian Federation was initially a secular nationalist one, like those of the Baltic republics or Ukraine.[26]

That demand, though, unlike in Ukraine and the Baltic, was refused: Chechnya was part of the new Russian Federation, and Russia's President Boris Yeltsin opted for war, claiming that it was necessary to save post-Soviet Russia itself from disintegrating. In 1994, Yeltsin sent troops into Chechnya. Grozny—mostly inhabited by ethnic Russians—was destroyed by indiscriminate bombing. The Russian army became quickly bogged down in a guerilla war. Its soldiers committed atrocities against Chechens, whom they saw through a fog of racial and religious prejudices. At the same time, drinking and demoralised, they sold their weapons to the Chechens. The campaign was a humiliating failure, and a peace agreement in 1996 led to Russian withdrawal. But in 1999 the war restarted. Vladimir Putin, an aggressive, but at the time relatively unpopular, new Russian prime minister, saw Chechnya as a "gangster enclave." Its reconquest offered an opportunity to make his mark as the new strongman of Russian national reassertion. After bombs exploded at two Moscow apartment blocks, Putin declared a "counter-terrorist" war, a term that Yeltsin had already used—and indeed there had been cross-border terrorist actions by Chechen guerillas during the 1994–96 war.[27]

Islamism did not drive the war in Chechnya; rather, it was empowered by it. The mid-nineties campaign had largely wrecked the country, and Putin's claim that by 1999, order had broken down and been replaced by Islamist radicals was not without foundation. The most prominent Islamist leader in Chechnya, Shamil Basayev, had apparently travelled to Osama Bin Laden's base in Khost, in Afghanistan, early in 1994, prior to the first outbreak of hostilities with Russia. He was later joined by a Saudi militant, thought to have been called Samir al-Suwaylim, who went by the *nom de guerre* of "al-Khattab," after the second caliph, Umar Ibn al-Khattab. These men and their followers gained prestige during the 1994–96 campaign through their military effectiveness. They attracted younger men to their ranks and began to promote a vision of building a North Caucasus caliphate rather than a free Chechnya.

In August 1999, two days before Putin's nomination as prime minister, Basayev and Khattab led several thousand guerillas in an incursion into Daghestan, in an attempt to provoke a regional Islamist insurrection. They failed, but they gave Russia a *casus belli*. Khattab would be assassinated by the FSB, the Russian secret services, who sent him a poisoned letter in 2002. Basayev was killed in 2006 by pro-Russian Chechens led by Ramzan Kadyrov, Putin's ally in the region who would become Chechnya's president the following year. In the meantime, they had led a jihadist radicalisation of the Chechen war, committing headline-grabbing terrorist atrocities. Most notably, in 2004, their followers took the staff and pupils of a school in Beslan, in North Ossetia, hostage, causing the deaths of nearly two hundred children. They split the independence movement, which became divided between their trans-regional, Wahhabi-influenced agenda and the more specifically Chechen nationalism of the movement's origins.

Over the course of the conflict, in response to the brutality of Russia's invasion, Chechen nationalism also increasingly evoked the legacy of Shamil and the moral authority of the region's Naqshbandi Sufism. Rather than being rooted in the region's Islamic heritage, what had begun as a secular nationalist war became Islamised—and visions of Islam became more warlike and more transnational—as the war spread and deepened. Already in early 2000, many of Chechnya's people were displaced refugees, "in the grip of cold, flu, lice, heart attacks, TB and psychiatric illness" as the journalist Anna Politkovskaya, who would be assassinated in 2006, wrote in her unsparing account of the war. In May 2000, Vladimir Putin swept into the presidency of Russia on the back of his government's "war on terror" in Chechnya. The war in Chechnya would run on for another nine years. Putin's power would last much longer.[28]

By the early 2000s, the violence in Algeria, the civil war in Bosnia, and Russia's "dirty war" in Chechnya all loomed large in the Islamist imagining of a global struggle between good and evil. Like the other wars of the late twentieth century, these conflicts had all arisen from their own specific circumstances, and developed according to their own logics. Like the ongoing struggle over Palestine, they were annexed to the apocalyptic vision of a global jihad, not—with the partial exception of the Second Chechen War—produced by it. The vantage point from which they came to be seen as aspects of a single struggle was also a particular place, with its own, particularly protracted, history of war: Afghanistan.

◇◇◇◇◇◇◇

1979 had been a dramatic year. The shah was overthrown in Iran; Egypt and Israel signed a peace treaty; the great mosque in Mecca was seized by Islamist radicals; and twenty-two-year-old Osama Bin Laden, son of a wealthy Saudi family with a successful construction business, left university. And on December 27, the Soviet Union invaded Afghanistan. In 1978, a faction of the Marxist People's Democratic Party of Afghanistan (PDPA), supported by the army, had seized power in a coup and launched a disastrous series of policies intended to wipe out Afghan "feudalism" and institute an egalitarian, collectivist society. Land reform was so mismanaged that agricultural production fell by one-third in the spring of 1979. A literacy campaign in the countryside, meant to spread education and combat religious "superstition," was seen as humiliating to locally respected elderly people (who were forced to attend classes) and as disrespectful of conservative gender boundaries (because almost all the teachers were men, and no separate classes were provided for girls). Villagers welcomed education, but deeply resented the impositions made by a high-handed and morally suspect urban elite on their self-respecting rural society. Revolt broke out rapidly, was met with repression, and spread. By the time the Soviet army invaded to prevent the regime's collapse, it had already lost control of two-thirds of the country.[29]

The Russians removed the unstable government in Kabul and replaced it with a rival faction. But Afghans were opposed to foreign intervention even if they supported the revolution: Maoist students in Kabul, both men and women, were among the first demonstrators against the new government. Then army officers deserted, government officials went into exile, and the whole country was effectively in a state of resistance. The war would last ten years, destroy the Soviet army's morale and its prestige at home, kill a million Afghans, and make refugees of three million more. It also became the crucible of a new kind of transnational jihad.

To some Islamist militants, Afghanistan was just the latest front in a global war against Muslims that was already raging. Now, it would become the foundation, the original "base" (in Arabic, *qaʿida*), for mobilising a fightback, a campaign to rouse the "sleeping" Muslim community from its apathy and avenge the Muslim dead everywhere from Palestine to Mindanao. This campaign's most prominent advocate would be an unassuming, quietly spoken Saudi millionaire militant, Osama Bin Laden. Bin Laden arrived in Peshawar, the frontier city in northern Pakistan that became the organising centre of the Afghan resistance, for the first time in 1980. Initially, his role was to aid and organise foreign Muslim volunteers joining the anti-Soviet struggle. He visited injured fighters, gave out generous sums of money, and travelled home to Saudi Arabia to raise funds and solidarity. In 1984, he joined forces with a militant preacher and lecturer, Abdallah Azzam, who set up a "services office" in Peshawar, a hub for funnelling money and volunteers from the Arab world into training camps and the war across the border.[30]

Born in Palestine in 1941, Azzam had joined the Muslim Brotherhood as a young man, and studied in Damascus and Cairo, where he was close to Sayyid Qutb's family and supporters. He moved to Saudi Arabia in 1978 before going to Pakistan to assist the Afghan mujahidin. Against the consensus of Sunni clerics, which held that jihad was a duty for the community as a whole (and therefore to be carried out only by some, on behalf of all, and subject to a ruler's prerogative), Azzam made waves by arguing that jihad, as armed struggle, was a duty for every individual Muslim capable of supporting or participating in it. It was also, he said, the highest form of worship. In a very influential tract entitled *Join the Caravan*, he claimed that "an hour of fighting" in the way of God "is better than sixty years of prayer." He also saw Afghanistan as only the first battle in a wider war that should be waged "so that Islam will reign again" from the Philippines to Andalusia. The Afghan jihad, he wrote, was a struggle directed by God, in which victories were won by miraculous intervention, fighters' hearts were purified, and martyrdom was to be sought and achieved as a blessed goal.[31]

Azzam was assassinated in Peshawar in 1989. But he was not the only ideological influence on Bin Laden and those around him. Another major figure was Ayman al-Zawahiri, an Egyptian medical doctor and militant who first went to Pakistan in 1980 to treat Afghan refugees. Zawahiri was imprisoned and tortured in Egypt after the assassination of Anwar al-Sadat in October 1981. He returned to Afghanistan in 1986, seeing it as a base to rebuild the Egyptian "Islamic Jihad" group. Influenced by the Afghan experience and the radicalisation of the transnational jihadi movement, Zawahiri too would move from focusing on his own country to embracing a global war against the "far enemy." He would later claim that the war in Afghanistan had been conscious preparation for the "awaited battle" against the superpower of the United States. In fact, the aim of turning the war against America would not emerge until the late 1990s, after the other superpower had been defeated—and it would be the fact that, in their eyes, they had defeated one superpower that made the jihadis believe they would be able to defeat the other. But to begin with, the mujahidin and the United States had a common enemy.[32]

Afghanistan became a major front in the Cold War, as well as a just cause in the eyes of Muslims incensed at Russia's aggression. By the mid-1980s, the various Afghan armed factions received funding and armament (including, crucially, portable anti-aircraft missiles) from the United States via Pakistan. Money was raised, especially in the Gulf states, to aid Afghan refugees. Young men, reportedly thirty-five thousand of them, from across the world but especially from Arab countries, came to help: to run aid organisations, tend the wounded, and join the armed struggle. After the Soviet withdrawal in 1989, the "Arab Afghans," whose relationship to the Afghans' own resistance had often been fraught, dispersed. Some, with Samir al-Suwaylim, went on to Chechnya. Some were said to be among the founders of the GIA in Algeria. In Afghanistan, meanwhile, a leftist Afghan government remained in place after the peace agreement and the evacuation of Soviet forces, but in 1992, it collapsed. Civil war ensued between the different factions of the resistance. There were ethnic and sectarian massacres, and the country was carved up by rival warlords.

The only education available for tens of thousands of Afghan boys and young men displaced by over a decade of war, especially Pashtuns from the south of Afghanistan, was in Deobandi-influenced schools set up for refugees along the border with Pakistan. These taught a basic, highly moralistic, stripped-down form of Islamic education that retained from the Deobandi tradition only its frugality, emphasis on ritual correctness, and desire to save the Muslim community from corrupting foreign ways. The *taliban* ("students") of such schools became the new force to be reckoned with in Afghanistan in the mid-1990s. The Taliban emerged in southern Afghanistan, seeing themselves as an incorruptible and purifying movement devoted to re-establishing godly rule in a country they saw as having fallen into anarchy. Supported by Pakistan, they took power in Qandahar in 1994, and in Kabul in 1996. They were resisted by an alliance of factions in the north, where Taliban forces carried out massacres of ethnic minorities and Shi'a, but were welcomed elsewhere as bringing security and restoring order. When the Taliban entered Kabul, their tanks were decorated with flowers.

But the order they brought was arid and merciless, combining patriarchal Pashtun customary codes with an impoverished, literalistic conception of sharia. Women were confined to their homes and had to be fully covered in the traditional burqa when outdoors; girls' schools were closed. Not only "vices" like alcohol and smoking but any signs of laxity or leisure in personal behaviour were banned. Making or listening to music (for centuries an important part of Afghan culture), "image-making" by taking photographs or watching television, and frivolities like keeping pigeons and flying kites were all forbidden. For more serious crimes, death sentences and amputations were carried out in public. The Taliban government was recognised only by Pakistan, Saudi Arabia, and the United Arab Emirates. Its eagerness to display an uncompromising zealotry found support among some Saudi clerics, who encouraged the destruction of the country's pre-Islamic heritage. Most infamously, two giant Buddhist statues carved into the rock face at Bamiyan, north of Kabul, dating to the sixth and seventh centuries, were denounced as idols. In 2001, in an act that was as much deliberate repudiation of international opinion as dutiful respect of the Qur'an's strictures on idolatry, the Taliban dynamited them.[33]

The Taliban's Afghanistan was a brutal, war-ravaged, and hyper-masculine version of an Islamic state. As such, it gave Bin Laden sanctuary after his return to the country, just as the Taliban were emerging as a major force, in 1996. The Iraqi invasion of Kuwait and Saddam Hussein's threat to Saudi Arabia in 1990 had led Bin Laden to propose a plan to form a multinational army of Islamist militants to defend, not so much the kingdom of Saudi Arabia, but the Prophet's Arabia. But the kingdom, more pragmatic than its ideological offspring, had accepted US military personnel and a multinational coalition under US leadership to defend it instead. Bin Laden was incensed that American soldiers should be allowed to set foot in the country the Prophet had trod, and where Islam's holiest places were located. He considered the US presence in the peninsula not as an alliance but as an occupation. He moved first to Khartoum, where the Sudanese military had established an Islamist-inclined government in 1989, and a few years later, when the Sudanese expelled him, he flew back to Jalalabad with his family and supporters.

From Afghanistan, in February 1998, Bin Laden, Zawahiri and others published a declaration of war against what they called "the Judeo-Crusader alliance" that "occupied the holiest parts of the Islamic lands." (The historical fact that Jews had been victims of the Crusades, well before the crusaders killed any Muslims, was irrelevant: Bin Laden and his colleagues shared with evangelical Christians in the US and Jewish supremacists in Israel a vision of history—unthinkable before the late twentieth century—in which a single "Judeo-Christian civilisation" stood against an equally monolithic Islam.) Invoking Qur'anic verses that called for aid for the oppressed, the self-declared World Islamic Front exhorted "everyone who believes in God and wants reward" to "launch the raid on the soldiers of Satan, the Americans, and whichever devil's supporters are allied with them."[34]

Just under four years later, in December 2001, the Taliban were driven from Kabul by another US-led coalition, and Bin Laden was in hiding, where he would remain until his assassination by US special forces in May 2011. Yet another war in Afghanistan had begun. It would last another twenty years.

16

THE MYTH OF CIVILISATIONS

Ruqia Hassan, a thirty-year-old Kurdish Syrian schoolteacher who had studied philosophy in Aleppo, was known on social media as Nissan Ibrahim. As Nissan, she posted brave, funny, romantic, defiant updates on Facebook and Twitter from her life in her hometown, Raqqa. On the Euphrates in northeast Syria, Raqqa was both a modest provincial town, and an ancient city that had seen it all. It was founded as Nikephorion—named after a festival of the goddess Athena, "bringer of victory"—in the fourth century BC, by one of Alexander the Great's Macedonian generals. Renamed Callinicum, it became a Byzantine fortress town. It was destroyed by the Sasanians in the mid-sixth century, and rebuilt by the Byzantine Emperor Justinian. The Battle of Siffin took place nearby in the mid-seventh century, and for twelve years at the turn of the eighth and ninth centuries, Raqqa was the residence of the Caliph Harun al-Rashid. It was also the seat of a bishop until the twelfth century and had four Christian monasteries.

Abandoned after the Mongol conquests in the 1200s, Raqqa was a garrison outpost for the Ottomans before being resettled again in the late 1800s. In the 1970s, it was a boomtown powered by development of the Tabqa hydroelectric dam upriver on the Euphrates, while the dictator Hafiz al-Assad was cementing his brutal personal rule over Syria. In 2011, in a moment of revolutionary hope, it was the first town in northern Syria to be freed from the Assad regime. Then, the Syrian revolution was overtaken by a vicious, sectarian civil war. Conservative Gulf monarchies provided arms to Sunni Islamist insurgents whose ideology was inspired by al-Qa'ida and anti-Shi'i sectarianism, while the Assad regime drew support from Shi'i Iran as well as from Vladimir Putin's resurgent Russia, for whom Syria was a strategic naval and communications base. Raqqa, like much of eastern Syria and northern Iraq, was overrun by Daesh, the so-called Islamic State (IS or ISIS) movement. In 2014 it became the capital of Daesh's "caliphate." Ruqia Hassan created an online identity to document Daesh's abusive rule and recount her own experiences. "I get threats all the time," she posted in July 2015, "whatever: they'll pick me up and cut my head off, so what, they'll be cutting off a head full of dignity, and I won't live in humiliation." Two months later, IS accused Ruqia of spying, and murdered her.[1]

Ruqia, and a collective of citizen-journalists who published the website Raqqa is Being Slaughtered Silently, risked their lives to get information on life in Raqqa to the outside world, and to make sure its dead—civilians killed by Daesh, and in the international coalition's airstrikes against Daesh—were not forgotten. In October 2017, when the city was finally retaken by mostly Kurdish militia groups after months of bombing, there was almost nothing left of Raqqa but the grey concrete shells of buildings, dust and rubble, and the carcasses of cars and pickup trucks. Reporters saw no civilian residents, but they were still there. Prevented from escaping by Daesh fighters, four thousand civilians are thought to have been killed in the battle for the city. As many as forty thousand may have been killed across the border in northern Iraq, in the battle to retake Mosul from Daesh three months earlier. Thousands of others, local people fleeing the war and the "caliphate," and the widows and orphans of foreign fighters who had flocked to join them, now lived in refugee camps on the road to the Turkish border, north of Raqqa, and beyond.

Some of these refugees, Sunnis from across the border in Iraq, had fled much earlier, from the violence that had torn their own country apart ever since the US-led invasion of Iraq in 2003. In 2014, when Daesh captured Mosul and came within thirty miles of Baghdad, forces of the Shiʻa-dominated Iraqi government had been shelling mostly Sunni cities like Fallujah. In Baghdad, people remembered how, in the 2006–7 civil war, Shiʻi militia had murdered Sunnis on the streets of the capital. Some Iraqi Sunnis sought refuge in the territory controlled by the self-proclaimed "Islamic State" from the sectarian violence further south. But this only became another nightmare. "The situation here is quite calm," one professional woman in Mosul wrote to a friend, the Irish journalist Patrick Cockburn, shortly after Daesh captured her city: "They seem to be courteous with the people and they protect all the government establishments against looters." But she already suspected that the calm was not to last: "But, we don't know what will happen.... May God protect everyone. Pray for us."[2]

◇◇◇◇◇◇◇

Just as al-Qaʻida had come unforeseeably out of Russia's war in Afghanistan, so Daesh ultimately came out of America's wars in Afghanistan and, especially, Iraq. The war in Afghanistan that began two months after 9/11 rapidly swept the Taliban's Islamic emirate from power, denied al-Qaʻida its safe haven, and forced its leaders into hiding. But the invading coalition would fail, despite the expense of blood, treasure, and best intentions, to install a credible and competent Afghan government that could win popular support. A Taliban insurgency persisted, and when international troops eventually withdrew in 2021, the Taliban swept back into power in a matter of weeks. In the meantime, far from disappearing, al-Qaʻida had expanded and diversified, particularly thanks to the US- and UK-led invasion and subsequent occupation of Iraq.

The rapidity of the Taliban's removal from Kabul encouraged the neoconservative faction of George W. Bush's administration—the so-called Vulcans—to extend the war beyond destroying the base that had incubated the 9/11 hijackers. Since the late 1990s, Republican Party hawks had sponsored national security doctrines that called for the unqualified, unilateral assertion of American military pre-eminence on a global scale, and the use of "shock and awe" to intimidate and overwhelm America's enemies. They objected to US interests being limited by international law, despised the United Nations, and generally signed up to a view of the world as defined by civilisational conflict. Saddam Hussein's Iraq, from being an ally against Iran at the end of the Cold War, had become their particular bugbear.[3]

The US-led campaign against Iraq's occupation of Kuwait, in the Gulf War of 1990–91, had stopped short of removing Saddam from power, much to their regret. The economic sanctions imposed on Iraq in 1991—which were supposed to be lifted when Iraq complied with international demands for the dismantling of its chemical, biological, and nuclear weapons programmes—did not have the catastrophic effect on child mortality that was reported, and widely believed, in the late 1990s. But they did contribute to the impoverishment of a country whose development had already been crashed by war with Iran, militarisation of the economy, dependence on imported food and medicine, and kleptocratic corruption. Saddam's regime was a danger, above all, to the people of Iraq; as British intelligence assessments repeatedly concluded, it was unlikely to become a danger to anyone else unless its survival was threatened.[4]

But after 9/11, and despite the overwhelming absence of any evidence to connect the ageing secular-nationalist dictator with the al-Qa'ida jihadists, both the Bush administration and Britain's Prime Minister Tony Blair repeatedly linked the threat of terrorism with "rogue states," specifically Iraq, and its alleged possession of weapons of mass destruction, to manufacture a case for war. In February 2003, British intelligence warned that the threat posed by al-Qa'ida and similar groups would only "be heightened by military action against Iraq." The following month, American and British troops invaded the country anyway. Saddam's regime fell (the dictator himself was tried for crimes against humanity and executed in 2006), but no weapons of mass destruction were found; Iraq collapsed into insurgency and sectarian civil war. The occupation would last until 2011, costing US taxpayers upwards of eight hundred billion dollars. At least 162,000 Iraqis were killed, almost three million were internally displaced, and two million more became refugees. As for al-Qaʻida, its brand spread from Southeast Asia to Northwest Africa, reinvigorating sometimes-moribund local Islamist groups with a renewed sense of participation in a global war. Soon, al-Qaʻida franchises or allies were the most active and dangerous Islamist guerilla groups in the West African Sahel and across the southern fringes of the Sahara, in Somalia and Yemen, and in Iraq itself, where a Jordanian who had spent time in Afghanistan and went by the name of Abu Musab al-Zarqawi saw an opportunity.[5]

The occupation of Iraq and the insurgency it provoked, Zarqawi wrote in a letter intended for the leadership of al-Qaʻida, had created the ideal conditions for "jihad in the Arab heartland." "We know," he wrote, "that the true, decisive battle between infidelity and Islam is in this land.... Therefore, we must spare no effort and strive urgently to establish a foothold.... Perhaps God may cause something to happen thereafter." The Americans, he thought, were in Iraq to establish a "State of Greater Israel from the Nile to the Euphrates," which would "accelerate the emergence of the Messiah." They were working with the Shiʻis, "the most evil of mankind," and Zarqawi planned a campaign of terror—or as he saw it, of "martyrdom operations," meaning suicide bombings, which his group had made central to their tactics— to set off a full-scale sectarian war. This, he believed, would force "the silent majority" to come out in support of the jihadi movement. For Zarqawi, the *umma* "cannot live without the aroma of martyrdom and the perfume of fragrant blood spilled on behalf of God." Muslims everywhere would not "awaken from their stupor unless talk of martyrdom and martyrs fills their days and nights."[6]

After Zarqawi was killed by a US airstrike in 2006, his movement, which had begun as "al-Qaʻida in Iraq," developed into a rival for al-Qaʻida itself, in the form of the caliphate-building project of Daesh in northern Iraq and Syria. In 2014, as the Iraqi government's army collapsed and Syria fragmented between competing, increasingly sectarian armed factions, Daesh found itself in control of a vast territory centred on the valley on the Euphrates, between the Turkish border in the north, the vicinity of Aleppo in the west, Mosul in the east and the approaches to Baghdad in the south. In this territory, which suddenly erased the Iraqi-Syrian border, Daesh attempted to create and rule a state, bringing to life the fantasy of a restored caliphate that Islamists had claimed to be working towards for the past century. Bringing the fantasy to life, perhaps inevitably, became a horror story.

Daesh's propaganda, especially that aimed at the outside world, sought to depict it as building "a state and caliphate" that would give oppressed Muslims back their "dignity, might, rights, and leadership." The group's leader, a forty-something Iraqi preacher and militant from Samarra known as Abu Bakr al-Baghdadi, claimed that in Daesh's territory, "the Arab and non-Arab, the white man and black man, the easterner and westerner are all brothers . . . loving each other . . . , standing in a single trench, defending and guarding each other, and sacrificing themselves for one another . . . under a single flag and goal." The group's black flags, and Baghdadi's black robes, evoked the revolutionary Abbasid movement and the last caliphate to be proclaimed in Iraq. Some, at least, in the populations of Mosul and other Iraqi cities initially welcomed its promise of godly rule. As had been true of the Taliban in Afghanistan twenty years earlier, for some at first Daesh's "moral order" came as a relief from the chaos and violence wrought by ten years of invasion, occupation, and civil war. Daesh tried to claim the historic mantle of universal Muslim rule against oppression and unbelief, creating a state in which all Muslims, from anywhere in the world, could be free and equal, and participate in establishing a righteous society on earth. Its ideologues and activists, its online influencers and those who bought into their narrative and travelled to "make hijra" to IS territory envisioned themselves as true believers re-creating the ideal Muslim community.[7]

This was a notion some young Muslims from Arab countries, and from Europe, North America, Australia and elsewhere, too, found irresistible. More than thirty thousand people are thought to have travelled to join Daesh between 2012 and 2016, as many as went to Afghanistan during the ten years of the anti-Soviet war in the 1980s. Young men and women alike travelled to IS-held territory out of a mix of conviction and delusion, naïveté and bravado, anger at the sufferings of Syrians under Assad's chemical attacks or frustration with discrimination and racism at home. Some had difficult home lives and vulnerable circumstances; others left supportive families and promising futures. They were attracted by the movement's slick online propaganda machine that devoted far more space to images of public health, the care of orphans, moral behaviour and fraternal bonding than to torture and beheading. They left behind families who felt loss and confusion, and who could not understand what they had done.[8]

Daesh's multilingual online media operation became noteworthy for its global reach and its "in-group"-promoting finesse as well as for its deliberately gruesome violence. The title of its English-language online magazine, *Dabiq*, evoked the location on the plains of northern Syria, near the early caliphate's frontier with Byzantium, where according to medieval eschatology Muslim armies would fight their final apocalyptic battle with the Romans. Propaganda aimed at outside audiences made much of the coming Armageddon, the zero-sum civilisational confrontation that would occur when the so-called "grey zone" of coexistence and compromise was extinguished, and true believers and unbelievers were forced by violence into their respective camps.

IS's Arabic-language newspaper intended for consumption within Iraq and Syria, at the same time, was more pragmatically focused on reporting the more local war it was actually fighting. And if men and women arrived from Germany, Britain, and Australia with dreams of building utopia—and, sometimes, with romantic Orientalist fantasies of camels, lions, and the desert—the movement's more significant local supporters, like Iraqi ex-Baʿthists, had a more immediate and pragmatic agenda. They saw Daesh as a vehicle to regain the power they had lost when the American occupation authorities purged the Iraqi army and administration after 2003; subsequent Shi'a-led governments had failed to build a national consensus that would reintegrate the Sunni Arab communities that had historically dominated the country.[9]

But the caliphate's capacity as a practical political project, let alone as a world-ending instrument of God's will, was limited. The imaginary utopia failed to materialise. Instead, its rule was quickly reduced to imposing discipline by extreme violence. Its claim to restore Muslim leadership actually meant the savage persecution and murder of Syrian and Iraqi Christians and other minorities. What it called adherence to the Prophet's way meant vandalising the region's ancient and early Islamic heritage, which like the Taliban it saw only as idolatrous. Its pretended restoration of a caliphal golden age was limited to symbolic gestures like the much-touted launch of a gold dinar currency, while its actual economy ran on extorting small businesses, selling cut-price oil, and hawking looted antiquities on the black market in the Gulf and Europe. Its claim to have reinstated true sharia came down to asserting the legality of enslavement, and staging public executions and corporal punishment.

Embracing a Muslim supremacism no less hateful than other kinds of supremacist politics elsewhere in the world, Daesh embarked on a genocidal campaign against the Kurdish-speaking Yazidi minority in northern Iraq, subjecting thousands of Yazidi women and girls to sexual slavery. Advocating an extreme Sunni sectarianism that was sharpened by the recent experience of civil war in Iraq and Syria, Daesh's spokesmen claimed that "nothing will work" with Shi'is "other than slicing their throats and striking their necks." There were suicide bombings at Shi'i mosques. In 2014, between 1,000 and 1,700 young Iraqi soldiers, apparently mostly Shi'is, were massacred when Daesh overran Tikrit, north of Baghdad.

Other Islamists—whether because they were more pragmatic, or because they were alarmed and offended by IS's pretensions—as well as Muslim religious authorities, both Sunni and Shi'i, emphatically refuted the so-called caliphate's claims to any kind of legitimacy. Many recruits to Daesh had been Saudis, and core principles of Wahhabi salafism—notably its insistence that devotion to God must mean separating oneself from anything and anyone associated with unbelief—were central to Daesh's ideology and propaganda. But Saudi clerics of all persuasions condemned Daesh as a gang of "Kharijites" dividing the community: "not jihadis but thugs and robbers." By 2015, both Iraqi Shi'i militia forces backed by Iran and Kurdish Sunni militia backed by the United States were fighting against Daesh on the ground, while a coalition of foreign nations' airpower bombed it from the sky. Neither Washington nor Tehran would admit it, but against this enemy, Iran and the US were effectively allies. Daesh, meanwhile, had become embroiled in intra-Islamist violence in Syria and had even incurred the hostility of Ayman al-Zawahiri's al-Qa'ida.[10]

While Daesh's spectacular violence exerted the terrible fascination on the world that its architects intended, less serious attention was paid to the way Muslims lived through its reign of terror. The market for generalised anti-Muslim prejudice in Europe and America flourished on the deliberate horror of its on-screen murders of journalists and aid workers, and its high-profile terrorist atrocities in European cities, feeding the equation of Islam with violence and aiding Daesh's own polarising agenda. Xenophobic and right-wing commentators rushed to find, or manufacture, evidence of Muslims' sympathy for the movement and to make hateful celebrities of anyone, whether knife-wielding sociopaths or influencer-groomed schoolgirls, who had left Western countries to join it.

In November 2015, following Daesh's suicide attacks in Paris that killed 130 people and injured more than four hundred, one British newspaper reported a "shock poll" with the headline "1 in 5 Brit Muslims' Sympathy for Jihadis." The paper was later forced to admit that the story was "significantly misleading," but it made no apology. The fact that a different survey carried out by the same polling company earlier the same year had come up with a slightly larger percentage of British *non*-Muslims expressing some "sympathy" with young

Muslims leaving the UK "to join fighters in Syria" did not trouble its editorial line. Yet another opinion poll run in 2015 had found that more than 80 per cent of a sample of British Muslims across all age groups thought Britain was a good place for Muslims to live, most did not support the project of an Islamic state (let alone that of Daesh), and only 4 (not 20) per cent had any sympathy for terrorism as a form of political action. This poll, which informed a TV documentary aired in April 2016, entitled *What British Muslims Really Think*, was itself much criticised as misleading and divisive. It was wittily lampooned on social media by Muslims using the documentary's title as a hashtag. Meanwhile, hate crimes against Muslims in Britain were reported to have increased by 300 per cent.[11]

The internal tensions between the utopian ideology, the limited state-building, and the apocalyptic rhetoric of the Islamic State movement might well have unravelled its "caliphate" in the end, even without the coalition bombing campaign against it, and so might the obscene atrocity of its rule that rapidly eroded whatever support it had in the areas under its control. Despite its pretensions to the contrary, Daesh was never able to mount a war of Islam against the West, for the simple reason that the vast majority of Muslims worldwide, as well as the most courageous of those living under its own brutal rule, rejected it and its propaganda. Daesh's jihad was, first of all, a war over Islam against other Muslims. It was only secondarily a war claiming to be for Islam against non-Muslims. It actively sought a global war: it claimed responsibility for terrorist attacks across Europe, and from the US and Canada to Israel, Mozambique, Australia, New Zealand, and the Philippines. The great majority of its victims, though, were other Muslims in predominantly Muslim countries. Its selective use of Islamic law and scripture, notably its references to the Qur'an and to medieval religious scholars, was driven not by fidelity to the faith's tradition, but by the movement's anti-intellectualism and its practical need to claim its own legitimacy by rejecting all other living Muslim authorities (including prominent salafi scholars who denounced it), and to justify its military and political positions.[12]

Daesh's deliberately curated image was a horror show of pseudo-medieval theatricality, intended to shock and provoke. But its ideology, strategy, and methods were all very much of its own time. Its radical eschatology and murderous extremism were not, as its spokesmen and some outside commentators equally hurried to claim, authentically "very Islamic." They were, rather, an Islamist variation on the politics of redemptive, utopian, and genocidal violence familiar from elsewhere in the global history of the twentieth century. Nazi Germany, Cambodia under the Khmer Rouge, and Hutu Power in Rwanda had in their ideologically different ways and in different contexts—but all, crucially, in the context of war and mobilising mass politics—similarly claimed to be saving their community from existential threat, obliterating their deadly enemies, and building a radiant future in the promised land. What was significant about Daesh was not the question of whether, and to what extent, it was "really" Islamic. It was the fact that it embodied just one, particularly hideous, possibility of what Islam, like other belief systems, could become in the conditions of the modern world's utopian politics, spectacle-hungry mass media, and unrestricted war.[13]

◇◇◇◇◇◇◇

For all their atrocity, and the attention they necessarily attracted, neither al-Qaʿida nor Daesh, which after 2017 lost its territorial base and became another amorphous global terrorist brand, could come close to monopolising the meaning of Islam in the early twenty-first century. Some of their own ideological influences, especially in the Gulf, distanced themselves forcefully from both their methods and their doctrines. Salafi scholars re-emphasised the importance of scholarly credentials for anyone giving legitimate rulings on sharia, repudiating the militants' claim to be interpreters of holy law in their own right. Saudi Arabia embarked on a lavish rebranding of the kingdom's image in the West that de-emphasised Wahhabism and promoted archaeology, the arts, sports, and tourism—while cracking down ever more harshly on political dissent. Other conservative Gulf monarchies promoted their importance as central nodes in the global circuits of finance, real estate, technology, and trade.

Meanwhile, other forms of Islam—as an artistic and intellectual heritage, a body of learning and devotional practice, and as individual identity, family ritual, community belonging and global solidarity—had multiplied and diversified everywhere from China and Southeast Asia through the Middle East to Europe and North America. Muslims cultivated *javanmardi* (an almost untranslatable ethic of manly chivalry) and subtly subversive femininity in gyms in Iran; expressed masculinity by "drifting" (high-speed skidding in stolen cars) on the suburban highways of Saudi Arabia; lived gay male lives in Lebanon; debated legacies of colonialism, women's rights, and public space in France; and pursued personal happiness while navigating racial and social injustice in the United States.[14]

In all of these places, being Muslim had come to mean particular things, overlapping with or expressed through ancestry, language, food, music, manners, clothing, neighbourhood and nationality, citizenship and opinion, while never losing its connections to the longer history of the faith and to the wider presence of a global community. The immense variety of Muslim life in the modern world made a mockery of the easy classification of Islam as a single cultural system, a distinct social order, or a separate civilisation destined to fight for its survival against the forces of unbelief, or for world domination against "the West." It resisted salafi disciplining into a uniform moral code just as it escaped from Western governments' clumsy and discriminatory racial profiling, generalised surveillance, and deradicalisation programs that often only heightened tensions with, and among, their own Muslim citizens. Muslim life was embodied in Muslim people, who lived their lives in different social and cultural worlds, in their own ways, just as they always had done, all over the world.

This variety of Muslim life was a product of both the connectedness and the fragmentation characterising the globalised world where Muslims now lived. Globalisation had been going on, albeit at a much slower pace, for a long time. By 1850 already, Arabic-speaking

Bedouin in Syria were wearing Lancashire cotton shirts, and by the 1870s, virtually everyone in Morocco was drinking black tea mixed with sugar, both commodities imported in great quantities on British ships. Muslims in Southeast Asia, India, and West Africa had been incorporated into an increasingly Euro-Atlantic-centred economy earlier still. By the 2000s, the ancient urban centres of Cairo, Fez, Isfahan and even Istanbul were themselves becoming peripheral to the skyrocketing cities of the Gulf in Abu Dhabi and Dubai, and to the networks of technology that connected mobile individuals to wider communities everywhere from Los Angeles to Shanghai. With no single, central source of teaching and no priesthood, religious authority in Islam had always been widely distributed. With the emergence of new media and the digital public sphere, ideas of what Islam should be and what it might mean to be Muslim proliferated as never before. Some commentators in the 1990s saw the increasing ability of individuals to define their faith, and themselves, as evidence of an "Islamic Reformation" like that of early modern Christianity. Again, this was not a wholly new idea. A "Reformation" in the Muslim world had first been anticipated in the 1890s by admirers of nineteenth-century reformers like Muhammad Abduh, who in his own time was already thought of as a potential Martin Luther of Islam. Before TV preachers, internet chatrooms, and online influencers, print and literacy had already been expected to have transformative effects on Muslim life.[15]

What was occurring a century later was not a belated Muslim replay of developments in sixteenth-century Christianity, but something much more in tune with its own time. In the post–Cold War apogee and subsequent crisis of globalisation, two apparently divergent but simultaneous trends were visible. On the one hand, as unifying political projects collapsed and sources of authority multiplied, markets for commodities of all kinds—ideological as well as material ones— proliferated, and individuals had greater choice over how to shape themselves and their lifestyles than ever before. On the other hand, their different spaces and societies were increasingly pulled together into a single, connected global public sphere, where an event in one place, or something written or spoken in one language, could almost instantly produce reactions in very different, distant contexts.

This was visible already in the 1980s. In September 1988, the British-Indian writer Salman Rushdie published his baroque, magical-realist novel *The Satanic Verses*. The book was a formally daring work of art, drawing irreverently on elements of the author's Muslim heritage. Its title referred to a highly contested, obscure episode in the biography of the Prophet and early anti-Muslim polemics. Controversy over the book's allegedly offensive portrayal of the Prophet Muhammad broke out almost as soon as it appeared. There were riots in Mumbai (Bombay), the city of Rushdie's birth and childhood, and the book was banned in India. Despite Rushdie's own antiracist politics, for some Muslims in Britain the book's treatment of themes from Islamic history seemed to reinforce a familiar message that their culture and beliefs could be mocked, and their dignity did not count. Muslim critics asked for an explanatory statement to be added to the book, and for it to be voluntarily withdrawn from further publication. But then, in January 1989, copies of the book were burned by protestors in the British city of Bradford. A month later, the ailing Ayatollah Khomeini issued a ruling (which popularised the Arabic word *fatwa*, a judicial opinion, in the West) calling for the author's assassination.

Responses to *The Satanic Verses* had little to do with the book itself, and everything to do with the contexts in which it became a lightning rod. In India, Rushdie's novel became a proxy for long-standing but increasingly severe communal tensions. To British Muslims, for whom a perceived insult to the Prophet was deeply injurious, it reinforced beliefs that establishment culture denigrated and discriminated against them. (Conservative government ministers lecturing them on how to be British only seemed to prove them right.) In Iran, the hard-line faction around Khomeini had been weakened by the failure to win the war against Iraq, which had ended in 1988, and reformist politicians within the regime were trying to re-establish relations with Europe. The notorious fatwa reasserted Khomeini's pre-eminence domestically as well as in international Islamist opinion, marginalising the reformers in Tehran. What became "the Rushdie affair" was opportunistically seized upon both by Khomeini and his hard-line supporters within Iran, and by anti-Muslim opinion-formers in the West, to pursue their own agendas within their own societies.

To many, the controversy seemed to crystallise a deep incompatibility between what one commentator called "our profoundest Western traditions" of free expression on the one hand, and the sensibilities of Muslims on the other. But in fact, free expression in Britain had rarely been unlimited: the end of official censorship in theatres had come only twenty years earlier. There was still a law against blasphemy in England (even if it was no longer practically enforceable, it would not be repealed until 2008): as the law's secularist critics pointed out, this was discriminatory as well as illiberal in that it specified offences only against Anglican Christianity. Muslims' beliefs clearly did not have parity of protection under the law. At the same time, Muslims and other artists and intellectuals from the Global South were among those defending Rushdie and denouncing the threat against him. Some British non-Muslims, meanwhile, supported Rushdie's right to free expression and condemned the threat of violence against him and his publishers, while also noting that demonstrators against the book themselves had "no other means of expression in public," and that their own protests, too, were "a legitimate form of expression." With the author forced into hiding amidst violent attacks on his publishers, the murder of one of the book's translators, and an outpouring of anxiety about free speech, the Rushdie affair exemplified the connected and contentious public sphere in which Muslims and others, Mumbai and Bradford, London and Tehran, were all bound up.[16]

While Khomeini's fatwa became symbolic of Islamist intolerance, within Iran itself things were changing. Khomeini died only four months after issuing his infamous ruling, in June 1989. Over the next decade, an Iranian "intellectual revolution" saw conservative and reformist clerics, and secular-modernist intellectuals, reopen the terrain of public and political debate within the country. Public space (parks, shopping malls, outdoor sports) had a revival too. A new generation of young, educated urban Iranians, including large numbers of young women from outside the major cities who now attended university, created their own subcultures in such new spaces, as well as in schools and universities that had lost the ideological radicalism of the early revolutionary years. For these young Iranians, as Iranian sociologist Asef Bayat put it, "God existed but did not prevent them from drinking alcohol or dating." By the early 2000s, there was a "dissonance and disconnect" between the way especially urban, middle-class Iranians lived their personal lives and the formal observances expected of them in public.[17]

By 2009, this dissonance had opened up a gulf between what some observers saw as a "post-Islamist" trend in Iran, and the "second Islamic republic" of the religious populist President Mahmoud Ahmadinejad, supported by those in the establishment committed to doubling down on patriarchal, ideological rule in the name of state security. It was this gulf between the regime and society, combined with the economic hardships caused by sanctions against the country, that produced the "Green Movement" of popular protests around the 2009 Iranian presidential election—the largest popular political mobilisation since the revolution thirty years earlier—and a subsequent wave of nationwide protests in 2017. When Mahsa Amini, a young Kurdish Iranian woman, was murdered in police custody in September 2022, having been arrested for allegedly violating dress code laws, there were more nationwide protests, led by women and schoolgirls under the slogan "Woman, life, freedom."

The Islamic republic was increasingly dominated less by the clerical leadership than by factional struggles within it, and by the generals of the *pasdaran* (the Revolutionary Guard Corps) and paramilitary forces. They resorted to violent repression and coercion, as the shah's regime once had, to crush dissent and maintain themselves in power. But they also sponsored new, not obviously "pro-regime" media to try to control the narrative of events in Iran and the wider world, and to reorient public opinion in support of the Islamic republic. Iran might still be imagined in Europe and the US as the model of a monolithic, civilisational otherness. But even there, not only could the diversity of ways of being Muslim, and arguments about the community and its future, not easily be stamped out; they were occurring both across society and within the regime itself.[18]

This multiplication of sources of religious authority, and of ways of living as a Muslim in the modern world, was no less apparent among Sunni Muslims. The conservative shaykh Yusuf al-Qaradawi was already highly influential across the Arabic-reading world when in 2004 he was elected, at a meeting held in Dublin, Ireland, to lead the "International Association of Muslim Scholars." The association brought together representatives of several doctrinal schools (Sunnis, Shi'is, Ibadis from Oman and Zaydis from Yemen) with the aim of providing a single authoritative source of guidance and legal rulings for Muslims of all backgrounds, anywhere in the world. Born in Egypt and trained at al-Azhar, Qaradawi was for a long time identified with the Muslim Brotherhood. Like other Egyptian Islamists, he was arrested during the Nasserist repression of the Brotherhood in the 1950s, and left the country in 1961. Qaradawi settled in Qatar, where he gave religious instruction to the country's ruler, and where by the early 2000s, aged in his seventies, he became famous as host of the popular satellite-TV show *Law and Life* (*Al-shari'a wa'l-hayat*).

Over a sixty-year career, until his death in 2022, Qaradawi gave legal opinions (fatwas) in his books and online in response to questions that arose in the daily life of Muslims young and old from all over the world. Drawing on the ideas of Hassan al-Banna, he advocated the "cultivation" (*tarbiya*) of properly religious, ethical individuality in the service of the regeneration of the community, the global *umma*, as a single whole. He was banned from entering the USA and the UK as an extremist and a supporter of terrorism, in particular because of his endorsement of Palestinian and Iraqi suicide bombings in the early 2000s. (He claimed that such attacks were legitimate acts of self-defence, though only when directed at military targets, not at civilians.) He also condemned the 9/11 attacks, and other Islamist atrocities, notably the March 2004 train bombings in Madrid and the bombings of July 7, 2005, in London.

Qaradawi sought to wrest legitimacy away from the self-appointed ideologues of al-Qaʿida and Daesh and put it back in the hands of legal scholars like himself. Adopting a Qurʾanic formula that describes Muslims as "a people of moderation" or "of the middle-ground," he sought to present his views as those of "the middle way," (*al-wasatiyya*). This, for Qaradawi, meant upholding an unchanging Islamic truth in changing times, and steering a "moderate" path between the most stringent conservatism and what he considered a too-permissive liberalism. (He advised, for example, that women should cover their heads, but not their face or hands.) He argued for educational and career opportunities for women, for democracy in the Arab world in place of orchestrated elections, which he called "a race with only one horse running," and for agreement between Christian and Muslim religious conservatives on the "immorality" of homosexuality. Qaradawi's conservative messages brought ideas of individual salvation, community belonging, and political purpose to global mass audiences through online and satellite media. Rather than allowing any individual believer to be his or her own interpreter of the faith, the new media landscape enabled the authority of the religious scholar to reassert itself, in some ways, more powerfully than ever before.[19]

While Qaradawi sought to create a single global Islamic authority, even his global pre-eminence was not uncontested. Other scholars, at the same time, promoted other views. Salafism claimed a more authentic, stringent return to the pristine tradition of the community to whom the Qurʾan was first revealed, often eschewing political activism entirely and focusing on individual ritual practice and the minutiae of the sharia as an inflexible rule for living. Conversely, other more progressive or radically liberationist perspectives sought to get behind the legal tradition, foregrounding a "Qurʾan-first" interpretation of Islam and reading God's word as a guide to action in contemporary contexts of patriarchal, racial or imperial oppression. Muslims mobilising against the apartheid regime in South Africa in the 1980s and early 1990s, and campaigning for gender and racial justice in the United States, drew on a nascent Islamic liberation theology, developed especially by a generation of commentators and activists born in the 1950s like the South African scholar and anti-apartheid campaigner Farid Esack, and the African American Qur'an scholar and gender justice advocate Amina Wadud. An earlier generation, drawing on both their Muslim heritage and their European academic disciplines, like the Tunisian historian Mohamed Talbi and the Algerian-born French philosopher Mohammed Arkoun, argued for a recentring of a shared Mediterranean space and heritage, against both the anti-migrant border policing of the European Union and the anti-Western rhetoric of North African Islamists. The noise and hostility of the global public sphere after 9/11 made such voices harder to hear, but did not silence them.[20]

◇◇◇◇◇◇◇◇

In this globalised and pluralistic public sphere, no one was any closer than they had been in the 1740s or the 1920s to unifying all Muslims around a single interpretation of the faith or a single vision for the community. But everyone involved in the debate was now plugged into the same globalised networks of mobility and communication. Often, this now meant adopting the idioms of the media and the market. When the Danish newspaper *Jyllands-Posten* published provocative cartoons depicting the Prophet Muhammad in 2005, claiming to be combating self-censorship and championing free expression, Qaradawi's response was to endorse a consumer boycott of Danish products. In 2002, amidst calls for Muslims to avoid buying American products as a gesture of support for Palestine, an entrepreneurial businessman in France set up "Mecca Cola" as an alternative to the US-owned global soft drink brands and announced a corporate ethics of donating 20 per cent of profits to charitable causes, split evenly between Palestinian and European NGOs. Mecca Cola was initially marketed with the politically engaged tagline "No more drinking stupid—drink with commitment," and later with the hashtag "Be different" and the slogan "Live the moment and discover the taste of freedom." Activist capitalism and consumer branding could be Muslim, too.

Beyond, or actively in conflict with, the ruling norms of the media and the market, individuals could also put the global environment in which Muslims now lived to more radical, rebellious, and revolutionary use. Protest could be staged both in the public space of the street and in the personal pages of the blogosphere, especially through the individual's physical body, which took on a new potency in this new context. The popular protests against authoritarianism, corruption and indignity that would overthrow the Tunisian dictator Zayn al-Abidin Ben Ali and spread across the Arab world in 2011 began in December 2010, after twenty-eight-year-old Mohamed Bouazizi set himself on fire in protest at the police's confiscation of the unlicensed fruit and vegetable cart that was his only means of making a living.

Self-immolations by citizens deprived of their rights, sometimes enacted as dramatic public statements in front of public buildings, were not infrequent across North Africa—several others occurred around the same time across the border in Algeria, without having a similar touch-paper effect. But Bouazizi's martyrdom—he died of his injuries after a few weeks' agony in hospital—became a focal point, and an expression of a more widely shared revolt. Almost a year later, in October 2011 and in the midst of an ongoing revolution in Egypt, nineteen-year-old Egyptian feminist student and blogger Alia al-Mahdy posted a nude photograph of herself in her blog *A Rebel's Diary*, with the captions "nude art" and "secularism is the solution," staking a claim to women's free expression and the liberation of women's bodies. Al-Mahdy, who later described herself as an atheist who was "never into politics," attracted worldwide attention and ignited a storm of controversy. Vilified in Egypt by secular leftists and religious conservatives alike, she was condemned for betraying the revolution as well as for licentious immodesty, received death threats, and was forced into exile.[21]

Al-Mahdy's offence was to uncover a young female body in protest at patriarchy and hypocrisy, in contrast to Bouazizi's sacrificing of a young male one in protest at poverty and authoritarianism. Egyptian security forces had taken to using so-called "virginity tests"—a form of licensed rape—to discipline and repress women demonstrators against the military regime. (The practice had also been used elsewhere against women, including in British immigration control in the 1960s and 1970s.) Her protest was both directed at such state-sanctioned sexual abuse—and at the rampant, everyday forms of sexual harassment experienced by women in Egypt—and criticised for playing into the very image of "debauchery" that the police used to accuse the women they arrested. Through the global media, ordinary people's individual bodies could become symbols for whole societies.

At the same time, the ways that people, especially women, chose to present their bodies and act in public space could also be a highly individual and personal way of expressing selfhood and belief. Some European governments, led by France and Belgium, moved to ban full face-veils (the *niqab*) in public and even, in France, modest Muslim women's swimwear (the so-called "burkini," which resembles nothing so much as a wetsuit with a swimming cap). Such signs of religious belonging were associated, in France, with anti-republican "separatism," and in Britain, with what the government took to calling "non-violent extremism." The argument, especially in France, usually ran that such forms of dress were coercively imposed, and evidence of Islam's oppression of women, depriving them of their social and political agency. In fact, the headscarves worn by Muslim women in the economically deprived high-rise Paris suburbs did not prevent them from organising politically when they felt their rights were being infringed upon, nor from using the state's own professed religious neutrality to point out when it was discriminating against them. Muslim women in Britain who became salafis were often converts, or from non-salafi Muslim family backgrounds. They generally chose their forms of veiling, just as non-salafi Muslim women did, as signs of their own spirituality, cultural preference, or self-expression—as a way to present themselves in public, where they were so often misrepresented.[22]

By the early 2000s, halal food, sharia-compliant banking, Islamic music videos, fashion-conscious headscarves and deliberately enveloping abayas (long, loose dresses) had all become icons of Islam as a global religious brand. In the twenty-first-century world, religious affiliation was becoming in some ways a commodity on offer in competition with other options in the market of identity-making. In the last quarter of the twentieth century and at the beginning of the twenty-first, being Muslim became bound up in the proliferating products of global capitalism. Many possible meanings of being Muslim could now be expressed in consumer choices, through Islamic-branded options from finance to food, dress, music, and dating, the identifiable styles of strict religiosity or their overt rejection. Being Muslim could be about personal belief and piety or it could be what one was by birth. It could be a conscious conversion or a cultural inheritance. It could be tied to a racialised identity and to the experience of being a minority subjected to varying degrees of toleration or intolerance. But whatever it was, it had become a part of the globalised world of capitalism, commodities, and consumer lifestyles. Even if it was defined by rejecting them, it could not escape from them.[23]

◇◇◇◇◇◇◇

Even as Muslims' lives everywhere were shaped by the same global forces as everyone else's, Muslims in many places were finding themselves penned in by others' definitions of Islam as a separate, threatening, alien presence. Especially from 2016 onwards, and in such different places as China, the United States, Myanmar, and India, a related series of fearful and violent fantasies about Muslims as inherently dangerous and subversive were amplified into public policy. Such policies, at a minimum, discriminated against Muslims as a whole, and at worst, subjected Muslims to overt and sometimes genocidal violence.

The right-wing Hindu-nationalist Indian People's Party (Bharatiya Janata Party, or BJP), the inheritor of the racialised Hindutva ideology of the 1930s, came to power in India in 2014 amidst ongoing communal tension, and following Islamist terror attacks in Mumbai in 2008 and 2011. In 2019, India's long-running conflict with Pakistan over Kashmir (the Muslim-majority but Hindu-ruled province that had been divided between India and Pakistan since partition) escalated. A lockdown was imposed in the Indian-administered parts of the province, and its autonomous constitutional status was revoked. The government's move, on the far side of the country that same year, to exclude Muslim residents and refugees in the northeastern state of Assam from citizenship similarly expressed and escalated anti-Muslim sentiment and violence in the country. A new citizenship law in 2019, ostensibly aiming to clarify voting rights and expose "illegal" immigrants, but clearly intended to advance the ultranationalist agenda for a Hindu-majoritarian state, excluded almost two million people in Assam from the national citizenship register. Lives were destroyed—some people committed suicide. Muslim communities established in Assam since at least the 1970s were now considered as "infiltrators" and "illegal encroachers" on the land. Police sent to evict them burned and bulldozed homes; people who got in the way were beaten and shot.[24]

Forty years earlier, in 1978, the nationalist military junta in Myanmar (Burma) had begun to strip its own Muslim minority of their citizenship rights, which had been unproblematically recognised between independence in 1948 and the coup that began military rule in 1962. The Rohingya community in northwest Burma, along the coast of the Bay of Bengal, sometimes traced their presence there as far back as the eighth century, to the Indian Ocean coastal trade that had involved Arab, Persian, and central Asian Muslims. Before the 1962 coup, Rohingya were referred to as Burmese, and there was Rohingya-language programming on national radio. But there was also unrest in the region, sometimes involving Muslim militants and communist insurgents, and a border with East Pakistan, later Bangladesh, whose security the Burmese military distrusted. The belief that Rohingya were illegal immigrants from Bengal—where, conversely, they were deemed not to be Bengali—took root. By the 1980s the junta had made the Rohingya into the world's largest stateless population. In 2017, they became the targets of genocidal violence, with the Myanmar army burning villages, killing some nine thousand men, subjecting women and girls to sexual violence, and forcing more than seven hundred thousand people to flee as refugees into camps in Bangladesh.[25]

Whether ideological or opportunistic, the use of anti-Muslim rhetoric served to bolster anxious, racialising nationalisms in very different contexts across the world. The rising trend of Islamophobia in the 2010s became a global phenomenon, but nowhere was it wholly new. Donald Trump's demand for a "total and complete shutdown of Muslims entering the United States," made on the campaign trail in 2015, ratcheted up Islamophobic rhetoric as a political tactic and prompted a spike in anti-Muslim hate crime. But it came on the heels of existing covert practices by US immigration and citizenship authorities and law enforcement agencies that already discriminated against Muslims. These programs had been instituted after 2001, when Muslims, from being a mostly invisible American minority, came under blanket suspicion as enemies and outsiders. They continued through the years when Barack Obama—who, from his East African heritage, shared a middle name with the Prophet's grandson, Hussein—was president.

Many Americans increasingly recognised the discrimination faced by their Muslim neighbours and were prepared to take a stand against it. In January 2017, when the first Trump administration's executive order barring refugees and citizens from six Muslim-majority countries from entering the US came into force, thousands of people protested at airports across the country. But it remained clear that demonising Muslims (despite, or perhaps because of, the fact that Muslims made up less than 2 per cent of the US population) was effective in rallying support on the American right. It was a powerful way of focusing anxiety and anger among all those who held, or were susceptible to, an older, white, conservative image of America, at odds with the country's changing demography and social liberalism, and fearing the end of their dominance over both the nation's politics and the definition of its identity.[26]

Trump spent much of his first term as president stoking tensions with China, too, but with respect to demonising Muslims, at least, his politics and China's had something in common. In China, though, the violence went much further. The Communist regime's campaign of mosque demolition, mass incarceration, "re-education," forced labour, sterilisation and enforced birth control against Uighurs and other Turkic Muslims in Xinjiang Province, in northwest China, was a massive escalation of state violence in the region. It too had its roots in older patterns of prejudice. Xinjiang's "emergency" developed from ways of classifying and governing that, since the foundation of the People's Republic in 1949, had seen Muslims (Hui who lived in Xi'an or Guangzhou as well as Uighur or Turkic Muslims from the edges of central Asia) as a racial rather than a religious group, a minority "nationality" (*minzu*), less "civilised" than Han Chinese, more inclined to "feudal" practices, and in need of guidance, and occasionally firm discipline, to bring them up to the speed of modern life.

During the Cultural Revolution in the late 1960s, mosques were attacked as relics of "old culture." Perceptions of Xinjiang, in particular, as a hotbed of violent dissent were inherited from a history of revolt that went back to the Qing Empire's conquest of East Turkestan in the eighteenth century. More recent unrest there had been caused, above all, by socioeconomic grievances that intersected with ethnic difference. The region's Han Chinese population had increased from 6 per cent in 1949 to 40 per cent in 1982, and the indigenous Uighur population felt disadvantaged and discriminated against. After 2001, just as Russia did in Chechnya, the Chinese state began to adopt the US rhetoric of "war on terror" to refer to what was often disproportionate state repression in response to protests and ethnic violence in Xinjiang. In the 2010s, as China's rulers worried about the spillover of instability from the Middle East and jihadi activism in Southeast Asia, the country's Muslims became targets of a campaign ostensibly against "terrorism, separatism, and religious extremism." The government identified Islam, not socioeconomic and political inequalities, as the cause of unrest in Xinjiang, and forcible Sinicization as the solution. As increasing evidence emerged of what was happening in Xinjiang, much of the rest of the world increasingly saw the so-called counter-terror campaign as a genocide.[27]

In their very different but simultaneous ways, and each for their own reactionary domestic political reasons, Indian, American, and Chinese nationalists all targeted Muslims as civilisational enemies and as threats to national security. While varying enormously in their intensity and violence, by 2019 such policies had all given practical shape to prejudices that dehumanised Muslims, seeing them uniformly as enemies to be excluded or contained. Less overtly violent, but hardly less dehumanising and insidious, politics flourished elsewhere, in the generally anti-migrant, particularly anti-Muslim rhetoric and policy platforms of the extreme right that mainstream conservative politicians were also increasingly adopting in Germany, the Netherlands, Sweden, France, Austria, and Britain.

Like other religious, racist, and xenophobic persecutions at other times, all of this had little to do with who most Muslims really were, what they actually thought or did, or what being Muslim meant to them. It stemmed, instead, from a fantasy about them created in others' imaginations. Just as antisemitism made actually-existing Jewish people the targets of its hatred on the basis of a belief in the existence of "the Jew"—a wholly fantastical, imagined figure spun out of religio-racial fears, conspiracies, and slanders—so Islamophobia made actual Muslim people its targets on the basis of an imaginary, ahistorical caricature of "Islam." This fantasy, in turn, grew out of a mythical view of history: history as a story of separate, unitary "civilisations," Western, Chinese, Hindu, and Buddhist (Russian nationalists would add a Slavic, Christian Orthodox one), each needing urgent protection from the imagined threat of an equally imaginary, unitary, and hostile Islamic civilisation.

Such ideas sold well, and easily, in the global marketplace. They made easy, and often convenient, sense of difficult and often discomforting problems. Politicians and ordinary people in many places signed up to them. They would only increase in currency through the crises that battered the global economy, the poorest in society, the post-1945 system of international law and order, and the complacency of democratic liberalism in the early twenty-first century. In a time of hyper-connectedness, the myth of civilisations was less useful than it had ever been for actually understanding the world. But it was also perhaps more powerful, more popular, and more widespread than ever in shaping perceptions of it.

◇◇◇◇◇◇◇

In September 2020, over several days, a special criminal court in Paris heard testimonies from survivors of the attack by two Islamist terrorists that had killed twelve people and injured eleven others at the office of the satirical magazine *Charlie Hebdo* in January 2015. A month before, on the other side of the world, a court in New Zealand had heard victim impact statements from families of the fifty-one people killed by a white supremacist terrorist at a mosque in Christchurch in March 2019. In both places, survivors of the violence talked about the human body: the voices and the physical presence of those who had died, the physical aftereffects of gunshot injuries. *Charlie*'s web designer explained that "none of us escaped," and told of the effects of the two bullets that hit him, leaving him with reduced mobility, constant trembling and tiredness, and a crutch that he propped against the witness stand, insisting on standing up to talk. One of the Christchurch survivors spoke of his lasting spinal injuries, his recurrent nightmares, the flashbacks experienced by his ten-year-old son, and his worries about his child's mental health. Another told the shooter in the dock, "You are…someone who's dumb enough not to realise that beyond the skin, all humans are the same."[28]

The fact that it had become necessary to point out something so obvious was perhaps a sign of how far the rhetoric of difference and dehumanisation had gone. The near simultaneity of the two hearings was a striking testimony to the common experiences of the victims of violence, whether Muslim or non-Muslim, inflicted by those, whether Islamists or Islamophobes, who put the rhetoric into action. The fact that they occurred on opposite sides of the world illustrated the global reach of such shared experiences, and of the processes of demonisation and violence that produced them. Despite the twentieth century's liberal and progressive efforts to enshrine a common recognition of universal human rights, and despite the atrocities of the twentieth century that had shown all too clearly where such dehumanisation, in denial of those rights, could lead, it seemed that in the first quarter of the twenty-first century such obvious things had become harder to see. The mythical narrative of civilisations at war, in which both the jihadists in Paris and the gunman in Christchurch believed, would account for their actions as manifestations of age-old, irreconcilable enmity. That narrative only added fuel to the fire, while failing to explain the real roots of the violence. It denied the reality of histories that had never been self-contained, but were always interwoven, and the shared human aspirations and experiences of those who made them.

From the very beginning, Muslims had made a distinctive world of Islam, with its own history and institutions, languages and laws, and they did so within other worlds with which they had much in common. They understood Islam both as a message for all humanity for all time, and as the way of life and worldview of a particular community in particular times and places. It would be impossible to understand Islam historically, as a monotheistic faith, a warning of God's judgment, and a claim to universal sovereignty, without the wider world of late antiquity, its empires and visions of God and man, into which the Prophet and his message came. It would be impossible to understand it as a legal and ethical system, a code of dynastic legitimacy, and a view of cosmic history, without the wider medieval and early modern worlds of conquering ambition, charismatic piety, and cross-continental trade of which Muslims became part and that they helped to build. And without the global pressures and transformations that Muslims experienced, and in which they participated, in the nineteenth and twentieth centuries, Islam would not have become what it was in 2020—a conservative program of social morality and a mobilising force of revolutionary change, a personal practice of devotion and a shared sense of identity, a claim to racialised difference and to nonracial universalism, a repressive demand for conformity and obedience and a generous vision of human liberation and flourishing.

Like other people, Muslims have always made their own history, but never just as they chose: they have always lived under material conditions determined by forces larger than themselves, as well as seeing their world, and how they might act in it, through imaginations given them by their own tradition. Their past has always been part of larger patterns. Now, more than ever, it can only be understood, not by generalisations about "civilisation identity," but as part of what the Palestinian American literary scholar Edward Said, writing in 2001, aptly called "the bewildering interdependence of our time."[29]

ACKNOWLEDGMENTS

The idea for this book first came out of my teaching in the history department at Princeton in 2004–7, so my first thanks are to my extraordinary colleagues there—especially the late Bob Tignor, Tony Grafton, Michael Cook, Peter Brown, Gyan Prakash, Molly Greene, John Haldon, Helen Tilley, Michael Gordin, Mike Laffan, Ishita Pande and Eileen Kane—and to the students who first made me think that someone needed to write a book like this. Students in my SOAS seminars on the history of northwest Africa in 2007–9, and those at Oxford who have taken papers with me on the global history of the nineteenth and twentieth centuries, or whose research I have been lucky enough to supervise, have been crucial in shaping my thinking about many of the themes explored here, as have other extraordinary colleagues, above all, Richard Reid, John Parker, Ben Fortna, Nelida Fuccaro, Charles Tripp, and Laleh Khalili (all then at SOAS), and in Oxford, the global history contingent at the History Faculty, the members of the Middle East Centre, and the fellowship of Trinity College.

I have also learned immensely over the past seventeen years from participants in the annual Arabic Pasts workshop at the Agha Khan University—Institute for the Study of Muslim Civilisations in London, and from the workshop's co-organisers, Sarah Bowen Savant, Konrad Hirschler, and Hugh Kennedy. (Their dinners are still the best.) Conversations with Gudrun Krämer, Catherine Mayeur-Jaouen, Augustin Jomier and Ismail Warscheid were invaluable when I was starting to think seriously about the book. Invitations from Akihito

Kudo to lecture in Tokyo, from Nils Riecken to give a paper in Berlin, and from Saul Dubow to speak to the world history seminar in Cambridge, and participants in discussions in all these places, helped to clarify things along the way. I am especially grateful for the generosity of friends and colleagues who have read and commented on parts of the book that touch on their areas of expertise: Jack Tannous, John Haldon, Fanny Bessard, Christopher Melchert, Mike Laffan, Raihan Ismail, Maryam Alemzadeh, Adeel Malik, Afifi al-Akiti, Faisal Devji, Jon Wilson, Eugene Rogan, John-Paul Ghobrial, Susan Slyomovics and Jillian Schwedler. All have improved the book and have saved me from making mistakes: none, of course, is responsible for any errors that remain. Thanks also to Debbie Usher and Jane Goodman who tracked down elusive references.

I would not have imagined that I could write a book on this scale were it not for the encouragement, once again, of Eugene Rogan and, this time, of my wonderful agents Catherine Clarke and George Lucas, and the late Felicity Bryan. Felicity's generous enthusiasm for the project, and early interest from Katie Lambright, then at Basic Books, were essential motivations. Eugene's and Catherine's advice made the book both much more ambitious and much more intelligible. My colleagues in the History Faculty and at Trinity College kindly allowed me the exceptional leave of absence without which it would never have been completed. I have been extraordinarily lucky to work with Stuart Proffitt at Penguin Allen Lane, and with Brandon Proia and Brian Distelberg at Basic, editors whose scrupulous attention to both the smallest detail and the bigger picture is second to none.

I have been luckiest of all in my wonderful (and patient) family. As ever, what I owe to Anna and Kate is more than I can put into words.

NOTES

The scholarly literature and available primary sources relevant to the subject of this book are immense, and I have referred to only a tiny fraction of them. References are restricted to providing sources for direct quotations or specific points of fact, and to specifying, especially where a point is contentious, whose work I have most followed. Titles given are those that most English-language readers are most likely to find useful and accessible in following up on points of interest. Specialists will see at once where I have followed or departed from consensus (where there is any), and in whose more expert footsteps in any of the subject's controversies I have followed.

Introduction

1. Ahmad Ibn Muhammad Ibn Idhari al-Marrakushi, *Al-Bayan al-mughrib fi akhbar muluk al-Andalus wa'l-Maghrib* [late 13th/early 14th century], ed. E. Lévi-Provençal et al., vol. 1 (Beirut, 1967), 27; Abdelmajid Hannoum, "Historiographie et légende au Maghreb: La Kâhina ou la production d'une mémoire," *Annales: Histoire, Sciences Sociales* 54, no. 3 (1999), 667–86; Allan Fromherz, "Kahina," in *Dictionary of African Biography* (Oxford, 2012).

2. Hugh Kennedy, ed., *Historical Atlas of Islam* (Leiden, 2002). Population figures are from "Mapping the Global Muslim Population," Pew Research Center, October 7, 2009, http://www.pewforum.org/2009/10/07/mapping-the-global-muslim-population/; "The Future of the Global Muslim Population," Pew Research Center, January 27, 2011, http://www.pewforum.org/2011/01/27/the-future-of-the-global-muslim-population/; and "Muslims," Pew Research Center, April 2, 2015, https://www.pewresearch.org/religion/2015/04/02/muslims/.

3. On the idea of a single "Muslim world," see Cemil Aydin, *The Idea of the Muslim World: A Global Intellectual History* (Cambridge, MA, 2017). On conventional ideas of a self-contained "West" and the "civilisational thinking" associated with it, see Josephine

Quinn, *How the World Made the West: A 4,000 Year History* (London, 2024), 10. On "Orientalism," see Edward Said, *Orientalism* (New York, 1978); Edward Said, *Covering Islam: How the Media and the Experts Determine How We See the Rest of the World* (New York, 1981); and Zachary Lockman, *Contending Visions of the Middle East: The History and Politics of Orientalism*, 2nd ed. (Cambridge, 2010); for a broader (and more positive) view of the "Orientalist" tradition of scholarship, see Robert Irwin, *For Lust of Knowing: The Orientalists and their Enemies* (London, 2007). Debate over Orientalism in the sense I use the term here has often centred on Said's 1978 book, reactions to it, and the post-colonial scholarship stemming from it, but earlier, often-overlooked historical work is equally important, especially Marshall G. S. Hodgson, "The Interrelations of Societies in History," *Comparative Studies in Society and History* 5, no. 2 (1963), 227–50, reprinted in Edmund Burke III, ed., *Rethinking World History: Essays on Europe, Islam, and World History* (Cambridge, 1993); Marshall G. S. Hodgson, "The Role of Islam in World History," *International Journal of Middle East Studies* 1, no. 2 (1970), 99–123; and Roger Owen, "Studying Islamic History," *Journal of Interdisciplinary History* 4, no. 2 (1973), 287–98. For more positive assessments of the relationship between Muslim societies (especially in the Middle East) and post-Enlightenment European ideas and science, see Albert Hourani, *Arabic Thought in the Liberal Age, 1798–1939*, 2nd ed. (Cambridge, 1983); Jens Hanssen and Max Weiss, eds., *Arabic Thought Beyond the Liberal Age: Towards an Intellectual History of the Nahda* (Cambridge, 2016); and Christopher de Bellaigue, *The Islamic Enlightenment: The Modern Struggle between Faith and Reason* (London, 2017).

4. For subtler accounts of world history, modernity, and the West, in addition to Quinn, *How the World Made the West*, see e.g., C. A. Bayly, *The Birth of the Modern World, 1780–1914* (Oxford, 2004); and David Scott, *Conscripts of Modernity* (Durham, NC, 2004). A magisterial intellectual history of Europe and Asia in the long eighteenth century is Jürgen Osterhammel, *Unfabling the East: The Enlightenment's Encounter with Asia* (Princeton, NJ, 2018).

5. For influential restatements of Eurocentric Orientalism, see Bernard Lewis, "The Roots of Muslim Rage," *Atlantic Monthly*, September 1990; Bernard Lewis, *What Went Wrong? The Clash Between Islam and Modernity in the Middle East* (London, 2002); Samuel P. Huntington, "The Clash of Civilizations?," *Foreign Affairs* 72, no. 3 (1993), 22–49; and Samuel P. Huntington, *The Clash of Civilizations and the Remaking of World Order* (New York, 1996).

6. Robert D. Kaplan, "Looking the World in the Eye," *Atlantic Monthly*, December 2001; Mahmood Mamdani, "Good Muslim, Bad Muslim, an African Perspective," November 1, 2001, https://items.ssrc.org/after-september-11/good-muslim-bad-muslim-an-african-perspective/; Mahmood Mamdani, "Good Muslim, Bad Muslim: A Political Perspective on Culture and Terrorism," *American Anthropologist* 104, no. 3 (2002), 766–75.

7. Shahab Ahmed, *What Is Islam? The Importance of Being Islamic* (Princeton, NJ, 2016), 102, 542. The aim of this book is in some ways the opposite of Ahmed's: if my concern is with how people who are Muslims have lived *as people* in the world, Ahmed's is to reach a more satisfactory definition of how people who are Muslims have lived *as Muslims*, "to provide a new language for the conceptualization of Islam." Ahmed, *What Is Islam?*, 108.

Chapter 1: A World among Others, a World in Itself

1. Qur'an 96:1–5.

2. Peter Brown, *The World of Late Antiquity*, 2nd ed. (London, 2018 [1971]); Glen Bowersock, *The Crucible of Islam* (Cambridge, MA, 2017); Chase Robinson, "The Rise of Islam, 600–705," ch. 5 in Chase Robinson, ed., *The New Cambridge History of Islam*, vol. 1 (Cambridge, 2010), 177.

3. The doctrinal dispute—no less serious than later ones between Catholic and Protestant theologies in the Western church—centred on the question of whether Christ had one nature or two (human and divine), and how these related to each other. Mark Whittow, "The Late Roman/Early Byzantine Near East," ch. 2 in Robinson, *New Cambridge History of Islam*, vol. 1, 80; Jack Tannous, *The Making of the Medieval Middle East: Religion, Society and Simple Believers* (Princeton, NJ, 2018), 497.

4. James Howard-Johnston, "State and Society in Late Antique Iran," in Vesta Sarkhosh Curtis and Sarah Stewart, eds., *The Idea of Iran*, vol. 3, *The Sasanian Era* (London, 2008); Ehsan Yarshater, ed., *The Cambridge History of Iran*, vol. 3, *The Seleucid, Parthian and Sasanian Periods* (Cambridge, 1983); Jonathan Berkey, *The Formation of Islam: Religion and Society in the Near East, 600–1800* (Cambridge, 2003), 26–32.

5. Nina Garsoian, "Byzantium and the Sasanians," ch. 15 in Yarshater, *Cambridge History of Iran*, vol. 3, 577; Bowersock, *Crucible of Islam*, 22n14; Garth Fowden, *Empire to Commonwealth: Consequences of Monotheism in Late Antiquity* (Princeton, NJ, 1993), ch. 1; Garth Fowden, *Before and After Muhammad: The First Millennium Refocused* (Princeton, NJ, 2014), 104.

6. Aziz al-Azmeh, *The Emergence of Islam in Late Antiquity: Allah and His People* (Cambridge, 2015), 128; Suzanne Pinckney Stetkevych, *The Mute Immortals Speak: Pre-Islamic Poetry and the Poetics of Ritual* (Ithaca, NY, 2010), 162.

7. Fred Donner, *The Early Islamic Conquests* (Princeton, NJ, 2014 [1981]), 11–37; on *tayyaye*, see Tannous, *Medieval Middle East*, 525–31.

8. R. B. Serjeant, "Haram and Hawtah: The Sacred Enclave in Arabia," in Abd al-Rahman Badawi, ed., *Mélanges Taha Husain* (Cairo, 1962), 41–58; Gene W. Heck, "Gold Mining in Arabia and the Rise of the Islamic State," *Journal of the Economic and Social History of the Orient* 42, no. 3 (1999), 364–95; Gene W. Heck, "Arabia Without Spices: An Alternate Hypothesis," *Journal of the American Oriental Society* 123, no. 3 (2003), 547–76; Patricia Crone, "Quraysh and the Roman Army: Making Sense of the Meccan Leather Trade," *Bulletin of the School of Oriental and African Studies* 70, no. 1 (2007), 63–88.

9. Qur'an 16:123, 2:135.

10. Qur'an 89:17–23.

11. Harry Munt, *The Holy City of Medina: Sacred Space in Early Islamic Arabia* (Cambridge, 2014).

12. John Haldon, "The Resources of Late Antiquity," ch. 1 in Robinson, *New Cambridge History of Islam*, vol. 1, 57–58; Robinson, "The Rise of Islam," 178–80; Patricia Crone, "The Religion of the Qur'anic Pagans: God and the Lesser Deities," *Arabica* 57 (2010), 151–200; Glen Bowersock, *Crucible of Islam*, ch. 2; Robert Hoyland, "The Jews of the Hijaz in the Qur'an and Their Inscriptions," ch. 4 in Gabriel Reynolds, ed., *New Perspectives on the Qur'an* (London, 2011).

13. Qur'an 81:1–4.

14. James Howard-Johnston, *Witnesses to a World Crisis: Historians and Histories of the Middle East in the Seventh Century* (Oxford, 2010). Quotes are from Robert Hoyland, *Seeing Islam as Others Saw It: A Survey and Evaluation of Christian, Jewish and Zoroastrian Writings on Early Islam*, 2nd ed. (Piscataway, NJ, 2019), 208, 212.

15. For a maximalist account of environmental factors within the "fall of Rome" paradigm, see Kyle Harper, *The Fate of Rome: Climate, Disease, and the End of an Empire* (Princeton, NJ, 2017). For a less "catastrophic" but still severe assessment, see Peter Sarris, *Empires of Faith: The Fall of Rome and the Rise of Islam, 500–700* (Oxford, 2011), chs. 4 and 7. For critiques, see John Haldon, Hugh Elton, Sabine R. Huebner, Adam Izdebski, Lee Mordechai, and Timothy P. Newfield, "Plagues, Climate Change, and the End of an Empire," *History Compass* 16 (2018); and the more cautious account of microclimatic variation in Haldon, "Resources of Late Antiquity," 22–25. On archaeological evidence, see Gideon Avni, *The Byzantine-Islamic Transition in Palestine: An Archaeological Approach* (Oxford, 2014); and Jodi Magness, *The Archaeology of the Early Islamic Settlement in Palestine* (Winona Lake, IN, 2003). On the Justinianic plague, see Merle Eisenberg and Lee Mordechai, "The Justinianic Plague: An Interdisciplinary Review," *Byzantine and Modern Greek Studies* 43, no. 2 (2019), 156–80; and Merle Eisenberg and Lee Mordechai, "Rejecting Catastrophe: The Case of the Justinianic Plague," *Past and Present* 244 (2019), 3–50.

16. Whittow, "Late Roman Near East," 72–73.

17. James Howard-Johnston, *The Last Great War of Antiquity* (Oxford, 2021); Qur'an 30:1–5.

18. Saïd Amir Arjomand, "The Constitution of Medina: A Sociolegal Interpretation of Muhammad's Acts of Foundation of the *umma*," *International Journal of Middle East Studies* 41 (2009), 555–75; Munt, *Holy City of Medina*, ch. 2; Michael Lecker, *The "Constitution of Medina": Muhammad's First Legal Document* (Princeton, NJ, 2004); Sarah Mirza, "*Dhimma* Agreements and Sanctuary Systems at Islamic Origins," *Journal of Near Eastern Studies* 77, no. 1 (2018), 99–117.

19. Arjomand, "The Constitution of Medina," uses this translation.

20. As Jack Tannous points out, "Most early Muslims...were late converts or members of tribes who had converted, *en masse*, at the end of the Prophet's life: most will likely have had only the most superficial understanding of the Prophet's message and its implications for their lives." Tannous, *Medieval Middle East*, 333.

21. Qur'an 2:131.

22. Tannous, *Medieval Middle East*.

23. For detailed discussion, see Hugh Kennedy, *The Prophet and the Age of the Caliphates* (Harlow, UK, 2004), 38–40; and Jacob Lassner, *Jews, Christians, and the Abode of Islam* (Chicago, 2012), 142–51.

24. Al-Azmeh, *Emergence of Islam*, ch. 4; Al Makin, "Re-Thinking Other Claims to Prophethood," *Al-Jamiah: Journal of Islamic Studies* 48, no. 1 (2010), 165–90; Gerald Hawting, "Were There Prophets in the Jahiliyya?," ch. 6 in Carol Bakhos and Michael Cook, eds., *Islam and its Past: Jahiliyya, Late Antiquity, and the Qur'an* (Oxford, 2017).

Chapter 2: Belonging and Believing

1. Kevin Jacques, "Muhammad's Mission and the *din* of Ibrahim According to Ibn Ishaq," ch. 6 in Patrick Gray, ed., *Varieties of Religious Invention* (Oxford, 2015).

2. Patricia Crone, *Slaves on Horses: The Evolution of the Islamic Polity* (Cambridge, 1980), 6–12. The idea of a "solid core" is William Montgomery Watt's: see William Montgomery Watt, *Muhammad at Mecca* (Oxford, 1953); and William Montgomery Watt, *Muhammad at Medina* (Oxford, 1956). The question of how to reconstruct early Islamic history has been extraordinarily complex and remains contentious. See part IV, "The Historiography of Early Islamic History," in Chase Robinson, ed., *The New Cambridge History of Islam*, vol. 1 (Cambridge, 2010); Robert Hoyland, "Writing the Biography of the Prophet Muhammad: Problems and Solutions," *History Compass* 5, no. 2 (2007), 581–602; appendix I, "Approaching the Sources," in Jack Tannous, *The Making of the Medieval Middle East: Religion, Society and Simple Believers* (Princeton, NJ, 2018); and Sean W. Anthony, "Introduction: The Making of the Historical Muhammad," in *Muhammad and the Empires of Faith: The Making of the Prophet of Islam* (Berkeley, CA, 2020).

3. Anthony, *Muhammad and Empires of Faith*, 26–29; Ali Ibn Ibrahim Ghabban and Robert Hoyland, trans., "The Inscription of Zuhayr, the Oldest Islamic Inscription (24 AH/AD 644–645), the Rise of the Arabic Script and the Nature of the Early Islamic State," *Arabian Archaeology and Epigraphy* 19, no. 2 (2008), 210–237; Mehdy Shaddel, "'The Year According to the Reckoning of the Believers.' Papyrus Louvre inv. J. David-Weill 20 and the Origins of the *hijri* Era," *Der Islam* 95, no. 2 (2018), 291–311.

4. Uncertainty as to when, according to existing calendars, the birth of Christ had actually occurred did not help. Judith Herrin, *The Formation of Christendom* (Princeton, NJ, 2021 [1987]), 3–6; Fowden, *Empire to Commonwealth: Consequences of Monotheism in Late Antiquity* (Princeton, NJ, 1993), 139–40.

5. Patricia Crone, *God's Rule: Government and Islam* (New York, 2004), 21–23; Linda T. Darling, "'The Vicegerent of God, from Him We Expect Rain': The Incorporation of the Pre-Islamic State in Early Islamic Political Culture," *Journal of the American Oriental Society* 134, no. 3 (2014), 407–29.

6. Qur'an 2:30, 38:26; Patricia Crone and Martin Hinds, *God's Caliph: Religious Authority in the First Centuries of Islam* (Cambridge, 1986); Andrew Marsham, "'God's Caliph' Revisited: Umayyad Political Thought in its Late Antique Context," ch. 1 in Alain George and Andrew Marsham, eds., *Power, Patronage, and Memory in Early Islam* (New York, 2018).

7. Crone, *God's Rule*, 23.

8. Qur'an 4:100; Crone, *God's Rule*, 54.

9. Abu Ja'far Muhammad Ibn Jarir Al-Tabari, *The History of Al-Tabari (Tarikh al-rusul wa'l-muluk)*, vol. 19, ed. and trans. I. K. A. Howard (Albany, NY, 1990), 164–66.

10. Fred M. Donner, *The Early Islamic Conquests* (Princeton, NJ, 2014 [1981]); Patricia Crone, "The First Century Concept of *hiğra*," *Arabica* 41, no. 3 (1994), 352–87; Abd al-Husain Zarrinkub, "The Arab Conquest of Iran and its Aftermath," in Richard N. Frye, ed., *The Cambridge History of Iran*, vol. 4, *The Period from the Arab Invasion to the Seljuqs* (Cambridge, 1975).

11. For Christianity, see Peter Brown, *Through the Eye of a Needle: Wealth, the Fall of Rome, and the Making of Christianity in the West, 350–550 AD* (Princeton, NJ, 2013).

12. Tannous, *Medieval Middle East*, chs. 13 and 14, p. 401 for al-Jahiz; Fanny Bessard, *Caliphs and Merchants: Cities and Economies of Power in the Near East, 700–950* (Oxford,

2020), 14–15; Arietta Papaconstantinou, "Between *umma* and *dhimma*: The Christians of the Middle East Under the Umayyads," *Annales islamologiques* 42 (2008), 127–56.

13. Chase Robinson, *Abd al-Malik* (Oxford, 2005).

14. Qur'an 4:171.

15. Oleg Grabar, "Kubbat al-sakhra," in *Encyclopaedia of Islam*, 2nd ed. (Leiden, 1960–2009), henceforward *EI2*; Marcus Milwright, "Dome of the Rock," in *Encyclopaedia of Islam*, 3rd ed. (Leiden, 2012), henceforward *EI3*; Oleg Grabar, with Muhammad al-Asad, Abeer Audeh, and Saïd Nuseibeh, *The Shape of the Holy: Early Islamic Jerusalem* (Princeton, NJ, 1996); Glen Bowersock, *The Crucible of Islam* (Cambridge, MA, 2017), chs. 5 and 9; Fowden, *Empire to Commonwealth*, 142–43; Robinson, *Abd al-Malik*.

16. Crone, *Slaves on Horses*; Crone, "Mawla," in *EI2*.

17. Saleh Said Agha, "Abu Muslim al-Khurasani," in *EI3*. Saled Said Agha, *The Revolution Which Toppled the Umayyads* (Leiden, 2003), quote at 56.

18. On Baghdad's foundation, see Justin Marozzi, *Baghdad: City of Peace, City of Blood* (London, 2014), ch. 1.

19. Abu Ja'far Muhammad Ibn Jarir Al-Tabari, *The History of Al-Tabari (Tarikh al-rusul wa'l-muluk)*, vol. 30, ed. and trans. C. E. Bosworth (Albany, NY, 1989), 307–8.

Chapter 3: The Book, the Law, and the Spirit

1. Shams al-Din Abu Abdallah Muhammad Ibn Battuta, *Tuhfat al-nuzzar fi ghara'ib al-amsar wa aja'ib al-asfar* [1358], trans. H. A. R. Gibb as *The Travels of Ibn Battuta, AD 1325–1354*, 5 vols. (London, 2011); Ross E. Dunn, *The Adventures of Ibn Battuta, a Muslim Traveler of the Fourteenth Century* (Berkeley, CA, 2012 [1986]), ch. 11 for China.

2. Muhyi al-Din Ibn Arabi, *Futuhat makkiyya* [12th cent.], quoted in Michel Chodkiewicz, *An Ocean Without Shore: Ibn Arabi, the Book, and the Law*, trans. David Streight (Albany, NY, 1993), 25.

3. Qur'an 2:1; Daniel Madigan, "Book," in Johanna Pink, ed., *Encyclopaedia of the Qur'an* (Leiden, 2001–2006). Jane Dammen McAuliffe, ed., *The Cambridge Companion to the Qur'an* (Cambridge, 2007).

4. For examples of Qur'anic use of *hudud allah*, see Qur'an 2:229, 58:4, 65:1 (divorce); and Qur'an 2:187 (fasting).

5. Qur'an 4:15, 24:2; Leviticus 20:10; Ezekiel 16:36–41. On how the death penalty (by stoning) came to replace the Qur'anic penalty for adultery, see John Burton, *The Sources of Islamic Law* (Edinburgh, 1990). On *hudud* in the Qur'an, in later jurisprudence, and in contemporary criminal law, see Mohammed Hashim Kamali, *Crime and Punishment in Islamic Law* (Oxford, 2019).

6. Qur'an 45:18; Norman Calder, "Shari'a," in *Encyclopaedia of Islam*, 2nd ed. (Leiden, 1960–2009), henceforward *EI2*; Wael B. Hallaq, *Shari'a: Theory, Practice, Transformations* (Cambridge, 2009).

7. Wael B. Hallaq, *The Origins and Evolution of Islamic Law* (Cambridge, 2005), 47–50.

8. Ibn al-Jawzi, *Manaqib al-imam Ahmad Ibn Hanbal* [12th cent.], trans. as *Virtues of the Imam Ahmad Ibn Hanbal*, ed. and trans. Michael Cooperson (New York, 2015), vol. 1, 100–101, 336–9 (9.1, 22.5, 22.8); Christopher Melchert, *Hadith, Piety and Law* (Atlanta, GA, 2015), 5; Christopher Melchert, *Ahmad Ibn Hanbal* (London, 2013), 16.

9. Ibn Hanbal, *Musnad al-Imam Ahmad Ibn Hanbal* [9th cent.], ed. Shuʿayb Arnaʾut et al., 50 vols. (Beirut, 1993–2001).

10. Hallaq, *Origins and Evolution of Islamic Law*, 122–40.

11. Melchert, *Ahmad Ibn Hanbal*, 17, 111–12.

12. Richard W. Bulliet, *The Patricians of Nishapur* (Cambridge, MA, 1972).

13. Ibn al-Jawzi, *Virtues of the Imam Ahmad Ibn Hanbal*, vol. 2, 508–9 (50.2).

14. Abu Jaʿfar Muhammad Ibn Jarir Al-Tabari, *The History of Al-Tabari (Tarikh al-rusul waʾl-muluk)*, vol. 32, ed. and trans. C. E. Bosworth (Albany, NY, 1987), 200, 202.

15. Al-Khatib al-Baghdadi, *Tarikh Baghdad aw madinat al-salam* [11th cent.], ed. Ahmad Ibn al-Siddiq, 14 vols. (Cairo, 1931), vol. 9, 243. Martin Hinds, "mihna," in *EI2*; Melchert, *Ahmad Ibn Hanbal*, 18–25.

16. Al-Tabari, *The History of Al-Tabari (Tarikh al-rusul waʾl-muluk)*, vol. 28, ed. and trans. Jane Dammen McAuliffe (Albany, NY, 1995), 167–9.

17. Najam Haider, *The Origins of the Shiʿa: Identity, Ritual, and Sacred Space in Eighth Century Kufa* (Cambridge, 2011); Najam Haider, *Shiʿi Islam* (Cambridge, 2014).

18. Vimal Patel, "A Lecturer Showed a Painting of the Prophet Muhammad. She Lost Her Job," *New York Times*, January 8, 2023. On the image, see Robert Hillenbrand, ed., *Persian Painting: From the Mongols to the Qajars* (London, 2000); Christiane Gruber, *The Praiseworthy One: The Prophet Muhammad in Islamic Texts and Images* (Bloomington, IN, 2018), 220–22; and more generally, Christiane Gruber, ed., *The Image Debate: Figural Representations in Islam and Across the World* (London, 2019).

19. Farhad Daftary, *The Ismaʿilis, Their History and Doctrines*, 2nd ed. (Cambridge, 2007), 828–9.

20. Ibn Battuta, *Tuhfat al-nuzzar*, vol. 3, 583.

21. Abuʾl-Hasan al-Masʿudi, *Muruj al-dhahab wa maʿadin al-jawhar* [10th cent.], ed. Charles Pellat (Beirut, 1966–79), vol. 5, 107–8, para. 3156.

22. Farid al-Din Attar, *Tadhkirat al-awliya* [13th cent.], quoted in Margaret Smith, *Rabia the Mystic and Her Fellow-Saints in Islam* (Cambridge, 2010 [1928]), 33–36, 97, 99; Margaret Smith and Charles Pellat, "Rabiʿa al-Adawiyya al-Kaysiyya," in *EI2*.

23. Vincent J. Cornell, ed. and trans., *The Way of Abu Madyan* (Cambridge, 1996), 136–7; Nelly Amri, "Le corps du saint dans l'hagiographie du Maghreb medieval," *Revue des mondes musulmans et de la Méditerranée* 113–4 (2006), 59–89.

24. Jonathan Berkey, *The Formation of Islam: Religion and Society in the Near East, 600–1800* (Cambridge, 2003), 152–8; Louis Massignon, *The Passion of al-Hallaj, Mystic and Martyr of Islam*, trans. Herbert Mason (Princeton, NJ, 1972), vol. 3, 26.

25. Al-Ghazali, *Al-Munqidh min al-dalal* [11th cent.], ed. and trans. Richard J. McCarthy as *Deliverance from Error* (Louisville, KY, 1999), 55, 78–9, 92.

26. Claude Addas, *Ibn Arabi et le voyage sans retour* (Paris, 1996), 12; Chodkiewicz, *An Ocean Without Shore*, 20; William C. Chittick, *Ibn Arabi: Heir to the Prophets* (Oxford, 2005).

27. Katia Boissevain, *Sainte parmi les saints* (Tunis, 2005); Boissevain, "Aʾisha al-Mannubiyya," in *Encyclopaedia of Islam*, 3rd ed. (Leiden, 2012); "En Tunisie, un commando détruit le mausolée d'une sainte très vénérée," Radio France Internationale, October 17, 2012, https://www.rfi.fr/fr/afrique/20121017-tunisie-commando-detruit-le-mausolee-une-sainte-tres-veneree; "Tunisie: Les Etats-Unis demandent l'arrestation des

auteurs de l'attaque contre leur ambassade," Radio France Internationale, October 14, 2012, https://www.rfi.fr/fr/afrique/20121014-tunisie-etats-unis-demandent-arrestation -auteurs-attentat-14-septembre.

Chapter 4: One God, Many Peoples

1. Nancy Shatzman Steinhardt, "China's Earliest Mosques," *Journal of the Society of Architectural Historians* 67, no. 3 (2008), 330–61; Geoff Wade, "Early Muslim Expansion in South-East Asia, Eighth to Fifteenth Centuries," ch. 10 in David O. Morgan and Anthony Reid, eds., *The New Cambridge History of Islam* (Cambridge, 2010), vol. 3, 368, 381. Kristian Petersen, *Interpreting Islam in China* (Oxford, 2017), 2.

2. Fanny Bessard, *Caliphs and Merchants: Cities and Economies of Power in the Near East (700–950)* (Oxford, 2020).

3. E.g., Qur'an 11:84–85.

4. Fanny Bessard, "The Politics of suqs in Early Islam," *Journal of the Economic and Social History of the Orient* 61, no. 4 (2018), 491–518; Amira Bennison, *The Great Caliphs: The Golden Age of the Abbasid Empire* (New Haven, CT, 2009), chs. 2 and 4; Olivia Remie Constable, "Muslim Trade in the Late Medieval Mediterranean World," ch. 22 in Maria Isabel Fiero, ed., *The New Cambridge History of Islam* (Cambridge, 2010), vol. 2, 634.

5. Bessard, *Caliphs and Merchants*, ch. 9; Hayyim J. Cohen, "The Economic Background and the Secular Occupations of Muslim Jurisprudents and Traditionists in the Classical Period of Islam," *Journal of the Economic and Social History of the Orient* 13, no. 1 (1970), 16–61; Gene W. Heck, *Charlemagne, Muhammad, and the Arab Roots of Capitalism* (New York, 2006).

6. *Akhbar al-Sin wa'l-Hind* [early 10th cent.], Tim Mackintosh-Smith, ed. and trans., *Accounts of China and India*, in Tim Mackintosh-Smith and James E. Montgomery, eds., *Two Arabic Travel Books* (New York, 2014), 68–69, 124–25; Nicholas Tackett, *The Destruction of the Medieval Chinese Aristocracy* (Cambridge, MA, 2014), ch. 5.

7. *Kitab Ahmad Ibn Fadlan* [10th cent.], James E. Montgomery, ed. and trans., *Mission to the Volga*, in Mackintosh-Smith and Montgomery, *Two Arabic Travel Books*, 196–97, 222–23, 228–92, 232–33, 236–37. The reference to the "infernal cold" (*al-zamharir*) of Hell echoes Qur'an 76:13.

8. Marek Jankowiak, "Dirhams for Slaves: Investigating the Slavic Slave Trade in the Tenth Century," medieval history seminar, All Souls College, Oxford, February 2012; Marek Jankowiak, "What Does the Slave Trade in the Saqaliba Tell Us About Early Islamic Slavery?," *International Journal of Middle East Studies* 49, no. 1 (2017), 169–72; Bessard, *Caliphs and Merchants*, 223–4; Michael McCormick, *Origins of the European Economy: Communications and Commerce, AD 300–900* (Cambridge, 2001), ch. 25; Hannah Barker, *That Most Precious Merchandise: The Mediterranean Trade in Black Sea Slaves, 1260–1500* (Philadelphia, PA, 2020); Felicia Roşu, ed., *Slavery in the Black Sea Region, c. 900–1900* (Leiden, 2022).

9. Abu'l-Hasan al-Mas'udi, *Muruj al-dhahab wa ma'adin al-jawhar* [10th cent.], ed. Charles Pellat (Beirut, 1966–79), vol. 5, 116–17, para. 3183.

10. Frederick Cooper, *Plantation Slavery on the East Coast of Africa* (New Haven CT, 1977); Gwyn Campbell, ed., *The Structure of Slavery in Indian Ocean Africa and Asia* (London, 2004); Gwyn Campbell, "East Africa in the Early Indian Ocean World Slave

Trade: The Zanj Revolt Reconsidered," ch. 12 in Gwyn Campbell, ed., *Early Exchange Between Africa and the Wider Indian Ocean World* (Cham, 2016); Reuven Amitai and Christoph Cluse, eds., *Slavery and the Slave Trade in the Eastern Mediterranean (c. 1000–1500 CE)* (Turnhout, Belgium, 2018); Aziz al-Azmeh, "Barbarians in Arab Eyes," *Past and Present* 134 (1992), 3–18; Lamia Belafrej, "Domestic Slavery, Skin Colour, and Image Dialectic in Thirteenth Century Arabic Manuscripts," *Art History* 44, no. 5 (2021), 1012–36.

11. Michael Brett and Elizabeth Fentress, *The Berbers* (Oxford, 1996); James McDougall, "Histories of Heresy and Salvation," ch. 1 in Katherine E. Hoffman and Susan Gilson Miller, eds., *Berbers and Others: Beyond Tribe and Nation in North Africa* (Bloomington, IN, 2010); Jennifer Vanz, "L'histoire en débats: Mémoires des premiers temps de l'Islam au Maghreb au début du VIIIè/XIVè siècle," *Revue des mondes musulmans et de la Méditerranée* 147 (2020), https://doi-org.ezproxy-prd.bodleian.ox.ac.uk/10.4000/remmm.14536.

12. Sarah Bowen Savant, *The New Muslims of Post-Conquest Iran: Tradition, Memory, and Conversion* (Cambridge, 2013), 120.

13. Hugh Kennedy, *The Prophet and the Age of the Caliphates* (Harlow, UK, 2004), 137, 140–43.

14. Qur'an 49:13.

15. Patricia Crone, *God's Rule* (New York, 2004), 244; Nizam al-Mulk, *Siyar al-Muluk* [1091–92], ed. and trans. Hubert Darke as *The Book of Government or Rules for Kings* (London, 2001 [1960]), 9, 12; Ira Lapidus, "State and Religion in Islamic Societies," *Past and Present* 151 (1996), 3–27.

16. Amira Bennison, *The Great Caliphs* (New Haven, CT, 2009), 180–81. For Abbasid Baghdad, see Marozzi, *Baghdad*, ch. 3.

17. Abu Ja'far Muhammad Ibn Jarir Al-Tabari, *The History of Al-Tabari (Tarikh al-rusul wa'l-muluk)*, vol. 30, ed. and trans. C. E. Bosworth (Albany, NY, 1989), 310; Christopher Melchert, *Hadith, Piety and Law* (Atlanta, GA, 2015), 155–6.

18. Michael Cooperson, trans., *Impostures* by al-Hariri: *Fifty Rogue's Tales Translated Fifty Ways* (New York, 2020).

19. Jawid Mojaddedi, *Beyond Dogma: Rumi's Teachings on Friendship with God and Early Sufi Theories* (Oxford, 2012), 159–60. Quotes are from *Masnavi*, ii, 1763, 1774.

20. Michael Cook, "The Origins of 'kalam,'" *Bulletin of the School of Oriental and African Studies* 43, no. 1 (1980), 32–43; Jack Tannous, *The Making of the Medieval Middle East* (Princeton, NJ, 2018), 421–22; Zvi Ben-Dor Benite, *The Dao of Muhammad* (Cambridge, MA, 2005); Kristian Petersen, *Interpreting Islam in China* (Oxford, 2017).

21. Robert Irwin, *Night and Horses and the Desert: An Anthology of Classical Arabic Literature* (London, 1999), ch. 6; Eric Calderwood, *On Earth or in Poems: The Many Lives of al-Andalus* (Cambridge, MA, 2023).

22. Hugh Kennedy, *Muslim Spain and Portugal: A Political History of al-Andalus* (London, 1996); Simon Barton and Richard Fletcher, *The World of El Cid: Chronicles of the Spanish Reconquest* (Manchester, 2013), 4, 90–94.

23. Kennedy, *Muslim Spain*, 145; Maria Rosa Menocal, "Visions of al-Andalus," ch. 1 in Maria Rosa Menocal, Raymond P. Scheindlin, and Michael Sells, eds., *The*

Literature of al-Andalus (Cambridge, 2012), 3; Janina M. Safran, *Defining Boundaries in al-Andalus: Muslims, Christians and Jews in Islamic Iberia* (Ithaca, NY, 2013), 168.

24. Mark R. Cohen, *Under Crescent and Cross: The Jews in the Middle Ages* (Princeton, NJ, 1994), ch.1.

25. Sarah Mirza, "*Dhimma* Agreements and Sanctuary Systems at Islamic Origins," *Journal of Near Eastern Studies* 77, no. 1 (2018), 99–117; Robert Hoyland, "The Earliest Attestation of the *Dhimma* of God and His Messenger, and the Rediscovery of P. Nessana 77 (60s AH/680s CE)," ch. 2 in Behnam Sadeghi et al., eds., *Islamic Cultures, Islamic Contexts* (Leiden, 2015).

26. Nimrod Hurvitz, ed., *Conversion to Islam in the Pre-Modern Age* (Berkeley, CA, 2020), 217; Christian Sahner, *Christian Martyrs under Islam* (Princeton, NJ, 2018); Tannous, *Medieval Middle East*, 318–32, quote at 327.

27. William Granara, *Narrating Muslim Sicily: War and Peace in the Medieval Mediterranean World* (London, 2019), 143.

28. Christophe Picard, *Sea of the Caliphs: The Mediterranean in the Medieval Islamic World* (Cambridge, MA, 2018), 13, 274–5; Chris Wickham, *The Inheritance of Rome: A History of Europe from 400 to 1000* (London, 2009), 349, 365–72; Olivia Remie Constable, "Muslim Trade in the Late Medieval Mediterranean World," ch. 22 in Fiero, *New Cambridge History of Islam*, vol. 2.

29. Niall Christie, *Muslims and Crusaders: Christianity's Wars in the Middle East, 1095–1382* (London, 2014), 19, 127–28.

30. Carole Hillenbrand, *The Crusades: Islamic Perspectives* (Edinburgh, 1999); Scott Moynihan, "Peacemaking and Holy War: Christian-Muslim Diplomacy, c. 1095–1291, in Crusades Historiography," *History Compass* 18 (2020).

Chapter 5: Heirs of the World-Conquerors

1. Hend Gilli-Elewy, "*Al-hawadith al-gami'a*: A Contemporary Account of the Mongol Conquest of Baghdad, 656/1258," *Arabica* 58 (2011), 353–71, quote at 367–68; Nassima Neggaz, "The Many Deaths of the Last Abbasid Caliph, al-Musta'sim bi-llah (d. 1258)," *Journal of the Royal Asiatic Society* (ser. 3) 30, no. 4 (2020), 585–612.

2. Mona Hassan, *Longing for the Lost Caliphate* (Princeton, NJ, 2017), ch. 1; Muhammad Faruque, "The Mongol Conquest of Baghdad: Medieval Accounts and Their Modern Assessments," *Islamic Quarterly* 32, no. 4 (1988), 194–206; Nahyan Fancy and Monica H. Green, "Plague and the Fall of Baghdad (1258)," *Medical History* 65, no. 2 (2021), 157–77.

3. Beatrice Forbes Manz, "The Rule of the Infidels: The Mongols and the Islamic World," ch. 4 in David O. Morgan and Anthony Reid, eds., *The New Cambridge History of Islam* (Cambridge, 2011), vol. 3, 143; Michal Biran, "Violence and Non-Violence in the Mongol Conquest of Baghdad (1258)," ch. 2 in Robert Gleave and Istvan Kristo-Nagy, eds., *Violence in Islamic Thought from the Mongols to European Imperialism* (Edinburgh, 2018); E. Neubauer, "Safi al-Din al-Urmawi," in *Encyclopaedia of Islam*, 2nd ed. (Leiden: Brill, 1960–2009), henceforward *EI2*.

4. Ahmad S. Dallal, *Islam, Science, and the Challenge of History* (New Haven, CT, 2010), 24–25, 42; F. J. Ragep, "Nasir al-Din al-Tusi," in *EI2*.

5. Biran, "Violence and Non-Violence," 28–29; E. Honigmann and C. E. Bosworth, "Nishapur," in *EI2*; R. N. Frye, "Balkh," in *EI2*; Katie Campbell, "The Impact of the Mongol Conquests on Earthen Cities in Central Asia," *International Journal of Islamic Architecture* 12, no. 2 (2023), 389–410.

6. Ala al-Din Ata-Malik al-Juvaini, *Ta'rikh-i jahan-gusha* [ca. 1260], trans. J. A. Boyle as *Genghis Khan: The History of the World Conqueror* (Manchester, 1997 [1958]), 103–5; Timothy May, "The Mongols as the Scourge of God in the Islamic World," ch. 3 in Gleave and Kristo-Nagy, *Violence in Islamic Thought*; George Lane, "Juwayni Family," in *Encyclopaedia of Islam*, 3rd ed. (Leiden, 2012); and George Lane, *Early Mongol Rule in Thirteenth Century Iran: A Persian Renaissance* (London, 2003).

7. Qur'an 3:26.

8. Judith Pfeiffer, "Reflections on a 'Double Rapprochement': Conversion to Islam Among the Mongol Elite During the Early Ilkhanate," in Linda Komaroff, ed., *Beyond the Legacy of Genghis Khan* (Leiden, 2006), 369–89; Rashid al-Din Tabib, *Jami'u-t-tawarikh* [14th cent.], ed. and trans. Wheeler M. Thackston, in *Persian Histories of the Mongol Dynasties*, vol. 3, *Jami'u' t-Tawarikh: Compendium of Chronicles*, 101 [288-9], 450 [1290]; Stefan Kamola, *Making Mongol History: Rashid al-Din and the Jami' al-Tawarikh* (Edinburgh, 2019); David Morgan, *Medieval Persia, 1040–1797* (Harlow, UK, 1988), ch. 8.

9. Peter Jackson, "The Mongol Age in Eastern Inner Asia," ch. 2 in Nicola Di Cosmo, Allen J. Frank, and Peter B. Golden, eds., *The Cambridge History of Inner Asia: The Chinggisid Age* (Cambridge, 2009), 42–43; Wonhee Cho, "Beyond Toleration: The Mongols' Religious Policies in Yuan-Dynasty China and Il-Khanate Iran, 1200–1368," PhD diss., Yale, 2014.

10. Muhammad Qasim Firishta, *Gulshan-i Ibrahimi* [16th cent.], ed. and trans. J. Briggs, *History of the Rise of Mohamedan Power in India till the Year AD 1612*, 2 vols. (Lahore, 1977 [London, 1829]), vol. 1, 494.

11. Walter Fischel, ed. and trans., *Ibn Khaldun and Tamerlane* (Berkeley, CA, 1952), 45, 47; Peter Jackson, *The Mongols and the West*, 2nd ed. (London, 2018), ch. 9; Marshall Hodgson, *The Venture of Islam* (Chicago, 1974), vol. 2, 428–36.

12. John Darwin, *After Tamerlane: The Rise and Fall of Global Empires, 1400–2000* (London, 2008); Morgan, *Medieval Persia*, ch. 9; Maria E. Subtelny, "Tamerlane and His Descendants: From Paladins to Patrons," ch. 5 in Morgan and Reid, *New Cambridge History of Islam*, vol. 3.

13. G. J. Ames, ed. and trans., *Em nome de Deus: The Journal of the First Voyage of Vasco da Gama to India, 1497–1499* (Leiden, 2009), 71–72.

14. André Wink, *Al-Hind: The Making of the Indo-Islamic World*, vol. 1 (Leiden, 1996), 69.

15. Richard M. Eaton, "Reconsidering 'Conversion to Islam' in Indian History," ch. 19 in Andrew Peacock, ed., *Islamisation: Comparative Perspectives from History* (Edinburgh, 2017).

16. Firishta, *Gulshan-i Ibrahimi*, vol. 1, 494.

17. Peter Jackson, "Muslim India: The Delhi Sultanate," ch. 3 in Morgan and Reid, *New Cambridge History of Islam*, vol. 3.

18. Firishta, *Gulshan-i Ibrahimi*, vol. 1, 217–22; Fouzia Farooq Ahmad, *Muslim Rule in Medieval India* (London, 2021), ch. 5.

19. Richard M. Eaton, "Temple Desecration and Indo-Muslim States," *Journal of Islamic Studies* 11, no. 3 (2000), 283–319; Richard M. Eaton, *India in the Persianate Age, 1000–1765* (London, 2019), 19–29.

20. Richard M. Eaton, *A Social History of the Deccan, 1300–1761* (Cambridge, 2005), 56; J. Burton-Page, "Niʿmat-Allahiyya," in *EI2*.

21. Richard M. Eaton, "Reconsidering 'Conversion to Islam,' " 385–87.

22. Carl Ernst and Bruce Lawrence, *Sufi Martyrs of Love: The Chishti Order in South Asia and Beyond* (New York, 2002), 4, 66; Tanvir Anjum, *Chishti Sufis in the Sultanate of Delhi, 1190–1400* (Oxford, 2011).

23. Michael Dols, *The Black Death in the Middle East* (Princeton, NJ, 1977), 161–62; Remi Jedwab, Noel. D. Johnson, and Mark Koyama, "The Economic Impact of the Black Death," *Journal of Economic Literature* 60, no. 1 (2022), 132–78.

24. James Belich, *The World the Plague Made* (Princeton, NJ, 2022), esp. part III; Robert Hymes and Monica H. Green, "New Evidence for the Dating and Impact of the Black Death in Asia," *Medieval Globe* 8, no. 1, special issue (2022); for the older view, see George D. Sussman, "Was the Black Death in India and China?," *Bulletin of the History of Medicine* 85, no. 3 (2011), 319–55; Şevket Pamuk and Maya Schatzmiller, "Plagues, Wages, and Economic Change in the Islamic Middle East, 700–1500," *Journal of Economic History* 74, no. 1 (March 2014), 196–229. Stuart Borsch, "Plague Depopulation and Irrigation Decay in Medieval Egypt," *Medieval Globe* 1 (2015), 125–56.

25. Ibn Hajar al-Asqalani [d. 1447], *Badhl al-maʿun fi fadl al-taʿun*, eds. and trans. Joel Blecher and Mairaj Syed as *Merits of the Plague* (London, 2023), 202–3, 165.

Chapter 6: Shadows of God

1. Marc David Baer, *The Ottomans: Khans, Caesars, and Caliphs* (New York, 2021), 23–27, 67; Cemal Kafadar, *Between Two Worlds: The Construction of the Ottoman State* (Berkeley, CA, 1995); Ahmet T. Karamustafa, *God's Unruly Friends: Dervish Groups in the Islamic Later Middle Period, 1200–1550* (Salt Lake City, 1994); J. Spencer Trimingham, *The Sufi Orders in Islam* (Oxford, 1971).

2. V. L. Ménage, "Some Notes on the *devshirme*," *Bulletin of the School of Oriental and African Studies* 29, no. 1 (1966), 64–78; H. Erdem Cipa, "Empire or Faith: Stretching the Boundaries of the Shariʿa in Ottoman Institutional Practice," *Journal of the Ottoman and Turkish Studies Association* 8, no. 2 (2021), 211–25.

3. R. C. Repp, "A Further Note on the *devshirme*," *Bulletin of the School of Oriental and African Studies* 31, no. 1 (1968), 137–9; Baer, *The Ottomans*, 208–12; Paul Rycaut, *The History of the Present State of the Ottoman Empire* (London, 1675), 14.

4. Giancarlo Casale, *The Ottoman Age of Exploration* (Oxford, 2015); James Belich, *The World the Plague Made* (Princeton, NJ, 2022), ch. 11; Fernando Cervantes, *Conquistadores: A New History* (London, 2020), 13–14.

5. Baer, *The Ottomans*, 80–81.

6. Marc David Baer, *Honoured by the Glory of Islam: Conversion and Conquest in Ottoman Europe* (Oxford, 2008); Karen Barkey, *Empire of Difference* (Cambridge, 2008), ch. 4.

7. Suraiya Faroqhi, "Political Activity Among Ottoman Taxpayers and the Problem of Sultanic Legitimation (1570–1650)," *Journal of the Economic and Social History of the Orient* 35, no. 1 (1992), 1–39; James E. Baldwin, "The Deposition of Defterdar Ahmed Pasha and the Rule of Law in Seventeenth Century Egypt," *Journal of Ottoman Studies* 46 (2015), 131–61.

8. Nathalie Clayer, "L'autorité religieuse dans l'islam ottoman sous le contrôle de l'état?," *Archives de sciences sociales des religions* 125 (2004), 45–62.

9. *The Great Turks terrible Challenge, this Yeare 1640 [. . .] To the tune of My bleeding heart, or Lets to the wars againe* (London, 1640), at Early English Books Online, www.proquest.com/books/great-turks-terrible-challenge-this-yeare-1640/docview /2240922737/se-2; Baer, *The Ottomans*, 143, 148.

10. Leslie P. Peirce, *Imperial Harem: Women and Sovereignty in the Ottoman Empire* (New York, 1993), 59.

11. Peirce, *Imperial Harem*, 59, 269; Leslie P. Peirce, *Empress of the East: How a Slave Girl Became Queen of the Ottoman Empire* (London, 2018).

12. Suraiya Faroqhi, *Women in the Ottoman Empire: A Social and Political History* (London, 2023), 21–22; Gülru Necipoğlu, *Architecture, Ceremonial, and Power: The Topkapi Palace in the Fifteenth and Sixteenth Centuries* (New York, 1991), ch. 8; Baer, *The Ottomans*, 212.

13. B. O'Kane, "Sinan," in *Encyclopaedia of Islam*, 2nd ed. (Leiden: Brill, 1960– 2009); Gülru Necipoğlu-Kafadar, "The Suleymaniye Complex in Istanbul: An Interpretation," *Muqarnas* 3 (1985), 92–117, quotes at 96, 98.

14. Baer, *The Ottomans*, 157–58; Stefan Winter, *The Shiites of Lebanon Under Ottoman Rule, 1516–1788* (Cambridge, 2010).

15. Homa Katouzian, *The Persians* (New Haven, 2009), 112–15; Kathryn Babayan, *Mystics, Monarchs, and Messiahs: Cultural Landscapes of Early Modern Iran* (Cambridge, MA, 2002), 26–39, 296.

16. Katouzian, *The Persians*, 118–20; Rudi Matthee, *The Pursuit of Pleasure: Drugs and Stimulants in Iranian History, 1500–1900* (Princeton, NJ, 2005), 75; Babayan, *Mystics, Monarchs, and Messiahs*, 319–23.

17. John Chardin, *A New and Accurate Description of Persia, and Other Eastern Nations* (London, 1724), 1, at Eighteenth Century Collections Online, link.gale.com/apps/doc /CW0100414303/ECCO?u=oxford&sid=gale_marc&xid=8cedddfa&pg=22; Farshid Emami, "Coffeehouses, Public Spaces, and the Formation of a Public Sphere in Safavid Isfahan," *Muqarnas* 33, no. 1 (2016), 177–220; Matthee, *Pursuit of Pleasure*, 165–66.

18. Daniel Goffman, *The Ottoman Empire and Early Modern Europe* (Cambridge, 2002), 68; Rifaat Ali Abu El Haj, "The Ottoman Vezir and Paşa Households, 1683–1703: A Preliminary Report," *Journal of the American Oriental Society* 94, no. 4 (1974), 438–47.

19. Stephen F. Dale, *Babur: Timurid Prince and Mughal Emperor, 1483–1530* (Cambridge, 2018), 140–41.

20. Dale, *Babur*, 73, 130–31.

21. Corinne Lefèvre, "In the Name of the Fathers: Mughal Genealogical Strategies from Babur to Shah Jahan," *Religions of South Asia* 5, no. 1–2 (2011), 409–42.

22. Audrey Truschke, *The Language of History: Sanskrit Narratives of Indo-Muslim Rule* (New York, 2021), 179–83; Truschke, *Aurangzeb* (Stanford, CA, 2017),

14; Truschke, "Hindu: A History," *Comparative Studies in Society and History* 65, no. 2 (2023), 246–71.

23. Stephen Dale, "India Under Mughal Rule," ch. 8 in David O. Morgan and Anthony Reid, eds., *The New Cambridge History of Islam* (Cambridge, 2011), vol. 3, 287–91; Stephen Dale, *The Muslim Empires of the Ottomans, Safavids, and Mughals* (Cambridge, 2009), ch. 4; Jahangir, *The Jahangirnama* [17th cent.], ed. and trans. Wheeler M. Thackston (Oxford, 1999), 22.

24. Qur'an 48:28.

25. A. Azfar Moin, "*Sulh-i kull* as an Oath of Peace: Mughal Political Theology in History, Theory, and Comparison," *Modern Asian Studies* 56 (2022), 721–48.

26. A. Azfar Moin, *The Millennial Sovereign: Sacred Kingship and Sainthood in Islam* (New York, 2012).

27. Moin, "*Sulh-i kull*," 730. For nineteenth century British accounts (and a corrective to them), see Richard M. Eaton, *India in the Persianate Age, 1000–1765* (London, 2019), 6–7.

28. Truschke, *Aurangzeb*, 72–3, 79–80; Jahangir, *Jahangirnama*, 26.

29. Ruby Lal, *Domesticity and Power in the Early Mughal World* (Cambridge, 2005); Carl Ernst and Bruce Lawrence, *Sufi Martyrs of Love: The Chishti Order in South Asia and Beyond* (New York, 2002), 88–89; Dale, "India Under Mughal Rule," 296–97.

Chapter 7: Shores of the Desert, Islands in the Sea

1. Abd al-Aziz Abd-Allah Batran, "A Contribution to the Biography of Shaikh Muhammad Ibn Abd al-Karim Ibn Muhammad (Umar-A'mar) al-Maghili, al-Tilimsani," *Journal of African History* 14, no. 3 (1973), 381–94; J. O. Hunwick, "Al-Maghili," in *Encyclopaedia of Islam*, 2nd ed. (Leiden, 1960–2009); Michael Laffan, *The Makings of Indonesian Islam* (Princeton, NJ, 2011), 8–9, 14; Kees Van Dijk, "Dakwah and Indigenous Culture: The Dissemination of Islam," *Bijdragen tot de Taal-, Land en Volkenkunde* 154, no. 2 (1998), 218–35.

2. Geoff Wade, "Early Muslim Expansion in South-East Asia, Eighth to Fifteenth Centuries," ch. 10 in David O. Morgan and Anthony Reid, eds., *The New Cambridge History of Islam* (Cambridge, 2011), vol. 3; R. Michael Feener and Michael F. Laffan, "Sufi Scents Across the Indian Ocean: Yemeni Hagiography and the Earliest History of Southeast Asian Islam," *Archipel* 70 (2005), 185–208.

3. Wade, "Early Muslim Expansion," 391–92.

4. Tomé Pires, *The Suma Oriental of Tomé Pires: An Account of the East, from the Red Sea to Japan* [1512–15], ed. and trans. Armando Cortesão, vol. 1 (London, 1944), 240–41.

5. Ross E. Dunn, *The Adventures of Ibn Battuta, a Muslim Traveler of the Fourteenth Century* (London, 1986), 116; Anthony Reid, "Islam in South-East Asia and the Indian Ocean Littoral, 1500–1800: Expansion, Polarisation, Synthesis," ch. 12 in Morgan and Reid, *New Cambridge History of Islam*, vol. 3, 428–29.

6. Mahdi Husain, ed., *The Rehla of Ibn Battuta (India, Maldive Islands and Ceylon): Translation and Commentary* (Baroda, India, 1976), 197, 203; Michael Pearson, "Islamic Trade, Shipping, Port States and Merchant Communities in the Indian Ocean, Seventh

to Sixteenth Centuries," ch. 9 in David O. Morgan and Reid, *New Cambridge History of Islam*, vol. 3, 339–41.

7. Ronit Ricci, "Conversion to Islam on Java and the 'Book of One Thousand Questions,'" *Bijdragen tot de Taal-, Land en Volkenkunde* 165, no. 1 (2009), 8–31; John Harvey D. Gamas et al., eds., *Mindanao Muslim History: Documentary Sources from the Advent of Islam to the 1800s* (Davao City, 2017), 8–10, 12–13, 34.

8. Barbara Watson Andaya, *The Flaming Womb: Repositioning Women in Early Modern Southeast Asia* (Honolulu, 2006), 86.

9. M. C. Ricklefs, *Mystic Synthesis in Java: A History of Islamization from the Fourteenth to the Early Nineteenth Centuries* (Norwalk, CT, 2006), 12–13, 46–47.

10. Ricklefs, *Mystic Synthesis*, 18–19, 25, 126–27.

11. Qur'an 12:31; Ricklefs, *Mystic Synthesis*, 44–45; Andaya, *Flaming Womb*, 72, 86–88.

12. Andaya, *Flaming Womb*, 73–74; Leonard Andaya, "The Bissu: Study of a Third Gender in Indonesia," ch. 2 in Andreea Zamfira, Christian de Montlibert, and Daniela Radu, eds., *Gender in Focus: Identities, Codes, Stereotypes and Politics* (Leverkusen, Germany, 2018); Jessica Hinchy, *Governing Gender and Sexuality in Colonial India: The Hijra, c. 1850–1900* (Cambridge, 2019); Sharyn Davies, *Gender Diversity in Indonesia: Sexuality, Islam, and Queer Selves* (London, 2010), 197–99.

13. Azyumardi Azra, *The Origins of Islamic Reformism in Southeast Asia* (Honolulu, 2004); Ricklefs, *Mystic Synthesis*, 11, 22.

14. G. W. J. Drewes and L. F. Brakel, eds. and trans., *The Poems of Hamzah Fansuri* (Dordrecht, Netherlands, 1986), 53, 64–65, 78–79, 133.

15. S. Soebardi, ed. and trans., *The Book of Cabolèk* (The Hague, Netherlands, 1975), 35; Reid, "Islam in South-East Asia," 449–50; Laffan, *Makings of Indonesian Islam*, 9.

16. Soebardi, *Cabolèk*, 66–68; M. C. Ricklefs, *The Seen and Unseen Worlds in Java: History, Literature, and Islam in the Court of Pakubuwana II* (St Leonards, NSW, 1998), 132; Ricklefs, *Mystic Synthesis*, 117–19.

17. R. Michael Feener, "South-East Asian Localisations of Islam and Participation Within a Global *umma*, 1500–1800," ch. 13 in Morgan and Reid, *New Cambridge History of Islam*, vol. 3, 490–92; Azra, *Origins of Islamic Reformism*, 64–65.

18. Ricci, "Conversion," 25–26.

19. John E. Willis, "Maritime Asia, 1500–1800: The Interactive Emergence of European Domination," *American Historical Review* 98, no. 1 (1993), 83–105; Reid, "Islam in South-East Asia," 430–31, 453–54.

20. Ismail Hakki Göksoy, "Ottoman-Aceh Relations as Documented in Turkish Sources," ch. 4 in R. Michael Feener, Patrick Daly, and Anthony Reid, eds., *Mapping the Acehnese Past* (Leiden, 2011), 68–69, 72–75, 79; Laffan, *Makings of Indonesian Islam*, 12.

21. Reid, "Islam in South-East Asia," 462; Sher Banu A. L. Khan, "The Jewel Affair: The Sultanah, Her *orang kaya*, and the Dutch Foreign Envoys," ch. 7, and Annabel Teh Gallop, "Gold, Silver, and Lapis Lazuli: Royal Letters from Aceh in the Seventeenth Century," ch. 6, in Feener et al., *Mapping the Acehnese Past*.

22. Azra, *Origins of Islamic Reformism*, 61; Feener, "South-East Asian Localisations," 489–91.

23. Sher Banu A. L. Khan, *Sovereign Women in a Muslim Kingdom: The Sultanahs of Aceh, 1641–1699* (Ithaca, NY, 2017).

24. Ricklefs, *Mystic Synthesis*, 39–40.

25. Ricklefs, *Mystic Synthesis*, 103, 110–15.

26. Lidwien Kapteijns, "Ethiopia and the Horn of Africa," ch. 11 in Nehemia Levtzion and Randall L. Pouwels, eds., *The History of Islam in Africa* (Oxford, 2000), 229–30; Haggai Ehrlich, *Ethiopia and the Middle East* (Boulder, CO, 1995), ch. 3.

27. Sam Nixon, ed., *Essouk-Tadmekka: An Early Islamic Trans-Saharan Market Town* (Leiden, 2017).

28. E. Ann McDougall, "The View from Awdaghust: War, Trade, and Social Change in the Southwestern Sahara, from the Eighth to the Fifteenth Century," *Journal of African History* 26, no. 1 (1985), 1–31; Chloé Capel, "Le tombeau à colonnes de Koumbi Saleh (Mauritanie, XIe–XIIe siècle)," *Revue des mondes musulmans et de la Méditerrannée* 149 (2021), 237–62.

29. John Wright, *The Trans-Saharan Slave Trade* (New York, 2007), 39, 167–68.

30. Michael Gomez, *African Dominion: A New History of Empire in Early and Medieval West Africa* (Princeton, NJ, 2018), ch. 4; Bruce Hall, *A History of Race in Muslim West Africa, 1600–1960* (Cambridge, 2011); Chouki El-Hamel, *Black Morocco: A History of Slavery, Race, and Islam* (Cambridge, 2013).

31. Gomez, *African Dominion*, 39; Ralph Austen, *Trans-Saharan Africa in World History* (Oxford, 2010), 32.

32. David C. Conrad, "Oral Traditions and Perceptions of History from the Manding Peoples of West Africa," ch. 4 in Emmanuel Kwaku Akyeampong, ed., *Themes in West Africa's History* (Oxford, 2006); Jan Jansen, "Beyond the Mali Empire: A New Paradigm for the Sunjata Epic," *International Journal of African Historical Studies* 51, no. 2 (2018), 317–40; Toby Green, *A Fistful of Shells: West Africa from the Rise of the Slave Trade to the Age of Revolution* (London, 2019), 44–45; Gomez, *African Dominion*, 68–70.

33. Leo Africanus, *The History and Description of Africa* [16th cent.], ed. Robert Brown, (Cambridge, 2010 [1896]), vol. 3, 823–25.

34. Abd al-Rahman al-Sa'di, *Ta'rikh al-sudan* [17th cent.], ed. and trans. John Hunwick, *Timbuktu and the Songhay Empire: Al-Sa'di's Ta'rikh al-sudan down to 1613 and Other Contemporary Documents* (Leiden, 2003), 10.

35. Ivor Wilks, "The Juula and the Expansion of Islam into the Forest," ch. 4 in Levtzion and Pouwels, *History of Islam in Africa*; Lamine Sanneh, *Beyond Jihad: The Pacifist Tradition in West African Islam* (Oxford, 2016).

36. Hunwick, *Timbuktu*, 38–80, quotes at 38, 49; Timothy Cleaveland, "Ahmad Baba al-Timbukti and his Islamic Critique of Racial Slavery in the Maghrib," *Journal of North African Studies* 20, no. 1 (2015), 42–64.

37. Hunwick, *Timbuktu*, 91, 96.

38. John Hunwick, *Shari'a in Songhay: The Replies of al-Maghili to the Questions of Askia al-Hajj Muhammad* (Oxford, 1985).

39. Sylviane A. Diouf, *Servants of Allah: African Muslims Enslaved in the Americas* (New York, 2013 [1998]), 100, 159; Ala Alryyes, ed. and trans., *A Muslim American Slave: The Life of Omar Ibn Said* (Madison, WI, 2011), 51, 61; Qur'an 67:1–2.

Chapter 8: Voices of Renewal

1. Boubacar Barry, *Le Royaume du Waalo, le Sénégal avant la conquête* (Paris, 1972).

2. Ahmad S. Dallal, *Islam Without Europe: Traditions of Reform in Eighteenth Century Islamic Thought* (Chapel Hill, NC, 2018), 18; Khaled El-Rouayheb, *Islamic Intellectual History in the Seventeenth Century* (Cambridge, 2015), 209.

3. Dallal, *Islam Without Europe*, 1–2, 19; El-Rouayheb, *Islamic Intellectual History*, 361.

4. Marc David Baer, *The Ottomans: Khans, Caesars, and Caliphs* (New York, 2021), ch. 15, quote at 290; El-Rouayheb, *Islamic Intellectual History*, 26, 352.

5. El-Rouayheb, *Islamic Intellectual History*.

6. Dallal, *Islam Without Europe*, 2; El-Rouayheb, *Islamic Intellectual History*, 200, 205.

7. Dallal, *Islam Without Europe*, ch. 3.

8. Julia Clancy-Smith, *Rebel and Saint: Muslim Notables, Populist Protest, Colonial Encounters (Algeria and Tunisia, 1800–1904)* (Berkeley, CA, 1994), ch. 7; Thierry Zarcone, "Soufis d'Asie centrale au Tibet aux XVIè et XVIIè siècles," *Cahiers d'Asie centrale* no. 1–2 (1996), 325–44; Zarcone, "Les confréries soufies en Sibérie (XIXè siècle et début du XXè siècle)," *Cahiers du monde russe* 41, no. 2–3 (2000), 279–96.

9. Ali al-Harazimi, *Jawhar al-ma'ani* [18th cent.], quoted in J. Spencer Trimingham, *The Sufi Orders in Islam* (Oxford, 1971), 107; Zachary Valentine Wright, *Realizing Islam: The Tijaniyya in North Africa and the Eighteenth Century Muslim World* (Chapel Hill, NC, 2020), 1–3, 7; Jamil Abun-Nasr, *The Tijaniyya: A Sufi Order in the Modern World* (Oxford, 1975).

10. David Robinson, "Revolutions in the Western Sudan," ch. 6 in Nehemia Levtzion and Randall L. Pouwels, eds., *The History of Islam in Africa* (Oxford, 2000), 140–43; David Robinson, *Paths of Accommodation: Muslim Societies and French Colonial Authorities in Senegal and Mauritania, 1880–1920* (Athens, OH, 2000).

11. Ahmad Dallal, "The Origins and Objectives of Islamic Revivalist Thought, 1750–1850," *Journal of the American Oriental Society* 113, no. 3 (1993), 341–59, quotes at 356–58.

12. Dallal, *Islam Without Europe*, 105–6; Trimingham, *Sufi Orders*, 118–20; Jean-Louis Triaud, *La légende noire de la Sanusiyya* (Paris, 1995); Jonathan M. Lohnes, "Reluctant Militants: Colonialism, Territory, and Sanusi Resistance on the Ottoman-Saharan Frontier," *Journal of Historical Sociology* 34 (2021), 466–78.

13. Dallal, "Origins and Objectives," 352–53.

14. Mervyn Hiskett, *The Sword of Truth: The Life and Times of the Shehu Usuman Dan Fodio* (Evanston, IL, 1994 [1973]); David Robinson, *Muslim Societies in African History* (Cambridge, 2004), ch. 10; Paul E. Lovejoy, *Transformations in Slavery*, 2nd ed. (Cambridge, 2000), 202; Jean Boyd and Beverley Mack, eds., *Collected Works of Nana Asma'u, Daughter of Usman 'dan Fodiyo (1793–1864)* (East Lansing, MI, 1997); Jean Boyd and Beverley Mack, *Educating Muslim Women: The West African Legacy of Nana Asma'u, 1793–1864* (Oxford, 2013).

15. Homa Katouzian, *The Persians* (New Haven, CT, 2009), 134.

16. Katouzian, *The Persians*, 129–40; David Morgan, *Medieval Persia, 1040–1797* (Harlow, UK, 1988), 149–55, 158–61; Haider, *Shi'i Islam*, 159–63.

17. Dale, "India Under Mugal Rule," 302, 309–12.

18. Robert Travers, "The Eighteenth Century in Indian History," *Eighteenth Century Studies* 14, 3 (2007), 492–508; P. J. Marshall, "Reappraisal: The Rise of British Power in Eighteenth Century India," *South Asia* 19, no. 1 (1996), 71–76.

19. Dallal, *Islam Without Europe*, 93; Dallal, "Origins and Objectives," 343–49, quote at 344.

20. Baki Tezcan, *The Second Ottoman Empire: Political and Social Transformation in the Early Modern World* (Cambridge, 2010); Marinos Sariyannis, "Ruler and State, State and Society in Ottoman Political Thought," *Turkish Historical Review* 4 (2013), 83–117; James McDougall, "Sovereignty, Governance, and Political Community in the Ottoman Empire and North Africa," ch. 5 in Joanna Innes and Mark Philp, eds., *Reimagining Democracy in the Mediterranean, 1780–1860* (Oxford, 2018).

21. H. Sükrü Ilicak, "A Radical Rethinking of Empire: Ottoman State and Society During the Greek War of Independence, 1821–1826," PhD diss., Harvard University, 2011; Ali Yaycioğlu, *Partners of Empire: The Crisis of the Ottoman Order in the Age of Revolutions* (Stanford, CA, 2016).

22. Ali Akyıldız and M. Şükrü Hanioğlu, "Negotiating the Power of the Sultan: The Ottoman Sened-i Ittifak (Deed of Agreement), 1808," doc. 4.1 in Camron M. Amin, Benjamin Fortna, and Elizabeth Frierson, eds., *The Modern Middle East: A Sourcebook for History* (Oxford, 2006), 24, 25, 27.

23. Dallal, "Origins and Objectives," 349–51; Cole Bunzel, *Wahhabism: The History of a Militant Islamic Movement* (Princeton, NJ, 2023), 59, 63.

24. Khaled Fahmy, *Mehmed Ali* (Oxford, 2009), 55–56, 58.

25. Bunzel, *Wahhabism,* 46; Dallal, *Islam Without Europe*, 6–7, and ch. 1; Dallal, "Origins and Objectives," 351.

Chapter 9: The Counsel of the Saints

1. H. T. Norris, ed. and trans., *The Pilgrimage of Ahmad, Son of the Little Bird of Paradise. An Account of a 19th Century Pilgrimage from Mauritania to Mecca* (Warminster, 1977), 71–72, 83–90, 91–93; René Caillié, *Journal d'un voyage à Temboctou et à Jenné, dans l'Afrique Centrale* (Brussels, 1830). An English translation appeared immediately as *Travels through Central Africa to Timbuctoo and Across the Great Desert, to Morocco, Performed in the Years 1824–1828* (London, 1830).

2. Joseph Desparmet, "Les réactions nationalitaires en Algérie," part 3, "La conquête racontée par les indigènes," *Bulletin de la Société de Géographie d'Alger* 130 (1932), 444–56; Peter Von Sivers, "The Realm of Justice: Apocalyptic Revolts in Algeria (1849–1879)," *Humaniora Islamica* 1 (1973), 47–60; James McDougall, *A History of Algeria* (Cambridge, 2017), ch. 2; Malek Bennabi, *Colonisabilité,* ed. Abderrahmane Benamara (Algiers, 2003).

3. James McDougall, "A World No Longer Shared: Losing the *droit de cité* in Nineteenth Century Algiers," *Journal of the Economic and Social History of the Orient* 60 (2017), 18–49, quotes at 29–30, 35; Jennifer Pitts, "Liberalism and Empire in a Nineteenth-Century Algerian Mirror," *Modern Intellectual History* 6, no. 2 (2009), 287–313.

4. Ian Coller, *Muslims and Citizens: Islam, Politics, and the French Revolution* (New Haven, CT, 2020); Jennifer Pitts, *A Turn to Empire: The Rise of Imperial Liberalism in Britain and France* (Princeton, NJ, 2009).

5. Alexis de Tocqueville, *Travail sur l'Algérie* [1841] in *De la colonie en Algérie*, ed. T. Todorov (Brussels, 1988), 77.

6. Amira Bennison, *Jihad and its Interpretations in Pre-Colonial Morocco* (London, 2002); McDougall, *History of Algeria*, 58–72, quote at 71; James McDougall, "Abd al-Qadir, al-Amir," in *Encyclopaedia of Islam*, 3rd ed. (Leiden, 2012).

7. Paul E. Lovejoy, *Transformations in Slavery*, 2nd ed. (Cambridge, 2000), 154.

8. P. M. Holt, *The Mahdist State in the Sudan, 1881–1898* (Oxford, 1970), 110; P. M. Holt, "Al-Mahdiyya," in *Encyclopaedia of Islam*, 2nd ed. (Leiden, 1960–2009); Aharon Layish, *Shari'a and the Islamic State in Nineteenth-Century Sudan* (Leiden, 2016), 64.

9. David Robinson, *Muslim Societies in African History* (Cambridge, 2004), 176; Ronald M. Lamothe, *Slaves of Fortune: Sudanese Soldiers and the River War, 1896–1898* (Woodbridge, UK, 2011); Kim A. Wagner, "Savage Warfare: Violence and the Rule of Colonial Difference in Early British Counterinsurgency," *History Workshop Journal* 85 (2018), 217–37.

10. "The Next War in the Light of Omdurman," *Saturday Review of Politics, Literature, Science and Art*, September 17, 1898, 369–70, https://www.proquest.com/historical-periodicals/next-war-light-omdurman/docview/9524255/se-2.

11. *Treaty of Commerce and Exchange between Great Britain and the Netherlands, signed at London, 17 March 1824* arts. 1–4, 10; Nurfadzilah Yahaya, "Legal Pluralism and the English East India Company in the Straits of Malacca During the Early Nineteenth Century," *Law and History Review* 33, no. 4 (2015), 945–64.

12. M. C. Ricklefs, *Islamisation and its Opponents in Java* (Singapore, 2012), 12; Michael Laffan, *The Makings of Indonesian Islam* (Princeton, NJ, 2011), 41–44, 91–92.

13. Peter Carey, *The Power of Prophecy: Prince Dipanagara and the End of an Old Order in Java, 1785–1855* (Leiden, 2007), 157, 161, 166–68, 170.

14. Laffan, *Makings of Indonesian Islam*, 45–46; Carey, *Power of Prophecy*, 131–50, quote at 146.

15. Carey, *Power of Prophecy*, 70, 72, 75–78, quote at 78.

16. Peter Carey, ed. and trans., *Babad Dipanagara: A Surakarta Court Poet's Account of the Outbreak of the Java War (1825–30)*, 2nd rev. ed. (Kuala Lumpur, 2019), 5, 7; Carey, *Power of Prophecy*, 512–15.

17. Carey, *Power of Prophecy*, 609, 611, 613–14, 653–54.

18. Amirul Hadi, "Exploring Acehnese Understandings of Jihad: A Study of the *Hikayat prang sabi*," ch. 9 in R. Michael Feener, Patrick Daly, and Anthony Reid, eds., *Mapping the Acehnese Past* (Leiden, 2011); David Kloos, "Dis/connection: Violence, Religion, and Geographical Imaginings in Aceh and Colonial Indonesia, 1890s–1920s," *Itinerario* 45, no. 3 (2021), 398–412; Kloos, "From Acting to Being: Expressions of Religious Individuality in Aceh, ca. 1600–1900," *Itinerario* 39, no. 3 (2016), 437–61.

19. Emmanuel Kreike, *Scorched Earth: Environmental Warfare as a Crime against Humanity and Nature* (Princeton, NJ, 2022), ch. 9; David Kloos, "A Crazy State: Violence, Psychiatry, and Colonialism in Aceh, Indonesia, ca. 1910–1942," *Bijdragen tot de Taal-, Land en Volkenkunde* 170, no. 1 (2014), 25–65.

20. Stuart Creighton Miller, *"Benevolent Assimilation": The American Conquest of the Philippines, 1899–1903* (New Haven, CT, 1982); Oliver Charbonneau, *Civilizational Imperatives: Americans, Moros, and the Colonial World* (Ithaca, NY, 2020); Kim A. Wagner, *Massacre in the Clouds: An American Atrocity and the Erasure of History* (New York, 2024).

21. Alexander Morrison, *The Russian Conquest of Central Asia: A Study in Imperial Expansion, 1814–1914* (Cambridge, 2021).

22. Moshe Gammer, *Muslim Resistance to the Tsar: Shamil and the Conquest of Chechnia and Daghestan* (Abingdon, 2004), 20, 34.

23. Gammer, *Muslim Resistance*, 90.

24. Adeeb Khalid, "Russia, Central Asia and the Caucasus to 1917," ch. 6 in Francis Robinson, ed., *The New Cambridge History of Islam*, vol. 5 (Cambridge, 2011), 184.

25. David Robinson, *Paths of Accommodation: Muslim Societies and French Colonial Authorities in Senegal and Mauritania, 1880–1920* (Athens, OH, 2000), 212.

26. James F. Searing, *God Alone Is King: Islam and Emancipation in Senegal* (Oxford, 2002), 251–52, 103.

27. Searing, *God Alone*, chs. 6 and 7; Robinson, *Muslim Societies in African History*, ch. 13; Rudolph T. Ware, *The Walking Qur'an: Islamic Education, Embodied Knowledge, and History in West Africa* (Chapel Hill, NC, 2014), 164.

Chapter 10: The Empire of Misrule

1. *Hansard*, vol. 151, 1655–59, July 19, 1858 (House of Lords).

2. William L. Ochsenwald, "The Jidda Massacre of 1858," *Middle Eastern Studies* 13, no. 3 (1977), 314–26; Ulrike Freitag, *A History of Jeddah* (Cambridge, 2020), 220–21; Michael Christopher Low, *Imperial Mecca: Ottoman Arabia and the Indian Ocean Hajj* (New York, 2020), 53–61.

3. Jon Wilson, *India Conquered: Britain's Raj and the Chaos of Empire* (London, 2017), 213, 203.

4. Lata Mani, *Contentious Traditions: The Debate on Sati in Colonial India* (Berkeley, CA, 1998); Wilson, *India Conquered*, 214.

5. Wilson, *India Conquered*, 113–16, chs. 7 and 8; Kim A. Wagner, *Rumours and Rebels: A New History of the Indian Uprising of 1857* (Oxford, 2017).

6. Wilson, *India Conquered*, 386, 258–59; Ayesha Jalal, *Partisans of Allah: Jihad in South Asia* (Cambridge, MA, 2008); Faisal Devji, "Islam and British Imperial Thought," ch. 12 in David Motadel, ed., *Islam and the European Empires* (Oxford, 2014); W. W. Hunter, *The Indian Musalmans*, 2nd ed. (London, 1872), 11, 43.

7. Jalal, *Partisans of Allah*, 67–69.

8. Devji, "Islam and British Imperial Thought," 264; Wilson, *India Conquered*, 246; Mirza Asmer Beg, "Understanding Sir Sayyid's Political Thought," ch. 9 in Yasmin Saikia and M. Raisur Rahman, eds., *The Cambridge Companion to Sayyid Ahmad Khan* (Cambridge, 2019), 184.

9. John Slight, *The British Empire and the Hajj, 1865–1956* (Cambridge, MA, 2015), 325n1; Muhammad Qasim Zaman, *The Ulama in Contemporary Islam* (Princeton, NJ, 2002), ch. 1.

10. Jürgen Osterhammel, *Unfabling the East: The Enlightenment's Encounter with Asia* (Princeton, NJ, 2018), 46; Daniel Goffman, *The Ottoman Empire and Early Modern Europe* (Cambridge, 2002); Lucette Valensi, *Birth of the Despot: Venice and the Sublime Porte* (Ithaca, NY, 1993); Chris Wickham, *The Inheritance of Rome* (London, 2009); David S. Katz, *The Shaping of Turkey in the British Imagination, 1776–1923* (London, 2016).

11. Marc David Baer, *The Ottomans: Khans, Caesars, and Caliphs* (New York, 2021), 339–41.

12. Baer, *The Ottomans*, 335, 342.

13. Davide Rodogno, *Against Massacre: Humanitarian Interventions in the Ottoman Empire, 1815–1914* (Princeton, NJ, 2012); Arnold Toynbee, *The Murderous Tyranny of the Turks* (London, 1917).

14. Khaled Fahmy, *Mehmed Ali* (Oxford, 2009), 12, 36.

15. Fahmy, *Mehmed Ali*, 13, 62; Paul Sedra, ed. and trans., "Observing Muhammad Ali Paşa and his administration at work, 1843–1846," doc. 1.6 in Camron Michael Amin, Benjamin Fortna, and Elizabeth Frierson, eds., *The Modern Middle East: A Sourcebook for History* (Oxford, 2006), 41.

16. Selim Deringil, *The Well-Protected Domains: Ideology and the Legitimation of Power in the Ottoman Empire, 1876–1909* (London, 1998).

17. Alp Eren Topal, "From Decline to Progress: Ottoman Concepts of Reform, 1600–1876," PhD diss., Bilkent University, Ankara, 2017; Topal, "Political Reforms as Religious Revival: Conceptual Foundations of *Tanzimat*," *Oriente Moderno* 101 (2021), 153–80; Halil Inalcik, trans., "The Hatt-i şerif of Gülhane, 3 November 1839," doc. 83 in J. C. Hurewitz, ed., *The Middle East and North Africa in World Politics*, vol. 1 (New Haven, CT, 1975), 269.

18. Inalcik, "Hatt-i şerif," 270–71; "Sultan Abdülmecid's *Islahat Fermani* Reaffirming the Privileges and Immunities of the non-Muslim Communities, 18 February 1856," doc. 104 in Hurewitz, *Middle East and North Africa*, vol. 1, 316–17.

19. "*Islahat Fermani*," 315.

20. Joanna Innes and Mark Philp, eds., *Re-Imagining Democracy in the Mediterranean, 1780–1860* (Oxford, 2018), 149; "Kanunu esasi" in A. Ş. Gözübüyük and S. Kili, eds., *Türk Anayasa Metinleri* (Ankara, 1982 [1876]), arts. 8, 10, 11, 17.

21. Ariel Salzmann, "Citizens in Search of a State: The Limits of Political Participation in the Late Ottoman Empire," in Michael P. Hanagan and Charles Tilly, eds., *Extending Citizenship, Reconfiguring States* (Lanham, MD, 1999); Ussama Makdisi, *The Culture of Sectarianism: Community, History and Violence in Nineteenth Century Ottoman Lebanon* (Berkeley, CA, 2000); Joel Beinin, *Workers and Peasants in the Modern Middle East* (Cambridge, 2001), ch. 2; Eugene Rogan, *The Damascus Events: The 1860 Massacre and the Destruction of the Old Ottoman World* (London, 2024).

22. Julia Phillips Cohen, *Becoming Ottomans: Sephardi Jews and Imperial Citizenship in the Modern Era* (Oxford, 2014); David Gutman, *The Politics of Armenian Migration to North America, 1885–1915* (Oxford, 2020); Zeynep Gürsel, "Portraits of Unbelonging," *Ottoman History Podcast*, episode 502, June 9, 2021, https://www.ottomanhistorypodcast.com/2021/06/gursel.html.

23. Osterhammel, *Unfabling the East*, 381; Baer, *The Ottomans*, 363.

24. Abd al-Rahman al-Kawakibi, *Taba'i' al-istibdad wa masari' al-isti'bad* (Cairo, 2007 [1900]), 23–24; Joseph G. Rahme, trans., "Abd al-Rahman al-Kawakibi: Summary of the Causes of Stagnation," doc. 19 in Charles Kurzman, ed., *Modernist Islam, 1840–1940: A Sourcebook* (Oxford, 2002), 155–56; Wael Abu-Uksa, *Freedom in the Arab World: Concepts and Ideologies in Arabic Thought in the Nineteenth Century* (Cambridge, 2018), 150–51.

25. Baer, *The Ottomans*, 406.

26. Selim Deringil, "'They Live in a State of Nomadism and Savagery': The Late Ottoman Empire and the Postcolonial Debate," *Comparative Studies in Society and History* 45, no. 2 (2003), 311–42; Eugene Rogan, *The Fall of the Ottomans: The Great War in the Middle*

East, 1914–1920 (London, 2015), 300, 164; Ronald Grigor Suny, *"They Can Live in the Desert but Nowhere Else": A History of the Armenian Genocide* (Princeton, NJ, 2015), 295.

27. Rogan, *Fall of the Ottomans*, 289, 291.

28. Baer, *The Ottomans*, 443; Rogan, *Fall of the Ottomans*, 183–84; Suny, *"They Can Live in the Desert,"* xx–xxi; Karnig Panian, *Goodbye, Antoura: A Memoir of the Armenian Genocide* (Stanford, CA, 2015).

Chapter 11: The Science of the Age

1. Selçuk Esenbel, "Abdürreşid Ibrahim Efendi," in *Encyclopaedia of Islam*, 3rd ed. (Leiden, 2012), henceforward *EI3*; Cemil Aydin, *The Politics of Anti-Westernism in Asia: Visions of World Order in Pan-Islamic and Pan-Asian Thought* (New York, 2007); Ulrich Brandenburg, "In His Father's Footsteps? Ahmed Münir Ibrahim's 1910 Journey from Harbin to Tokyo," *Global Perspectives on Japan* 2 (2019), 106–26.

2. Augustin Jomier, *Islam, réforme, et colonisation: Une histoire de l'ibadisme en Algérie (1882–1962)* (Paris, 2020); Amal Ghazal, *Islamic Reform and Arab Nationalism: Expanding the Crescent from the Mediterranean to the Indian Ocean (1880s–1930s)* (New York, 2010); Hilary Kalmbach, *Islamic Knowledge and the Making of Modern Egypt* (Cambridge, 2020); Farida Makar, "Progressive Education, Modern Schools, and Egyptian Teachers, 1922–1956," DPhil diss., University of Oxford, 2023; Zvi Ben-Dor Benite, "Taking Abduh to China," ch. 12 in James L. Gelvin and Nile Green, eds., *Global Muslims in the Age of Steam and Print* (Berkeley, CA, 2014); Michael Laffan, *Islamic Nationhood and Colonial Indonesia: The Umma Below the Winds* (London, 2007).

3. Tassadit Yacine, ed., *Poésie berbère et identité: Qasi Udifella, héraut des At Sidi Braham* (Paris, 1987), poem 11:line 16, poem 23:line 15; Arthur Asseraf, *Electric News in Colonial Algeria* (Oxford, 2019); Fanny Colonna, *Les versets de l'invincibilité: Permanences et changements religieux dans l'Algérie contemporaine* (Paris, 1995); James McDougall, *History and the Culture of Nationalism in Algeria* (Cambridge, 2006), ch. 3; James McDougall, *A History of Algeria* (Cambridge, 2017), 162.

4. Sayyid Ahmad Khan, "Lecture on Islam" (Lahore, 1884), trans. Christian W. Troll, doc. 40 in Charles Kurzman, ed., *Modernist Islam, 1840–1940: A Sourcebook* (Oxford, 2002), 296.

5. David Lelyveld, *Aligarh's First Generation: Muslim Solidarity in British India* (Princeton, NJ, 1978), 105–8, quote at 107.

6. Barbara D. Metcalf, *Muslim Revival in British India: Deoband, 1860–1900* (Princeton, NJ, 1982), 98; Muhammad Qasim Zaman, *The Ulama in Contemporary Islam* (Princeton, NJ, 2002).

7. Nikkie R. Keddie, *Sayyid Jamal al-Din "al-Afghani," a Political Biography* (Berkeley, CA, 1972), 63–64, 128, 144, 222, 250–51.

8. Albert Hourani, *Arabic Thought in the Liberal Age, 1798–1939*, 2nd ed. (Cambridge, 1983); Cemil Aydin, *The Idea of the Muslim World: A Global Intellectual History* (Cambridge, MA, 2017); Wael Abu-Uksa, *Freedom in the Arab World: Concepts and Ideologies in Arabic Thought in the Nineteenth Century* (Cambridge, 2018), ch. 2; Monica M. Ringer, *Islamic Modernism and the Re-Enchantment of the Sacred in the Age of History* (Edinburgh, 2022).

9. Sayyid Jamal al-Din al-Afghani, "Lecture on Teaching and Learning" [Calcutta, 1882], trans. Nikkie Keddie, doc. 11 in Kurzman, *Modernist Islam*, 104–6.

10. Muhammad Abduh, *Risalat al-Tawhid*, 10th ed. (Cairo, 1942 [1897]), 26–27; Muhammad Abduh, "Law Should Change in Accordance with the Conditions of Nations and the Theology of Unity," doc. 3 in Kurzman, *Modernist Islam*, 59; Hourani, *Arabic Thought*, ch. 6.

11. Anke Von Kügelgen, "Muhammad Abduh," in *EI3*; Ben-Dor Benite, "Taking Abduh to China."

12. Michael Provence, *The Last Ottoman Generation and the Making of the Modern Middle East* (Cambridge, 2017).

13. Eugene Rogan, *The Fall of the Ottomans: The Great War in the Middle East, 1914–1920* (London, 2015); Kyle J. Anderson, *The Egyptian Labor Corps* (Austin, TX, 2021).

14. Aaron Jakes, *Egypt's Occupation: Colonial Economism and the Crises of Capitalism* (Stanford, CA, 2020), 248–50; Anderson, *Egyptian Labor Corps*, ch. 8, quotes at 164, 165.

15. Jon Wilson, *India Conquered: Britain's Raj and the Chaos of Empire* (London, 2017), 244, 368–69; M. Naeem Qureshi, *Pan-Islam in British Indian Politics: A Study of the Khilafat Movement, 1918–1924* (Leiden, 1999), 94.

16. Wilson, *India Conquered*, 398–99; Kim A. Wagner, *Amritsar 1919: An Empire of Fear and the Making of a Massacre* (New Haven, CT, 2019).

17. Qureshi, *Pan-Islam*, 110, 175–232; Aydin, *Idea of the Muslim World*, 127.

18. Qureshi, *Pan-Islam*, 226–27.

19. *The Covenant of the League of Nations*, art. 22 (available at the Avalon Project, Yale Law School, https://avalon.law.yale.edu/20th_century/leagcov.asp); Hussein Omar, "The Arab Spring of 1919," *London Review of Books* (blog), April 4, 2019, https://www.lrb.co.uk/blog/2019/april/the-arab-spring-of-1919; Mahfoud Kaddache, ed., *L'Emir Khaled: Documents et témoignages pour servir à l'étude du nationalisme algérien* (Algiers, 1987), 121–24.

20. Abd al-Aziz Tha'alibi, *L'esprit libéral du Coran* (Paris, 1905), 4, 93, 98–99; Mushir Husain Kidwa'i, *Islam and Socialism* (London, 1912), iv–v; Faridah Zaman, "The Future of Islam, 1672–1924," *Modern Intellectual History* 16, no. 3 (2019), 961–91.

21. Omnia El-Shakry, *The Arabic Freud: Psychoanalysis and Islam in Modern Egypt* (Princeton, NJ, 2017).

22. Nikkie R. Keddie, *Modern Iran: Roots and Results of Revolution* (New Haven, CT, 2003), ch. 5.

23. *The Daily Mail* (London), November 11, 1938.

24. *The Incredible Turk*, CBS, 1958; James McDougall, "The British and French Empires in the Arab World: Some Problems of Colonial State-Formation and Its Legacy," ch. 3 in Raymond A. Hinnebusch and Sally N. Cummings, eds., *Sovereignty After Empire: Comparing the Middle East and Central Asia* (Edinburgh, 2011).

Chapter 12: The Community of Faith

1. William L. Cleveland, *Islam Against the West: Shakib Arslan and the Campaign for Islamic Nationalism* (Austin, TX, 1985), 68, 74, 76, 79; Shakib Arslan, *Li-madha ta'akhkharra'l-muslimum wa li-madha taqaddama ghayruhum*, trans. M. A. Shakoor, *Our Decline and Its Causes* (Lahore, 1952), 51, 55, 83.

2. Ayesha Jalal, *The Sole Spokesman: Jinnah, the Muslim League, and the Demand for Pakistan* (Cambridge, 1985).

3. *La Nation Arabe* no. 1 (March 1930), 1, 41.

4. James Piscatori and Amin Saikal, *Islam Beyond Borders: The Umma in World Politics* (Cambridge, 2019).

5. Ali Abd al-Raziq, *Al-Islam wa usul al-hukm: Bahth fi'l-khilafa wa'l-hukuma fi'l-islam* (Cairo, 1925), 64, 38; *Islam and the Foundations of Political Power*, trans. Maryam Loutfi, ed. Abdou Filali Ansari (Edinburgh, 2012).

6. Hamid Enayat, *Modern Islamic Political Thought* (Austin, TX, 1982), ch. 2; Reza Pankhurst, *The Inevitable Caliphate? A History of the Struggle for Global Islamic Union, 1924 to the Present* (London, 2013), 53–58; Madawi Al-Rasheed, Carool Kersten, and Marat Shterin, eds., *Demystifying the Caliphate* (London, 2013).

7. Elizabeth F. Thompson, *How the West Stole Democracy from the Arabs: The Syrian Arab Congress of 1920 and the Destruction of Its Historic Liberal-Islamic Alliance* (New York, 2020); James L. Gelvin, *Divided Loyalties: Nationalism and Mass Politics at the Close of Empire* (Berkeley, CA, 1998).

8. Rashid Rida, *Al-Khilafa aw al-imama al-uzma: Mabahith shar'iyya siyasiyya ijtima'iyya islahiyya* (Cairo, 1922), 15–17; Enayat, *Modern Islamic Political Thought*, 69–83.

9. Dyala Hamzah, *The Making of the Arab Intellectual: Empire, Public Sphere and the Colonial Coordinates of Selfhood* (London, 2012), ch. 5, quote at 98.

10. Ahmad Dallal, "Appropriating the Past: Twentieth Century Reconstruction of Pre-Modern Islamic Thought," *Islamic Law and Society* 7, no. 1 (2000), 325–58.

11. Richard P. Mitchell, *The Society of the Muslim Brothers* (Oxford, 1993 [1969]), 6; Roxanne L. Euben and Muhammad Qasim Zaman, eds., *Princeton Readings in Islamist Thought: Texts and Contexts from Al-Banna to Bin Laden* (Princeton, NJ, 2010), 57.

12. Gudrun Krämer, *Hassan al-Banna* (Oxford, 2010), 28–29, 31; Euben and Qasim Zaman, *Princeton Readings in Islamist Thought*, 58–59.

13. Euben and Qasim Zaman, *Princeton Readings in Islamist Thought*, 60–62, 74–78.

14. Krämer, *Hassan al-Banna*; Mitchell, *Society of Muslim Brothers*; Hazem Kandil, *Inside the Brotherhood* (Cambridge, 2015).

15. Nabil Mouline, *Les clercs de l'Islam: Autorité religieuse et pouvoir politique en Arabie saoudite, XVIIIè–XXIè siècle* (Paris, 2011); Madawi Al-Rasheed, *A History of Saudi Arabia* (Cambridge, 2002), 46, 61.

16. Mouline, *Les clercs*, 133–41; Al-Rasheed, *History of Saudi Arabia*, 66–71.

17. Jeff Eden, "Did Ibn Saud's Militants Cause 400,000 Casualties? Myths and Evidence About the Wahhabi Conquests, 1902–1925," *British Journal of Middle Eastern Studies* 46, no. 4 (2019), 519–34.

18. *La Nation Arabe* no. 1 (March 1930), 31, 35; Mouline, *Les clercs*, 18–19.

19. Thompson, *How the West Stole Democracy*, 214; Rashid Rida, "Renewal, Renewing, and Renewers," *Al-Manar*, July 1931, doc. 6 in Charles Kurzman, ed., *Modernist Islam, 1840–1940: A Sourcebook* (Oxford, 2002), 78.

20. Qasim Amin, *The Liberation of Women; and, The New Woman: Two Documents in the History of Egyptian Feminism*, trans. Samiha Sidhom Peterson (Cairo, 2000).

21. Beth Baron, *Egypt as a Woman: Nationalism, Gender, and Politics* (Berkeley, CA, 2005), 110, 113.

22. Beth Baron, *The Women's Awakening in Egypt: Culture, Society, and the Press* (New Haven, CT, 1994), 1, 14; Marilyn Booth, *"May Her Likes Be Multiplied": Biography and Gender Politics in Egypt* (Berkeley, CA, 2001).

23. Booth, *"May Her Likes be Multiplied"*; Marilyn Booth, *Classes of Ladies of Cloistered Spaces: Writing Feminist History Through Biography in Fin-de-Siècle Egypt* (Edinburgh, 2015); Marilyn Booth, "Fawwaz, Zaynab," in *Encyclopaedia of Islam*, 3rd ed. (Leiden, 2012); Sara Rahnama, *The Future is Feminist: Women and Social Change in Interwar Algeria* (Ithaca, NY, 2023).

24. Mervat F. Hatem, *Literature, Gender, and Nation-Building in Nineteenth -Century Egypt: The Life and Work of A'isha Taymur* (New York, 2011), 21, 118.

25. Abd al-Aziz Tha'alibi, *L'esprit libéral du Coran* (Paris, 1905), 11–13; Margot Badran and Miriam Cooke, eds., *Opening the Gates: An Anthology of Arab Feminist Writing*, 2nd ed. (Bloomington, IN, 2004), 270–71, 273.

26. Suraiya Faroqhi, *Women in the Ottoman Empire: A Social and Political History* (London, 2023), 145; Kaitlin Staudt, "(In)visible Beauty Queens: Literary Modernism and the Politics of Women's Visibility in Nezihe Muhiddin's *Güzellik Kraliçesi*," *Feminist Modernist Studies* 2, no. 3 (2019), 287–303.

27. *Memoirs of an Early Arab Feminist: The Life and Activism of Anbara Salam Khalidi*, trans. Tarif Khalidi (London, 2013), 1.

28. David Motadel, *Islam and Nazi Germany's War* (Cambridge, MA, 2014), 136, 221, 224.

29. Motadel, *Islam and Nazi Germany's War*, 7; Michael Laffan, *Under Empire: Muslim Lives and Loyalties Across the Indian Ocean World, 1775–1945* (New York, 2022), 309, 311, 315, 319.

30. Euben and Qasim Zaman, *Princeton Readings in Islamist Thought*, 74; Israel Gershoni and James Jankowski, *Confronting Fascism in Egypt: Dictatorship Versus Democracy in the 1930s* (Stanford, CA, 2010).

31. Jalal, *Sole Spokesman*; Yasmin Khan, *The Great Partition: The Making of India and Pakistan* (New Haven, CT, 2007).

32. Minutes of the War Cabinet, October 31, 1917, and Balfour Declaration, November 2, 1917, docs 25.6 and 25.7 in J. C. Hurewitz, ed., *The Middle East and North Africa in World Politics: A Documentary Reader,* vol. 2, *British-French Supremacy, 1914–1945* (New Haven, CT, 1979), 105–6.

33. Eugene Rogan and Avi Shlaim, *The War for Palestine: Rewriting the History of 1948*, 2nd ed. (Cambridge, 2007); Bernard Wasserstein, *The British in Palestine*, 2nd ed. (Oxford, 1991); Matthew Hughes, *Britain's Pacification of Palestine: The British Army, the Colonial State, and the Arab Revolt, 1936–39* (Cambridge, 2019); James Sunderland, "When Terror Works: The Case of Jewish Terrorism in Mandate Palestine, 1944–1948," DPhil diss., University of Oxford, 2024; Rashid Khalidi, *The Hundred Years' War on Palestine: A History of Settler Colonial Conquest and Resistance* (London, 2020); Colin Shindler, *A History of Modern Israel* (Cambridge, 2008); Benny Morris, *1948: A History of the First Arab-Israeli War* (New Haven, CT, 2008).

Chapter 13: The Wretched of the Earth

1. Roy Mottahedeh, *The Mantle of the Prophet: Religion and Politics in Iran* (London, 1985), 60, 226–27.

2. Mottahedeh, *Mantle of the Prophet*, 124, 126, 132; Homa Katouzian, *Musaddiq and the Struggle for Power in Iran* (London, 1990).

3. Homa Katouzian, *The Persians* (New Haven, CT, 2009), ch. 10; Mark J. Gasiorowski and Malcolm Byrne, eds., *Mohammad Mosaddeq and the 1953 Coup in Iran* (Syracuse, NY, 2004).

4. Jalal Al-e Ahmad, *Gharbzadegi, Weststruckness*, trans. John Green and Ahmad Alizadeh (Lexington, KY, 1982).

5. Hamid Dabashi, *The Last Muslim Intellectual: The Life and Legacy of Jalal Al-e Ahmad* (Edinburgh, 2021), 65; Mottahedeh, *Mantle of the Prophet*, 296–303.

6. Ruhollah Khomeini, "Islamic Government," in Hamid Algar, ed. and trans., *Islam and Revolution I: Writings and Declarations of Imam Khomeini (1941–1980)* (Berkeley, CA, 1981), 49.

7. Kermit Roosevelt, *Countercoup: The Struggle for the Control of Iran* (New York, 1979), v, ix; Mark Gasiorowski, *US Foreign Policy and the Shah: Building a Client State in Iran* (Ithaca, NY, 1991).

8. Papers of John F. Kennedy: Pre-Presidential Papers, Senate Files, Box 784, "Algeria Speech" (July 2, 1957), John F. Kennedy Presidential Library, Boston, MA, https://www.jfklibrary.org/archives/other-resources/john-f-kennedy-speeches/united-states-senate-imperialism-19570702.

9. Daniel Lerner, *The Passing of Traditional Society: Modernizing the Middle East* (Glencoe, IL, 1958); Hemant Shah, *The Production of Modernization: Daniel Lerner, Mass Media, and "The Passing of Traditional Society"* (Philadelphia, PA, 2011).

10. Frantz Fanon, *Les damnés de la terre* (Paris, 1961), 44; Elaine Mokhtefi, *Algiers, Third World Capital: Black Panthers, Freedom Fighters, Revolutionaries* (London, 2018); Jeffrey James Byrne, *Mecca of Revolution: Algeria, Decolonization, and the Third World Order* (Oxford, 2019).

11. Ali Shariati, *Marxism and Other Western Fallacies: An Islamic Critique*, trans. R. Campbell (Berkeley, CA, 1980), 50.

12. Rizal Sukma, *Islam in Indonesian Foreign Policy* (London, 2003), 27.

13. Kevin W. Fogg, *Indonesia's Islamic Revolution* (Cambridge, 2019); Chiara Formichi, *Islam and the Making of the Nation: Kartosuwiryo and Political Islam in Twentieth Century Indonesia* (Leiden, 2012); Naoko Shimazu, "Diplomacy as Theatre: Staging the Bandung Conference of 1955," *Modern Asian Studies* 48, no. 1 (2014), 225–52.

14. Khairudin Aljunied, *Islam in Malaysia* (Oxford, 2019), 120–21; Anthony Milner, *The Invention of Politics in Colonial Malaya* (Cambridge, 1995), 90; Meredith L. Weiss, "Legacies of the Cold War in Malaysia: Anything but Communism," *Journal of Contemporary Asia* 50, no. 4 (2020), 511–29; Karl Hack, *The Malayan Emergency: Revolution and Counterinsurgency at the End of Empire* (Cambridge, 2022).

15. Toyin Falola and Matthew M. Heaton, *A History of Nigeria* (Cambridge, 2008); Elizabeth Isichei, "The Maitatsine Risings in Nigeria, 1980–85: A Revolt of the Disinherited," *Journal of Religion in Africa* 17, no. 3 (1987), 194–208; Michael Watts, "Black Gold, White Heat: State Violence, Local Resistance and the National Question in Nigeria," ch. 2 in Michael Keith and Steven Pile, eds., *Geographies of Resistance* (London, 1997); Virginia Comolli, *Boko Haram: Nigeria's Islamist Insurgency* (London, 2015), 38–42.

16. Eric Pace, "Ahmed Sékou Touré, a Radical Hero," *New York Times*, March 28, 1984; Muhamed Kamil, "Ahmed Sékou Touré: The Tyrant Hero," ch. 3 in Baba Galleh Jallow, ed., *Leadership in Postcolonial Africa* (London, 2014).

17. Elizabeth Schmidt, *Mobilising the Masses: Gender, Ethnicity and Class in the Nationalist Movement in Guinea, 1939–1958* (Portsmouth, NH, 2004).

18. Mike McGovern, *Unmasking the State: Making Guinea Modern* (Chicago, IL, 2013), 148–51.

19. Gregory J. Massell, *The Surrogate Proletariat: Moslem Women and Revolutionary Strategies in Soviet Central Asia* (Princeton, NJ, 1974), 258.

20. Massell, *Surrogate Proletariat*, 281; Marianne Kamp, *The New Woman in Uzbekistan: Islam, Modernity, and Unveiling Under Communism* (Seattle, WA, 2006); Adeeb Khalid, *Central Asia: A New History from the Imperial Conquests to the Present* (Princeton, NJ, 2021), 220–23.

21. Yaacov Ro'i, *Islam in the Soviet Union, from World War II to Perestroika* (New York, 2000), 544–45; Khalid, *Central Asia*, 308.

22. Khalid, *Central Asia*, 313–15.

23. Christian Noack and Stéphane A. Dudoignon, eds., *Allah's Kolkhozes: Migration, De-Stalinisation, Privatisation, and the New Muslim Congregations in the Soviet Realm (1950s–2000s)* (Berlin, 2014); Stéphane A. Dudoignon, "Gnosis as Dissent? In Soviet and Present-Day Tajikistan," *Journal of Central Asian History* 1 (2022), 273–308.

24. Usaama al-Azami, "Locating *hakimiyya* in Global History: The Concept of Sovereignty in Premodern Islam and Its Reception After Mawdudi and Qutb," *Journal of the Royal Asiatic Society* (ser. 3) 32, no. 2 (2022), 355–76, quote at 363.

25. Hamid Enayat, *Modern Islamic Political Thought* (Austin, TX, 1982), 41–51; Rainer Brunner, *Islamic Ecumenism in the Twentieth Century: The Azhar and Shiism Between Rapprochement and Restraint* (Leiden, 2004); Kate Zebiri, *Maḥmūd Shaltūt and Islamic Modernism* (Oxford, 1993).

26. Muhammad Asad, *The Principles of State and Government in Islam* (Berkeley, CA, 1961), ix, xii.

27. Abu'l Ala Mawdudi, *Khutubat* (1940), ed. and trans. Khurram Murad as *Let Us Be Muslims* (Leicester, 1985), 296–97; Andrew F. March, *The Caliphate of Man: Popular Sovereignty in Modern Islamic Thought* (Cambridge, MA, 2019).

28. Abu'l Ala Mawdudi, *The Islamic Law and Constitution*, ed. and trans. Khurshid Ahmad, 2nd ed. (Lahore, 1960), 3, 53, 55–56; Seyed Vali Reza Nasr, *Vanguard of the Islamic Revolution: The Jamaat-i Islami of Pakistan* (Berkeley, CA, 1994); Seyed Vali Reza Nasr, *Mawdudi and the Making of Islamic Revivalism* (Oxford, 1996).

29. John Calvert, *Sayyid Qutb and the Origins of Radical Islamism* (Oxford, 2009), 150, 154.

30. Calvert, *Sayyid Qutb*, 9; Sayyid Qutb, *Social Justice in Islam*, trans. John B. Hardie, ed., rev. Hamid Algar (Oneonta, NY, 2000), 261; Albert Bergeson, ed., *The Sayyid Qutb Reader: Selected Writings on Politics, Religion, and Society* (New York, 2008), 50.

31. Bergeson, *Sayyid Qutb Reader*, 49.

Chapter 14: The Homes of Islam

1. Umar b. Sliman Naji to H. S. B. Philby, September 17, 1930, GB165-0229 Philby Collection, Middle East Centre Archive, St Antony's College, Oxford, ref. no. 6/5/1, Philby's Conversion to Islam, folios 12–14. Thanks to Mike Laffan for drawing this source to my attention, and to Debbie Usher for locating it.

2. "Mr St John Philby: Reported Conversion to Islam," *Manchester Guardian*, August 18, 1930; Elizabeth Monroe, *Philby of Arabia* (London, 1973), 2, 16–17, 151–53.

3. Jamie Gilham, *Loyal Enemies: British Converts to Islam, 1850–1950* (Oxford, 2014), 56, 92–93, 98; Tom Griffin, "The Problem with the Quilliam Foundation," *OpenDemocracy*, November 7, 2016, https://www.opendemocracy.net/en/opendemocracyuk /problem-with-quilliam-foundation/; Abdullah Quilliam Society (Liverpool, founded 1997), http://www.abdullahquilliam.org/; Rumeana Jahangir, "Mosque Leaders Find Moments of Hope After Violent Disorder," *BBC News* online, August 5, 2024, https:// www.bbc.co.uk/news/articles/c84jjv7kp1wo.

4. Patrick Weil, "Le statut des musulmans en Algérie colonial, une nationalité française dénaturée," *Histoire de la Justice* 16 (2005), 95–109; Sariya Cheruvallil-Contractor and Jamie Gilham, eds., *Muslim Women in Britain, 1850–1950: 100 Years of Hidden History* (London, 2023), 18, 22.

5. Fred Halliday, "The *millet* of Manchester: Arab Merchants and Cotton Trade," *British Journal of Middle Eastern Studies* 19, no. 2 (1992), 159–76; Jane I. Smith, *Islam in America* (New York, 1999), ix–x; Yvonne Yazbeck Haddad and Jane I. Smith, eds., *Muslim Minorities in the West: Visible and Invisible* (Lanham, MD, 2002).

6. Smith, *Islam in America*, 78–80; Hisham Aidi, "'Let us be Moors.' Islam, Race, and 'Connected Histories,'" *Middle East Report* 229 (2003), 42–53.

7. Malcolm X with Alex Haley, *The Autobiography of Malcolm X* (New York, 1992 [1966]), 315; Edward E. Curtis IV, *Black Muslim Religion in the Nation of Islam, 1960–1975* (Chapel Hill, NC, 2006), 22.

8. Smith, *Islam in America*; Curtis, *Black Muslim Religion*; Mattias Gardell, *In the Name of Elijah Muhammad: Louis Farrakhan and the Nation of Islam* (Durham, NC, 1996).

9. Malcolm X, *Autobiography*, 349, 351, 380.

10. Jonathan Eig, "The Real Reason Muhammad Ali Converted to Islam," *Washington Post*, October 26, 2017.

11. Dawn-Marie Gibson and Jamillah Karim, *Women of the Nation: Between Black Protest and Sunni Islam* (New York, 2014), 228; Edward E. Curtis IV, "Embodying the Nation of Islam," *Modern American History* 1 (2018), 425–29; Dawn-Marie Gibson, "Making Original Men: Elijah Muhammad, the Nation of Islam, and the Fruit of Islam," *Journal of Religious History* 44, no. 3 (2020), 319–37; Haddad and Smith, *Muslim Minorities*, vi.

12. Moustafa Bayoumi, "East of the Sun (West of the Moon): Islam, the Ahmadis, and African America," ch. 4 in M. Marable and Hisham Aidi, eds., *Black Routes to Islam* (New York, 2009), 71; Islamic Republic of Pakistan, Act (no. XLIX) further to amend the Constitution (arts. 106, 260), 1974; Smith, *Islam in America*, 74.

13. Gilham, *Loyal Enemies*, 127; Ron Greaves, *Islam and Britain: Muslim Mission in an Age of Empire* (London, 2017), 81–82.

14. John H. Hanson, *The Ahmadiyya in the Gold Coast: Muslim Cosmopolitans in the British Empire* (Indianapolis, IN, 2017); Greaves, *Islam and Britain*.

15. Barbara Daly Metcalf, "New Medinas: The Tablighi Jama'at in America and Europe," ch. 6 in Barbara Daly Metcalf, ed., *Making Muslim Space in North America and Europe* (Berkeley, CA, 1996), quotes at 118, 120; Dietrich Reetz, "Global Islam 'Made

in South Asia': The Tablighi Jamaʿat and its Universalized Preaching Mission," ch. 11 in Itzchak Weismann and Jamal Malik, eds., *Culture of Daʿwa: Islamic Preaching in the Modern World* (Salt Lake City, UT, 2020); Farish A. Noor, *Islam on the Move: The Tablighi Jamaʿat in Southeast Asia* (Amsterdam, 2012); Marloes Janson, *Islam, Youth, and Modernity in the Gambia: The Tablighi Jamaʿat* (Cambridge, 2013).

16. Tamara Sonn, "Muslims in South Africa: A Very Visible Minority," ch. 14 in Haddad and Smith, *Muslim Minorities*, 256; Anthony H. Johns and Abdullah Saeed, "Muslims in Australia, the Building of a Community," ch. 11 in Haddad and Smith, *Muslim Minorities*, 197.

17. Abdelmalek Sayad, *La double absence: Des illusions de l'émigré aux souffrances de l'immigré* (Paris, 1999); "Ya rayah," song by Dahmane El-Harrachi, 1973.

18. Jim House and Neil MacMaster, *Paris 1961: Algerians, State Terror, and Memory* (Oxford, 2006).

19. Marcel Maussen, *Constructing Mosques: The Governance of Islam in France and the Netherlands* (Amsterdam, 2009), 168–69 [translation amended]; John R. Bowen, *Why the French Don't Like Headscarves: Islam, the State, and Public Space* (Princeton, NJ, 2007); Emile Chabal, *A Divided Republic: Nation, State and Citizenship in Contemporary France* (Cambridge, 2015); Nedjib Sidi Moussa, *La fabrique du musulman: Essai sur la racialisation et la confessionalisation de la question sociale* (Paris, 2017); Leyla Arslan, *Enfants d'Islam et de Marianne: Des banlieues à l'Université* (Paris, 2010).

20. Jacqueline Jenkinson, *Black 1919: Riots, Racism and Resistance in Imperial Britain* (Liverpool, 2009), 95.

21. Martin Pugh, *Britain and Islam: A History from 622 to the Present Day* (New Haven, CT, 2019), 224–25; "Religion; England and Wales," UK National Census 2021, https://www.ons.gov.uk/peoplepopulationandcommunity/culturalidentity/religion/bulletins/religionenglandandwales/census2021; Andy Ngo, "A Visit to Islamic England," *Wall Street Journal*, August 29, 2018.

22. Khadijah Elshayyal, *Muslim Identity Politics: Islam, Activism and Equality in Britain* (London, 2018); Tariq Modood, *Multicultural Politics: Racism, Ethnicity, and Muslims in Britain* (Edinburgh, 2012).

23. Patrick Haenni, *L'islam de marché: L'autre révolution conservatrice* (Paris, 2005); Charles Tripp, *Islam and the Moral Economy: The Challenge of Capitalism* (Cambridge, 2006); Humeira Iqtidar, "Secularism Beyond the State: The 'State' and the 'Market' in Islamist Imagination," *Modern Asian Studies* 45, no. 3 (2011), 535–64; Salwa Ismail, "Piety, Profit, and the Market in Cairo: A Political Economy of Islamisation," *Contemporary Islam* 7, no. 1 (2013), 107–28; Patricia Sloane-White, *Corporate Islam: Sharia and the Modern Workplace* (Cambridge, 2018).

24. Michael Farquhar, *Circuits of Faith: Migration, Education, and the Wahhabi Mission* (Stanford, CA, 2016).

25. Madawi Al-Rasheed, *A History of Saudi Arabia* (Cambridge, 2002), 144–45.

26. Pascal Menoret, *Graveyard of Clerics: Everyday Activism in Saudi Arabia* (Stanford, CA, 2020).

27. Mohamed-Ali Adraoui, *Du golfe aux banlieues: Le salafisme mondialisé* (Paris, 2013); Sadek Hamid, "Islamic Political Mobilization in Britain: The Case of Hizb-ut-Tahrir," ch. 11 in Tahir Abbas, ed., *Islamic Political Radicalism: A European Perspective* (Edinburgh, 2007).

Chapter 15: The War Process

1. "Will Gives a Window into Suspect's Mind," *Washington Post*, October 6, 2001; Roxanne L. Euben and Muhammad Qasim Zaman, eds., *Princeton Readings in Islamist Thought: Texts and Contexts from Al-Banna to Bin Laden* (Princeton, NJ, 2010), ch. 19.

2. Jason Burke, *Al-Qaeda: The True Story of Radical Islam* (London, 2004), 239–42; National Commission on Terrorist Attacks upon the United States, *The 9/11 Report* (New York, 2004), 161; Faisal Devji, *Landscapes of the Jihad: Militancy, Morality, Modernity* (London, 2005), 3–4; Bruce Lawrence, ed., *Messages to the World: The Statements of Osama Bin Laden* (London, 2005), 61; Euben and Qasim Zaman, *Princeton Readings in Islamist Thought*, 469–70; Fred Halliday, *Two Hours that Shook the World: September 11, 2001, Causes and Consequences* (London, 2002); Lawrence Wright, *The Looming Tower: Al-Qaeda's Road to 9/11* (London, 2006).

3. Carrie Rosefsky Wickham, *The Muslim Brotherhood: Evolution of an Islamist Movement* (Princeton, NJ, 2013), 30.

4. Charles D. Smith, *Palestine and the Arab-Israeli Conflict*, 4th ed. (New York, 2001), 449, 451; Jeroen Gunning, *Hamas in Politics: Democracy, Religion, Violence* (London, 2009), 36–39.

5. Vishvini Sakthivel, "The Movement for a Society of Peace: Islamism and Political Sense-Making in Post-Conflict Algeria," DPhil diss., University of Oxford, 2019; James McDougall, *A History of Algeria* (Cambridge, 2017), 306.

6. Jillian Schwedler, *Faith in Moderation: Islamist Parties in Jordan and Yemen* (Cambridge, 2006); Jillian Schwedler, "Can Islamists Become Moderates? Rethinking the Inclusion-Moderation Hypothesis," *World Politics* 63, no. 2 (2011), 347–76.

7. Jenny B. White, *Islamist Mobilization in Turkey: A Study in Vernacular Politics* (Seattle, WA, 2002); Nathan J. Brown, *When Victory Is Not an Option: Islamist Movements in Arab Politics* (Ithaca, NY, 2012); Hendrik Kraetzschmar and Paola Rivetti, eds., *Islamists and the Politics of the Arab Uprisings* (Edinburgh, 2018).

8. Olivier Roy, *The Failure of Political Islam*, trans. Carol Volk (Cambridge, MA, 1994); Salwa Ismail, *The Rule of Violence: Subjectivity, Memory, and Government in Syria* (Cambridge, 2018); McDougall, *History of Algeria*, ch. 7; Luis Martinez, *La guerre civile en Algérie, 1990–98* (Paris, 1998).

9. Burke, *Al-Qaeda*, 119, 135; Ahmed Rashid, *Taliban: Militant Islam, Oil, and Fundamentalism in Central Asia* (New Haven, CT, 2001), 93–94, 139–40.

10. Fawaz A. Gerges, *The Far Enemy: Why Jihad Went Global*, 2nd ed. (Cambridge, 2009); Faisal Devji, *The Terrorist in Search of Humanity: Militant Islam and Global Politics* (London, 2008).

11. Samuel P. Huntington, "The Clash of Civilizations?," *Foreign Affairs* 72, no. 3 (1993), 31; Samuel P. Huntington, *The Clash of Civilizations and the Remaking of World Order* (New York, 1996); Bernard Lewis, "The Roots of Muslim Rage," *Atlantic Monthly*, September 1990, 47–60; Marshall Hodgson, "The Interrelations of Societies in History," *Comparative Studies in Society and History* 5, no. 2 (1963), 227–50; Akira Iriye, "The Second Clash: Huntington, Mahan, and Civilizations," *Harvard International Review* 19, no. 2 (1997), 44–70; Edward Said, "The Clash of Ignorance," *The Nation*, October 22, 2001; Fred Halliday, *Islam and the Myth of Confrontation*, 2nd ed. (London, 2003).

12. Willem Van Schendel, *A History of Bangladesh* (Cambridge, 2020), ch. 17; Nayanika Mookherjee, *The Spectral Wound: Sexual Violence, Public Memories, and the Bangladesh War of 1971* (Durham, NC, 2015).

13. Pierre Razoux, *The Iran-Iraq War*, trans. Nicholas Elliott (Cambridge, MA, 2015); Charles Tripp, *A History of Iraq*, 2nd ed. (Cambridge, 2007), 236–39.

14. Karool Kersten, *A History of Islam in Indonesia* (Edinburgh, 2017); Robert Cribb, "Unresolved Problems in the Indonesian Killings of 1965–66," *Asian Survey* 42, no. 4 (2002), 550–63.

15. Edward Aspinall, *Islam and Nation: Separatist Rebellion in Aceh, Indonesia* (Stanford, CA, 2009).

16. Aspinall, *Islam and Nation*, 193, 201; Noorhaidi Hasan, *Laskar Jihad: Islam, Militancy and the Quest for Identity in Post–New Order Indonesia* (Ithaca, NY, 2006).

17. Thomas McKenna, *Muslim Rulers and Rebels: Everyday Politics and Armed Separatism in the Southern Philippines* (Berkeley, CA, 1998), 86.

18. McKenna, *Muslim Rulers and Rebels*, 114, 139; Jeroen Adam, "Bringing Grievances Back In: Towards an Alternative Understanding of the Rise of the Moro Islamic Liberation Front in the Philippines," *Bijdragen tot de Taal-, Land en Volkenkunde* 174, no. 1 (2018), 1–23.

19. Adam, "Bringing Grievances," 4–5.

20. Huntington, "Clash of Civilizations?," 35; Lawrence, *Messages to the World*, 124, 113, 61.

21. United Nations General Assembly, Resolution 194 (III), art. 11, December 11, 1948.

22. Rashid Khalidi, *The Hundred Years' War on Palestine: A History of Settler Colonial Conquest and Resistance* (London, 2020); Avi Shlaim, *Collusion Across the Jordan: King Abdallah, the Zionist Movement, and the Partition of Palestine* (Oxford, 1988); Avi Shlaim, *The Iron Wall: Israel and the Arab World*, rev. ed. (London, 2014); Eugene Rogan, *The Arabs: A History*, 3rd ed. (London, 2018); Yezid Sayigh, *Armed Struggle and the Search for State: The Palestinian National Movement, 1949–1993* (Oxford, 1997); Michael Oren, *Six Days of War: June 1967 and the Making of the Modern Middle East* (London, 2003); Robert Fisk, *Pity the Nation: Lebanon at War*, 3rd ed. (Oxford, 2001); Ian Lustick, *For the Land and the Lord: Jewish Fundamentalism in Israel* (New York, 1988); Graham Usher, *Dispatches from Palestine: The Rise and Fall of the Oslo Peace Process* (London, 1999); appendix A.6, "Various Organizations: Losses on the Five-Year Anniversary of the Al-Aqsa Intifada," *Journal of Palestine Studies* 35, no. 2 (2006), 194–99.

23. Lawrence, *Messages to the World*, 107; Arab Barometer, Public Opinion Survey Reports and Palestine Country Reports, 2006–2022, https://www.arabbarometer.org/countries/palestine/; Hamas Charter (2017) at "Hamas in 2017: The Document in Full," *Middle East Eye*, May 2, 2017, https://www.middleeasteye.net/news/hamas-2017-document-full.

24. McDougall, *History of Algeria*, 384–317; Martinez, *La guerre civile*; Abderrahmane Moussaoui, *De la violence en Algérie: Les lois du chaos* (Paris, 2006).

25. Mark Mazower, *The Balkans* (London, 2000); Vjekoslav Perica, *Balkan Idols: Religion and Nationalism in Yugoslav States* (Oxford, 2004); Lara J. Nettelfield and Sarah E. Wagner, *Srebrenica in the Aftermath of Genocide* (Cambridge, 2014).

26. James Hughes, *Chechnya: From Nationalism to Jihad* (Philadelphia, PA, 2007).

27. Hughes, *Chechnya*, 111.

28. Hughes, *Chechnya*; Anna Politkovskaya, *A Dirty War: A Russian Reporter in Chechnya* (London, 2001), 147.

29. Olivier Roy, *Islam and Resistance in Afghanistan* (Cambridge, 1986), 89, 94, 118.

30. Roy, *Islam and Resistance*, 118; Thomas Barfield, *Afghanistan: A Cultural and Political History*, 2nd ed. (Princeton, NJ, 2023), 171.

31. Burke, *Al-Qaeda*, 73; Thomas Hegghammer, *The Caravan: Abdallah Azzam and the Rise of Global Jihad* (Cambridge, 2020), 293.

32. Gerges, *Far Enemy*, 13, 87–98.

33. Rashid, *Taliban*; Burke, *Al-Qaeda*, 196.

34. Lawrence, *Messages to the World*, 58–62.

Chapter 16: The Myth of Civilisations

1. Nissan Ibrahim [Ruqia Hassan], Facebook post, July 20, 2015, 7:49am, tweeted by Hussam Eesa, @HussamEesa, January 2, 2016, at 8:09pm; "Ruqia Hassan, the Woman Who Was Killed for Telling the Truth about Isis," *The Guardian*, January 13, 2016; Hala Kodmani, *Seule dans Raqqa* (Paris, 2017); "Al-Rakka," in *Encyclopaedia of Islam*, 2nd ed. (Leiden, 1960–2009).

2. "Raqqa Recaptured from Islamic State by US-Backed Forces," *The Guardian*, October 17, 2017; "Raqqa: A Journey into the Destroyed Heart of the Islamic State Capital," *The Guardian*, October 10, 2017; "Raqqa Is Being Slaughtered Silently," https://www.raqqa-sl.com/en/; Michael J. McNerney et al., "Understanding Civilian Harm in Raqqa and its Implications for Future Conflicts," RAND Corp. research report (2022), 35; "The Massacre of Mosul: 40,000 Feared Dead in Battle to Take Back City from ISIS as Scale of Civilian Casualties Revealed," *The Independent*, July 19, 2017; Patrick Cockburn, *The Rise of Islamic State: ISIS and the New Sunni Revolution* (London, 2015), 20, 24, 17.

3. Project for the New American Century, *Rebuilding America's Defenses* (Washington, DC, 2000); Harlan K. Ullman and James P. Wade, *Shock and Awe: Achieving Rapid Dominance* (Washington, DC, 1996); Jim Mann, *Rise of the Vulcans: The History of Bush's War Cabinet* (New York, 2004).

4. Abbas Alnasrawi, "Iraq: Economic Sanctions and Consequences, 1990–2000," *Third World Quarterly* 22, no. 2 (2001), 205–18; Tim Dyson and Valeria Cetorelli, "Changing Views on Child Mortality and Economic Sanctions in Iraq: A History of Lies, Damned Lies, and Statistics," *BMJ Global Health* 2, no. 2 (2017); *The Report of the Iraq Inquiry* (Chilcot Inquiry report), executive summary, July 6, 2016, 41–44, https://webarchive.nationalarchives.gov.uk/ukgwa/20171123122743/, http://www.iraqinquiry.org.uk/the-report/.

5. Chilcot Inquiry report, 48, para. 344; Benjamin Isakhan, ed., *The Legacy of Iraq: From the 2003 War to the "Islamic State"* (Edinburgh, 2015), 11–12; Patrick Cockburn, *The Occupation: War and Resistance in Iraq* (London, 2007).

6. Haroro J. Ingram, Craig Whiteside, and Charlie Winter, eds., *The ISIS Reader: Milestone Texts of the Islamic State Movement* (London, 2020), 38–39, 41, 43.

7. Ingram et al., *The ISIS Reader*, 164.

8. Azadeh Moaveni, *Guest House for Young Widows: Among the Women of ISIS* (London, 2019); Shiraz Maher and Peter R. Neumann, *Pain, Confusion, Anger and Shame: The Stories of Islamic State Families* (London, 2016); Shahira S. Fahmy, "The Age of

Terrorism Media: The Visual Narratives of the Islamic State Group's *Dabiq* Magazine," *International Communication Gazette* 82, no. 3 (2020), 260–88.

9. Dounia Mahlouly and Charlie Winter, *A Tale of Two Caliphates: Comparing the Islamic State's Internal and External Messaging Priorities*, ICSR Vox-Pol report (London, 2018); Moaveni, *Guest House*, 152–53, 178.

10. Ingram et al., *The ISIS Reader*, 183; Raihan Ismail, "Reclaiming Saudi Salafism: The Saudi Religious Circles and the Threat of ISIS," *Journal of Arabian Studies* 9, no. 2 (2019), 164–81, quote at 168.

11. Moaveni, *Guest House*, 214–15; "Does *The Sun*'s Claim about UK Muslims' Sympathy for Jihadis Stack Up?," *The Guardian*, November 23, 2015. "Statement on Survation's Poll of Muslims for *The Sun*," November 2015, https://www.survation.com /statement-on-survations-poll-of-muslims-for-the-sun/; ICM, C4/Juniper Survey of Muslims [in the UK], April 25 to May 31, 2015; Miqdaad Versi, "What Do Muslims Really Think? This Skewed Poll Certainly Won't Tell Us," *The Guardian*, April 12, 2016; "What British Muslims Really Think About Poll That Asked, 'What Do British Muslims Really Think?,'" *The Independent*, April 12, 2016; "A Decade of Anti-Muslim Hate," Tell MAMA report, July 2023, 19–21.

12. Tim Jacoby, "Islam and the Islamic State's Magazine, *Dabiq*," *Politics and Religion* 12 (2019), 32–54.

13. Graeme Wood, "What ISIS Really Wants," *The Atlantic*, March 2015.

14. Fariba Adelkhah, *Being Modern in Iran*, trans. Jonathan Derrick (London, 1999), ch. 2; Azadeh Moaveni, *Lipstick Jihad: A Memoir of Growing up Iranian in America and American in Iran* (New York, 2005); Pascal Menoret, *Joyriding in Riyadh: Oil, Urbanism, and Road Revolt* (Cambridge, 2014); Sofiane Merabet, *Queer Beirut* (Austin, TX, 2014); Moustafa Bayoumi, *How Does It Feel to Be a Problem? Being Young and Arab in America* (New York, 2009).

15. Albert Hourani, *A History of the Arab Peoples* (London, 1991), 267; C. R. Pennell, *Morocco Since 1830: A History* (London, 2000), 76; Dale F. Eickelman, "Inside the Muslim Reformation," *Wilson Quarterly* 22, no. 1 (1998), 80–89.

16. Nikkie R. Keddie, *Modern Iran: Roots and Results of Revolution* (New Haven, CT, 2003), 262; Lucinda Maer, "The Abolition of the Blasphemy Offences," UK House of Commons Library standard note SN/PC/04597, May 9, 2008, https://researchbriefings .files.parliament.uk/documents/SN04597/SN04597.pdf; Paul Weller, *A Mirror for Our Times: The Rushdie Affair and the Future of Multiculturalism* (London, 2009), 19, 21; Talal Asad, *Genealogies of Religion: Discipline and Reasons of Power in Christianity and Islam* (Baltimore, MD, 1993), ch. 7.

17. Asef Bayat, "The Making of Post-Islamist Iran," ch. 2 in Asef Bayat, ed. *Post-Islamism: The Changing Faces of Political Islam* (Oxford, 2013), quote at 40; Mehran Kamrava, *Iran's Intellectual Revolution* (Cambridge, 2008), 223; Moaveni, *Lipstick Jihad*.

18. Adelkhah, *Being Modern in Iran*; Narges Bajoghli, *Iran Reframed: Anxieties of Power in the Islamic Republic* (Stanford, CA, 2019).

19. Qur'an 2:143. Jakob Skovgaard-Petersen and Bettina Gräf, eds., *Global Mufti: The Phenomenon of Yusuf al-Qaradawi* (London, 2009); Bettina Gräf, "In Search of a Global Islamic Authority," *ISIM Review* 15 (Spring 2005), 47; "Friendly Fire. Madeleine Bunting Meets Sheikh Yusuf al-Qaradawi in Qatar," *The Guardian*, October 29, 2005.

20. Farid Esack, *On Being a Muslim* (Oxford, 1999); Amina Wadud, *Qur'an and Woman* (New York, 1999); Shadaab Rahemtulla, *Qur'an of the Oppressed: Liberation Theology and Gender Justice in Islam* (Oxford, 2017); John Cooper, Ronald Nettler and Mohamed Mahmoud, eds., *Islam and Modernity: Muslim Intellectuals Respond* (London, 2000), chs. 6 and 8.

21. Marwan M. Kraidy, *The Naked Blogger of Cairo: Creative Insurgency in the Arab World* (Cambridge, MA, 2016); Mohamed Fadel Fahmy, "Egyptian Blogger Aalia El-mahdy: Why I Posed Naked," *CNN*, November 19, 2011, https://www.cnn.com/2011/11/19/world/meast/nude-blogger-aliaa-magda-elmahdy.

22. Jennifer Selby, "French Secularism as a 'Guarantor' of Women's Rights? Muslim Women and Gender Politics in a Parisian *banlieue*," *Culture and Religion* 12, no. 4 (2011), 441–62; Anabel Inge, *The Making of a Salafi Muslim Woman: Paths to Conversion* (Oxford, 2016).

23. Amel Boubekeur and Olivier Roy, eds., *Whatever Happened to the Islamists? Salafis, Heavy Metal Muslims, and the Lure of Consumerist Islam* (London, 2012); Patrick Haenni, *L'islam de marché: L'autre révolution conservatrice* (Paris, 2005).

24. "'Muslims Are Foreigners': Inside India's Campaign to Decide Who Is a Citizen," *New York Times*, April 4, 2020; "'Do We Not Have Any Rights?' Indian Muslims' Fear After Assam Evictions," *The Guardian*, October 18, 2021; Angana P. Chatterji et al., *Breaking Worlds: Religion, Law and Citizenship in Majoritarian India: The Story of Assam* (Berkeley, CA, 2021).

25. Ronan Lee, *Myanmar's Rohingya Genocide: Identity, History, and Hate Speech* (London, 2021); Nasir Uddin, *The Rohingya: An Ethnography of "Subhuman" Life* (Oxford, 2020).

26. Bayoumi, *How Does It Feel?*, "Afterword for 2018," 272–76, 278; "Inside the Huge JFK Airport Protest over Trump's Muslim Ban," *Rolling Stone*, January 29, 2017; Moustafa Bayoumi, *This Muslim American Life: Dispatches from the War on Terror* (New York, 2015), ch. 11.

27. Chiara Formichi, *Islam and Asia: A History* (Cambridge, 2020), 233; Jonathan Lipman, *Familiar Strangers: A History of Muslims in Northwest China* (Seattle, WA, 1998); Maris B. Gillette, *Between Mecca and Beijing: Modernization and Consumption among Urban Chinese Muslims* (Stanford, CA, 2000); Sean R. Roberts, *The War on the Uyghurs: China's Internal Campaign Against a Muslim Minority* (Princeton, NJ, 2020); Joanne Smith Finley, "Why Scholars and Activists Increasingly Fear a Uyghur Genocide in Xinjiang," *Journal of Genocide Research* 23, no. 3 (2021), 348–70; David Tobin, "Genocidal Processes: Social Death in Xinjiang," *Ethnic and Racial Studies* 45, no. 16 (2022), 93–121.

28. Simon Fieschi, statement quoted in "Au procès de l'attentat contre *Charlie Hebdo*: 'Cette balle ne m'a pas raté, mais elle ne m'a pas eu,'" *Le Monde*, September 10, 2020; Rahimi Bin Ahmad and Mustafa Boztas, statements quoted in "The Christchurch Testimonies: Survivors and the Bereaved Give Their Accounts of New Zealand's Worst Terror Attack," *The Guardian*, September 2, 2020.

29. Edward Said, "The Clash of Ignorance," *The Nation*, October 22, 2001.

INDEX